Lecture Notes in Computer Scie
Edited by G. Goos, J. Hartmanis, and J. van l

Springer
Berlin
Heidelberg
New York
Hong Kong
London
Milan
Paris
Tokyo

Kurt Bauknecht   A Min Tjoa
Gerald Quirchmayr (Eds.)

E-Commerce and Web Technologies

4th International Conference, EC-Web
Prague, Czech Repbulic, September 2-5, 2003
Proceedings

 Springer

Series Editors

Gerhard Goos, Karlsruhe University, Germany
Juris Hartmanis, Cornell University, NY, USA
Jan van Leeuwen, Utrecht University, The Netherlands

Volume Editors

Kurt Bauknecht
University of Zürich
IFI
Winterthurer Str. 190, 8057 Zürich, Switzerland
E-mail: baukn@ifi.unizh.ch

A Min Tjoa
Vienna University of Technology
Institute of Software Technology and Interactive Systems
Favoritenstr. 9-11/188, 1040 Vienna, Austria
E-mail: tjoa@ifs.tuwien.ac.at

Gerald Quirchmayr
University of Vienna
Institute of Computer Science and Business Informatics
Liebiggasse 4, 1010 Vienna, Austria
Gerald.Quirchmayr@univie.ac.at

Cataloging-in-Publication Data applied for

A catalog record for this book is available from the Library of Congress

Bibliographic information published by Die Deutsche Bibliothek
Die Deutsche Bibliothek lists this publication in the Deutsche Nationalbibliografie;
detailed bibliographic data is available in the Internet at <http://dnb.ddb.de>.

CR Subject Classification (1998): K.4.4, H.4, J.1, H.5, H.3, H.2, K.6.5

ISSN 0302-9743
ISBN 3-540-40808-8 Springer-Verlag Berlin Heidelberg New York

Springer-Verlag Berlin Heidelberg New York
a member of BertelsmannSpringer Science+Business Media GmbH

http://www.springer.de

© Springer-Verlag Berlin Heidelberg 2003
Printed in Germany

Typesetting: Camera-ready by author, data conversion by DA-TeX Gerd Blumenstein
Printed on acid-free paper   SPIN 10929162   06/3142   5 4 3 2 1 0

Preface

We welcome you to the 4th International Conference on E-Commerce and Web Technology (EC-Web 2003) held in conjunction with DEXA 2003 in Prague, Czech Republic. This conference, first held in Greenwich, UK in 2000, is now in its fourth year and is very well established. As in the three previous years, it served as a forum to bring together researchers from academia and commercial developers from industry to discuss the current state of the art in e-commerce and Web technology. Inspirations and new ideas emerged from intensive discussions during formal sessions and social events.

The keynote addresses, research presentations and discussions during the conference helped to further develop the exchange of ideas among the researchers, developers and practitioners who attended.

The conference attracted 108 submissions and each paper was reviewed by at least three program committee members. The program committee selected 42 papers for presentation and publication, a task which was not easy due to the high quality of the submitted papers.

We would like to express our thanks to our colleagues who helped with putting together the technical program: the program committee members and external reviewers for their timely and rigorous reviews of the papers, and the organizing committee for their help in administrative work and support. We owe special thanks to Gabriela Wagner and Maria Schweikert for always being available when their helping hand was needed.

Finally, we would like to thank all the authors who submitted papers, authors who presented papers, and the participants who together made this conference an intellectually stimulating event through their active contributions.

We hope that you enjoyed the conference and the hospitality of Prague.

September 2003

A Min Tjoa
Gerald Quirchmayr

Program Committee

General Chairperson

Kurt Bauknecht, University of Zurich, Switzerland

Conference Program Chairpersons

Gerald Quirchmayr, University of Vienna, Austria and
University of South Australia
A Min Tjoa, Vienna University of Technology, Austria

Program Committee Members

Karl Aberer, EPFL Lausanne, Switzerland
Antonio Badia, University of Louisville, USA
Bharat Bhargava, Purdue University, USA
Sourav Saha Bhowmick, Nanyang Technological University, Singapore
Martin Bichler, Technical University of Munich, Germany
Walter Brenner, University of St. Gallen, Switzerland
Stephane Bressan, National University of Singapore, Singapore
Wojciech Cellary, Poznan University of Economics, Poland
Asuman Dogac, Middle East Technical University, Turkey
Eduardo Fernandez, Florida Atlantic University, USA
Elena Ferrari, University of Milan, Italy
Yongjian Fu, University of Missouri-Rolla, USA
Chanan Glezer, Ben Gurion University, Beer Sheva, Israel
Rüdiger Grimm, Technical University Ilmenau, Germany
Hiroyuki Kitagawa, University of Tsukuba, Japan
Wolfgang Koenig, University of Frankfurt, Germany
Vijay Kumar, University of Missouri-Kansas City, USA
Karl Kurbel, Europe University, Frankfurt (Oder), Germany
Alberto Laender, Federal University of Minas Gerais, Brazil
Winfried Lamersdorf, University of Hamburg, Germany
Tan Kian Lee, National University of Singapore, Singapore
Juhnyoung Lee, IBM T.J. Watson Research Center, USA
Lilien Leszek, Purdue University, USA
Ee Peng Lim, Nanyang Technological University, Singapore
Huan Liu, Arizona State University, USA
Sanjay Kumar Madria, University of Missouri-Rolla, USA
Michael Merz, Ponton GmbH, Germany
Natwar Modani, IBM India Research Lab, India

External Reviewers

Christian Zirpins
Alexander Pokahr
Iryna Kozlova
Harald Weinreich
Toby Baier
Umit Altintakan
K. Alpay Erturkmen
Arif Tumer
Ilhami Gorgun
Baris Uz
Sait Pektas
Lutz Kolbe
Ruediger Zarnekow
Axel Hochstein
Ragnar Schierholz
Malte Dous
Jarogniew Rykowski
Adriano Pereira
Renato Ferreira
Wagner Meira, Jr.
Zissis Palaskas
Thomi Pilioura
George-Dimitrios Kapos
George Athanasopoulos
Indrajit Ray
Tai Xin
Anwitaman Datta
Jie Wu
Vicente Pelechano
Juan Sanchez
Jörg Gilberg
Aixin Sun
Yoshiharu Ishikawa
Atsuyuki Morishima

Table of Contents

Modeling and Technology

XML

Case Studies

Modeling, Design and Performance

Business Processes

Brokering and Recommender Systems

Position Paper

Trust for Digital Products

Günther Pernul

Lehrstuhl für Wirtschaftsinformatik I – Department of Information Systems
University of Regensburg, Germany

1   Introduction

Digital goods are bitstrings, sequences of 0s and 1s, that have economic value. Increasingly the Internet is used for their distribution, examples include digital versions of books, articles, music, and images. Obviously, trading digital goods over the Internet offers lots of advantages. For example, digital goods have in common, that transaction costs are minimal (in comparison to conventional goods) since all logistic processes may happen consistent without changing the media of the Internet. This includes costs for information, arrangements, transaction, controlling and adapting of the bargain.

Saving costs is only one side of the picture. Parties being involved in trading and using digital goods must deal with the question whether they can "trust" the digital good and the underlying trading infrastructure. The ease with which digital goods can be copied and redistributed makes the Internet well suited for unauthorized copying, modification and redistribution. The digital distribution network is not limited to online computers alone. Mobile devices, DVD players, MP3 players, game consoles, television decoders and a number of other new appliances, in combination with communication networks have already caught up in the digitalization wave. With the increasing use of digital products comes the need to protect that content from unauthorized use once it is outside the control of the supplier, demander or legitimate user.

In this extended abstract we look at the trust issues of digital products. Trust is an interdisciplinary issue, involving at least sociological, psychological, but also technical issues. Our concern will be on the technical aspects mainly with a focus on security and privacy. The remainder of this paper is structured as follows: in section 2 categories of digital products are given and the properties that influence trust are discussed. In section 3 we describe a technical infrastructure with focus on security and privacy for trading digital products. In section 4 - as an example of an innovative digital product and the use of the infrastructure mentioned above - we introduce digital emission permits. Emission permits are very up-to-date because their use is demanded in the Kyoto protocol as a means to reduce the greenhouse gas emissions. This protocol was passed at the conference of the UN Framework Convention on Climate Change in Kyoto and signed and ratified by the industrial countries. It will come into effect in 2005.

K. Bauknecht, A Min Tjoa, G. Quirchmayr (Eds.): EC-Web 2003, LNCS 2738, pp. 1-5, 2003.
© Springer-Verlag Berlin Heidelberg 2003

2   Digital Products and Properties

Digital products occur in different forms: They may refer to "information", that can be found in databases or encyclopaedias. Digital products may be products of the entertainment industries, like movies, whole digital TV channels, audio and video services. Digital products may refer to general services, like distance teaching and learning, online banking and brokerage, telemedicine, or services of public administrations, e-government. Digital products may also be symbols, that refer to some right or privilege. Examples are credit cards, which offer the right to spend some money up to a specified limit or tickets offering the right to take a certain seat on a given flight. The emission permits, which will be discussed later, fall in this category, too.

Digital products, by their nature, have properties in common which influence the development of trust. They are transmutable, nonrival, indestructible, infinitely reproducible, discrete, virtual, and invaluable. A product is *transmutable* if by slightly changing it or by combining it with others produces a new good with features absent in the original. In many cases this is even possible at low costs and without any remaining signs on the original good. A product is *nonrival* if its use by one agent does not degrade its usefulness to any other. It is *indestructible* if after usage it does not show any sign of wear. It may happen that the storage media shows such signs, however, it may be changed without effecting the product. A digital good is infinitely reproducible, i.e. its quantity can be made arbitrarily large and this quickly and at low cost. The original and each of its copies are identical. This leads to a further property of digital goods. They are *discrete*, in the sense that their quantity can only be 0, 1, 2,... As a result most digital goods are indivisible, i.e. the first half of the string of 1s and 0s may not be worth anything. Even robust digital goods remain of value only for "small" consumption. Digital products are *virtual*, i.e. they are at the same time both nowhere and everywhere. Because of its distribution over networks digital products may uniformly and immediately spread over the globe. Finally they are *invaluable*, i.e. it is difficult to estimate their monetary value. For example, what is the value of the stock of a digital product?

Let us now discuss what are technical properties necessary to develop trust. The most important property is the *integrity* of the digital product. Integrity refers to the value of the digital product, i.e. that it keeps its value, for both supplier and demander after being traded over the Internet. Obviously, this is dependent on the type of the digital product. As an example consider a digital coin, which only keeps its integrity as an original. A copy of the coin is of no value. This is different from a digitally represented piece of music. For the listener it is of no importance whether he listens to the master piece or to an identical digital copy. In this case integrity is kept only if the listener has the corresponding right to listen (only once or several times depending on the right). Other necessary properties are the existence of a corresponding legal framework, including intellectual property rights involved in digital goods like authorship, ownership, copyright, or right to use; services for legal binding, mutual dependencies, non-repudiation; services which are generally understood under the term security, like confidentiality, integrity, availability; and last but not least that the underlying technical infrastructure for all parties involved supports fairness and if desired anonymity. Additional information about COPS may be found in [1], [2], and [3].

3   COPS - An Infrastructure for Secure and Fair E-commerce

COPS has the goal to develop and implement a prototype of a generic market infrastructure for trading digital products with its main focus on security and fairness. Each market participant in each phase of a business transaction (trading the digital good) is defined (1) by a set of services offered by the infrastructure, (2) by its communication relationships to other market participants, and (3) by a set of actions, conditions and events which are characteristic for this part of the business transaction.

In figure 1 we give a graphical model of COPS. The three levels (I,N,E) show three phases of the business transactions, while the corner elements are representing the different participants in a COPS market: demander, supplier, electronic intermediary (cybermediary), trusted third party, and information services.

4   Digital Emission Permits

Due to the increasing need for control of greenhouse gas emissions the Kyoto protocol was passed by the parties of the UN Framework Convention on Climate Change in 1997. The protocol includes massive reduction of emissions in the participating (industrial) countries by an average of 5.2 per cent compared to the rates of 1990. The launch period of the protocol and the belonging mechanisms begin in 2005; until 2008, the introduction shall be finished, so that reduction goals can be reached within the final period (2008 - 2012).

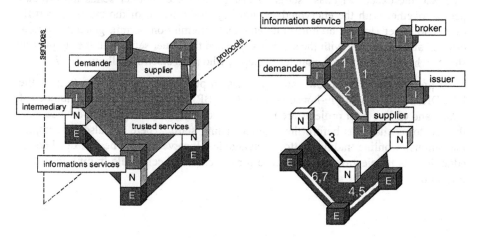

Fig. 1. COPS Market Model   **Fig.2.** COPS business transactions

In order to realise the Kyoto protocol the European Union will establish a uniform trading system for carbon dioxide (CO_2) by allowing direct business-to-business trading between companies beginning in 2005. Within the first three years, participation is voluntary. From 2008 on, the participation will then be mandatory for specific kinds of companies (e.g. power and heat generation, steel and paper industry).

In the general model of transferable emission permits [4], [5] a coordinating institution defines a specific environmental quality target for a certain environmental system, e.g. a lake or a geographic region, by using certain criteria. Having fixed the environmental target, the corresponding maximum emission quantity can be defined. This emission quantity is divided into emission contingents which are documented in emission permits and licenses. Emission is only allowed for owners of corresponding permits which exactly define the allowed quantity of pollution, the affected region and the period of time.

In Fig. 2 we sketch an electronic market for digital represented emission permits. Each permit in this model allows its owner emission of a certain amount of toxins. Permits can be traded freely. When the permit is traded it has to be digitally represented, it must not be possible to forge or to copy it and finally the market should be anonymous. The example shows how the market may be realised in COPS and additionally how trusted authorities (in this example the issuer) can be used for guaranteeing originality and anonymity of digital goods. The example and the underlying cryptographic protocols are further described in [3].

Trading the digital good "emission permit" is carried out in different steps. During the steps marked with 1 the demander and supplier search for each other. In step 2 the demander gets a binding offer from the supplier. This concludes the information phase of the transaction. In step 3, the contract terms are discussed, the contract is completed, and the demander sends a session key which is encrypted by using the public key of the issuer to the supplier. This is necessary for establishing the connection to the emission certificate and for preparing anonymity. The negotiation phase ends and the execution phase starts. During step 4 the supplier sends his original permit together with the encrypted session key to the issuer of the emission certificate. The issuer (trusted authority) deletes the old emission permit, generates a new original and encrypts it with the session key. Then the issuer sends it to the supplier in step 5, who gives it to the demander in step 6, who pays electronically in step 7.

At present, there are a few national emission permit trading schemes (e.g. in the UK, DK, Germany) and in-house systems (e.g. BP) already in use. But a number of online and offline pilot projects are being conducted in order to gain experience with the Kyoto mechanisms before the official trading starts. There are also first implementations of online trading platforms available. However, to the best of our knowledge there is no electronic marketplace for direct (B2B) certificate trading in operation so far.

References

[1]   Röhm, A. W., Pernul, G. COPS: a model and infrastructure for secure and fair electronic markets. *Decision Support Systems Journal,* Vol. 29, Nr. 4 (2000) pp. 343-355. Elsevier Science.

[2]   Pernul, G., Röhm, A. W., Hermann, G. Trusted Electronic Market Transactions - a macro- and a micro-level view. In: *The E-Business Handbook* (Paul B. Lowry, Ronald J. Watson, J. Owen Cherrington, Eds.), pp. 365 - 378. CRC Press, 2002.

[3]   Röhm, A. W., Gerhard, M.: A secure electronic market for anonymous transferable emission permits. *Proc. of 31st Hawaii International Conference on System Sciences,* HICSS-31; (1998).

[4]   Crocker, T. D.: The Structuring of Atmospheric Pollution Controll Systems. In: Wolozin, H. (Ed.): *The Economics of Air Pollution*; New York; 1966; p. 61-86.

[5]   Dales, J. H.: Land, Water and Ownership. *Canadian Journal of Economics* 1; Vol. 1.

e-Procurement Using Goal Programming*

S. Kameshwaran and Y. Narahari

eEnterprises Laboratory, Department of CSA
Indian Institute of Science
Bangalore-560012, India
{kameshn,hari}@csa.iisc.ernet.in
http://lcm.csa.iisc.ernet.in

Abstract. e-Procurement is an Internet-based business process for obtaining materials and services and managing their inflow into the organization. In this paper we develop multiattribute e-Procurement systems with configurable bids and formulate the bid evaluation problem as a linear integer multiple criteria optimization problem. Configurable bids allow multiple values for each attribute and for each value the bidder can specify price as a piecewise linear function of quantity. The suppliers can express volume discount bargaining strategy and economies of scale, using the above price function. The buyer can include several business rules and purchasing policies as side constraints in the optimization problem to evaluate the winning bids. We propose the use of goal programming techniques to solve the bid evaluation problem.

1 Introduction

The Internet and Internet-based technologies are impacting businesses in many ways. With the increasing pressure that companies are experiencing as markets become more global, Internet continues to play a critical role to speed up operations and to cut costs. e-Procurement is an Internet-based business process for obtaining materials and services and managing their inflow into the organization. This involves identifying, evaluating, negotiating and configuring optimal groupings of suppliers' bids, which are received in response to the buying organization's Request-for-Quote (RFQ).

The business logic used in current e-Procurement systems can be broadly categorized as: *reverse auctions, multiattribute auctions, optimization techniques,* and *configurable bids.* Reverse auctions select the supplier with the lowest bid price. They are simple, inexpensive and many commercial systems like SpeedBuy (http://www.edeal.com) can be deployed within hours. Though reverse auctions are successful in various cases [7], competing on price alone make the suppliers feel de-branded and commoditized. Moreover, as sourced goods increase in complexity, several aspects of supplier performance, such as quality, lead time, on-time delivery, etc. also need to be addressed.

---

* This research is supported in part by IBM Research Fellowship awarded to the first author by IBM India Research Laboratory, New Delhi.

K. Bauknecht, A Min Tjoa, G. Quirchmayr (Eds.): EC-Web 2003, LNCS 2738, pp. 6–15, 2003.

Multiattribute auctions based on multiattribute utility theory (MAUT) [8] for e-Procurement were first proposed in [1]. Multicriteria decision analysis techniques like MAUT are also used in bid analysis products from Frictionless Commerce (http://www.frictionless.com) and Moai Technologies (http://www.moai.čom). The buyer assigns weights to the attributes indicating their relative importance and has a scoring function for each attribute. A bid is scored by combining the weights and the scoring function in the weighted additive fashion [1, 3] and the bids are ranked according to their score. IBM Research's ABSolute decision engine [5] provides to buyers, in addition to standard scoring mechanisms, an interactive visual analysis capability that enable buyers to view, explore, search, compare and classify submitted bids. An English auction protocol for multiattribute items was proposed in [3], which again uses a weighted additive scoring function to rank the bids. *Multicriteria auction* proposed in [4] is an iterative auction which allows incomparability between bids and the sellers *increment* their bid value by bidding *more* in at least one attribute. To automate negotiations in multiattribute auctions, *configurable bids* were proposed in [2]. In configurable bids of [2], bidders can specify multiple values for each attribute and price markups for each attribute value, and the buyer can configure the bid optimally by choosing appropriate values for the attributes.

e-Procurement systems that promise a productive strategic sourcing should also take into account various business rules and purchasing policies like *exclusion constraints* (e.g. goods of supplier X cannot be received from location A), *aggregation constraints* (e.g. at least two and at most five winning suppliers), *exposure constraints* (e.g. at most forty percentage of total business to any supplier), *business objective constraints* (e.g. overall quality factor must at least be seven), etc. The above mentioned multiattribute auction mechanisms cannot handle such policies. Many commercial bid analysis products from companies like Emptoris (http://www.emptoris.com), Rapt (http://www.rapt.com), and Mindflow (http://www.mindflow.com) use optimization techniques like linear programming and constraint programming, where the business rules are added as constraints to the optimization problem. However, they are limited by their inability to express multiple objectives of the buyer in the bid evaluation process. The general objective considered in these models is *minimizing cost*, whereas other possible objectives like *minimizing lead time, maximizing on-time delivery*, and *minimizing part failure rate* are not considered.

From the above discussion, we can infer that the important requirements of an e-Procurement system are: (1) allowing bidders to bid on *multiple attributes*, (2) a rich bidding language like *configurable bids* to automate negotiations across multiple bids, (3) flexibility for allowing *business rules* and *purchasing logic* in bid evaluation, and (4) bid evaluation using *multiple criteria*. The current solutions satisfy only some of the above requirements. Bid optimization and analysis tool from Perfect (http://www.perfect.com) provides flexibility for incorporating business rules and uses multicriteria decision analysis technique for handling multiple attributes, whereas the multiattribute auctions proposed in [2] uses in addition configurable bids. In this paper, we develop an e-Procurement system for trading multiple units of a single good (not combinatorial) that meets all the above requirements. Our proposal differs from the current approaches in the following ways: (1) the configurable bids are more general, namely piecewise linear functions of price on quantity for each value of each attribute, (2) the bid evaluation problem is modeled as a multiple criteria optimization problem, and (3) the use of goal programming (GP) techniques for bid evaluation.

2   The Model

The e-Procurement system considered in this paper consists of the following phases: (1) *RFQ generation* and distribution by the buyer, (2) sealed *bid submission* by the suppliers during a predefined bidding interval, and (3) *bid evaluation* by the buyer (after the expiration of the bidding interval) to determine the winning bids and their optimal configuration. To illustrate the practical applicability of the model, we will use the procurement of single lens reflexive cameras as an example procurement scenario.

2.1   RFQ Generation

The RFQ consists of two parts: the header and the feature [5]. The header part contains relevant information such as an identifier, product name, issue date, quote due date, and the buyer information. The feature part specifies the set of attributes U and the admissible domain of E_u of each attribute $u \in U$.

RFQ Notation

$[\underline{b}, \overline{b}]$	Requested quantity range $(\underline{b} \le \overline{b})$
U	Set of attributes
E_u	Admissible domain of values for attribute $u \in U$

The attributes can consist of product features (like lens focus, flash), service features (like lead time, warranty), and supplier features (like stock values, manufacturing capacity). We allow for goods to be sourced from multiple suppliers. The domain E_u of attribute u can be either discrete (like varieties of flashes) or continuous (like on-time delivery probability).

2.2   Bid Submission

Configurable bids proposed in [2] allow bidders to specify multiple values for each attribute and markup prices (unit price) for each attribute value. The buyer can configure the product by choosing appropriate attribute values that suits his interests and demand. In this paper we consider configurable bids of following nature: for each attribute u, the bid j can specify a set of values $W_u \subseteq E_u$ and

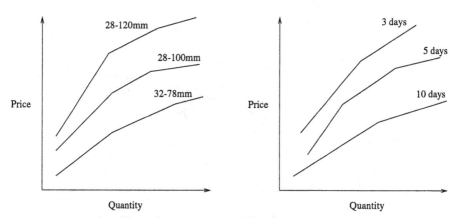

Fig. 1. Configurable bids for attributes *Lens Focus* and *Lead Time*

a continuous piecewise linear price function Q_{juw} defined over quantity range $[\underline{a}_{juw}, \overline{a}_{juw}]$ for each value $w \in W_u$. In [2] the price function of any attribute is linear with quantity, whereas we generalize it to piecewise linear. This generalization is reasonable as the cost structure of product features like accessories (lens focus and flash) and service features like lead time (transportation mode) depend on quantity. The supplier can easily express the volume discount bargaining strategy and the economies of scale using the above structure. Figure 1 illustrates the possible cost functions for attributes lens focus and lead time, for the camera procurement example.

Notation for Bid j

W_u	Set of values for each attribute $u \in U$
$[\underline{a}_{juw}, \overline{a}_{juw}]$	Supply quantity range available for attribute u with value w
Q_{juw}	Piecewise linear cost function for attribute u with value w defined over $[\underline{a}_{juw}, \overline{a}_{juw}]$
Q_{juw}	$\equiv ((\delta^0_{juw}, \dots, \delta^{l(juw)}_{juw}), (\beta^1_{juw}, \dots, \beta^{l(juw)}_{juw}), n_{juw})$
$l(juw)$	Number of piecewise linear segments in Q_{juw}
δ^*_{juw}	Breakpoints at which the slope of Q_{juw} changes
β^s_{juw}	Slope of Q_{juw} on $(\delta^{s-1}_{juw}, \delta^s_{juw})$
n_{juw}	Price at $\underline{a}_{juw}$

The price function Q_{juw} shown in Figure 2 is the total price (not the unit price) at which the bidder is willing to trade as the function of quantity. The function shown in the figure can be compactly represented by tuples of break points and slopes $((\delta^0_{juw}, \dots, \delta^{l(juw)}_{juw}), (\beta^1_{juw}, \dots, \beta^{l(juw)}_{juw}), n_{juw})$ where $l(juw)$ is the number of linear segments and n_{juw} is the price at $\delta^0_{juw} = \underline{a}_{juw}$. The break points $\delta^0_{juw} (= \underline{a}_{juw}), \delta^1_{juw}, \dots, \delta^{l(juw)}_{juw} (= \overline{a}_{juw})$ denote the points where the slope

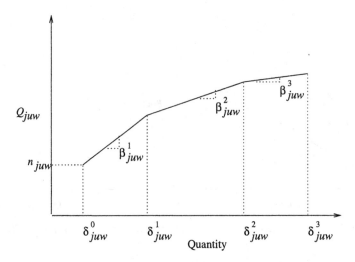

Fig. 2. Piecewise linear price function Q_{juw}

changes and the corresponding slopes are $\beta^1_{juw}, \ldots, \beta^{l(juw)}_{juw}$. The set W_u is assumed to be always finite even if the domain E_u is infinite. For example the attribute *on-time delivery probability* can have $E_u = [0.8, 1]$, but the bidder can specify only finite possible values $W_u = \{0.8, 0.85, 0.9\}$. The Q_{juw} shown in Figure 2 is for only one value w of attribute u. The bidder specifies such function for each $w \in W_u$ as shown in Figure 1. If the buyer configures the bid j with q_{juw} units for $w \in W_u$ and $u \in U$, then the total cost of procurement from bid j is:

$$Cost_j = \sum_{u \in U} \sum_{w \in W_u} Q_{juw}(q_{juw}) \tag{1}$$

The implicit assumption in the above cost structure is that the attributes are independent of each other except with the quantity procured.

2.3   Bid Evaluation

Multiple attributes can be used both in bid definition and bid evaluation. Multiple attributes in bid definition (or RFQ) provides a means to specify complex product or service. In bid evaluation, the buyer can use multiple attributes to select the winning bidders. We will use the phrases *criteria* for bid evaluation and *attributes* for bid definition. In our camera procurement example, the *attributes* defined in the RFQ are like lens focus, flash, lead time, and warranty, and the *criteria* used by the buyer for evaluating the bids can be like total cost, lead time and supplier credibility. With the above norm established, a criterion for evaluating the bids may consist of zero, one or many attributes defined in the RFQ. For example, the criterion that the winning supplier should have high *credibility*, is not an attribute defined in the RFQ but a private information known to the buyer. On the other hand, minimizing cost of procurement is a function of many attributes defined in the RFQ.

Evaluating the bids by taking into account different factors is a multiple criteria decision making (MCDM) problem. MCDM has two parts: *multiattribute decision analysis* and *multiple criteria optimization*. Multiattribute decision analysis techniques like MAUT [8] are often applicable to problems with a small number of alternatives that are to be ordered according to different attributes. In MAUT, a multiattribute utility function representing the preferences of the decision maker is elicited and is used to order the set of feasible alternatives. When the decision space has very large or infinite number of alternatives, the practical possibility of obtaining a reliable representation of the decision maker's multiattribute utility function is limited. Multiple criteria optimization [10] techniques are used in such scenarios where explicit knowledge of the utility function is not available. The bid evaluation problem of [1, 3] to rank the bids was solved by MAUT of multiattribute decision analysis. In our case, the decision space is large (many winning bids and multiple possible configurations for each winning bid) and it is difficult for the buyer to explicitly specify his utility function over such a large space. We model the bid evaluation problem as a linear integer multiple criteria optimization problem.

Decision Variables in Bid Evaluation

$x^s_{juw} \in \mathcal{Z}^+$, amount of goods bought from bid j with value w for attribute u
with unit cost β^s_{juw}

$X_j \quad \in \mathcal{Z}^+$, amount of goods bought from bid j

$z_j \quad \in \{0,1\}$, indicator variable that selects/rejects bid j

$d^s_{juw} \in \{0,1\}$, binary variable that assumes 1 if goods are bought from linear
segment s of Q_{juw}

$D_{juw} \in \{0,1\}$, indicator variable for choosing value w for attribute u of bid j

Constraints We first formulate the constraints in configuring the bids. The amount of goods from bid j with value w for attribute u has to be chosen considering the price function Q_{juw}. As shown in Figure 1, this function can be nonlinear. Using the piecewise linear nature, we can represent them using linear inequalities. The quantity range $[\underline{a}_{juw}, \overline{a}_{juw}]$ is split into $l(juw)$ segments, where the quantity range in segment s is $[0, \delta^s_{juw} - \delta^{s-1}_{juw}]$. For the above conversion to make sense, whenever $x^s_{juw} > 0$, then $d^{s'}_{juw} = 1$ and $x^{s'}_{juw} = \delta^{s'}_{juw} - \delta^{s'-1}_{juw}$ for $s' < s$. The following are the set of linear constraints that handle the quantity selection:

$$x^s_{juw} \leq d^s_{juw} \left(\delta^s_{juw} - \delta^{s-1}_{juw}\right) \quad s = 1, \ldots, l(juw) \tag{2}$$

$$x^s_{juw} \geq d^{s+1}_{juw} \left(\delta^s_{juw} - \delta^{s-1}_{juw}\right) \quad s = 1, \ldots, l(juw) - 1 \tag{3}$$

The above set of constraints are for each $w \in W_u$ of every attribute $u \in U$ of every bid j. Following constraints handle the consistency and logical relationships among the variables, and the demand requirements:

$$\sum_{s=1}^{l(juw)} d_{juw}^s \leq l(juw) D_{juw} \; \forall w \in W_u, \; \forall u \in U, \; \forall j \tag{4}$$

$$\sum_{w \in W_u} D_{juw} = z_j \qquad \forall u \in U, \; \forall j \tag{5}$$

$$\sum_{w \in W_u} \sum_{s=1}^{l(juw)} x_{juw}^s = X_j \; \forall u \in U, \; \forall j \tag{6}$$

$$\underline{b} \leq \sum_j X_j \leq \overline{b} \tag{7}$$

There may be several business rules and purchasing policies like restriction on the number of suppliers, allowable quantity in a single shipment, homogeneity of attributes [2], etc. Such business rules can be added as side constraints. Furthermore, we have not considered any interaction effects between the attributes for simplicity. There may be logical restrictions on the allowable combination of the attribute values and the supplier may give special discounts on certain attribute combinations. These logical constraints were modeled as linear constraints in [2] which can be added with the above set of constraints.

Objectives Let $\mathbf{X}$ denote the vector of decision variables. Then the bid evaluation problem is the following multiple criteria optimization problem with G linear objectives:

$$\min \{\mathbf{c_1 X} = f_1\}$$
$$\min \{\mathbf{c_2 X} = f_2\}$$
$$\vdots$$
$$\min \{\mathbf{c_G X} = f_G\}$$
$$\text{s.t.} \quad \mathbf{X} \in F$$

where F is the set of feasible solutions defined by the constraints. Without loss of generality all the objectives considered were of minimization type. The objectives of the buyer can be like *minimize total-cost, minimize lead-time, maximize on-time-delivery probability*, etc. For example, the objective of minimizing total cost is:

$$\min \sum_j \sum_{u \in U} \sum_{w \in W_u} (n_{juw} D_{juw} + \sum_{s=1}^{l(juw)} \beta_{juw}^s x_{juw}^s)$$

3   Bid Evaluation Using Goal Programming

Multiple criteria optimization problems can be solved using various techniques like GP, vector maximization, and compromise programming [9, 10]. The idea of GP is to establish a goal level of achievement for each criterion. For example, the cost minimization criterion can be converted to the goal: $cost \leq \$20,000$, where $\$20,000$ is the target or aspiration level. When the target levels are set for all criteria, GP finds a solution that simultaneously satisfies all the goals as *closely* as possible: it is more of a *satisficing* technique than an *optimizing* technique. The goal g can be any of the following types: *greater than or equal to* ($\geq t_g$), *less than or equal to* ($\leq t_g$), *equality* ($= t_g$), and *range* ($\in [\underline{t}_g, \overline{t}_g]$), where t_g's are the target or aspiration levels. Without loss of generality let us assume the *less than or equal to* goal structure for the procurement problem:

$$\text{goal } \{\mathbf{c_1 X} = f_1\} \qquad (f_1 \leq t_1)$$
$$\vdots \tag{8}$$
$$\text{goal } \{\mathbf{c_G X} = f_G\} \qquad (f_G \leq t_G)$$
$$\text{s.t.} \quad \mathbf{X} \in F$$

For each goal, there will be a deviational variable that measures the deviation from the target level and these give rise to new goal constraints:

$$\mathbf{c_1 X} - \gamma_1 \leq t_1$$
$$\vdots \tag{9}$$
$$\mathbf{c_G X} - \gamma_G \leq t_G$$
$$\gamma_g \geq 0 \quad g = 1, \ldots, G$$

The γ_g measures the deviation away from the goal g. The above goal constraints do not restrict the original feasible region F. In effect, they augment the feasible region by casting F into a higher dimensional space [10]. The GP techniques vary by the way the deviational variables are used to find the final solution. We present in this paper three popular GP techniques for solving the bid evaluation problem.

3.1 Weighted GP

Weighted GP (WGP) or *Archimedian* GP uses weights, given by the decision maker, to penalize the *undesirable* deviational variables. The GP [8] will then be the following single objective programming problem:

$$\min \sum_g w_g \gamma_g \tag{10}$$
$$\text{s.t. [9] and } \mathbf{X} \in F$$

The goals are generally incommensurable (for example, cost minimization is measured in currency whereas minimizing lead time is measured in days) and the above objective function is meaningless as the weighted summation includes different units. The most intuitive and simplest way would be to express γ_g as percentage rather than as absolute value [9]. For e-Procurement, the buyer can specify minimum and maximum deviations allowed for a goal and then use the percentage of deviation in the objective function.

3.2   Lexicographic GP

In lexicographic GP (LGP) or *preemptive* GP, the goals are grouped according to priorities. The goals at level l are considered to be infinitely more important than the goals at level $l+1$. First the problem is solved only for the goal(s) at the highest level (if there are more than one goal at a level, then they are aggregated as in WGP). If there are alternate optimal solutions, then the next level goals are optimized over the alternate optimal solutions. This procedure stops when all levels are optimized or at some level which has no alternate optimal solutions. Unlike WGP, LGP requires several iterations.

3.3   Interactive Sequential GP

The main aim of multiple criteria optimization techniques is to work without the explicit knowledge of the utility function and to search the *space of trade-offs* among the conflicting objectives. The *interactive procedures* that involve human intervention have proven to be most effective in searching trade-off space for a final solution [10]. Interactive sequential GP (ISGP), proposed in [6], combines and extends the attractive features of both GP and interactive solution approaches. ISGP is based on the implicit assumption that the decision maker can adjust the desired goals through an iterative learning process based on information in a set of solutions. The information provided in each iteration is contained in a current best compromise solution (solution provided by GP solved using the goals given in previous iteration), and a set of alternate solutions which are compromise solutions obtained if each goal is satisfied serially. Using this information, the decision maker can set new goal levels. The algorithm terminates when a satisfactory solution is found. If the goal levels are changed in a consistent manner then the number of iterations is expected to be small (refer to [6] for a detailed algorithm).

4   Conclusions and Future Work

e-Procurement is an Internet-based business process for obtaining materials and services and managing their inflow into the organization. In this paper we proposed an e-Procurement system with the following properties: (1) allowing the bidders to bid on multiple attributes, (2) a rich bidding language to automate negotiations across multiple bids, (3) flexibility for allowing business rules and purchasing logic in bid evaluation, and (4) bid evaluation using multiple criteria. The proposed piecewise linear cost structure of the configurable bids allows bidders to specify price functions that closely capture their volume discount bargaining strategy and also the economies of scale. The bid evaluation problem is formulated as a multiple criteria linear integer programming problem, where the criteria for bid evaluation are formulated as objectives and the business rules can be included as side constraints. We proposed the use of goal programming to solve the above optimization problem. The approach is practically appealing as it does not demand explicit knowledge of utility functions but simple aspiration or target levels for each criterion. Moreover, the GP techniques proposed can be solved using the existing commercial integer optimization solvers. The immediate requirement is the investigation of computational complexity and implementation feasibility of the above system. Another prospective research direction is the use of game theoretic and experimental analysis to determine whether the information about goal levels, allowable deviations, and weights for the different criteria should be disclosed by the buyer.

References

[1] Bichler, M., Kaukal, M., and Segev, A.: Multi-attribute Auctions for Electronic Procurement. In: Proceedings of the First IBM IAC Workshop on Internet Based Negotiation Technologies, Yorktown Heights, NY, USA, (March 1999) 18-19

[2] Bichler, M., Kalagnanam, J., and Lee, H. S.: RECO: Representation and Evaluation of Configurable Offers. IBM Research Report RC 22288 (2002)

[3] David, E., Azoulay-Schwartz, R., and Kraus, S.: An English Auction Protocol for Multi-Attribute Items. In: Padget, J. A., Shehory, O., *et. al* (eds.): Agent-Mediated Electronic Commerce. Lecture Notes in Computer Science, Vol. 2531. Springer-Verlag (2002) 52-68

[4] De Smet, Y.: Multicriteria Auctions: an introduction. In: Proceedings of the 14th Mini-EURO Conference, HCP 2003 (2003)

[5] Lee, J., Bichler, M., Verma, S., and Lee, H. S.: Design and Implementation of an Interactive Visual Analysis System for e-Sourcing (2001)

[6] Masud, A. S. and Hwang, C. L.: Interactive Sequential Goal Programming. Journal of Operational Research Society. 32 (1981) 391-400

[7] Moser, E. P.: E-Procurement – Successfully Using and Managing Reverse Auctions. Pharmaceutical Technology (April 2002) 101-105

[8] Raiffa H., Keeney R.: Decisions with Multiple Objectives. Wiley, New York (1976)

[9] Romero, C.: Handbook of Critical Issues in Goal Programming. Pergamon Press, Oxford (1991)

[10] Steuer, R. E.: Multiple Criteria Optimization: Theory, Computation and Application. John Wiley and Sons, New York (1986)

Increasing Realized Revenue via Profit Redistribution: A Variant of Online Dutch Auction

Marin Markov[1], Penka Markova[2], Mukesh Mohania[3] and Yahiko Kambayashi[4]

[1] Computer Science Department
Purdue University, West Lafayette, IN, USA
markovm@cs.purdue.edu
[2] Departments of Electrical Engineering and Computer Science
Stanford University, Stanford, CA, USA
penka@stanford.edu
[3] IBM – India Research Laboratory
Block I – IIT Hauz Khas, New Delhi – 110016, India
mkmukesh@in.ibm.com
[4] Department of Social Informatics
Kyoto University, Kyoto, Japan
yahiko@kuis.kyoto-u.ac.jp

Abstract. In this paper we propose a new variant of a Dutch auction with the aim of maximizing the revenue realized from the auctioneer by shifting to him some of the profits from the highest bidders, while at the same time preserving the allocative efficiency achieved in the Dutch auctions. We then develop and analyze a model for this variant that corresponds to a multi-unit, progressively ascending, lowest winning bid open auction. The proposed model achieves the objective through the use of coupons, which may be introduced during the auction and drive up the lowest winning price and respectively the total revenue. This variant of a Dutch auction guarantees that the sum of the face value of all used coupons will be less than (or equal to) the increase in the revenue caused by their use. As a result the realized revenue will be higher than the revenue received in a typical Dutch auction with the same settings.

1   Introduction

The demand for greater consumer influence on the price setting process had brought profound changes to the existing business-to-consumer (B2C) relations in recent years. One expression of these metamorphoses has been the development of online auctions and their strong growth in popularity as a means of doing business in the electronic marketplace. One particular kind in that growing category had been the so-called Dutch auction.

The Dutch auction is a multi-item, progressively ascending, uniform price, lowest winning bid, open auction, and is ooffered by e-commerce sites such as eBay[1],

K. Bauknecht, A Min Tjoa, G. Quirchmayr (Eds.): EC-Web 2003, LNCS 2738, pp. 16–25, 2003.
© Springer-Verlag Berlin Heidelberg 2003

Amazon and others[4,5]. Typically, the auctioneer or the seller has a number of identical items to be auctioned. The customers or the bidders engage in a continuous process of bidding over the items until the time for the auction expires. At the end of the auction, all winning bidders purchase their items at the lowest winning bid price. The realized revenue R is given by

$$R = Q \times P_w$$

where Q is the quantity of the items and P_w is the lowest winning price.

For example, lets assume that there are 4 items (Q = 4) and 5 bidders each of whom bids with a corresponding tuple (Price, Quantity), and that at the end of the auction the sorted final price bids are $\{(6, 1)_1, (5.5, 2)_2, (5, 1)_3, (4.8, 2)_4, (4, 1)_5\}$. In this particular case the 4 items will be sold to the top three bidders. The price paid for each of the items will be $5, since this is the lowest winning bid (bidder 3). The total revenue realized by the auctioneer is $R = Q \times P_w = 4 \times \$5 = \$20$.

In overview, Dutch auctions benefit the buyer more than any other auction format in that they allow all buyers to buy the same item at the lowest successful bid price. That said, not only would a buyer not regret bidding higher than someone else, but he would also have a stronger sense of equality and satisfaction. However, it is also a zero-sum game - any surplus for the customer leads to a revenue loss for the auctioneer. And although customer satisfaction is central in the seller's goals, revenue growth is not at a lower priority. Therefore there is an incentive to increase the revenue even if it comes for the price of somewhat lower customer satisfaction.

In this paper we present a variation of the Dutch auction which increases the revenue of the seller by shifting to him some of the profits normally realized by the buyers with the highest bids. That shift of the profit is achieved by the use of bid price coupons, which may be offered to the bidders during the auction. The significant novelty is that depending on the coupon value some of the bidders would have no incentives to use them. Since the winning price is expected to shift by the coupon value, this would lead to an overall increase in the revenue of the auctioneer.

Another aspect of our model is that we achieve the goal of increasing the revenue with minimum impact on customer satisfaction. The reason for such minimized impact is that only a minority of the bidders would incur differences in the final outcome compared to their ordinary Dutch auction results. Furthermore, since we are targeting the highest bidders, their loss of surplus will be comparatively the smallest possible among all the buyers.

During the rest of the paper we will make a generalization concerning the number of items a customer bids on, in that we will assume he only bids for 1 item. The number of items a buyer bids for is irrelevant to our study, in the sense that multiple items can be divided and seen as different bids. The assumption allows us to avoid getting into the details of how the auction is set - whether bidders can bid with one price for certain number of items, or they can put different bids on each item they desire, etc. Similarly we will ignore the issue of the last winning bid order (when there are not enough units to satisfy the last bid quantity). There are different rules governing the handling of such special cases, and they might or might not influence the winning price. However, in either case they do not directly affect the improved performance of our model over the original Dutch auction model.

There has been little previous work on the use of coupons in auctions, especially on their use in Dutch auctions. As far as we are aware there is no previous work on a bid price coupons for auctions. The closest research done on the topic is described in [7]. However, it uses a winning price coupon and has a very different approach for redistributing the surplus. The assumption of the authors in [7] (based on market analysis) is that some of the customers would act rather irrationally and not use the coupons, thus losing revenue by doing so. In our approach we rely on the fact that rational bidders would use the coupons to improve their chances at getting the desired item(s). The increase in revenue will come from bidders who will not be able to use the coupons because of their high bids. The introduction of coupons could also trigger the so-called deal-effect (promotions affect sales positively) and result in higher than the coupon value bid increases [6]. In case some of the bidders do not use the coupons, that would further increase the auctioneer surplus.

We have laid out the rest of the paper as follows. In the next section we detail the specifics of the auction customer interface. Section 3 presents the model for issuing the coupons and illustrates the benefits of such action. A simple realistic example is presented in Section 4, and we conclude in Section 5.

2   The Auction Customer Interface

The auction customer interface consists of an online "auction page" and a coupon repository. The online "auction page" is a web page specifically created for a certain product type and auction. The user navigates through the page where textual and/or pictorial description of the product along with other information appears. The bidding history is also visible on the page, or there is a direct link to it. Also on that page, there is a link to the coupon repository, or possibly directly to the coupon available for the particular auction.

The "coupon repository" is a web page containing all coupons that are applicable at the time of loading the page, as well as coupons which will be used for auctions starting later on. The users can acquire coupons (free of charge) by clicking on the coupon buttons. Once acquired, the coupon would either be redeemed automatically from the auctioneer at the end of the particular auction, or would expire worthlessly if the bidder has not won. The coupon would also be worthless if the bidding price of the user is greater than the sum of the lowest winning bid price and the coupon value. The final price paid per unit is the minimum of the lowest winning bid price and the bidder's price minus the coupon value. It is also possible, but not mandatory, that the coupon value might increase during the auction. Such an increase would automatically increase all the bids that at that time use the coupons. Decreasing the coupon value is not allowed once the auction has started.

If at a certain point a losing bidder who does not use a coupon could potentially become a winning bidder by acquiring one, the auctioneer has the incentive and might remind the buyer that he could increase his chances to have a winning bid by using the coupon for that auction. As we will see in the next section, it is in the seller's best interest that most of the bidders do use the coupons.

3   The Model

As stated above, the Dutch auction benefits the buyer but this leads to a certain disadvantage for the seller. Our variant of Dutch auction achieves further redistribution of the surplus, thus increasing the revenue for the seller and correspondingly decreasing the surplus for some of the bidders. Since the outcome of the model is the same for most of the customers, their behavior is not expected to change compared to their behavior in ordinary Dutch auction, with the only exception that here some of the bidders would acquire and use a coupon for the item they bid on.

As we saw earlier in the Dutch auction model the revenue is determined by the formula $R = Q \times P_w$. Since the quantity Q is fixed, the only way to increase the revenue is by increasing the winning price P_w, i.e. the winning price bid has to go up. Let P_i be the i-th highest bid in the bidding history. Without loss of generality we will use only the bid price to distinguish between the bidders – if certain record needs to be kept, we could simply add another number to indicate the bidder id.

The usefullness of the coupons becomes obvious once a somewhat stable state can be observed in the bid history. As soon as the auction reaches some kind of equilibrium, say $P_1 \geq P_2 \geq \ldots \geq P_k$, then as long as $P_1 > P_w$ there would exist an incentive for the auctioneer to introduce a coupon. If at that moment he introduces a coupon **on the bidding price** with a face value of $C < P_1 - P_w$, then upon rational play the bidders would increase their bids by C, thus effectively shifting all the revenue significant bids by C. Since many of the bids would be much higher than $P_w + C$, some of the bidders would not be able to use the coupon at the end, therefore increasing the realized revenue of the seller.

The details of the reasoning for the bids increase is as follows:

- We will consider specifically 2 sets of bidders: set U consisting of the bidders with bids lower than P_w, but within range C from P_w, and set M consisting of the bidders with bids higher than P_w, but within range C from it.
- The players in set U (all of whom are currently non-winning) would use their coupons in hope of increasing their chances to win, i.e. they would increase their bids by the coupon value C so that they could potentially displace a currently winning bid. Since they would use the coupon at the end, their final price would be the same as what they have already bid. (For example, if the current bids are the ones on Table 1 in Section 4, if a $2 coupon is made available bidder #6 would use it, thus increasing his effective bid to $27.00 and displacing bidder #5 as long as bidder #5 doesn't use the coupon.)
- The players in set M (all of whom are currently winning) would also use the coupon and increase their bids in order to preserve the status quo, i.e. to retain their winning position. By increasing their bid by C their cost on the item would remain the same, so they have no reason not to bid higher. A consideration is to increase the bid less than the coupon value, but that would pose the risk of someone else outbidding them, so this is highly unlikely to be the case.

- The winning bidders with bids higher or equal to $P_w + C$ do not need to use the coupon, however it is likely that many of them might do so, in order to preserve their ranking in the winning bids.
- The non-winning bidders that have bid prices lower than $P_w - C$ would not benefit even if they use the coupons, therefore they are excluded from further considerations.

Finally, after the players have increased their bids, the new revenue will be calculated using the following formula:

$$R' = Q \times Pw + \sum_{i=1}^{Q-1} \min(C, Pi - Pw - C) > R$$

Or, the new revenue R' would equals the previous revenue plus the additional revenue obtained from the bidders that had bids much higher than the winning price and were not able to use the coupon or at least part of its value.

[Note: $Pi \geq Pw + C$, i.e. $Pi - Pw - C \geq 0$ in the general case. The only possibility to have it negative would be if the current lowest winning bid does not bid higher. However that is unlikely, given that the bidders in M will always bid higher in order not to be outbid from the bidders in U]

In order to maximize the revenue, the coupon value has to be very carefully chosen. The coupon value analysis is as follow:

Lets denote the average of player $i's$ bid and the winning price to be M_i:

$$Mi = \frac{Pi - Pw}{2}$$

The revenue increase for player i will be denoted by δi.

For each individual player, we have 3 general cases for the C value:

1) $C = Mi$

   In this case the surplus is evenly split between the seller and the buyer, therefore the revenue will increase by C.

   $$\delta i = C$$

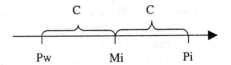

2) $C > Mi$

   There are two subcases:

   - $C > Pi-Pw$

     in this case the bidder will bid $\lambda i = C - (Pi-Pw)$ higher, i.e. he would be guaranteed to be at the last winning bid position, have the other players not raised their bids more than C. In this case the bidder will use the coupon, thus again he will pay Pw, i.e. he will not trigger revenue increase.

$$\delta i = 0$$

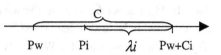

- $C < Pi-Pw$

  the bidder has no incentive to bid higher, since he would still have a winning bid. Once he uses the coupon, the revenue increase will be

$$\delta i = (Pi - Pw) - C$$

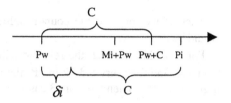

3) $C < Mi$

   In that case the auctioneer clearly does not maximize the surplus he could realize from this player, since any coupon value greater than C but smaller than Mi will increase the revenue. Nevertheless the increase of revenue in this case is

$$\delta i = C$$

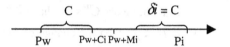

As we see, the maximum possible revenue increased realized for any winning player Pi is achieved for coupon value equal to Mi. For any value of C greater than M_i we will have lower revenue than we could achieve. Analogously for any value smaller than M_i we know that we could improve by increasing the coupon value. Since P_1 is the highest and P_{w-1} the lowest winning bids different than P_w, then the maximizing value for the coupon used in the auction is between M_1 and M_w.

The function for the increase of revenue therefore has domain $[M_1, M_w]$ and the increase is:

$$I = \sum_{i=1}^{Q-1} \min(C, Pi - Pw - C) > 0$$

To maximize the revenue, we find the coupon value that will yield the largest increase. We first proof that there exist maximizing coupon value $C' = Mj$ where $j \in [1, w-1]$ and then we show how to find it.

Proof: Assume that there exists C' such that $C' \notin Mk$ where $k \in [1, w-1]$.

Since the domain is $[M_1, M_w]$, then C' lies between two averages Mi and Mj such that Mi<Mj. Let set Ω contain the winning bids higher than Pw+C', and Ψ contain the winning bids lower than Pw+C'. With α we denote the size of set Ω and β would be the size of Ψ. We let $\Delta = Mj - C'$ be the increase needed for C' to equals Mj and $\Theta = C' - Mi$ be the decrease needed for the coupon to equal Mi.

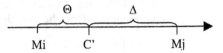

Then if we increase the coupon value by Δ to $Ci' = \Delta + C' = Mi$ the effect would be as follows:

For any bid Pk in Ω the revenue will increase because the coupon value is less than Mk, and for every bid Pk in Ψ the revenue will decrease because value of C' is higher than Mk. Then there are 3 cases:

1) If $\alpha = \beta$ then the overall change is $I = \alpha \cdot \Delta - \beta \cdot \Delta = 0$, thus Ci'=C', i.e. $\exists\, C'$ such that $C' \in Mk$ for $k \in [1, w-1]$.

2) If $\alpha > \beta$ then the change in the revenue will be $I = \alpha \cdot \Delta - \beta \cdot \Delta > 0$ which would cause an increase in the revenue. However, that is a contradiction on the claim that C' is the maximizing coupon value, thus for $\alpha > \beta$ there could not exist C' such that $C' \notin Mk$ values.

3) If $\alpha < \beta$ then the change of revenue will be $I = \alpha \cdot \Delta - \beta \cdot \Delta < 0$ which is consistent with the claim that C' is a maximum. However, if we subtract Θ from C', i.e. we decrease the coupon value, the change in revenue will be $I = \beta \cdot \Theta - \alpha \cdot \Theta > 0$ which causes increase, therefore contradicting the claim that C' is the maximizing coupon value. Thus there could not exist C' outside Mk for $\alpha < \beta$.

From the three cases above we see that any maximizing value C' will be equal to some average Mk where $k \in [1, w-1]$. □

As we proved that there always exist $C' \in Mk$, we can find it by calculating the revenue change for all possible coupon values such that $C' \in Mi, i \in [1, w-1]$. Then we find the maximum of those values and that is the maximizing coupon value for the auction [See example in section 5].

The allocative efficiency for the auction as defined in [5] is:

$$\eta = \frac{(\text{Total auction revenue} + \text{Total consumer surplus})}{(\text{Benchmark revenue assuming full demand revelation})}$$

Since there is a direct transferring of surplus from the highest bidders to the auctioneer the sum of the revenue and consumer surplus remains the same. The revenue assuming full demand revelation also does not change thus η remains constant. Therefore the allocation efficiency achieved for the Dutch auction will be preserved in the variant we developed.

In this model rather than relying on irrational behavior of the bidders (not used coupons, etc.), we assume a 'rational' behavior, i.e. it is in their best interest that they get the coupons and raise their bids accordingly. Since the bidding price distribution is most dense around the winning price, the currently losing bidders in that range will all use the coupons with the goal of outbidding the currently winning bidders immediately above the winning price, which in turn will bid in order to preserve the status quo. That competition effectively leads to the shift of the winning price by the coupon value. In the case that some of the winning bidders do not increase their bids or make increase with less than the coupon value that could lead to lower efficiency, but those bids would also mean losses of winning bids for some of those bidders. Therefore that is unfavorable outcome and such behavior is highly unlikely. As mentioned earlier, in such cases the auctioneer do has interest that the bidders bid higher, and appropriate reminders would be send to those that could use the coupons and remain with winning bids.

4   A Realistic Example

We use data taken from [1] to evaluate the gains using the proposed model.

Table 1. Time bids at time t. Total items being auctioned is Q = 5

Bidder ID	Bid price (in $)	Quantity
1	30.50	1
2	30.07	1
3	26.00	1
4	25.01	1
5	25.01	1
6	25.00	1
7	25.00	1
8	24.50	1
9	24.00	1
10	24.00	1
11	23.50	1
12	22.50	1

In this example the first five bidders will win and the revenue will be R=P5*Q = 25.01*5 = $125.05.

Since bidders 4 and 5 have the winning price, they could not contribute to the bid increase, thus they have been omitted from the calculations.

As described by the model in last section, we find the coupon values for the corresponding bids by calculating the Pi-Pw for each winning bid greater than Pw (the Pw bids would not increase the revenue since they will increase to Pw' but will use the coupon for the same value of the increase) and then calculating Ci to be half of that – Ci = (Pi-Pw)/2. The revenue increase for each coupon is equal to the old revenue plus the value of the coupons that have not been used by the players, including those that have been used with part of their value. The coupon value chosen for the auction is the on that will produce the greatest increase of the revenue.

Bidder ID	Bid Price	Pi-Pw	Coupon value	New Revenue
1	30.50	5.49	2.75	R' = R + 2.75+2.31 = 125.05 + 5.06 = $130.11 (+4.05%)
2	30.07	5.06	2.53	R' = R + 2.32+2.32 = 125.05 + 4.64 = $129.69 (+3.71%)
3	26.00	0.99	0.45	R' = R + 3*0.45 = 125.05 + 1.35 = $126.40 (+1.08%)

As we could see, the maximizing coupon value is C = 2.75, i.e. a 4.05% increase in the realized revenue of the auctioneer.

That said, the seller will issue a coupon of value C = 2.75 and the bidding history would change as follows:

Bidder Id	Original Bid Price (in $)	New Bid Price	Original Final Price paid	New Final Price paid	Revenue Increase
1	30.50	30.50	25.01	30.50-2.75=27.75	2.74
2	30.07	30.07	25.01	30.07-2.75=27.32	2.31
3	26.00	27.76	25.01	27.76-2.75=25.01	0
4	25.01	27.76	25.01	27.76-2.75=25.01	0
5	25.01	27.76	25.01	27.76-2.75=25.01	0
Total			125.05	130.11	5.05

5   Conclusion

Dutch auctions are considered to be one of the most beneficial multi-item auction types for the customers. Their model brings greater revenue that other multi-item auctions and at the same time the customers are more satisfied with their purchases. However, the auctioneer receives lower revenue due to the uniform price that all the customers pay. We proposed a variant of the Dutch auction that shifts to the seller some of that excessive surplus realized by the buyers. The reallocation of the profit is achieved by the use of a bid price coupon, which may be introduced during the auction. By facilitating this coupon the winning price for the particular auction effectively increases by the coupon value, thus driving up the revenue. Since part of the winning bidders would use the coupon at the end of the auction, the total realized revenue increase comes from the fraction of the bidders who had too high bids and do not use the coupon, as well as from those who used only part of its value. However, most of the buyers pay the same price and the increase in the price paid by the highest bidders is still small, therefore there will be little if any dissatisfaction from the customers.

In this paper we presented a model for using the bid price coupon as a tool in increasing the revenue of the seller. We also outlined the algorithm to determine the coupon value maximizing that increase. Other approaches and uses of the bid price coupons will be examined in detail in future research.

References

[1] http://www.ebay.com

[2] L. Ausubel and J. Schwartz: The Ascending Auction Paradox. Working Paper, University of Maryland , 1999.

[3] V. Bansal, R. Garg: Efficiency and Price Discovery in Multi-item Auctions. ACM SigEcom Exchanges, Vol. 2(1), pp. 26-32, 2001.

[4] R. Bapna, P. Goes, and A. Gupta: A theoretical and empirical investigation of multi-item online auctions. Information Technology and Management, Vol. 1, pp. 1-23, 2000.

[5] R. Bapna, P. Goes, and A, Gupta: Comparative analysis of multi-item online auctions: evidence from the laboratory. Decision Support Systems, Vol. 32, pp. 135-153, 2001.

[6] P.K. Kopalle, C.F. Mela, and L. Marsh: The dynamic effect of discounting of auction under single and multi-unit demand. Marketing Science, Vol. 18, No. 3, 1999.

[7] R. Kothari, M. Mohania, and Y. Kambayashi: Increasing Realized Revenue in a Web Based Dutch Auction. Lecture Notes in Computer Science, Vol. 2455, pp. 7-16, 2002. Springer-Verlag, Berlin Heidelberg New York.

[8] A.M. Manelli, M. Sefton and B.S. Wilner: Multi-Unit Auctions: A Comparison of Static and Dynamic Mechanisms. Working Paper, University of Nottingham, September 2000.

[9] P. Milgrom: Auctions and bidding: A primer. Journal of Economic Perspectives, Vol. 3, pp. 3-22, 1989.

[10] W. Vickrey: Counter-speculation, auctions, and competitive sealed tenders. Journal of Finance, Vol. 41, pp. 8-37, 1961.

[11] G. Demange, D. Gale, and M. Sotomayor: Multi-item Auctions. Journal of Political Economy, Vol. 94, pp.863-872, 1986

A Combinatorial Exchange
for Autonomous Traders

Andreas Tanner and Gero Mühl

Intelligent Networks and Management of Distributed Systems
Faculty for Electrical Engineering and Computer Science
Berlin University of Technology
10587 Berlin, Germany
{tanner,gmuehl}@ivs.tu-berlin.de

Abstract. Combinatorial exchanges have attracted much attention recently. However, to this point there is no generally accepted payment allocation algorithm capable of clearing combinatorial exchanges. The Vickrey-Groves-Clarke mechanism, which has been successfully applied in the case of one-sided combinatorial auctions, is not budget-balanced when generalized to two-sided auctions.

We present a new model for an auction market with autonomous traders and conjunctive combinatorial bids that allows formulation of some fairness properties applicable when pricing is based solely on the buyer's bids. We then give an example payment allocation algorithm that implements these properties.

Keywords: Combinatorial Exchanges

1 Introduction

Internet auctions are one of the success stories of electronic commerce. Retrospectively, this is altogether not surprising, as modern economy produces a large turnover of goods; and a large quantity of high value goods is not allocated by traditional retail commerce. Apparently, there is a demand for a highly efficient secondary retail market, which specializes in transactions between partners that participate in the exchange market spontaneously. Auctions are an elegant way to tackle the problem of pricing and, properly used, can lead to efficient allocation of goods.

Bidding on single goods reflects utilities without interdependencies. If bundling goods increases utility (*complementary utility*), or goods can substitute each other, bidding on single goods involves a risk of incomplete or redundant purchases. Combinatorial auctions allow bidders to express more complex utility functions. Winner determination and payment allocation for one-sided combinatorial auctions is possible using the Vickrey-Grove-Clarke (VGC) mechanism. There is much work about complexity issues of VGC mechanism [3, 7, 9, 10]. While the exact problem is computationally intractable, there are approximation

K. Bauknecht, A Min Tjoa, G. Quirchmayr (Eds.): EC-Web 2003, LNCS 2738, pp. 26–36, 2003.
© Springer-Verlag Berlin Heidelberg 2003

algorithms [14] with good stochastic performance and accuracy whose availability encourages us to leave complexity issues aside in this paper. VGC leads to efficient, budget-balanced, individual rational, and even incentive compatible goods and payment distributions [7]. However, revealing true utilities looses much attractivity if bids under false names are possible. Sakurai et al. [8] and Yokoo et al. [12] show that there is no protocol with the properties stated above that is robust against false name bids. With these results in mind, Yokoo et al. [13] present a protocol which is budget-balanced, individual rational, and robust against false name bids, giving up on efficiency.

One-sided combinatorial auctions allocate goods from *one seller* to *many bidders*. For Internet auctions, we need to model a market with *many sellers* and *many bidders*. This is a special case of a *combinatorial exchange* or *double auction* [11]. The Vickrey-Groves-Clarke mechanism (VGC) when applied to combinatorial exchanges preserves all above properties except budget balance. Unfortunately, there is a grave negative result [5, 6] about protocols for combinatorial exchanges stating that there is no protocol for double auctions that is efficient, budget-balanced, and individual rational.

Internet auctions have a couple of peculiarities that are so far rarely considered in connection with double sided auctions: Both sellers and buyers enter their bids continuously, sellers specify auction clearing times (there is no market inherent clearing rhythm), there is virtually no mean against false name bids, sellers may wish to leave the pricing completely to the buyer's side, i.e., offer their goods without asking any specific price, and winner determination and payment allocation should benefit all individual traders. We present protocols and algorithms for clearing, winner determination, and pricing double auctions in this setting which exhibit the following properties: They allow auctioneers to start auctions at *any time* and determine their life span, bids can be *aggregated* over some time, a price for every successful auction is based *solely on the collected bids*, bidding under false names is possible only with a *risk of forfeiting trade*, and pricing is *budget-balanced* and *individual rational*.

The rest of the paper is structured as follows: Sect. 2 deals with winner determination and pricing algorithms. In subsection 2.1 we present a model that serves as the basis for further discussion. In subsection 2.2 we suggest some properties of payment allocation we consider necessary in the context of auctions with autonomous traders. We then present an algorithm that incorporates these properties. In Sect. 3 we develop a complete auction protocol capable of clearing combinatorial auctions with autonomous traders, including policies for submittable bids, clearing times, winner determination, and pricing.

2 Winner Determination and Pricing

2.1 The Model

We now introduce the notation used by our model in detail. Our market trades with n goods. The state of the market is comprised by an arbitrary number of *bids* which are tuples $b = (k_1^b, \ldots, k_n^b, p^b)$ with $k_i^b \in \{-1, 0, 1\}$ and $p^b \in \mathbb{R}$. We distinguish between *auction bids* (or *auctions*) and *buying bids*, respectively:

Auction bids represent the offered goods. For auction bids all k_i^b's are 0 except one, and this one has value -1. An auction bid b is *offering good i* if $k_i^b = -1$. Furthermore, we impose $p^b = 0$ for auction bids as any pricing is left to the buyers. This means that b is auctioning the good "with no price limits". As goods are unique, we assume that for any good i, there is exactly one auction bid a_i offering i.

Buying bids represent the demanded goods. For buying bids all k_i^b's have either value 0 or 1. A buying bid b is *bidding for goods* $\{i_1, \ldots, i_x\}$ if $k_i^b = 1$ for all $i \in \{i_1, \ldots, i_x\}$ and $k_i^b = 0$ otherwise. Here, p^b is always positive (due to the free disposal requirement negative bids are not reasonable) and represents the amount the buyer is willing to pay for the goods he is bidding for. For example, the buying bid $(0, 1, 1, 20)$ means that a buyer is willing to pay a maximum of 20 for goods 2 and 3.

Let $\mathcal{A}$ and $\mathcal{B}$ be the sets of auction and buying bids in the market, respectively.

Definition 1 (Winner Determination Algorithm). *A winner determination algorithm takes as input a set $\mathcal{A}$ of auction bids and a set $\mathcal{B}$ of buying bids. From this, it computes an* acceptance function $\chi : \mathcal{B} \mapsto \{0, 1\}$ *with*

$$\sum_{b = (k_1^b, \ldots, k_n^b, p^b) \in \mathcal{B}} \chi(b) \cdot k_i^b \leq 1 \tag{1}$$

for all $i = 1, \ldots, n$. A bid $b \in \mathcal{B}$ is accepted *by the algorithm if $\chi(b) = 1$, and* rejected *otherwise.*

Informally spoken, a winner determination algorithm determines for each offered good at most one buying bid that is accepted.

Definition 2 (Payment Allocation Algorithm). *A payment allocation algorithm takes as input a set $\mathcal{A}$ of auction bids, a set $\mathcal{B}$ of buying bids, and an acceptance function χ. From this, the algorithm computes a* payment allocation function $p : \mathcal{A} \cup \mathcal{B} \mapsto \mathbb{R}$.

A payment allocation function p satisfies budget-balance *if*

$$\sum_{c \in \mathcal{A} \cup \mathcal{B}} p(c) \geq 0$$

It is individual rational, *iff for all bids b with $\chi(b) = 1$ we have $p(b) \leq p^b$, and for all b with $\chi(b) = 0$ we have $p(b) = 0$.*

Hence, a payment allocation algorithm assigns to each accepted bid its corresponding revenue which is positive for a buying bid and negative for an auction bid. The following example describes the well-known two-sided VGC mechanism in our setting:

Example 1 (Two-sided Vickrey-Groves-Clarke). Let χ be maximizing the sum of revenues

$$V^* = \sum_{b \in \mathcal{B}} \chi(b) \cdot p^b \tag{2}$$

subject to condition (1). Let for $c \in \mathcal{A} \cup \mathcal{B}$ be $(V_{-c})^*$ be the maximized sum of revenues for auctions and bids $\mathcal{A} \cup \mathcal{B} \setminus \{c\}$, and let

$$\Delta_{\text{vick},c} = V^* - (V_{-c})^* \tag{3}$$

be the *Vickrey discount* for c. Let the payment function p be defined by

$$p(a) = -\Delta_{\text{vick},a} \quad \text{for } a \in \mathcal{A} \tag{4}$$
$$p(b) = p^b - \Delta_{\text{vick},b} \quad \text{for } b \in \mathcal{B}. \tag{5}$$

Our model describes a variant of a *clearing house* or *periodic double auction* that admits combinatorial bids. However, we impose a number of additional constraints that reduce the complexity of the model to make it more feasible in practice:

- uniqueness of goods: exactly one copy of every good is being auctioned
- no substitutions – no OR-connected bids
- only pure offers and pure buying bids
- only buying bids can be combinatorial
- free disposal is possible (i.e., the seller can keep his good)
- price is computed only from buying bids, i.e., sellers do not specify any price

We do not consider OR-connected bids because it is hard to mediate between interest conflicts arising between auctioneers when there are not enough bids to sell all items.

No Minimum Prices. The last constraint implies that sellers cannot specify a minimum price as precondition for selling their good. Note that while two-sided VGC does allow sellers to specify a negative utility for the sale of a good, this is not really a *minimum price condition* because specification of negative utility from a sale changes payment allocation even when more than the lost utility is given to the seller anyway, as demonstrated by the following example:

Example 2. Let there be two auctions and one bid of 10 for both items together. Suppose first that the auctions are without minimum price.

According to VGC, all auctions and bids would be matched, the following payments would be allocated: the auctioneers would receive a payment of 10 each, while the bidder's payment would be 0.

Suppose now that the first auctioneer would demand a minimum price of 7. VGC would then allocate a payment of 10 to this auctioneer, while the other one's payment would shrink to 7.

This contrasts with one-sided Vickrey payment or plain pay-your-bid payment for single item auctions where specifying a minimum price does not change payment allocation once the payment surpasses the minimum price.

In many settings, specification of minimum prices is not required by the sellers. In particular, this holds when the market has sufficient liquidity, or when the fixed - variable cost ratio is high. In this paper, we therefore refrain from considering minimum prices. We nevertheless acknowledge the problem of respecting minimum prices in the above sense, while preserving other desired properties of the payment allocation algorithm, an interesting question for further research.

2.2 Pricing

Pricing in a combinatorial exchange is far from being trivial. Following [6] and [4], we take individual rationality and budget-balance as hard constraints that our payment allocation algorithm must satisfy. Besides these two constraints, we consider a couple of other properties being useful which are discussed in the following.

Respecting Single Item Bids. By accepting combinatorial bids, we expect more willingness from the bidders to bid and therefore an increased total revenue. Thus, a reasonable constraint for the payment allocation is that no bidder looses from combinatorial bids:

Definition 3. *A payment allocation function p respects single item bids, if for all auctions a and for all buying bids b that bid only for a, we have $p(a) \geq p^b$.*

Proposition 1. *VGC respects single item bids.*

Proof. Let a be an auction bid, and b_a be a bid bidding for a only. Let V_{-a} be the maximized revenue of all auctions except a. By accepting bid b_a, the revenue increased by p^{b_a}. So a increases the total revenue by at least p^{b_a}, and therefore a's Vickrey discount is at least p^{b_a}.   □

Parkes et al. [6] present some VGC-based budget-balanced payment rules. The rules are generated by minimizing the deviation from the Vickrey payments measured in various distance function. Practically, they divide the available revenue [1] between all traders, using various division rules:

- The *Equal* payment rule splits the available surplus equally among all sellers and buyers.
- The *Fractional* payment rule splits the available surplus according to the fractional share from the total Vickrey discount of every agent
- *Small* starts awarding discounts to the traders with small Δ_{vick} and proceeds until the available discount is used up.

---

[1] Remember that we have no minimum prices in our setting

While VGC does respect single item bids, these variants of VGC do not as is illustrated in the following example:

Example 3. Let there be auctions and bids

$$a_1 : (-1, 0, 0)$$
$$a_2 : (0, -1, 0)$$
$$b_1 : (1, 1, 60)$$
$$b_2 : (1, 0, 50)$$
$$b_3 : (1, 0, 49)$$

a_1, a_2 and b_1 are accepted. The available surplus is 60. The Vickrey discounts for the agents are:

$$a_1 : 60$$
$$a_2 : 10$$
$$b_1 : 10$$

The *Equal* payment rule splits the available surplus equally, so a_1 and a_2 receive 20 each, and b_1 pay 40. However, a_1 would prefer to accept bid b_2 with a surplus of 50, leaving a_1 with a share of 25 under the *Equal* payment rule. The *Fractional* payment rule leads to the following payments: a_1 receives $60 \cdot 60/80 = 45$, a_2 receives $10 \cdot 60/80 = 7.5$, b_1 pays $60 - 10 \cdot 60/80 = 52.5$. If however a_1 accepts bid b_2, a surplus of 50 results. The Vickrey discount of a_1 is 50, of b_2 is only 1, and a_1 receives a payment of $50 \cdot 49/50 = 49$ under the *Fractional* rule. Similarly, examples for the other payment rules (*Threshold, Small, Large,* and *Reverse* payment) can be constructed showing that they do not respect single item bids.

We are tempted to generalize single item bid respect to "all bids respect" by demanding that for all bids b

$$\sum_{1 \le i \le n} k_i^b \cdot p(a_i) \ge p^b \tag{6}$$

where a_i is the auctioning bid of the auction offering good i. Basically, this would mean that every auction can choose its favorite bid to be accepted. However, we can easily see that this is incompatible with budget-balance:

Example 4. Let there be three auctions, and let there be bids as follows:

$$b_1 : (1, 1, 0, 10)$$
$$b_2 : (1, 0, 1, 10)$$
$$b_3 : (0, 1, 1, 10)$$

The maximal revenue is 10 as only one bid can be accepted. To satisfy the three inequalities resulting from (6), we would need a revenue of 15, however.

No Loss from a Bid. Next, we desire that no auctioneer ever looses from a bid for his good. Formally, that means:

Definition 4. *A payment allocation algorithm has the* no loss from a bid *property if the following holds: Let $\mathcal{A}$ be a set of auctions and let $\mathcal{B}$ be a set of bids. Let $a \in \mathcal{A}$ be an auction offering good i and let $b = (k_1^b, \ldots, k_n^b, p^b)$ be a bid with $k_i^b = 1$. Let p be the payment allocation function for $(\mathcal{A}, \mathcal{B})$ and let p' be the payment allocation function of $(\mathcal{A}, \mathcal{B} \cup \{b\})$. Then $p'(a) \geq p(a)$.*

Note that VGC does satisfy the no loss from a bid property. However, the *Small* rule of [6] does not:

Example 5. Let there be two auctions a_1 and a_2, and bids as follows:

$$b_1 : (1, 1, 100)$$
$$b_2 : (1, 1, 99)$$
$$b_3 : (1, 0, 1)$$

Then bid b_1 is accepted, $V^* = 100$, and

$$\Delta_{\text{vick},a_1} = 100$$
$$\Delta_{\text{vick},a_2} = 99$$
$$\Delta_{\text{vick},b_1} = 1$$

and the *Small* rule allocated discounts to b_1 and a_2, leaving a_2 with a payment of 99 and a_1 with no payment. Suppose now that there is an additional bid

$$b_4 : (0, 1, 2)$$

Now the discount goes to b_1 and a_1, leaving a_2 with no payment. So a_2 suffered from an additional bid.

Our Payment Allocation Algorithm Now, we present a budget-balanced, individual rational, single item bid respecting payment allocation algorithm with the no loss from a bid property.

Algorithm SBNL

Input: $\mathcal{A}$ – a set of auctions, $\mathcal{B}$ – a set of bids
Output: a payment allocation function $p : \mathcal{A} \mapsto \mathbb{R}$.

- *Step 1.* Compute the item allocation that maximizes revenue. Let V be the maximized revenue.
- *Step 2.* For an auction a offering good i, let $b_a = (0, \ldots, 0, 1, \ldots, 0, p^{b_a})$ be the highest bid bidding for good i only. If there is no such a bid, define $p^{b_a} = 0$. Let $V_{\text{single}} = \sum_{a \in \mathcal{A}} p^{b_a}$.

- *Step 3.* Solve the linear programming problem

$$\text{Minimize } Y = \sum_{1 \le i \le n} y^i$$

such that

$$(\forall_{b \in \mathcal{B}}) \sum_{1 \le i \le n} k_i^b \cdot y^i \ge p^b$$

Among all optimal $(y^i : 1 \le i \le n)$, choose the one that minimizes $\sum_i (y^i)^2$.
- *Step 4.* Let $Q = \frac{V - V_{\text{single}}}{Y - V_{\text{single}}}$.
- *Step 5.* For all auctions $a \in \mathcal{A}$, let $p(a) = p^{b_a} + (y^i - p^{b_a}) \cdot Q$, where a is offering good i.

Our pricing mechanism let successful buyers pay exactly the amount of their bid. Winner determination takes place subject to maximizing total revenue. The pricing mechanism distributes this revenue among the sellers.

Proposition 2. *Algorithm SBNL satisfies budget-balance and individual rationality, respects single item bids, and has the no loss from a bid property.*

Proof. Obviously the algorithm is individual rational. The sum of the payments is

$$\sum_a p(a) = \sum_a p^{b_a} + Q \cdot \left(\sum_i y^i - \sum_a p^{b_a} \right) = V_{\text{single}} + Q \cdot (Y - V_{\text{single}}) = V$$

and this proves budget-balance. Step 2 ensures single item bid respect. For the no loss from a bid property, note that we always have $Y \ge V$, and this implies $Q < 1$. Thus an additional single item bid for a can only increase a's payment. The argument for an additional combinatorial bid is similar.   □

3   Auction Protocols

After developing a pricing scheme, we will now turn our attention to the *clearing policy* of an auction protocol which defines at what times auction and buying bids are being matched.

3.1   Clearing Policies

Our market model allows continuous publication of new auctions. There are various clearing strategies in use for continuous double auction markets [1, 2]:

- *Continuous clearing.* The trade occurs as soon matching bids and asks arrive.
- *Periodic or random clearing.* The trade occurs at certain times (periodic, random, or a combination of both), bids and asks are matched subject to certain optimality conditions (e.g. maximizing surplus or throughput).

The first policy does not make any sense in an multiple round auction without minimum prices as simply any bid matches. Both random and periodic clearing result in auctions with diverging time spans during which they invite bids. We find it desirable to allow the auctioneer to control the live span of his auction. Therefore, we use another clearing policy that we now describe.

Every auction announcement $\mathbf{a} = (a^{\mathbf{a}}, t^{\mathbf{a}}_{\text{earliest}}, t^{\mathbf{a}}_{\text{latest}})$ contains the following information:

- the auction bid $a^{\mathbf{a}}$, i.e. identity of the good
- the earliest commit time $t^{\mathbf{a}}_{\text{earliest}}$
- the latest commit time $t^{\mathbf{a}}_{\text{latest}}$

Every auction goes through the following sequential phases:

- *Pre-commit*. Bids for this auction can be submitted. The auction will not commit to accepting any of them.
- *Allow-commit*. Bids for this auction can be submitted. The auction house can request that the auction commits to a bid if that bid wins by the winner determination algorithm applied by the auction house. In this case, all unsuccessful bids for this auction are uncommited, and the auction transits into Expired state.
- *Force-commit*. No bids can be submitted anymore for this auction. The winner determination algorithm determines the winner among all bids that bid for auctions in Allow-commit or Force-commit stage. Non-accepted bids for this auction are uncommitted. Transit into Expired state.
- *Expired*. The auction is finished, the winner was determined and the payment computed.

A bid is *committable* if all auctions the bid is bidding for are in Allow-commit or Force-commit state. Pre-commit for an auction $\mathbf{a}$ is the time before $t^{\mathbf{a}}_{\text{earliest}}$. The Allow-commit phase lasts from $t^{\mathbf{a}}_{\text{earliest}}$ to $t^{\mathbf{a}}_{\text{latest}}$ and are followed by the Force-commit and Expired phases. This policy lets the auctioneer control the live span of his auction. A combinatorial bid can be accepted if the commit phases of all auctions bidden for do overlap. The larger the Allow-commit phase, the more inviting his auction will be toward combinatorial bids.

3.2 Putting Things Together

Now, we present our protocol for implementation of combinatorial auctions for autonomous traders.

- At any time t, auctions $\mathbf{a} = (a^{\mathbf{a}}, t^{\mathbf{a}}_{\text{earliest}}, t^{\mathbf{a}}_{\text{latest}})$ can be announced, as long as $t < t^{\mathbf{a}}_{\text{earliest}} \leq t^{\mathbf{a}}_{\text{latest}}$.
- Bids can be submitted at any time as long all auctions the bid is bidding for are in Pre-commit or in Allow-commit phase, and the bid is qualified in the sense that at the time when the bid is submitted, there is a possible continuation of the auction in which this bid will win. The latter condition prohibits risklessly "pushing up" prices.

– For any auction **a**: At Force-commit time, define $\mathcal{B}$ to be the set of all committable bids for **a**, and let $\mathcal{A}$ be the set of the corresponding auctions. Compute the revenue-maximizing allocation. Request commit from all auctions with a winning bid. Apply algorithm SBNL to compute payments.

4   Conclusion and Future Work

In this paper we have presented a new model for combinatorial exchanges with autonomous traders and conjunctive bids that exhibits some properties useful for implementing E-commerce platforms for autonomous traders. In particular, we have given an example pricing scheme satisfying these properties. However, we are still looking for a pricing scheme applicable to combinatorial exchanges with autonomous traders, based solely on buyer's bids, that allows specification of minimum prices.

Currently, we are implementing a prototype of an auction platform that incorporates several pricing strategies including the one proposed in this paper. Based upon this implementation we will carry out simulations to corroborate the validity of our approach.

Acknowledgments

The authors wish to thank Kurt Geihs and Andreas Ulbrich for fruitful discussion.

References

[1] Deutsche Börse Group. *Xetra Stock Market Model*, 2001. http://www.xetra.de.
[2] Deutsche Börse Group. *Xetra Warrant Market Model*, 2001. http://www.xetra.de.
[3] S. DeVries and R. Vohra. Combinatorial auctions: A survey. *INFORMS Journal on Computing*, 15, 2003.
[4] S. Kameshwaran and Y. Narahari. A new approach to the design of electronic exchanges. In *EC-Web 2002*, pages 27–36. LNCS 2455, 2002.
[5] Robert B. Myerson and Mark A. Satterthwaite. Efficient mechanisms for bilateral trading. *Journal of Economic Theory*, 28:265–281, 1983.
[6] David C. Parkes, Jayant Kalagnanam, and Marta Eso. Achieving budget-balance with vickrey-based payment schemes in exchanges. Technical report, IBM Research Report, MAR 2002.
[7] Michael H. Rothkopf, Alexander Pekec, and Ronald M. Harstad. Computationally managable combinatorial auctions. *Management Science*, 44:1131–1147, 1998.
[8] Y Sakurai, M. Yokoo, and S. Matsubara. A limitation of the generalized vickrey auction in electronic commerce. In *Proc. AAAI-99*, pages 86–92, Orlando, FL, 1999.
[9] T. Sandholm, S. Suri, A. Gilpin, and D. Levine. Winner determination in combinatorial auction generalizations, 2001.

[10] Tuomas Sandholm and Subhash Suri. Improved algorithms for optimal winner determination in combinatorial auctions and generalizations. In *AAAI/IAAI*, pages 90–97, 2000.

[11] P. Wurman, W. Walsh, and M. Wellman. Flexible double auctions for electronic commerce: Theory and implementation. *Decision Support Systems*, 24:17–27, 1998.

[12] M. Yokoo, Y. Sakurai, and S. Matsubara. The effect of false name declarations in mechanism design: Towards collective decision making on the internet. In *Proc. 20th International Conference on Distributed Computing Systems (ICDCS-2000)*, pages 146–153, 2000.

[13] Makoto Yokoo, Yuko Sakurai, and Shigeo Matsubara. Robust combinatorial auction protocol against false-name bids. *Artificial Intelligence*, 130:167–181, 2001.

[14] Edo Zurel and Noam Nisan. An efficient approximate allocation algorithm for combinatorial auctions. In *Proceedings of the 3rd ACM conference on Electronic Commerce*, pages 125–136. ACM Press, 2001.

A Web Services Matchmaking Engine for Web Services

Christian Facciorusso[1], Simon Field[2], Rainer Hauser[1], Yigal Hoffner[1],
Robert Humbel[1], René Pawlitzek[1], Walid Rjaibi[3] and Christine Siminitz[4]

[1] IBM Research, Zurich Research Laboratory, 8803 Rüschlikon, Switzerland
yho@zurich.ibm.com
[2] Matching Systems Ltd., Switzerland
spf@matchingsystems.com
[3] IBM Toronto Software Laboratory, Canada
wrjaibi@ca.ibm.com
[4] IBM Storage Software Products Division, NC, USA
csi@us.ibm.com

Abstract. This paper concentrates on the issue of matchmaking in the context of web services. It provides a brief review of the difference between directory services and matchmaking facilities and explains why directories such as UDDI are important but insufficient for web services and need to be complemented with advanced matchmaking facilities. It discusses the requirements that web services place on matchmaking, namely symmetry of information exchange, the ability of each party to specify requirements of the other party, rich languages to describe services and their consumers as well as their demands, and the ability to dynamically update and configure what is being offered. These requirements are addressed by the **Web Services Matchmaking Engine (WSME)** - a powerful matchmaking engine capable of matching complex entities, and a Data Dictionary Tool for defining the language of the corresponding matchmaking process. The WSME matchmaking process and property and rules languages are described. An example of how a dynamic market for selling and buying Capacitors can be created with WSME is given. Finally, conclusions and possible future avenues of work are presented.

1   Finding Compatible Web Services and Consumers

Ensuring that web service providers and consumers are compatible business partners will become increasingly important as web service technology and its exploitation for serious business purposes become more pervasive. In this context, several issues are of paramount importance:

- Facilitating the specification of complex information models by developing appropriate languages for describing services as well as consumers.

K. Bauknecht, A Min Tjoa, G. Quirchmayr (Eds.): EC-Web 2003, LNCS 2738, pp. 37–49, 2003.

- Reaching agreements in specific domains on service and consumer definitions that can be used to create internal or external markets.
- Building matchmaking facilities that can deal with the complexity of service and consumer descriptions and the two-way relationship between them.

This paper concentrates on the issue of matchmaking in the context of web services. It provides a brief review of the difference between directory services and matchmaking facilities and explains why directories such as UDDI are important but insufficient for web services and need to be complemented with advanced matchmaking facilities. It discusses the requirements that web services place on matchmaking, namely symmetry of information exchange, the ability of each party to specify requirements of the other party, rich languages to describe services and their consumers as well as their demands, and the ability to dynamically update and configure what is being offered. These requirements are addressed by the **Web Services Matchmaking Engine** (WSME) - a powerful Matchmaking Engine capable of matching complex entities, and a *Data Dictionary Tool* for defining the language of the corresponding matchmaking process. The WSME matchmaking process and property and rules languages are described. An example of how a dynamic market for selling and buying Capacitors can be created with WSME is given. Finally, conclusions and possible future avenues of work are presented.

2   Directories and Matchmaking Facilities

Most early directories provided a mapping from a name to an address. With work on distributed system in the 80's, directories changed to a more advanced form where the search is not carried out for a specific entry by name but rather based on its attributes. In other words, it is possible to search for something of a certain 'type' with certain attributes, rather than having to know its name.

Along with the notions of searching by attribute rather than by name, came the idea of qualifying the search with an expression, referring to the description of the service and acting as a requirement. This was the basis of the ANSAware Trader [ANSAware 93] and the CORBA/ODP Trading Service [OMG 96, ODP 95]. Such services can be regarded as an advanced form of a directory, a 'Yellow Pages' in an electronic form. One shortcoming of those directories is that they provide an asymmetric form of selection, where the selection criteria are provided entirely by the potential consumer.

Work on advanced **Matchmaking Engines (MMEs)** extended these ideas by introducing symmetry into the selection process [HOFFNER 00]. Here, the potential consumer is able to provide a description of themselves and what they offer as consumers. This allows the service provider to specify their demands of the potential consumer, thereby being able to select them, just as the consumer selects the service. This advanced form of matchmaking opened up ways of dynamically updating the description of the service at matchmaking rather than advertising time. By coupling this with the notion of symmetry, directories can be more dynamic and facilitate the configuration of what is being offered to suit the needs of the specific consumer, thus introducing dynamic customisation.

To summarise - it is possible to discern a spectrum ranging from the simplest form of a directory, implemented as a simple query to a database, and the matchmaking process with its multi-dimensions: symmetry, rich description and requirement languages, dynamic configuration, etc. [FIELD 02].

A service often put forward as a directory for web services, is the **Universal Description, Discovery and Integration** or **UDDI** [UDDI 2002] [Graham 01a, b]. UDDI is an example of a directory aimed at to publishing and discovering information about Web services and serves as a repository for web service descriptions with a limited search capability. UDDI is an 'open' directory, in the sense that the contents are available to everybody who has access to the directory. Restrictions can be placed on the availability of advertisements, but only on the basis of the identity of the consumer, not by using any attributes that may describe them. The search is thus asymmetric - only consumers have the ability to express their requirements of the service and its provider, but not vice versa. UDDI is a static directory - its content is specified at advertising time and can only be updated if an advertisement is replaced by a new one.

We claim that if web services are to be used as the building blocks for creating internal as well as cross organisational business processes, then UDDI may serve as a basic introduction service but lacks the matchmaking capability essential for selecting the right web services and consumers.

3   Requirements of Web Service Matchmaking

3.1   Symmetry of Information Exchange and Selection

The process of finding the right service for a given service consumer is not necessarily a one-way process of having the consumer state their requirements and select a winner from the matching services. Service providers may wish to receive information from the consumer before deciding to make a particular service available to that consumer. The input to the matchmaking process (Figure 1) therefore needs to take account of the demands of both service consumers and providers, relating these demands to information provided by both parties - resulting in a symmetric exchange by service consumers and providers of both information and demands.

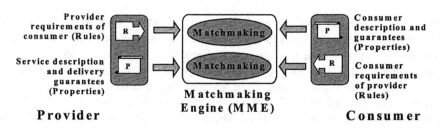

Fig. 1. The two-way exchange of information and selection in the symmetric matchmaking process

3.2   Powerful Description and Requirement Language

Powerful languages are needed to describe complex services and similarly, powerful languages are needed to describe complex compatibility criteria, i.e. requirements relating to the description of the other party. The matchmaking language has to be sufficiently powerful to express the type of properties that organisations are looking for when selecting a partner. The descriptions created with this language should be capable of using complex data structures to express complex attributes such as delivery dates with price tags attached and associated Quality of Service parameters, etc. Similarly there is a need to be able to access these complex data structures and extract the relevant information from them within a specification of requirements or rules.

3.3   Dynamic Service Configuration

Matchmaking should allow a provider to describe its offer as a skeleton or a generating function that can be used to offer different service configurations. This can be done in the form of a reference to an external system as shown in Figure 2 or alternatively by supplying a script that the MME can evaluate locally. Thus, the MME can generate the specific service offer dynamically at the time of searching. Input to the process that provides the specific value can contain information from the potential consumer, each service configuration can be tailored to the circumstances of the specific consumer. This is needed for several reasons:

- It facilitates an up-to-date description of the service where service properties such as the cost, availability or quality of service may be subject to variations. Such variations can for example be due to load, maintenance, etc.
- It provides a way to specify a range of services without having to enumerate all the options associated with them in the MME as this may overload the MME.
- It provides a way to configure the service and the consumer application according to the needs and properties of the both parties. This facilitates personalisation of the service.
- It provides a way to integrate existing applications that reside on back-end systems (legacy problem).

4   The WSME Matchmaking Process

The rest of this article contains a description of **WSME - Web Services Matchmaking Engine.** It is deployed as a web service that can receive queries and advertisements and also provide management and auxiliary functionality. **WSME** combines Internet and web-technology to create, operate and manage an arena where advertisements can be placed and where searches can be conducted with the aim of pairing compatible entities. WSME is a web service supplied as part of the IBM **Web Services Tool Kit (WSTK)** [ALPHAWORKS 02] and can be downloaded and used for experimentation.

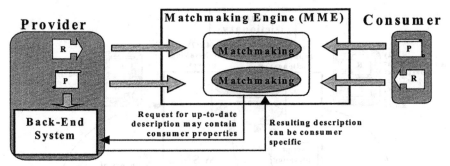

Fig. 2. Dynamic properties can be updated when needed during the matchmaking process either by the script provided to the MME or by calling a Back-end system on the provider side

The WSME has its origins in ANSAware [ANSAWare 93], and the CORBA/ODP Trading Service standard [OMG 96] [ODP 95]. It addresses all the requirements discussed in Section 3.

The WSME matchmaking process is a two-way or symmetric process: each party to the process submits a description of itself and the requirements it has of the other party. The evaluation of those demands against the descriptions of the two parties during the matchmaking process, allows both parties to "select" each other.

The WSME matchmaking process is shown in Figure 3:

1. The Data Dictionary is injected into the WSME through one of its web service operations, so that the WSME can check the correctness of properties and rules submitted to it.
2. The **Advertisement submission** is sent from the provider to the WSME and is long lived, remaining in the WSME until it is explicitly withdrawn by the provider or until the application server is stopped. The advertisement contains the following information:

   - **MyType**: this specifies the advertisement record-type.
   - **YourType**: this specifies the record-type expected to be submitted by the consumer query.
   - **Properties**: a list of the properties defined as MyType. Some of those properties may be defined as dynamic properties by the provider. In this case, the provider will have to supply a script to evaluate the property in the WSME, or alternatively, a reference to a location where the value of the property can be obtained, e.g. a back-end system. The specification of the dynamic property may define the consumer properties that have to be supplied for it to be resolved.
   - **Rules**: what the provider requires from the consumer.

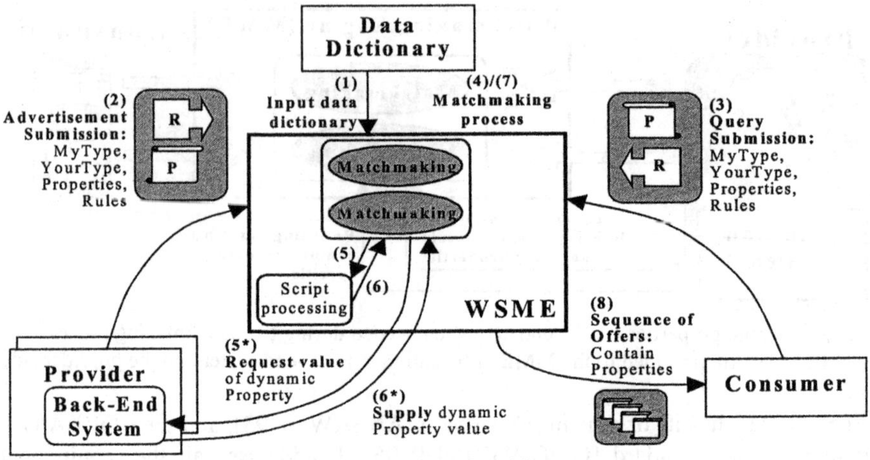

Fig- 3. The WSME matchmaking process

3. A **Query submission** is sent from the consumer to the WSME and is transient, terminating after initiating the matchmaking process and bringing it to its conclusion. The query contains the following information:

- **MyType**: this specifies the query record-type.
- **YourType**: this specifies the provider's advertisement record-type that the query is looking for.
- **Properties**: a list of the properties defined as MyType.
- **Rules**: what the consumer requires from the provider.

4. The **Matchmaking Process** brings together matching advertisements and queries by applying the rules of each party to the description of the other party. The WSME matchmaking process is a two-way or symmetric process carrying out the evaluation of the demands of each party against the descriptions of the other parties, thus allowing both parties to 'select' each other.

5. If during the matchmaking process, a rule that contains a reference to a provider **dynamic property** is evaluated, a call will be made to resolve the property's value. Depending on what the advertisement contained, this will either be a call to a script in the WSME, or an external call to a provider back-end system, for example (5*). In either case, the input to the request may contain details of the consumer query currently being matched. This allows the reply to be specially tailored to that particular consumer.

6. The value of the dynamic property is returned to the matchmaking process, either from the local script or from the external location (6*).

7. The matchmaking process can now continue. If more dynamic properties are encountered, steps (5) and (6) are repeated. A matching advertisement is called an offer. If more than one offer is available, they are collected together.

8. Zero, one or more matching **offers** are sent to the consumer.

The exchange of information coupled with the ability to apply rules to the submitted information requires that the parties in a matchmaking space agree on a common language and terminology. The results of this agreement are data dictionary definitions, which will be discussed later.

5   WSME Data-Structure and Script Languages

This section describes the WSME languages used to describe the matchmaking parties, what they offer and require of each other. This requires the creation of **Properties** and **Rules**. The two languages that are used to construct properties and rules are the **WSME Data-Structure** language and the **WSME Script** language.

5.1   Properties

The **WSME Property Language** provides the building blocks for describing entities such as products, services, components and descriptions of the providers and consumers. Those descriptions are contained in the advertising and query submissions sent to the WSME. A **Property** is a 'name-value' pair, where the name consists of a string and the value can be: One of a set of pre-defined basic types, a sequence of basic types or a user defined record type. A property can be defined as one of the following:

- **Static property** contains the appropriate value associated with the property at the point of submitting it to the WSME. The value of a static property does not change during the life of a submission.
- **Dynamic property** does not contain the value at the point of submission. Instead, a reference is provided, either to a local **Script** (an executable program that can calculate the required value) or alternatively, a reference to an external service that can be called to provide the value.

For example, the following properties can be defined: `Age, StockLevel, QuantityRequired, QuantityAvail` can be defined as integers, and `Price` and `Payment` as floats.

To facilitate the symmetric matchmaking process described in Section 4, each party has to be able to relate to the other party's properties as well as to its own. Therefore, when a property is referred to, it is prefaced by an indication of the side it is coming from as in `'my.property-name'` and `'your.property-name'`. For example: `my.QuantityRequired` and `your.QuantityAvail` can be compared in a rule as explained below. The prefix 'my' and 'yours' is relative to the originator of the rule in which the expression is found.

5.2   Rules

The **WSME Rules** allow one party to define requirements from the other party by referring to the properties of both parties. Rules allow both sides to select the other party they wish to deal with by specifying their eligibility. A rule is a WSME script that is evaluated at matchmaking time, resulting in a Boolean value. A rule can refer to the properties of the two parties whose advertisement and query are involved in the matchmaking process. Example of a possible provider rule is the following:

```
boolean result = false;
if (my.QuantityRequired <= your.QuantityAvail)
result = true;
return result;
```

A problem arises if a rule refers to a property that was not supplied. To avoid such a situation, the WSME Type system defines the mandatory list of properties that a submission must provide; the data dictionary contains those definitions.

The use of the type system in the matchmaking process is shown in Figure 4. The figure shows how the rules of each side can refer to the properties of the other party as well as to the properties of their own side, thus allowing comparisons to be made between the two parties.

The matchmaking process applies the rules of the submission of one party to (an instance of) the properties of the submission of the other and vice versa as shown in Figure 4. Only if the result of the evaluation of all submission-rules is 'true', will the advertisement-query be considered a matching pair. An **Offer** (to be returned to the query submitter) is an advertisement submission that matches the query with **all** its dynamic properties resolved.

5.3   WSME Data-Structure Language

The **WSME Data-Structure Language** provides the building blocks and composition instructions for defining the value of a property. The value of a property can be any of the following: One of a set of pre-defined basic types - *boolean, integer, float, string,* and *date,* a sequence of these basic types or of record types, or a user defined record type made of any combination of the above. In other words, it is possible to create records of sequences and sequences of records with any combination of the basic and composite record-types.

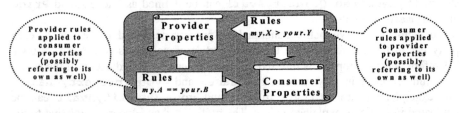

Fig. 4. The *'typed' matchmaking process* - applying the rules of one party to the properties of the other, within the confines of the Data Dictionary definitions. Each party can refer to its own properties as well as those of the other party.

5.4   WSME Script Language

The **WSME Script (Programming) Language** provides the building blocks and composition instructions for writing logical expressions or programs. Scripts can be used for:

- **Dynamic Properties**: Properties that may include a script at advertising time, to be evaluated at matchmaking time. Scripts may return any of the simple or complex types of the property language.
- **Rules:** These define requirements from the other party using a script containing a logical expression or a program that is evaluated to a Boolean value at matchmaking time.
- The **WSME Script Language** can be regarded as a simplified programming language consisting of Data structures (as defined by the Data-Structure Language), temporary variables and value assignments, Logical expressions, Arithmetic expressions, Conditional expressions, Control flow expressions and Built in functions.

6   A Capacitor Market Example

The **WSME Capacitor Market** example specifies a matchmaking space where providers can advertise their Capacitors with the aim of finding suitable buyers, and where buyers can search for Capacitors that are appropriate for their needs. The translation of a business model into a list of properties (name-value pairs) is an important part of creating the matchmaking space.

6.1   The Capacitor Market Data Dictionary

The Capacitor Market data dictionary definition is shown in Figure 5.

Provider/product description:

- *ProviderDetails* (record): *Name* (string) and *Email* (string).
- *CapacitorTypes* (sequence of string): a list of any combination of the following - Tantalum, Aluminium or Ceramic.
- *Capacitance* (float): expressed in micro Farad.
- *QuantityAvail* (integer): shows the current stock level.
- *TotalPrice* (float): this is a dynamic property - the price of the capacitors requested by a buyer is calculated at matchmaking time and is dependent of the quantity requested and the price of a single unit. The example script shown here is calculated at matchmaking time and is dependent on the quantity requested and the price of a single unit:

```
float sum;
if (your.CapacitorType == "Ceramic") sum =
your.QuantityRequired * .55;

if (your.CapacitorType == "Tantalum") sum =
your.QuantityRequired * .65;

if (your.CapacitorType == "Aluminium") sum =
your.QuantityRequired * .75;
return sum;
```

The dynamic property will be evaluated in case either a provider or a consumer rule refers to it. If a dynamic property has not been evaluated earlier, it will be evaluated before the advertisement is made into an offer and sent to the consumer.

- *WSBindingInfo* (record): *WebService_URL* - this is the URL of the service used to order the capacitors; *WSDL_URL* - this is the URL where the WSDL description of the ordering service can be found.

Buyer description:

- *BuyerDetails* (record): *Name* (string), and *Email* (string).
- *CapacitorType* (string): Tantalum, Aluminium or Ceramic.
- *Capacitance* (float): expressed in micro Farad.
- QuantityRequired (integer):
- *DaysToDelivery* (integer): indicates the expected speed of delivery of capacitors.

6.2   Buyer and Provider Rules

An example of a rule from the provider side could be:

```
boolean result = false;
if ( your.CapacitorType in my.CapacitorTypes
      && your.Capacitance == my.Capacitance )
{ result = true; }

return result;
```

Similarly, a rule from the consumer could look like this:

```
return ( my.QuantityRequired <= your.QuantityAvail
      && yourDaysToDelivery < 7 ) ;
```

The matchmaking process with instances of the data dictionary definition of Figure 5 is shown in Figure 6. Using the rules shown above and the values of the properties shown in Figure 6, the matchmaking process would result in a match between the advertisement and query submissions.

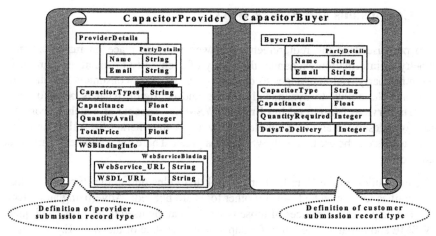

Fig. 5. The two parts of the data dictionary define the properties expected to be included in the submissions from the Capacitor provider and buyer

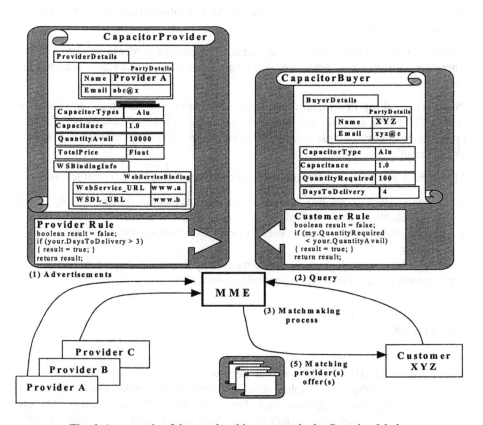

Fig. 6. An example of the matchmaking process in the Capacitor Market

7   Conclusions and Future Work

This paper discussed the requirements that web services place on matchmaking - symmetry of information exchange, the ability of each party to specify requirements of the other party, rich languages to describe services, their consumers and their demands, and the ability to dynamically update and configure what is being offered. The **Web Services Matchmaking Engine (WSME)** - capable of matching complex entities was described and an example of how a dynamic market for selling and buying Capacitors can be created with WSME was given. There are a number of areas for future work:

Tools: in addition to the Data Dictionary tool that helps define the (type of) properties of entities to be matched, several other tools are needed: Advertising and querying tool to help create instances of those types that can be used to advertise and query the WSME and a management tool for supervising the state of the WSME.

Distributed Matchmaking Spaces: in some complex matchmaking spaces, it may be desirable to divide the information between different matchmaking engines. This can result if an extended dialogue conducted between the consumer and multiple WSMEs. Each WSME may contain different type of information, related to a different stage in the dialogue.

N-party Matchmaking Process: the current matchmaking process has two parties. There are some business scenarios which call for more parties to the matchmaking process.

Post-matchmaking Processing: once several matching offers to a query are found, it is possible to compare them and rank them according to some criteria. Ways of specifying and evaluating complex utility functions may use the script languages or extensions thereof.

Monitoring and Statistics Derivation: this can be envisaged at different levels:

- When a matchmaking process fails, it is sometimes useful to know exactly where in the rule the failure occurred.
- Overall statistics may provide useful marketing information and insight.

Long-Lived Queries: If queries can be made long-lived in a similar manner to advertisements, a host of interesting possibilities opens up.

References

[ALPHAWORKS 02] Alphaworks, Web Services Toolkit,
http://www.alphaworks.ibm.com/tech/webservicestoolkit, 2002.
[ANSAware 93] *"The ANSAware 4.1 Reference Manual"*, Architecture Projects Management (APM), http://www.ansa.co.uk/, Poseidon House, Castle Park, Cambridge, UK, 1993.

[Field 02]   Field, S., Hoffner, Y.: In Search of the Right Partner. In: Camarinha-Matos, L. (ed): Collaborative Business Ecosystems and Virtual Enterprises, PRO-VE'02, 3rd IFIP Working Conference on Infrastructures for Virtual Enterprises. Kluwer, Dordrecht (2002) 56-62.

[Graham 01a]   Graham, S.: The Role of Private UDDI Nodes in Web Services, Part 1: Six Species of UDDI. Web Services Architect, IBM Emerging Internet Technologies, May 2001a.

[Graham 02b]   Graham, S.: The Role of Private UDDI Nodes, Part 2: Private Nodes and Operator Nodes. Web Services Architect, IBM Emerging Internet Technologies, May 2001b.

[Hoffner 00]   Hoffner, Y., Facciorusso, C., Field, S., Schade, A.: Distribution Issues in the Design and Implementation of a Virtual Market Place. Computer Networks 32 (2000) 717-730.

[Hoffner 01]   Hoffner, Y., Field, S., Grefen, P., Ludwig, H.: Contract-Driven Creation and Operation of Virtual Enterprises. Computer Networks 37 (2001) 111-136.

[ODP 95]   ODP, Open Distributed Processing Reference Model. ISO/IEC 10476. ITU-T Recommendation X.900, Parts 1–3 (1995).

[OMG 96]   OMG, Object Management Group and X/Open Standard: CORBA Trading Object Service. Document orbos/96-05–6, 1996.

[FELLER 02]   Feller, J.: IBM Web Services ToolKit - A Showcase for Emerging Web Services Technologies. http://www-3.ibm.com/software/solutions/webservices/wstk-info.html, 2002.

[UDDI 2002]   The UDDI Version 3 Specification, 19 July 2002, http://www.uddi.org/.

A Secure Electronic Payment Scheme for Charity Donations

Mansour A. Al-Meaither* and Chris J. Mitchell

Information Security Group
Royal Holloway, University of London, Egham, Surrey, TW20 0EX, United Kingdom
{m.al-meaither,c.mitchell}@rhul.ac.uk

Abstract. Although many charities have a web presence, almost all of them have been designed to accept credit cards as the only means for making donations. The anonymity requirements of many donors, however, make the existing means of donation inappropriate for them. In this paper we investigate the business need for an internet charity donation scheme, identify the security requirements such a scheme should fulfill, and propose a scheme that uses an anonymous electronic cash technique to make donations, and that employs smart cards for donation distribution. Finally, we analyse how the proposed scheme matches the identified security requirements.

Keywords: charity, e-commerce security, payment systems, anonymity, smart cards

1 Introduction

Giving charity is a common activity for many individuals; for instance giving charity is an integral part of the Islamic faith. One occasion for making charitable donations is the month of Ramadan, where, after completing a month of fasting, Muslims celebrate Eid, the festival of the breaking of the fast. It is also an occasion to make a special donation to the poor. All Muslims who have enough money to take care of their own family's needs must make this donation. The amount of donation is the same regardless of their income.

On the other hand, the Internet and e-commerce are changing individual lives considerably. The Internet excels at facilitating the exchange of information and goods, and what better use for this exchange than giving to those in need? With the ever growing popularity of the Internet, the transition from traditional commerce to electronic commerce is becoming a reality. This transition is supported by the convenience, speed and ease of use of the new commerce scenarios. Electronic payments are a crucial component in the development of e-commerce.

Although the necessary technology is already in place, most charities do not take advantage of the ubiquity of the Internet and recent developments in smart

---

* This author's work is supported by the Saudi Arabian Government

K. Bauknecht, A Min Tjoa, G. Quirchmayr (Eds.): EC-Web 2003, LNCS 2738, pp. 50–61, 2003.

card technology. However, individuals are increasingly prepared to donate online. According to [3], of those Internet users who are likely to make a donation online, 52% have purchased a product or service over the Internet, making online buyers more likely to give online than other Internet users.

Currently, almost all online donation mechanisms found on charity Web sites are based on electronic credit card transactions. This is a potential problem since these systems do not provide any anonymity to the donor. Privacy concerns are a barrier to online donations just as they have been for e-commerce transactions. According to [3], concerns about privacy and credit card security remain high. 71% of donors said they were concerned about the security of their personal information online. Nearly 90% said they would never give their credit card information out to a charity. The current situation could be changed if a new electronic payment scheme for charity donations can be devised.

In this paper, we introduce the concept of e-donation, the electronic counterpart of a charity donation. We propose a scheme that allows donations to be made anonymously and distributed to recipients using smart cards, allowing recipients to redeem their e-donations directly from a shop. In particular the scheme involves the donor contributing a specific amount of money to the charity, which then arranges for the recipient to receive goods of precisely the value contributed by the donor. Moreover the donor can specify the nature of the goods to be made available to the recipient. Whilst this is not a model of charitable donation of general applicability, it matches the particular requirements of certain scenarios, e.g. the obligation on Muslims to make donations during Eid (as described above).

2   System Model

In this section, we describe our model for Internet charity transactions. The model identifies the entities involved and includes a brief description of their interactions.

2.1   Participants

We now examine each of the participants in an electronic payment scheme for charitable donations.

- **Donor**: A person who wishes to donate to a charity anonymously using the Internet.
- **Charity**: A charity is an intermediary between the donor and the recipient. It generates and issues e-donations to the recipients. It trusts the Pseudonym Server to issue valid electronic coins to the donors.
- **Recipient**: A recipient is the entity that receives goods when redeeming an e-donation from a participating store. Each recipient has a smart card supplied by his charity. This card holds e-donations (specifying particular goods) issued by the charity which the holder can redeem from a participating store at a convenient time.

- **Store**: A store is an entity willing to promote its goods through participation in the scheme. It has an agreement with a charity to exchange e-donations generated by that charity for goods described in the e-donations. It uses a terminal to receive e-donations from the recipient smart card.
- **Certification authority (CA)**: A trusted entity that generates public key certificates for charities, stores, and the pseudonym server.
- **Pseudonym server (PS)**: A trusted entity that will bind cryptographic data to participants. It provides an infrastructure for issuing anonymous identities and electronic coins to donors. It is trusted not to revoke the anonymity of a donor at any time except under certain conditions agreed upon by all participants. It is trusted by all other parties and should be managed in such a way that fraud is very unlikely. To cover the operational costs of providing this kind of service, the PS might make a charge to the donor and/or the charity.

Trust is a critical issue in payment systems. In our model, we assume that the store and the charity trust each other. This trust is explicit as the store and the charity have a formally established agreement that defines the trust and liability relationship. The donor trusts the charity to deliver his donation to a deserving recipient. The donor might need a receipt for his donation from the charity to prove it has been issued to a recipient. All participants trust the CA and the PS to be honest.

2.2   Interactions

E-donation will provide a recipient of charity with the digital representation of a right to claim goods of a specified type from a participating store. A participating store will first need to decide which types of goods it will make available for distribution via charitable means — for each such item it will generate an e-donation token. Each such token is a simple data structure containing a description of the goods to be purchased. Associated with each token will also be the cost for a donor to purchase a right for a recipient to receive the goods specified in the token. The charity publishes these e-donation tokens via its web site. When a donor wishes to donate, he first contacts the PS to get an electronic cash coin which can only be used to donate to a charity, and an anonymous identity (pseudonym) used when communicating with a charity. After selecting the kind of donation he wishes to make at a charity web site, the donor makes the donation using the electronic cash coin received earlier from the PS. In response the charity generates an e-donation that satisfies the donor requirements and keeps it in a database.

When the charity decides to issue an e-donation to a recipient, it retrieves this e-donation from the database and loads it into the recipient's smart card. The recipient collects the goods from a participating store in exchange for the e-donation contained in the smart card. At a later stage, the store sends all the redeemed e-donations to their respective charities for clearing.

A great advantage of our scheme is transparency, i.e. the donor knows that a recipient will receive goods exactly as specified by the donor. Moreover, the charity does not need to be contacted during each redemption.

3 Security Requirements

The purpose of the scheme is to facilitate the transfer of donations from donors to recipients. However, the scheme provides the potential for considerable financial gains for those who attack it successfully. Therefore security measures must be provided to protect the e-donation transactions. We discuss the security requirements that our scheme should satisfy.

3.1 Donor Anonymity

When it comes to charity donations, donor privacy is important. This is especially important in an internet environment where information may travel through network segments that are not necessarily trusted. The donor wants anonymity for his donation; neither the charity nor the recipient should be able to learn the donor's real identity. There are many reasons why anonymity might be required in a payment system [2]; in this case, the donor might not wish charities to be able to link different donations together and build a profile of his/her behaviour.

However, there are situations where anonymous payments can be misused for criminal activities [6]. Furthermore, there may be regulatory and legal constraints limiting anonymous donations. In order to make an anonymous electronic charity payment system acceptable to both donors and governments, a mechanism for limiting donor anonymity may also be needed.

3.2 Double Spending

Double spending refers to the possibility of fraudulently spending the same e-donation more than once. Since e-donations are in digital form, they can readily be duplicated by the store or by the recipient, who may also blame each other for any fraudulent behaviour. If double spending does take place, the charity will not know this until the stores send the redeemed e-donations for clearing.

The scheme should protect against recipients attempting to redeem the same e-donation more than once and from stores attempting to deposit an e-donation multiple times. Ideally such double-spending or double-depositing should be prevented, although detection must be possible where prevention is not. Moreover, only the holder should be able to initiate a redemption transaction. Stores must be able to detect attempted double-spending without requiring any online verification from charities.

3.3   Integrity

Integrity ensures that information is not altered by unauthorised participants during storage or transmission, without detection by the scheme participants. E-donation data may be manipulated to attack the system. For example, a dishonest recipient may try to change an e-donation to extend its validity period or increase its value. Alternatively, an operator of a false or manipulated store terminal may interrogate the recipient's card and extract information which can later be used to obtain goods from a genuine store (at the expense of the genuine recipient).

To combat the above threats, it must not be possible to successfully fake or modify an e-donation.

4   Anonymous Public Keys

The proposed scheme uses anonymous public keys (APKs), i.e. certified public keys where the owner is anonymous to the verifier [5]. These public keys can be used in the same way as true public keys. Although the PS knows the user's identity, the PS cannot eavesdrop on the user's encrypted communication or forge a digital signature of the user.

We now sketch one method of implementing APKs (as described by Oishi et al. [5]), which applies to public keys for a discrete logarithm based signature scheme.

1. A user X registers his identity id_X and public key P_X with the PS, where P_X is generated using a discrete logarithm base g.
2. First, the PS convert the pair (g, P_X) to another pair (g', P'_X). These two pairs, however, are associated with the same private key S_X.
3. Next, the PS generates an anonymous public key certificate that consists of the converted public key P'_X, additional information (e.g. identity of the PS, validity period, etc.) and a signature on them generated by the PS.
4. Finally, the PS sends the anonymous public key certificate $\text{Cert}_{P'_X}$ to X.

5   Proposed Scheme

We now present a secure electronic payment scheme for charity donations.

5.1   System Set Up

When initially establishing the system, the PS must decide on a number of fundamental system parameters, which must be reliably communicated to all parties within the system. These include selecting:

– A signature algorithm, where $s_{S_X}(M)$ denotes the signature on message M using the private signing key of entity X,

- A Message Authentication Code (MAC) algorithm, where $\text{MAC}_K(M)$ denotes the MAC computed on message M using secret key K,
- A scheme for generating Anonymous Public Keys, and
- An anonymous electronic cash system with revocable anonymity that the PS must operate; an example of such a system is given in [4].

The CA must also generate its own signature key pair, used for generating public key certificates, where the CA-generated certificate for public key P_X is written as Cert_{P_X}.

Prior to use of the system every participating charity and store must generate and securely store their own secret MAC keys, denoted KC and KS respectively. Additionally, the participating organisations (charities, stores, and the PS) must register with the CA operating the system. Registration will involve the organisation (X say):

- Generating a signature key pair, with private key S_X and public key P_X,
- Obtaining a certificate Cert_{P_X} for P_X from the CA, and
- Obtaining a reliable copy of the public certificate verification key of the CA.

Each donor must be issued with a smart card by a charity, where smart card personalisation and issue involve the following steps.

1. The recipient card must be equipped with a signature key pair.
2. During smart card personalisation, the charity stores in the card a copy of the CA public key, the card expiry date, the charity public key certificate Cert_{P_C}, the card public key certificate Cert_{P_R} signed by the charity, and the recipient unique identifier id_R.
3. To prevent misuse of stolen or borrowed cards, we assume that PIN entry by the authorised cardholder is required to use a recipient card.

The proposed scheme is composed of five phases: the *Initialization phase*, in which the store provides the charity with e-donation tokens that can be redeemed from the store during a specified interval of time, the *Anonymity phase*, in which the donor obtains an anonymous identity and an electronic coin from the PS, the *E-donation definition phase* wherein the donor selects an e-donation token to donate and pays for it, the *Donation phase* during which the charity loads the e-donation into a recipient smart card for redemption from a participating store, and the *Redemption phase* wherein the recipient pays an e-donation to a participating store in exchange for the described goods. In the scheme description, $X\|Y$ denotes the concatenation of data items X and Y.

5.2   Initialization Phase

The store provides the charity with a token for generating e-donations that can be redeemed from the store during a specified interval of time. I.e.

$$token = s\_data\|\text{MAC}_{KS}(s\_data)$$

where
$$s\_data = Item||Value||Expiry||id_S||id_C$$
and where *Item* specifies the goods, *Value* denotes the cost of the goods, *Expiry* indicates the expiry date of the token, and id_S and id_C are identifiers for the store and the charity respectively.

The MAC protects the integrity of the token. The charity publishes the received e-donation tokens on its web site. This gives the donors choices for the donations.

5.3   Anonymity Phase

This phase involves the donor and the PS. A donor must first obtain an APK certificate from the PS. Donors then withdraw electronic coins from the PS which can only be used to purchase e-donations from a participating charity. The electronic cash system is operated by the PS which acts as a bank to donors and charities. The charity scheme requires the e-cash system to possess three main functions (typically involving special purpose exchanges of messages):

- Withdraw(val): A donor withdraws a coin c of value val from the PS.
- Payment(c): A donor pays a charity a coin c to make an e-donation.
- Deposit(c'): A charity deposits a spent coin c' with the PS which credits the charity account with the amount of val.

We now describe the anonymity phase:

1. If the donor D does not have an APK certificate from a previous donation, the donor generates a signature key pair (with private key S_D).
2. The donor visits the PS web site and submits: the donor identity id_D, the amount val to be donated, payment information (e.g. an account number), and the public key to be anonymously certified.
3. After collection of the payment from the donor using the specified payment information, the PS uses the provided donor public key to create the anonymised donor public key P_D, and generates an APK certificate $Cert_{P_D}$ for P_D.
4. The donor uses the PS withdraw function to obtain a coin c of value val. The donor can use this coin to make an anonymous e-donation to a participating charity.

5.4   E-donation Definition Phase

This phase starts when a donor visits a charity web site and decides to donate through this charity. After browsing through the available e-donation tokens provided by participating stores, he selects the token that satisfy his requirements for value, donation type (e.g. food or clothing), validity period, and location where the e-donation will be spent. Then the donor sends an e-donation request to the charity. To construct the request, the donor signs a message that contains the selected charity token and a time stamp T to ensure message freshness. The donor send the message, along with his APK certificate $Cert_{P_D}$, to the charity.

$$Donor \longrightarrow Charity : s_{S_D}(\,token||T)||Cert_{P_D}$$

After successful verification of the donor certificate, the signature on the message, and the expiry date within *token*, the charity creates an entry *c_data* in a donation requests database. We assume that the charity keeps a database of all donation requests received and awaiting use for generation of an e-donation. I.e. it generates

$$c\_data = token||Serial\_number||Creation\_time$$

where *Serial_number* is a number that uniquely identifies this entry and *Creation_time* indicates the date/time that the entry was created by the charity.

On generating the entry, the charity signs and sends a response message to the donor. The message contains a signed copy of the generated entry along with the charity certificate $Cert_{P_C}$

$$Charity \longrightarrow Donor : c\_data||s_{S_C}(\,c\_data)||Cert_{P_C}$$

On receiving the above message, the donor verifies the signature and that the entry was generated according to the donor requirements. If successful the donor and the charity engage in an electronic cash payment protocol that allows the donor to pay the coin c to the charity for the generated entry.

$$Donor \longleftrightarrow Charity: \text{Payment } (c)$$

Upon receiving the payment from the donor, the charity interacts with the PS in an electronic cash deposit protocol to deposit the received coin c'.

$$Charity \longleftrightarrow PS: \text{Deposit } (c')$$

If successful the charity adds the generated entry *c_data* to its database of donation requests. The donor must trust the charity to spend the donated coin in the way requested.

5.5   Donation Phase

In this phase, the recipient smart card and the charity terminal engage in an authentication protocol during which the recipient smart card receives e-donations. This protocol conforms to the mutual entity authentication mechanism specified in clause 5.2.2 of ISO/IEC 9798-3 [1].

This phase begins when the recipient presents his card to receive e-donations. First, the charity terminal reads the recipient's identity id_R and the recipient card public key certificate $Cert_{P_R}$ from the card. Then, the charity generates a random number $r2$ and sends it to the recipient card along with its unique identifier id_C.

    1. *Charity* $\longrightarrow$ *Recipient* : $r2 \,\|id_C$

After receiving the message in step 1, the recipient card generates a random number $r3$ as a challenge to the charity. It then creates a signed message that contains $r3$, the charity identity id_C and the received random number $r2$. The recipient card sends the generated signature to the charity terminal along with $r3$.

    2. *Recipient* $\longrightarrow$ *Charity* : $r3\|s_{S_R}(r2 \,\| \, r3\|id_C)$

After receiving the message in step 2, the charity terminal uses the recipient card public key certificate Cert_{P_R} to verify the received signature. If the verification fails, the process is terminated and the card is rejected. Otherwise, the charity terminal generates a response message that contains an $e-donation$ and sends it to the recipient card.

When a charity chooses to issue an $e-donation$ to a recipient, it retrieves an entry c_data from the donation requests database and adds $Issuance\_time$, the date/time this $e-donation$ is issued, and the recipient unique identity id_R to that entry. Then, using its secret key KC, the charity terminal computes and adds $\text{MAC}_{KC}(c\_data\|Issuance\_time\|id_R))$ to the retrieved entry. Thus,

$$e-donation{=}c\_data\|Issuance\_time\|id_R\|\text{MAC}_{KC}(c\_data\|Issuance\_time\|id_R)$$

The charity terminal now creates a signed message that contains the random numbers received in step 2, the recipient identifier id_R, and the $e-donation$. The charity sends the $e-donation$ and the generated signature to the recipient card.

    3. *Charity* $\longrightarrow$ *Recipient* : $e-donation\|s_{S_C}(r3\| r2\|id_R\| e-donation)$

Upon receiving the message in step 3, the recipient card uses the stored charity public key certificate to verify the charity signature. If the check fails, the process is terminated and the card does not accept any information from the terminal. Otherwise the card updates its stored list of e-donations. We assume that the charity keeps a database of all e-donations issued during a specific period. The charity also deletes the c_data used in the $e-donation$ generation from the donation requests database, and adds an entry to the e-donations database.

5.6   Redemption Phase

In this phase, the recipient card and the store terminal engage in an authentication protocol during which the store terminal retrieves e-donations stored in the recipient card in exchange for goods. The recipient must trust the store terminal not to remove e-donations not authorised by the recipient.

First, the store terminal reads the recipient unique identity id_R, the card expiry date, the charity public key certificate, the recipient card public key certificate and the list of e-donations. If the card has not expired, then the store terminal verifies the recipient card public key certificate using the charity public key certificate, which in turn can be verified using the CA's public key known to the store terminal. If successful, then the store terminal displays to the recipient a list of unredeemed e-donations, from which the recipient selects the one that is to be redeemed. Moreover, the store terminal asks the recipient card for a challenge.

The recipient card responds by generating a random number $r4$ and sends it to the store terminal.

1. *Recipient* $\longrightarrow$ *Store* : $r4$

After receiving the message in step 1, the store terminal generates a random number $r5$ as a challenge to the recipient card. It then creates a signed message that contains $r5$, the store identity id_S and the received random number $r4$. The store terminal sends the generated signature to the recipient card along with $r5$, id_S and the store public key certificate $Cert_{P_S}$.

2. *Store* $\longrightarrow$ *Recipient* : $r5||id_S||s_{S_S}(r5||id_S||r4)||Cert_{P_S}$

When the recipient card receives the message in step 2, it uses the stored CA public key to verify the store's public key certificate. If successful the card uses it to verify the received signature. If the signature verifies successfully, the recipient card responds with a message that contains the selected unspent e-donation and a signature computed over the concatenation of that $e - donation$, $r5$, and the identities of both the recipient and the store.

3. *Recipient* $\longrightarrow$ *Store* : $e - donation||s_{S_R}(e - donation||r5||id_R||id_S)$

Upon receipt of the message in step 3, the store verifies the recipient card signature. If the signature verifies successfully, then the store uses its secret key KS to recompute $MAC_{KS}(s\_data)$ and then checks the result against the received $e - donation$. If the check succeeds then it accepts the $e - donation$ as valid and proceeds with providing the goods specified in the $e - donation$ to the recipient. Moreover, the recipient card marks the $e - donation$ used in message 3 as spent.

To help protect the card against fraud by the store, the recipient card logs message 3 for later settlement by the charity.

Similarly, protection of the store against the recipient is provided by exchanging the goods stated in the $e - donation$ for the message in step 3. The store later uses message 3 to collect the corresponding monetary amount from the charity.

Typically, the transactions would be sent in a batch, signed by the store so that the charity can verify the integrity and authenticity of the transaction batch.

6   Security Analysis

In this section, we examine to what extent the generic security requirements outlined in section 3 are met by our scheme.

6.1   Donor Anonymity

The anonymity of the donor is protected from the charity using the APK certificate, which allows a donation to be made to a charity without revealing the donor's real identity. Although the donor is not anonymous to the PS, since the donor makes a payment in exchange for an APK certificate and an electronic cash coin, it is not possible for the PS to know what donation a donor makes because the coin used to make the donation is anonymous. The PS would need to deanonymize the coin deposited by a charity to reveal the identity of the withdrawer.

6.2   Double-Spending

Protection from e-donation double spending is provided by means of smart cards. Our e-donation scheme is an offline system, i.e. the store does not need to contact the charity for every redemption performed by a recipient. Instead, the scheme relies on a tamper-resistant recipient card that uses cryptographic means to recognize when it is communicating with a member of the scheme (e.g. charity or store). The charity and the recipient trust the recipient card to update its list of e-donations every time it is involved in a donation or redemption transaction with a member of the scheme. Moreover, since the recipient card is tamper-resistant, an attacker cannot modify the card contents without permanently damaging the card. Therefore, the recipient cannot benefit more than once from the same e-donation. The disadvantages of using the smart card approach is that no card is completely tamper resistant, and the cost associated with setting up the scheme may be significant.

On the other hand, the charity maintains a database of all e-donations which have been issued. The charity uses the redeemed e-donations received from stores and recipient cards logs to detect and punish double spending afterwards.

Typically, an e-donation would have a limited validity (days) to limit the problems of forgery, and to limit the size of the e-donation database. This database will be large, but not infeasibly so. There will need to be one database record per generated e-donation.

6.3   Integrity

Integrity protection for the e-donation data is accomplished using message authentication codes and digital signatures. Calculating a message authentication code over parts of the messages exchanged using a key known only to the authorised parties provides evidence to the verifier that the message content has not been altered or destroyed, accidentally or with malicious intent, since it was created.

For example, if an attacker decided to change the *Item* field found in the *s_data* part of $e - donation$ to his benefit, the attacker would need to modify $MAC_{KS}(s\_data)$ to reflect the new value of the *Item* field. However, our scheme assumes that no one other than the store who computed the original $MAC_{KS}(s\_data)$ knows the key KS. Moreover, we assume that the MAC function used is secure. The use of a MAC thus prevents such an attack.

On the other hand, theft of e-donations paid to a store is prevented by making such e-donations depositable only by that store. This is done by including the identity of the store in the signature $s_{S_R}(e - donation||r5||id_R||id_S)$, which is created by the recipient card in step 3 of the *Redemption phase*.

7   Conclusion

In this paper we have proposed a scheme to make and distribute charitable donations electronically using the Internet and smart cards. We described the scheme in detail, and explained how it meets the identified security requirements. In the future, a prototype implementation of the scheme will be built using a Java servelet and Java Card technology. The purpose of the prototype will be to examine the efficiency of a possible practical deployment of the scheme.

It would be interesting to investigate how the proposed scheme could be modified to allow the recipient to receive and redeem e-donations using a mobile phone instead of a smart card.

References

[1] ISO/IEC 9798-3. *Information technology — Security techniques — Entity authentication mechanisms — Part 3: Mechanisms using asymmetric signature techniques.* International Organization for Standardization, Geneva, Switzerland, 1998.

[2] D. Chaum. Blind signatures for untraceable payments. In D. Chaum, R. L. Rivest, and A. T. Sherman, editors, *Advances in Cryptology—CRYPTO '82*, pages 199–203. Plenum Press, August 1983.

[3] Smith Craver, Mathews and Company. Socially engaged internet users: Prospects for online philanthropy and activism, 1999. available at http://www.craveronline.com.

[4] D. Kugler and H. Vogt. Fair tracing without trustees. In Paul Syverson, editor, *Proceedings of Financial Cryptology 2001*, number 2339 in Lecture Notes in Computer Science, pages 136–148, Springer-Verlag, Berlin, 2001.

[5] K. Oishi, M. Mambo, and E. Okamoto. Anonymous public key certificates and their applications. *IEICE Transactions on Fundamentals of Electronics, Communications, and Computer Sciences*, E81-A(1):56–64, January 1998.

[6] S. von Solms and D. Naccache. On blind signatures and perfect crimes. *Computers & Security*, 11(6):581–583, 1992.

Smart Card Based Mobile Payment with Fairness Revocation Mechanism

Hyung-Woo Lee[1], Im-Yeong Lee[2], and Dong-iK Oh[2]

[1] Dept. of Software
Hanshin University, Osan, Gyunggi, Korea, 447-791
hwlee@hanshin.ac.kr
http://netsec.hanshin.ac.kr
[2] Div. of Information Technology Engineering
Soonchunhyang University, Chungnam, Korea, 336-745
imylee@sch.ac.kr,dohdoh@sch.ac.kr

Abstract. A *mobile payment* is a business driven transaction to pay for goods, services or digital content using a combination of mobile devices, mobile delivery networks, and the Internet. Secure mechanism must be provided in mobile payment system. However, the anonymity and privacy of transaction is a serious problem on existing mobile secure mechanism, because anonymity on mobile payment transaction can be misused by attacker. Therefore, we propose tamper-proof smart card based efficient secure mobile e-coins with *fairness revocation mechanism*.

1 Introduction

A *mobile payment* is a business driven transaction to pay for goods, services or digital content using a combination of mobile devices, mobile delivery networks, and the Internet. Nowadays the *m-Commerce* is established with diverse payment service using SMS-based payment gateway system. In the final steps of *m-Commerce*, payment step will be one of the main services deployed in mobile communication networks. However, mobile payments face a number of problems, both from a technical and theoretical point of view. First of all, the mobile system does not inter-operate with existing payment system. Thus, it is not possible to access the existing payment infrastructure[1].

In case of multimedia applications, a special device known as the set-top box should be installed by subscribers, which receives the encrypted signal from a premium channel, decrypts and decodes the compressed digital video and passes the signal to the common display console. Such *Pay-Per-View(PPV)*[2] service has advantages over common open services in that it can offer greater efficiency and flexibility to customer and also provide greater benefit to the service providers. For doing it, appropriate billing mechanisms are required for widely spreading the important of digital contents providing services[3].

A critical issue on billing mechanism is to make provision for settling possible dispute over provided digital services, especially in the cast that the illegal or abnormal usage in the middle of a session. In order for the *m-Commerce* based

K. Bauknecht, A Min Tjoa, G. Quirchmayr (Eds.): EC-Web 2003, LNCS 2738, pp. 62–71, 2003.

digital contents service to be widely accepted, it is important that the common mobile users can use secure payment mechanism over a strongly reliable medium such as tamper-proof devices. For provide secure mobile payment system, we must use traditional digital signature for secure transaction. Therefore, digital signature is a very important primitive in cryptographic mobile protocols.

Both the *anonymity* and *atomic function* must be considered for implementing secure mobile payment system[1,3]. However, the existing payment systems provide perfect anonymity, they could be illegally used. As perfect unlinkability by anonymity on mobile payment transaction also bring it possible for a illegal user can doublly spend e-coins and service provider illegally reuse user's payment message. So, it would be useful that the fairness and anonymity on mobile system must be removed if illegal transactions are happen on payment system. For doing it, A judge as a trusted entity can verify the mobile payment message-signature pair if necessary. In this paper, we propose mobile payment system with fairness revocation mechanism.

We first review the existing model and consider fairness on mobile payment system in section 2. We then propose smart card based mobile payment system with fairness revocation and propose counter based payment procedure with secure module in section 3. Furthermore, we compare suggested scheme with existing one in section 4 and conclude this study with the consideration of the future works in final section.

2   Smart Card on Mobile Payment

2.1   Security of Mobile Payment System

Mobile Payment is a point-of-sale (POS) payment made through a mobile device, such as a cellular telephone, a smart phone, or a personal digital assistant (PDA). Using moblie payment method, a person with a wireless device could pay for items in a store or settle a restaurant bill without interacting with any staff member. This ability makes it a potential *e-Commerce* and *m-Commerce* application. Mobile payments are used to pay not only for merchandise purchased via mobile channel but also for transactions in the physical world such as vending machines, passport photo machines, car wash machines etc.

The lack of security has been a major obstacle for the success of business to consumer *m-Commerce*. The evolution of payment services has been hampered by the absence of a ubiquitous security standard. Secure payment standards are essential if *m-Commerce* has to become a mass market pheonomenon. Mobile commerce began with the appearance of mobile phones equipped with smart cards, because they offer security functions not available through other methods of *e-Commerce*. When mobile phones are equipped with a device to protect personal information, the security level of an entire service, including the network, improves considerably. Data on a smart card is said to be relatively secure because it is difficult to extract encrypted data from the outside and difficult to alter it. The mobile phone with its integrated SIM card is an ideal bearer for the private key digital signature of a PKI system. Thus, the mobile device can become a security tool, for example for secure payment in *e-Commerce* and *m-Commerce*.

Smart cards will be the preferred way of gaining access to a secure system. The smart cards in third-generation (3G) mobile phones will include a processor for encryption and other processing, an electrically-erasable programmable read-only memory(EEPROM) to store user information, a program ROM, and random access memory (RAM) work space. Data on the smart card is said to be relatively secure because it is difficult to extract encrypted data from the outside and difficult to alter it. The EEPROM in the smart card stores a variety of information that requires protection, including the terminal information needed during communication, the electronic authentication certificate issued by the certifying authority to verify the identity of the user and the encryption program itself.

2.2   Signature Scheme for Mobile Payment

Special-purpose digital signature[5] providing anonymous primitive is a protocol for obtaining a signature from a signer such that the signer's view of the protocol cannot be linked to the resulting message-signature pair. Unlinkability means that we can't find any relations for linking the message and its signature between the signer and the sender by whom transaction of signature is done. Therefore it is an important cryptographic tool for realizing systems with which the signer B can issue such a credential without obtaining any useful information about neither the pseudonym of sender A nor the issued credential.

Although the key generation algorithm is similar with common signature signature scheme, the interactive protocol provides additional message recovery functions itself. Fairness scheme provides publicly verifiable process on signed message if the trusted entity want to certificate this signature. The concrete processes of registration protocol and the fairness mechanism is as follows.

2.3   Fairness Revocation

Publicly verifiable functions must be provided by the trusted entity. Therefore, the sender A does the pre-registration processes to the trusted entity and receive the secrets used for fair signature. The signer performs signature generation on sender's message and returns this signed message to the sender. Using pre-registration protocol, the trusted entity allocates the secrets for fairness to the sender. And by the key generation algorithm, the signer receives his secret key. Additionally, a verifiable fair function can be defined by this suggested interactive signature protocol with message recovering facility.

Definition Revocation Mechanism.

- SKG: Public/secret key generation algorithm based on the registration protocol RP.

- FIP_{MR}: An interactive fair signature issuing protocol involving a sender and a signer for message recovery. The sender's inputs are a value v generated in registration process and a message m and a public key y. The signer's inputs are the information c for fair protocol and a corresponding secret key x. The signer sends his blinded message $s = sender(v, m, y)_{signer(c,x)}$ to the sender.
- R: A revocation algorithm on signature with one or both of the following properties, r_I on $type_I$ and r_{II} on $type_{II}$.
  - r_I: From the signer's signature (m^*, s^*), the trusted entity J can associate the sender's message (m, s).
  - r_{II}: From the sender's signature (m, s), the trusted judge J can associate the signer's message (m^*, s^*).
- $FVer_{MR}(r, y, m, s)$: A fairness verification algorithm that confirms the overall blinded signature if s is a valid signature of the message m with respect to the revocation information r and the public key y.

The sender A performs the registration with the trusted entity J as follow sequences.

Step 1: Request for registration.
  - The sender A generates random secret $s_A \in Z_q$.
  - A sends both a $\delta \equiv g^{s_A} \bmod p$ and identity information ID_A to the trusted entity J for requesting his registration.

Step 2: Registration.
  - Trusted entity J generates both a $v_j, v_{1-j} \in Z_q$ used for fair signature process and random $w_J \in Z_q$, which satisfies $t_j \bmod g^{w_J} \bmod p$.
  - J stores the A's ID_A, δ and revocation keys v_j, v_{1-j} in his database.
  - J computes $c = h(\delta \cdot v_j \parallel \delta \cdot v_{1-j} \parallel t_J)$ using hash function on the keys v_j, v_{1-j}.
  - Trusted entity generates s_J and sends the message $(\delta \cdot v_j, \delta \cdot v_{1-j}, s_j, c)$ to A.

Step 3: Verification of registration.
  - A verifies J's message using his own random δ and gets the revocation keys v_j, v_{1-j} on it.
  - As the value c will be used in the β_j, β_{1-j} of oblivious transfer protocol, we can fairly verify the message-signature pair in the end.

3   Proposed Fairness Revocation Scheme

We propose *smart card based payment scheme with fairness revocation mechanism*, which uses mobile phone account information to authentication consumer-driven payment transactions. Developed with a flexible architecture, it addresses the needs of proxy server card publisher, contents provider. Proposed mechanism features flexible deployment options to suit the requirements of multiple *m-Commerce* types. Among them, suggested scheme would be used to process transactions from mobile service subscribers purchasing digital content and services as MP3 files, location services, digital games, electronic books and other

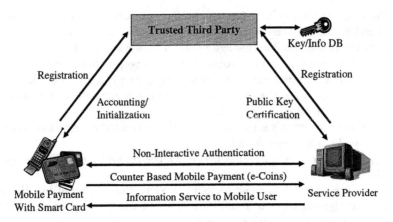

Fig. 1. Model of Proposed Mobile Payment System

media. Typically proposed scheme would provide an aggregation of content from one or multiple content providers through a connection to a content server.

We propose fair protocol that enhances the function of existing electronic payment system[7,8]. As we want to provide micropayment schemes, we adopt *counter based mobile cash* with advanced entity authentication technique and fairness primitive. Suggested protocol can detect doubly spent coins and verify overall fairness on mobile transactions. Therefore, if any mobile user does illegal pay, *trusted authority* can point out an injustice entity. We first propose a registration process on proxy server. The detailed procedure on mobile payment systems are as follow Fig. 1.

3.1 Registration Step

Registration step is as follows.

Step 1: The mobile user U generates his own secret key $s_U \in Z_q^*$ and random $\sigma \equiv g^{s_U} \bmod p$ and mobile phone account information ID_U and then sends them to the *TPS(Trusted Registration Server)*.

Step 2: The server(*judge J*) generates his own random secret nonce $\omega_J \in G(q)$ and additional two secret revocation key $v_i, v_{1-i} \in Z_q^*$ ($i \in \{0, 1\}$) for mobile user U, which is used for fairness revocation scheme.

Step 3: The J can calculates $t_J \equiv g^{\omega_J} \bmod p$ for ω_J and generates $c = H(\sigma \cdot v_i || \sigma \cdot v_{1-i} || t_J)$ by using common hashing function H. For the hashed string c, the J signs on it by using his own secret key x_J (public key $y_J \equiv g^{x_J} \bmod p$) like this equation $s_J \equiv x_J \cdot c + \omega_J \bmod q$ and he send overall registration results $(\sigma \cdot v_i, \sigma \cdot v_{1-i}, s_J, c)$ to the mobile user U.

Step 4: And then the mobile user U verities this registration string by checking $c' = H(\sigma \cdot v_i || \sigma \cdot v_{1-i} || u_J)$ on . If $c = c'$, registration process will be completed.

3.2 Initialization Step

After the registration process, the mobile user sends initialization messages to the service provider B for mobile payment.

Step 1: The mobile user gets service provider $B's$ public key $y_B \equiv g^{x_B} \bmod p$ on $B's$ own secret key x_B. And then, the mobile user U sends oblivious message β_i, β_{1-i} to the service provider B by using the received random values v_I, v_{1-i} and c as follow equation (1).

$$\beta_i \equiv g^{v_i + v_{1-i}} \bmod p, \beta_{1-i} \equiv c \cdot (g^{v_i + v_{1-i}})^{-1} \bmod p \qquad (1)$$

About this oblivious message, the service provider can get the value c , which is generated from the trusted proxy server as $c \equiv \beta_i \cdot \beta_{1-i} \bmod p$.

Step 2: And then, the mobile gateway generated his own random nonce z_i^*, z_{1-i}^* for generating oblivious challenges strings γ_i, γ_{1-i} on λ_i, λ_{1-i} as follow equation (2).

$$\gamma_i \equiv \beta_i^{z_i^*} \bmod p, \gamma_{1-i} \equiv \beta_{1-i}^{z_{1-i}^*} \bmod p, \lambda_i^* \equiv g^{z_i^*} \bmod p, \lambda_{1-i}^* \equiv g^{z_{1-i}^*} \bmod p \quad (2)$$

By using this initialization process, the mobile user can send oblivious message to the service provider and checks mobile gateway's identification on γ_i, γ_{1-i} and c γ_i, γ_{1-i} as $(\lambda_i^*)^{v_i} \equiv \gamma_i \bmod p$ $(i \in \{0,1\})$. This oblivious transfer will be used for fairness revocation processes in later billing protocol with blinded parameter λ_i, λ_{1-i} in fair signature protocol.

Step 3: After this, mobile user authenticates the service provider as a non-interactive form. Proposed scheme works as a ElGamal[6] like protocol, which also uses shared (divided) secret $s_0, s_1 < p - 1$. Service provider finally sends y_i to the mobile user, which is generated from the ElGamal like authentication and verification equation using $s_i, t_i (0 \leq i \leq 1)$, etc.

3.3 Issuing Account on Smart Card

After the initialization process, the mobile user issues his account on the service provider system.

Step 1: The mobile user U generates $h_u \equiv g^{u_1} \bmod p$ on mobile user's own additional random secret $u_1 \in Z_q$ and sends it to the mobile gateway with σ.

Step 2: Then, the service provider calculates $h_0 \equiv g^{o_1} \bmod p$ on service provider's random nonce $o_1 \in Z_q$. And the B can store the value h_0 and I in mobile gateway's database and sent them to the mobile user, and then it is computed as $I \equiv h_0 \cdot h_1 \equiv g^{(o_1 + u_1) \bmod p}$. Returned value I can be used for the identification information on mobile user's smart card as it is issued from the service provider to the mobile user.

Step 3: The mobile user stores $\{h_0, I, h_u, u_1, \sigma\}$ on his database. As the mobile user does not know the service provider's value o_1, he can't spend same coin several times. If he spends it twice, the mobile gateway can calculate u_1 from this values.

Step 4: The service provider issues smart card T to the mobile user U. And then the issued smart card stores initial public values $T' \equiv \{\sigma, g, o_1, p, q, balance, Seq\}$ with some amount of electronic *coins(balance)* with transaction sequence number(*Seq*) for fair billing protocol.

3.4   Request for Payment

We propose smart card based protocol by using counter scheme on e-coins.

Step 1: If the mobile user want to withdraw some coins(*amount*), then the service provider decrease total amount of cash in mobile user's account (*balance = balance' − amount*) and send them to $U's$ smart card for satisfying initial withdrawal. The service provider applies one-way hash function H on the *amount* with transaction sequence number Seq.

Step 2: When the mobile user want to pay some amount of e-coins(*amount'*) to the digital contents provider(S), he re-withdraws it from the smart card. The detailed protocol between the smart card and its owner U is as follows.

In this protocol, the means that the mobile user want to bill some *amount* of e-coin to the digital contents provider S of ID_S at some transaction *date* and *time*.

3.5   Payment Step on Smart Card

Service provider blindly signs on the *amount'* message which the mobile user want to bill to the digital service provider S. By this signature, the service provider can provide publicly verifiable property on e-coins.

Step 1: The mobile user must send enveloped e-coin(m_i^*) using $B's$ blinded parameter(λ_i^*) to the service provider on $U's$ own *amount*. Then B signs on this envelop and send signed s_i^* to the mobile user. Proposed signature scheme provides fairness revocation on illegal billing transactions.

Step 2: On mobile gateway's signature, the mobile user develops it and can get the e-coin recovery facility on verification process, $amount' \equiv g_i^s y_i^r r_i^{-1} \bmod p$. The signed e-coin is $(amount', (r_i, s_i))$.

Step 3: The mobile user can spend these signed e-coins to the service provider S by calculating r and r^* satisfying follows equations $r \equiv u \cdot (r_1^0 + d \cdot u_1) + u' \bmod q$, $r^* \equiv u \cdot d + u' \bmod q$ and send final payment ($Counter = \{\mu, \theta, r, r^*, (r_i, s_i), spec\}$) to S.

The mobile user's *Counter* contains signed e-coin (r_i, s_i) on his *amount'* with additional parameters. On this payment, S generates $d \equiv H'(\mu, \theta, spec)$ from the *Counter* and accepts this e-coin as correct one when $\mu^d \cdot \theta \equiv g^r \bmod p$ is hold.

The service provider sends *Counter* message to the service provider for updating his account. Then the service provider can detect the doubly spent e-coins with fairness revocation functionality.

Step 4: If the e-coins are already stored in the service provider's database, they can be fabricated or doubly spent by U. When we assume that the fabricated billing is $\{\mu, \theta, r', r^{*'}, (r_i', s_i'), spec'\}$, the service provider can detect it by using by follows equations (3).

$$\frac{(r - r')}{(r^* - r^{*'})} = \frac{u \cdot d \cdot (o_1 + u_1) - u \cdot d' \cdot (o_1 + u_1)}{u \cdot d - u \cdot d'} = (o_1 + u_1) \tag{3}$$

Therefore, the service provider can detect the illegal mobile user in his database by using I information, such as $I \equiv g^{o_1 + u_1} \bmod p$. Service provider can calculate the o_1 as he knows the value $u_1 \equiv log_g(I) \bmod p$. It is possible for B to detect the doubly spent e-coin.

4   Performance Evaluation and Discussions

4.1   Safety of Proposed System

In this section, we evaluate the performance and properties of proposed mechanism. Both the anonymity and prevention of secure payment must be considered for implementing mobile cash on public key cryptosystem. However, as a common scheme[7,9,12,13] prevents linking the withdrawal of money and the payment made by the same customer, the anonymity could be misused by criminal. Therefore, it would be useful if the anonymity could be removed with the help of a trusted entity, when this is required for legal reasons.

Fairness: A service provider as a trusted entity can verify the fairness if necessary. By running the link-recovery protocol, the signer obtains information from the judge and he can recognize the corresponding protocol view and message-signature pair. Verifying the fairness of proposed scheme, we overview each revocation procedures.

Security: Proposed schemes are also based on the intractability of the discrete logarithm problem, and it is similar with existing electronic payment protocols. But proposed scheme generalizes the interactive fair protocol by using tamper-proof smart card. However, as the proposed scheme sends secret shared oblivious message, the computed registration and initialization procedures provide a lot of complexity.

For optimization, we use only two random secrets. As proposed scheme is based on the counter-type blinded e-coin, it is very easily applicable to the micropayment scheme in large distributed Internet services such as digital contents provider framework.

4.2   Privacy and Atomic Function

We can propose a complicated protocol that allows for authenticated but publicly verifiable messages in case of accruing abnormal transactions.

Privacy: Mobile user can transfer anonymous bill to the service provider so that his identity can be blinded on the service provider. With the growing use of the Internet for commercial transactions, there is more call for network-based privacy and anonymity in business. On the other hand, trusted proxy server seem unwilling to give up the control that the current audit trail scheme.

Proposed protocol prevents mobile user from paying e-coins for more than the mobile user claims to, and it prevent mobile user from photocopying the billing order and spending it twice. And the service provider knows if the person who retrieved e-coins tried to cheat the service provider or if the service provider tried to cheat the service provider.

In suggested protocol, there is an observer with tamper-proof chips such as smart card. The observer chip keeps a mini database of all the pieces of e-coins spent by that smart card. If the mobile user attempts to copy some e-coins and spend it twice, the imbedded observer chip would detect the attempt and would not allow the requesting transaction. Since the observer chip is tamper-proof, smart card holder cannot erase the mini-database without permanently damaging the smart card.

Atomic Function: Atomic function in proposed mobile payment system is achieved through a sequence log in the smart card and service providers system. These entities are originally introduced to reduce the computational load or communication cost in a mobile payment system. But, mobile gateway checks e-coins with the smart card for legal payments.

The proxy maintains a minimum amount of information in order for it to ensure this atomic function. One of the main goal is to develop a efficient mobile payment system for a *m-Commerce* environment, where the most important issue is the mobility of the hosts and the characteristics of the wireless interfaces that these hosts use. The basic principle for structuring a efficient system for mobile hosts is to reduce their computational load and communication costs.

5   Conclusions

Proposed counter based payment protocol has the following merits compared with the existing common payment systems. Mobile users can use counter-based secure billing procedure that they want to pay for. And mobile users can use anonymous digital services from the service provider by using common signature scheme. Mobile users only need to pay what they have received digital services. Service provider can revoke the fairness of digital billing transactions. Service provider can provide anonymous secure billing to the digital contents providers. Service provider can check the counterfeit of Counter by using fairness revocation scheme. This protocol can also be applicable to the diverse *m-Commerce* systems.

References

1. Konrad Wrona, Marko Schuba, Guido Zavagli, "Mobile Payments - State of the Art and Open Problems", WELCOM2001 Lecture Notes in Computer Science, Spronger-Verlag, Vol. 2232, pp. 88-100, 2001.
2. Jianying Zhou, Kwok-Yan Lam, "A Secure Pay-per View Scheme for Web-Based Video Service", Public Key Cryptography, Lecture Notes in Computer Science, Spronger-Verlag, pp. 315-326, 1999.
3. Michael Peirce, Donal O'Mahony, "Flexible Real-Time Payment Methods for Mobile Communications", IEEE Personal Communications, Dec, pp. 44-55, 1999.
4. Aphrodite Tsalgatidou, Jari Veijalainen, "Mobile Electronic Commerce : Emerging Issues", EC-WEB2000 Lecture Notes in Computer Science, Spronger-Verlag, Vol. 1875, pp. 477-486, 2000.
5. D. Chaum: Blind Signature for Untraceable Payments, Advances in Cryptology - Crypto'82, Lecture Notes in Computer Science, Springer-Verlag, (1982) 199-203.
6. Jan L. Camenisch, Jean-Marc Piveteau, Markus A. Stadler, "An Efficient Fair Payment System", 3rd ACM Conference on Computer Communication Security, ACM Press, pp. 88-94, 1996.
7. T. ElGamal, "A Public Key Cryptosystem and a Signature Scheme based on Discrete Logarithm", IEEE Transactions on Information Theory, Vol. IT-30, No. 4, pp.469-472, 1985.
8. Rui Zhang, Michiharu Kudoh, Kanta Matsuura, Hideki ImaiInstance, "Revocation of Digital Signature and Its Applications", The 2002 Symposium on Cryptography and Information Security Shirahama, SCIS2002, Japan, Jan.29-Feb.1, 2002.
9. Markus Stadler, Jean-Marc Piveteau, Jan Camenisch, "Fair Blind Signature", Advances in Cryptology, Proceedings of Eurocrypt'95, Lecture Notes in Computer Science, Springer-Verlag, pp. 209-219, 1995.
10. Alfred J. Menezed, Paul C. van Oorschot, Scott A. Vanstone (ed.), "Handbook of Applied Cryptography", CRC Press, 1996.
11. B. Schneier, "Applied Cryptography", Second Edition, Wiley, 1996.
12. Holger Petersen, Guillaume Poupard, "Efficient Scalable Fair Cash with Off-line Extortion Prevention," Technical Report LIENS-97-7, Ecole Normale Superieure, May, 1997.
13. Greg Maitland and Colin Boyd, "Fair Electronic Cash Based on a Group Signature Scheme," Advances in Cryptology, Proceedings of ICICS'2001, Lecture Notes in Computer Science, Springer-Verlag, pp. 209-219, 2001.
14. Dong-Guk Han, Hye-Young Park, Yong-Ho Park, Sangjin Lee, Dong Hoon Lee and Hyung-Jin Yang, "A Practical Approach Defeating Blackmailing." Advances in Cryptology, Proceedings of ACISP'2002, Lecture Notes in Computer Science, Springer-Verlag, pp. 119-132, 2002.

Enhancing E-commerce Security Using GSM Authentication

Vorapranee Khu-smith and Chris J. Mitchell

Information Security Group
Royal Holloway, University of London, Egham, Surrey, TW20 0EX, United Kingdom
{v.khu-smith,c.mitchell}@rhul.ac.uk

Abstract. Today, e-commerce transactions are typically protected using SSL/TLS. However, there are risks in such use of SSL/TLS, notably threats arising from the fact that information is stored in clear at the end point of the communication link and the lack of user authentication. Although SSL/TLS does offer the latter, it is optional and usually omitted since users typically do not have the necessary asymmetric key pair. In this paper, we propose a payment protocol in which user authentication is provided using GSM 'subscriber identity authentication'. In the protocol, a consumer is required to possess a GSM mobile station registered under a subscriber name corresponding to that on his/her debit/credit card. The cardholder identity is combined with the GSM subscriber identity in such a way that without a mobile station, in particular the SIM, and the corresponding debit/credit card, an unscrupulous user will find it difficult to make a fraudulent payment at the expense of the legitimate cardholder. This is achieved in such a way that no management overhead is imposed on the user.

Keywords: E-commerce transactions security; payment protocol; GSM security

1 Introduction

In an e-commerce transaction, a consumer typically makes a payment using a debit/credit card. The communications link between the consumer PC and the merchant server is usually protected against eavesdropping using Secure Socket Layer (SSL) or Transport Layer Security (TLS). Even so, a number of security threats remain. One reason for these remaining vulnerabilities is that SSL/TLS does not obligate client authentication. As a result, it is not easy to verify if the person who is making a payment is the legitimate cardholder. A malicious user, who may have obtained card details by some means, may then be able to use them to make payments over the Internet at the expense of the legitimate cardholder. Consequently, a way to reduce the risk of such frauds is to perform user authentication.

Apart from the lack of client authentication, using SSL/TLS to protect an e-commerce transaction poses another threat. Since SSL/TLS was designed to

K. Bauknecht, A Min Tjoa, G. Quirchmayr (Eds.): EC-Web 2003, LNCS 2738, pp. 72–83, 2003.

secure the communication link, the information is available in clear text at the destination. As a result, merchant servers have become a target for attackers who wish to obtain card numbers.

If client authentication is to be provided using public key cryptography (as supported by SSL/TLS), then the user must first establish a public key pair. He/she will also need a secure place to store the private part of the key. Usually the key is stored in the user PC and hence the user has to use the particular machine every time a payment is to be made. Although a smart card could be employed to store the key and hence enhance mobility, not many user PCs are equipped with smart card readers. By contrast, very large numbers of users across the world now possess a GSM mobile phone.

In this paper we propose a payment protocol in which user authentication is enhanced using a GSM mobile phone (or in classic authentication model terms, something the user has). The protocol also indirectly reduces the threat posed by the storage of unencrypted card numbers in a merchant server by reducing the value of stolen card numbers to a fraudster. This is achieved by requiring the user to possess both a debit/credit card and a Mobile Station (MS), i.e. a Mobile Equipment (ME) and a Subscriber Identification Module (SIM), which must be registered under the name that appears on the card. In short, the protocol makes use of MS portability and the GSM authentication mechanism to provide user authentication in a way that also supports user mobility.

In this paper, GSM subscriber identity authentication is first described, followed by the proposed protocol. A threat analysis, and a discussion of the advantages and disadvantages of the scheme are subsequently given, followed by an overview of and comparisons with related work.

2   Subscriber Identity Authentication

Three main security services are provided by the GSM air interface protocol. They are subscriber identity confidentiality, subscriber identity authentication, and data confidentiality. However, subscriber identity authentication is the only security service used in the proposed protocol and hence will be the only issue described here. Details of the other security services can be found in [3, 4, 8].

In every SIM, there exists a long-term secret key, K_i, which is unique and known only to the SIM and Authentication Centre (AuC) of the home network operator of the subscriber. The home network operator is the organisation with whom the subscriber has some kind of contractual arrangement for the provision of service, and which the subscriber pays for this service.

To authenticate a SIM, the visited network needs two parameters, namely a random number ($RAND$) and a expected response ($XRES$). The ($RAND$, $XRES$) pair enables the network to verify the authenticity of the SIM without having the K_i. To compute the ($RAND$, $XRES$) pair, the AuC generates a $RAND$ and passes it with K_i as parameters to algorithm $A3$ which is specific to a network operator. The output of $A3$ is $XRES$.

$$(RAND, K_i) \xrightarrow{A3} XRES$$

The AuC generates the ($RAND$, $XRES$) pair as required, and passes them to whichever network needs them. When a SIM is requested to authenticate itself to a network, a $RAND$ is sent from the network to the SIM. Since the SIM is equipped with the function $A3$ and the secret key K_i, it can generate the Signed Response ($SRES$) using $RAND$ and K_i as inputs. The SIM then sends the $SRES$ to the network where it is compared with the $XRES$. If they match, SIM verification is successful.

3   Using GSM Authentication for Electronic Transactions

In this section, an e-commerce user authentication protocol which makes use of the GSM authentication service is described. In the proposed scheme, a consumer is required to have a GSM Mobile Equipment and a SIM registered under the name that appears on the debit/credit card. It is important to note that the protocol does not need the SIM to be modified in any way. However, the ME does need to have the means to take a $RAND$ value from a PC, pass it to the SIM, and pass the $SRES$ value from the SIM back to the PC.

In this section, the system components required are first described, followed by the transaction processing procedure.

3.1   System Components

Three main system components are involved in our payment protocol. These are a User System, a merchant server, and an AuC.

User System. The User System consists of an MS and a PC. The MS (in fact the SIM) is responsible for outputing the $SRES$. Therefore, although an ME is needed to interact with the SIM, the protocol can work without an ME if there is an alternative means for the SIM to communicate with the user PC. The means of communication used between the MS and the user PC is not specified in this paper. However, Infrared, a cable, or Bluetooth[1] could be employed for the purpose (such means of communication are becoming commonplace as mobile devices are increasingly being used for data transfer). In a recent version of the SIM Toolkit (U-SIM Application Toolkit) [1], there exists a command called 'AT command' which enables a U-SIM to tell an ME to open an infrared or bluetooth channel. The U-SIM Application Toolkit (USAT), therefore, could be used to implement the proposed protocol. However, it is worth noting that such use of USIM Toolkit requires both the SIM and the ME to support USIM Toolkit commands.

In the remainder of this paper the scheme is described in the context of a User System in which the PC provides the main platform for conducting user e-commerce, and the MS simply acts to support user authentication. However, in environments where the MS has sophisticated user interfaces and processing

---

[1] http://www.bluetooth.com

capabilities, e.g. a WAP or 3G phone, the MS could take on some or all of the PC's tasks.

Merchant Server and Authentication Centre. The merchant server is the component that interacts with the User System to support electronic transactions. The merchant server also interacts with the AuC in order to retrieve values required in the user authentication process.

The Authentication Centre (AuC) is required to supply the merchant server with values necessary for the GSM identity authentication process. It takes inputs from the merchant server and produces the values used for identity authentication. The choice of the communication link between the two is again not an issue here. However, it could be the Internet or a special-purpose link provided by the mobile network operator.

As discussed in Section 4.2, we suppose that the integrity and confidentiality of the merchant server/AuC link is protected in some way, e.g. via encryption and MACs or signatures; however, the means by which this is achieved is outside the scope of the discussion here.

3.2   Transaction Processing

The proposed payment protocol starts after a consumer has decided to make a payment. The decision about which purchase to make is outside the scope of this paper — we simply assume that the consumer and the merchant wish to perform a specified transaction.

The consumer first fills in a typical Internet purchase form using the PC. In this protocol however, the form is required to contain a field for a mobile phone number. Upon receipt of the form, the merchant server extracts the mobile number from the form and the identity authentication process begins. The procedure is illustrated in Figure 1.

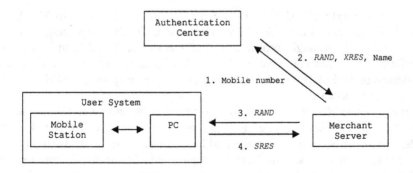

Fig. 1. GSM-e-commerce identity authentication process

The merchant server first sends the consumer's mobile number to the AuC in order to retrieve three values: a random number ($RAND$), an expected response ($XRES$), and the subscriber name. This corresponds to message 1 in the figure.

Upon receipt of the merchant server request, the AuC generates the ($RAND$, $XRES$) pair using the key K_i of the requested mobile number and algorithm $A3$. It then sends the ($RAND$, $XRES$) pair along with the name of the subscriber to the merchant server as shown in message 2 in the figure. Upon receipt of message 2, the merchant server first compares the name of the cardholder with the subscriber name received from the AuC. If they match, the $RAND$ will be sent to the PC as in message 3 of the figure. Otherwise, the identity authentication process fails and the protocol ends.

After having received the $RAND$, the user PC forwards it to the ME. The ME then sends the $RAND$ value to the SIM, just as it would if the $RAND$ was sent via the radio interface by a GSM base station. The SIM now generates an $SRES$ using the received $RAND$ and its stored K_i as inputs to algorithm $A3$. The SIM then passes the generated $SRES$ back to the ME, again just as it would normally (i.e. the SIM is not required to have any special functionality). The ME then sends the $SRES$ to the PC which again forwards the value to the merchant server (message 4). At the merchant server, the $SRES$ is compared with the $XRES$. If they match, the consumer is deemed to have been authenticated. The Internet transaction processing may now continue.

4   Threat Analysis

In this section, we consider threats to the proposed protocol. The threats can be divided into three categories: threats to the User System, threats to the two communications links (user system/merchant server and merchant server/AuC), and threats in the merchant server and the AuC.

4.1   Threats in the User System

As stated previously, the User System consists of a user PC and an MS. Since the user PC does not contain sensitive information, the threats arising from the PC are minimal. Although information that passes via the PC can be cached, this information is not confidential. A debit/credit card number can be cached and compromised but the protocol still requires a corresponding SIM to make an electronic transaction.

Threats to the MS are divided into two scenarios depending on the amount of information an attacker has. Clearly, if he/she has neither the SIM nor the card details, a transaction cannot be made and hence there is no threat. It should also be clear that if the attacker has both a complete set of card details and a stolen SIM for the cardholder, then the system cannot prevent an attack — unless, of course, the SIM has been reported stolen and blacklisted by the network. We therefore consider the two main 'intermediate' scenarios.

- Scenario 1: Attacker has a stolen SIM without the corresponding card details. In this scenario, if an attacker has stolen a SIM and the subscriber name of the stolen SIM is unknown, although a valid *SRES* can be generated, he/she will not be able to create a matched cardholder name necessary to pass the authentication process.

  By contrast, if the subscriber name is known to the attacker, it is possible for him/her to fabricate a complete set of cardholder details including a cardholder name corresponding to the subscriber name. However, the fraud becomes clear soon after the merchant tries to charge the card. In the most typical case for an e-commerce transaction, the merchant will try to charge the specified payment card before the goods are dispatched. Hence in such a case, the threat is small. Nevertheless, the threat can be more serious if the goods are, for example, information or music which will be delivered instantly via the Internet. However, even in this case, the threat can be avoided if, as is often the case, the merchant server seeks payment authorisation before authorising delivery of the goods. If the card details are fabricated then the card issuer will, of course, reject the payment.
- Scenario 2: Attacker has stolen card details without the corresponding SIM. If an attacker has only card details, without the SIM, it will not be possible to generate a valid *SRES*. This threat is therefore addressed by the scheme described above.

Thus, to be successful, an attack on the user system needs both the victim's SIM and the corresponding debit/credit card details to complete a fraudulent transaction.

4.2   Threats to the Communications Links

If any of the information transferred across either of the links is modified, then the protocol will fail. Hence, a theoretical denial of service attack exists, although there are many simpler ways to prevent the completion of a transaction. We now consider other threats arising to the two links.

Threats on the PC/Merchant Server Link. The 'usual' confidentiality and integrity issues apply to the payment information transferred across this link. However we can assume that, as would typically be the case today, this link is protected using SSL/TLS. Indeed, the whole purpose of the scheme described here is to enhance the security provided by SSL/TLS rather than seeking to design a completely new and comprehensive security system. This is based on the belief that security for e-commerce must be introduced in ways which minimise the overheads for all parties, and in particular for the e-consumer.

Note that a possible alternative to the protocol described in this paper would be to use GSM authentication to enhance the security of the SSL/TLS initialisation process. However, if such an approach is followed, it is not clear how to achieve the desired link between the GSM subscriber name and the cardholder name — such an analysis is outside the scope of this paper.

Threats on the Merchant Server/AuC Link. Threats on this link can be further divided into two types, namely integrity threats and confidentiality threats.

Integrity threats: There are a number of ways in which an attacker could manipulate this link in order to persuade the merchant server to accept an impostor. Perhaps the simplest method would involve the attacker using an arbitrary (valid) SIM and ME in combination with stolen card details (which, of course, will not match the GSM subscription name). In message 2 the AuC will provide a valid $RAND$ and $XRES$ for the attacker's SIM, and will return the name associated with the attacker's GSM subscription. An active attacker could change this name to the name associated with the stolen card details, and the merchant server will accept message 2. The remainder of the protocol will complete correctly, and the account for which the details were stolen will be charged for the transaction.

An alternative attack, again using stolen card details, does not require the attacker to have a valid SIM at all. The attacker supplies an arbitrary (but valid) GSM number with the stolen card details. In message 2, the AuC will send a $(RAND, XRES)$ pair for the arbitrarily chosen GSM subscription, along with the subscriber name. The active attacker can then replace the contents of message 2 with the name for the stolen card details, along with an arbitrary $(RAND, XRES)$ pair. The merchant server will accept message 2 because the names match, and will send the manipulated $RAND$ to the attacker in message 3. The attacker simply returns the manipulated $XRES$ value in message 4, and again the attack will succeed. The existence of these attacks means that it is vital that the integrity of the link between AuC and merchant server is protected.

Confidentiality threats: There are also a number of serious confidentiality threats. First note that a passive eavesdropper can perform an attack similar to the second integrity attack described above. Suppose an attacker has a set of stolen card details and also knows the GSM number for the owner of the stolen card details. The attacker initiates the protocol using the stolen card details and the known GSM number. Message 2 will be accepted by the Merchant server because the GSM number belongs to the valid cardholder. However, if the attacker can intercept message 2, then the $XRES$ value can be obtained. The attacker then simply inserts this value into message 4 and the protocol will complete successfully.

Also note that, in the absence of integrity and confidentiality, the merchant server/AuC protocol could also be used to find the subscriber name corresponding to any GSM number. This would be a significant breach of GSM subscriber confidentiality.

These attacks mean that it is also important to provide confidentiality for this link, and this is why we assume throughout the paper that this link is both confidentiality and integrity protected.

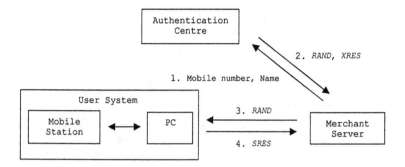

Fig. 2. Revised protocol

4.3   Threats in the Merchant Server and the AuC

Since the merchant server is responsible for the identity authentication process, in particular the comparison of the names and *XRES* with *SRES*, it is important to protect the server against any attack which might cause the protocol to be bypassed.

Over and above the integrity of the user authentication process, the merchant server will have access to large volumes of potentially sensitive subscriber information. As part of the user authentication process, the merchant server retrieves from the AuC the account holder name for any GSM telephone number. Not only is this a sensitive privacy issue, but requiring the AuC to supply such information may potentially be in breach of its license and/or data privacy legislation. It is therefore vital that the merchant server be protected so that this information cannot be abused.

One way of mitigating this security issue is to make a slight modification to the protocol of Section 3.2. In the revised protocol, shown in Figure 2, in message 1 the merchant server supplies the cardholder name as well as the mobile number. The AuC is then required to perform the matching between the name supplied in message 1 with the name it has associated with the GSM number. If they do not match the protocol should not proceed. If they do match, in message 2 the AuC simply provides a *(RAND, XRES)* pair.

Another way to reduce this threat is for the merchant server to create and send a *RAND* to the User System and thence the SIM. Upon the receipt of the *RAND*, the SIM generates the *SRES* and sends it to the merchant server via the user PC. The merchant server subsequently sends the cardholder's name, his/her mobile number, the *RAND*, and the *SRES* to the AuC to verify. The protocol is shown in Figure 3.

These modified protocols have the advantage that the AuC retains control of sensitive subscriber information. However, they have the disadvantage of requiring additional processing by the AuC.

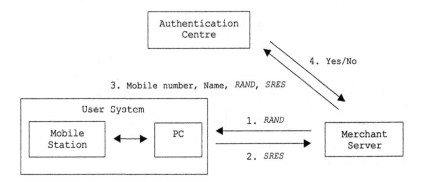

Fig. 3. Another revised protocol

If the integrity of the AuC could be compromised, then there are possible attacks to the security of the user authentication process. However, in such an event there are also many other serious attacks to the security of the GSM network itself, and so we assume that the AuC is well-protected.

5　Advantages and Disadvantages

In this section, the advantages and disadvantages of the proposed protocol are considered.

5.1　Advantages

The following advantages arise from use of the proposed GSM-based user authentication.

1. The protocol provides user authentication based on GSM subscriber authentication. As a result, stolen credit card details cannot be used to launch a successful e-commerce transaction.
2. Since stolen credit card details cannot be used to launch a successful e-commerce transaction, the threat arising from the storage of unencrypted credit card numbers in merchant servers is accordingly reduced.
3. The protocol supports user mobility. The user authentication process requires only the correct software to be loaded on the PC, and for there to exist a means to connect the MS to the PC. In the authentication process, the PC is simply responsible for forwarding messages between the MS and the merchant server. Moreover, since the protocol does not involve storing any secrets on the PC, the risks in using untrusted PCs are minimised.
4. From the merchant point of view, the protocol will lessen fraudulent transactions and hence reduce the cost of 'card not present' chargebacks.

5.2   Disadvantages

The following disadvantages arise from use of the proposed GSM-based user authentication.

1. Prior agreement is required between the merchant and the mobile phone service provider to support the protocol between AuC and merchant server. To avoid the need for many individual arrangements between merchants and mobile network operators, a Trusted Third Party (TTP) could be introduced to act as a 'broker' between the two parties. This broker could simply route messages between merchant servers and the AuC. In such a scenario, merchant servers and mobile network operators would only need to have a contractual agreement with the broker. One possible candidate for the broker would be the card brand.
2. Merchants may be charged for the AuC services. This cost therefore has to be weighed against the cost of 'card not present' chargebacks which may vary from merchant to merchant. Of course, this is not a disadvantage for the GSM network provider, who may find this a useful additional revenue stream.
3. If the U-SIM Toolkit is to be used, the proposed protocol may require an ME and a SIM that support the functionality.

6   Related Work

There exist other GSM-based payment systems which we now briefly review.

- The payment scheme proposed by Claessens et al. [2] provides user authentication using GSM. However, unlike the scheme discussed above, it makes extensive use of SMS messaging.
- The GiSMo (G i(nternet) S M o(pen)) scheme was developed by Millicom International Cellular in 1999. In this scheme, consumers must first open an electronic wallet over the Internet and supply their mobile phone number. Every Internet transaction is then validated with a password sent over the mobile phone using an SMS message. The GiSMo project, however, ended in 2001.
- Mint[2] and Paybox[3] are both GSM-based payment systems. They too require consumers to first open an e-wallet. Transactions in the two protocols involve either making or receiving calls using the delegated mobile phone.
- The 3-D Secure Protocol has been developed by Visa [5, 7]. The protocol aims to provide cardholder authentication for merchants using a central server called the Access Control Server (ACS). The cardholder must enroll before using the service. When a transaction is to be made, he/she will be required to enter a Personal Account Number (PAN) in addition to other information used in a traditional purchase form. The merchant then requests

---

[2] http://www.mint.nu
[3] http://www.paybox.co.uk

cardholder authentication from the ACS. The cardholder is now required to enter a password or PIN to authenticate him/herself to the ACS. The protocol can be extended to be used in mobile Internet devices such as a WAP phone [6] and the transaction flow remains similar to the one specified in [5].

Broadly speaking, the other proposed GSM-based payment systems either use SMS messaging, require e-consumers to open an e-wallet, or require them to make or receive phone calls using a GSM phone. The protocol proposed here, however, does not use any such measures. It simply utilises the GSM subscriber identity authentication process. The Visa 3-D Secure Protocol is similar to the proposed protocol in the way that they both aim to provide cardholder authentication. However, the Visa protocol is a complete payment security system, and is therefore much more complex than the scheme proposed here.

7   Conclusions

Today most e-commerce transactions are protected in a rather ad hoc way using SSL/TLS — this gives rise to threats, notably because of the lack of user authentication.

In this paper, we have proposed the use of GSM identity authentication to enhance e-commerce security. The protocol provides user authentication and hence significantly reduces threats arising from misuse of misappropriated card details. It therefore also indirectly reduces the risk of storing card details in unencrypted form in merchant servers. The protocol works with a 'standard' GSM SIM and requires only an appropriate equipped Mobile Equipment and a user PC. It therefore imposes minimal overheads on the user, thus increasing the likelihood of successful use. The gains for the merchant in terms of reduced chargebacks also appear significant, and the possibility of an increased revenue stream may also make the system attractive to the GSM operators.

Acknowledgement

We would like to thank Dr. Keith Martin, Dr. Scarlet Schwiderski-Grosche, and the anonymous referees for their helpful comments that have significantly improved the quality of this paper.

References

[1] 3GPP. *Technical Specification Group Terminals; USIM Applicaiton Toolkit (USAT) version 5.1.0.* Third Generation Partnership Project, June 2002.

[2] J. Claessens, B. Preneel, and J. Vandewalle. Combining World Wide Web and wireless security. In B. De Decker, F. Piessens, J. Smits, and E. Van Herreweghen, editors, *Advances in Network and Distributed Systems Security*, Proceedings of IFIP TC11 WG11.4 First Annual Working Conference on Network Security, pages 153–171, Boston, 2001. Kluwer Academic Publishers.

[3] ETSI. *Digital cellular telecommunications system (Phase 2+); Security aspects (GSM 02.09 version 8.0.1)*. European Telecommunications Standards Institution (ETSI), June 2001.

[4] ETSI. *Digital cellular telecommunications system (Phase 2+); Security related network functions (GSM 03.20 version 8.1.0)*. European Telecommunications Standards Institution (ETSI), July 2001.

[5] Visa. *3-D Secure Protocol Specification: core functions version 1.0.1*. Visa International Service Association, November 2001.

[6] Visa. *3-D Secure Protocol Specification: extension for mobile Internet devices version 1.0.1*. Visa International Service Association, November 2001.

[7] Visa. *3-D Secure Protocol Specification: system overview version 1.0.3*. Visa International Service Association, December 2001.

[8] M. Walker and T. Wright. Security. In F. Hillebrand, editor, *GSM and UMTS: The Creation of Global Mobile Communication*, pages 385–406. John Wiley & Sons Ltd., 2002.

The ET-RBAC Based Privilege Management Infrastructure for Wireless Networks*

Dong-Gue Park and You-Ri Lee

Department of Information and Technology Engineering
College of Engineering, SoonChunHyang University
San 53-1, Eupnae-ri, Shinchang-myun Asan-si Choongnam, Korea
{dgpark,thisglass}@sch.ac.kr

Abstract. M-commerce have grown rapidly, it is very important to determine whether an identity is permitted to access a resource in mobile environments. In this paper we propose ET-RBAC based Wireless Privilege Management Infrastructure(WPMI) model and Wireless Attribute Certificate(WAC) for authorization in mobile communication. All access control decisions are driven by an authorization policy, which is itself stored in an WAC. Authorization policies are written in XML according to a DTD that has been published at XML.org. Finally we show the effectiveness of the proposed ET-RBAC by applying it to an example of M-commerce service.

1 Introduction

With the rapid development of wireless internet technology, it is very important to determine whether an identity is permitted to access a resource in mobile environments.

Digital certificates are used to support integrity services by conforming that the information in a certificate has not been altered by unauthorized methods and belongs to the proper subject. Currently, there are two kinds of information which are supported by certificates: identity and attributes. While identity certificate is used for authentication services to verify the subjects of the certificates, an attributes certificate contains the subject's attribute information such as a role, access identity, group, or clearance and is used for authorization in order to determine whether an identity is permitted to access a resource.[10]

A PKI supports the issuing and management of public-key certificates which identify and authenticate authorized users. A PMI provides attribute certificates particularly suitable for authorization purposes.[19]

WPKI has become one of the most outstanding proposals referring to authentication in wireless environments, and several applications have been based on WPKI certificates in order to provide authentication services to well-known

---

* This work is supported in part by the Ministry of Information & Communication of Korea and in pary by Institute for Industrial Technology of Soonchunhyang University.

K. Bauknecht, A Min Tjoa, G. Quirchmayr (Eds.): EC-Web 2003, LNCS 2738, pp. 84–93, 2003.

scenarios in mobile systems. But WPKI certificates do not support for authorization service to determine whether authorized users have the rights to access a resource in wireless environments, although they support for authentication of authorized users in wireless environments.[6] WPMI model and WAC structure were proposed in order to support authorization service for authorized users in wireless environments.[18]

Role-Based Access Control(RBAC) has recently received considerable attention as a promising alternative to traditional discretionary and mandatory access controls. RBAC ensures that only authorized users are given access to protected data or resources. A successful marriage of Web and RBAC technology can support effective security in large scale enterprise-wide systems.[16] But this model does not support the complex work processes associated with dynamic separation of duty requirements, particularly with user-user conflicts. The ET-RBAC, extended model of T-RBAC for enterprise environment, is an integration of the task role based access control model and the "conflicting entities" administration paradigm for the specification of static and dynamic separation of duty requirements in the workflow environment.[20]

In this paper we propose ET-RBAC based WPMI model and WAC for authorization in mobile communication. All access control decisions are driven by an authorization policy, which is itself stored in an Wireless attribute certificate. Authorization policies are written in XML according to a DTD that has been published at XML.org.

WPMI can support simple ET-RBAC by defining role-specification ACs that hold the permissions granted to each role, and role-assignment ACs that assign various roles to the users. In the former case, the AC holder is the role, and the privilege attributes are permissions granted to the role. In the latter case, the AC holder is the user, and the privilege attributes are the roles assigned to the user. WPMI can support hierarchical ET-RBAC by allowing both roles and privileges to be inserted as attributes in a role-specification AC so that the latter role inherits the privileges of the encapsulated roles.[17] And WPMI can support constraint ET-RBAC by allowing roles for separation of duty to be inserted as attributes in a role-specification AC.

The rest of this paper is organized as follows. Next, in Section 2, we describe the technologies related in our approach. In Section 3, we propose the ET-RBAC policy. In Section 4, we provides an example about using ET-RBAC based WPMI for mobile application. This is followed by our conclusion in Section 5.

2 Related Technologies

2.1 Public Key Infrastructure and Wireless Public Key Infrastructure

PKI is the fundamental structure of public key management and offers five basis security services such as privacy, access control, integrity, certification and Non-repudiation.[1][2] The basic structure of PKI consists of certification authority, registration authority, directory and user. Certification Authority(CA) is the pivot subject of the basic structure of public key, which can produce or nullify certificate according to the certification policy and make own coupled keys and user's key selectively. Registration Authority(RA) can certify user's identification and utilize application based on the basic structure of public key. Directory is the cache of logs including relevant information and is allowed to be searched. User is the person within basic structure and takes advantage of the system. [3][4]

WPKI was proposed for authentication service in wireless environments. WPKI is composed of CA, RA, wireless handset and mobile contents provider. A major difference between PKI and WPKI is to verify certificates. Verifying certificates in wireless is very difficult according to the limit of computing power and memory in wireless environments and consuming cost and time occurred by downloading CRL periodically. To solve these problems, Online Certificate Status Protocol(OCSP) is used or certificate having short lived format is used. The certificate having short lived format has 48 hours as validity duration. And ECDSA algorithm having 160bit is used instead of RSA by limited performance of wireless handset.[7]

2.2 Privilege Management Infrastructure and Wireless Privilege Management Infrastructure

PMI is the infrastructure for issuing, storing and managing AC. An attribute-certificate based PMI is a mechanism that can be used to support enterprise authority structures. PMI comprises Source of Authority(SOA), Attribute Authority(AA), Privilege Holder and Privilege Verifier. [8][9] An AC in PMI is a separate structure from a PKC. A user may have multiple AC associated with each of its PKC. While the PKC is issued by CA, the AC is issued by AA. The use of AC, issued by an AA, provides a flexible PMI which can be established and managed independently from a PKI. [9]

WPMI is the infrastructure for issuing, storing and managing WAC and can be used to support authorization service for authorized users in wireless environments. A WAC Structure is proposed by modifying previous AC structures in order to determine whether an identity is permitted to access a resource in mobile environments. The format of WAC includes the base fields, Attribute Type, privilege revocation extensions, roles extensions and delegation extensions. Role attribute type and roles extensions in the proposed WAC structure are used for roles model and delegation extensions are used for delegation model. [18]

Revocation of AC may or may not be needed. An AC does not contain authentication information such as public key. Therefore Attributes must be coupled with the corresponding identities. There should be a mechanism to link attributes to proper identities. [12][14] Since the autonomic signature supports higher reusability of PKC than do tightly coupled mechanism, the autonomic signature is used to support individual CAs or different lifetimes for identity and attributes in WPMI model. [18]

Verifying certificates in WPMI is very difficult according to the limit of computing power and memory in wireless environments like as WPKI. To solve these problems, Online Certificate Status Protocol(OCSP) may be used or certificate having short validity duration may be used. And cryptographic algorithms used in WPMI should be selected by considering limited performance of wireless handset and wireless environments.

3   The Policy of ET-RBAC Based Wireless Privilege Management Infrastructure

The authorization policy specifies who has what type of access to which targets, and under what conditions. The separate access control lists configured into each target, is hard to manage and duplicates the effort of the administrators, since the task has to be repeated for each target. Policy based authorization on the other hand allows the domain administrator (the SOA) to specify the authorization policy for the whole domain, and all targets will then be controlled by the same set of rules. Domain wide policy authorization is far more preferable than having separate access control lists configured into each target. [15]

We have specified an ET-RBAC policy specifically designed for use with an wireless attribute certificate based WPMI. The WPMI ET-RBAC Policy is composed of a number of sub-policies. The domain of the WPMI Policy is the union of all the domains of the sub-policies. Each policy is given a unique object identifier (OID) that globally unambiguously identifies it. This OID is used in order to guarantee that the correct policy will be used in all the subsequent access control decisions made by the implementation.

The concept of session in ET-RBAC is classified into two classes such as WSession and session. A WSession exists only while the user is busy with a particular task, during the time from when a user starts to work on a task in the his worklist to when that user stops or suspends work on the same task. If a user selects an item from the his worklist,the user takes responsibility for the corresponding task instance and must complete that task instance. And when the user suspends or completes the task instance, all permissions for the task instance are revoked from the user, and the WSession for the task instance is destroyed. [20]

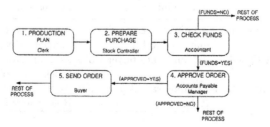

Fig. 1. An Example of Workflow in M-Commerce System

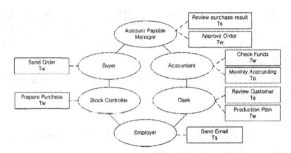

Fig. 2. Example of Role Hierarchy for M-Commerce Systems

Figure 1 graphically describes a portion of a typical purchasing workflow.

Figure 2 depicts a role hierarchy relating to the example workflow in M-Commerce System. Some tasks, which belong to class S, are inherited upwards in the hierarchy. But some tasks, which belong to class P, are private and don't be inherited to higher roles.

Table 1 shows an example of the administrative role definitions and permissions in M-commerce system. The Role Hierarchy Policy defines the role hierarchies that are supported by this ET-RBAC policy. Table 2 is an example of permission role assignment policy for M-commerce system. The permission role assignment policy comprises actions (privileges) assigned to each role. Table 3 is an example of role hierarchy policy for M-commerce system. Each role hierarchy (RoleSpec in the DTD) supports multiple superior roles inheriting the privileges of a common subordinate role.

The SOD Policy defines Separation of Duty(SOD) in role-based system. Constrained ET-RBAC is supported by this ET-RBAC policy. Table 4 is an example of SOD Policy for M-commerce system. SOD is a time honored technique for reducing the possibility of fraud and accidental damage. These include static SOD(based on user-role assignment) and dynamic SOD(based on role activation).

Table 1. Administrative Role Definitions and Permissions in M-commerce system

role name	role definition	permission
Senior Security Officer	Administrate account manager Roles	Administrate account manager Roles
Buyer Security Officer	Administrate buyer Roles	Administrate buyer Role, Stock Controller Role
Account Security Officer	Administrate Accountant Roles	Administrate Accountant Role, Clerk Role.

Table 2. An Example of Permission Role Assignment Policy

```
<PermissionroleassignPolicy>
            <Role name="Account_manager">
                        <Definition Value="Account Manager Shopping Mall"/>
                        <Permission Value="Manage Accounts"/>
            </Role>
            <Role name="Buyer">
                        <Definition Value="Goods buy in Shopping Mall"/>
                        <Permission Value="Retrieve Goods"/>
            </Role>
</PermissionroleassignPolicy>
```

Table 3. An Example of Role Hierarchy Policy

```
<RoleHierarchyPolicy>
            <RoleSpec Type="shoppingRole" OID="1.2.826.0.1.3344810.1.1.14">
                        <SupRole Value="Account_manager">
                                    <SubRole1 Value="Buyer">
                                                <SubRole2 Value="Stock_controller"/ />
                                                <SubRole3 Value="Employer"/ >
                                    <SubRole1>
                        </SupRole>
            </RoleSpec>
</RoleHierarchyPolicy>
```

Table 4. An Example of Separation of Duty Policy

```
<SeparationofDutyPolicy>
            <SodRoleList Type="SSD">
                        <Role Type="shoppingRole" Value="Buyer"/>
                        <Role Type="shoppingRole" Value="Accountant"/>
            </SodRoleList>
            <SodRoleList Type="DSD">
                        <Session>
                                    <Role Type="shoppingRole" Value="Accountant"/>
                                    <Role Type="shoppingRole" Value="Account_manager"/>
                        </Session>
                        <WSession>
                                    <Role Type="shoppingRole" Value="Account_manager"/>
                                    <Role Type="shoppingRole" Value="Stock_controller "/>
                        </WSession>
            </SodRoleList>
</SeparationofDutyPolicy>
```

The user role assignment policy specifies which roles can be assigned to which subjects by which SOAs. For each role assignment, it is specified in this policy whether the assigned roles can be delegated or not (see above), and whether there are any time constraints on the assignment. Table 5 is an example of user role assignment policy for M-commerce system.

Table 5. An Example of User Role Assignment Policy

```
<ConstrainRoleAssignmentPolicy>
            <ConstrainRoleAssignment>
                        <SubjectDomain ID="Alice"/>
                        <Role Type="shoppingRole" Value="Account_manager"/>
                        <Delegate Depth="0"/>
                        <SOA ID="PolicyOwner"/>
                        <Validity>
                                    <Absolute Start="2003-2-21T12:00:00"/>
                        </Validity>
            </ConstrainRoleAssignment>
<///ConstrainRoleAssignmentPolicy>
```

4   The Example of ET-RBAC Based Wireless Privilege Management Infrastructure

Figure 3 shows an example of M-commerce system. WPKI and WPMI is used for authentication and authorization of M-commerce system. Mobile user visits bank by off-line and receives ID/Password from the bank. The bank provides user information to Korea Financial Telecommunications and Clearings Institute(KFTC). Mobile user requests a WPKC to the KFTC by a gateway of the mobile company.

KFTC verifies the identity of the mobile user and issues the WPKC for user and deposits it to directory server and transmits it to the mobile user. Also, shopping mall receive his own WPKC through these processes like the mobile user. As a result, a secure channel between the mobile user and shopping mall is established based on WPKI. When the mobile user wants to control a stock on M-commerce system, he must be authorized by the system whether he has a membership of it. Accordingly, he requests a WAC to AA with his WPKC.

AA authenticates him with its own WPKC and assigns him to a stockcontroller role like Fig. 4 and issues WAC to him. If he and other mobile user, alice are the same family member and he gained stock controller role and alice wants to enter a account manager role at a shopping mall, she sends her own WAC to

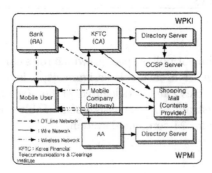

Fig. 3. An Example of M-Commerce System

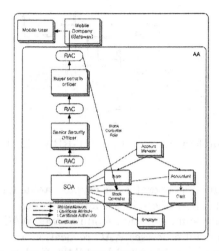

Fig. 4. An Example of User Role Assignment in AA

the shopping mall and can be verified her privilege about the membership by shopping mall. But stock controller role and account manager can be specified as dynamically conflicting tasks by the business rule, "an order may not be approved by its initiator." in shopping mall. Therefore alice can not be assigned to account manager by w-session in DSD.

Figure 4 shows an example of hybrid model, which is mixed roles model and delegation model, based on WAC in order to assign stock controller role to the mobile user. It is assumed in the Figure 4 that the diagram has been simplified and certificates associated with this are not shown. The delegation of authority to individuals is made by issuing role assignment certificates(RAC). The modelling of the actual role hierarchy in an organization for role-based model is made by issuing role specification certificates(RSC).

When an end entity tries to access a controlled object, the privilege verifier can ensure that the end entity possesses the privilege/security attribute required to access by ensuring that the chain of trust is not broken between the SOA and the end entity of the attribute. Even though the complexity of delegation chains results from attempting to mirror the distribution of privilege within a real organization, the complexity due to processing paths and retrieving certificates may be mitigated through the use of a cache within the verifier components and the flexibility of being able to model the actual privilege delegation paths in an organization is an advantage of this task role-based model.[13]

Figure 5 shows the implementation of the ET-RBAC in the WPMI. The WAA was implemented to create WAC in the Windows 2000 environment. AA administration module controls AA functions. It authenticates user by user's WPKC and accepts user's request and allocate privileges to users by authorization policy. Policy module creates policy ACs according to XML policy created by SOA and is used by AA administration module to allocates privileges to

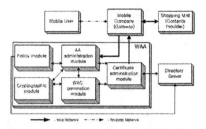

Fig. 5. Implementation of the ET-RBAC in the WPMI

users. Cryptographic module operates the cryptographic functions relating with the creation and verification of certificate and WAC generation module creates user's WAC. Certificate administration module saves WAC in database and issues WAC to Gateway and processes WAC revocation and verification.

Our implementation was developed by J2ME, EJB components to provide effectively RBAC for wireless environments. The EJB components were implemented by using JBuilder6, Inprise Application Server 4.5. And the ET-RBAC databases were implemented by using Oracle9i.

5   Conclusion

In this paper we proposed ET-RBAC based WPMI model in order to support authorization service for authorized users in wireless environments. ET-RBAC model support elaborate separation of duty policy to tasks in enterprise environment through the classification of enterprise sessions according to their characteristics. All access control decisions are driven by an authorization policy, which is itself stored in an Wireless attribute certificate. Authorization policies are written in XML according to a DTD that has been published at XML.org. Finally we showed the effectiveness of the proposed RBAC by applying it to an example of M-commerce service.

References

[1] Alfred Arsenault, S. Turner : Internet X.509 Public Key Infrastructure PKIX Roadmap Work in Progress. Internet-draft 05, March 2000 <http://www.ietf.org/internet -drafts/ draft-ietf-pkix-roadmap-05.txt>

[2] Adams, C and Lloyd, S. : Understanding Public-Key Infrastructure: Concepts, Standards, and Deployment Considerationsíí.Macmillan Technical Publishing 1999

[3] ITU-T Rec. : X.509 2000 |ISO/IEC 9594-8 The Directory: Authentication Framework

[4] Russell Housley, Warwick Ford, Tim Polk, David Solo. : Internet X.509 Public Key Infrastructure Certificate and CRL Profile. RFC 2459, IETF PKIX Working Group, January 1999 <http://www.ietf.org/rfc/rfc2459.txt>

[5] A. Aresenault, S. Tuner : Internet X.509 Public Key Infrastructure, Internet Draft, November 2000

[6] J. I.Lee, J. H.Park, J. S.Song : Domestic PKI model for WAP, Institute of Information Security & Cryptology Journal, October 2000

[7] Wireless Application Protocol Wireless Transport Layer Security, WAP Forum 6th of April 2001

[8] S. H.Jin, D. S.Choi, Y. S.Cho, E. J.Yoon : Attribute Authentication technology & PMI, Institute of Information Security & Cryptology Journal, December 2000

[9] S. Farrell, R. Housley : An Internet Attribute Certificate Profile for Authorization, Internet Draft, June 2001

[10] S. Farrell, R. Housley : "An Internet Attribute Certificate Profile for Authorization", RFC 3281, April 2002. available on
line at http://www.ietf.org/rfc/rfc3281.txt

[11] ISO/IEC 9594-8/ITU-T Recommendation X.509, "Information Technology-Open System Interconnection: The Directory: Authentication Framework" 2002

[12] D. G.Park, Y. D.Hwang : "RBAC in Distributed Retrieving Systems by Attribute Certificates", IC2001

[13] Scott Knight, Chris Grandy : "Scalability Issues in PMI Delegation", 1st Annual PKI Research Workshop-proceedings, April 2002

[14] J. S. Park,R. Sandhu : " Binding Identities and Attributes Using Digitally Signed Certificates" ACSAC 2000

[15] D. W.Chadwick, O.Otenko : "The PERMIS X.509 Role based Privilege Management Infrastructure" SACMAT 2002

[16] D. W.Chadwick, A.Otenko : "RBAC Polices in XML for X.509 based Privilege Management" Sec 2000

[17] D. W.Chadwick : "Privilege Management Infrastructure" Business Briefing: Global Security Systems Reference Section

[18] D. G.Park, Y. R.Lee : "The PMI model for the wireless environment" KOCIES Conference 2002

[19] Toni Nykanen : "Attribute Certificate in X.509" HUT TML 2000, Tik-110.501 Seminar on Network Security

[20] D. G.Park and Y. D.Hwang : "AExtended Task-Role-Based access control model for access control enforcement in Enterprise Environments" EALPIIT 2002

Efficient Signature Validation Based on a New PKI

Jianying Zhou

Institute for Infocomm Research
21 Heng Mui Keng Terrace, Singapore 119613
jyzhou@i2r.a-star.edu.sg

Abstract. Digital signatures usually serve as irrefutable cryptographic evidence to support dispute resolution in electronic transactions. Trusted time-stamping and certificate revocation services, although very costly in practice, must be available to prevent big loss due to compromising of the signing key. In this paper, we employ a revocation-free public-key framework to improve the efficiency in maintaining the validity of digital signatures as non-repudiation evidence. The new PKI allows an end user to control the validity of his own public-key certificate and enables certificate verification without retrieving the revocation information from the CA. Based on this new PKI, we could validate *generic* digital signatures using a TSA only. Moreover, we could validate *forward-secure* digital signatures without the TTP's involvement.

1 Introduction

Digital signature is a fundamental security mechanism for authentication and non-repudiation services. A signer can generate a digital signature of a message using his private key. A verifier can check the origin and integrity of the message by verifying the signature with the corresponding public key. Moreover, the signer cannot deny originating the signature because others are unable to forge the signature without the private key. To determine the origin of a signed message, the verifier first needs to make sure what is the claimed signer's public key. Public-key certificates play an important role in binding the public key with the identity of the owner of the corresponding private key [ISO13888-1]. To ensure the authenticated binding, the certificate needs to be issued by a *trusted third party* (TTP) called the *certification authority* (CA).

However, a private key might be compromised before the corresponding public-key certificate's scheduled expiry date. Then, any party holding the compromised key could forge the signatures. A straightforward solution is to request the issuing CA to revoke the certificate. The certificate revocation information will be accessible to the public thus the relevant users will be aware that an apparently valid certificate is no longer valid.

K. Bauknecht, A Min Tjoa, G. Quirchmayr (Eds.): EC-Web 2003, LNCS 2738, pp. 94–103, 2003.

The *public-key infrastructure* (PKI) provides a framework on services related to issuing public-key certificates and distributing revocation information. However, efficient and timely distribution of certificate revocation information is a big challenge facing the PKI providers. The efficiency could be significantly improved if a user can control the validity of his own certificate and others can check the validity of such a certificate without retrieving the revocation information from the CA (or the designated directory).

Digital signature is one of the most important types of cryptographic evidence that could be used to support settlement of disputes in electronic transactions [Zh01]. As disputes may arise at a time well after the end of a transaction, it should be able to prove that a signature remains valid as long as it was valid at the time of generation, even if the corresponding certificate has expired or been revoked at the time of dispute resolution.

A number of mechanisms exist for maintaining the validity of digital signatures as non-repudiation evidence. However, most of them (e.g., [Bo81, ZL99]) rely on trusted time-stamping and certificate revocation services. Some mechanisms (e.g., [IR02, Zh02]) may not require those supporting services from the TTP. But the *one-way sequential link* mechanism [Zh02] is only limited to B2B applications, where the transacting parties usually have a regular business relationship and both sides maintain a long-term transaction log. The *intrusion-resilient* signature [IR02] is fragile in real applications as loss of synchronization between the signer and the home base can cause the signer unable to generate valid signatures any more.

In this paper, we employ a *revocation-free* public-key framework [ZBD02] to improve the efficiency in maintaining the validity of digital signatures as non-repudiation evidence. The new PKI allows an end user to control the validity of his own certificate and enables certificate verification without retrieving the revocation information from the CA. Based on this new PKI, we could validate *generic* digital signatures using a *trusted time-stamping authority* (TSA) only. Moreover, we could validate *forward-secure* digital signatures without the TTP's involvement.

2   Certificate Revocation

Certificate revocation is one of the major issues in PKI. There are two standardized certificate revocation mechanisms in the IETF.

- CRL – Certificate Revocation List [RFC2459], which provides periodic revocation information.
- OCSP – On-line Certificate Status Protocol [RFC2560], which provides timely revocation information.

A CRL is a time-stamped list of serial numbers or other certificate identifiers for those certificates that have been revoked by a particular CA. It is signed by the relevant CA and made freely available in a public repository. Updates should be issued regularly, even if the list has not been changed (thus enabling users possessing a CRL to check that it is the current one). The revoked certificates should remain on the list until their scheduled expiry date.

A disadvantage of the CRL-based mechanism is that the time granularity of revocation is limited to the CRL issue period. For example, if a revocation is reported now, it will not be reliably notified to certificate verifiers until the next periodic CRL is issued – this may be up to one hour, one day, or one week depending on the frequency that the CA issues CRLs.

As a supplement to checking against a periodic CRL, the OCSP-based mechanism enables applications to determine the status of a certificate timely but with a much higher operational cost. An OCSP client issues a status request to an OCSP responder and suspends acceptance of the certificate in question until the responder provides a response. Upon receipt of a request, the OCSP responder either returns a definitive response, or produces an error message. All definitive response messages should be digitally signed.

Both of the above mechanisms require the certificate verifier to obtain the revocation information from a trusted third party to check the status of a public-key certificate. That could place a considerable processing, communication, and storage overheads on the CA as well as the relying parties.

Many efforts have been devoted to improve the efficiency of certificate revocation. The use of *certificate revocation tree* (CRT) was suggested in [Ko98] to enable the verifier to get a short proof that the certificate was not revoked. A *windowed revocation* mechanism was proposed in [MJ00] to reduce the burden on certificate servers and network resources. A certificate revocation system was presented in [Mi01] to improve the CRL communication costs. More work on efficient certificate revocation can be found in [ALO98, Co00, NN98, WLM00]. Unfortunately, there is no scheme that exempts the CA from certificate revocation.

3   A Revocation-Free PKI

The new PKI [ZBD02] is a revocation-free public-key framework in which the maximum lifetime of a certificate is divided into short periods and the certificate could expire at the end of any period under the control of the certificate owner (or his manager in a corporate environment). The verifier can check the certificate status without retrieving the revocation information from the CA. This is based on a security building block "one-way hash chain".

A one-way hash chain is constructed by recursively applying an input string to a one-way hash function [La81], which can be denoted as $H^i(r) = H(H^{i-1}(r))$ (i = 1,2, ...) where $H^0(r) = r$ is the root of the hash chain. According to the feature of one-way hash function, if r is chosen randomly and the hash chain is kept secret, given $H^i(r)$ it is computationally infeasible to find the input $H^{i-1}(r)$ except for the originator of the hash chain.

As a basic security building block, one-way hash chain has been seen in many applications including one-time password authentication and micro-payment. The one-way hash chain generated in the above way can also be bound to a public-key certificate. In [Mi01], the CA generates a one-way hash chain for each user requesting a public-key certificate, and includes each user's last chained hash value in their certificate. The CA updates the status of users' certificates regularly by releasing the corresponding hash values instead of the CRL. The performance is improved in such a system. However, the CA still needs to be constantly involved to provide the revocation information to certificate verifiers.

The new PKI is intended to exempt the CA from testifying the validity of a public-key certificate once the certificate has been issued by the CA. The exclusion of the CA's involvement is based on the assumptions that the CA's private key is well protected against compromise and the certificates issued by the CA are error-free.

3.1   Generation of Revocation-Free Certificate

Suppose $SIGN_A(M)$ denotes party A's signature on message M. A user U's revocation-free public-key certificate could be generated in the following way.

Actions by U
1. Generate a pair of keys:
   SK_U – private key
   PK_U – public key
2. Define the certificate parameters:
   T – maximum lifetime
   D – starting valid date
   L – time period for refreshing validity of the certificate
   Suppose $j = T/L$ is an integer. The refreshing points are denoted as $D_1 = D+L$, $D_2 = D+2*L$, ..., $D_j = D+j*L$.
3. Generate a one-way hash chain $H^i(r) = H(H^{i-1}(r))$ $(i = 1, 2, ..., j)$, where r is a random number known only to U.
4. Send $(PK_U, D, H^j(r), j, L)$ to the CA.

Actions by the CA
1. Authenticate U's request in an out-of-band method.
2. Generate a certificate $CERT_U = SIGN_{CA}(U, PK_U, D, H^j(r), j, L)$.[1]
3. Issue $CERT_U$ to U.

Compared with an ordinary public-key certificate, $CERT_U$ contains extra data $(H^j(r), j, L)$.[2] They will be used to control the validity of $CERT_U$.

3.2   Use of Revocation-Free Certificate

Once $CERT_U$ is generated, it could either be delivered by the certificate owner U during a transaction, or be retrieved from a public directory maintained by a third party. At the starting valid date D, U can release $H^{j-1}(r)$ to initialize the validity of $CERT_U$, which then has an expiry date $D_1 = D+L$.

Suppose the next refreshing point of $CERT_U$ is D_e. When U generates a digital signature with SK_U, he will attach $(H^i(r), i)$, where $i = j - (D_e-D)/L$, to the signature.[3]

---

[1] For simplicity, other less related information is omitted in $CERT_U$.
[2] $CERT_U$ should also include an identifier of the hash function used to generate and verify the hash chain.

Note that it is entirely up to U for the hash value release at a refreshing point. For example, if U does not generate any signature in the period between D_{e-1} and D_e, U need not release $H^i(r)$. But later if U wants to generate signatures in the period between D_e and D_{e+1}, U can directly release $H^{i-1}(r)$. Furthermore, U can even release $H^{i-2}(r)$ in the period between D_e and D_{e+1} if U thinks it is safe to extend the expiry date of $CERT_U$ beyond the forthcoming refreshing point.

When a transacting party V wants to verify U's signatures, he first needs to check the status of $CERT_U$. Suppose V holds the CA's public verification key, the latest hash value that V received from U is $H^i(r)$, and the current time that V verifies $CERT_U$ is D_v. V can take the following steps to check the status of $CERT_U$.

1. V verifies the CA's signature on $(U, PK_U, D, H^j(r), j, L)$. If true, V believes that U's public key is PK_U, the starting valid date is D, the maximum lifetime is $T = j*L$, the refreshing time period is L, and the last hash value in the one-way hash chain is $H^j(r)$.
2. V checks that $0 \leq i < j$ and $H^{j-i}(H^i(r)) = H^j(r)$. If true, V believes that $H^i(r)$ is a valid hash value in the one-way hash chain ended with $H^j(r)$.
3. V checks that $D_v \leq D + (j-i)*L$. If true, V concludes that $CERT_U$ is valid now, and remains valid until $D_e = D + (j-i)*L$.

In such a way, U can control the validity of $CERT_U$ by releasing the corresponding $H^i(r)$ when generating digital signatures. V can check the status of $CERT_U$ without retrieving the revocation information from the CA. Thus, the CA is got rid of certificate revocation in the new PKI.

3.3   Protection of Hash Chain Root

The certificate owner U relies on the hash chain root r to control the expiry date of his public-key certificate $CERT_U$. There is an advantage on the use of a separate secret r to protect the private key SK_U. The system remains secure as long as either r or SK_U is not compromised. If SK_U is compromised, U could destroy r then $CERT_U$ will expire shortly at the next refreshing point. Similarly, if r is compromised, U could destroy SK_U and stop using it for signing.

It might be at the same risk, however, if r and SK_U are stored in the same computer system. If the system is broken, both r and SK_U will be compromised. Then, a hacker holding r and SK_U can always generate valid signatures by refreshing the validity of $CERT_U$ until its maximum lifetime T. Therefore r and SK_U need to be protected separately.

The hash chain root r can be protected in a way different from the signing key SK_U because of the following reasons.

*   r is needed only at the refreshing points while SK_U might be used at any time. That means SK_U should be highly available in a system while r could be kept "off-line".

---

[3] $(H^i(r), i)$ need not be a part of message to be signed. Instead, it is only the data that will be stored or transmitted together with the signature.

- A signing key usually has a length of 1024 bit or above while the hash chain root can be as short as 128 bits. That implies SK_U is usually beyond the human's capability to memorize while r might be memorized.

For *individual users*, the most straightforward approach is to remember the hash chain root r and manually input r at the time of refreshing $CERT_U$. After the hash value needed for refreshing is generated, r will be erased from the local computer system. That will minimize the possibility of compromise caused by system break-in.

For *corporate users*, the hash chain root r could be stored in a security server, which releases the corresponding hash value to the certificate owner U at each refreshing point. The role of the security server is fundamentally different from the CA's role in certificate revocation.

- The CA needs to make the revocation information available to any potential certificate verifier over the Internet, which may lead to the higher risk of denial of service attacks. On the other hand, the security server only needs to communicate with the internal certificate owners, and there could be a set of security servers, each of which manages the hash chain roots for a group of clients and restricts its connections within a specified sub-domain to minimize the risk of system break-in and denial of service attacks.
- The authenticity and integrity of the revocation information released by the CA need to be protected while the chained hash values released by the security server need no protection.

4   Efficient Signature Validation

With the above new PKI, we have two effective approaches to maintain the validity of digital signatures as non-repudiation evidence. We could validate *generic* signatures only using the TSA. Moreover, we could validate *forward-secure* signatures without the TTP's involvement.

4.1   Validating Generic Signatures Using TSA Only

Suppose the signer U generates a digital signature σ using his private key SK_U. U then obtains a trusted time-stamp D_g on σ, denoted as $SIGN_{TSA}(D_g, \sigma)$, from the TSA [RFC3161]. Suppose the next refreshing date of $CERT_U$ is D_e. U sends $SIGN_{TSA}(D_g, \sigma)$ and $(H^i(r), i)$, where $i = j - (D_e-D)/L$, to a transacting party V as non-repudiation evidence.

As discussed in Section 3.2, with $(H^i(r), i)$, it is easy for V to check whether $CERT_U$ is valid until the date D_e. Suppose V holds the TSA's public verification key.[4] Then, V could use $SIGN_{TSA}(D_g, \sigma)$ to further check whether σ is U's signature generated before D_e, i.e., $D_g \leq D_e$. If so, V could accept $SIGN_{TSA}(D_g, \sigma)$, $(H^i(r), i)$, $CERT_U$

---

[4] V might contact the TSA to check the status of its public key. The TSA might maintain an auditing log to testify the validity of its time-stamping in case of private key compromise.

safely as valid non-repudiation evidence. They could be used to prove to any third party that U's signature σ was generated while the corresponding certificate $CERT_U$ was still valid, and thus undeniable.

U could further extend the expiry date of $CERT_U$ to D_e+L by releasing $(H^{i-1}(r), i-1)$ when $D_e < D_j$, or let $CERT_U$ to expire at D_e by destroying the unreleased one-way hash chain. In either case, it will not affect the validity status of σ.

This approach avoids the CA's involvement for certificate revocation. Nevertheless, it still relies on the TSA to provide a trusted time-stamping service. The approach below is more attractive in that it eliminates the involvement of both the CA and the TSA.

4.2   Validating Forward-Secure Signatures without TTP

Forward-secure digital signature schemes [AR00, BM99, IR01, Kr00] update the private signing key at a regular interval while keeping the public key fixed throughout the lifetime of the certificate. The compromise of the current signing key will not lead to the compromise of the past signing keys. However, it will result in the compromise of subsequent signing keys and thus the forgery of signatures generated in the subsequent time periods. This problem could be solved with the support of the new PKI.

A forward-secure digital signature scheme contains four components: FWKG for key generation, FWUPD for private key update, FWSIGN for signing, and FWVER for signature verification. FWKG generates the public key PK and the root private key SK_0. PK, together with $(H^j(r), j, L)$, will be certificated by the CA. FWUPD updates the private key at each refreshing point as follows: $SK_1 = FWUPD(SK_0)$ at point D, $SK_2 = FWUPD(SK_1)$ at point D_1, ..., $SK_j = FWUPD(SK_{j-1})$ at point D_{j-1} (see Figure 1). FWUPD is a one-way function in the sense that no one can derive SK_{j-1} from SK_j but computing SK_j from SK_{j-1} is easy. Once the private key is updated, the old private key must be erased, thus nobody can derive any past private keys from the current one.

According to the time of signature generation, the digital signatures generated with this mechanism can be classified into three types as illustrated in Figure 1: signatures of past time periods, signatures of current time period, and signatures of subsequent time periods.

Suppose the current private key is SK_c. The signer U must attach the current time D_g to the message M that is to be signed,[5] denoted as $FWSIGN(M, D_g, SK_c)$. Suppose the next refreshing point of $CERT_U$ is D_e. U attaches $(H^i(r), i)$, where $i = j - (D_e-D)/L$, to the signature.

When the verifier V receives $FWSIGN(M, D_g, SK_c)$, $(H^i(r), i)$, and $CERT_U$, V could make the following checks.

---

[5] Here D_g need not be a trusted time stamp. Its main purpose is to indicate at which time period the signature was generated. The verification will fail if D_g is not within the time period that SK_c is valid for signing.

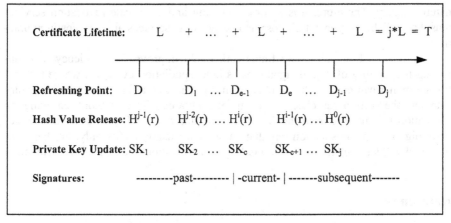

Fig. 1. Validating Forward-Secure Signatures without TTP

1. V checks U's signature $FWSIGN(M, D_g, SK_c)$ which requires D_g as an input of FWVER. If the signing time D_g is not within the valid period of SK_c, i.e., $D_g \leq D_{e-1}$ or $D_g > D_e$, the verification will fail. Otherwise, V believes that $FWSIGN(M, D_g, SK_c)$ is U's signature generated at a time between D_{e-1} and D_e.

2. With $(H^i(r), i)$, V further checks whether $CERT_U$ is valid until D_e. If so, V believes that $FWSIGN(M, D_g, SK_c)$ is U's signature generated at a time that $CERT_U$ was still valid.

If the above checks are successful, $FWSIGN(M, D_g, SK_c)$, $(H^i(r), i)$, and $CERT_U$ could be accepted safely as valid non-repudiation evidence. Signature generation and verification are not necessarily to be taken in the same time period.

If U suspects the compromise of his current private key SK_c, he could let $CERT_U$ to expire at D_e by destroying the unreleased one-way hash chain. The attacker cannot derive past private keys from the compromised current one, and thus cannot forge valid signatures of past time periods. Although the attacker could derive the subsequent private keys from the compromised current one, he cannot use them to forge valid signatures of subsequent time periods since $CERT_U$ has expired. More importantly, as the time periods of private key update and certificate expiry date extension are synchronized, and their frequency could be defined according to the individual's security requirement, the risk of signature forgery in the current time period could be well controlled. This is more flexible and secure than the CRL-based revocation mechanism where the update interval must be unified and acceptable to all certificate users.

5   Conclusion

Signature validation is one of the major topics in non-repudiation. Digital signatures usually serve as irrefutable cryptographic evidence to support dispute resolution in electronic transactions. As a signing key might be compromised, it could lead to signature forgery. Therefore, trusted time-stamping and certificate revocation services must be available to prevent big loss. However, these services are very costly in practice.

A revocation-free public-key framework could improve the efficiency in maintaining the validity of digital signatures as non-repudiation evidence, where the certificate owner can control the validity of his certificate that has an extensible expiry date, and the verifier can check the status of such a certificate without retrieving the revocation information from the CA. Based on this new PKI, we could validate *generic* digital signatures as non-repudiation evidence using a TSA only. Furthermore, we could validate *forward-secure* digital signatures without the TTP's involvement.

References

[ALO98]   W. Aiello, S. Lodha, and R. Ostrovsky. *"Fast digital identity revocation"*. Lecture Notes in Computer Science 1462, Advances in Cryptology: Proceedings of Crypto'98, pages 137--152, Santa Barbara, California, August 1998.

[AR00]   M. Abdalla and L. Reyzin. *"A new forward-secure digital signature scheme"*. Lecture Notes in Computer Science 1976, Advances in Cryptology: Proceedings of Asiacrypt'2000, pages 116--129, Kyoto, Japan, December 2000.

[BM99]   M. Bellare and S. Miner. *"A forward-secure digital signature scheme"*. Lecture Notes in Computer Science 1666, Advances in Cryptology: Proceedings of Crypto'99, pages 431--438, Santa Barbara, California, August 1999.

[Bo81]   K. S. Booth. *"Authentication of signatures using public key encryption"*. Communications of the ACM, 24(11):772--774, November 1981.

[Co00]   D. Cooper. *"A more efficient use of delta-CRLs"*. Proceedings of 2000 IEEE Symposium on Security and Privacy, pages 190--202, Oakland, California, May 2000.

[ISO13888-1] ISO/IEC 13888-1. "Information technology - Security techniques - Non-repudiation - Part 1: General". ISO/IEC, 1997.

[IR01]   G. Itkis and L. Reyzin. *"Forward-secure signatures with optimal signing and verifying"*. Lecture Notes in Computer Science 2139, Advances in Cryptology: Proceedings of Crypto'2001, pages 332--354, Santa Barbara, California, August 2001.

[IR02]   G. Itkis and L. Reyzin. *"SiBIR: Signer-base intrusion-resilient signatures"*. Lecture Notes in Computer Science 2442, Advances in Cryptology: Proceedings of Crypto'02, pages 499--514, Santa Barbara, California, August 2002.

[Ko98]   P. Kocher. *"On certificate revocation and validation"*. Lecture Notes in Computer Science 1465, Proceedings of 1998 Financial Cryptography, pages 172--177, Anguilla BWI, February 1998.

[Kr00]   H. Krawczyk. *"Simple forward-secure signatures from any signature scheme"*. Proceedings of 7th ACM Conference on Computer and Communications Security, pages 108--115, Athens, Greece, November 2000.

[La81]   L. Lamport. *"Password authentication with insecure communication"*. Communications of the ACM, 24(11):770--772, November 1981.

[Mi01]   S. Micali. *"Certificate revocation system"*. US Patent 6292893, September 2001.

[MJ00]   P. McDaniel and S. Jamin. *"Windowed certificate revocation"*. Proceedings of IEEE INFOCOM'2000, pages 1406--1414, Tel-Aviv, Israel, March 2000.

[NN98]   M. Naor and K. Nissim. *"Certificate revocation and certificate update"*. Proceedings 7th USENIX Security Symposium, San Antonio, Texas, January 1998.

[RFC2459]   R. Housley, W. Ford, W. Polk, and D. Solo. *"Internet X.509 public key infrastructure certificate and CRL profile"*. RFC 2459, January 1999.

[RFC2560]   M. Myers, R. Ankney, A. Malpani, S. Galperin, and C. Adams. *"X.509 Internet public key infrastructure on-line certificate status protocol (OCSP)"*. RFC 2560, June 1999.

[RFC3161]   C. Admas, P. Cain, D. Pinkas, and R. Zuccherato. *"Internet X.509 public key infrastructure time-stamp protocol (TSP)"*. RFC 3161, August, 2001.

[WLM00]   R. Wright, P. Lincoln, and J. Millen. *"Efficient fault-tolerant certificate revocation"*, Proceedings of 7th ACM Conference on Computer and Communications Security, pages 19--24, Athens, Greece, November 2000.

[Zh01]   J. Zhou. *"Non-repudiation in electronic commerce"*. Computer Security Series, Artech House, 2001.

[Zh02]   J. Zhou. *"Maintaining the validity of digital signatures in B2B applications"*. Lecture Notes in Computer Science, Proceedings of 2002 Australasian Conference on Information Security and Privacy, pages 303--315, Melbourne, Australia, July 2002.

[ZBD02]   J. Zhou, F. Bao, and R. Deng. *"NewPKI"*. Internal document, 2002.

[ZL99]   J. Zhou and K. Y. Lam. *"Securing digital signatures for non-repudiation"*. Computer Communications, 22(8):710--716, Elsevier, May 1999.

An Anonymous Asymmetric Public Key Traitor Tracing Scheme*

Choi, Jung Yeon Hwang, and Dong Hoon Lee

Center for Information Security Technologies (CIST)
Korea University, 1, 5-Ka, Anam-dong, Sungbuk-ku, Seoul, 136-701, Korea
{bluecey,hjy}@cist.korea.ac.kr
donghlee@korea.ac.kr

Abstract. In broadcast encryption schemes, traceability is a useful property to trace authorized subscribers, called *traitors*, who collude for manufacturing a pirate decoder. Unfortunately, this is usually achieved with a sacrifice of a privacy. Most traitor tracing schemes in the literature have been developed without considering a subscriber's anonymity, which is one of important requirements for electronic marketplaces to offer similar privacy as current marketplace. It would be unsatisfactory for the subscriber to reveal his/her identity to purchase multimedia contents. In this paper we propose an anonymous broadcast encryption scheme, where a user can subscribe anonymously, but anonymity control is provided, i.e., a data supplier can trace traitors. Our scheme is constructed based on an asymmetric public-key traitor tracing scheme with one trustee.

1 Introduction

Recently, broadcast encryption schemes are applied to distribution of digital contents −multimedia, software, or pay TV− on the network. In the broadcast encryption schemes it is important that only authorized subscribers can access digital contents and any malicious subscriber should not obtain digital contents from broadcast encryption messages. In general, to achieve this confidentiality, broadcast messages are encrypted by a session key which is encrypted again by subscriber's personal keys. Each subscriber decrypts broadcast messages with his personal key to find the session key.

Another important requirement in the broadcast encryption schemes is *traitor tracing*. The concept was introduced by Chor et al. [5] and enables to trace authorized subscribers, called *traitors*, who collude for manufacturing a pirate's device, called *pirate decoder* by offering a personal key. (Note that leaking the session keys themselves, constantly all the time, is typically considered in the literature not to be an economically viable option.) The traitor tracing scheme in [2] is *symmetric*, in which each subscriber shares a secret key with his data supplier (DS). But it is possible in the symmetric setting that DS frames an innocent

---

* This work was supported by grant No. R01 − 2001 − 000 − 00537 − 0 from the Korea Science & Engineering Foundation.

K. Bauknecht, A Min Tjoa, G. Quirchmayr (Eds.): EC-Web 2003, LNCS 2738, pp. 104–114, 2003.
© Springer-Verlag Berlin Heidelberg 2003

subscriber in the construction of a pirate decoder because DS can generates each subscriber's secret key. This may cause unsettled disputes. Pfitzmann proposed the *asymmetric traitor tracing scheme* [14] where secret keys are known only to subscribers, not to DS. This resolves a framing attack problem in the symmetric setting. Thereafter Boneh and Franklin (based on a preliminary suggestion of [9]) initiated the study of *public key traitor tracing scheme* [2], where DS encrypts a session key using only one public encryption key and each subscriber decrypts the session key using a distinct personal key. In view of applicability, a public key scheme allows digital contents to be sent by many content providers. This gives a scalable design of content distribution schemes with many content sources.

Anonymous Traitor Tracing Scheme. Anonymity becomes more important when one purchases multimedia contents giving a lot of information about his lifestyle, habits, and etc. Various researches about anonymity have been done in anonymous payment systems and communication systems [3, 4, 10]. It is a great pity that a buyer's anonymity is destroyed for the purpose of obtaining multimedia contents. However, this requirement might be conceptually conflicting with traceability of traitors. Namely, while buyers can purchase contents anonymously, DS can identify traitors in case of illegal redistribution. Hence it is not easy to design an anonymous traitor tracing scheme.

Recently, one anonymous traitor tracing scheme [11] has been proposed, where time-lock puzzles [13] and blind signatures [6] are used in order to provide anonymity. Unfortunately it has a flaw and does not provide anonymity as shown in Section 3. To the best of our knowledge, no anonymous traitor tracing scheme has been presented.

Our Contributions. First, we show that the anonymous scheme of [11] is actually not anonymous. That is, a dishonest DS can break anonymity protection for all honest subscribers. Next, we construct two anonymous schemes with Trusted Agent. The first scheme is the modification of the scheme in [11] by adopting Proving in Zero-knowledge from [7] and a bulletin board to provide anonymity. An amount of data transmission is reduced, compared to the scheme in [11]. The second scheme is a public key version of the first one by adopting asymmetric traitor tracing scheme from [8]. Our scheme is efficient since it needs no cut-and-choose technique to confirm the correctness of a personal key distributed by DS. Furthermore, our scheme achieves anonymity protection and provides full tracing. That is, given a pirate decoder, the tracing algorithm finds all keys that were used in the construction of the decoder, while in the scheme in [11] only one key is guaranteed to be found.

Organization of the Paper. This paper is organized as follows. In Section 2, we recall the basic building blocks required for our anonymous asymmetric scheme. In Section 3, we show a flaw of the previous proposal [11] and propose a solution achieving anonymity. In Section 4, we construct an anonymous asymmetric scheme using asymmetric public key traitor tracing [8]. Finally, we conclude in Section 5.

2   Building Blocks

Notations. The encryption of a message m with a key ek is denoted by $E_{ek}(m)$ and $E_{ek}(m', m) = E_{ek}(m')\|E_{ek}(m)$. The message m signed with a key sk is denoted by $m_{sign(sk)}$. We assume that G_q is a multiplicative subgroup of order q of $\mathbb{Z}_p^*$ where p and q are primes and $q \mid (p-1)$.

Oblivious Polynomial Evaluation. An OPE protocol [12] allows receiver B to compute the evaluation of sender A's polynomial P over its secret value α such that :

- Sender A can not extract any non-trivial information about α.
- Receiver B cannot extract any information about the polynomial P over a finite field, other than about the value $P(\alpha)$.

$\mathsf{OPE}(\alpha)$ denotes the data transmitted by B to A in the first flow, $\mathsf{OPE}(P(\alpha))$ denotes the data transmitted by A to B in the second flow. OPE has additional property; it is malleable, i.e., given $\mathsf{OPE}(\alpha)$ A can easily compute $\mathsf{OPE}(\alpha + \alpha')$ in the underlying finite field.

Asymmetric Public Key Traitor Tracing [8]. Kiayias and Yung proposed an efficient asymmetric public key traitor tracing scheme which can prove the implication of all traitors that participate in the construction of a pirate decoder. This scheme consists of the following six processes.

Initialization. The system-manager chooses one random polynomial $Q_1(x) = a_0 + a_1 x + a_2 x^2 + \ldots + a_{2v} x^{2v}$ over $\mathbb{Z}_q$ and a random $b \in \mathbb{Z}_q$, and computes $y = g^{a_0}, h_0 = g, h_1 = g^{-a_1}, \ldots, h_{2v} = g^{-a_{2v}}, h' = g^{-b}$. The tuple $< y, h_0, \ldots, h_{2v}, h' >$ is published as the public-key of the system. The system-manager computes $Q(x, y') := Q_1(x) + by'$ for two variables x and y' and keep it secret.

Join. The system-manager chooses random z_u, and $\alpha_u = \alpha_u^C + \alpha_u^R$ where α_u^C is a value selected and committed by a subscriber, and α_u^R is a value selected by the system-manager. The commitment of value α_u^C of the subscriber u is of the form $< C_u = g^{\alpha_u^C}, sign_u(C_u) >$. The join protocol is implemented by a Malleable OPE over a committed value. The subscriber's personal key is set to the vector $\overrightarrow{k_u} :=< Q(z_u, \alpha_u), z_u, z_u^2, \ldots, z_u^{2v}, \alpha_u >$.

Encryption. DS encrypts a message (content) M using a random r and encryption key $ek :=< y, h_0, \ldots, h_{2v}, h' >$ as follows.

$$\mathcal{E}(ek, M) =< y^r \cdot M, h_0^r, \ldots, h_{2v}^r, (h')^r >$$

Decryption. Subscribers decrypt a ciphertext $\widetilde{G} :=< G, G_0, G_1, \ldots, G_{2v}, G' >$ using their personal key $\overrightarrow{k} :=< \delta_0, \ldots \delta_{2v}, \delta' >$ as follows.

$$D(\widetilde{G}, \overrightarrow{k}) = G/((G')^{\delta'} \prod_{j=0}^{2v} (G_j)^{\delta_j})$$

Traitor-Tracing. The system-manager reveals the identities of the traitors by using a traitor tracing algorithm which is based on Decoding of Algebraic Codes. The algorithm detects non-repudiated information of all traitors which can be verified by a judge.

- Input : the pirate-decoder $\overrightarrow{K}$ and integers $z_1, \ldots, z_n$.
$\overrightarrow{K} = \sum_{\ell=1}^{t} \mu_\ell \overrightarrow{k}_{u_\ell}$, where $\{u_1, \ldots, u_t\} \subseteq \{1, 2, \ldots, n\}$, $t(< 2v + 2)$ is the set of traitor subscribers and n is the number of all subscribers in the system.
- Output : the vector $\overrightarrow{\nu} =< \nu_1, \ldots, \nu_t >$, where $\nu_{u_\ell} = \mu_\ell$ for $\ell = 1, \ldots, t$ and $\nu_i = 0$ for all $i \in \{1, \ldots, n\} - \{u_1, \ldots, u_t\}$.

The Trial. The system-manager transmits to the judge the vector $\overrightarrow{\nu}$, the pirate-decoder $\overrightarrow{K}$, the value $\alpha_{u_1}^R, \ldots, \alpha_{u_t}^R$, the commitments of the subscribers C_{u_1}; $sign_{u_1}(C_{u_1}), \ldots, C_{u_t}; sign_{u_t}(C_{u_t})$. Then the judge tests whether

$$\prod_{\ell=1}^{t} (C_{u_\ell} g^{\alpha_{u_\ell}^R})^{\nu_{u_\ell}} =^? g^{\overrightarrow{K}}.$$

If the test is passed, the judge assures that the subscribers $\{u_1, \ldots, u_t\}$ were implicated in the construction of the pirate-decoder $\overrightarrow{K}$.

Proving in Zero-Knowledge [7]. Let us briefly recall one of various proof-protocols in [7] proving the knowledge of a discrete logarithm x of a group element y to base g. The prover chooses a random $r \in_R \mathbb{Z}_q$ and computes $t = g^r$ and sends t to the verifier. The verifier picks a random challenge $c \in_R \{0,1\}^k$ and sends it to the prover. The prover computes $s = r - cx \bmod q$ and sends s to the verifier. If $g^s y^c = t$ holds, the verifier accepts.

Non-interactive Oblivious Transfer (nOT). A $(n,1)$-oblivious transfer protocol (OT_1^n) [1] is a data transferring method such that a receiver using her secret key can extract from $OT(\{s_i \mid 1 \leq i \leq n\})$ exactly one of n strings $\{s_i \mid 1 \leq i \leq n\}$ but a sender does not know which of n strings a receiver got. If there is no interaction between a sender and a receiver this OT_1^n is called non-interactive, denoted by nOT_1^n. We briefly recall nOT_1^2 presented by Bellare and Micali[1]. Let g be a generator of G_q. Suppose that some element C of $\mathbb{Z}_q^*$ are known to all the subscribers in the system, but nobody knows the discrete log of C.

How to Get keys: Receiver B picks $i \in \{0,1\}$ at random, $x_i \in \mathbb{Z}_{q-1}$ at random, and sets $\beta_i = g^{x_i}, \beta_{1-i} = C \cdot (g^{x_i})^{-1}$. His public key is (β_0, β_1) and his secret key is (i, x_i).

nOT(s_0, s_1): Sender A picks at random $y_i \in \mathbb{Z}_{q-1}$, $i \in \{0, 1\}$ and sends $\alpha_0 = g^{y_0}$, $\alpha_1 = g^{y_1}$ to B. Then A computes $\gamma_0 = \beta_0^{y_0}$ and $\gamma_1 = \beta_1^{y_1}$, and sends $r_i = s_i \oplus \gamma_i$, $i \in \{0, 1\}$ to B. B uses his secret key to compute $\alpha_i^{x_i} = \gamma_i$. Then he computes $\gamma_i \oplus r_i = s_i$. This protocol is based on the Diffie-Hellman assumption. Therefore, he cannot compute s_{1-i}, which means that A has succeeded in obliviously transferring the pair of strings (s_0, s_1).

3 A Flaw in Previous Proposal[11] and Anonymity Solution

In this section we show that anonymity of [11] is not achieved and propose a modification with Trusted Agent(TA). Though this modification requires a trusted entity, it reduces the amount of data transmission.

3.1 The Scheme of [11] is Flawed

The scheme of [11] is an asymmetric modification of the proposal [9] by Kurosawa and Desmedt. The authors of [11] made use of *non-interactive oblivious transfer* for an asymmetric setting. DS cannot determine the subscriber's decryption key which is one of two keys that were obliviously transfered. They also used *time-lock puzzle* to provide traceability. With a time-lock puzzle, a subscriber encrypts a message (a real identity of the subscriber) with an appropriately large symmetric key so that a receiver, DS, can decrypt it after a period of T seconds. When a pirate decoder is confiscated, the private decryption key of an unknown subscriber u is exposed. DS solves the time-lock puzzle assigned with the decryption key, identifies the subscriber and decides that u is a traitor. But we note that this technique is also used to achieve anonymity protection for all honest subscribers. If a malicious DS computes a time-lock puzzle with both possible decryption keys, it can reveal an innocent subscriber's identity. Therefore anonymity is not achieved.

3.2 Anonymous Traceability Scheme with Trusted Agent

We propose an anonymity solution using Trusted Agent(TA), based on zero-knowledge proof technique in [7] and a bulletin board. The bulletin board is used for DS to check whether a value given by a subscriber is valid or not. Later, it is possible for TA to find the traitors' identity.

In the following scheme, we assume that collusion between DS and TA can not occur. The protocol consists of two phases, initialization and key-generation.

Initialization

- Step 1. TA generates a key pair (ek_A, dk_A); dk_A is the secret decryption key of TA and ek_A is the public encryption key of TA. TA also generates a generator g of G_q at random and publishes (g, ek_A) as its public key.

Subscriber(sk_u; vk_u)		TA(dk_A; (g, ek_A))
$x \in_R \mathbb{Z}_q, PI = g^x$		
$w_b \in_R \mathbb{Z}_{q-1}, \ (b = 0 \ or \ 1)$		
$a_b = g^{w_b}, a_{1-b} = C \cdot (g^{w_b})^{-1}$	$\xrightarrow{\quad E_{ek_A}(PI_{sign(sk_u)}), \text{ID} \quad}$	Publish $(PI, (a_0, a_1))$
$< w_b, (a_0, a_1) >$	$\xrightarrow{\quad E_{ek_A}((a_0, a_1)_{sign(sk_u)}) \quad}$	on the bulletin board

Fig. 1. Initialization

- Step 2. A subscriber generates a key pair (vk_u, sk_u); sk_u is the secret signing key and vk_u is the public verification key. The subscriber chooses a random $x \in_R \mathbb{Z}_q$, computes $PI = g^x$ and signs the value PI with her signing key. We define the value PI as the *pseudo-identity*. The subscriber generates a key pair $< w_b, (a_0, a_1) >$ for nOT$_1^2$ and signs (a_0, a_1). The subscriber sends $E_{ek_A}(PI_{sign(sk_u)})$, the subscriber's identity ID and $E_{ek_A}((a_0, a_1)_{sign(sk_u)})$ to TA.
- Step 3. TA checks the key pair (a_0, a_1) and publishes $(PI, (a_0, a_1))$ on the bulletin board. TA then stores (ID, $PI_{sign(sk_u)}$, $(a_0, a_1)_{sign(sk_u)}$) in its database.

Key-Generation. Key generation phase consists of two steps as follows.

- *Setup.* DS generates a random polynomial $f(x) = c_0 + c_1 x + \ldots + c_k x^k$ over $\mathbb{Z}_q$ as an encryption key, where q is a prime with $q > n$ for a set of n authorized subscribers. DS associates a subscriber with two unique decryption keys, i.e., $S_0 = < u_0, f(u_0) >, S_1 = < u_1, f(u_1) >$ for two random numbers u_0 and u_1.
- *Key Generation.* The subscriber chooses $r \in_R \mathbb{Z}_q$, computes $t = g^r$ and transmits (PI, t) to DS. DS checks the correctness of the subscriber's public-key for nOT$_1^2$ and the subscriber's value on the bulletin board, obtains the subscriber's public-key (a_0, a_1). Then DS chooses $c \in_R \{0, 1\}^k$ and sends it to the subscriber. The subscriber computes $s = r - cx \mod q$ and sends s to DS. DS verifies whether the subscriber generates PI by checking $g^s (PI)^c =^? t$. If the test is passed, DS executes nOT$_1^2$ = nOT(S_0, S_1) protocol. The subscriber obtain exactly one of two decryption keys $\{S_0, S_1\}$, while DS can not determine which key the subscriber has extracted.

Anonymity. This scheme ensures anonymity protection of all honest subscribers since DS only knows the *pseudo-identity*. After a session, the subscriber should fresh *pseudo-identity* PI to avoid the leakage of linking information as follows.

- Step 1. The subscriber chooses a random number d and computes a new *pseudo-identity* $PI' = PI^d$ and the encryption key (a_0', a_1') for an oblivious transfer.

Setup : DS

$f(x) = c_0 + c_1x+, \ldots, +c_kx^k$: broadcast public key

$(S_0, S_1)-$ possible decryption key pairs

$S_0 = <u_0, f(u_0)>, S_1 = <u_1, f(u_1)>$

Key-Generation

Subscriber		DS
	$\xrightarrow{\quad (PI,\ t) \quad}$	Check $(PI, (a_0, a_1))$
$r \in_R \mathbb{Z}_q \; t = g^r$		on the bulletin board
	$\xleftarrow{\qquad c \qquad}$	$c \in_R \{0,1\}^k$
$s = r - cx \; mod \; q$	$\xrightarrow{\qquad s \qquad}$	Check $g^s(PI)^c =^? t$
$r_i \oplus \gamma_i = S_i$		$\beta_i = g^{y_i}, y_i \in_R \mathbb{Z}_{q-1}, i \in \{0,1\}$
Obtain	$\xleftarrow{OT(S_0,S_1)=\beta_0,\beta_1,r_0,r_1}$	$\gamma_0 = (a_0)^{y_0}, \gamma_1 = (a_1)^{y_1}$
one decryption key		$r_0 = S_0 \oplus \gamma_0, r_1 = S_1 \oplus \gamma_1$

Fig. 2. Key-Generation protocol

- Step 2. The subscriber signs them with the signature key sk_u and sends $E_{ek_A}(PI'_{sign(sk_u)})$, ID, $E_{ek_A}((a'_0, a'_1)_{sign(sk_u)})$ to TA. If a new session starts, the subscriber creates $r' \in_R \mathbb{Z}_q, t' = g^{r'}$ and sends (PI', t') to DS.
- Step 3. TA checks the subscriber's signature and stores in the database, then he publishes $(PI', (a'_0, a'_1))$. Therefore DS can not link various purchases made by a subscriber.

Traitor Tracing. When a pirate decoder is confiscated, the pirate decryption key $S_b = <u_b, f(u_b)>$ is exposed. DS finds out the subscriber's *pseudo-identity* and transmits it to TA. TA finds out the subscriber who was implicated in the construction of the pirate decoder and provides the subscriber's identity to DS. DS can decide the traitor.

Security. In the proposed this scheme, TA knows the identity of a subscriber. Therefore, if DS wants to frame an innocent subscriber in the construction (of the pirate decoder), then it must select one of two decryption keys that were transmitted to the subscriber. DS is able to incriminate the subscriber with a success probability $\frac{1}{2}$. After all, DS must run the risk of making a false accusation.

Compared to [11], an amount of data transmission is reduced in the scheme since DS just checks the *pseudo-identity* on the bulletin board instead of executing *cut-and-choose* technique for checking the correctness of the blinded

Subscriber(sk_u; vk_u)		TA(dk_A; (g, ek_A))
choose random a α_u^C		
$< C_u = g^{\alpha_u^C}, C_{u_{sign(sk_u)}} >$	$E_{ek_A}(PI_{sign(sk_u)})$, ID	Publish PI
$x \in_R \mathbb{Z}_q, PI = g^x$	$E_{ek_A}(<C_u = g^{\alpha_u^C}, C_{u_{sign(sk_u)}}>)$	on the bulletin board

Fig. 3. Initialization

message. In [11], a number of interaction is 3, while in the protocol presented above, a number of interaction is 2 including TA.

At the end of the protocol, the subscriber still execute cut-and-choose technique which makes DS choose correct decryption keys. The following conditions [11] are important for the security of the system.

Condition 1. For each subscriber i ($i = 1, \ldots, n$), an instance of $OT_i(S_{i,0}, S_{i,1})$ must contain two different decryption keys $S_{i,0}$ and $S_{i,1}$ such that $S_{i,0} \neq S_{i,1}$.

- DS creates two instances $OT_i =< E_{k_i}(S_{i,0}), E_{k_i}(S_{i,1}) > (i = 0, 1)$ of the oblivious transfer protocol, where K_1 and K_2 are two encryption keys of a symmetric encryption scheme. We define a commitment of the key K_i as C_{k_i}. Then DS signs ($OT_0, C_{k_0} \parallel OT_1, C_{k_1}$) and sends it to the subscriber. The subscriber can check the correctness of the encryptions by checking $E_{k_i}(S_{i,0}) =^? E_{k_i}(S_{i,1})$. The subscriber can also check the correctness of the symmetric key using C_{k_i} and K_i given by DS.

Condition 2. For any two different subscribers i and j, two instances of $OT_i(S_{i,0}, S_{i,1})$ and $OT_j(S_{j,0}, S_{j,1})$ must contain four different decryption keys.

- DS creates two instances $OT_i(=< C_{k_i}, E_{k_i}(S_{i,0}), E_{k_i}(S_{i,1}), hash(S_{i,0}), hash(S_{i,1}) >)$, $OT_j(=< C_{k_j}, E_{k_j}(S_{j,0}), E_{k_j}(S_{j,1}), hash(S_{j,0}), hash(S_{j,1}) >)$ for $i, j \in \{0, 1\}$ of the oblivious transfer protocol. The subscribers register the hash value on the bulletin board. Therefore, each joining subscriber always checks whether the hash values have been registered in the bulletin board or not. If not, DS is honest.

4   An Anonymous Asymmetric Public-Key Traitor Tracing Scheme

In this section we propose an anonymous asymmetric traitor tracing using public-key traitor tracing [8] with TA. This scheme consists of two phases; initialization and key generation.

TA stores ($ID, PI_{sign(sk_u)}, < C_u = g^{\alpha_u^C}, C_{u_{sign(sk_u)}} >$) in the database. DS makes use of the encryption key dk_D, ek_D.

Setup : DS
Choose $Q_1(x) = a_0 + a_1x + a_2x^2 + \ldots + a_{2v}x^{2v}$ over $\mathbb{Z}_q$ and a random $b \in \mathbb{Z}_q$.
Compute $Q(x, y') := Q_1(x) + by'$, the secret key and
$$y = g^{a_0}, h_0 = g, h_1 = g^{-a_1}, \ldots, h_{2v} = g^{-a_{2v}}, h' = g^{-b}.$$
Publish $< y, h_0, \ldots, h_{2v}, h' >$: the public key

Key – Generation

Subscriber		DS($dk_D; ek_D$)
	$\xrightarrow{\quad (PI, t) \quad}$	Check PI
$r \in_R \mathbb{Z}_q, \ t = g^r$		on the bulletin board
		Choose random z_u, α_u^R
	$\xleftarrow{c, \ z_u, \ \mathrm{OPE}(\alpha_u^R)}$	$c \in_R \{0,1\}^k$
$s = r - cx \ mod \ q$	$\xrightarrow{E_{ek_D}(s, \mathrm{OPE}(\alpha_u^R + \alpha_u^C))}$	Check $g^s(PI)^c =^? t$
Obtain		$\alpha_u = \alpha_u^R + \alpha_u^C$
$\overrightarrow{k_u} := < z_u, \alpha_u, Q(z_u, \alpha_u) >$	$\xleftarrow{\mathrm{OPE}(Q(z_u, \ \alpha_u))}$	

Fig. 4. Key-generation protocol of an anonymous asymmetric scheme

It is obvious that the scheme ensures *anonymity*. Contrary to a non-interactive oblivious transfer technique used the protocol presented in section 3, the subscriber's personal key $\overrightarrow{k_u}$ is verified by his own public-key $< y, h_0, \ldots, h_{2v}, h' >$ since $(h_0)^{Q(z_u, \alpha_u)} (h_1)^{z_u} \ldots (h_{2v})^{z_u^{2v}} (h')^{\alpha_u} = g^{Q(z_u, \alpha_u) - a_1 z_u - \ldots - a_{2v} z_u^{2v} - b\alpha_u} = g^{a_0} = y$.

Traitor Tracing and Trial. When a pirate decoder $(\overrightarrow{K} = \sum_{\ell=1}^{t} \mu_\ell \overrightarrow{k}_{u_\ell}$, where $\{u_1, \ldots, u_t\} \subseteq \{1, 2, \ldots, n\})$ is confiscated, DS inputs integers $z_1, \ldots, z_n$ to the algorithm. The output of the algorithm is the vector $\overrightarrow{\nu} = < \nu_1, \ldots, \nu_t >$, where $\nu_{u_\ell} = \mu_\ell$ for $\ell = 1, \ldots, t$ and $\nu_i = 0$ for all $i \in \{1, \ldots, n\} - \{u_1, \ldots, u_t\}$. Then DS sends the *pseudo-identity* PI, $\overrightarrow{\nu}$, $\overrightarrow{K}$, $\alpha_{u_1}^R, \ldots, \alpha_{u_t}^R$ to TA. Nezt TA finds out a commitments of $\alpha_{u_1}^C, \ldots, \alpha_{u_t}^C$ and checks if $\prod_{\ell=1}^{t} (C_{u_\ell} g^{\alpha_{u_\ell}^R})^{\nu_{u_\ell}} =^? g^{\overrightarrow{K}}$ for identifying the correctness of DS's claim. Then TA gives their identity to DS.

Security. This scheme imposes an limitation on the structure of pirate decoder. It is based on the hardness of the discrete logarithm problem. If the pirate decoder is not a linear combination of the vectors $< Q(z_u, \alpha_u), z_u, z_u^2, \ldots, z_u^{2v}, \alpha_u >$, then the discrete-log problem over *Group* is easily solved. Therefore, if the number of the coalition is t $(< 2v + 2)$, our scheme can find all subscribers that were implicated in the construction of the pirate key, while the scheme in [11] guarantees that only one traitor is traced.

5   Conclusion

In this paper, we showed that the anonymous scheme of [11] is actually not anonymous because of misuse of *Time-Lock Puzzles*. That is, a dishonest *DS* could break anonymity protection for all honest subscribers using again *Time-Lock Puzzles*, which is used to design traceability. We constructed two anonymous schemes with TA. The first scheme was the modification of the scheme in [11] by adopting Proving in Zero-knowledge from [7] and a bulletin board to provide anonymity. An amount of data transmission is reduced, compared to the scheme in [11]. The second scheme is a public key version of the first one by adopting asymmetric traitor tracing scheme from [8]. Our scheme is efficient since it needs no inefficient cut-and-choose technique to confirm the correctness of a personal key distributed by DS. Furthermore, our scheme achieves anonymity protection and provides full tracing. That is, given a pirate decoder, the tracing algorithm finds all keys that were used in the construction of the decoder, while in the scheme in [11] only one key is guaranteed to be found.

References

[1] M. Bellare, S. Micali, *Non-Interactive Oblivious Transfer and Applications*, Advances in cryptology – CRYPTO'89, LNCS 435, Springer-Verlag, 1990, pp.544-557.

[2] D. Boneh and M. Franklin. *An efficient public key traitor tracing scheme*. Advances in cryptology – CRYPTO'99, LNCS 1666, Springer-Verlag, 1999, pp.338-353.

[3] S. Brands, *Untraceable off-line cash in Wallets with observers*, Advances in cryptology – CRYPTO'93, LNCS 0773, Springer-Verlag, 1993, pp.302-318.

[4] D. Chaum, A. Fiat and M. Naor, *Untraceable Electronic Cash*, Advances in cryptology – CRYPTO'88, 1990, pp 319-327.

[5] B.Chor, A.Fait and M.Naor. *Tracing traitors*. Advances in cryptology – CRYPTO'94, LNCS 839 ,Springer-Verlag, 1994, pp. 257-270.

[6] D. Chaum, *Blind Signatures for Untraceable Payments*, Advances in cryptology – CRYPTO'82, Plenum Press, 1982, pp. 199-203.

[7] J. Camenisch and M. Michels, *Proving in Zero-Knowledge that a Number Is the Product of Two Safe Primes*, Advancen in cryptology–EUROCRYPT'99, LNCS 1592, 1999, pp 107-122.

[8] A. Kiayias and M.Yung, *Breaking and repairing asymmetric public-key traitor tacing*, ACM Conference on Computer and Communication Security, ACM, 2002.

[9] K. Kurosawa and Y. Desmedt ,*Optimum traitor tracing and asymmetric scheme*, Advances in cryptology – EUROCYRYPT '98, LNCS 1403, Springer-Verlag, 1998, pp.145-157.

[10] A. Lysyanskaya, R. L. Rivest, A. Sahia, and S. Wolf, *Pseudonym systems*, http://theory.lcs.mit.edu/anna/lrsw99.ps, 1999.

[11] E. Magkos, P. Kotzanikolaou, V. Chrissikopoulod, *An asymmetric traceability scheme for copyright protection without trust assumptions*, Advances in cryptology – EC_Web'2001, LNCS 2115, Springer-Verlag, 2001, pp.186-195.

[12] M.Naor and B. Pinkas, *Oblivious Transfer and Polynomial Evaluation*, the 31th ACM Conference on Computer and Communication Security, ACM, 1999.

[13] R. Rivest, A. Shamir, and D. Wagner, *Time-Lock Puzzles and Timed-Released Crypto.*, LCS Techinical Mono MIT/LCS/TR-684, 1996.

[14] B. Pfitzmann. *Trials of traced traitors*, Information Hiding'96, LNCS 1174, Springer-Verlag, 1996, pp 49-64 .

Toward a Security EC Transaction on Web

Whe Dar Lin

The Overseas Chinese Institute of Technology, Dept of Information Management
No. 100, Chiao Kwang Road Taichung 40721, Taiwan

Abstract. In this article, we present the way toward a security EC transaction on Web. The Internet and electronic commerce offer endless possibilities and opportunities to business of all sizes as well as convenience to consumers. These benefits are not reaped without danger for merchants and consumers. When a purchase list or an invoice is created it may get infected with some modification by intruder before the signature is attached to it. We proposed a signature scheme that let one can sign right in atomic step after creation for a security EC transaction on Web protocol. We have seen how electronic commerce accommodates the increasing consumer appetite for online shopping and Internet trade using the EC-Web server as the enabler. The data with some modification by intruder can be detected by EC-Web server or mobile agent. Besides that, we also proposed the message recovery capability to recover the original purchase list to save the infected files. The most natural extension of our protocol scheme that the mobile agent with anonymous property for mobile agent. The mobile agent use random id to purchase on EC Web. The EC-Web server can check random id is legal group member or not, with EC application packages will allow mobile agent and EC-Web server to commit themselves to one another. Security is the critical backdrop that must be in the place for our EC transaction on Web protocol.

1   Introduction

We know the important new economy aspect has been the creation of the Internet as a relative low-cost, easily accessible connection for all users. Consumer data communications from a mobile agent is routed to an EC-Web server, the information goes into EC-Web server, which store and service. Theft of confidential, propriety, technology, or mobile agent information belonging to the firm or to the customer. An intruder may disclose such information to a third party, resulting in damage to a customer, a mobile agent, or EC-Web server itself.

In this paper, we use a verifier to detect all infections caused after the completed digital service code, use a digital service transaction order manufacturer and an EC-Web server to specify the origin of the infection, the proposed system keep confidentiality, knowing ensuring that information in the network remains private for mobile agent, the proposed system keep authentication, based on a public key scheme

K. Bauknecht, A Min Tjoa, G. Quirchmayr (Eds.): EC-Web 2003, LNCS 2738, pp. 115-124, 2003.
© Springer-Verlag Berlin Heidelberg 2003

making sure that message senders or principals are who they say they are, and the proposed system keep integrity, making sure that transfer information is not accidentally or maliciously altered or corrupted in transit.

2   Backgrounds

The World Wide Web is fundamentally an application running over the Internet and TCP/IP intranet. Computer and communication technologies have encouraged the mobile agent and the distribution of electronic commerce information. We provide a digital service manufacturer, EC-Web server and mobile agent security in our protocol. We proposed the security model and approach discussed the issue of Web security. Therefore, the problem of our discussion in Web security is extremely important nowadays and in the future of electronic commerce. [1], [4]

In formally, Our proposed scheme relies on the existence of a hash function h. Specifically, We assume there exist a function h such that, On random input (r_i, m_i), it is difficult to generate (e_i) such that $h(r_i, m_i) = (e_i)$. More generally, it is difficult to generate such (e_i) on input (r_i, m_i) and samples of signature on random messages signed with EC-based platforms. [7]

The EC-Web server is vulnerable to attacks on EC transactions over the Internet. In generally, intruder can infect and incubate library files and text files. Intruder can damage both library files and text files. The EC-Web server for logistical partake to corporate, product information, consumer behavior and as the platform for EC transactions. Reputations can be damaged and money can be lost if the EC-Web server are subverted. [5], [8]

Our proposed signature scheme of protection against intruder works upon the following security assumptions. Solving the discrete logarithm problem is difficult, so we use in cryptographic protocols. Inverse calculation of one-way hash functions is difficult that we use assumption is often made in cryptographic protocols. Distributed operating system in Web-based executes a verification program properly. This assumption is important because improper events must be ruled out in the verification procedure so that one can rely on the results of the verification. The size of the largest primes for which discrete logs can be computed has usually been approximately the same size as the largest integers that could be factored both of these refer to computations that would work for arbitrary numbers of these sizes. [2], [3], [6], [9]

3   Our Proposed Toward a Security EC Transaction on Web Protocol

Let p and q be two large prime, such a prime p with $2^{511} < p < 2^{512}$, a prime divisor q|p – 1, a generator g with order q over GF(p). The security information of the digital service manufacturer u_m is x_m and the public information of the digital service manufacturer u_m is y_m ($y_m \equiv g^{x_m} \bmod p$). The security information of the EC-Web server u_s is x_s and the public information of the EC-Web server u_s is y_s

$(y_s \equiv g^{x_s} \bmod p)$. The security information of the mobile agent u_a is x_a and the public information of the mobile agent u_a is y_a ($y_a \equiv g^{x_a} \bmod p$).In this section, we shall illustrate the structure of our proposed method.

In our proposed protocol, the digital service manufacturer is denoted by u_m, the EC-Web server u_s and the mobile agent u_a. They follow the steps below. Step 1: The EC-Web server u_s sends the request Bit_vendor_produt$_{sm}$ to the digital service manufacturer u_m. Step 2: The digital service manufacturer u_m sends the E_tailer$_{ms}$ platform to the EC-Web server u_s. Step 3: The mobile agent u_a sends the transaction order Purchase_list$_{as}$ to the EC-Web server u_s. Step 4: The EC-Web server u_s sends the executable digital service invoice code Invoice$_{sa}$ to the mobile agent u_a.

3.1   The Mobile Agent Gets the Anonymous License

When mobile agent u_a wants to get an anonymous digital service, u_a must purchase an anonymous license from digital service manufacturer u_m. The digital service manufacturer u_m deducts a fixed amount of money from u_a's account. This anonymous license will allow mobile agent u_a authentication on EC-Web server. The protocol is as follows:

In step1, mobile agent u_a sends his ID$_a$, a nonce word N_1, his authentication information Cert$_{am}$, where a time stamp T, an expire time day T_e, and the certificate

$$Cert_{am} = (ID_a, T, T_e)_{K_{am}}$$

In step 2, the r is a random number. The digital service manufacturer u_m computes

$$Ran_a = g^r \bmod P \tag{1}$$

$$Cert_a = x_m * f(T_e) + r * T_e \bmod Q \tag{2}$$

where x_m is the secret key of digital service manufacturer u_m, y_m ($y_m = g^{x_m} \bmod P$) is the public key of the digital service manufacturer.

3.2   The EC-Web Server Requests the Bit_vendor_produt

When an EC-Web server u_s requests the delivery of the Bit_vendor_produt$_{sm}$. The computation is as follows.

(1) Generate a random number α_{sm} satisfying $0 < \alpha_{sm} < q-1$
(2) Compute

$$\beta_{sm} \equiv g^{\alpha_{sm}} \bmod p \tag{3}$$

$$m_{sm} \equiv con(u_s, Bit\_vendor\_product_{sm}) \tag{4}$$

$$r_{sm} \equiv h(\beta_{sm}, m_{sm}) \bmod q \tag{5}$$

$$R_{sm} \equiv \alpha_{sm} - x_s * r_{sm} \quad \bmod q \tag{6}$$

where h is a one-way function and con denotes concatenation function.

(3) Send $(u_s, Bit\_vendor\_product_{sm}, r_{sm}, R_{sm})$ with the request to the digital service manufacturer u_m .

3.3   The Digital Service Manufacturer Sends E_tailer Web-Based Platform

When the digital service manufacturer u_m receives the integers $(u_s, Bit\_vendor\_product_{sm}, r_{sm}, R_{sm})$, he verifies by computing the equations.

$$\beta^* \equiv g^{R_{sm}} y_s^{r_{sm}} \quad \bmod p \tag{7}$$

$$r_{sm} = h(\beta^*, con(u_s, Bit\_vendor\_product_{sm})) \tag{8}$$

check whether the congruence holds. If it holds, the digital service manufacturer u_m does as follow.

(2).   Generate a random number α_{ms} satisfying $0 < \alpha_{ms} < q\text{-}1$

(3).   Compute

$$\beta_{ms} \equiv g^{\alpha_{ms}} \quad \bmod p \tag{9}$$

$$check_{ms} \equiv x_m + \alpha_{ms} * \beta_{ms} \quad \bmod q \tag{10}$$

$$m_{ms} \equiv con(E\_tailer_{ms}, check_{ms}) \tag{11}$$

$$r_{ms} \equiv h(\beta_{ms}, m_{ms}) \quad \bmod q \tag{12}$$

$$R_{ms} \equiv \alpha_{ms} - x_m * r_{ms} \quad \bmod q \tag{13}$$

(4)   Send the E_tailer$_{ms}$ Web-based platform and its signature $(E\_tailer_{ms}, check_{ms}, r_{ms}, R_{ms})$ to u_s.

3.4   The Mobile Agent Requests to Process a Purchase List Order

A mobile agent u_a wants to order a purchase list, and the EC-Web server creates an executable digital service invoice code Invoice$_{sa}$. The EC-Web server u_s verifies $(E\_tailer_{ms}, check_{ms}, r_{ms}, R_{ms})$ by computing the following equations.

(1)   Compute

$$\beta^* \equiv g^{R_{ms}} y_m^{r_{ms}} \quad \bmod p \tag{14}$$

$$r_{ms} \equiv h(\beta^*, con(E\_tailer_{ms}, check_{ms})) \tag{15}$$

check whether the congruence holds. If it holds, the EC-Web server u_s does as the mobile agent wishes.

In the process of calculating a signature, the mobile agent executes the following steps:

(2). Generate a random number α_{as} satisfying $0 < \alpha_{as} < q-1$

(3). Compute

$$\beta_{as} \equiv g^{\alpha_{as}} \mod p \tag{16}$$

$$m_{as} \equiv con(Random\_ID_{as}, Purchase\_list_{as}) \tag{17}$$

$$r_{as} \equiv h(\beta_{as}, m_{as}) \mod q \tag{18}$$

$$R_{as} \equiv Randon\_ID_{as}^{-1}(\alpha_{as} - Purchase\_list_{as} * r_{as}) \mod q \tag{19}$$

$$check_\alpha \equiv Cert_a + \alpha_{as} * T_e + Random\_ID * R_{as} + Purchase\_list_{as} * r_{as} \quad \text{m} \tag{20}$$

$$check_\beta \equiv \beta_{as} * Ran_a \mod q \tag{21}$$

(4). Send $(Random\_ID_{as}, Purchase\_list_{as}, r_{as}, Check_\alpha, Check_\beta, T_e)$ with the request to the EC-Web server u_s.

3.5   The EC-Web Server Sends the Executive Digital Service Invoice

When the EC-Web server u_s receives the integers $(Random\_ID_{as}, Purchase\_list_{as}, r_{as}, Check_\alpha, Check_\beta, T_e)$, he verifies by computing the following equations

(1)   Compute

$$\beta^* \equiv g^{Check_\alpha} y_m^{-f(T_e)} Check_\beta^{-T_e} \mod p \tag{22}$$

$$r_{as} \equiv h(\beta^*, con(Random\_ID_{as}, Purchase\_list_{as})) \mod q \tag{23}$$

check whether the congruence holds. If it holds, executes the following steps:

(2)   Generate a random number α_{sa}, satisfying $0 < \alpha_{sa} < q-1$

(3)   Compute

$$\beta_{sa} \equiv Purchase\_list_{as} * g^{-\alpha_{sa}} \mod p \tag{24}$$

$$R_{sa} \equiv (\alpha_{sa} - \beta_{sa} * x_s) \mod q \tag{25}$$

$$Invoice_{sa} \equiv E\_tailer_{ms}(Purchase\_list_{as}) \tag{26}$$

$$Check_{sa} \equiv h^{-1}(Invoice_{sa})(Check_{ms} + \beta_{ms} * x_s) \mod q \tag{27}$$

$$\beta_{ms} \equiv g^{R_{ms}} y_m^{r_{ms}} \mod p \tag{28}$$

(4)   Send $(\beta_{sa}, R_{sa}, Check_{sa}, Invoice_{sa})$ satisfy digital service invoice to mobile agent u_a.

The E_tailer$_{ms}$ Web-based platform can be used only by the EC-Web server u_s because the integer check$_{ms}$ is the proxy key of the digital service manufacturer u_m. We support the message recovery capability to recover the original transaction order back to rescue the infected transaction order Purchase_list$_{as}$.

3.6   Signature Verification

When a mobile agent executes a digital service invoice code, Invoice made by u_s , the use verifies the signature with the digital service manufacturer's public key and server's public key.

$$g^{Check_{sa} * h(Invoice_{sa})} \equiv y_m (\beta_{ms} * y_s)^{\beta_{ms}} \mod p \tag{29}$$

In this verification process, the digital service manufacturer's public key is needed. Although the verifier can identify this signer us, he can check whether Invoice is modified or not. Since the signature $(\beta_{sa}, R_{sa}, Check_{sa}, Invoice_{sa})$ is automatically created, in this case, the infection can be detected by the verification. We can determine who causes the injection.

4   Correctness of Our Scheme

Theorem 1: The mobile agent u_a can get the correctness anonymous license from digital service manufacturer u_m. The EC-Web server u_s can processes the correctness transaction order request from the agent u_a. When an executable digital service code Invoice$_{sa}$ has been infected, the digital signature has message recovery capability to recover the original transaction order.

Proof:
The mobile agent u_a, receiving $(Cert_a, Ran_a, T_e)$ from digital service manufacturer u_m can compute

$$g^{Cert_a} = y_m^{f(T_e)} Ran_a^{T_e} \mod P \; where$$
$$g^{Cert_a} = g^{x_m * f(T_e) + r * T_e} = (g^{x_m})^{f(T_e)} (g^r)^{T_e} = y_m^{f(T_e)} Ran_a^{T_e} \tag{30}$$

If the above equations hold, the anonymous license $(Cert_a, Ran_a, T_e)$ is validly issued by digital service manufacturer u_m, has secret key x_m and public key y_m.

The agent u_a, receiving $(\beta_{sa}, R_{sa}, Check_{sa}, Invoice_{sa})$ from server u_s can compute

$$g^{Check_{sa}*h(Invoice_{sa})} \equiv y_m(\beta_{ms}*y_s)^{\beta_{ms}} \mod p$$

$$where \quad g^{Check_{sa}*h(Invoice_{sa})} \equiv g^{h^{-1}(Invoice_{sa})(Check_{ms}+\beta_{ms}*x_s)h(Invoice_{sa})}$$

$$\equiv g^{Check_{ms}+\beta_{ms}*x_s} \equiv g^{x_m+\alpha_{ms}*\beta_{ms}+\beta_{ms}*x_s} \tag{31}$$

$$\equiv g^{x_m}g^{(\alpha_{ms}+x_s)\beta_{ms}} \equiv y_m(\beta_{ms}*y_s)^{\beta_{ms}} \mod p$$

Then we can be sure the signature $(\beta_{sa},R_{sa},Check_{sa},Invoice_{sa})$ and use the public key of digital service manufacturer y_m and EC-Web server y_s.

$$g^{R_{sa}}y_s^{\beta_{sa}}\beta_{sa} \equiv g^{(\alpha_{sa}-\beta_{sa}*x_s)}(g^{x_s})^{\beta_{sa}}\beta_{sa} \equiv g^{\alpha_{sa}-\beta_{sa}*x_s+x_s*\beta_{sa}}\beta_{sa}$$

$$\equiv g^{\alpha_{sa}}*Purchase\_list_{as}*g^{-\alpha_{sa}} \equiv Purchase\_list_{as} \text{ m} \tag{32}$$

We will sure the signature of $(\beta_{sa},R_{sa},Check_{sa},Invoice_{sa})$ is Purchase_list$_{as}$ and when an executable digital service code Invoice$_{sa}$ has been infected, the digital signature has message recovery capability to recover the original transaction order Purchase_list$_{as}$.

5   Security Considerations

Theorem 2: The malicious agents want to forger the signature from the proposed scheme is computing impossible.

Proof:
Let G be a finite cyclic group with generate g. The crackers want to from the public key $y_m \equiv g^{x_m} \mod p$, $y_s \equiv g^{x_s} \mod p$, and $y_a \equiv g^{x_a} \mod p$ to reveal x_m, x_s, and x_a, they have to solve the discrete logarithm problem. For a fixed prime factor q of the order $|G|$ of G, consider the group element $a^{|G|/q}=a^{x\cdot|G|/q}$. Because $(a^{|G|/q})^q=a^{|G|}=e$ where e is the element of G, the q different q-th roots $g^0=e,g^{|G|/q},...,g^{(q-1)|G|/q}$ of e. We define $x \equiv i \pmod q$ as $a^{|G|/q}=g^{i\cdot|G|/q}$. The q is a prime factor of $|G|$ the representation $x \equiv x_0+x_1q+\cdots+x_{f-1}q^{f-1} \pmod{q^f}$. Because $(a\cdot g^{-x_0})^{|G|/q^2}=g^{x_1|G|/q}$ the group element is again equal to the q-th root of element. The complexity of the protocol for a group G with $|G|=\prod q_i^{f_i}$ is $O(\sum f_i(\log|G|+q_i))$.

The server u_s gets the receive $(E\_tailer_{ms},check_{ms},r_{ms},R_{ms})$ from u_m can compute

$$\beta^* \equiv g^{R_{ms}} y_m^{r_{ms}} \equiv g^{\alpha_{ms} - x_m * r_{ms}} (g^{x_m})^{r_{ms}}$$
$$\equiv g^{\alpha_{ms} - x_m * r_{ms} + x_m * r_{ms}} \equiv g^{\alpha_{ms}} \equiv \beta_{ms} \quad \mathrm{mod}\, p \tag{33}$$

$$h(\beta^*, con(E\_tailer_{ms}, check_{ms}))$$
$$= h(\beta_{ms}, con(E\_tailer_{ms}, check_{ms})) = h(\beta_{ms}, m_{ms}) = r_{ms} \tag{34}$$

holds. We will sure the signature of $(E\_tailer_{ms}, check_{ms})$ is (r_{ms}, R_{ms}).

I: The malicious agents use the false $(E\_tailer'_{ms}, check_{ms}, r_{ms}, R_{ms})$ signature send to server u_s

$$\beta^* \equiv g^{R_{ms}} y_m^{r_{ms}} \equiv g^{\alpha_{ms} - x_m * r_{ms}} (g^{x_m})^{r_{ms}}$$
$$\equiv g^{\alpha_{ms} - x_m * r_{ms} + x_m * r_{ms}} \equiv g^{\alpha_{ms}} \equiv \beta_{ms} \quad \mathrm{mod}\, p \tag{35}$$

$$h(\beta^*, con(E\_tailer'_{ms}, check_{ms}))$$
$$= h(\beta_{ms}, con(E\_tailer'_{ms}, check_{ms})) = h(\beta_{ms}, m'_{ms}) = r'_{ms} \neq r_{ms} \tag{36}$$

We will sure the signature of $(E\_tailer'_{ms}, check_{ms}, r_{ms}, R_{ms})$ is false signature.

II: The malicious agents use the false $(E\_tailer_{ms}, check'_{ms}, r_{ms}, R_{ms})$ signature send to EC-Web server u_s

$$\beta^* \equiv g^{R_{ms}} y_m^{r_{ms}} \equiv g^{\alpha_{ms} - x_m * r_{ms}} (g^{x_m})^{r_{ms}}$$
$$\equiv g^{\alpha_{ms} - x_m * r_{ms} + x_m * r_{ms}} \equiv g^{\alpha_{ms}} \equiv \beta_{ms} \quad \mathrm{mod}\, p \tag{37}$$

$$h(\beta^*, con(E\_tailer_{ms}, check'_{ms}))$$
$$= h(\beta_{ms}, con(E\_tailer_{ms}, check'_{ms})) = h(\beta_{ms}, m'_{ms}) = r'_{ms} \neq r_{ms} \tag{38}$$

We will sure the signature of $(E\_tailer_{ms}, check'_{ms}, r_{ms}, R_{ms})$ is false signature.

III: The malicious agents use the false $(E\_tailer'_{ms}, check'_{ms}, r'_{ms}, R'_{ms})$ signature send to server us

$$\beta^* \equiv g^{R'_{ms}} y_m^{r'_{ms}} \equiv \beta'_{ms} \quad \mathrm{mod}\, p \tag{39}$$

$$h(\beta^*, con(E\_tailer'_{ms}, check'_{ms}))$$
$$= h(\beta'_{ms}, con(E\_tailer'_{ms}, check'_{ms})) = h(\beta'_{ms}, m'_{ms}) = r'_{ms} \tag{40}$$

But the malicious agents choose another Web-based platform $E\_tailer'_{ms}$ and another proxy key $check'_{ms}$ tm' without know x_m, the congruence equation that they have to solve the discrete logarithm problem.

6   Performance

In this section, we shall calculate performance of our new method.

I: The computation cost on verifying the signature of an executable digital service code Invoice$_{sa}$

In our proposed method verifies the signature.

$$g^{Check_{sa}*h(Invoice_{sa})} \equiv y_m(\beta_{ms}*y_s)^{\beta_{ms}} \mod p$$

Our method uses 2 modular exponentiation computing time and 1 hash function computing time.

II: When an executable digital service code Invoice$_{sa}$ has been infected by viruses:

We have the message recovery ability for such digital service code.

We will sure the signature of $(\beta_{sa}, R_{sa}, Check_{sa}, Invoice_{sa})$ and public key of EC-Web server y_s that the digital signature has message recovery capability to recover the original Purchase_list$_{as}$.

$$g^{R_{sa}}y_s^{\beta_{sa}}\beta_{sa} \equiv g^{(\alpha_{sa}-\beta_{sa}*x_s)}(g^{x_s})^{\beta_{sa}}\beta_{sa} \equiv g^{\alpha_{sa}-\beta_{sa}*x_s+x_s*\beta_{sa}}\beta_{sa}$$
$$\equiv g^{\alpha_{sa}} * Purchase\_list_{as} * g^{-\alpha_{sa}} \equiv Purchase\_list_{as}$$

We will sure the signature of $(\beta_{sa}, R_{sa}, Check_{sa}, Invoice_{sa})$ is Purchase_list$_{as}$ and when an executable digital service code Invoice$_{sa}$ has been infected, the digital signature has message recovery capability to recover the original transaction order Purchase_list$_{as}$ toward a security EC transaction on Web.

7   Conclusion

In traditional ways of doing business, there are practical and legal differences between traditional paper-based commerce and Web-based commerce. In this paper, we proposed protocol used toward a security EC transaction on Web to process an EC transaction order which a signature scheme which enabled a verifier to detect all infections caused after the produce digital service invoice and a transaction order manufacturer to describe the origin of the infection.

The issue of security surfaces, privacy is also involved. A secure EC-Web site implies a site that ensures the privacy and confidentiality of the mobile agent identification. This means that an EC-Web site should keep anonymous policy for the member of clubs or group. Many people fears with respect to show of personal information in an EC-Web site.

In our design protocol, our security policies cover the threads against which EC transactions information must be protected in order to ensure integrity, and privacy. In our design toward a security EC transaction on Web, involves a good EC service require, EC-Web site security need, and structuring the security environment the EC system. We proposed the message recovery capability to recover the original purchase list to save the infected files.

In the future, the EC security perimeter generally has firewall, authentication, anonymous, virtual private network, and intruder detection. That means capturing processing EC service operating within the security policy, and verifying that attacks by intruder or hacker.

References

[1]   A. Ginige and S. Murugesan, "Web Engineering: An Introduction," J. of IEEE MultiMedia, January 2001, pp.14-18.

[2]   A. Young and Moti Yung, "Auto-Recoverable Auto-Certifiable Cryptosystems," Advances in Cryptology-EUROCRYP'FO'98, LNCS 1403, pp.17-31, Springer-Veriag, 1991.

[3]   Berry Schoenmakers, "A Simple Publicly Verifiable Secret Sharing Scheme and Its Application to Electronic Voting," Advances in Cryptology-CRYPTO'99, LNCS 1666, pp148-164, Springer-Veriag, 1999.

[4]   D. W. Manchala, "E-Commerce Trust Metrics and Models," J. of IEEE Internet Computing, March 2000, pp. 36-44.

[5]   J. B. Lim and A. R. Hurson, "Transaction order processing in Mobile, Heterogeneous Database Systems," IEEE Trans. On Knowledge and data Engineering, Vol. 14, No. 6, 2002, pp.1330-1346.

[6]   K. Nyberg, R.A. Rueppel, "Message recovery for signature scheme based on the discrete logarithm problem," Designs, Codes and Cryptography, No 7, pp.61-81, 1996.

[7]   K. Usuda, M. Mambo, T. Uyematsu and E. Okamoto "Proposal of an automatic signature scheme using a Web-based platform", IEICE Trans. Fundamentals E79-A (1) (1996) 94-101.

[8]   R. Sherwood, B. Bhattacharjee and A. Srinivasan, "A Protocol for Scalable Anonymous Communication," Proc. the IEEE Symposium on Security and Privacy, 2002, pp.1-12.

[9]   Ueli Maurer, "Information-Theoretic Cryptography," Advances in Cryptology-CRYPTO'99, LNCS 1666, pp47-65, Springer-Veriag, 1999.

Genetic Local Search
in an Automated Contracting Environment

Ma. Fe R. Alvarez[1] and Remedios de Dios Bulos[2]

[1]College of Computer Studies, De La Salle University, Manila, Philippines
mra1217@yahoo.com
[2]College of Computer Studies, De La Salle University, Manila, Philippines
remedios@ccs.dlsu.edu.ph

Abstract. In automated contracting, bid evaluation is a complex process because the task of finding the optimal set of bids requires the consideration of several factors such as time constraints, risk estimates and price. There have been attempts in the recent past (such as the use of simulated-annealing) to solve the bid evaluation problem in an automated contracting environment. This research endeavors to offer a better alternative to the solution of the bid evaluation problem by adopting the genetic local search (GLS) method.

1   Introduction

Markets play an essential role in the economy by facilitating the exchange of information, goods, and services [3]. And there is growing evidence that software agents will play an increasing role as mediators in electronic markets [14, 23]. Mediators typically provide services such as searching for a product or supplier, negotiating the terms of a deal, providing payment services, and ensuring delivery of goods. Automated negotiation, particularly bid evaluation [2, 13] is one market function where software agents' capability can be explored.

Bid evaluation is a costly optimization problem. It involves the examination of all possible combination of bids and subsequently the selection of the best combination based on factors such as price, supplier reliability, schedule risk, etc. If an exhaustive search approach is used to derive the optimum solution, the generation of possible bid combinations will explode combinatorially as the number of bids (input) grow.

In the recent past, several attempts have been made to improve search performance of combinatorial problems, among which include classical local search algorithms [21], simulated annealing [24], threshold accepting [9], tabu search [8], elastic nets [7], neural networks [1], genetic algorithms [12, 15], and ant colonies [11]. Although some of these approaches may have yielded limited success when applied individually, better solutions, however, have been achieved by integrating several methods. Genetic local search (GLS), which is a combination of local search and genetic algorithms, is one example.

K. Bauknecht, A Min Tjoa, G. Quirchmayr (Eds.): EC-Web 2003, LNCS 2738, pp. 125–134, 2003.
© Springer-Verlag Berlin Heidelberg 2003

The use of GLS is found to be effective in finding near-optimum solutions to combinatorial optimization problems such as the traveling salesman problem (TSP) [16], the graph bi-partitioning problem (GBP) [20], NK-Landscapes [17], and binary quadratic programming [19]. Ulder et al. [23] have even compared and consequently proven the superiority of GLS with other methods such as simulated annealing and multi-start local search.

This research, with the main purpose of offering a better alternative, adopts the genetic local search (GLS) method to the bid evaluation problem in a multi-agent automated contracting environment [2].

2   MAGNET Protocol

Basically, automated contracting involves negotiation among agents, who are assumed to be self-interested and possess limited rationality. This research adopts the *MAGNET* automated contracting protocol [5], which involves two types of agents: the *customer* and the *supplier*. To successfully execute a plan, the customer agent requests for resources or services. The supplier agent(s) may fulfill the request by offering resources or services for specified prices over specified periods. During negotiation, the supplier agent attempts to gain the highest possible price while the contractor agent endeavors to bargain for the lowest price [6].

The MAGNET protocol consists of five steps, which are plan formulation, issuance of call-for-bids, submission of bids, evaluation of bids, and awarding and delivery of bids. Figure 1 (using AUML [25]) illustrates an example of a contracting situation using MAGNET for a fictitious company (ACME). In this example, the customer agent issues a call-for-bids for a plan that consists of nine subtasks (S0, S1, S2, S3, S4, S5, S6, S7 and S8). For each subtask, a time window (start time and finish time of the task) is specified.

The supplier agent(s) formulates and submits sealed bids (Bid 0, Bid 1, Bid 2 and Bid 3) for the subtasks. Upon receiving the bids, the customer agent then evaluates the bids based on factors such as price, supplier reliability, schedule risk, etc. Subsequently, it awards the tasks to the lowest bidder. The customer agent has the option of either awarding the whole task (all subtasks) to a specific supplier or granting individual bid components (specific subtasks) to different suppliers. As shown in the figure, the customer agent opts to award components of the bid to different suppliers (that is, S6 is awarded to bid 0, subtasks S0 and S3 are awarded to bid 1, subtasks S1, S5 and S7 are awarded to bid 2, and subtasks S2, S4 and S8 are awarded to bid 3).

3   Bid Cost Estimation

The bid evaluation procedure adopted in this study involves the estimation of the total cost of the bid-task combination (Tc) by getting the weighted sum of the bid-task price (P_k), supplier reliability (S_k), and schedule risk (C_k), that is,

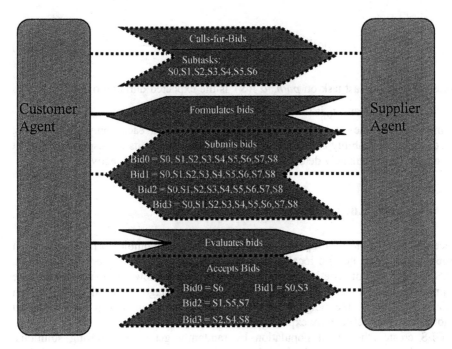

Fig. 1. An Example of a Contracting Situation (ACME Corporation)

$$Tc = P_k + S_k + C_k \tag{1}$$

where, k is the path,

$$P_k = total\_bid\_prices * weight\_factor \tag{2}$$

$$S_k = average\_splier\_reliability * weight\_factor\_splier \tag{3}$$

$$C_k = total\_sked\_risk * weight\_factor\_sked \tag{4}$$

A bid may incur some risks, such as recovery cost, loss of value due to delays and cost of plan failure. In this study, two types of risks are considered: supplier reliability and schedule risk. Supplier reliability refers to the reputation of the supplier. Schedule risk is related to constraint-tightness, which is determined according to the slack available along each partial path through the task network [6]. When the schedule becomes tighter, the value of constraint-tightness becomes lower and the schedule risks become higher.

Constraint-tightness is measured by path (k), where a path is a sequence of tasks starting at the beginning of the plan and extending toward the goal along successor relations. Partial paths and complete paths are used for the calculation because tasks can be constrained both by their precedence relationships and by the time windows specified in the bids. Along each path, constraint tightness is measured as the ratio of slack to expected duration, that is,

$$k(path) = \frac{t_{lf}(s_{last}) - t_0 - \sum_{s \in path} d_e(s)}{\sum_{s \in path} d_e(s)} \tag{5}$$

where, s_{last} is the last task on *path*, $d_e(s)$ is the expected duration of task s, t_{lf} is the late finish time and t_0 is the start time.

In estimating the total cost of a bid–task combination, each component (that is, price, supplier reliability and schedule risk) is multiplied by its corresponding weight factor, which is ultimately determined by the customer agent (subjective).

4   Genetic Local Search (GLS)

Recently, approaches for optimal solutions to various combinatorial optimization problems based on genetic local search (GLS) (e.g. [23], [10]) have been proposed. GLS is a variation of genetic algorithm (GA) in which the new candidate solutions are improved by local search (LS). It combines the advantages of local search, which efficiently exploits the neighborhood of a single solution and population-based algorithms, which efficiently explore the search space.

GLS creates the initial population by randomly generating starting solutions, without incorporating domain knowledge. Genetic operators are then applied to randomly selected members of the population for a predefined number of times. Since the genetic operators are generally not able to produce locally optimum solutions, the local search algorithm is applied to the offspring before they are added to the population. For survival, the selection of the best individuals from the extended population should form a new generation. The search process is said to have converged when the probability for generating new solutions with better fitness has approached zero.

Application of GLS to the bid evaluation problem can be best described through the discussion of the representation of individuals and the initial population, fitness function, the local search, and the genetic operators used.

4.1   Representation

The solution to the bid evaluation problem is represented as a vector of bids, such that the value j of the ith component in the vector indicates that bid j is assigned to task i. For example, in a solution vector: bid 4 is assigned to task 0, bid 2 is assigned to task 1, bid 0 is assigned to task 2, and so on.

4.2   Evaluation Function

The fitness function returns a single numerical "fitness" or "figure of merit" which should be proportional to the "utility" or "ability" of the individual. In the bid evaluation problem, the fitness of a solution vector is calculated as:

$$\min f(x) = P_k + S_k + C_k \qquad (6)$$

where $f(x)$ is equal to the total cost (see equation 1).

4.3   Initialization and Selection

The initial population is randomly generated. The genetic algorithm (GA) is then applied to discover the most promising members. The solutions with high fitness values (using equation 6) are chosen as offspring for the next generation.

4.4   Genetic Algorithm Operators

In the GLS approach adopted in this study, two operators, namely, *crossover* and mutation are applied. During crossover, all common bid-task assignments held by both parents are copied to the offspring. The remaining unassigned tasks are then randomly filled with bids. However, during this process, it should be ensured that the assigned bid should not duplicate the bids of the parents.

Mutation, which randomly alters each gene, is applied to a child after crossover. In bid evaluation, mutation involves the reversing the order of entries of a substring (of length l) in the genome (bid-task assignment), which leads to a solution that has a distance l to the original solution, if l is even, and a distance of $l-1$, if l is odd [18]. The following steps are executed during mutation: selection of an individual from the population at random; selection of positions k and l at random; and inversion of the sub string from position k to position l.

4.5   Local Search Heuristic

The local search used in this study is a variant of the *1-opt neighborhood* search. It can be described as the generation of possible solutions by iteratively changing a single element in the current solution. It requires the entire neighborhood to be searched at each step. The solution in the neighborhood with the best fitness is chosen.

4.6   GLS Algorithm for Bid Evaluation

Below, is the genetic local search algorithm code for bid evaluation.

5   Implementation

The GLS approach to the bid evaluation problem was implemented in Java and runs on an Intel Pentium 4 workstation (1.16 GHz). To illustrate an example of the GLS approach, a set of tasks (or plan) for a fictitious company (ACME) was used and is shown in Table 1. This plan together with the bids (see Table 2 for sample bids) from the suppliers and parameter settings comprises the main input required to execute GLS method. The run time parameters used are: number of generations (tmax) is 10, population size (pop-size) is 4, convergence factor (dmax) is 20, number of crossovers (C_{max}) is 2, number of mutations (M_{max}) is 2, number of bids (bid-size) is 4 and number of tasks (task-size) is 9.

Listing 1. The Genetic Local Search Algorithm For Bid Evaluation

```
procedure GLS-BEP
begin
initialize population P;
for each individual i ∈ P do i: = Local-Search(i);
repeat
    for i := 1 to #crossovers do
        select two parents ia, ib ∈ P randomly;
        ic := Crossover(ia, ib);
        ic := Local-Search(ic);
        add individual ic to P;
    end for;
    for i := 1 to #mutations do
        select an individual i ∈ P randomly;
        im := Mutate(im);
        im := Local-Search(im);
        add individual im to P;
    end for;
    P := select(P);
until time limit is reached or population has
converged;
end;
```

The initial step entails the estimation of total cost of each bid-task combination (using equation 1). For example, for the bid-task combination V0 = [2 0 2 0 2 3 1 2 3], the total cost calculated is 590.6953. Subsequently, the GLS steps are executed. The initial population randomly generated consisted of: V0 = [2 0 2 0 2 3 1 2 3] = 590.6953; V1 = [3 0 1 3 1 3 1 0 2] = 567.7455; V2 = [3 0 2 0 1 3 1 0 2] = 593.2456;V3 = [2 0 2 3 0 2 1 0 2] = 638.0028.

Table 1. A Plan for ACME Construction

k	Activity	Duration (days)	Predecessor Activities	Early Start	Late Finish
0	Foundation	16	-	0	16
1	Rough Plumbing	10	-	0	10
2	Concrete slab	14	0,1	16	30
3	Structural members	8	2	30	38
4	Roof	10	3	38	48
5	Rough electrical	14	3	38	52
6	Heating and air conditioning	14	1, 3	38	52
7	Walls	28	3, 5, 6	52	80
8	Interior finish	38	4, 7	80	118

Table 2. Example of Bids Offered by A Supplier

Bid	Task	Price	Early Start	Duration	Late Finish	Reliability
B0	S0	26.401127	1	15	16	83
	S1	56.20806	5	2	7	
	S2	39.880566	25	4	29	
	S3	35.30115	34	2	37	
	S4	71.93485	40	7	48	
	S5	58.74893	40	7	48	
	S6	23.21508	39	13	52	
	S7	71.58414	52	18	70	
	S8	95.28641	80	17	116	

Local search is then performed for each individual in the initial population to obtain a population of local minima. For example, local minimum at task 4 is the permutation P2 = [2 0 2 0 2 3 1 2 3] = 590.6953. The initial population after the local search is applied becomes: V0 = [2 0 2 0 3 3 1 2 3] = 560.6377; V1 = [3 2 1 3 1 3 1 0 2] = 540.4933; V2 = [3 0 2 0 1 3 1 0 3] = 583.0978;V3 = [2 0 2 3 3 2 1 0 2] = 608.5564;

If the population has converged (d = d_{max}) or the number of maximum generations has been reached (t = t_{max}), the best solution of the current population is selected; otherwise the GA operators are applied.

Two crossover operations (with local search) are applied to randomly chosen individuals for a predefined number of times (C_{max}). For the first crossover operation, a new individual (V4 = [1 2 0 3 3 0 1 0 3] = 482.5218) is added to the population. For the second crossover operation another individual (V5 = [3 2 3 1 1 2 1 0 3] = 385.6329 is added.

Two mutation operations are subsequently applied to randomly chosen individuals for a predefined number of times (M_{max}). For the first mutation operation, a new individual (V6 = [1 2 3 3 3 2 1 0 2] = 423.9372) is added to the population. For the second mutation operation another individual (V7 = [1 2 3 0 3 3 3 0 3] = 422.2546) is added.

The individuals with high fitness values (low costs) are chosen as offspring for the next generation in order to keep the population size constant. The individuals chosen are: V0 = [1 2 0 3 3 0 1 0 3] = 482.5218; V1 = [3 2 3 1 1 2 1 0 3] = 385.6329; V2 = [1 2 3 3 3 2 1 0 2] = 423.9372; V3 = [1 2 3 0 3 3 3 0 3] = 422.2546

When the population has converged or the number of maximum generations has been reached, the best solution of the current population is reported. Otherwise, the process of crossover and mutation is again performed. The best solution obtained from a random run of GLS with 10 generations for the ACME example is: VB = [1 2 3 1 3 2 0 2 3] = 225.0814.

6   Results and Analysis

To test the efficiency and effectiveness of the GLS approach adopted in this study, experiments were conducted. These experiments compare the performance of the GLS with the simulated annealing method.

A total of four tests were conducted and each test has a different problem size. In both simulated annealing (SA) and GLS methods, identical plans and bid sets for each problem size were used. For each test, run time parameters were setup for both SA and GLS. In the simulated-annealing method [6], the initial temperature is 0.35; it is reduced by 0.0095 every iteration; the patience factor (number of iterations without improvement) is 50, and the time limit (loop passes) is 500. The stopping criterion is either time limit or failure of the solution to improve when the number of iterations is equal to the patience factor.

In GLS, the population size 10, the number of crossovers is 5, the number of mutations is 2, the convergence factor (number of iterations without improvement) is 50 and the number of generations is 70. The stopping criterion is either time limit (number of generations) or failure to improve when the number of iterations is equal to the convergence factor.

The comparative results for the experiments are presented in Table 3. Each test involved 10 runs. The Solutions/Problem column shows the number of distinct nodes or solutions generated before the optimum or best value was found. The Best Value Found column contains the average final value of the best solution over 10 runs. The Optimal Solution column shows the value of the optimum or best-known solution. The Problems Solved column gives the number of runs (out of 10 runs) in which the optimum solution was found. The average running time for both procedures are shown in the Run Time column. The # Iterations column shows the number of loop passes or generations in which the optimum solution was found.

Based on the results, it can be said that for all the test instances, the use of GLS in producing the optimal solution(s) relatively required smaller number of iterations and shorter time. And as indicated by the average values, the GLS method obtained the optimal solutions in the majority of runs. Explicitly, it can be said that GLS method yields better results than the simulated annealing procedure for the varying problem sets used in the experiments.

Table 3. Comparative Results of SA and GLS

Problem Size		Solutions/Problem		Best Value Found		Optimal Solution	Problems Solved		Run Time						#Iterations	
		SA	GLS	SA	GLS		SA	GLS	SA hh	mm	ss	GLS hh	mm	ss	SA	GLS
# bids	# tasks															
50	20	31.6	12.8	65.6344	62.4896	62.4896	9	10	0	0	14	0	0	5.7	253.7	75
100	30	46.4	18.8	57.8075	56.2220	56.2220	7	10	0	0	38	0	0	13.8	341.4	91.9
2000	20	31.8	13.8	21.4979	21.3672	18.6568	6	9	0	2.7	18.4	0	0.5	32.8	250.9	53.4
5000	30	44.2	19.8	40.11974	21.2347	21.2347	2	10	0	0.4	28.5	37.9	0	21.3	31.6	298.8	111.9

7   Conclusion and Recommendations

The genetic local search technique presented in this paper solves the problem of bid evaluation more efficiently than simulated annealing. For future research, an alternative local search (such as simulated annealing) may be investigated to further enhance the performance of the GLS approach. Also, it will be worthwhile to examine whether the GLS will still perform respectably in more complex bid evaluation problems, which involve relatively wide and possibly overlapping time windows.

References

[1]   Aarts, E., Stehouwer, H.P.: Neural Networks and the Travelling Salesman Problem.   In Proceedings International Conference on Artificial Neural Networks, Springer-Verlag (1993) 960-966

[2]   Alvarez, M. F. R.: A Genetic Local Search Approach To The Bid Evaluation Problem In An Automated Contracting Environment. A Thesis Presented to the Faculty of the Graduate School of the College of Computer Studies, De La Salle University (2002)

[3]   Bakos, Y.: The Emerging Role of Electronic Marketplaces on the Internet. In Communications of the ACM (1998) 33-42

[4]   Beam, C., Segev, A.: Automated Negotiations: A Survey of the State of the Art. Technical Report CITM Working Paper 96-WP-1022, Walter A. Hass School of Business (1997)

[5]   Collins, J., Sundareswara, R., Tsvetovat, M., Gini, M., Mobasher, B.: Search Strategies for Bid Selection in Multi-Agent Contracting.   Agent-mediated Electronic Commerce. Proceedings of IJCAI '99, Stockholm, Sweden, (1999)

[6]   Collins, J., Sundareswara, R., Tsvetovat, M., Gini, M., Mobasher, B.: Multi-Agent Contracting for Supply-Chain Management. Technical Report 00-010, University of Minnesota (2000)

[7]   Durbin, R., Sacliski, R., Yuille, A.: An Analysis of the Elastic Net Approach to the Traveling Salesman Problem. Neural Computation, Vol. 1 (1989) 348-358.

[8]   Fiechter, L.: A Parallel Tabu Seach Algorithm for Large Traveling Salesman Problems.   Discrete Applied Mathematics and Combinatorial Operations Research and Computer Science (1994) 243-267

[9]   Freisleben, B., Schulte, M: Combinatorial Optimization with Parallel Adaptive Threshold Accepting. In Proceedings of 1992 European Workshop on Parallel Computing, Barcelona, TOS Press, (1992) 176-179

[10] Freisleben, B., Merz, P.: A Genetic Local Search Algorithm for Solving Symmetric and Asymmetric Traveling Salesman Problems. In Proceedings of the 1996 IEEE International Conference on Evolutionary Computation, Nagoya, Japan, (1996) 616-621

[11] Gambardella, L.M., M. Dorigo, M.: Ant-Q: A Reinforcement Learning Approach to the Travelling Salesman Problem. In Proceedings of 18th International. Conference on Machine Learning, Morgan Kaufman (1996) 252-260

[12] Goldberg, D.E.: Genetic Algorithms in Search, Optimization and Machine Learning. Addison-Wesley (1989)

[13] Guttman, R. Maes, P.: Cooperative vs. Competitive Multi-agent Negotiations in Retail Electronic Commerce. In 2nd International Workshop on Cooperative Information Agents (1998).

[14] Guttman, R., Moukas, A., Maes, P.: Agent-mediated Electronic Commerce: A Survey, In Knowledge Engineering Review (1998)

[15] Homaifar, L., Guan, C., Liepins, G.: A New Approach to the Travelling Salesman Problem by Genetic Algorithms. In Proc. 5th International Conference on Genetic Algorithms, Morgan Kaufmann (1993) 460-466

[16] Merz, P., Freisleben, B.: Genetic Local Search for the TSP: New Results. In Proceedings of the 1997 IEEE International Conference on Evolutionary Computation, IEEE Press, (1997) 159-164

[17] Merz, P. Freisleben, B.: On the Effectiveness of Evolutionary Search in High-Dimensional NK-Landscapes. In Proceedings of the 1998 IEEE International Conference on Evolutionary Computation, IEEE Press (1998) 741-745

[18] Merz, P., Freisleben, B.: A Genetic Local Search Approach to the Quadratic Assignment Problem", a manuscript (1999)

[19] Merz, P. Freisleben, B.: Fitness Landscapes, Memetic Algorithms and Greedy Operators for Graph Bi-Partitioning. Evolutionary Computation (1999)

[20] Merz, P., Freisleben, B.: Genetic Algorithms for Binary Quadratic Programming. In Proceedings of the Genetic and Evolutionary Computation Conference, Morgan Kaufman (1999)

[21] Reinelt, G.: The Traveling Salesman: Computational Solutions for TSP Applications. Lecture Notes in Computer Science, Vol 840. Springer-Verlag (1994)

[22] Sycara, K. Decker, K., Williamson, M.: Middle-agents for the Internet, In Proceedings. of the 15th Joint Conference on Artificial Intelligence (1997)

[23] Ulder, N., Aarts, E., Bandelt, H., van Laarhoven, P., Pesch, E.: Genetic Local Search Algorithms for the Traveling Salesman Problem. In Parallel Problem Solving from Nature – Proceedings of 1st Workshop, PPSN I, Springer-Verlag, (1991), 109-116

[24] Van Laarhoven, P. Aarts, E.H.L Simulated Annealing: Theory and Applications. Kluwer Academic Publishers (1987)

[25] Wagner, G. A UML Profile for External AOR Models, *Proc. of Agent-Oriented Software Engineering (AOSE) 2002*, AAMAS 2002, Bologna, (2002), 99-110

Mobile Agents for Web Service Composition

Juan R. Velasco[1] and Sergio F. Castillo[2]

[1] Universidad de Alcalá
Escuela Politécnica, Departamento de Automática
Crtra. N–II, Km 31,600, 28871 Alcalá de Henares, Madrid, Spain
juanra@aut.uah.es
[2] Universidad Industrial de Santander
Ciudad Universitaria
Bucaramanga, Colombia
scastillo@uis.edu.co

Abstract. Web services are supposed to be designed as software components for an intercommunicated business world. In this way, they are published to be used by any other software process or person that needs them. The exchange information format is also defined. In addition to this, one of the added value capabilities is the possibility of web service integration, federation or composition. The idea of service composition is not new, as it has been studied in the telecommunication world. In this field, technologies are needed to be as independent as possible. Mobile agents, as proposed in this paper, may be one of these technologies.

1 Introduction

Service composition can be easily defined as the creation of a new service through the combination of other existing services. This composition offers an added value to the original service and is a very important business activity for any web site. It is not unusual to locate a web site that offers information or products to the visitors, by combining these elements from different sources. In this way, the visitor obtains an added value, because he or she does not have to surf the network to obtain this information.

Web services are specially created having this idea in mind. A given company offers some information or products, and a way to access them. This access way is published in a known place, so every user who wants to offer this information or products can do it easily (sometimes, after signing a contract). The key problem here is to assure that all services can understand all the messages they receive. In order to solve this, it is necessary to agree on a common ontology that could be used by any server. This paper presents two different ways to implement web service composition by using mobile agents: on one hand, mobile agents can represent the user or the main web service and can navigate around the network contacting interesting web services that are useful for them. On the other hand, the ontology problem can be partially solved by means of an *Ontos* agent [3], which is able to translate messages and data among several different (but related) ontologies.

K. Bauknecht, A Min Tjoa, G. Quirchmayr (Eds.): EC-Web 2003, LNCS 2738, pp. 135–144, 2003.
© Springer-Verlag Berlin Heidelberg 2003

Next section will talk about the elements that are going to be combined: composition of services, a brief description of web services and how they work, and a subsection for agents and mobile agents, as they are going to be a key element on this work.

Section 3 presents how mobile agents can be used for web service composition in both senses: for service interaction and for ontology translation.

Finally, the conclusions and research lines will be presented.

2   The Starting Point

2.1   Composition of Services

Despite its importance, the issue of service composition has received little attention in literature. One of the most remarkable works can be found in the telecommunication field: the service composition and federation mechanism defined by the TINA consortium for TINA (telecommunications information networking architecture) [11]. Although TINA consortium is not live any more, some important ideas can be used from that work. In this way, TINA service composition is based on the following four principles [10]:

1. Identification and location of services among different domains.
2. Separation between access and service usage (this is a main characteristic of TINA.)
3. Consistent management of compound services over multiple domains (a compound service maintains a consistent management environment.)
4. Session and interaction support.

The common principles for federation are: mutual agreement between involved partners, decentralization (administration is carried out in a distributed way) and autonomy of the partners.

Authors have been involved in a research project (the SCARAB project [9] and [1]), where one of the main technical contributions was "the structuring of service composition in a distributed environment". Within that project, a mobile agent based architecture was developed to implement service composition in a TINA environment [2]. Learnt lessons from that project were the starting point for the work on mobile agent based web services.

In order to clarify what the composition of services is, an example will be described. This example will be used along all the paper. Let's consider that a given user wants to access to an On-line Travel Agency (OTA) service. OTA may offer its own product, but it is possible (and this is usually the way), that it will look for travel service suppliers which give what it is looking for its client. For instance, let's suppose that OTA service is a compound service of an Airline Ticket service, a Hotel Reservation service, a Medical Assistance service and an Opera Ticket service. Figure 1 shows a user who requests a service from SP_A (Service Provider A is the Travel Agency), and for any reason, the SP_A has to request a service composition with a wholesaler, in this case the SP_B (Service Provider B, that may be any of the OTA suppliers).

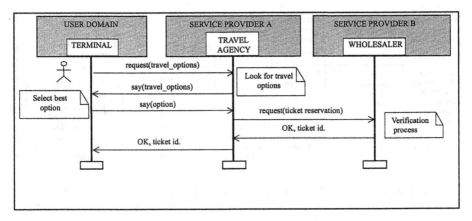

Fig. 1. Service composition

2.2 Web Services

A Web service is "a platform and implementation independent software component that can be: described using a service description language, published in a registry of services, discovered through a standard mechanism, invoked through a declared API, and compound with other services" [4]. The services are described by using WSDL (Web Service Description Language), are invoked by using SOAP (Simple Object Application Protocol), and are discovered through a UDDI-based mechanism (UDDI stands for Universal Description, Discovery and Integration).

The three roles of the Web service model are as follows:

- The service provider: The entity that hosts one or more Web services. The service providers publish their services in the service registry.
- The service requester: The entity that invokes the Web services using SOAP. A service requester seeks the services in the service registry.
- The service registry: The entity where the service definitions and binding information are kept and made available for searching. The service provider publishes its services in the service registries.

Figure 2 shows the interactions between the three roles of the Web service model. As the goal of this paper is to deal with service composition, the figure shows how a service provider A, looks for a new service by using the UDDI, and then starts the service interaction with Service Provider B.

One important aspect for this communication between web services is that all of them have to share the same ontology. An ontology can be seen as a common data description, so every ontology user uses the same syntaxis and semantic for data. In figure 3, a main web service, accessed by the user, looks for the peer web service that can solve any of the user requests. As all of them share the same ontology, the main web service may ask all the other web services for the

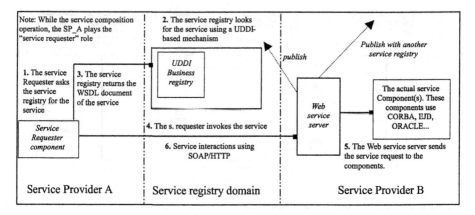

Fig. 2. Web service roles

particular question. When it receives back the information from them, it selects which one will be finally used. Coming back to the online travel agency example, the user connects to his or her usual travel agency (OTA), and asks for a given travel to any country or area. If OTA has not reserved free seats for that possible travel, it asks travel suppliers (the wholesalers) in order to locate possible travels that satisfy its customer. Once the suppliers give the answers, OTA may use one or several wholesalers to provide the final travel for the user.

This solution, with a shared ontology, is adapted from the W3C initial mechanism for web service composition, as can be found in [13]. In any case, there are two main disadvantages of this mechanism:

1. The assumption of having an ontology that is shared by all the entities is not realistic. Even if all the entities manage a shared set of concepts and relationships about the domain, in general, entities represent these concepts and relationships in different ways. For example, a service provider can use the "exotic travel" concept while another service provider uses the "adventure travel" or "high risk travel" concept for a similar idea[1].
2. The mechanism lacks important functionalities. As it is detailed in [5] , the entities at the Web service model know nothing about the users: they are neither autonomous nor proactive. They do not work in a natural fashion with the ontologies.

2.3   Agents and Mobile Agents

Agent based systems [12] facilitate the deployment of a widely distributed architecture, with high capabilities for communication and negotiation among all the components. From a not formal point of view, an agent is a piece of software that receives and stores information from the environment, is allowed to make

---

[1] This different names for similar ideas can be chosen for marketing or cultural reasons.

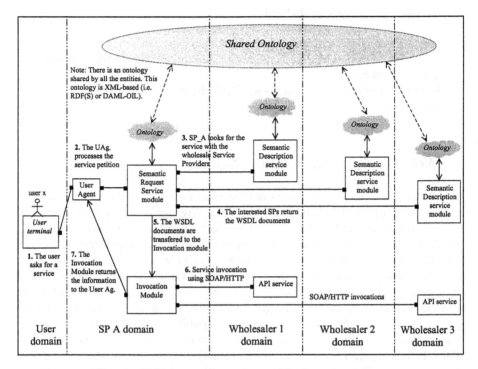

Fig. 3. Different web services with shared ontology

decisions, may act in a proactive way and is able to communicate with other agents for, on one hand, asking them to do any activity they can perform or, on the other hand, doing one of its own activities for other agents.

The key hallmarks of agenthood are [6]:

- Autonomy: agents should be able to perform the majority of their problem solving tasks without the direct intervention of humans or other agents.
- Social ability: agents should be able to interact with other software agents and humans in order to complete their own problem solving and to help others.
- Responsiveness: agents should perceive their environment and respond to changes.
- Proactiveness: agents should not only act in response to the environment, but they should also be able to take the initiative when appropriate.

Mobile agents are a special kind of agents. The mobile agent model is the result of the convergence of remote procesing (RPC, process migration, mobile objects, ...) and multi-agent systems. An informal definition of mobile agent could be a piece of software that can move or be moved to a different computer or platform where it continues running, and which acts as a representative of the user or another entity.

The main advantages of the mobile agent paradigm are:

- A better use of the available bandwidth.
- Useful for mobile devices (usually with limited resources for computation and communication.)
- Facility to distribute services to multiple clients or computers.
- Scalability.
- Good remote interaction.

3   Web Services and Mobile Agents

As it has been said, mobile agents can be used for two main activities on web services composition. First, by using their mobility, agents can surf the network contacting the different services that have to be composed of, acting as representatives of the main web service. This situation is shown in figure 4. In this case, the main web service (in our example, OTA) launches a mobile agent to the network to negotiate with other web services. Once the agent has contacted all the web services that could be interesting for its user, it starts the negotiation to obtain the service, and then it goes to the user terminal with the travel suggestion. In the example, due to the decision capability of the mobile agent, once it has collected all the information, it decides to negotiate with the third wholesaler (the one where it is at that moment) and moves to the first one to finish the negotiation. Then it goes to the user terminal with the travel information.

This situation is rather different from the one shown in figure 3. In that case, the main web service contacts the three wholesalers and then obtains the service from the first and the third, being the SP_A (OTA) which selects the best wholesalers.

With the mobile agent approach, the benefits of service composition are still valid, and there are some advantages that may be taken into account:

1. SP_A, once it starts the negotiation by creating the mobile agent and sending it to the wholesaler domains, is free to attend new users, redirecting its workload to the compound web services
2. All the interactions are made in a local way, so possible important data do not travel on the network. If some data are not going to be used (for instance, because the travel option is more expensive than others), they are even not stored into the agent.
3. 3. It is possible that the user terminal launches the agent (in the figure it is created by the SP_A, but this is not a must). In that case, user preferences could travel with the agent, so negotiation is more user oriented that in the conventional case.

Of course, there are some disadvantages, being the security aspects the most important [7]. When mobile agents are used, there are two different security problems. First, the well-known problem of the security for the platform that

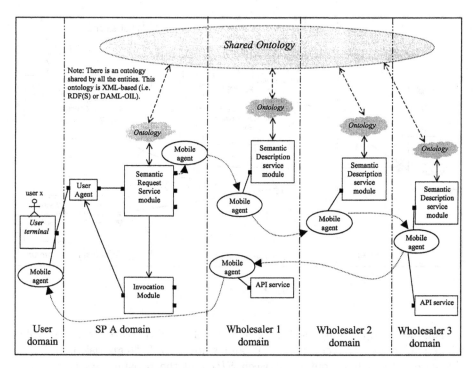

Fig. 4. Mobile agent contacting different web services

allows the execution of a piece of code (the mobile agent) that comes from a foreign system. This problem may be solved in the same way that conventional
downloaded code: signatures, certificates, sandboxes for execution, etc. The second situation is different and completely new: mobile agents have to prevent
themselves from their execution environment. In other words: the system has to
assure that agent platforms, distributed on the web service servers, are not going
to corrupt the code or the execution of the mobile agents they accept into. This
is a research line, and some ideas have been advanced, like in [8]. The main ideas
are related to encripting/signing every data stored by the agent in a separated
way, by both, the agent and the platform. In this way, when the mobile agent
arrives to a new server, it keeps the information from a bad use. In the case that
the server destroys the agent replacing it by a new one with information that
it wants to distribute (for instance its own travel fares, maybe more expensive
than other wholesalers), when the mobile agent goes back to the SP_A or the
user terminal, it will be uncovered, as original data are not signed by the mobile
agent creator.

The second main use for mobile agents (compatible with the first) is the possibility of acting as ontology translators. This case, shown in figure 5, represents
several systems, each of them using a different ontology.

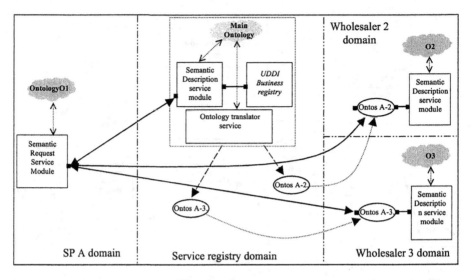

Fig. 5. *Ontos* agent

For the example being used, SP_A may use the "exotic travel" concept while wholesaler 2 uses "adventure travel" and wholesaler 3 "high risk travel". In this case, after a first contact between SP_A and the register server, two new *Ontos* agents are created. Each one of them are prepared to translate similar concepts between a couple of ontologies (A-2 and A-3). These agents move to the web service servers and wait until SP_A performs the communication. The main advantage of this idea is that every web service may have its own ontology (related to a reference or main ontology, but different from others), and it is not necessary for every web service to know how to translate all the ontologies. This translation activity is something that is given by the distributed system.

When both mobile agent uses are combined, the result is shown in figure 6. In this case, the mobile agent that travels from the SP_A to the wholesalers is able to communicate with them thanks to the existence of an *Ontos* agent that translates the concepts in order to make them understandable for both systems.

The main characteristics of the proposed use of mobile agents for web service composition are as follows:

- Each entity may use a different ontology (O1, O2, O3 in figure 6).
- In order to communicate the different concepts and relationships of two different ontologies, a mediator *Ontos* agent is used in each service provider domain. The main goal of this agent is to "translate" the requests and the replies.
- Because the *Ontos* entity is a mobile agent, it will appear on the web service platform when it is needed, and it can extend the web services in important ways offering a better level of interoperability and cooperation to other web services.

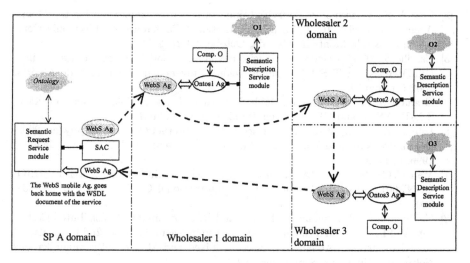

Fig. 6. *Ontos* agent and a mobile agent that looks for information or products

- The service requester (in our example, service provider A) uses a WebS mobile agent. This agent manages the service composition through its interactions with the *Ontos* agent at each service provider domain. This mobile interaction allows the service requester to perform other activities, reducing its workload thanks to service composition.

4   Conclusions and Research Line

Mobile agents may be used in the web service domain to provide a better way for composition of services. On one hand, the main web service (the one that is being used by the user) may send mobile agents to the network in order to locate better information or products for its user. On the other hand, it is not necessary that all web services use the same exact ontology, allowing some variations due to market or cultural reasons. Of course there is a lot of work in some research lines: security is a key aspect, and assuring that the mobile agent is not going to be corrupted and that the information it brings back is the right one is a fundamental issue. A second aspect is the user preferences, which can be managed by the agent, allowing it to select how and where to move and which kind of information is relevant or not for its user.

References

[1] Bos, L., Ciminiera, L., De Blieck, E., Sisto, R., Exploiting smart cards and mobile agents for personalised service provisioning: A case study in Proc. CLIMATE Workshop on Advanced Services in Fixed and Mobile Telecommunications Networks, Singapore, September 1999.

[2] Castillo S., Velasco J. R.: "Service Composition in m-commerce using the Mobile Agents approach", ICECR-5 5th International Conference on Electronic Commerce Research, Montreal, Canada, October 23-27, 2002.

[3] Castillo S.: "Composición de servicios mediante el modelo de los agentes móviles" (Ph.D. tesis), E. T. S. I.Telecomunicación, Universidad Politécnica de Madrid, 2002 (in Spanish).

[4] Graham S. et. al.: "Building Web Services with Java: Making Sense of XML, SOAP, WSDL and UDDI", Sams Publishing, USA, 2001.

[5] Huhns M. N.: "Agents as Web Services", IEEE Internet Computing, july/ag. 2002.

[6] Jennnings, N. R. and Wooldridge, M., Software Agents, In IEE Review, January 1996, pp17-20.

[7] Man M. C., Wei V. K.: "A Taxonomy for Attacks on Mobile Agent", IEEE EUROCON'2001 Trends in Communications, International Conference on, p. 385-388, 2001.

[8] C. Ruland, O. Weissmann, A. Friesen and N. Oikonomidis. A distributed Certificate and Profile Management System for use in Agent Systems. 2nd international ACTS workshop: "Advanced Services in Fixed and Mobile Telecommunikations Networks" (Singapur, September, 1999).

[9] SCARAB consortium: The SCARAB Software Architecture. Semi-public document available from authors (1999).

[10] TINA consortium: ôOverall Concepts and Principles of TINAö, version 1.0, feb. 1995.

[11] TINA consortium: Telecommunications Information Networking Architecture-Service Architecture, version 5.0 (1996).

[12] Wooldridge, M. and Jennnings, N. R. (eds). Proceedings of the 1994 workshop on Agent Theories, Architectures and Languages (ATAL 94), The Netherlands, August, 1994.

[13] World Wide Web Consortium: "Web service use case: Travel reservation - Use case 5 May 2002", (http://www.w3.org/2002/06/ws-example), 2002.

Development of an ebXML Conformance Test System for e-Business Solutions

Dongsoo Kim[1] and Jung-Hee Yun[2]

[1] Graduate School of Healthcare Management and Policy
The Catholic University of Korea,
505 Banpo-Dong, Seocho-Gu, Seoul 137-701, Republic of Korea
dskim@catholic.ac.kr
[2] Department of e-Business Research, National Computerization Agency
NCA Bldg. 77, Mugyo-Dong, Jung-Gu, Seoul 100-775, Republic of Korea
yunjh@nca.or.kr

Abstract. This research has designed and implemented a standard conformance test system for e-Business solutions that support the ebXML, which is currently being focused on as the leading electronic commerce framework. The adoption of standards such as ebXML is probably the best way to achieve interoperability among electronic commerce systems, and more and more e-Business solutions around the world are supporting ebXML. This work primarily discusses the concept and needs for the standard conformance tests on e-Business solutions. The standard conformance test system is developed based on the detailed specifications of the ebXML framework. This system has been used to test commercial e-Business solutions. The system implemented in this research will provide a significant basis for the standard conformance certification of e-Business solutions, and could also provide clear decision criteria for e-Business solutions currently in market, thus activate the overall e-Business market.

1   Introduction

Recently, the size of inter-enterprise e-commerce is becoming larger, resulting in the wide adoption of e-commerce systems by enterprises. For the e-commerce systems among various firms to acquire interoperability and integrate to each other, standardizations should be met in the areas of trading business processes, electronic documents, electronic catalogues, enterprise information descriptions and repositories, messaging protocols, security mechanisms, electronic payment systems and so forth.

B2B trading not only is expanding beyond local commerce, but also is reaching global market beyond the national boundaries. To enable the dynamic trading in an international scale, a standard that defines international specification is required, and ebXML (electronic business using eXtensible Markup Language), with its numerous conformant solutions, could be considered as such standard.

K. Bauknecht, A Min Tjoa, G. Quirchmayr (Eds.): EC-Web 2003, LNCS 2738, pp. 145-154, 2003.

For the functions described in the standard to be implemented properly and to be used, a solution should undergo a standard conformance test. The conformance is the level of requirements met by a solution that adopts a standard, and the process of testing such conformance is called the standard conformance test [3]. The standard conformance test is a process needed to evaluate the quality of a solution, and further on, is a requirement for interoperability among different solutions.

A standard conformance test of an e-Business solution is the process of testing e-Business solutions of how well it follows the e-Business standards. As the volume of B2B e-commerce increases and more and more firms adopt the e-commerce systems, the need for a standard conformance test of solutions is a necessity. This paper addresses the need for standard conformance test in the e-Business solution domain, and has designed and implemented an e-Business standard conformance test system supporting the ebXML, a most well-known e-commerce framework. The standard conformance test system is designed to test commercial e-Business solutions, focusing on the core specifications of ebXML, such as the Messaging Service Specifications, Reg/Rep (Registry and Repository), and CPP/CPA (Collaboration Protocol Profile/Agreement) specification.

The standard conformance test system presented in this research provides the following results. It enables the early detection of errors in a solution under development, and provides confidence to the users that the solution will provide a reliable result, and will work in a manner that it is supposed to. The conformance test also provided confidence to the users that the solution would generate a proper result, and would operate in a manner that it is expected to do so. Further on, the test system developed in this work will be used as a milestone for the preparation for a certification system.

This paper is composed of the following sections. Section 2 introduces the ebXML, a framework for e-Business standards, along with the standard conformance test and the certification system. Section 3 presents the checklists and modular functionalities of the e-Business standard conformance test system. Section 4 describes the procedure of the ebXML test system using the messaging conformance test module as an example. Section 5 concludes this research.

2   e-Business Standard and Conformance

In this section, the ebXML, a leading framework for e-Business standardization is introduced along with its current trends. Concepts and needs for a standard conformance test and certification process are also presented.

2.1   ebXML as a Standard e-Business Framework

As the size of e-commerce expands day by day, various movements concerning the standardization of e-commerce framework is a hot issue. Many e-commerce frameworks such as eCo, cXML, xCBL, BizTalk, RosettaNet, and ebXML have been introduced to the market, and ebXML is receiving much attentions [1][2]. Among these, the UN/CEFACT (United Nations/Center for the Trade Facilitation and e-Business) and OASIS (Organization for the Advancement of Structured Information

Standards) are establishing and promoting the ebXML. The motto of ebXML is to construct a single global electronic market using an open standard based on XML. Various documents, business processes, and messaging protocols are standardized using XML to construct an effective e-commerce environment for inter-enterprise operations.

As a result of an 18 month long project that lasted from November of 1999, 7 major parts of the ebXML specifications were completed, resulting in the completion of the 1st phase standardization task, and the 2nd phase is currently being carried out. 4 technology areas - Registry, Messaging Services, CPP/A, and Implement, Interoperability and Conformance - are being carried out by OASIS through formulating dedicated Technical Committees (TCs) for each technical domain. UN/CEFACT is responsible for the standardization of core components and business processes.

2.2   Standard Conformance Testing

A standard is an agreement among designers, developers, and users of a product. The designer and the developer consider a standard as a framework that is used to construct a product, and the users may refer to a standard as a user's manual. A standard holds its position only when solutions are developed according to the given set of requirements in the standard, and the degree of requirements followed by a solution is called the standard conformance. Also, the process of checking the conformance of a solution to a given standard is called the standard conformance test [3][4][5].

A standard conformance test is a necessary step in order for a solution to operate properly, and is a mandatory for the interoperability among various solutions. It enables the early detection of errors in a solution under development, and provides confidence to the users that the solution will provide a reliable result, and will work in a manner that it is supposed to.

The conformance test is executed using the standard specification and the test suite. The conformance clause in the standard specification explicitly describes the conditions the solution being tested should meet. The test suite is used to directly check the conformance to the standard, and is composed of a test case and a test document. A test case can be a test tool or a document according to the type of standard specifications, and the method and test procedures should be explicitly described in a test document.

2.3   Conformance Certification System

The standard conformance, which consists of specifications and test suites, is effective when it is officially agreed upon and certified. The process of testing the standard conformance of a specification using an official test suite is called validation. When an authority acknowledges - based on the result of validation - that the given specification conforms to a given set of requirements, this activity is called certification. Generally, a standard conformance test procedure consists of conformance testing, validation, and certification by an authority. Official organizations in charge of each process should exist [3][4]. Fig. 1 depicts a general standard conformance testing procedure and associated organizations.

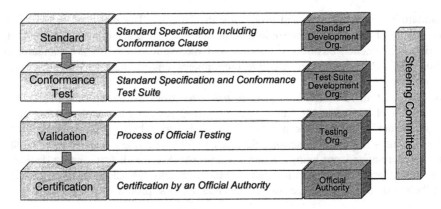

Fig. 1. Conformance testing procedure and associated organizations

The standard conformance certification system refers to various administrative and policy issues concerning testing, validation and certification of a given standard. The establishment of a standard conformance system promotes the development of reliable solutions, and contributes to market activation.

3   System Design of ebXML Conformance Testing

The standard conformance test system developed in this research handles the ebXML standard, and is composed of Registry conformance test, Messaging conformance test, and CPP/CPA conformance test modules. This section describes the architecture of the ebXML standard conformance test system and the checklists for the conformance testing.

3.1   System Architecture

The structural diagram of the entire test system is depicted in Fig. 2. It consists of modules that test standard specifications of Registry, Messaging, and CPP/CPA. The test module that is used to check the interoperability among different solutions is also included. The 'Test Scenario Bank' could be seen as the most important part of the entire system. This part stores the 'Reference Result' information. The 'Reference Result' information is the test scenarios of each module, and the correct results expected to be acquired from the scenarios. The scenarios being stored in the 'Test Scenario Bank' is based on the checklists that lists up mandatory test procedures required for each test modules. The checklist required for the standard conformance test could be drafted based on the standard specifications, and should include the mandatory test for each test module. Each test module such as Messaging, CPP/CPA, and Registry test modules has its own checklists, which are used as base information during the conformance testing.

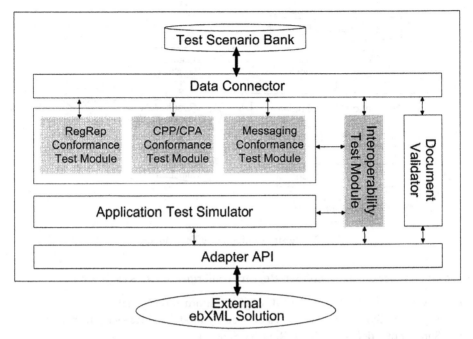

Fig. 2. Configuration of ebXML Standard Conformance Test System

The 'Data Connector' in the configuration diagram is composed of API's that support search and modification of data in the 'Test Scenario Bank' (i.e. Test Case Documents) by the test modules. In other words, the 'Data Connector' connects the 'Test Scenario Bank' and the test modules. The 'Application Test Simulator' activates the external ebXML solution being tested. At this point, the 'Adapter API' acts as the connector of the external ebXML solution. The 'Document Validator' acts as a parser that validates the schema of the input and output of the specimen solution.

The three modules of the ebXML standard conformance test modules, and the role and detailed structure of the Interoperability test module is described in the following sections.

3.2   Conformance Test Module for Registry System

The Registry Conformance Test module has been drafted based on the ebXML Registry Information Model v2.0 [6] and Registry Services Interface v2.0 [7]. Tests are conducted based on the conformance criteria described in each specification. Fig. 3 depicts the scheme of the Registry conformance test module.

According the test scenario stored in the 'Test Scenario Bank', the 'Application Test Simulator' activates the external registry solution. The results of the activation are compared to the 'Reference Results' (i.e. the desired results of the external solution), and the level of conformance is checked to flag the external solution as either 'Pass' or 'Fail'.

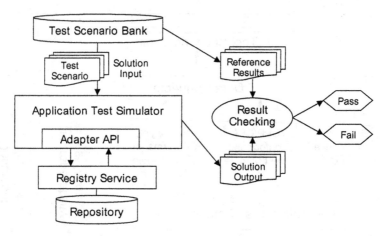

Fig. 3. Registry Conformance Test Module

The criteria checked in the ebXML Registry conformance test is as follows.

- Level of conformance of ebXML Registry Information Model
- Support of Syntax and Semantics of Security Model and Registry Interfaces
- Support of a defined ebXML Registry Schema
- Support of Syntax and Semantics of SQL Query Support (optional)

3.3   Messaging Module Conformance Testing

Since all electronic commerce systems are based on the exchange of messages among two or more business partners, the messaging part of the ebXML standard is principal, and yet very important.

The Messaging conformance test module is based on the ebXML Message Service Specification v2.0 [8], and the test is carried out according to the conformance criteria explicitly described in the specification. Fig. 4 depicts the modular structure of the Messaging conformance test module. This structure is to test the messaging conformance of the solution itself, and the 'Message Test Simulator' acts as an external messaging solution. When the 'Message Test Simulator' is replaced with another solution or an 'Application Test Simulator' of another solution, the conformance of message exchange with other messaging solutions can be tested. All other functions are similar to those of the Registry conformance test module.

Areas that are checked in the ebXML Messaging conformance test module are as follows

- Level of conformance of messaging standards: Based on SOAP (Simple Object Access Protocol) 1.1 and SOAP with Attachment specification
- XML syntax packaging validation element: Payload container definition basis, usage of SOAP Extension using Namespace, usage of Version Attribute within SOAP extension, usage of signature element (XMLDSIG) for security

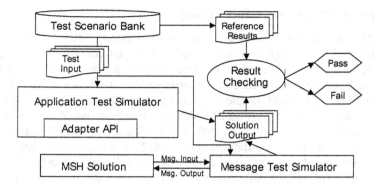

Fig. 4. Conformance Test for MSH (Messaging Service Handler) Solution

3.4   CPP/CPA Conformance Test Module

The CPP/CPA conformance test module is based on the ebXML Collaboration Protocol Profile and Agreement Specification v2.0 [9], and the test is carried out according
to the conformance criteria explicitly described in the specification. The structure of
CPP/CPA conformance test module is relatively simple compared to that of other test
modules. This test module basically acts as a 'Document Validator' depicted in Fig. 1.
The XML schemas of CPP or CPA documents, which are the results given by the
specimen solution through the 'Document Validator', are checked for validation, and
comparison with the 'Reference Result' is made.
Areas that are checked in the ebXML CPP/CPA conformance test module are as
follows.

- Support of interface requirements and functions described in the specification
- Validity of the XML schema definition in CPP or CPA

3.5   Interoperability Testing

The Interoperability test validates whether distinct ebXML solutions are capable of
performing transactions electronically without any trouble. In this work we have
tested the ebXML MSH to validate the interoperability. In the Interoperability test
module, the results acquired through APIs' of each ebXML MSH products were used.

4   Test Procedure

As mentioned in Chapter 3, the conformance test system developed in this research is
composed of the Registry conformance test module, Messaging conformance test
module, CPP/CPA conformance test module, and Interoperability test module. In this
section, due to the limited amount of pages, procedures concerning the conformance
test are described using the example of ebXML MSH solution.

4.1   Procedure of MSH Conformance Testing

The ebXML MSH is a software module that sends/receives messages to/from partners according to the ebXML Message Service Specification. For the conformance testing of MSH, we need a test driver that would receive/send messages from/to the external ebXML MSH and test the conformance of the message. A test driver is a type of a simulator for ebXML, and should be able to receive and send messages according to the ebXML Message Service Specification. Also, the recipient should be able to send/receive ebXML messages using ebXML MSH. However, the API between ebXML MSH and Application is not defined in the ebXML Message Service Specification. Each solution developers are put in a situation where they should define their own API between ebXML MSH and Applications, or in some cases, omit the APIs. Therefore, in order to approach the specimen ebXML MSH in a unified manner, we have developed an Adapter API. The developer of the specimen ebXML MSH has to develop an adapter that could be conformant to the Adapter API.

Fig. 5 depicts the process of conducting the conformance test for ebXML MSH.

The test performer should use the ebXML MSH conformance test tools to set the specimen product and test scenario information in the Test Driver. Appropriate types of ebXML messages are sent or received according to the test scenario, and the response results are used for the conformance test for each scenario.

The conformance test and the interoperability of the ebXML MSH product are carried out by repeating the exchange of messages between the Application Driver and the Test Driver of the test system. The process of message transmission and reception is as follows.

- Setup: Set up of test scenario, test cases (Checklists), and CPP/CPA
- Start: Test start by the test performer (Receiving type, Sending type)
- Proceed: Carrying out scenarios according to the test cases
- Shutdown: 'Normal shutdown'- Completion of all test cases; 'Abnormal shutdown'- Occurrence of 'Fatal' or 'Warning' exception from the Test Driver
- Restart: Restart in case of 'Abnormal shutdown' ('Warning' exception)
- Wrap-up: Log final error information in case of 'Fatal' exception, and log 'Normal termination' in case of 'Normal shutdown'. Terminate test log recording and terminate the Test Driver
- Stop: Termination of test due to 'Fatal' exception or 'Normal shutdown'.

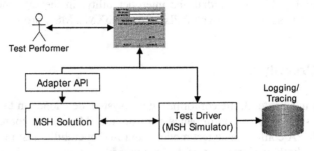

Fig. 5. MSH Conformance Test procedure

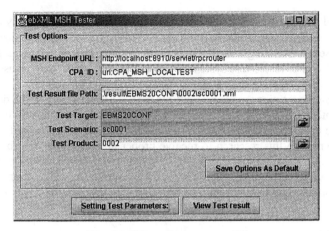

Fig. 6. MSH conformance test UI

4.2   Structure of the Test Program and Execution of the Test

The Test Driver for the ebXML MSH conformance test is developed using Java Servlets. Fig. 6 shows the environment setup and test scenario selection user interface for the ebXML MSH conformance test.

The test performer uses the UI depicted in Fig. 6 to set the information for the specimen product and to set the test scenario information. Initial setup processes such as assigning the CPA for the test MSH and Test Driver is also made using this interface.

A Web based users interface is used to send messages and receive results of the Test Driver. The user can select the registered CPA, check the information in the CPA summary, configure Service, Action, and Payload elements, and send the message using the Web based UI.

If the conformance test for a scenario is completed, or when an error occurs, the test is halted and the result is logged. If the test is terminated due to 'Normal Shutdown', the test is terminated after logging the normal shutdown log, and if the test is terminated due to 'Fatal' exceptions, the test is terminated after logging the final error. The test performer drafts the final result after analyzing the log and trace information when the test is over.

5   Conclusion

This research presented the need for a standard conformation test in the e-Business solution domain, and has designed and implemented a standard conformance test system supporting the ebXML, a framework highlighted by many parties. The structures of standard conformance test modules concerning the specifications of ebXML have been addressed in details, and have shown an actual evaluation of a commercial e-Business solution using the standard conformance test system.

The standard conformance test system presented in this research not only enables the suppliers to produce more reliable products, but also provide concrete decision criteria for the users in selecting a commercial product supporting the ebXML. Further on, the standard conformance test system presented in this work may be used as milestone for the completion of the validation and certification processes.

Since multiple transactions made by multiple parties are necessary in the domain of e-Business, inter-operation among solutions is vital, and the standard conformance stands in the center of attention for interoperability. In order for the conformance test system presented in this research to receive proper attention, it should be developed beyond a simple test program, into a test suite that could be acknowledged officially, and should evolve into an e-Business standard conformance certification system that could test, validate and certify solutions based on official authority.

References

[1]   ebXML Technical Architecture Project Team, ebXML Technical Architecture Specification v1.0.4, February 16, 2001.
[2]   ebXML Requirements Team, ebXML Requirements Specification v1.06, May 8, 2001.
[3]   L. Rosenthal, M. Skall, and L. Carnahan, Conformance Testing and Certification Framework, June 25, 2001.
[4]   OASIS ebXML Implementation, Interoperability and Conformance TC, ebXML Test Framework v0.3, July 17, 2002.
[5]   L. Rosenthal and M. Skall, Conformance Requirements for Specification v1.0, March 15, 2002.
[6]   ebXML Registry TC, Registry Information Model v2.0, December 5, 2001.
[7]   ebXML Registry TC, Registry Services Specification v2.0, December 6, 2001.
[8]   ebXML Messaging Services TC, Message Service Specification v2.0, April 1, 2002.
[9]   ebXML Collaboration Protocol Profile and Agreement TC, Collaboration Protocol Profile and Agreement Specification v2.0, June 5, 2002.

ebIOP: An ebXML Compliant B2B Interoperability Platform

Yusuf Tambag[1] and Ahmet Cosar[2]

[1] The Scientific and Technical Research Council of Turkey
06100 Ankara, Turkey
yusuf.tambag@ceng.metu.edu.tr
[2] Middle East Technical University
Department of Computer Engineering
06531 Ankara, Turkey
cosar@ceng.metu.edu.tr

Abstract. Interoperability has become one of the big problems of e-commerce since it was born. A number of B2B standards like ebXML, UDDI, RosettaNet, xCBL, etc. emerged recently to solve the interoperability problem. UDDI and ebXML are the leading standards in the area of e-commerce that provide different solutions for interoperability. UDDI standard provides a service based solution that proposes a registry standard for companies to publish their services on the web. On the other hand, ebXML provides a process based solution. It proposes several standard specifications like ebXML Messaging Service Specification (ebMSS) to achieve messaging interoperability, ebXML Business Process Specification (ebBPSS) and ebXML Collaboration Protocol Profile/Aggreement (ebCPP/A) to provide business process and partner profile interoperability, ebXML Registry Service Specification (ebRSS) and ebXML Registry Information Model (ebRIM) to describe a registry/repository that provides a classification mechanism to achieve partner discovery.

Currently, there exists many B2B standards each provide competing and complementary solutions to B2B interoperability. So, there is a need for serving implementation of these standards from a single, central point to ease the use and management of the implementations. In this paper, we present our system ebIOP, an ebXML compliant B2B Interoperability platform. ebIOP is designed to provide a central store for implementations of ebXML specifications to be able to use and configure the implementations of ebXML specifications from a single, central point. It defines the term *ebIOP Component* which corresponds to plug&play ebXML applications that are stored in the ebIOP.

1 Introduction

Interoperability has become the most important and challenging problem in the area of e-commerce. A number of standars are proposed to solve the interoperability problem like XML, XSL, SOAP etc. XML has emerged as the leading textual language for representing and exchanging data on the web. As a result,

K. Bauknecht, A Min Tjoa, G. Quirchmayr (Eds.): EC-Web 2003, LNCS 2738, pp. 155–164, 2003.

more and more companies started using XML. Also standard bodies like xCBL and RosettaNet made use of XML to define standards for business documents and/or business processes to solve the interoperability problem. Currently, two competing solutions of such e-commerce problems are emerging namely Universal Description, Discovery and Integration (UDDI) and ebXML. UDDI [1] provides three categorization schemes namely UNSPSC, NAICS and ISO 3166 (a Geographical Taxonomy). Other than these, UDDI Version 2 also supports publishing of an external taxonomy. Using the registry service provided by UDDI, a company can publish its services using any language (e.g., WSDL or plain English etc.) and these three schemes. On the other hand, ebXML [2] does not impose any restrictions on the classification scheme to be used. Any authorized user could publish a taxonomy by grouping *ClassificationNode* instances as a tree structure. ebXML also defines standards for defining business processes and company profiles.

Since many specifications appeared that provide different solutions for various e-commerce problems, companies tend to support more than one specification [4]. By supporting more than one specification, a company will be able to combine complementary aspects of the specifications to provide better services and the availability of the services supported by the company will be increased (i.e., if implementation of a specification is unavailable, the company may use the implementation provided by another specification that provide solution for the same problems). So, there is a need for an engine that will store and serve implementations of these specifications from a single, central point. The engine should also be easily customizable to enable addition/removal of these implementations. ebIOP provides a start for implementation of such an engine. ebIOP aims to provide such an engine for ebXML. It defines the term *ebIOP Component* to be an ebXML application which is an implementation of an ebXML specification or a client to an implementation of an ebXML specification. ebIOP provides implementation of three *ebIOP Components* namely *Messaging Service Handler (MSH) Component* that implements *ebXML Messaging Service Specification*, *Registry Client Component* that provides a GUI for the user to browse ebXML Registries and a *B2BServer Component* that implements ebXML Business Process Specification and ebXML Collaboration Protocol Profile and Agreement (CPP/A) specification. In this paper, we describe ebIOP to show how the business lifecycle (discover, create aggrement and do business) could be managed using the *ebIOP Components* defined.

The rest of the paper is organized as follows: Section 2 provides some background on ebXML and discusses related work, Section 3 describes the architecture of ebIOP, Section 4 provides implementation details with example application of the system to the RosettaNet PIPs [5] and finally, Section 5 concludes the paper.

2   Background and Related Work

2.1   Background

ebXML is a non-profit initiative established by the United Nations Centre for Trade Facilitation and Electronic Business (UN / CEFACT) [6] and the Organization for the Advancement of Structured Information Standards (OASIS) [7]. Vision of ebXML is to create a single set of internationally agreed upon technical specifications that consists of common XML semantics and related document structures to facilitate global trade. ebXML provides following specification for various e-commerce problems:

1. **ebXML Registry / Repository Specifications**
   ebXML provides two specifications namely ebXML Registry Information Model (ebRIM) and ebXML Registry Services Specification (ebRSS) that describe the ebXML Registry / Repository. ebRIM defines an information model for the ebXML Registry / Repository by providing UML class diagrams for the model. *RegistryObject* provides a common base interface for almost all objects in the information model like *ExtrinsicObject* that describes the registry content submitted (e.g., a CPP) and *ClassificationScheme* that describes a registered taxonomy. ebRSS provides a set of services that enable sharing of information between interested parties. *LifecycleManager* service defines the set of methods that is used to submit/change the registry content and *QueryManager* defines the methods used to process user queries. ebRSS also defines the *RegistryClient* interface that will be used to communicate with the registry service.

2. **ebXML Messaging Service Specification (ebMSS)**
   ebMS aims to facilitate the exchange of electronic business messages within an XML framework. It focuses on defining a communication-protocol neutral method for exchanging electronic business messages and provides specific enveloping constructs that support reliable, secure delivery of business information. ebXML message packaging complies with Simple Object Access Protocol (SOAP) and SOAP Messages with Attachments (SOAPAttach). ebMSS proposes some extensions to the SOAP header (e.g., "eb:MessageHeader" element) and SOAP body (e.g., "eb:Manifest" element) elements of the SOAP Envelope. These are packaged within a MIME multipart message to allow payloads or attachments to be included in the message.

3. **ebXML Business Process Specification (ebBPSS)**
   ebBPSS provides a standard framework for business process specification. As such, it works with the ebXML Collaboration Protocol Profile and Agreement (CPP/A) specification to bridge the gap between Business Process Modeling and the configuration of ebXML compliant e-commerce software. Using ebBPSS, one can define choreography of business activities and documents to be generated as a result of activities between two or more trading parties.

2.2   Related Work

ebXML specifications are implemented and currently being implemented by a number of companies or individuals. A list of all implementations could be found at [8]. All ebXML implementations could be plugged into the ebIOP by coding suitable wrappers.

HP provides a web services platform [9] that provide similar services like ebIOP does. The platform provides technology to enable the easy creation, publication, discovery, and invocation of web services. It supports creation of web services from existing J2EE components, discovery and invocation of web services using standards-based service registries, easy addition of plug-and-play components that support the requirements of higher-level B2B protocols (e.g., **ebXML**, RosettaNet). The platform provides "plug and play" components for receiving and processing messages and application processing.

The biggest difference of the systems is that, ebIOP proposes a component based architecture for ebXML framework whereas, HP web services platform provides tools for web services that will ease the business lifecycle and designed to mainly support UDDI framework. ebIOP also standardizes the "plug and play" components to be integrated into the platform. So, *ebIOP Components* could easily be integrated into the platform by making a small change in the configuration file of the ebIOP without changing the code.

3   System Architecture

Currently many XML based specifications appeared that provide solutions for various e-commerce problems and many companies are supporting more than one specification. As a result, there is a need for using and managing implementations of these specifications from a single central point. ebIOP provides a prototype implementation of a platform that provides such functionalities for ebXML framework.

ebIOP contains a server that listens to a port for requests coming from the MSHs of other companies and contains one or more *ebIOP Components* and zero or more utilities (small software packages) that the components use. Figure 1 shows the interoperability platform architecture. The platform basically has three components namely *B2BServer Component* to handle business processes, *ebIOP Messaging Service Handler (MSH) Component* which is written to wrap the ebXML MSH described in section 3.2 and a *Registry Client Component* which handles all the communication with the known ebXML Registries. ebIOP provides a number of software components that are shared by *ebIOP Components* to achieve their jobs. These software components and their responsibilities are explained in the following subsection:

3.1   Shared Software Components

Shared software components performs some small key tasks to help the components to achieve their jobs. All of the shared software components extend

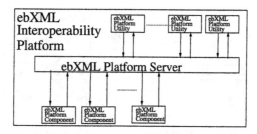

Fig. 1. Interoperability Platform Architecture

EbXMLUtility base class and provide a set of abstract methods to be implemented by the vendors. At least one implementation of these components are provided in the prototype [3]. The responsibility of each component is briefly explained below:

- **UniqueIDGenerator:** Using this component, *ebIOP Components* generate unique identifiers (e.g., a conversationId in B2BServer) as needed.
- **UniqueIDResolver:** *ebIOP Components* may use this software component to resolve the unique id that they receive from the other parties trough the ebXML MSH.
- **CPAResolver:** A *CPAResolver* is used to load the requested CPA from a resource (e.g., a URL).
- **BusinessProcessResolver:** Like *CPAResolver*, a *BusinessProcessResolver* is used by *ebIOP Components* to load the requested business process specification from a resource.

3.2   ebIOP Components

Before ebIOP starts, it reads its configuration file, creates and initializes all components and utilities it is configured to have and puts them to the related lookup tables. ebIOP contains three utilities that the components use. These utilities and their functionalities are briefly explained below:

- **DocumentManagerUtility:** A *DocumentManager* provides a mechanism for storing and retrieving the documents exchanged in collaboration executions.
- **ExpressionEvaluatorUtility:** Provides a way to execute expressions specified by *ebIOP Components*. It is currently used only for evaluation of *ConditionExpressions* in ebXML business processes.
- **KeyManagerUtility:** This utility manages the keystore of the company. *KeyManagerUtility* is used for security support in ebXML messaging.

ebIOP provides following components:

1. **ebIOP MSH Component:** *MSH Component* is implemented to be JAXM (Java XML Messaging) [11] compliant. Figure 2 shows a high level view

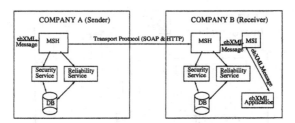

Fig. 2. ebIOP Messaging Service Architecture

of the MSH. Architecture provides two types of communication between the sender and the receiver. In the first case, sender prepares an ebXML message and directly sends the message to the receiver over a transport protocol (e.g., HTTP). In the second case, the message is send over a service provider. As shown in Figure 2, *EbXMLMessagingServiceHandler* uses a number of internal services to achieve its job. *EbXMLReliableMessagingService* is used to save the message to a persistent storage using a *MessageQueue* and *EbXMLSecureMessagingService* provides encryption and decryption services for the ebXML messages.

2. **ebIOP Registry Client Component:** The component contains one or more *RegistryRequestor*s to form, send and display the results of the registry requests (e.g., submitObjects, approveObjects, etc.). If a *RegistryObject* is returned as a result of a query, a button named "Find Matching Objects" appears on the GUI that shows the detailed information of the *Registry-Object* which is used to locate *RegistryObject*s that are compatible with the classifications of the *RegistryObject*. Compatible *RegistryObject*s are located by the *ClassificationRecognizerManager*. A *ClassificationRecognizerManager* has a list of *ClassificationRecognizer*s and given a list of classifications connected with logical predicates (i.e., "and", "or"), it queries and locates the *RegistryObject*s that are compatible with the provided classifications.

3. **ebIOP B2BServer Component:** *B2BServer Component* implements ebXML Business Process Specification (ebBPSS) v1.0.1 and manages the execution of the business processes. Figure 3 shows the execution of a single business transaction which summarizes the work done by the *B2BServer Component*. Initiating party starts an instance of the business process and upon receiving the instance request, *B2BServer Component* starts a new instance of the specified business process by starting the first business transaction in the business process. In order for a company to be able to start an instance of a business process, the company should play the *Initiating* role of the first business transaction in the business process. Usually, a company needs to execute legacy (existing) application for business transaction activities in a business process. B2BServer's *LegacyApplicationHandler* provides a mechanism for execution of legacy applications. A *LegacyApplicationManager* includes one or more *LegacyApplicationHandler*s. A *LegacyAp-*

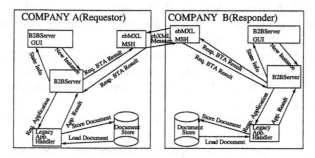

Fig. 3. Execution of a single Business Transaction

plicationHandler is a wrapper that handles the communication between the B2BServer and legacy application(s) of the company.

B2BServer Component and *RegistryRequestor*s of the *Registry Client Component* locate and use the *MSH Component* to send the ebXML messages. ebIOP receives the ebXML messages coming from other parties that are targeted to a component on the platform. It resolves the message and locates the component to which the message is targeted to and passes the message to the component for further processing.

4   Implementation

The system is implemeted in Java JDK 1.4.1-rc. Jakarta tomcat 4.1.12-LE-jdk14 is used as servlet engine that hosts the MSH and ebXML Registry Service. JAXM API 1.1 is used to implement ebXML Messaging Service, Apache log4j 1.2.6 is used for logging purpose, Apache-XML-Security-J 1.0.2 is used for XML Digital Signature support, JAXP 1.2 is used together with Apache Xerces 2.2 to parse necessary XML documents and Apache Xalan 2.3.1 is used to execute xpath expressions.

The prototype is implemented using a component-based methodology and implementers could easily plug-in their implementation of components to the ebIOP without modifying the code trough configuration files of ebIOP or "ebxml.properties" (determines the class names of software components used by ebIOP) file. Following section shows how the business lifecycle could be managed using ebIOP with an example.

4.1   Example Scenario

Following steps briefly describes the example scenario:

1. A part of RosettaNet classification scheme is registered to an ebXML Registry.

2. Companies that browse the ebXML Registry see the classification scheme and register/update their CPPs to the ebXML Registry and classify their CPPs with the PIPs that they support.
3. A customer combines some of the RosettaNet PIPs in logical order and forms a multiparty collaboration to buy some products from a seller.
4. Then, the customer locates the possible partners that matches with the PIPs supported by the customer.
5. After locating selected parties, customer contacts them manually and forms a CPA with three sellers, a bank and a shipper.
6. Customer then starts the multiparty collaboration to buy some products from the one of the sellers.

The scenario is started by a *ClassificationScheme* provider (e.g., RosettaNet) registering the RosettaNet PIPs as a classification scheme to the ebXML Registry. Figure 4 shows the RosettaNet Classification Scheme. As shown in the figure, the scheme is defined to be an internal classification scheme, and each role in a PIP is identified by a unique path in the scheme (e.g., path '/PIP/3/B/13/I' represents the Initiating role in RosettaNet PIP 3B13, NotifyOfShipmentConfirmation). Representation of this scheme and mapping of RosettaNet PIPs to the ebBPSS binary collaboration is borrowed form [10]. The frame shown in the figure is a GUI interface for "submitObjectsRequest" in ebRSS and can be accessed from the *ebIOP Registry Client Component*. The request is send to the ebXML Registry using the *ebIOP MSH Component*.

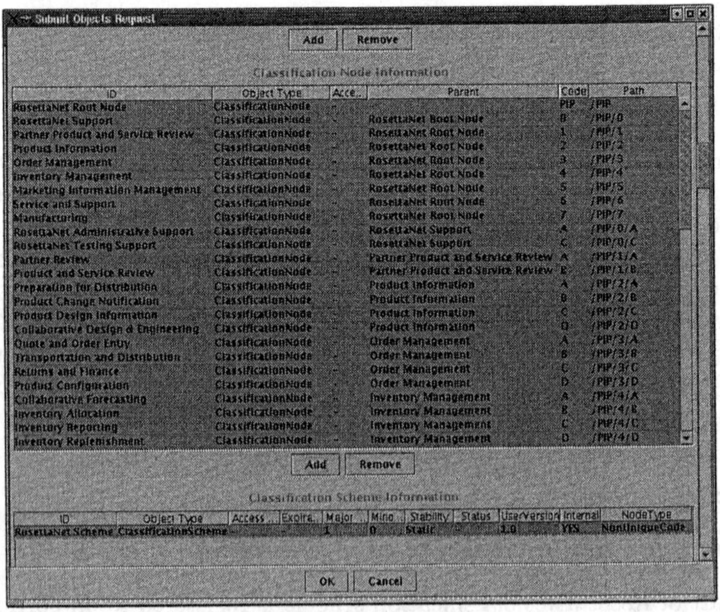

Fig. 4. RosettaNet Classification Scheme implemented in ebXML

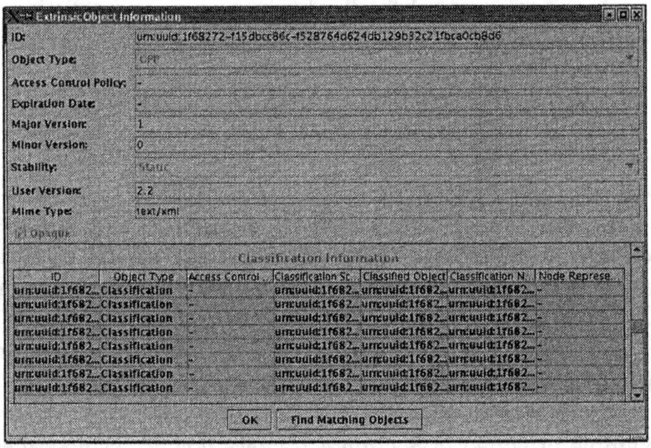

Fig. 5. ExtrinsicObject attributes and Classifications that identifies the CPP of the Customer

After the scheme is loaded, companies starts browsing the registry and they submit their CPPs to the ebXML Registry along with the suitable classifications. Submitted CPPs are stored in the ebXML Registry as *ExtrinsicObjects* and *ExternalLink* child elements under these *ExtrinsicObjects* identify the locations of the CPPs. The company that plays the customer role in the business process queries its CPP from the registry. After locating its CPP, the customer then presses the "FindMatchingObjects" button on the resulting window shown in Figure 5 to locate the possible trading partners. Required queries to locate the possible trading partners are then fired by the *PIPClassificationRecognizer*. As a result of this request, CPPs of all the companies that support compliant role in any PIP which is supported by the customer are located. The customer then creates a suitable multiparty collaboration to buy some products from the seller and contacts related parties manually to create an aggrement. After the aggreements completed, customer starts the multiparty collaboration using the *B2BServer Component* of the ebIOP. The instance is started by the *B2BServer Component* that runs at the customer's site by starting the first PIP in the collaboration named PIP 2A2 (Query Product Information). After PIP 2A2, PIP 3A2 (Request Price and Availability), PIP 3A4 (Request Purchase Order), PIP 3C2 (Request Financing Approval), PIP 3C3 (Notify of Invoice), PIP 3C6 (Notify of Remittance Advice), PIP 3B11 (Notify of Shipping Order), PIP 3B13 (Notify of Shipment Confirmation), PIP 3C5 (Notify of Billing Statement) are executed in the given order between the customer, the seller, the shipper and the bank.

This scenario shows how ebIOP could be used together with *ebIOP Components* through the business lifecycle (i.e., a classification scheme provided, then companies configured their run-time systems and created profiles for themselves, afterwards, the companies located their possible trading parties and created a common business process and finally, business process execution is started). More information on demo and the prototype could be found at [3].

5   Conclusions and Future Work

In this paper, we presented architecture of our ebXML Compliant Interoperability Platform (ebIOP). ebIOP provides a common platform for ebXML applications to make businesses easily integrate and use ebXML applications from a single, central point. ebIOP achieves this by providing a common base class namely *EbXMLPlatformComponent*. During the implementation of the prototype, a component based methodology is used and the implementors could replace or add/remove software components (e.g., *CPAResolver*, *ebIOPComponent*) to/from the ebIOP easily only by making a small change in the configuration. The example provided in Section 4.1 shows how a business lifecycle could be managed by ebIOP using *ebIOP Components*.

Future work includes extension of the ebIOP to host all kind of software components and we will name it IOP. We also plan to provide support for remote components that are on different machine than that the IOP resides and a web interface for managing the IOP easily over the web. For this reason we will provide a message format for IOP to communicate with the remote software components and the web interface. We also plan to provide support for UDDI in the future versions of the platform to compare the two standards.

References

[1] Universal Discovery, Description and Integration (UDDI), http://www.uddi.org
[2] ebXML Home Page, http://www.ebxml.org
[3] ebIOP Home Page, http://www.ceng.metu.edu.tr/~e102830/ebXML
[4] Jean-Jacques Dubray and Carl Sjogreen. Be ready to support more than one XML-based B2B specification. Unisys World Technical Whitepaper, July 2000. http://www.unisysworld.com/webpapers/2000/07_excelon.shtml
[5] RosettaNet Home Page, http://www.rosettanet.org/
[6] United Nations for Trade Facilitation and Electronic Business (UN/CEFACT). http://www.diffuse.org/fora.html#CEFACT
[7] Organization of the Advancement of Structured Information Standards (OASIS). http://www.oasis-open.org/
[8] ebXML Implementations Home Page, http://www.ebxml.org/implementations/
[9] HP Web Services Platform, http://www.hp.com/go/webservices/
[10] Dogac, A., Tambag, Y., Pembecioglu, P., Pektas, S., Laleci, G. B., Kurt, G., Toprak, S., Kabak, Y., "An ebXML Infrastructure Implementation through UDDI Registries and RosettaNet PIPs", ACM SIGMOD International Conference on Management of Data, Madison, Wisconsin, USA, June 2002
[11] Java XML Messaging (JAXM), http://java.sun.com/jaxm

A Watermarking Method for Halftone Images
Based on Iterative Halftoning Method*

In-Gook Chun and Sangho Ha

School of Information Technology Engineering, Soonchunhyang University
Asan-si, Choongchungnam-do, Republic of Korea
{chunik,hsh}@sch.ac.kr

Abstract. This paper proposes a new watermarking method to embed invisible data in halftone images. Halftone images are binary images appearing in printed matters such as books. The embedded data in halftone images can be used for copyright protection. The data hiding is integrated into halftoning operation. Watermark bits are hidden at pseudo-random locations within a halftone image during halftoning process. In order to minimize the distortions due to the inserted watermark, the proposed method tries to find the best neighborhood pattern using iterative binary search method. In order to cope with unintentional attacks such as cropping and distortions, the watermark is inserted periodically in halftone images. Experiments show that the proposed method can hide the relatively large amount of data within a halftone image without causing noticeable artifacts and the watermark is robust to crop and geometrical distortion.

1   Introduction

Recently digital images are widely used within home computers and Internet. Nevertheless one critical drawback of digital images is that they may be copied and distributed through Internet very easily. So the copyright protection of digital images becomes an important issue. Digital watermarking is one of such techniques to protect the copyright of digital images by embedding of copyright information into the images. There are a lot of watermarking methods. The common approaches of watermarking are to embed watermark in the spatial domain or frequency domain. Watermarking techniques previously developed mainly deal with on-line digital data. In this paper, we deal with printed image rather than on-line data. Printed image watermarking can be used widely for preventing forgery of on-line tickets, coupons, documents on Internet. In the proposed method, watermarking is performed by exploiting the printing process itself i.e. halftoning. Halftoning is a process to convert continu-

* This work is supported by in part by the Ministry of Information & Communication of Korea("Support Project of University Information Technology Research Center" supervised by KIPA).

K. Bauknecht, A Min Tjoa, G. Quirchmayr (Eds.): EC-Web 2003, LNCS 2738, pp. 165-175, 2003.
© Springer-Verlag Berlin Heidelberg 2003

ous-tone images to two-tone images [1]. It is widely used in printing process because most printers have limited numbers of colors. Most previous watermarking methods were designed for grayscale images and they can not be applied directly to halftone images because halftone images have only two tones: black and white.

There are a lot of halftoning methods, but most popular methods are ordered dithering, error diffusion and iterative halftoning method like DBS (direct binary search) [2]. Ordered dithering uses a threshold pattern and needs only simple computation. Error diffusion is a computationally complicated but its visual quality is fairly good. In error diffusion, the halftone error between the actual pixel intensity and halftone value is fed back to its neighboring pixels. There is another halftoning method called iterative halftoning method. Iterative halftoning method refines the initial halftone by iterative procedure [2]. DBS(Direct Binary Search) is one of the iterative halftoning methods. It requires several passes to determine the final halftone image. It is computationally expensive method but its visual quality is quite good compared with other halftoning methods. And it is an attractive halftoning method for watermarking because the error-minimizing iteration of DBS makes the watermark not-detectable. In this paper, a DBS-based watermarking method for halftone images is proposed.

There are some researches on this field. There are two popular methods. The first method is to use two dither matrices (instead of one) to encode the watermark information [3], [4], [5]. The problem here is how to design an optimal dither matrix pair. The second method is to change directly the pixel of the halftone image according to the watermark information. Ming and Oscar have proposed a data hiding method for halftone image generated by error diffusion method [6], [7], [8], [9]. Data Hiding Error Diffusion (DHED) integrates the data hiding into the error diffusion operation. DHED hides data by forced complementary toggling at pseudo-random locations within a halftone image. But their method shows some artifacts due to the watermark insertion. The main reason is that the data hiding error is only compensated by the future pixel, that is, the next pixels in the scanning order.

In this paper, a robust watermarking method for halftone image using DBS halftoning method is described. The proposed method generates good visual quality halftone image containing watermark because of the iterative search property of DBS. And the watermark is designed to be robust to cropping and geometric distortion. Its disadvantage is the computation overhead. But from our experiment, it is observed that after a few iterations, the proposed method quickly converged to its final halftone image.

2   Iterative Halftoning Method

Iterative halftoning method like DBS requires several passes to determine the final halftone image [2]. It starts with an initial halftone image and tries to find the best halftone image for a given continuous-tone image during iterations. The best halftone is defined as the one when examined from a distance it matches the grayscale image the most. During iterations, DBS minimizes a cost function between the perceived continuous-tone image and perceived halftone image.

The perceived image is the one that our eye sees from a distance. When we see a picture from a distance, we do not perceive the exact picture. Our eye functions as a low-pass filter and this Human Visual System (HVS) functions are extensively used recently in watermarking field. The halftoning error is defined as follows:

$$E = \sum_m \sum_n \left| h(m,n) * * g(m,n) - h(m,n) * * f(m,n) \right|^2 \tag{1}$$

where $h(m,n)$ represents the point spread function(PSF) of the HVS, $f(m,n)$ is the continuous-tone original image, which is assumed to lie between 0.0(white) and 1.0(black), $g(m,n)$ is the halftone image and $**$ denotes 2D convolution. In the above equation, $h(m,n) ** g(m,n)$ is the perceived halftone image, $h(m,n) ** f(m,n)$ is the perceived continuous-tone image and $|h(m,n) ** g(m,n) - h(m,n) ** f(m,n)|$ means the perceived halftoning error for a particular pixel.

To minimize the error, DBS uses direct binary pixel search like toggling or swapping. The whole halftone image is scanned one by one from left-top location to right-bottom. At the particular location, possible candidate patterns are generated by toggling and swapping. The error function of each binary pattern is calculated and the minimum error pattern is chosen. DBS is a computation-intensive algorithm. Recently computationally simpler algorithms have appeared such as lookup table method [2].

Figure 1 shows the intermediate halftoning results. Here the random dot is used as an initial halftone pattern. DBS has converged to its final halftone image after 7 iterations.

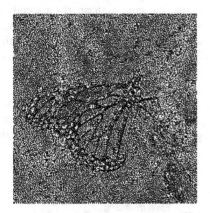 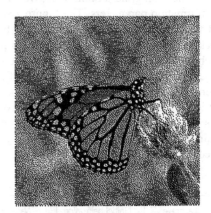

(a) 1th iteration result   (b) 7th iteration result

Fig. 1. The results of DBS halftoning method

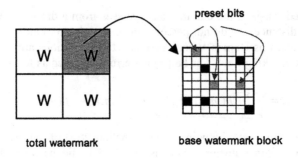

Fig. 2. Periodic watermark with preset bits

3   Watermarking Algorithm

3.1   Watermark Embedding

In order to provide robustness to cropping and geometrical robustness, the same watermarks are inserted multiple times at periodic shifted locations. This redundancy can be used to identify the parameters of geometrical affine transformation [12]. Since the watermark has been embedded multiple times, the autocorrelation of watermarked image has multiple peaks. If the image has undergone a geometrical transformation, the peaks in the autocorrelation function will reflect the same transformation. Hence using these point pairs, we can compute the parameter of the geometrical transformation parameters. The Figure 2 shows that the same watermarks are embedded four times in four non-overlapping blocks. The first P bits of base watermark block are preset to known values. These preset bits act like a reference mark which can be used in order to compute the amount of   translation. Note that the values of preset bits are known but the positions of preset bits are not preset. The positions are determined according to the secret key.

Figure 3 is the detailed block diagram of the watermark embedding system. It consists of three stages, initial halftoning stage, watermark-embedding stage, error-minimizing stage. In the initial halftoning stage, the original grayscale image is halftoned with a predefined threshold matrix.

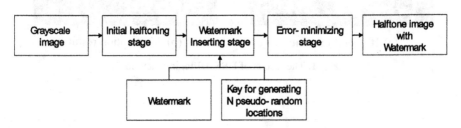

Fig. 3. The block diagram of watermark embedding system

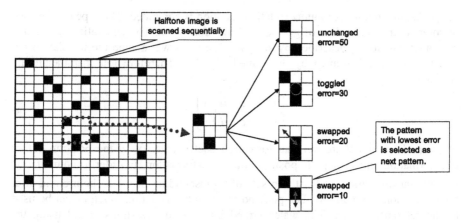

Fig. 4. Error minimizing procedure. Each pattern is generated by toggling or swapping

In the watermark embedding stage, we use a symmetric key cryptography. N pseudo-random locations are generated by a secret key known to both encoder and decoder. Watermark data is hidden at these pseudo-random locations. Data can be any kinds of binary bit data, namely raw binary data or data with error correction codes. One bit of data is hidden at each of the N pseudo-random locations by forcing the pixel value at those locations to be zero or one according to the watermark data.

In the error-minimizing stage, the initial halftone image generated from the previous stage is enhanced by error minimizing pattern search iteratively. It consists of several passes through halftone image to determine final halftone image. For one iteration, halftone image is scanned from left-top to right-bottom location. For each pixel, It checks whether the location is one of the N pseudo random locations containing the watermark data or not. If the pixel location is the one of the N pseudo random locations, the pixel value is not changed. If the pixel is not the one of the N pseudo random locations, it checks whether toggling the pixel value or swapping the pixel value with neighbor pixels reduces the perceived halftoning error. If toggling or swapping reduces the error, the pixel value is changed; otherwise the pixel value is not changed. The halftone image is iterated until the pixel values are not changed at all or until the predefined number of iterations. Generally after a few iterations, most pixel values are not changed anymore. Figure 4 illustrates the binary search method of DBS [10].

3.2 Watermark Extraction

In order to determine the parameters of geometrical transformation, autocorrelation function is computed using the following equation

$$R_{g,g}(u,v) = \sum_{m}\sum_{n} g(m,n)g(m+u,n+v) \tag{2}$$

where $g(m,n)$ is the watermarked image. If there are any periodic data in the watermarked image, there would be multiple peaks in autocorrelation function. To detect the peaks, the gradient of autocorrelation function is computed. These peaks are used to compute the parameters of geometrical transformation. The generalized geometrical transformation is described by six parameters but we assume the translation parameter can be determined by other methods [12]. Therefore four parameters are sufficient.

$$\begin{bmatrix} x' \\ y' \end{bmatrix} = \begin{bmatrix} a & b \\ c & d \end{bmatrix} \begin{bmatrix} x \\ y \end{bmatrix} \tag{3}$$

where a, b, c, and d are the transformation coefficients, (x, y) the position before transformation and (x', y') the position after transformation. In order to compute the inverse transformation, at least two sets of corresponding positions before and after transformation are required. The peak points of autocorrelation function can be used as the reference points. The watermarked image is inverse-transformed using the computed transformation parameters.

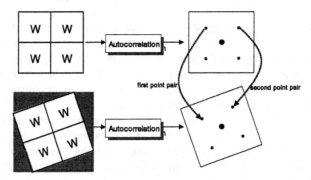

Fig. 5. The peaks of autocorrelation function can be used as reference points in computing transformation parameters

   N pseudo-random locations are generated by a same key which was used in the embedding process. Knowing the information of these random locations, the corrected image is scanned sequentially to find the preset bits of the watermark. The concept of preset bits is used in order to be robust to translation and cropping. The first P bits of watermark are preset to known values. After finding the preset bits, the remaining watermark bits can be recovered simply by reading the pixel values at next random locations. Figure 6 shows the block diagram of watermark extraction system.

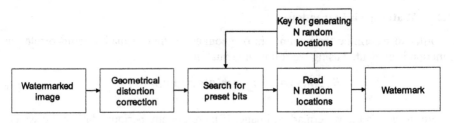

Fig. 6. The block diagram of watermark extraction system

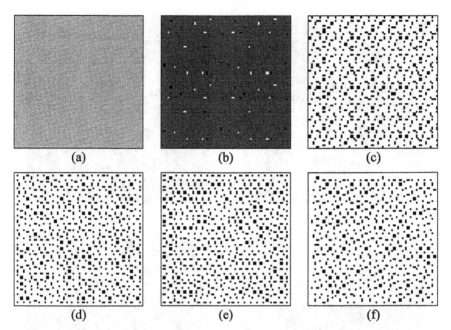

Fig. 7. The results of "constant" image watermarking. (a) original image (b) watermark image (c) initial halftone image (d) final halftone image with watermark (e) final halftone image without watermark (f) final halftone image using DHED

4   Experimental Results and Discussion

The proposed algorithm is tested with test images in order verify its performance. The results were compared with that of Ming [7] [8]. Ming proposed DHED (Data Hiding Error Diffusion) method which inserted watermark by toggling the pixel value of halftone image. In DHED, the data hiding error is only compensated by the future pixel, that is, the next pixels in the scanning order, but in the proposed method, the error is spread out to its neighbor pixels by the HVS filtering more uniformly than DHED.

The first test image is a 64x64 8-bit grayscale image "constant" shown in Figure 7(a). Figure 7(b) is the watermark image consisting of four non-overlapping blocks containing 16 bits. The watermark bit "0" is shown as a black dot and "1" as a white dot. Figure 7(c) shows the initial halftone image generated by ordered dithering. It shows the salt and pepper type artifacts and the distribution of black and white pixels is not uniform. It is mainly due to the watermark bits which are forced at the pseudo-random locations. Figure 7(d) is the final halftone image generated by the proposed algorithm. As you can see, the black and white pixel distributions are more uniform than the initial halftone image and the number of salt and pepper type artifacts is significantly decreased. Moreover it is difficult to identify the watermark pixels.

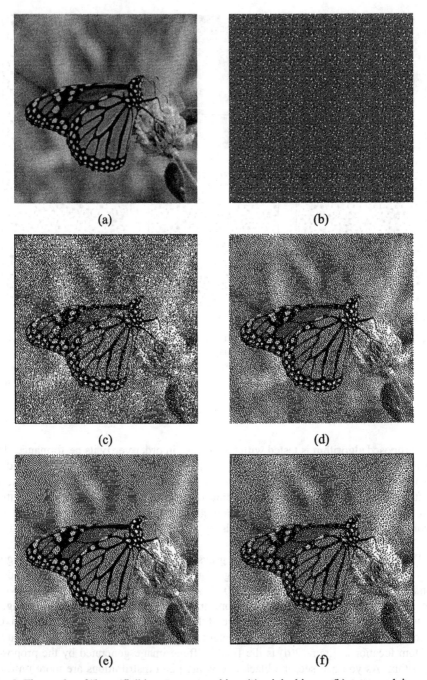

(a)

(b)

(c)

(d)

(e)

(f)

Fig. 8. The results of "butterfly" image watermarking. (a) original image (b) watermark image (c) initial halftone image (d) final halftone image with watermark (e) final halftone image without watermark (f) final halftone image using DHED

Figure 7(e) is the final halftone image without watermark data. Note that there is nosignificant visual difference between Figure 7(d) and (e). Figure 7(f) is the final result of DHED algorithm. As you can see, the result of the proposed algorithm is better than that of DHED.

The second image is a 256x256, 8-bit grayscale image "butterfly" shown in Figure 8(a). Figure 8(b) is the watermark image consisting of 16 non-overlapping blocks which contains 128 bits per each block. The reason for this large amount of watermark data is to prove the performance of the proposed method to remove the artifacts. From Figure 8(c)-(f), it is observed that it is difficult to find out any abnormal artifacts and the visual quality is relatively high in spite of the large amount of watermark data.

To test the robustness of the proposed algorithm, the final halftone was rotated by 20° in Figure 9(a). In order to compute the parameters of geometrical transformation, the autocorrelation function of the rotated halftone image is calculated as shown in Figure 9(b). As you can see, the peaks can be identified and the parameters of geometrical transformation can be determined.

To compare the results of the proposed method with that of DHED, we use MPSNR (Modified Peak Signal-to-Noise Ratio) between the original continuous-tone image and halftone image [8]. The idea is that we apply a lowpass filtering to the halftone image before computing the normal PSNR. Table 1 shows the MPSNR values. Generally MPSNR of the results of the proposed method is higher than that of results of DHED.

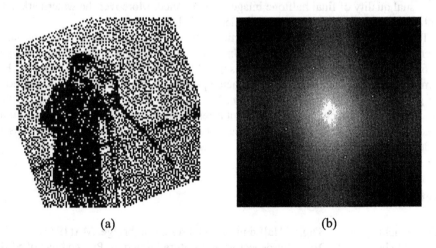

(a)   (b)

Fig. 9. The results of watermark extraction in the case of distorted "cameraman" halftone image. (a) rotated halftone image with watermark (b) autocorrelation function of the rotated halftone image. The watermark pixels should be at least 10% of total pixels if the peaks can be identified reliably

Table 1: MPSNR of haltone images

	"constant" image	"butterfly" image	"cameraman" image
DHED	17.74dB	20.81dB	19.00dB
Proposed method	23.63dB	22.17dB	20.72dB

5   Conclusion

In this paper, a watermarking method for halftone images is proposed. The proposed method is based on iterative halftoning technique. It hides data at pseudo-random locations within a halftone image. The major problem of this method is to remove the artifacts and distortions due to the embedded watermark data effectively. The proposed method achieves the improved visual quality by using the property of iterative error minimizing technique. The proposed method tries to find the best halftone image which has the least perceived halftoning error by iterative direct binary search method. It checks whether toggling the pixel value or swapping the values of pixels nearby reduce the halftoning error for each pixel. The artifacts due to the inserted watermark are removed by finding the best neighborhood pixel pattern which decreases the halftoning error the most. By integrating data hiding into halftoning operation, relatively large amount of data can be hidden within a halftone image while the visual quality of final halftone image is maintained. Moreover the watermark data within the halftone images is not easily detectable by the eye.

To be robust to cropping and distortion, the watermark consists of several non-overlapping blocks. Each block contains the same watermark data. This multiple embedding of the watermark results in several peaks in autocorrelation function. By comparing the configuration of the extracted peaks with their expected configuration, the geometrical distortion can be determined. The distortion can be inverted and the watermark can be recovered. Experimental results show that the proposed algorithm generates halftone images with good visual quality. The proposed method can be used widely for preventing forgery of on-line tickets, coupons, documents on Internet.

References

[1]   Ulichney, R. A.: Digital Halftoning. MIT Press, Cambridge, MA(1987)
[2]   Allebach, J. P.: DBS: Retrospective and Future Direction. Proceedings of SPIE Vol. 4300 (2001) 358-376
[3]   Hel-Or, H. Z.: Copyright Labeling of Printed Images. Proceedings of IEEE Int. Conf. on Image Processing (2000) 702-705
[4]   Wang, S.G. and Knox, K.T.: Embedding digital watermarks in halftone screens. Proceedings of SPIE Vol. 3971(2000) 218-227
[5]   Baharav, Z. and Shaked, D.: Watermarking of dither halftoned images. Proceedings of SPIE Vol.3657(1999) 307-316

[6]   Fu, M.S. and Au, O.C.: Data Hiding in Halftone Images by Stochastic Error Diffusion. Proceedings of IEEE Int. Conf. on Acoustics, Speech, and Signal Processing (2001) 1965-1968

[7]   Fu, M.S. and Au, O.C.: Hiding Data in Halftone Image using Modified Data Hiding Error Diffusion. Proceedings of SPIE Vol. 4067 (2000) 1671-1680

[8]   Fu, M.S. and Au, O.C.: Data Hiding for Halftone Images. Proceedings of SPIE Vol.3971, (2000) 228-236

[9]   Fu, M.S. and Au, O.C.: Halftone image data hiding with intensity selection and connection selection. Signal Proceeding: Image Communication 16(2001) 909-930

[10] Kacker, D. and Allebach, J. P.: Joint Halftoning and Watermarking. Proceedings of IEEE Int. Conf. on Image Processing (2000) 69-72

[11] Mese, M., Vaidyanathan, P. P.: Look-Up Table (LUT) Method for Inverse Halftoning. IEEE Trans. on Image Processing, Vol. 10 (2001) 1566-1578

[12] Kutter, M.: Watermarking Resisting to Translation, Rotation, and Scaling. Proceedings of SPIE Vol. 3528 (1998) 423-431

A Security Architecture for Reputation Systems[*]

Roslan Ismail[1], Colin Boyd[1], Audun Josang[2], and Selywn Russell[1]

[1] Information Security Research Centre
Queensland University of Technology
Brisbane Qld 4001, Australia
{roslan,boyd,russell}@isrc.qut.edu.au
[2] Distributed Systems Technology Centre
Queensland University of Technology
Brisbane Qld 4001, Australia
ajosang@dstc.edu.au

Abstract. Reputation systems are emerging as a promising means to assist users to make a right decision about their counterparts before embarking on a business transaction with them in the e-commerce environment. Thus, it is extremely important to ensure that reputation systems are securely implemented and protected from manipulation. Motivated by such needs a security architecture for reputation systems is proposed. Within the architecture several services are identified. In addition, the mechanisms and parameters to support the identified services are also determined.

1 Introduction

E-commerce has created many new opportunities for users to explore. However, plenty of uncertainties have arisen as there are many unknown users involved. Reputation systems have emerged as a means which allows those uncertainties to be reduced to a reasonable level. A reputation system is specifically developed to collect, analyse and produce users' reputation which later can be used to determine their level of trustworthiness before e-commerce business transactions can commence.

There has been extensive research undertaken to develop reputation systems [7, 8, 9]. However, these concentrate more on developing an effective calculation engine. There is no doubt that this effort is vital but leaving security out of the main agenda may place the system in jeopardy. The system may not be able to produce a correct result, and consequently affects the process of decision making. Hence, security should be considered as crucial as other aspects, and not as an extra option to be added after the system is completed.

[*] The work reported in this paper has been funded in part by the Co-operative Research Centre for Enterprise Distributed Systems Technology (DSTC) through the Australian Federal Government's CRC Programme (Department of Industry, Science & Resources).

K. Bauknecht, A Min Tjoa, G. Quirchmayr (Eds.): EC-Web 2003, LNCS 2738, pp. 176–185, 2003.

Table 1. The entities and their symbols used throughout the paper

FT	A feedback target is the entity who is being evaluated and gained the reputation rating based on the feedback given by a feedback provider.
FP	A feedback provider is the entity who provides a feedback about *FT* based on transactions made between *FP* and *FT*.
RP	A relying party is the entity who uses the reputation rating produced to make a decision whether to proceed in a transaction with *FT* or not.
TI	The token issuer manages the registration of *FP* and *FT*, records transactions made between *FP* and *FT*, signs the token to produce a legitimate token.
CC/CA	The collection centre/certificate authority collects the valid feedbacks and uses them to calculate reputation rating and then issue the certificates for *FT*.

Motivated by the argument above, a security architecture for reputation systems is presented. To our knowledge there is no such architecture proposed in the literature. Although there are some initiatives [6, 2, 3, 1, 4] they cannot be considered as a complete security architecture. Many of the schemes proposed attempted to tackle problems without looking at the whole picture of the reputation system. As a result the designed solutions only manage to solve a part of the problems. To fill this gap a global view approach is employed in the process of developing the new security architecture. This approach views the system from a top down perspective which enables us to identify the entities participating in the system and consequently focus on the main issues of the system.

Notation Table 1 outlines the description of the roles of each entity and the symbols used throughout the paper.

Organisation of the Paper The remainder of the paper is organized as follows. Section 2 lists the threats that have been addressed. Section 3 presents the model used as the foundation to describe the new security architecture. Section 4 highlights the events that take place between one entity and another. Section 5 concludes the paper with some remarks.

2   Threats

The new architecture is expected to overcome several threats through services and mechanisms identified. Among the threats are those described below.

- *Lack of Privacy of Feedback Provider* This specifically threatens the privacy of feedback provider. The identity of the feedback provider is disclosed to the feedback target.

- *Lack of Privacy of Feedback Target* This specifically threatens the privacy of feedback target. The reputation rating of feedback target is known publicly.
- *Tampering of Feedback* This threat enables the attackers to read and change the original content of the feedback to one favorable to them. Thus, integrity of the submitted feedback is defeated.
- *Masquerading of Identity* This threat enables attackers to use other users' identity and subsequently provide a phantom feedback. This threat becomes more dangerous especially if the attacker uses the identity of the reputable feedback provider when submitting a feedback.
- *Intercept of Feedback* Although this threat does not allow change to the content of the submitted feedback it enables the attackers to read the value of given feedback and consequently may allow them to know the produced reputation rating of feedback target.
- *Repudiation of Feedback* This threat causes repudiation of receiver. The feedback provider may claim that he never received the legitimate token sent by the token issuer and subsequently deny that he sent the feedback on the feedback target.
- *Shilling Attack* This threat concerns a large number of positive feedbacks which are submitted to increase the reputation of certain entities dramatically. This threat is often effective when there is collusion among feedback providers. Besides increasing reputation rating, decreasing of reputation rating can also be the intention of colluders when launching this attack.

3   Background Security Architecture

Before going further, the definition of the security architecture which will be used throughout the paper is given.

Definition 1. *A security architecture identifies security services and mechanisms needed throughout a system to fullfil the requirements for creating a secure reputation system.*

There are two types of structures currently employed in reputation system implementations; the centralized and the decentralized. In the centralized structure transactions are normally brokered or mediated by a centralised authority. A similar entity, called a monitor, is described in Milosevic et al [5]. The entities participating in the centralized systems are required to register with the central authority. All feedbacks are submitted to the central authority for calculation of the reputation rating and these values can be obtained from the central authority without restriction. Generally most of the practical reputation systems are centralized. Although the centralized systems provide an elegant solution such as being more manageable they have several shortcomings. One of the major shortcomings of the central system is that privacy of participants is not fully achieved. In addition, these systems only provide a minimum level of security. They are designed for a basic purpose which is to produce reputation rating without the burden of taking security measures into consideration.

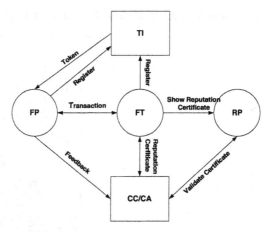

Fig. 1. Abstract View of Security

The decentralized structure, on the other hand, does not require the central authority for brokering transactions. Each transaction is executed between one entity and another. Feedback is given one to another and the value will be kept by each entity. This reputation rating will only be communicated to other parties upon request and if the feedback provider is willing to release it. The main limitation of this structure is how to determine the genuineness of reputation rating. There are many possibilities that the reputation given may not be the actual experience of the feedback provider himself but of the value given by another recommender. It is also possible that the feedback target himself forwards his reputation using a different identity. Due to this uncertainty a decentralized structure seems not suitable to be considered for our security architecture development.

3.1   Abstract View

The desired architecture is developed with careful consideration of the points highlighted above. Figure 1 depicts the abstract view of the security architecture for reputation systems. This architecture is centralized because the token issuer and the collection centre/certificate authority are arranged in the centralized manner. However, a separation of functions (registration and calculation) is proposed. This arrangement is vital to ensure that the monitoring process can be undertaken easily to certify the validity of transactions made and consequently assures the submitted feedback is genuine. In addition, it also allows a standard procedure to be used in issuing and calculating reputation ratings. For example, the produced reputation rating is calculated using the same engine even though the feedbacks come from various feedback providers.

The process of interaction in the architecture commences when a legitimate token (includes of the signature of token issuer on it) is sent to FP. This allows

Table 2. Summary of Mechanisms Required for Each Entity

	Anonymity	Unlinkability of Feedback	Integrity of Feedback & Reputation Rating	Correctness of Reputation Rating	Validity of Feedback & Reputation	Updating of Reputation Rating	Authentication of Feedback Provider
Feedback Provider	★	★	★				
Feedback Target			★	★	★		
Collection Centre/Certificate Authority					★	★	★
Token Issuer					★		★
Relying Party					★		

FP to submit his feedback to CA/CC. The legitimate token may consist of fields such as the identification and signature of TI, the identification of FT, the feedback value and the expiry date of the token. The producing of the legitimate token is strictly controlled to prevent an illegal production. It can only be produced after meeting two conditions as follows; a transaction between FP and FT has already taken place, and FP is a registered user. These two conditions aim to block a phantom feedback to enter into the system and to omit an unregistered user's feedback.

The CC/CA will check the validity of the legitimate token received before counting it to produce a reputation rating. After receiving a certain number of feedbacks for a specific target only then the CC/CA will issue a reputation certificate for that particular feedback target. The reputation certificate contains several essential fields so that RP can depend on it and consequently making a decision to trust or not the feedback target's reputation. Those fields are feedback target identification, certificate authority identification and signature, reputation value and expiry date of the certificate.

There are several mechanisms required for each entity. Table 2 presents these mechanisms with regard to each entity. They are anonymity, unlinkability of feedback, integrity of feedback and reputation, the correctness of reputation rating, validity of feedback and reputation, updating of reputation rating and authentication of feedback provider. Anonymity will ensure that the identity of FP is hidden from CC/CA while unlinkability of feedback causes CC/CA cannot learn

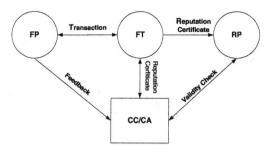

Fig. 2. Abstract View of Security without Token Issuer

a relationship between FP and feedback. The integrity of feedback and reputation rating protects from modification. The correctness of reputation rating will ensure that the reputation rating is calculated correctly. The validity of feedback and reputation provides an assurance on the genuineness of the produced information. Updating of the reputation rating means the reputation rating will be frequently updated. The authentication of feedback povider authenticates FP before giving a legitimate token.

Although the above architecture is ideal in the sense of defining the structure processes, it lacks scalability. There are difficulties in establishing many token issuers due to an extra cost and increased complexity of architecture. Hence, we would like to explore two other options of architectures which may produce some fruitful solutions for a secure reputation system.

3.2   Simplified Options

The first option is to take out the token issuer from the architecture. Now, the feedback provider does not have to obtain the legitimate token in order to submit a feedback to the collection centre. However, this option maintains the collection centre/certificate authority entity in its architecture. Thus, the feedback target can obtain a reputation certificate from the collection centre. The collection centre manages the process of collecting feedback and calculating reputation. It is assumed to be a trusted entity, and does not expose the submitted feedback and the reputation rating produced publicly. The privacy of feedback provider is achieved provided the collection centre is honest while the privacy of feedback targets is still the same as the previous architecture. Figure 2 shows the complete view of this architecture.

As there is no token issuer involved this architecture faces the problem of accountability of the feedback given. There is no assurance that the transaction has actually taken place between a feedback provider and a feedback target. As a result the given feedback may not be genuine. To overcome this problem, both entities (feedback provider and feedback target) are required to submit the particulars of any transaction to the collection centre to prove that the transaction has taken place. With this condition the submitted feedback will

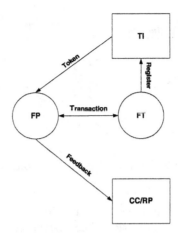

Fig. 3. Abstract View of Security with CC and RP are combined

only be counted if the particulars of the transaction made are provided by the feedback target.

The second option is to combine the collection centre and the relying party to become one entity and maintain the token issuer in the system. In general this architecture is similar to the decentralized structure. However, here a feedback is certified by the token issuer. Thus, the collection centre/relying party can ensure that the submitted feedback is genuine. In this architecture, the relying party broadcasts several requests to obtain the reputation of a feedback target. On receiving the request, the feedback providers submit an anonymous token (consisting of feedback value) to the relying party. Based on the received feedback the relying party then calculates and produces the reputation rating for the specific feedback target. We are aware that this architecture has a limitation, namely lacking of privacy of the feedback target to have control over his reputation. Figure 3 shows the complete view of this architecture.

4   Interactions of Entities

The abstract view of the system presented above identifies several security interactions of the entities participating in reputation systems. Figure 4 illustrates these interactions using the message sequence diagram approach.

- **1: Registration** FP and FT are required to register with TI before both of them can conduct transactions and then take part in submitting a feedback. There are two ways that registration can be undertaken; FP or FT himself comes to the office of the token issuer or the particulars are sent through the email. For the former way, verification can be conducted immediately by token issuer whereas the latter requires verification to be conducted in a more comprehensive way. Manipulation may occur in the latter as information is vulnerable to intercepting and tampering activities due to insecure

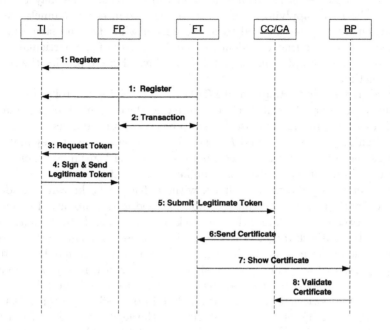

Fig. 4. Message sequence diagram of the proposed architecture

channels used. To ensure that confidentiality and integrity of these particulars are preserved the use of cryptographic means may be appropriate. An enforcement for a unique identity is conducted. This is achieved through a substantial examination of particulars sent to find any duplication to the previous created data prior to completing the registration.

– **2: Transaction** This is the stage where a transaction between two entities, feedback provider and feedback target, takes place. The completed transaction is important because the submitted feedback is based on such transaction. Each transaction partner can play both the role of feedback provider and feedback target. Before a transaction can commence both entities involved must register with the token issuer so that they transactions can be recorded. They also must agree on some conditions such as price and the condition of products in the transaction. As the transactions between feedback provider and feedback target need be monitored, it is suggested that a database to record such transactions may be introduced and maintained, and this database should be always updated to reflect the current transaction events.

– **3: Request Token** In this stage FP requests a legitimate token from TI to enable him to submit feedback. To start the process FP sends the particulars of the transaction made between him and FT. These particulars can be the identity of feedback provider, the identity of feedback target, the date of transaction is taken place and the feedback value may be hidden from the TI by applying a hash function. Due to insecure channels used, the particulars may be exposed to manipulation while transmission. Hence, it is vital to ensure that confidentiality and integrity of the particulars is protected. Cryptographic means could be employed here to provide the required protection.

- **4: Sign and Send Legitimate Token** On receiving the token of the feedback particulars, TI will check to ensure that the content of token is matched with the ones in the database. The database typically consists of transaction particulars between FP and FT including time and date. If they match, TI signs the token to create a legitimate token. The legitimate token reflects that the submitted feedback is genuine. To protect the interest of feedback provider to express their feedback without fear to be known, the identity of feedback provider is commonly not included in the submitted token. The link between feedback and the feedback provider should also be untraceable either by feedback target or the collection centre. To facilitate this need, an anonymous token could be implemented. Due to a huge number of tokens to be issued, the issuing process should be controlled in a proper manner. It can be achieved by maintaining a database to record the tokens issued. It is also important to encode expiry date into a legitimate token issued so that the time limits apply. This prevents the legitimate token from being kept for a long time. In addition, requests made should be monitored so that the issuing of the legitimate token for the same feedback in a short time cannot happen. Due to insecure channels used, confidentiality and integrity are needed here besides non-repudiation of the receiver.

- **5: Submit Legitimate Token** Upon receiving the legitimate token from CC/CA, FP uses this token to submit a valid feedback about FT to CC/CA. It is essential for each submitted feedback to use the legitimate token otherwise the feedback will not be counted for the reputation rating calculation.

- **6: Send Certificate** CC/CA calculates the submitted feedbacks and use them to produce the reputation rating for FT. He then issues the reputation certificate to allow reputation to be used offline. To prevent the reputation rating to be publicly known the certificates will only be given to the registered feedback targets. Thus, authentication of the identity of the feedback targets is required prior the certificates are issued to them.

- **7: Show Certificate** The interaction between FT and RP involves the process of showing the reputation certificate by a feedback target. Based on this certificate the relying party will decide to proceed or not to conduct a transaction with the feedback target. Thus, the certificate has to be updated to reflect the current reputation rating. To limit the distribution of the reputation certificates publicly, it can only be given to the intended RP determined by FT.

- **8: Validate Certificate** RP may contact CA/CC to verify the freshness of certificate shown to them in case any doubt arising about the certificate especially on its validity. However, due to a requirement that a certificate can be accessed only by FT, privacy of reputation certificate is applied. Thus the restricted access is implemented. Any request from RP without obtaining consent from the related FT is not permitted and this can be implemented through an access control mechanism.

5   Conclusion

A security architecture for reputation systems is presented using the top down approach. This approach generally assists us to identify the interface services needed by the entities involved in a reputation system, and consequently determines the mechanisms required to implement the interface services identified. In addition, it also helps us to identify the parameters required for each entity in the process of developing the architecture. Since this attempt is considered an early stage to formalise the security architecture in the security research of reputation systems we believe there is a room for improvement and expansion before developing an adequate and accepted security architecture for reputation systems.

References

[1] J. Carbo, J. M. Molina, and J. Davila. A BDI agent architecture for reasoning about reputation. In *IEEE International Conference on Systems, Man and Cybernetics*, volume 2, pages 817–822, 2001.

[2] F. Cornelli, E. Damiani, S. de Capitani di Vimercati, S. Paraboschi, and P. Samarati. Choosing reputable servents in a P2P network. In *The eleventh international conference on World Wide Web*, pages 376–386. ACM Press, 2002.

[3] E. Damiani, D. C. di Vimercati, S. Paraboschi, P. Samarati, and F. Violante. A reputation-based approach for choosing reliable resources in peer-to-peer networks. In *Proceedings of the 9th ACM conference on Computer and communications security*, pages 207–216. ACM Press, 2002.

[4] C. Dellarocas. Mechanisms for coping with unfair ratings and discriminatory behavior in online reputation reporting systems. In *Proceedings of the twenty first international conference on Information systems*, pages 520–525. Association for Information Systems, 2000.

[5] Z. Milosevic, A. Josang, T. Dimitrakos, and M. A. Patton. Discretionary enforcement of electronic contracts. In *6th IEEE International Enterprice Distributed Object Computing Conference EDOC 2002*, 17-20 September 2002.

[6] OpenPrivacy. www.openprivacy.org.

[7] A. A. Rahman and S. Hailes. Supporting trust in virtual communities. In *Proceedings of the 33rd Hawaii International Conference on System Sciences*, pages 1769–1777, 2000.

[8] J. Sabater and C. Sierra. Regret: A reputation model for gregarious societies. In *Proceedings of the 4th Workshop on Deception, Fraud and Trust in Agent Societies, in the 5th International Conference on Autonomous Agents (AGENTS'01)*, pages 61–69, 2001.

[9] G. Zacharia, A. Moukas, and P. Maes. Collaborative reputation mechanisms in electronic marketplaces. In *Proceedings of the 32nd Hawaii International Conference on System Science*. IEEE, 1999.

TY*SecureWS: An Integrated Web Service Security Solution Based on Java

Sung-Min Lee, O-Sik Kwon, Jae-Ho Lee, Chan-Joo Oh, Sung-Hoon Ko

R&D Center, Tong Yang SYSTEMS Corp.
24 Ogum-dong, Songpa-gu, Seoul 138-855 Korea
{lsm, oskwon, jholee, cjoh, shko}@tysystems.com

Abstract. In this paper we propose an integrated XML web service security solution based on Java. The goal of the proposed solution is guaranteeing confidentiality, integrity, and non-repudiation in using web services. It provides flexibility as its security functions are implemented in security handlers instead of modifying web services engine. It also supports extensibility since it has been developed based on international standards such as WS-Security, XKMS, XML Encryption, and XML Signature specifications. The proposed solution provides clients and servers in the business to business environments with confidence and security.

1 Introduction

A web service is an XML object comprised of content, application code, process logic, or any combination of these, that can be accessed over any TCP/IP network using the Simple Object Access Protocol (SOAP) standard for integration, the Web Services Definition Language (WSDL) standard for self-description, and the Universal Description, Discovery, and Integration (UDDI) standard for registry and discovery within a public or private directory[1].

Many distributed technologies such as Unix RPC, CORBA, RMI, and DCOM had failed on the Internet because they strongly coupled the endpoints and therefore could not become pervasive[2]. However, web service can supplement weakness because it places no restrictions on the endpoint implementation technology by using SOAP, which is the XML-based platform-neutral choice. Security is, in most environments, the most important aspect of web service. Despite the importance of securing web services, security solution for web services has not been integrated but only partial security solutions have been integrated (i.e., only providing authentication or encryption). The specifications related to web services security are just emerging. According to Gartner Group, web service architecture will represent the next generation of platform middleware by 2003[3]. Therefore, it is necessary to provide trusted web service solution as soon as possible.

In this paper, we propose an integrated security solution for web services. The objective of our solution is not only providing authentication between client and server but also guaranteeing confidentiality, integrity, and non-repudiation. Namely, it provides an integrated solution for trusted web services. Proposed solution has been

K. Bauknecht, A Min Tjoa, G. Quirchmayr (Eds.): EC-Web 2003, LNCS 2738, pp. 186–195, 2003.

implemented with Java to provide high portability. It provides flexibility as its security functions are implemented in security handlers instead of modifying web service engine. It also supports extensibility because it has been developed based on international standards such as WS-Security[9], XKMS[8], XML Encryption[6], and XML Signature[7] specifications. In addition, it supports one-way and two-way security checks; in one-way security check, only the server is authenticated by the client and in two-way security check, both the server and the client are authenticated by each other. Thus, if we perform one-way security check, system will provide high-speed web services with low security rate and vice-versa. It is important to make a good tradeoff between the levels of security and performance. In addition, we can use all security handlers to provide maximum security. However, for the efficiency, we can use as few handlers as needed. Therefore, it supports various security options by configuring its security handlers. The proposed solution provides clients and servers in the business to business environments with confidence, security, and efficiency.

The rest of this paper is organized as follows. Section 2 describes a secure web services framework and our goals. Section 3 presents the integrated security solution for web services. Section4 reviews the feature of our solution and the results of our performance evaluation. Finally the paper concludes with Section 5.

2 Secure Web Services Framework and Our Goals

In this section we define secure web service framework and describe its components. We also discuss our goals and coverage.

2.1 Secure Web Services Framework

Web Services are based on the extensible Markup Language (XML). The related specifications for XML applications can be thought of as the web services framework. The secure web service framework takes a layered approach, with core technologies such as XML syntax, schema, and transformation underlying higher-level application specifications such as those relevant to security.

The first layer indicates XML-related specifications. XML is a form of self-describing data that creates common information formats in order to share both the format and the data across the Internet. They are core technologies of web service concept. The characteristics of XML make web services be implemented heterogeneous environments.

The second layer indicates web service standards to provide interoperability – the ability from components created in different programming languages to work together as if they were implemented using the same language. Three major web service standards are SOAP, WSDL, and UDDI. These standards are based on XML. SOAP is a key standard for delivering web services. It is an XML-based protocol that consists of three parts: the SOAP envelope construct defines an overall framework for expressing what is in a message; who should deal with it, and whether it is optional or mandatory, the SOAP encoding rules define a serialization mechanism that can be used to exchange instances of application-defined data-types, the SOAP Remote Procedure Call (RPC) defines a convention that can be used to represent remote procedure calls and responses[4]. WSDL is an XML format meta-data for describing network services as a set of endpoints operating on messages. UDDI is a platform-independent, open framework for describing services, discovering businesses, and integrating business services using the Internet. A SOAP message is an XML document that consists of a mandatory SOAP envelope, an optional SOAP header, and a mandatory SOAP body[4]. The header is a generic mechanism for adding features to a SOAP message in a decentralized manner without prior agreement between the communication parties. Our security information for trusted web services has been implemented in the soap header.

The third layer is for securing web services. There are many emerging specifications for web service security. WS-Security specification describes enhancements to SOAP messaging to provide quality of protection through message integrity, message confidentiality, and single message authentication. Actually, IBM, Microsoft, and VeriSign have proposed this specification. XML encryption specification defines an XML schema for encrypting data. The encrypted data may consist of a complete XML document, individual elements in an XML document, or an external data object referenced by an XML document. XML signature specification defines an XML schema for cryptographically authenticating data, providing non-repudiation. XML Key Management Specification (XKMS) provides trusted web services for managing cryptographic keys, including public keys. The specification defines XML messages that allow applications to register key pairs, locate keys for later use, and validate information associated with a key. VeriSign has built the first implementation of the trust web service[10,11]. Security Assertions Markup Language (SAML) is a framework for specifying and sharing trust assertions in XML. A trust assertion can be any data used to determine authorization, such as credentials, credit ratings, approved roles, and so on.

The secure web services can be deployed only through combination of the three layers. Our solution has been designed based on the following framework.

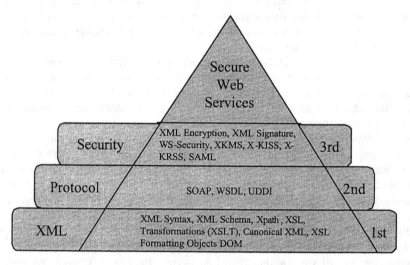

Figure 1 Secure Web Services Framework

2.1 Our Goals and Coverage

Our goal is to offer enterprises an easy way to deploy secure web services. Such services need the following characteristics:

- Availability: web services must be easy to invoke.
- Authentication: the sender is positively identified for sending the message.
- Confidentiality: the data are not available to unauthorized individuals, entities, or processes.
- Integrity: the data have not been modified.
- Non-repudiation: the originator of the data cannot deny that it was sent from their system (Undeniable proof of the origin, delivery, submission, or transmission of a message).

For secure web services, we must consider all the security of SOAP, WSDL, and UDDI protocol. However, in this paper we focus on only SOAP security. WSDL and UDDI security are out of scope in the proposed paper.

3 Proposed Web Services Security Solution

In this section we describe the overall architecture of the proposed solution. In addition, we provide our flexible security handlers and secure web service invocation process.

3.1 Overall Architecture

Ty*SecureWS has been designed, based on web service security standards. It uses Apache AXIS as a web service engine. In order to provide secure web service, we have implemented security handler chains for the web service engine. Figure 2 shows the overall architecture of Ty*SecureWS.

Ty*SecureWS consists of two parts: secure SOAP message generator and security handlers. The client first generates a SOAP message which may contain authentication information, encrypted data field, and digital signature to invoke web services securely. The secure SOAP message is issued based on WS-Security, XML encryption, XML signature, and XKMS specification.

Once a secure SOAP message is issued, the client invokes a web service using the message. Then, the server receives the secure SOAP message and translates it. Before web service invocation, request security handlers intercept the SOAP message and process it. If the client is authenticated and the signature of the client is valid, the server invokes the web service. After invocation, response security handlers start to work. Lastly, the server first signs the response SOAP message using its private key. Then, the server encrypts the SOAP message using a session key and sends it.

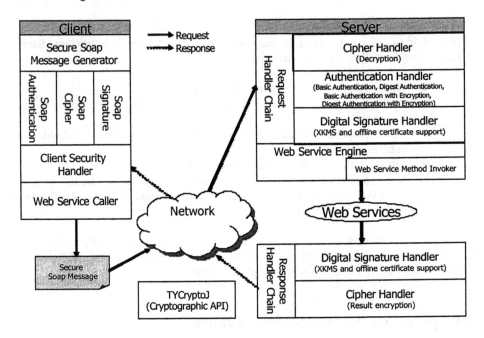

Figure 2 Overall Architecture

3.2 Security Handler Chain

It is necessary to embed security modules into web service engine to invoke web services securely by an authorized user. Disadvantage of this approach is that it ties the security services tightly to web service engine. Every time the engine changes, the security implementations must be carefully considered, and frequently the security functions must be modified as well. However, we don't have to modify web service engine to provide web service security because we have implemented security handlers. The security handlers, consist of request security handler and response security handlers, are the essential part in Ty*SecureWS. The request security handlers intercept SOAP message sent by the client, decrypt it, and then authenticate the client and receive message. The response handlers generate SOAP message, which contains web service invocation result. They add the information that proves the authenticity of the server and the message. Lastly, the server encrypts the SOAP message and sends it to the client.

The request security handlers are comprised of cipher handler, signature handler, and authentication handler. The response security handlers consist of signature handler and cipher handler. Figure 4 shows the security handler chain of the Ty*SecureWS.

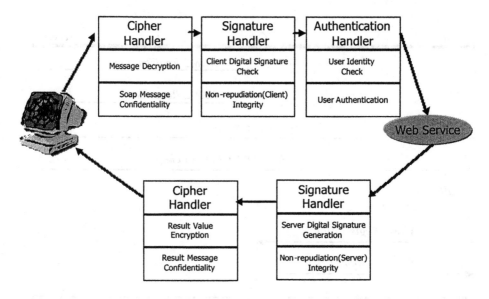

Figure 4. Security Handler Chain

The Request cipher handler intercepts the secure SOAP message, decrypts the message, and passes it to the request signature handler. The request signature handler then verifies the digital signature in the SOAP message. If the signature is valid, passes the SOAP message to the authentication handler, otherwise throws exception and stops. In order to verify the signature, we can use off-line certificate and client public key of obtained through using XKMS. The authentication handler supports basic and digest authentication. If the user authentication is valid, it invokes the web services otherwise throws exception and stops.

The Response signature handler signs the result of the web service invocation using its private key and passes it to the response cipher handler. The response cipher handler then encrypts the SOAP message using a session key and sends it to the client.

The Cipher handler guarantees confidentiality, signature handler guarantees integrity and non-repudiation, and authentication handler supports user identification. We can use all 5 security handlers to provide maximum security. However, for the efficiency and optimization of the system, we can use as few handlers as needed.

3.3 Secure Web Services Invocation Process

Three types of principals are involved in our protocol: client, server, and certificate authority (CA). Proposed invocation process for secure web service consists of two parts: initialization protocol and invocation protocol. The initialization protocol is prerequisite for invoking web services securely. Through the initialization protocol, all principals in our protocol set up security environments for their web services, as shown in Figure 5.

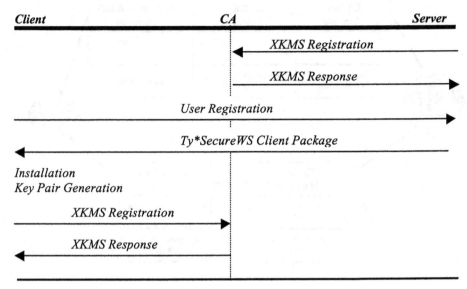

Figure 5 Initialization Protocol

The flow of setting up security environments is as follows. The server first registers its public key that will be used for verifying its digital signature to a CA through using XKMS. The client first registers its information for using web services, and then gets its id/password that will be used for verifying its identity when it calls web services via secure channel. Then, the client downloads Ty*SecureWS client package and installs it to configure its security environments and to make a secure SOAP message. It then generates a key pair for digital signature, and registers its public key to a CA. Ty*SecureWS supports both XKMS and offline-certificate-based signature. Therefore, principals in our protocol can choose a signature scheme that is more suitable for their objective.

Figure 6 shows the invocation protocol for secure web service. The client creates a SOAP message, containing authentication information, method information, and digital signature, encrypts it, and then sends it to a server. The message is in following form: $Enc_{session}(Envelope(Header(SecurityParameters, Sig_{client}(Body)) + Body(Method, Parameters))))$, where $Sig_x(y)$ denotes the result of applying x's private key function (that is, the signature generation function) to y. Ty*SecureWS provides two encryption methods: bulk encryption like SSL and specific field encryption. The protocol shown in Figure 6 shows the use of end-to-end bulk encryption. The security handlers in server receive the message, decrypt it, and translate it by referencing security parameters in the SOAP header. To verify the validity of the SOAP message and authenticity of the client, the server first examines the validity of the client's public key using XKMS. If the public key is valid, the server receives it from CA and verifies the signature. The server invokes web services after completion of examining the security of the SOAP message. It creates a SOAP message, which contains result, signature, and other security parameters. Then, it encrypts the message using a session key and sends it back to the client. Lastly, the Client examines the validity of the SOAP message and server, and then receives the result.

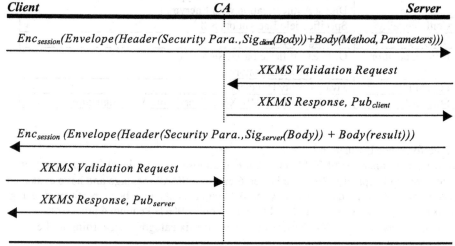

Figure 6 Secure Web Service Invocation Protocol

4 Analysis

In this section, we analyze the Ty*SecureWS and evaluate its performance.

4.1 Characteristics

The characteristics of Ty*SecureWS are shown in Table 1. The items have been reviewed including authentication, confidentiality, integrity, non-repudiation, portability, and standards. Our solution provides four authentication modes: basic authentication, digest authentication, basic authentication with encryption, and digest authentication with encryption. The user's credential information for authentication is created based on WS-Security specification. Also, it supports specific SOAP message field encryption and use of SSL to provide confidentiality - It uses strong encryption algorithm such as AES, SEED, and so on. In order to support the integrity of SOAP message, it generates a message digest of the SOAP message and inserts it into the message. To guarantee non-repudiation, it signs the message digest using its private key. It can use two signing methods: offline-certificate-based signature and XKMS-based signature. In order to provide portability, we have developed Ty*SecureWS under Java, using security handlers without modifying the web service engine. Therefore, it can be used on any java-based platforms. Lastly, it supports extensibility because it has been developed based on international standards for XML web services.

Table 1 Characteristics of the Proposed Solution

Characteristics	Description
Authentication	Basic Authentication, Digest Authentication Basic Authentication with Encryption Digest Authentication with Encryption
Confidentiality	Specific Field Encryption, SSL
Integrity	Message Digest
Non-repudiation	Offline Certificate-based Signature XKMS-based Signature
Portability	Java, Security Handlers
Standards	WS-Security, XKMS, XML Encryption, XML Signature

4.2 Performance Evaluation

Security administrator of Ty*SecureWS can choose security level based on system's objectives and capacity. We have issued 6 cases of SOAP message and have evaluated performance in regards to each type. All experiments had been performed using j2sdk1.4.1, Apache Axis 1.0, and WebLogic 6.1 on 1.69GHz Pentium 4 processor.

We have classified the SOAP message cases into six categories according to the security modes:

- Case A: the non-secured SOAP message.
- Case B: the SOAP message containing basic authentication function.
- Case C: the SOAP message providing digest authentication.
- Case D: the SOAP message applied digest authentication with encryption.
- Case E and Case F: the SOAP message containing signature with case D message.

Table 2 Performance Evaluation

	Authentication		confiden tiality	integrity	Non-repudiation		Time (sec.)	Size (Kbytes)
	basic	digest			Certificate	XKMS		
Case A							3.6	0.28
Case B	●						3.9	0.78
Case C		●					4.1	0.81
Case D		●	●				5.1	1.77
Case E		●	●	●	●		6.2	2.82
Case F		●	●			●	10	2.11

As shown in Table 2, run-time results were derived from our application, Ty*SecureWS, when first executed. The executed program is cumulative. If the program is executed again without stopping server, the xml information in the source will be loaded into memory (cache memory). Since the previously executed xml information in the source is added to the results of the previous run(s), the run-time performance will be improved.

In all three cases, A, B, and C, there are only slight differences in run-time performance. In case E and type F, the SOAP messages yield high-level security and low run-time performance because they satisfy all security requirements. In addition, since the SOAP message in case E is containing Base64-encoded certificate, the size of SOAP message in case E is greater than the size of SOAP message in case F.

5. Conclusion

Although there are diverse efforts for enhancing XML web service technologies, security solutions available to use web services have been rarely developed. In this paper, we have proposed an integrated security solution for web services. Not only providing authentication between client and server but also guaranteeing confidentiality, integrity, and non-repudiation is the purpose of our solution. In order to provide high portability and flexibility, we have implemented our solution in Java using security handlers instead of modifying web services engine. It also supports extensibility because it has been developed based on international standards such as WS-Security, XKMS, XML Encryption, and XML Signature specifications. In addition, the proposed solution provides clients and servers in the business to business environments with confidence, security, and efficiency.

References

1. A Delphi Group, "Web Services 2002:Market Milestone Report," A Delphi Group White Paper, IBM, 2002.
2. Steve Holbrook, "Web Services Architecture: Technical Overview of the Pieces," IBM, 2002
3. Ray Wagner, "Web Services Security: New Dog, Old Tricks," Gartner Symposium ITXPO, 2002.
4. W3C Note, "SOAP: Simple Object Access Protocol 1.1," May 2000.
5. W3C Recommendation, "Canonical XML Version 1.0," March 2001.
6. W3C Recommendation, "XML Encryption Syntax and Processing," March 2002.
7. W3C Proposed Recommendation, "XML Signature Syntax and Processing," August 2001.
8. W3C Note, "XML Key Management Specification (XKMS)," March 2001.
9. Bob Atkinson, Stoshi Hada, Phillip Hallam-Baker, and et. "Web Services Security (WS-Security),", April, 2002.
10. VeriSign, "Using VeriSign's Trust Services Integration Kit with XKMS," VeriSign Inc., March 2002.
11. VeriSign, "VeriSign Digital Trust Services: Enabling Trusted Web Services," February 2002.
12. A Joint White Paper from IBM Corp. and Microsoft Corp., "Security in a Web Services World: A Proposed Architecture and Roadmap," April 2002.

Protecting Intellectual Property by Guessing Secrets*

Marcel Fernandez and Miguel Soriano

Department of Telematics Engineering, Universitat Politècnica de Catalunya
C/ Jordi Girona 1 i 3, Campus Nord, Mod C3, UPC, 08034 Barcelona, Spain
{marcelf,soriano}@mat.upc.es

Abstract. In the guessing secrets problem defined by Chung, Graham and Leighton [9], player **B** has to unveil a set of $k > 1$ secrets that player **A** has chosen from a pool of N secrets. To discover the secrets, player **B** is allowed to ask a series of boolean questions. For each question asked, **A** can adversarially choose one of the secrets but once he has made his choice he must answer truthfully. In this paper we first present a solution to the $k = 2$ guessing secrets problem consisting in an error correcting code equipped with a tracing algorithm that efficiently recovers the secrets. Next, we show how with a slight modification in the tracing algorithm our approach to the guessing secrets problem also provides a solution to the collusion secure fingerprinting problem.

1 Introduction

In the original "I've got a secret" TV game show [9] a contestant with a secret was questioned by four panelists. The questions were directed towards guessing the secret. A prize money was given to the contestant if the secret could not be guessed by the panel.

In this paper we consider a variant of the game defined by Chung, Graham and Leighton [4]. In this variant, called "guessing secrets", there are two players **A** and **B**. Player **A** draws a subset of $k \geq 2$ secrets from a set of N secrets. Player **B** asks a series of questions in order discover the secrets. For each question asked **A** can adversarially choose a secret among the k secrets, but once the choice is made he must answer truthfully.

Using the same approach as Alon, Guruswami, Kaufman and Sudan discussed in [1], we present a solution to the guessing secrets problem consisting in the concatenation of a dual binary Hamming code with a Reed-Solomon code. We also design a tracing algorithm that recovers the secrets using soft-decision decoding techniques.

The problem of guessing secrets is related to several topics in computer science such as separating systems [11], efficient delivery of Internet content [4] and the construction of schemes for the copyright protection of digital data [1]. We

---

* This work has been supported in part by the Spanish Research Council (CICYT) Project TIC2002-00818 (DISQET).

K. Bauknecht, A Min Tjoa, G. Quirchmayr (Eds.): EC-Web 2003, LNCS 2738, pp. 196–205, 2003.

exploit this relationship with copyright protection schemes and show how with a minor modification our solution to the guessing secrets problem can also be used in fingerprinting schemes.

The fingerprinting technique consists in the embedding of marks into a digital object in order have protection against illegal redistribution.

The paper is organized as follows. In Section 2 a formal description of the game of guessing secrets for the case of $k = 2$ secrets is presented. Section 3 gives an overview of IPP and (2,2)-separating codes. A first approach to solve the guessing secrets problem using dual binary Hamming code is given in Section 4. This solution is improved using code concatenation in Section 5. Finally in Section 6 this last solution is transformed in order to be applied in collusion secure fingerprinting.

2 Guessing Two Secrets with Binary Answers

In this section we present a formal description of the game of guessing secrets for the case of $k = 2$ secrets.

Let $S = \{s_1, s_2\}$ be the two secrets drawn by **A** from the pool of N secrets. We first note that there's no way to guarantee that player **B** can learn both secrets since if all replies apply to just one of the two secrets, then **B** cannot learn nothing about the other.

Note also that **B** can never assert that a certain secret is one of **A**'s secrets, since **A** can always take three secrets $\{s_1, s_2, s_3\}$ and answer using a majority strategy. In this case the answer that **B** provides will be feasible for the three sets of secrets $\{s_1, s_2\}$, $\{s_1, s_3\}$ and $\{s_2, s_3\}$.

Using the above reasoning, we see that for a given answer we have the following possible configurations for the sets of secrewe givets: A *star* configuration, when all pairs of secrets have a common element. A *degenerated star* configuration, when there is a single pair of secrets. And a *triangle* configuration, when there are three possible disjoint pairs secrets.

The solution for the $k = 2$ secrets problem will then consist in finding the appropriate star or triangle configuration for a given sequence of answers.

When considering the set of questions to be asked, there are two possible strategies that one can use: *adaptive* and *oblivious*. In an adaptive strategy a given question depends on the answers to the previous questions. On the other hand in an oblivious strategy the questions are fixed at the beginning of the game. Although adaptive strategies seem more natural one can do surprisingly well by simply using oblivious strategies [1], so will focus on the later.

3 IPP Codes and (2,2)-Separating Codes

In this section we give a description of IPP codes and (2,2)-separating codes in terms of error correcting codes.

Let $\mathbf{F}_q^n$ be a vector space, then $C \subseteq \mathbf{F}_q^n$ is called a *code*. The set of scalars, $\mathbf{F}_q$ is called the *code alphabet*. A code C is called a *linear code* if it forms a subspace of $\mathbf{F}_q^n$. If the dimension of the subspace is k, then we call C an $[n,k,d]$-code.

For any two words $\mathbf{a}$, $\mathbf{b}$ in $\mathbf{F}_q^n$ we define the *set of descendants* $D(\mathbf{a},\mathbf{b})$ as $D(\mathbf{a},\mathbf{b}) := \{x \in \mathbf{F}_q^n : x_i \in \{a_i,b_i\}, 1 \leq i \leq n\}$. For a code C, the *descendant code* C^* is defined as: $C^* := \bigcup_{\mathbf{a} \in C, \mathbf{b} \in C} D(\mathbf{a},\mathbf{b})$.

If $\mathbf{c} \in C^*$ is a descendant of $\mathbf{a}$ and $\mathbf{b}$, then we call $\mathbf{a}$ and $\mathbf{b}$ *parents* of $\mathbf{c}$. If for every descendant in C^*, at least one of the parents can be identified, we say that code C has the *Identifiable Parent Property* (IPP)[8]. Usually a word in C^* has several pairs of parents so if the code has IPP then the intersection of those pairs will be non-empty. The IPP decoding algorithm consists in finding all possible pairs of parents of a given descendant.

Next theorem gives an explicit way to construct IPP codes.

Theorem 1 ([8]). *Let q be a prime power. If $q \geq n - 1$ then a Reed-Solomon code over $\mathbf{F}_q$ with parameters $[n, \lceil n/4 \rceil, n - \lceil n/4 \rceil + 1]$ exists and has IPP.*

Theorem 2 below, provides a useful condition for a codeword to be a parent.

Theorem 2. *Let C be a $[n, k, d]$ Reed-Solomon code with IPP, if a codeword agrees in more than $2(n-d)$ positions with a given descendant then this codeword is a parent of the descendant.*

Proof. If the code has minimum distance d, then two codewords can agree in at most $n - d$ positions, therefore a parent pair is only able to produce a descendant that agrees in at most $2(n - d)$ positions with any other codeword. Then any codeword that agrees with a descendant in at least $2(n - d) + 1$ positions is a parent. □

A weaker form of parent identification is given by $(2,2)$-*separating* codes [11]. A code C is $(2,2)$-*separating*, if for any two disjoint subsets of codewords of size two, $\{\mathbf{a},\mathbf{b}\}$ and $\{\mathbf{c},\mathbf{d}\}$, where $\{\mathbf{a},\mathbf{b}\} \cap \{\mathbf{c},\mathbf{d}\} = \emptyset$, their respective sets of descendants are also disjoint, $D(\mathbf{a},\mathbf{b}) \cap D(\mathbf{c},\mathbf{d}) = \emptyset$.

4   Guessing Secrets Using Dual Binary Hamming Codes

In this section we show how a binary $(2,2)$-*separating* code defines an explicit set of questions that solves the $k = 2$ guessing secrets problem. Moreover, we also present a strategy based on the Chase decoding algorithms that efficiently recovers the secrets.

4.1   Explicit Construction of the Strategy

Following the notation in [1] we denote the questions in an oblivious strategy as a sequence $\mathcal{G}$ of n boolean functions $g_i : \{1, \ldots, N\} \to \{0,1\}$. For a given secret $\mathbf{x}$ the sequence of answers to the questions g_i will then be $C(\mathbf{x}) = \langle g_1(\mathbf{x}), g_2(\mathbf{x}), \ldots, g_n(\mathbf{x}) \rangle$.

Without loss of generality we suppose that $\log_2 N$ is an integer. In this case, using the binary representation for $\{1, \ldots, N\}$ we can redefine C as the mapping $C : \{0,1\}^{\log_2 N} \to \{0,1\}^n$. From this point of view C can be seen as an error-correcting code. From now on we will refer to a given strategy $\mathcal{G}$ using its associated code C, and to the sequence of answers to a given secret using its associated codeword.

The question now is: which properties an error-correcting code must possess in order to solve the guessing secrets problem?. From the definition of (2,2)-separating codes in Section 3 we infer that if a code is (2,2)-separating then for every four distinct codewords (secrets) s_1, s_2, s_3 and s_4 there exists at least one value i, $i \in \{1, \ldots, n\}$, called the *discriminating index* for which $C(s_1)_i = C(s_2)_i \neq C(s_3)_i = C(s_4)_i$. So if **B** asks questions according to a (2,2)-separating code, then using the answer on the i'th question, he is able for every two disjoint pairs of secrets to rule out one of them. This is stated formally in the the following lemma.

Lemma 1 ([1]). *There exists a (2,2)-separating code $C : \{0,1\}^{\log_2 N} \to \{0,1\}^n$ if and only if there exists an oblivious strategy for **B** to solve the 2-secrets guessing problem for a universe size of N that uses n questions.*

From Lemma 1 it follows that the problem of guessing secrets is reduced to constructing (2,2)-separating codes. Next corollary from [5] gives a sufficient condition for a linear code to be (2,2)-separating.

Corollary 1 ([5]). *All linear, equidistant codes are (2,2)-separating.*

Therefore, the dual binary Hamming $[2^r - 1, r, 2^{r-1}]$ code S_r, that consists of **0** and $2^r - 1$ codewords of weight 2^{r-1}, with every pair of codewords the same distance apart, is readily seen to solve the guessing secrets problem.

4.2   Efficient Recover of the Secrets

We now tackle the problem of how to efficiently recover the secrets, when the strategy used is a dual binary Hamming code. To recover the secrets we need a way to relate the word associated to a sequence of answers with the codewords corresponding to these secrets. This is done in the following lemma.

Lemma 2. *Suppose a dual binary Hamming code is used as the strategy to solve the $k = 2$ guessing secrets problem. Let s_1 and s_2 be a pair of secrets and let x_1 and x_2 be its associated codewords. The set of possible sequences of answers of **A** according to the secrets s_1 and s_2 is precisely $D(x_1, x_2)$, the descendant set of x_1 and x_2.*

If we denote by **v** the word corresponding to the sequence of answers, then as it was shown in Section 2 we have that:

1. In a star configuration, for the common secret, say **x**, we have that $d(x, v) \leq 2^{r-2} - 1$.

2. In a "degenerated" star configuration, for the single pair of secrets, say $\{\mathbf{x}, \mathbf{y}\}$, we have that $d(\mathbf{x}, \mathbf{v}) = d(\mathbf{y}, \mathbf{v}) = 2^{r-2}$.
3. In a triangle configuration, for the three possible pairs of secrets, say $\{\mathbf{x}, \mathbf{y}\}$, $\{\mathbf{x}, \mathbf{z}\}$ and $\{\mathbf{y}, \mathbf{z}\}$, we have that $d(\mathbf{x}, \mathbf{v}) = d(\mathbf{y}, \mathbf{v}) = d(\mathbf{z}, \mathbf{v}) = 2^{r-2}$.

Therefore, we need an algorithm that outputs all codewords of a dual binary Hamming code within distance 2^{r-2} of $\mathbf{v}$. The algorithm we discuss is based on the Chase decoding algorithms [3]. As it is assumed in [3], we suppose that we have a binary decoder that corrects up to $\lfloor (d-1)/2 \rfloor = 2^{r-2} - 1$ errors.

If the closest codeword to $\mathbf{v}$ lies at a distance at least 2^{r-2}, then the binary decoder fails to decode. But in this case, note that the word $\mathbf{v}'$, obtained by applying a test pattern $\mathbf{p}$ of weight 1 to $\mathbf{v}$ ($\mathbf{v}' = \mathbf{v} \oplus \mathbf{p}$), is within distance $2^{r-2} - 1$ of a codeword. So, using the appropriate test pattern, we are allowed to correct 2^{r-2} errors.

The idea of the algorithm is to efficiently find the right test pattern, using the already found secrets. To see how this is done, note that once the codeword corresponding to a secret is found, the support of the test pattern that helps to find another secret, lies in the matching positions between the codeword associated to the secret and the word associated to the answers.

Simplified Chase Algorithm:

The algorithm uses:

- A function called *binary_decoder*($\mathbf{v}$) that outputs, if it exists, the unique codeword within distance $2^{r-2} - 1$ of $\mathbf{v}$.
- A function called *right_shift*($\mathbf{p}$), that takes as its argument a test pattern $\mathbf{p}$ of weight 1, and outputs a test pattern with its support shifted one position to the right with respect to $\mathbf{p}$, i.e., *right_shift*$((0,1,0,0)) = (0,0,1,0)$.
- A *list* that maintains all the already used test patterns that, when applied to $\mathbf{v}$, failed to decode into a codeword.
- Take $\mathbf{u} = (u_1, \dots, u_r)$ and $\mathbf{v} = (v_1, \dots, v_r)$, then $\mathbf{u} \oplus \mathbf{v}$ denotes the bitwise *exclusive or*, $\mathbf{u} \oplus \mathbf{v} = (u_1 \oplus v_1, \dots, u_r \oplus v_r)$.

Input: S_r, Dual binary Hamming code of dimension r; word $\mathbf{v}$ associated to a secret.
Output: All codewords within distance 2^{r-2} of $\mathbf{v}$.

1. Set $\mathbf{u}_1 := binary\_decoder(\mathbf{v})$. If $\mathbf{u}_1 \neq \emptyset$ then output $\mathbf{u}_1$ and quit.
2. Initialization: $\mathbf{p} := (1,0,0,\dots,0)$, *list* $:= \{\emptyset\}$.
3. Set $\mathbf{v}' := \mathbf{v} \oplus \mathbf{p}$ and run the binary decoder. Set $\mathbf{u}_1 := binary\_decoder(\mathbf{v}')$.
4. If $\mathbf{u}_1 \neq \emptyset$ then go to step 5.
   Else add $\mathbf{p}$ to *list*. Set $\mathbf{p} := right\_shift(\mathbf{p})$. Go to step 3.
5. Construct a new test pattern $\mathbf{p}$ of weight 1 that:
   - is different from all the patterns in *list*.
   - its support is one of the matching positions between $\mathbf{v}$ and $\mathbf{u}_1$.
6. Set $\mathbf{v}' := \mathbf{v} \oplus \mathbf{p}$ and run the binary decoder, $\mathbf{u}_2 := binary\_decoder(\mathbf{v}')$.
7. If $\mathbf{u}_2 \neq \emptyset$ then go to step 8.
   Else add $\mathbf{p}$ to *list* and go to step 5.

8. Construct a new test pattern $\mathbf{p}$ of weight 1 that:
   - is different from all the patterns in *list*.
   - its support is one of the matching positions between $\mathbf{v}$, $\mathbf{u}_1$ and $\mathbf{u}_2$.
   If there are no more test patterns available, output codewords $\mathbf{u}_1$, $\mathbf{u}_2$ and quit.
9. Set $\mathbf{v}' := \mathbf{v} \oplus \mathbf{p}$ and run the binary decoder, $\mathbf{u}_3 := binary\_decoder(\mathbf{v}')$.
10. If $\mathbf{u}_3 \neq \emptyset$ then goto step 11.
    Else add $\mathbf{p}$ to *list* and go to step 8.
11. Output codewords $\mathbf{u}_1$, $\mathbf{u}_2$ and $\mathbf{u}_3$ and quit.

5   Guessing Secrets Using Concatenated Codes

In channel coding, code concatenation is used to improve the rate of a code. In this section we improve the rate of the (2,2)-separating code of Section 4 (and therefore reduce the number of questions in the guessing secrets problem) by using code concatenation.

A concatenated code is the combination of an *inner* $[n_i, k_i, d_i]$ q_i-ary code $(q_i \geq 2)$ with an *outter* $[n_o, k_o, d_o]$ code over $\mathbf{F}_{q_i^{k_i}}$. The combination consists in mapping the codewords of the inner code to the elements of $\mathbf{F}_{q_i^{k_i}}$, that results in a q_i-ary code of length $n_i n_o$ and dimension $k_i k_o$. Note that the size of the concatenated code is the same as the size of the outer code, therefore from now on we will identify each secret with its associated codeword in the outter code.

To construct a (2,2)-separating binary code $\mathcal{C}$, we use code concatenation taking:

- as inner code, a $[2^r - 1, r, 2^{r-1}]$ dual binary Hamming code S_r,
- as outer code, a $[n, \lceil n/4 \rceil, n - \lceil n/4 \rceil + 1]$ IPP Reed-Solomon code over $\mathbf{F}_{2^r}$,
- together with a mapping $\phi : \mathbf{F}_{2^r} \to S_r$.

The codewords of $\mathcal{C}$ are obtained as follows, take a codeword $\mathbf{x} = (x_1, \ldots, x_n)$ from the Reed-Solomon code and compute $\mathbf{c}_i = \phi(x_i)$, $1 \leq i \leq n$. The concatenation of the $\mathbf{c}_i$'s forms a codeword $\mathbf{c} \in \mathcal{C}$, where, $\mathbf{c} = (\mathbf{c}_1, \ldots, \mathbf{c}_n)$ such that $\mathbf{c}_i = \phi(x_i)$.

Note that the size of the outer code and the size of the resulting concatenated code are identical, therefore from now on we will refer to a given secret using the associated codeword of the outter code.

Before discussing the algorithm that recovers the secrets, we first present the Guruswami-Sudan soft-decision list decoding algorithm.

5.1   The Guruswami-Sudan Soft-Decision List Decoding Algorithm

The concept of *list decoding* [7] is a relaxation of the classical unique decoding. Instead of trying to deliver a single codeword, a list decoder outputs a small list of all codewords within distance beyond the error correction bound of the code.

The *soft-decision* decoding technique applies to the cases where the decoding process takes advantage of "side information" generated by the receiver and

instead of using the received word symbols, the decoder uses probabilistic reliability information about these received symbols.

Next theorem is a powerful result due to Guruswami and Sudan (GS algorithm) [7] that says that there exists a soft-decision list decoding algorithm that
given a set of weights corresponding to the reliability of the symbols of the received word, we can find in polynomial time a small list of potential candidates
to be the sent codeword.

Theorem 3 ([7]). *Consider an $[n, k, n-k+1]$ Reed-Solomon code with messages
being polynomials f over $\mathbf{F}_q$ of degree at most $k - 1$. Let the encoding function
be $f \longmapsto \langle f(x_1), f(x_2), \ldots, f(x_n) \rangle$ where $x_1, \ldots, x_n$ are distinct elements of $\mathbf{F}_q$.
Let $\epsilon > 0$ be an arbitrary constant. For $1 \le i \le n$ and $\alpha \in \mathbf{F}_q$, let $r_{i,\alpha}$ be
a non-negative rational number. Then, there exists a deterministic algorithm with
runtime polynomial in n, q and $1/\epsilon$ that, when given as input the weights $r_{i,\alpha}$
for $1 \le i \le n$ and $\alpha \in \mathbf{F}_q$, finds a list of all polynomials $p(x) \in \mathbf{F}_q[x]$ of degree
at most $k - 1$ that satisfy*

$$\sum_{i=1}^{n} r_{i,f(x_i)} \ge \sqrt{(k-1) \sum_{i=1}^{n} \sum_{\alpha \in \mathbf{F}_q} r_{i,\alpha}^2 + \epsilon \max_{i,\alpha} r_{i,\alpha}} \tag{1}$$

5.2   Efficient Recover of the Secrets

We now are in position to describe the algorithm in full detail. The algorithm
takes as its input a word $\mathbf{y} = (\mathbf{y}_1, \mathbf{y}_2, \ldots, \mathbf{y}_n)$, that corresponds to the answers
of player $\mathbf{B}$, and outputs the codewords corresponding to the secrets.

We first perform the inner decoding consisting in the decoding of each sub-
word $\mathbf{y}_i$ using the Simplified Chase Algorithm. The output, as seen in Section 4,
will be a single codeword $\{\mathbf{h}_1\}$, a pair of codewords $\{\mathbf{h}_1, \mathbf{h}_2\}$ or three codewords
$\{\mathbf{h}_1, \mathbf{h}_2, \mathbf{h}_3\}$.

Then, for $i = 1, \ldots, n$ we use the mapping $\phi(s_m) = \mathbf{h}_m$ to obtain the
set $S_i^{(j)} = \{s_{i_1}, \ldots, s_{i_j}\}$, where the superscript $j \in \{1, 2, 3\}$ indicates the cardinality of the set. Note that the elements of the $S_i^{(j)}$'s are symbols from $\mathbf{F}_{2^r}$. We
denote by $\mathcal{S}^{(1)}$ the set of the $S^{(1)}$'s, by $\mathcal{S}^{(2)}$ the set of the $S^{(2)}$'s and by $\mathcal{S}^{(3)}$ the
set of the $S^{(3)}$'s.

Finally, we define the n-tuple of sets $\mathcal{S} = (S_1^{(j)}, \ldots, S_n^{(j)})$, that is used to set
up the weights that will be the input to the GS soft-decision decoding algorithm.
From the output list of the algorithm we can easily recover the secrets.

1. For $i := 1$ to n:
   (a) Decode the inner word $\mathbf{y}_i$ using the Simplified Chase Algorithm to obtain
       a list of at most 3 codewords $\{\mathbf{h}_1, \ldots, \mathbf{h}_j\}$, $j \in \{1, 2, 3\}$.
   (b) Define $S_i^{(j)} = \{s_{i_1}, \ldots, s_{i_j}\}$, where $\phi(s_m) = \mathbf{h}_m$, $1 \le m \le j$ and $j \in$
       $\{1, 2, 3\}$ depending on the output of step 1a.
2. Initialize $\mathcal{S} = (S_1^{(j)}, \ldots, S_n^{(j)})$. Define the subsets $\mathcal{S}^{(1)} = \{S_p^{(j)} \in \mathcal{S} : j = 1\}$,
   $\mathcal{S}^{(2)} = \{S_p^{(j)} \in \mathcal{S} : j = 2\}$ and $\mathcal{S}^{(3)} = \{S_p^{(j)} \in \mathcal{S} : j = 3\}$.

3. For $p := 1$ to n, set the weights r_{p,α_l} as follows:

$$r_{p,\alpha_l} := \begin{cases} \dfrac{1}{j} & \text{if } s_{p_m} = \alpha_l, \ s_{p_m} \in S_p^{(j)}, \ 1 \le m \le j \\ 0 & \text{otherwise} \end{cases}$$

4. Run the GS algorithm using r_{p,α_l}, obtaining a list of codewords U.
5. If $(|\mathcal{S}^{(1)}| + |\mathcal{S}^{(2)}|) > 2(n - d)$ then compute
   $U_{1,2} = \{\mathbf{u} \in U : |\{p : u_p \in S_p^{(1)} \vee u_p \in S_p^{(2)}\}| > 2(n - d)\}$. Note that $|U_{1,2}| \le 2$.
   - If $|U_{1,2}| = 2$ then output $U_{1,2}$ and quit.
   - If $U_{1,2} = \{\mathbf{u}^1\}$ then define $S_p^{(1)'} = \{s_{p_i} : s_{p_i} \in S_p^{(2)} \wedge s_{p_i} \ne u_p^1\}$ and
     construct the set $\mathcal{P} = \{S_p^{(1)} : u_p^1 \notin S_p^{(1)}\} \cup \{S_p^{(1)'}\}$.
     • If $|\mathcal{P}| = 0$, then output $\mathbf{u}^1$ and quit.
     • If $|\mathcal{P}| \ge k$, then take any k of the symbols in $\mathcal{P}$ and re-encode to find
       $\mathbf{u}^2$. Output $\{\mathbf{u}^1, \mathbf{u}^2\}$ and quit.
     • If $|\mathcal{P}| < k$, then taking the symbols in $\mathcal{P}$ and using every possible
       combination of alphabet symbols for the remaining up to k positions
       and re-encoding, yields all possible codewords associated with a se-
       cret, one for each combination, that together with $\mathbf{u}^1$ conform the
       star configuration.
6. Find a list U_3, of all codewords $\mathbf{u}^l \in U$ such that $|u_p^l \in S_p^{(3)}| \ge 2(n - d) + 1$.
   Note that $|U_3| \le 3$. Output $|U_3|$ and quit.

The re-encoding process in Step 5 can be performed because Reed-Solomon
codes are *maximum distance separable* codes ([10] Chapter 11) and therefore
any k symbols of the received word can be taken as information symbols.

6 A Fingerprinting Scheme Based on Guessing Secrets

A fingerprinting code is a set of codewords ("fingerprints"), where each codeword
is to be embedded in a different copy of a digital object. The codewords must
be chosen in a way that it must be possible to identify at least one guilty user
in case of a collusion attack.

In a collusion attack, a coalition of users compare their copies and create
a new *pirate* copy by changing some of the marks that they can detect. Under
the assumption that the coalition can only change the marks where their copies
differ, the set of potential pirate copies that the coalition is able to create, is
precisely the set of descendants of the codewords belonging to the members of
the coalition.

Therefore the task of the tracing algorithm is to identify the parents of a given
descendant. The tracing algorithm is almost identical to the algorithm in Section 5.2 that recovers the secrets given a sequence of answers. However, since in
a fingerprinting scheme we do not want to accuse any innocent users, we have
to make the following restrictions: In case of a star configuration we only output
the common codeword (parent) of the star. In case of a triangle configuration
we call a tracing failure.

The algorithm takes as its input a word $\mathbf{y} = (\mathbf{y}_1, \mathbf{y}_2, \ldots, \mathbf{y}_n)$ of the concatenated code, and outputs the positive parents of this word in the form of codewords of the outter code. We only need to replace steps 5 and 6 of the algorithm in Section 5.2 with the following steps:

5. If $(|\mathcal{S}^{(1)}| + |\mathcal{S}^{(2)}|) > 2(n-d)$ then compute $U_{1,2} = \{\mathbf{u} \in U : |\{p : u_p \in S_p^{(1)} \vee u_p \in S_p^{(2)}\}| > 2(n-d)\}$. Note that $|U_{1,2}| \le 2$.
   If $|U_{1,2}| = 0$ then go to Step 6, else output $|U_{1,2}|$ and quit.

6. Find a list U_3, of all codewords $\mathbf{u}^l \in U$ such that $u_p^l \in S_p^{(3)}$ for all $S_p^{(3)} \in \mathcal{S}$.

   a. For each $S_p^{(2)} \in \mathcal{S}$ do:
      If there is an $S_p^{(2)} = \{s_{p_1}, s_{p_2}\}$ for which there are exactly 2 codewords $\{\mathbf{u}^1, \mathbf{u}^2\} \in U_3$ such that $u_p^1 = s_{p_1}$ and $u_p^2 = s_{p_2}$, then output $\{\mathbf{u}^1, \mathbf{u}^2\}$ and quit.

   b. For each $S_p^{(1)} \in \mathcal{S}$ do:
      If there is an $S_p^{(1)} = \{s_{p_1}\}$ for which there is exactly 1 codeword $\mathbf{u}^1 \in U_3$ such that $u_p^1 = s_{p_1}$, then output $\mathbf{u}^1$ and quit.

   c. Decoding Fails.

Intuitively, the reason why the concatenated code of Section 5 works in fingerprinting schemes is because if the codewords are embedded in a digital object then they are unknown to the colluders, and so they can only detect the positions were they differ. In this case we can make the probability of creating a descendant that "decodes" into a triangle configuration arbitrarily small by increasing the code length. In [6] dual binary Hamming codes are were first proposed as fingerprinting codes, however one of the major drawbacks of that scheme is that the number of codewords grows linearly with the length of the code. To overcome this situation we use as a fingerprinting code a concatenated construction.

Note that if the algorithm succeeds it outputs at least one of the parents and it never accuses innocent users. Next, we will show that the probability that the algorithm fails can be made arbitrarily small. To see this, we first recall a Proposition from [6].

Proposition 1 ([6]). *Given* $\mathbf{x}, \mathbf{y} \in S_r$. *The probability that the coalition* $\{\mathbf{x}, \mathbf{y}\}$ *constructs a descendant word* $\mathbf{v}$, *such that there exists a* $\mathbf{z} \in S_r$ *with* $\mathbf{d}(\mathbf{v}, \mathbf{z}) = 2^{r-2}$ *is* $p \le (1/2)^{2^{r-1}}$.

Next theorem shows that the probability that the tracing algorithm fails, decreases exponentially with the length of the code.

Theorem 4. *Given the code from Section 5 and given a descendant word* $\mathbf{y} = (\mathbf{y}_1, \mathbf{y}_2, \ldots, \mathbf{y}_n)$ *created by a coalition of at most size two. The probability that the tracing algorithm fails is given by* $p \le 2^{-[2^{r-1}[n-2(n-d)]-kr]}$, *where* $d = n - \lceil n/4 \rceil + 1$ *is the minimum distance of the outter code and* k *its dimension.*

Proof. From the decoding algorithm, it can be seen that decoding can only fail if $(|\mathcal{S}^{(3)}| \ge n - 2(n-d))$. Using Proposition 1, the probability that this happens is $(2^{-2^{r-1}})^{[n-2(n-d)]}$.

No codeword will be identified if there is a codeword in the outter code that matches all the parents positions in $\mathcal{S}^{(1)} \cup \mathcal{S}^{(2)}$. The outter code is a Reed-Solomon code over $\mathbf{F}_{2^r}$, so there are $2^r \binom{n}{k-1}$ of such codewords. Since we have that $2^r \binom{n}{k-1} < 2^{rk}$, the theorem follows. $\square$

7   Conclusions

In this paper we first present an explicit set of questions that solves the $k = 2$ guessing secrets problem together with an efficient algorithm to recover the secrets. Since the explicit set of questions is based on a concatenated binary (2,2)-separating code, the recovering of the secrets consists in the decoding of a concatenated code, where both the inner and the outter code are decoded beyond the error correction bound. For the decoding of the inner code, we present a modification of the Chase algorithms, that taking advantage of the structure of the descendant code of a dual binary Hamming code, allows to efficiently search for all codewords within distance 2^{r-2}. The outter code is decoded with the Guruswami-Sudan soft-decision decoding algorithm.

Furthermore, using the conceptual relationship between the guessing secrets game and collusion secure fingerprinting of digital data we transform the guessing secrets solution to a fingerprinting scheme equipped with an efficient tracing algorithm. The tracing algorithm never accuses an innocent user and the probability that tracing fails can be made arbitrarily small.

References

[1] N. Alon, V. Guruswami, T. Kaufman and M. Sudan. Guessing secrets efficiently via list-decoding. *Proc. of the 13th Annual ACM-SIAM SODA*, 254–262, 2002.

[2] D. Boneh and J. Shaw. Collusion-secure fingerprinting for digital data. *Lecture Notes in Computer Science*, 963:452–465, 1995.

[3] D. Chase. A class of algorithms for decoding block codes with channel measurement information. *IEEE Trans. Inform. Theory*, 18:170–182, 1972.

[4] F. Chung, R. Graham and T. Leighton. Guessing secrets. *The Electronic Journal of Combinatorics*, 8(1):R13, 2001.

[5] G. Cohen, S. Encheva, and H. G. Schaathun. On separating codes. Technical report, ENST, Paris, 2001.

[6] J. Domingo-Ferrer and J. Herrera-Joancomartí. Simple collusion-secure fingerprinting schemes for images. *Proceedings of the Information Technology: Coding and Computing ITCC'00*, pages 128–132, 2000.

[7] V. Guruswami and M. Sudan. Improved decoding of Reed-Solomon and algebraic-geometry codes. *IEEE Trans. Inform. Theory*, 45(6):1757–1767, 1999.

[8] H. D. L. Hollmann, J . H. van Lint, J. P. Linnartz, and L. M. G. M. Tolhuizen. On codes with the Identifiable Parent Property. *J. Comb. Theory*, 82(2):121–133, 1998.

[9] I've got a secret. A classic TV gameshow. http://www.timvp.com/ivegotse.html.

[10] F. J. MacWilliams and N. J. A. Sloane. The Theory of Error-Correcting Codes. *North Holland*, 1977.

[11] Y. L. Sagalovich. Separating systems. *Probl. Inform. Trans.*, 30(2):14–35, 1994.

A Privacy-Enhanced Peer-to-Peer
Reputation System*

Michael Kinateder[1] and Siani Pearson[2]

[1] University of Stuttgart
Institute of Parallel and Distributed Systems (IPVS)
Universitätsstr. 38, 70569 Stuttgart, Germany
Phone +49-711-7816-230
michael.kinateder@informatik.uni-stuttgart.de
[2] Hewlett-Packard Research Laboratories Bristol
Filton Road, Stoke Gifford, Bristol BS34 8QZ, UK
Phone +44-117-312-8438
Siani_Pearson@hp.com

Abstract. In this paper, a method is described for providing a distributed reputation system with enhanced privacy and security as a design feature. This is achieved using a network of trusted agents on each client platform that exploit Trusted Computing Platform Alliance (TCPA) technology [1].

1 Introduction

A lack of trust in electronic services and the uncertainty of potential buyers about the *reputation* of online sellers is among the most prominent inhibiting elements [2] for successful B2C e-commerce. It is therefore most important that *trustworthy reputation systems* [3] are developed that are acceptable to end-users; using a privacy-enhancing peer-to-peer approach [4, 5] is especially appropriate since this improves the attractiveness to users of such systems.

In this paper we present such a system by introducing a trusted mechanism within the recommender's *Trusted Platform* (TP) for forming and collecting sensitive recommendations. A trusted agent forms recommendations and decides what is appropriate to send out, depending upon who is asking for it. This, or another such trusted agent, can be used to formulate queries asking for recommendations from others in a peer-to-peer network and process the responses. Furthermore, the system is designed such that the agents are independent and may be trusted by entities other than the owner of the platform on which they are running, and the integrity of these agents is protected by the TP against unauthorized modification.

The first generation of TCPA platforms that are currently available are aimed at the corporate market, and therefore the application of our approach to generic p2p applications may be restricted; however, other forms of trusted computing

---

* This work has been funded by Hewlett-Packard Limited.

K. Bauknecht, A Min Tjoa, G. Quirchmayr (Eds.): EC-Web 2003, LNCS 2738, pp. 206–215, 2003.
© Springer-Verlag Berlin Heidelberg 2003

(such as Microsoft's NGSCB) can be used in an analogous way to that described in this paper to bring similar benefits.

2 Motivation

In this section we list the possible threats and security requirements that will be addressed by our system.

2.1 Possible Threats

The following are a number of possible threats relating to running reputation systems over peer-to-peer networks, including the Internet:

T1: anyone can join the "reputation net" to provide malicious content
T2: recommendations can be modified en route to a requester
T3: recommendations can be accessed in an unauthorized manner
T4: people are too worried about their comments being attributed to them personally to want to engage in the system
T5: there is no legal redress if the system allows false recommendations to be provided and using these causes business loss

2.2 Security Requirements

We now list general requirements for providing a trusted peer-to-peer reputation system, based on our analysis above:

S1: wrongful recommendations must be detected (addressing T1)
S2: reputation information about the reliability of recommenders must be protected against unauthorized modification (T1)
S3: existing recommendations must not be altered without the creator's authorization (T2)
S4: recommendations should be protected by tamper-resistant hardware such that they are only accessible to authorized parties (T3)
S5: participants' privacy (identity) protection (T4)
S6: technological method for finding recommenders' identity given sufficient legal justification (T5)

3 Background

In this section we give background information about core technologies relating to our system, namely an overview about related work in trust modelling, reputation systems and TCPA technology.

3.1   Trust Modelling and Reputation Systems

Work has been published that is dealing with *trust modelling*, and we will put our focus on the distributed trust modelling approaches that have been taken so far. Jonker and Treur [6] propose a formal framework for the notion of trust within distributed agent systems. They are investigating trust developed through experiences and define properties of what they call trust evolution and trust update functions. Our developed models and algorithms fit into their framework.

Abdul-Rahman et al. are working in the area of *trust* development *based on experiences* and describe in [7] a trust model and several algorithms about how trust is created, distributed and combined. The trustworthiness of an agent is determined based on direct experiences of an agent and recommendations from other agents. Mui et al. are also working in this field and have shown in [8] a computational model of trust and reputation. Neither Abdul-Rahman's nor Mui's work however gives insights about context respectively different categories of reputation.

The area of *reputation systems* can be categorized in the *centralized* and *distributed* approaches and furthermore in *commercial applications* and *research work*. Here, we will focus again on the distributed approaches.

Noteworthy among the commercial works is the Poblano project (see [9]), SUN's work on reputation in their JXTA peer-to-peer architecture. Poblano introduces a decentralized trust model with trust relationships not only between peers but also between peers and content (what they refer to as "codat", code or data). "Trust" in a peer is calculated here based on the content this peer has stored in addition to its performance and reliability.

Scientific work in distributed recommendation systems is also still relatively rare. The trust modelling work of Abdul-Rahman et al. can be implemented in a distributed fashion as Aberer and Despotovic mention in [10]. They are furthermore proposing a model where they focus completely on negative recommendations (complaints) to derive trust in an agent and describe distributed storage issues and trust calculation algorithms for their model.

To summarize the related work presented so far it can be concluded that there are reputation systems out there, but they are either depending on a single merchant or specific product category or under control of one company. Comparably little work has been done in the area of distributed recommendation systems.

3.2   TCPA Technology

A *Trusted Platform* (TP) - sometimes also called a *Trusted Computing Platform* - provides most of the basic features of a secure computer, but does so using the smallest possible changes to standard platform architectures. However, a TP must include cost-effective security hardware (roughly equivalent to a smart card chip) that acts as the *"root of trust"* in a platform. This device is called a *Trusted Platform Module* (TPM). The TPM, as described in [1], is physical to prevent forgery, tamper-resistant to prevent counterfeiting, and has cryptographic functions to provide authenticity, integrity, confidentiality, guard against replay attacks, make digital signatures, and use digital certificates as required (further explanation of such terms is given in [11]).

Essentially, a TP is a normal open computer platform that has been modified to maintain privacy. It does this by providing the following basic functionalities:

Protected Storage. Protection against theft and misuse of secrets held on the platform. Such secrets are rendered unintelligible unless the correct access information is presented and the correct programs are running.

Integrity Checking. A mechanism for a platform to show that it is executing the expected software: the integrity of a TP, including the integrity of many components of the platform (such as BIOS, OS loader and so on) can be checked by both local users and remote entities. This mechanism is used to provide the information needed to deduce the level of trust in the platform. The trust decision itself can only be made by the entity that desires to use the platform, and will change according to the intended use of the platform, even if the platform remains unchanged. The entity needs to rely on statements by trusted individuals or organizations about the proper behavior of a platform.

TCPA Pseudonymous Identities. A mechanism for the platform to prove that it is a TP while maintaining anonymity. Proof that a platform is a genuine TP is provided by cryptographic *attestation identities*. Each identity is created on the individual TP, with attestation from a PKI Certification Authority (CA). Key features (further discussion in [12]) are:

- The TPM has control over multiple pseudonymous attestation identities; the platform owner may choose different CAs to certify each TPM identity in order to prevent correlation.
- A TPM attestation identity does not contain any owner/user related information: it is a platform identity to attest to platform properties.
- No unique TPM "identity" is ever divulged to arbitrary third parties or used to digitally sign data – in order to give privacy protection, a TPM will only use attestation identities to prove to a third party that it is a genuine (TCPA-conformant) TPM.

To summarize, this paper builds upon existing privacy technologies to provide a flexible and trustworthy method that allows dynamic development and reporting of recommendations. It deals with a different problem context to other methods for protecting privacy while revealing data. Instead of a centralized approach such as using a privacy infomediary (c.f. [13]), we concentrate on a peer-to-peer approach. In particular, TCPA protected storage, trusted attestation and integrity checking mechanisms are used to enhance the security of a peer-to-peer reputation system in a cost-effective and flexible manner.

4   A General Approach for Providing Trusted Peer-to-Peer Recommendations

We will focus in this chapter mainly on the system model on which we base our work and the means by which we protect the software agents that allow the functioning of the system against misuse and fraud. In order to allow better understanding of the interactions, we will then give a brief introduction to our notion of a trust model and will then cover the contents of recommendations.

4.1   System Model

The system model of our reputation system consists of *trusted agents* running in a specific *entity's* context on a particular computing platform as shown in Fig. 1. The trusted agents have connectivity to other agents on other entities' platforms in a peer-to-peer manner and are employing pseudonymous attestation identities during the communication. The system is greatly strengthened if these platforms are TPs as argued below. The entities can act in the roles of *recommender*, *requester* and *accumulator* and will most likely fulfill several of these roles in a running system.

Recommender: Upon having made own experiences, the recommender creates a recommendation (as described in Section 4.3), publishes it (see Section 5.2) and announces his expertise to interested parties regularly. If the recommender's platform were to be compromised, wrongful recommendations could be created or existing recommendations could be altered or released inappropriately in the recommender's name. To counter this, it is possible for a recommendation to only be sent out if the recommender platform's software environment is in the expected state (e.g. has not been hacked); this is possible because TCPA provides *protected storage functionality* for sealing data to a platform and software environment in this way.

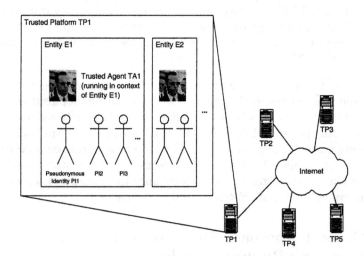

Fig. 1. Trusted Agents operating on a Trusted Platform in a certain Entity's Context

Requester: When uncertain whether to buy a product or to use a service etc. a user formulates a query with his trusted agent which queries a set of reliable sources and presents the received recommendations back to the user. Feedback is given to the agent about what recommender gave a fitting recommendation and which one should not be queried on further occasions. If the requester's agent is not reliable, then the feedback given to the system by the requester about the information received might have been tampered with, and this can completely change the trust decisions based on those recommendations. It would even be possible to change the reputation information about already known recommenders or add strong trust in new (malicious) recommenders, with potentially disastrous results.

Accumulator: The accumulator is – unlike the recommender – an entity that is creating recommendations based not on direct first-hand experiences but instead on multiple experiences from other entities accumulated in a meaningful way. Therefore the accumulator has not necessarily a high *authority rating* (describing the expertise in an area) but instead the accumulator has a high *hub rating*, meaning that he is very well connected and knows many recommenders with (hopefully) high expertise. The dangers for the accumulator's system to be corrupted are similar to the ones of the recommender in giving out wrongful (accumulated) recommendations, causing definitely a loss of reputation and more than likely connected to that financial damage to requesters trusting the judgment of this accumulator.

4.2   Trust Model

There exists no *general* trust of an entity A towards entity B but instead B is trusted differently depending on the *area in question*. In order to model trust we therefore need to model the different *categories* that an entity could be trusted in. Our model (see [14] for more details) consists of a set of categories with one *trust value* and one corresponding *confidence vector* for each category.

The *trust values* are in the range from 0..1 with 0 indicating either no previous experiences or just bad experiences with that entity in the category and 1 indicating the maximum trust. We assume that having no previous experiences is similar to having made only bad experiences since it is relatively simple to obtain a new pseudonym when the old one got a bad reputation. The initial default trust in each category of 0 can be set manually to a different value for known trusted entities to transfer real-world trust into the system.

The *confidence vector* stores meta-information used to judge the quality of the trust value and contains the number of experiences with the expertise of a recommender in that category and a trail of the last n experiences (n depends on the storage capacities of the system the agent is running on) with the associated recommender confidences (see following Section 4.3).

4.3   Recommendations

Recommendations in our initial system consist of the following three main components: *target*, *rating information* and a *digital signature* of the recommender.

The *target information item* identifies the recommendation target (another entity, a certain product or service, digital content) by specifying a descriptive name in addition to the recommendation's category. The first target option refers to the case where a recommender is judging e.g. the expertise or reliability of another entity in giving out recommendations in a certain area.

There are various types of *rating information* that can be included in the recommendation, like binary ratings, percentage values, multiple attribute-rating pairs and textual reviews. We found it to be important to add a confidence value to the rating specifying the recommender's own confidence in the given statement. This influences the impact of this recommendation for the trust update when processing the requestor's feedback.

As mentioned before we do add the *recommender's identity* to the recommendation, however not the real world identity but instead the pseudonymous attestation identity that the recommender is using for recommendations of the category in question. In order to prove the authenticity of the recommendation, a *digital signature* is added under the appropriate pseudonym. A recommendation identifier and time of creation is added to facilitate recommendation handling and timeliness checks.

The recommender's privacy is protected via protection of the stored recommendation using encryption and hardware-based storage of the decryption key(s) (preferably, using the TCPA protected storage functionality). *Authorization data* is needed in order to gain access to data stored via the TPM, and this cannot be overridden even by the platform owner or administrator, so the recommendation will only be accessible with the say-so of the recommender (or, more practically, the agent acting on behalf of the recommender). This is useful because the user may want only selected groups to see sensitive recommendations.

5   Interactions within this System

5.1   Requesting Recommendations

An entity seeking advice about a recommendation target uses the agent on its platform to formulate a *query for recommendations* about that target; this agent returns recommendations that are *locally* available and accessible and on his or her behalf requests recommendations from *other entities* with expertise in the area in question (each acting under pseudonymous identities) as shown in Fig. 2. For each category in the trust model this group of experts (or *neighborhood*) is being identified over time (e.g. $PI5$, $PI7$ and $PI9$ for identity $PI4$) by adapting the trust values according to successful or not so successful previous encounters. Upon receipt of the query the receiving entity checks whether suitable recommendations are available and decides whether or not to forward the query further to its own group of experts for the category in question.

The received recommendations are weighted according to the *resulting reputation* of their recommenders and *accumulated* if possible (depending on the type of received recommendations). This result is *presented* to the requester, who

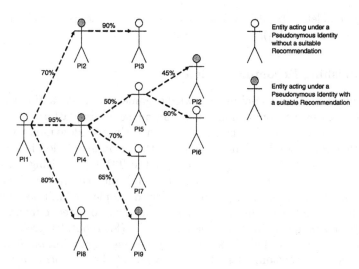

Fig. 2. Dissemination of a Recommendation Request to Members of the Neighborhood for the Category of the Recommendation Target in Question

then decides whether or not to strike the deal/use the service etc. If the deal has been stricken and own experiences have been made, the user decides about whether it was a good or bad deal and delivers *feedback* to the system regarding which recommenders were giving out a fitting and which ones a non-fitting recommendation. Their *reputation is updated* accordingly.

In a TP, the TPM would protect this trusted mechanism. Each agent may be *integrity checked* by the user of the platform or a remote party to ensure that the agent is operating as expected and has not been modified or substituted in an unauthorized manner. This process would involve a trusted third party (usually the vendor of the agent software) publishing or otherwise making available a signed version of the integrity measurements that should correspond to a genuine agent. Upon boot, the integrity of each agent can be measured as an extension to the platform boot integrity checking process [1]; a challenger may then check the software state of the platform by comparing the measured integrity metrics with the certified correct metrics and, based on this information, decide whether to trust the agent. The agents themselves can be protected further by running within a protected environment such as a suitably isolated compartment.

Nevertheless, there is still a link between the requester's platform's IP address and the recorded holder registered with this address. This issue can be addressed by MIX cascades [15], which may be used to provide anonymity on the IP layer. In order to allow communication between the requester and the recommender without revealing their identities to each other, additional techniques may be used such as anonymous web-posting (where for example messages are posted in 'anonymous letter boxes' associated with keys that are potentially set up for this specific purpose [16]).

5.2 Publishing Recommendations

An entity that is about to publish knowledge gained from interacting with a second entity creates a recommendation via an agent on its platform as described above. This recommendation is associated with the pseudonymous attestation identity that corresponds to the category of the recommendation in question.

The recommendations are protected via the TPM (exploiting TCPA protected storage mechanisms binding data to a TP and sealing it to its software environment) so that for example, unauthorized people couldn't see them. It is advantageous to allow having recommendations from one recommender stored on multiple hosts, for instance for load balancing (for reputable recommenders) or availability reasons. This is achieved by storing *authorization information* with the recommendation, such that the owner of the platform on which the recommendation were stored would not necessarily be able to access that recommendation (in the sense of reading an unencrypted version of it), although he/she could delete it.

6   Conclusions

We have proposed a distributed reputation system that has the following advantages in that the security requirements S1-S8 are addressed as follows:

S1: Protection Against False Recommendations.   The recommender's platform can be integrity checked and trusted identities can be used to link recommendations. Nobody may recommend in another person's name since the recommendations are protected by the digital signature of their recommender. The trust mechanisms ensure, that wrongful recommenders are detected and prevent them from being queried in future transactions.

S2: Reputation Protection. If the recommender's platform were to be compromised, wrongful recommendations could be created or existing recommendations could be altered or released inappropriately in the recommender's name. To counter this, it is possible for a recommendation to only be sent out or forwarded on if the recommender platform's software environment is in the expected state (e.g. has not been hacked); this is possible because TCPA provides functionality for sealing data to a platform and software environment in this way.

S3, S4: Recommendation Protection. The TPM protects against unauthorized access using TCPA protected storage mechanisms. Furthermore recommenders are protected against malicious requesters through integrity checking of the requester's platform (if this platform is a TP), possibly coupled with other policy-level checks on the corresponding enquirer, before the recommender's platform releases recommendation information.

S5: Participant's Privacy Ensured (Identity Protection).   All parties may engage in the system without having to say who they really are via the use of trustworthy pseudonyms.

S6: Redress for Unreliable Recommendation. Potentially, if entity A receives a recommendation from entity B that proves to be false and results in A making a financial loss, could that entity could go to entity B's privacy-CA to find out their real identity? The answer will depend upon the circumstances: whether your privacy-CA reveals your real identity in such a situation will depend upon the policy of that CA as well as legal reasons, such as whether you are suspected of breaking the law.

References

[1] Trusted Computing Platform Alliance: TCPA main specification, version 1.1 (2001) Available via *http://www.trustedcomputing.org*

[2] Cheskin Research: Trust in the wired americas (2000) Available via *http://www.cheskin.com/*

[3] Crawford, D., ed.: Special issue on recommender systems. Communications of the ACM **40** (1997)

[4] Andy, O.: Peer-to-Peer, Harnessing the Power of Disruptive Technology. O'Reilly (2001)

[5] Korba, L.: Privacy in distributed electronic commerce. In: Proc. 35th Hawaii International Conference on System Sciences, Big Island, Hawaii, IEEE (2002)

[6] Jonker, C., Treur, J.: Formal analysis of models for the dynamics of trust based on experiences. In: Proc. 9th European Workshop on Modelling Autonomous Agents in a Multi-Agent World. Volume 1647 of LNAI., Valencia, Springer-Verlag (1999)

[7] Abdul-Rahman, A., Hailes, S.: Supporting trust in virtual communities. In: Proc. 33rd Hawaii International Conference on System Sciences, Maui Hawaii (2000)

[8] Mui, L., Mohtashemi, M., Halberstadt, A.: A computational model of trust and reputation. In: Proc. 35th Hawaii International Conference on System Sciences, Big Island, Hawaii, IEEE (2002)

[9] Chen, R., Yeager, W.: Poblano – a distributed trust model for peer-to-peer networks. Technical report, Sun Microsystems, Inc. (2001)

[10] Aberer, K., Despotovic, Z.: Managing trust in a peer-2-peer information system. In: Proc. 9th International Conference on Information and Knowledge Management (CIKM 2001), Atlanta (2001)

[11] Schneier, B.: Applied Cryptography. Second edn. John Wiley & Sons, New York (1996)

[12] Pearson, S., ed.: Trusted Computing Platforms: TCPA Technology in Context. Prentice Hall (2002)

[13] Grritzalis, D., Kyrloglou, N.: Consumer online-privacy and anonymity protection using infomediary schemes. In: Proc. SCCC 2001, IEEE Computer Society (2001)

[14] Kinateder, M., Rothermel, K.: Architecture and Algorithms for a Distributed Reputation System. In: Proc. First International Conference on Trust Management. Volume 2692 of LNCS., Crete, Springer-Verlag (2003)

[15] Chaum, D.: Untraceable electronic mail, return addresses and digital pseudonyms. Communications of the ACM **24** (1981)

[16] Huberman, B., Hogg, T.: Protecting privacy while revealing data. Nature Biotech **20** (2002)

Profiting from Untrusted Parties in Web-Based Applications*

Claus Boyens and Matthias Fischmann

Institute of Information Systems, Humboldt University Berlin
Spandauer Str. 1, 10178 Berlin, Germany
{boyens,fis}@wiwi.hu-berlin.de
http://www.wiwi.hu-berlin.de/iwi

Abstract. Privacy Homomorphisms (PHs) are encryption functions that allow for a limited processing of encrypted data. They are of particular importance for the transformation of sensitive data that is given away to untrusted third parties for computation purposes. In this paper, we analyze the theoretical foundations of this class of functions and mark out its limitations in terms of security and functionality. We then propose the employment of PHs in two different usage environments. First, a single user wants an untrusted service provider to perform operations on encrypted data that she lacks the power or ability to compute herself. Second, a group of peers uses the services of a semi-trusted mediator who cannot be relied on in principle but who is assumed not to collude with either of the peers. In both cases, privacy is preserved by encrypting sensitive data with a PH before transferring it to the untrusted party. The results show that PHs can be usefully employed in both situations although their firm theoretical limitations inhibit general-purpose use.

1   Introduction

As the number of services offered on the Internet steadily increases, sensitive user data is spread widely across sites that often were not the target of the original data release. In other words, many people get access to others' personal information via channels that are impossible to track and control. A trivial way to solve this problem from a user's perspective would be to not release any personal information at all. Yet often the use of online services requires at least some input data. If the user does not entirely trust the service provider to handle this information confidentially, then the following question arises:

How Can the User Profit from the Offered Service when He Is not Willing to Release Any Personal Information?

This question is independent from access control and confidentiality of the communication channel. Rather, it aims at the fact that the service provider almost always needs to possess the plaintext input data in order to execute a specific operation. These data are not only threatened by attacks to the provider's

---

* This research was supported by the Deutsche Forschungsgemeinschaft, GRK 316/3.

K. Bauknecht, A Min Tjoa, G. Quirchmayr (Eds.): EC-Web 2003, LNCS 2738, pp. 216–226, 2003.

database, but also by incompetent or malicious staff on the provider's part and by insecurity about data property once the provider has gone bankrupt or has been acquired by another company. Abstracting from juristic and organizational approaches, a technical solution to the question above can be structured in several dimensions. These include hardware- or software orientation, level of trust towards the service provider, number of users involved, and the kind of privacy breaches to be limited.

- *Hardware vs. Software*

Proposed hardware solutions are based on a tamper-proof device that is the only place where confidential information is viewable outside the user's machine [6, 13, 1]. Major drawbacks are the limited processing and memory capabilities of these devices. The seminal software solution was proposed by [11] by using so-called *privacy homomorphisms*, encryption functions that allow for a limited processing of encrypted data.

- *Untrusted vs. Semi-Trusted Service Providers*

The lack of trust in online service providers has been studied in [3]. Users are hesitant or even refuse to release personal information if the provider is not assumed to treat data confidentially. Semi-trusted servers were first introduced by [2] as commodity servers. They cannot be relied on in principle either, but they are assumed to adhere to the agreed protocol and not to collude with any of the trusted parties involved in the service creation process. It is difficult to find a trusted peer; it is much easier to find semi-trusted parties.

- *Single User vs. Group of Peers*

In a hostile environment, a single user would usually not trust anybody and therefore not share his sensitive data. In contrast, a larger number of peers may cooperate with each other to a certain degree if they are protected against the untrusted central facility they use as the means of communication. Privacy problems in peer-to-peer (P2P) networks have been studied in [9].

- *Direct vs. Inferential Disclosure*

Direct disclosure occurs when a specific value can be read in plaintext without further efforts, whereas inferential disclosure means deriving the sensitive value or its statistical estimate from publicly available information [7, 16, 15].

This paper omits the deployment of supporting hardware and develops a purely *software-oriented* approach to prevent service providers from *directly* breaching users' privacy. Privacy Homomorphisms as the central tool are analyzed with regard to their security and functional properties. We present two different scenarios for the usage of these functions.

First, we review a service model that allows a *single user* to use a number of services from an *untrusted* provider without revealing the plain input data. We propose application areas that our approach is especially useful for and mark out its limitations.

Second, we propose a privacy-preserving architecture for a *group of peers* who want to cooperate via a *semi-trusted* central facility. We discuss the example of a file-sharing P2P network, where the peers want to share information about availability in specific file categories without revealing their personal file tree.

The remainder of this paper is structured as follows. Section 2 presents the formal framework for the proposed service architecture. Section 3 is dedicated to the single-user case dealing with an untrusted service provider. A group of peers creating and sharing aggregate information via a semi-trusted service provider is described in section 4. We conclude with a discussion of general implications for electronic commerce and open research questions.

2   The Central Tool: Privacy Homomorphisms

2.1   Processing Encrypted Data

Privacy Homomorphisms (PHs) are "encryption functions that permit encrypted data to be worked with without preliminary decryption of the operands" [11]. In other words, a user can apply a Privacy Homomorphism to sensitive data before transmitting it to the untrusted service provider. Although he cannot read the original datum, the service provider can still process it in a useful way. The pseudo-result, which is still of no value for the service provider, is then returned to the user who decrypts it to see the plain result of the requested service. We introduce the following terminology:

$d_i, i = 1(1)n$	Sensitive data to be processed
p	Private key (only known to the user)
q	Public key (given to the service provider)
$S : (d_i, d_j) \mapsto S(d_i, d_j)$	Operation/Service on plaintext data
$T_p : d_i \mapsto T_p(d_i) = t_i$	Encryption function
$S' : (t_i, t_j) \mapsto S'(t_i, t_j)$	Operation/Service on encrypted data
$T_p^{-1} : t_i \mapsto T_p^{-1}(t_i)$	Decryption function

The pair of functions $\{T_p, T_p^{-1}\}$ is called a privacy homomorphism iff

$$T_p^{-1}(S'(T_p(d_i), T_p(d_j))) \overset{!}{=} S(d_i, d_j) \ \forall d_i, d_j \in dom(T_p).$$

p denotes the private key of the user which is necessary for encryption and decryption. The service provider is given the public key q which allows him to process the encrypted data.

Figure 1 describes the basic idea of a privacy homomorphism.

We will now describe some inherent characteristics of these particular functions and derive implications for the feasible services S that can be outsourced to a service provider.

2.2   Inherent Characteristics

Clearly, working with encrypted data imposes significant restrictions on the extent of feasible operations on the underlying data. The following is a collection of fundamental findings and implications.

- *A Secure Encryption Scheme Can Never Preserve Order*

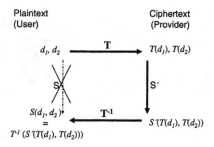

Fig. 1. The basic idea of a Privacy Homomorphism

This means that for a given set of attribute values as e.g. $\{3, 17, 31, 35, 42\}$, no secure encryption scheme allows for determining the order $(T_p(3),\ T_p(17),\ T_p(31),\ T_p(35),\ T_p(42))$ on the ciphertexts [11]. An important conclusion is that attributes in encrypted databases cannot be sorted at all.

- *Multiplication Can Be Preserved at a Higher Level of Security than Addition*

On the scale that measures the security of encryption schemes [14], the maximum level attainable for addition-preserving encryption schemes is below the maximum level for multiplication-preserving ones [5]. This implies that encryption schemes that preserve all basic arithmetic operations can reach at most the lower additive security level.

The PH employed in the remainder of this paper is based on the one proposed in [8]. It maps integers $\in \mathbb{Z}_p$ to encrypted integers $\in \mathbb{Z}_q$ preserving all field operations (addition, subtraction, multiplication and division). Furthermore, it is a non-deterministic encryption scheme, i.e. the same plaintexts are not necessarily mapped to identical ciphertexts, yet the decrypted results of the operation always stay the same.

We will now propose the employment of this PH in two different scenarios.

3   An Untrusted Service Provider for a Single User

3.1   The Basic Idea

We consider the case of a single user who wants to use the services of an untrusted party for one or more of the following reasons:

- He lacks the computing power to perform the service himself.
- He wants to dispose of database and computer maintenance tasks.
- The service offered is simply faster or cheaper when outsourced.

We presented in [4] an architecture that allows for secure outsourcing of a limited number of services. Following the idea of public key infrastructure [12], the basic

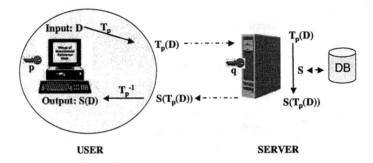

Fig. 2. A single user communicating with an untrusted service provider [4]

idea is to transform the sensitive data with the help of a secret key only known to the user. The service provider uses the corresponding public key to process the encrypted data. This general idea is depicted in Figure 2.

After the installation of the key infrastructure, the service procedure includes the following steps:

1. The user encrypts the sensitive data d_i with the PH T_p and transmits it to the service provider.
2. The service provider carries out the Service S on the transformed data.
3. The user receives and decrypts the encrypted pseudo-result $S(T_p(d_i))$ to obtain $S(d_i)$.

3.2 A Sample Service

The most useful way to employ our approach is to calculate aggregate figures. Suppose a company wants to know the mean monthly absent hours in its departments. The service provider can calculate this figure with only little additional effort required from the user.

Let $d_1^F, \ldots, d_n^F$ denote the plain absent hours in the company's Finance department. Before sending it to the service provider, the company applies the PH on the data and obtains $T_p(d_1^F), \ldots, T_p(d_n^F)$. The service provider, who stores this information in his database, can retrieve the corresponding records and calculate $s' = \sum_{i=1}^{n} T_p(d_i^F)$. Unfortunately, linearity is not preserved by the deployed PH, i.e.

$$T_p(\lambda d_i) \neq \lambda T_p(d_i)$$

for practically all $\lambda \in \mathbb{Z}$, $d_i \in dom(T_p)$. Therefore the provider cannot simply divide the sum by the number of data sets n but must transfer both the encrypted sum and the plain number back to the client, who then has $\mu_{Finance} = \frac{1}{n} T_p^{-1}(s')$.

3.3 Implementation Issues

We suggest two different implementation approaches. In the first case, the service provider could deliver a certified browser plug-in that contains the encryption logic and that can be parametrized by the user (e.g. with the private key). On the other hand, larger firms could employ a proxy server that checks every outgoing packet for marked up sensitive data and, if necessary, employs the adequate transformation. A sample implementation shows that, compared to a standard non-secured procedure, the service performance time increases only slightly, whereas the space requirements in the provider's database steps up significantly [4].

3.4   Limits and Opportunities

The discussed approach allows a single user to profit from a number of online services without revealing any plain information. It is especially well-suited for large datasets and for services that require only basic arithmetic and database operations. It is not suited as a one-size-fits-all approach for arbitrary outsourced services. Nevertheless, it may be usefully employed in hybrid service architectures if only part of the sensitive data is processed in an encrypted state.

4   A Semi-trusted Service Provider for a Group of Peers

4.1   The Basic Idea

We now consider the case of multiple peers who have an interest in aggregate information about a network/system to which they belong. The local information would be sent to a central facility who generates and manages the aggregate figures. Some examples are stated below.

1. Schools share statistics about absent students with the ministry of education without revealing their individual data. However, each school is interested in learning how it performs compared to the average of all participating institutes.
2. Hospitals share statistics about treatment outcomes with a research group. While not willing to reveal its individual data, each hospital has a strong interest in learning which treatment is the most successful.
3. Users of file-sharing Peer-to-Peer (P2P) networks want to know the general availability of files in the entire network. Nevertheless they may be unwilling to expose their personal file tree to a mediator.

As the single piece of information that each peer contributes to the entire picture is considered sensitive, our approach is to encrypt these data with a privacy homomorphism before sending it. The untrusted mediator must then be able to gather and process encrypted data from all the network participants. Furthermore, the peers must be able to access and read the results created by the mediator.

Contrary to recent approaches in zero-knowledge multi-party computation [10], the system we propose is built around a *semi-trusted* mediator [2]. This central

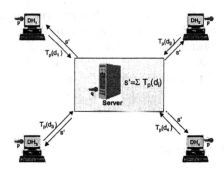

Fig. 3. Peers communicating with an untrusted mediator

mediator is not trusted to keep the peers' data confidential but does not collude with any of the involved peers. The participating peers all share a common *peer key* p, whereas the mediator is provided with the public key q. Each peer sends his encrypted piece of information $T_p(d_i)$ to the mediator who calculates an aggregate value, e.g. the sum of the encrypted values. He then provides every peer with the result s'. This approach is especially useful in very decentralized environments where the central facility cannot be trusted in general. The basic idea of our framework is depicted in Figure 3. $\mathcal{DH} = \{DH_1, \ldots, DH_4\}$ is the set of data holders involved in the network, whereas $s' = S'(T_p(d_1), T_p(d_2), T_p(d_3), T_p(d_4))$ is the result of the mediator's computation.

In the next section we discuss sample services S' that a mediator is able to provide.

4.2   Totals Provided by the Mediator

The main task of the mediator is to provide the peers with the aggregates to which they contributed. An exemplary service that is conducted on encrypted peer data is the calculations of totals.

1. Service S_1: Totals $(\sum_{i=1}^{N} T_p(d_i))$

   (a) $\forall i : DH_i$ sends $T_p(d_i)$ to the service provider.
   (b) The service provider calculates $s'_1 = \sum_{i=1}^{N} T_p(d_i)$.
   (c) The provider sends s'_1 to all the data holders DH_i.
   (d) All peers obtain the plaintext result by decrypting s'_1.

Besides their importance as part of more complex calculations, total sums are very useful with regard to count data. For example, the number of absent hours, the number of disease occurrences and the number of files in a specific category would be relevant calculations for our previous examples.

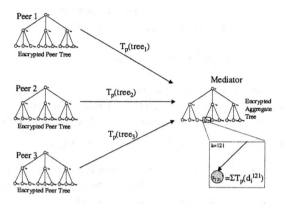

Fig. 4. Calculating the aggregate tree from encrypted peer trees

4.3 An Example: Sharing File Information via a Semi-trusted Mediator

Referring to the third application example from section 4.1, we assume a middleware software for peer-to-peer (P2P) file-sharing systems that provides the total number of available files in different categories. Participants in that network may want to know how many files of a specific category are available in the whole system, but do not want to allow the mediating software to sketch a detailed tree of their individual file directory. An example for such a file tree is given in Figure 4.

Privacy homomorphisms can now come in as a means of protecting the privacy of every individual user towards the mediator while still allowing the users to obtain the total number of files of a specific type. The homomorphic property of the transformation function results in the decrypted sum of encrypted numbers being equivalent to the sum of the clear text numbers. The communication between mediator and peers can be described as follows.

1. Install key infrastructure
   Generate and distribute the private key p among the peers.
   Generate and give the public key q to the mediator.

2. Ensure tree coherence
   Every single node value d^{cat_k} in the graph corresponds to a specific category cat_k of files. Every node value must be equal to the sum of all child node values, unless it is a leaf node. The micro-tree coherence is important because the mediator will later not be able to correct it. (If he could, the PH would not be secure.)

3. Encrypt peer trees
   Use PH T_p to map every single node value d^{cat_k} to $T_p(d^{cat_k})$. The exemplary node scheme is mapped from

```
node(node_id, child_id, node_name, value) to
node(node_id, child_id, node_name, tp_value).
```

4. Transfer encrypted values to the mediator

5. Calculate the master tree (`master_node`)
   The mediator uses the underlying tree structure in order to calculate the
   encrypted sum of the single node values for all categories cat_k.
   $$s'_k = S^{cat_k}(T_p(d_1^{cat_k}), \ldots, T_p(d_N^{cat_k})) = \sum_{i=1}^{N} T_p(d_i^{cat_k}), \; \forall k$$

6. Pose queries for single master values and decrypt the results
   The peers may now pose queries for single `master_node` values to the medi-
   ator and obtain the actual values via decryption.
   No. of Files in category cat_7:
   $T_p^{-1}($`SELECT tp_value FROM master_node WHERE (node_id = 7)`$)$

In addition to the employment of PHs, the traffic from the peers to the mediator
is protected using a public/private key pair held by the mediator. In practice, we
suggest that all traffic to the mediator be SSL-protected. If peers submit their
data encrypted only using their shared key p, a passive attacker on the network
could redistribute the inputs among all peers, and all peers could decrypt it.

4.4   Evaluation

Though not delivering ultimate privacy protection, the presented approach
makes it significantly harder for the service mediator to see sensitive information. Specifically, the employment of a non-deterministic encryption scheme contributes to an additional level of security. The major difference to the single-user
case discussed in section 3 is the fact that the peer key resides on multiple hosts.
This is in part accounted for by the assumption that the mediator does not collude with any of the peers in the sense of "trading individual information" but
still, the loss of the peer key to the mediator represents a major threat.

5   Conclusions

For the case that users of an online service do not want to release any personal
information to their service provider, we presented a software-based approach
that both preserves user privacy and facilitates the use of some elementary services. We propose the employment of privacy homomorphisms, a specific class
of encryption functions, in two particular usage environments.

   If a single user outsources data for lack of computational power or for economic reasons, he can use privacy homomorphisms to encrypt sensitive data
while still obtaining useful aggregates such as e.g. averages over specific attribute
values in the encrypted database. This procedure is beneficial especially if the
underlying dataset is large and if the extent of the computation is limited to
basic arithmetic operations.

A group of peers who want to create and share aggregate information about the network they belong to via an untrusted mediator can employ privacy homomorphisms to encrypt their personal datum before sending it. The mediator collects the single encrypted data and computes an encrypted pseudo-aggregate that is still of no use to him. Yet all the peers can decrypt and see the aggregate result while maintaining the privacy of every single peer. We gave an example of a file-sharing network where peers contribute encrypted information about their personal file structure and in turn, obtain plain information about the total file availability in the entire network.

In both cases, clear limits are set to the extent of the provided services. Some fundamental database operations and more complex calculations are impossible to perform on encrypted data. The proposed architectures are thus not suited for arbitrary operations, but rather for customized solutions that consider these limitations. Nevertheless we believe that the presented methods can be usefully employed as part of hybrid frameworks.

Future research could thus be directed to the integration of the discussed methods into more general service architectures. Especially when it comes to the extensive use of basic arithmetic operations or to the aggregation of sensitive data in general, privacy homomorphisms are a suitable tool to enhance privacy protection. Another interesting question in this context is in how far the computational problems can be partitioned into a public and a private component. Any fragmentation that reduces the service complexity increases the suitability of the methods discussed in this paper.

Acknowledgments

The authors would like to thank Sarah Aerni, Ramayya Krishnan and Rema Padman for helpful comments on earlier versions of this paper.

References

[1] D. Asonov and J. C. Freytag. Almost optimal private information retrieval. In *Proceedings of the 2nd Workshop on Privacy Enhancing Technologies (PET '02)*, San Francisco, 2002.

[2] D. Beaver. Commodity-based cryptography. In *Proceedings of the ACM STOC Conference*, El Paso, USA, 1997.

[3] C. Boyens and O. Günther. Trust is not enough: Privacy and security in ASP and web service environments. In *Advances in Database and Information Systems (ADBIS 2002)*. Springer Verlag, Heidelberg, 2002.

[4] C. Boyens and O. Günther. Using online services in untrusted environments - a privacy-preserving architecture. In *Proceedings of the European Conference on Information Systems (ECIS)*, Naples, Italy, to appear in 2003.

[5] E. Brickell and Y. Yacobi. On privacy homomorphisms. In *Eurocrypt '87*. Springer Verlag, Berlin, Heidelberg, New York, 1987.

[6] B. Chor, O. Goldreich, E. Kushilevitz, and M. Sudan. Private information retrieval. In *Proceedings of the 36th IEEE Conference on Foundations of Computer Science*, pages 41–50. IEEE Press, New York, 1995.

[7] S. D. Chowdhury, G. Duncan, R. Krishnan, S. Roehrig, and S. Mukherjee. Disclosure detection in multivariate categorical databases: auditing confidentiality protection through two new matrix operators. In *Management Science*, Vol. 45, No. 12, December 1999.

[8] J. Domingo-Ferrer and J. Herrera-Joancomarti. A privacy homomorphism allowing field operations on encrypted data. In *Jornades de Matematica Discreta i Algorismica*, Barcelona, 1999.

[9] J. Feigenbaum, M. Freedman, T. Sander, and A. Shostack. Privacy engineering for digital rights management systems. In *Digital Rights Management Workshop*, pages 76–105, 2001.

[10] O. Goldreich. Secure multi-party computation. Working Draft, 1998.

[11] R. Rivest, L. Adleman, and M. Dertouzos. On data banks and privacy homomorphisms. In *Foundations of Secure Computation*. Academic Press, New York, 1978.

[12] R. Rivest, A. Shamir, and L. Adleman. A method for obtaining digital signatures and public key cryptosystems. In *Communications of the ACM*, volume 21,2, 1978.

[13] S. W. Smith and S. H. Weingart. Building a high-performance, programmable secure coprocessor. In *Computer Networks, Special Issue on Computer Network Security*, volume 31:831-860, 1999.

[14] W. Stallings. *Cryptography and Network Security: Principles and Practice*. Prentice Hall, 1999.

[15] L. Sweeney. *Computational Disclosure Control: A Primer on Data Privacy Protection*. PhD thesis, Massachusetts Institute of Technology, 2001.

[16] L. Willenborg and T. de Waal. *Elements of Statistical Disclosure Control*. Addison Wesley, 2001.

An Access Scheduling Tree
to Achieve Optimal Freshness in Local Repositories

Li Qin and Vijayalakshmi Atluri

MSIS Department and
Center for Information Management, Integration and Connectivity (CIMIC)
Rutgers University
180 University Avenue, Newark NJ 07102
{liqin,atluri}@cimic.rutgers.edu

Abstract. To achieve improved availability and performance, often, local copies of remote data from autonomous sources are maintained. Examples of such local copies include data warehouses and repositories
managed by web search engines. As the size of the local data grows, it
is not always feasible to maintain the *freshness* (up-to-dateness) of the
entire data due to resource limitations. Previous contributions to maintaining freshness of local data use a freshness metric as the proportion
of fresh documents within the total repository (we denote this as *average freshness*). As a result, even though updates to more frequently
changing data are not captured, the average freshness measure may still
be high. In this paper, we argue that, in addition to average freshness, it
is important that the freshness metric should also include the proportion
of changes captured for each document, which we call *object freshness*.
The latter is particularly important when both the current and historical
versions of information sources are queried or mined. We propose an
approach by building an *access scheduling tree* (AST) to precisely
schedule access to remote sources that achieves optimal freshness of the
local data under limited availability of resources. We show, via experiments, the performance of our approach is significantly higher than a
linear priority queue.

1 Introduction

To achieve improved availability and performance, often, local copies of remote data
from autonomous sources are maintained. Examples of such local copies include data
warehouses and repositories managed by web search engines. Synchronization of the
local data with that of remote data, often referred to as change detection, is accomplished by determining whether and what changes have taken place to data of interest.
Change detection can be accomplished relatively easily if the sources are structured
databases where changes can be extracted by setting up triggers, querying the sources
or analyzing logs. However, legacy systems usually cannot provide such functions.

K. Bauknecht, A Min Tjoa, G. Quirchmayr (Eds.): EC-Web 2003, LNCS 2738, pp. 227–236, 2003.

More importantly, many information sources are autonomous and uncooperative. As a result, data sources are updated independently of the local data repositories that maintain copies of their data. In these cases, changes are detected by polling the source data periodically and then comparing their successive snapshots. For example, there exist around 350 genome databases around the world that frequently change, and at least two warehouses that systematically cache this information. The changes are both to the structure as well as to the data itself.

As the size of the local repository grows, it is not always feasible to maintain the freshness (up-to-dateness) of the entire data, due to resource limitations. Experimental studies [6, 3] show that data sources on the web change at varied frequencies. Thus, to make the synchronization process more efficient, it is essential to determine how often and when to revisit the data sources to maintain the freshness of the local repository. Assuming the change frequency can be estimated with certain accuracy, and based on the importance of the data source, we can determine the frequency at which the data source needs to be revisited (the *access frequency*).

Cho et al. [4] discuss how access frequencies are determined to maximize the freshness of a fixed size local repository under resource constraints. They use freshness measure as the proportion of fresh documents within the total repository (we denote this as *average freshness*). As a result, the average freshness measure may still be high, even though updates to more frequently changing data are not captured. Using this freshness metric, they demonstrate that a uniform policy in which all the web pages are revisited at the same frequency always achieves higher freshness compared with the proportional policy in which the access frequencies are proportional to their change frequencies. The justification that Cho et al. make for having such a metric is that it is not important to capture the changes to more frequently changing data. In this paper, we argue that, in addition to average freshness, it is important that the freshness metric should also include the proportion of changes caught for each document, which we call *object freshness*. The latter freshness measure is essential to correctly portray the measure of freshness when more frequently changing object is also more important, which is often the case with many electronic commerce applications. Also, object freshness metric is significant when both the current and historical versions of information sources are queried or mined, e.g., the WebArchive project (http://webarchive.cs.ucla.edu), which is intended to store the history and the evolution of the web for archiving human knowledge, web surveillance and other purposes. Therefore, for many applications, it is not only important that a large proportion of the local data are up-to-date (measured by *average freshness*), but also there is a need to capture the changes to every document as much as possible (measured by our proposed *object freshness*), so that the archive can represent a more complete history of these data.

Cho et al. [5] prioritize web pages to be crawled based on a number of importance metrics, such as PageRank, backlink count and similarity to a driving query, and organize the URLs of the web pages as a priority queue. According to this approach, the page with the highest importance is visited first, dequeued from the front of the URL queue, and appended to another queue. The URL queue is reordered whenever newly discovered URLs in the visited page are inserted or the importance of a web page in the URL queue is updated. A cycle is complete when all the pages in the URL queue are visited once, and another cycle is started with the newly built queue. The basic idea of this approach is that web pages are visited in the order of their importance. However, under this approach, each web page in the queue is given an equal chance to be visited exactly once during each cycle irrespective of their importance, and their change frequencies are completely ignored. If one uses the change frequency as the metric to prioritize web pages in the queue, the simple method of dequeueing does not work as higher change frequency web pages need to be visited more than once in a cycle. As a result, this approach cannot be employed if both average freshness and object freshness are desired.

In this paper, we propose an approach that employs a binary tree structure, called *access scheduling tree* (AST), and reorganizes the tree such that the items that need to be visited next are pushed to the root of the tree. AST is capable of indicating precisely at what time each source has to be revisited. Our idea is to construct the AST using a *priority queue*, and implement it as a *heap*. Though we focus much of our discussion on the web data, the proposed approaches are applicable to any change detection scheduling scenario.

This paper is organized as follows. In section 2, we present preliminaries on priority queue and its implementation, the heap. In section 3, we discuss how access frequencies are determined to improve the data freshness. We present the algorithm that details the operation of the access scheduling tree in section 4. Our experimental results are presented in section 5. We conclude this paper and provide insight into ongoing research in section 6.

2   Preliminaries

In this section, we give a brief overview of the priority queue [2] and its implementation, as our approach relies on these two.

Essentially, a priority queue is a list of items in which each item has associated with it a priority. The priority is set at the time each item is added to the queue. Items are withdrawn from a priority queue in the order of their priorities starting with the highest priority item first. We often want to promote the priority of a particular item and demote the priority of others. In these cases, we would want to reorder the items in the priority queue.

A priority queue can be implemented in a number of ways. One way is to use the sorted linear implementation, where items are ordered based on their priorities. The complexity of deleting the node of the highest priority for sorted linear implementation is $O(1)$. However, for an insertion operation, array-based implementation will involve $O(n)$ data movements, and pointer-based linear implementation will involve $O(n)$ comparisons. Though the complexity for insertion is $O(1)$ for an unsorted linear implementation, the complexity for deleting the item with the highest priority is linear. A more efficient way to implement a priority queue, whose insertion and deletion are both $O(\log n)$, is to use a *heap* having the following properties: (1) It is a complete binary tree. A complete binary tree is a binary tree of height h that is full to level $h-1$ and has level h filled in from left to right. This means there are no "holes" in the binary tree. (2) Either it is empty or the priority for each node in the tree is no less than that for either of its children. This implies that the priority of every node is greater than or equal to the priorities of all its descendants.

A heap can be built incrementally by inserting new elements into the leftmost open spot in the tree. If the priority of the new element is greater than that of its parent, their positions are swapped and this process is repeated. If we start with an unsorted array, we can start from the $\lfloor n/2 \rfloor th$ element, treat it as the root of a subtree and heapify this subtree, then work backwards to the root. The complexity of building a heap is $O(n\ log(n))$, where n is the number of items.

As mentioned earlier, the root of a heap always has the highest priority in the tree and thus the root will always be the next node due for deletion or dequeuing. When the root is deleted, the rightmost value from the bottom level will be moved to the root. Since the heap property may be violated, the tree needs to be rebuilt. The complexity for deleting the node with the highest priority and rebuilding the heap is $O(log\ n)$.

When a new node is inserted into a heap, it is inserted at the bottom of the tree and then it trickles up to its proper place. The complexity of inserting a node into the heap is $O(log\ n)$.

3   Determining the Access Frequency

Given the change frequency for each object, we need to determine how often we access each of them under certain resource constraint. Since a Poisson process has been widely accepted for modeling web page changes [1, 4], we assume object i changes by a Poisson process with change frequency λ_i, and is accessed with access frequency f_i. Here, we specifically discuss how access frequencies are determined for a local repository with a fixed number of data objects. The optimal access frequency for each object is the solution to an optimization problem with its goal of improving the overall data freshness of the local repository. We start our discussion with defining the overall data freshness of the local repository in terms of two freshness metrics, *average freshness* and *object freshness*. Then, we present how freshness of the local repository changes with different access frequencies. After that, we discuss how to cater to different levels of freshness requirements desired by the applications and formulate the optimization problem to compute the access frequencies. We also discuss the assumptions and conditions to capture all the changes to all the data objects.

Freshness Metrics

We define the following two metrics to measure the freshness of the local repository. Let N be the number of data objects, and λ_i and f_i be the change frequency and access frequency of data object i, respectively. (1) **Average freshness**: The average freshness of the local repository, which is the proportion of data objects that are up-to-date[1]. (2) **Object freshness**: This is the proportion of the expected number of changes detected to the expected total number of changes within any time period. Object freshness ranges between 0 and 1.

The average freshness and object freshness can be computed as (af) and (of), respectively.

---

[1]   This is the same as the definition by Cho in [4].

$$\frac{1}{N}\sum_{i=1}^{N}\frac{1-e^{-\frac{\lambda_i}{f_i}}}{\frac{\lambda_i}{f_i}} \qquad (af) \qquad\qquad \frac{\sum_{i=1}^{N} f_i \cdot (1-e^{-\frac{\lambda_i}{f_i}})}{\sum_{i=1}^{N}\lambda_i} \qquad (of)$$

Theorem 1: Given the change frequency for each data object i, λ_i, $i =1,2,...N$, the access frequency to each data object, f_i, should satisfy $\lambda_1/f_1 = \lambda_2/f_2 = ... = \lambda_N/f_N$ to achieve the highest object freshness. *(See [8] for proof)*

Comparison of the Freshness Metrics

The following example depicts how the overall freshness of the local repository changes with different resource allocations. To illustrate, we consider a simple hypothetical example with two data objects: object 1 changes once a day and object 2 changes 4 times a day. Fig. 1 shows how the average freshness and object freshness change as we increase the access frequency for object 1 *(the x-axis represents the access frequency for object 1)* under the constraint that we have resources to access 5 objects/day, 10 objects/day and 20 objects/day, respectively. From Fig. 1, it is evident that both average freshness and object freshness have been improved as we increase the availability of resources, which is not surprising. Under each resource constraint, the average freshness and the object freshness reach their maximum at different access frequencies. When compared with the object freshness, the average freshness reaches its peak when more resources are allocated to the object that changes less frequently *(object 1 in the above example)*. This helps us gain some intuition on resource consumption for a certain required average freshness and/or object freshness. We also compare the freshness for two objects with different change frequencies and we find that it is more significant to distinguish between average freshness and object freshness when the objects have a wider range of change frequencies.

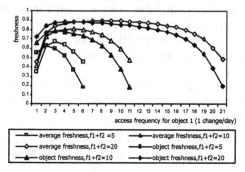

Fig. 1. Average freshness & object freshness when $f_1 + f_4 = 5$, 10 and 20 with $\lambda_1 = 1$ and $\lambda_2 = 4$

Achieving Optimal Overall Freshness

When we determine the access frequencies, we take into consideration the following three factors: (1) The average freshness of the local repository, computed as (af). (2) The object freshness of the local repository, computed as (of). (3) The resource constraint, $\sum_{i=1}^{N} f_i = \frac{N}{I}$, where N objects can be accessed in I time units.

The application under consideration usually has certain requirement about at least one of the two metrics. Then, our goal will be to maximize the other metric of overall freshness while satisfying the constraints of this specific requirement and resource consumption. We encounter the following two cases.

Case 1: Let the desired object freshness be at least η, where $0 < \eta < 1$. Now, given change frequencies λ_i's of all the N data objects, and assuming the resources capable of accessing N objects within I time units, the problem of achieving optimal values for access frequencies f_i 's of N data objects can be found by maximizing (af) such that f_i's satisfy the constraints $\sum_{i=1}^{N} f_i = \dfrac{N}{I}, f_i \geq 0$ and (of) $\geq \eta$.

Case 2: Alternatively, we can find the resource consumption for a certain desired average freshness and/or object freshness. This can be formulated as follows: Given change frequencies λ_i's, we can find the values for access frequencies f_i's which minimize $\dfrac{1}{N} \sum_{i}^{N} f_i$ when f_i's satisfy the constraints $f_i \geq 0$, (of) $\geq \eta$ and/or (af) $\geq \gamma$.

The above can be generalized to take into account the importance of objects, where optimization problem can be formulated with minor modifications.

Can we capture all the changes?

Assuming that we have no resource constraints (i.e., infinite resources), now, let us examine the possibility of capturing all the changes by accessing the objects periodically. First, we assume that the data objects change by a Poisson process. If T is the time it takes for the occurence of the next change in a Poisson process with rate λ, the probability density function for T, $f_T(t) = \lambda e^{-\lambda t}$ for $t > 0$, and 0 for $t \leq 0$. This indicates that the next change can occur at any time with probability greater than zero. Under this assumption, we cannot guarantee capturing all the changes. However, in practice, we can usually find the maximum value for the change frequency of each object based on its change history or domain knowledge. If we assume that each object will never change more frequently than its specified maximum change frequency, then we can prove that we can capture all the changes under no resource constraints. This can be formalized as follows.

We use t_{access_n} and t_{change_n} to denote the time when the nth access is done and the time when the nth change occurs, respectively, where $n = 1, 2, 3...M$, and M is the maximum number of changes.

Definition 1: We say i^{th} access catches j^{th} change if $t_{change\_j} < t_{access\_i}$ and no p can be found such that $t_{change\_j} < t_{access\_p} < t_{access\_i}$ and no q can be found such that $t_{change\_j} < t_{change\_q} < t_{access\_i}$.

Definition 2: If i^{th} access catches j^{th} change, we say i^{th} access does not miss any changes if r can be found such that $t_{change\_j-1} < t_{access\_r} < t_{change\_j}$.

The following theorem states that, suppose that the time between successive changes for an object is no smaller than t, which is the reciprocal of its maximum change frequency, we can capture all the changes to this object by accessing it at every t.

Theorem 2: Suppose a data object does not change more frequently than λ_{max}. By accessing it every $t = 1/\lambda_{max}$, we can guarantee that for each $k > 0$, we can find an m where $t_{change\_k} < t_{access\_m} < t_{change\_k+1}$. *(See [8] for proof)*

Note that even if all the changes can be captured under our assumption, the delay between the time when the change occurs and the time when the access is done to capture the change still cannot be avoided because information sources are autonomous, and there is always a delay between the time the change occurs and the time the object is accessed. So, even if we can catch all the changes, the local repository may still suffer from some staleness due to this delay. The delay should be no longer than t if the object is accessed every t time and it can be shortened if we can access the object more frequently.

4   Access Scheduling Tree

Our approach begins with by grouping data objects into partitions based on their access frequencies. The attributes associated with each partition and the properties of our access scheduling tree based on the general heap properties in combination with our scenario are discussed. Since we need to update the priority values as time elapses, we discuss when and how priority values are updated. Finally, we present the operation of our AST.

Partitions and their Attributes

We assume that data objects change independently of one another, and we access each object at regular intervals. To be general, we use data objects to refer to data sources or portions of data sources since multiple data granularity may be considered. We group the objects into different partitions based on how often we access them. Each partition may contain a queue of data objects.

Definition 3: We characterize each partition p_i as a tuple, $p_i = \{t_i, c_i, oq_i\}$, where (1) t_i is the time between successive accesses. $t_i = 1/f_i$ where f_i denotes its access frequency. (2) A counter c_i, expressed as an integer or decimal number. The counter is initialized as t_i and decremented when a partition needs to be accessed. Since objects in each partition need to be revisited, c_i is re-initialized to t_i once it reaches zero. Thus, $0 \leq c_i \leq t_i$. (3) A queue of data objects oq_i, each of which is identified by its object ID and revisited every t_i.

Properties of the Access Scheduling Tree

Our access scheduling tree is a priority queue with each partition as a node in the heap. Although intuitively one can imagine using t_i as the priority value, it cannot be adopted directly since some nodes need to be accessed several times before others are accessed once, and the node to be accessed next can be anywhere in the priority queue. Instead, we use the counter c_i as the priority value because c_i captures the value of time before the next access, and therefore determines the next node to be accessed. Since the partition with the smallest c_i is the next to be accessed, the smaller the c_i, the higher its priority. Essentially, our AST is nothing but this priority queue implemented using a tree structure to schedule the accesses over time.

Definition 4: Our access scheduling tree is defined as following: (1) It is a complete binary tree with a partition p_i $\{t_i, c_i, oq_i\}$ as its item type. (2) Each node's c_i is no greater than that of either of its children. By transitivity, each node's c_i is no greater than the counters of all of its descendents.

Updating the Priorities

Since the counter c_i counts down the time left for the next access, we need to update the counters as time elapses. Since the root is the next node we need to access, we know exactly when the next access would occur by retrieving the counter for the root, c_{root}. When the root is accessed, the counter for each node in the tree should be decremented by c_{root} since c_{root} time has elapsed. Any node whose counter decrements to zero should be scheduled for access and its counter is reinitialized to its t_i since each node needs to be accessed repeatedly every t_i time. Then the tree is rebuilt and the counter for the root is retrieved again to see whether it needs to be accessed. We keep reinitializing the counter, rebuilding the tree and retrieving the counter for the root as long as the counter for the root stays zero. When the counter for the root is greater than zero, we will repeat the above procedure after c_{root} time elapses.

Algorithm for the Operation of Access Scheduling Tree

We present the algorithm on how the access scheduling tree operates in Fig. 2.

```
Algorithm Operation of access scheduling tree
Input At t_current = t_0, partitions p_i{t_i, c_i, oq_i}, each with
its t_i, its counter c_i = t_i and an object queue oq_i.
Output An access queue aq_k, which includes the objects
scheduled for access during the time window
Procedure
[1] Build a heap satisfying the properties in Defini-
tion 4
[2] for(t_current = t_0 + c_root; ;t_current = t_next)
[3]     t_last = t_current
[4]     c_i = c_i - c_root
[5]     while (c_root = 0)
[6]         aq_k = aq_k∪oq_root
[7]         c_root = t_root
[8]         rebuild the tree
[9]         t_next = t_last + c_root
```

Fig. 2. Algorithm for the operation of access scheduling tree

5   Experimental Results and Discussion

To study the performance of our scheduling algorithms, we have implemented the AST and compared its running time with the implementation of a linear queue over up to 300,000 data objects on a Sun ULTRA 80 workstation. The programs are written in C++. We have simulated the input with access frequencies designed as follows: 23% of the data objects have access frequency as every 1 day, 15% as every 2 - 7 days, 16% as every 8 - 30 days, 17% as every 31 - 120 days and 29% as every 121 - 400 days. These access frequencies are chosen to reflect the experimental results of change frequencies given in [3].

We implemented the scheduling using a linear queue and our AST. We have included only one data object in each node of the tree. Fig. 3 presents their performance for scheduling 500,000 accesses over different data sizes. Each point in the experiments is obtained by averaging the time (in seconds) for five runs. Fig. 4 is specifically to show the performance of AST.

Obviously, the implementation of the heap is much more efficient than the linear queue. The efficiency of a tree structure over a linear queue is not new. Here, we just present their difference in terms of their scheduling efficiency. With reference to the downloading time of 34-112 docs/second [7] and change detection time of at least 0.1 second for comparing 10KB documents over 1% change [9], the above AST implementation is quite efficient and uses much less time. Due to system limitations, we were unable to conduct experiments for larger data sets.

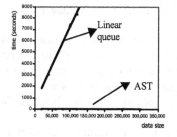
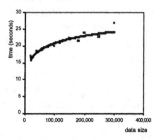

Fig. 3. Performance of a linear queue and AST   **Fig. 4.** Performance of AST

6   Conclusions and Future Research

Earlier work on maintaining freshness of local data use a freshness metric (called *average freshness* in this paper) as the proportion of fresh documents within the total repository. As a result, even though updates to more frequently changing data are not captured, the average freshness measure may still be high. However, in many applications, it is important that the freshness metric should also include the proportion of changes captured for each document. To capture this, in this paper, we have introduced a new freshness metric, called *object freshness*. We have proposed an approach by building an *access scheduling tree* (AST), which can precisely schedule access to remote sources that achieves optimal freshness of the local data under limited availability of resources. We have presented the formalism to determine the optimal access frequency to improve the overall freshness of the local repository, especially when the application has a certain requirement about one of the metrics.

In this paper, we have assumed that each object changes independently from others. In fact, their changes could be correlated in some way. For example, changes to some data objects may lead to changes to other semantically related data objects. We are currently working on incorporating the semantic relationships among groups of data objects into our study of their change behavior. Another assumption we made in this paper is that the change frequencies are static in nature. In our future work, we will examine the scenarios when the change frequencies themselves change, and as a result how the scheduling can be adaptively adjusted in an efficient way.

References

[1]   Brian E. Brewington and George Cybenko. How Dynamic is the Web? 9th World Wide Web Conference (WWW9), 2000.

[2]   Frank M. Carrano and Janet J. Prichard. Data Abstraction and Problem Solving with C++. Addison Wesley. 3rd edition, 2001.

[3]   Junghoo Cho and Hector Garcia-Molina. The Evolution of the Web and Implications for an Incremental Crawler, 26th International Conference on Very Large Databases (VLDB), pages 200-209, 2000.

[4]   Junghoo Cho and Hector Garcia-Molina. Synchronizing a Database to Improve Freshness. ACM SIGMOD International Conference on Management of Data, pages 117-128, 2000.

[5]   Junghoo Cho, Hector Garcia-Molina and Lawrence Page. Efficient Crawling Through URL Ordering. 7th World Wide Web Conference (WWW7), 1998.

[6]   Fred Douglis, Anja Feldmann, Balachander Krishnamurthy and Jeffrey Mogul. Rate of Change and Other Metrics: A Live Study of the World Wide Web. USENIX Symposium on Internetworking Technologies and Systems, December 1997.

[7]   Allan Heydon and Marc Najork. Mercator: A Scalable, Extensible Web Crawler. World Wide Web, 2(4):219-229, 1999.

[8]   Li Qin and Vijayalakshmi Atluri. An Access Scheduling Tree to Achieve Optimal Freshness in Local Repositories. Technical report, 2002.

[9]   Yuan Wang, David J. DeWitt and Jin-Yi Cai. X-Diff: An Effective Change Detection Algorithm for XML Documents. 19th International Conference on Data Engineering (ICDE), 2003.

Cooperative Queries in Semistructured Data Model

Kartik Menon[1], Sanjay Madria[1], and A. Badia[2]

[1] Department of Computer Science, University of Missouri-Rolla, MO 65401
[2] Computer Engineering and Computer Science Department, Speed Scientific School
University of Louisville, Louisville KY 40292
{kartik,madrias}@umr.edu
abadia@louisville.edu

Abstract: Traditional query languages proposed for semistructured data models such as OEM (Object Exchange Model) require queries to find exact matches. These queries fail to return the results in case the query paths specified do not completely match the paths in the database. In other words, a query, whose paths are *over- or under-specified,* fails to retrieve results. It is possible that the users may not be aware of the structure or schema of the semistructured data or schema may have been changed since it was queried last time. In this paper, we discuss the cooperative query processing techniques in case of semistructured data. We explore our ideas with the help of examples and provide some overview of the algorithms to process such queries.

1   Introduction

New research aims at getting semistructured data into the database realm [FLM], so that it can benefit from the years of database research on the issues like query processing, schema management, indexing and efficient access to large amount of data. The strategy usually pursued in semistructured data management is to design the more flexible data models, query languages and storage structures.

Since semistructured data [FLM] is accessed by many kinds of users, including casual (non expert) users, the chances of formulating a query incorrectly are higher than in the traditional databases. The lack of a completely regular structure also increases the likelihood of making a mistake when writing a query. Thus, current semistructured query languages are inflexible and require exact matches between the query specification and the data in the database, and are unable to retrieve closely related information to the user. The queries to semistructured data that slightly deviate from the databases do not retrieve answers.

Semistructured data model OEM (Object Exchange Model) [AQMW] handles irregular and not completely structured data, and LORE system [GMW, AQMW] provides a query language to query OEM data. However, the query needs to be exact and cannot handle incompelete queries due to the lack of complete knowledge of the schema or associated data. In this paper, we restrict our discussion to OEM. However, the techniques proposed work well with XML Query languages such as XML-QL

K. Bauknecht, A Min Tjoa, G. Quirchmayr (Eds.): EC-Web 2003, LNCS 2738, pp. 237–247, 2003.

[DFFS], XQL[BC], Xquery [CCF+] which can not handle queries which are not complete. Note that the regular expressions can handle only some of those incomplete queries, but not the type of over- and under-specified queries discussed in this paper. Most techniques for CQA have been developed in the context of traditional databases [CC, GGM].

This paper defines new methods to achieve cooperative query answering in the context of semistructured data model OEM. The goal is to make the semistructured database OEM behave in a way that maximizes the information exchange by devising strategies in which the system does not merely respond to the queries, but tries to collaborate with the user. Instead of literally answering a query, the system tries to provide related data that may help the user obtain the information(s) she needs. This is useful when the user does not have a good (or detailed) idea about the structure of the data in the OEM database. In particular, we relax the condition that data must match exactly the query specifications in order to qualify for an answer, and describe methods by which to find the data that is reasonably close to what was asked for.

1.1   Related Work

Recently some efforts have been made in the direction of similarity based approximate queries in XML environment [S1, TW]. In [S1], an approximate pattern matching language ApproXQL is proposed to handle queries which are not exact. In [TW], a language called XXL is presented where similarity operators have been introduced and are applied to element names and to text sequences. Another language ELIXIL [CK] is comparable to XXL but additionally also supports similarity joins. Both languages however do not allow partial structural matches. Another work to solve the incomplete information problem in semistructured environment was introduced by Abiteboul *at el.* [ASV] where authors represent partial information about the source document acquired by successive queries, and that can be used to intelligently answer new queries. The framework provides a model for XML documents and DTDs, a simple XML query language, and a representation system for XML with incomplete information. However, the model's focus is different than ours, for example, we assume that semistructured data is complete but queries are incomplete.

2   Co-operative Query Answering and Categorization

An example of a query in Lore is as follows:

> Select R.name
> From guide.hotel.restaurant R
> Where R.zipcode = "65409";

Consider the OEM in Figure 1, the Where and From clauses in the query look for branches with nodes guide.hotel.restaurant.zipcode = "65409" and among those branches, it selects the restaurant name with the given zipcode. In this case, the query returns the value "El maguey" restaurant with zipcode 65409.

Here, we discuss different types of queries that are incomplete. There are several examples of queries unanswerable with the existing LORE system. These queries can have paths that are broadly classified as over- or under-specified depending on the various branches (paths) in the OEM. These paths can occur in Select, Where, or From clause of the queries. Over-specified queries are those in which the query has more nodes than present in the database path. Under-specified queries are those in which the query has fewer nodes than present in the database.

2.1   Over- and Under-Specified Queries

Here, we present some examples of queries which are over-specified either in Select, From or Where clause.

1)   Select R.restaurant
      From guide R
      Where guide.hotel.restaurant.address.zipcode = "65409";

This is an example of over-specified query path in the 'Where' clause with respect to the path guide.hotel.restaurant.zipcode in the OEM database because the label 'address' is not there.

2)   Select R
      From guide.restaurant.city R
      Where guide.restaurant.zipcode = "65401";

This is an example of over-specified query path in the 'From' clause with respect to the path guide.restaurant in the OEM database because the label 'city' is not there.

3)   Select R.street
      From guide.hotel.restaurant.address R
      Where guide.hotel.restaurant.name="great wall";

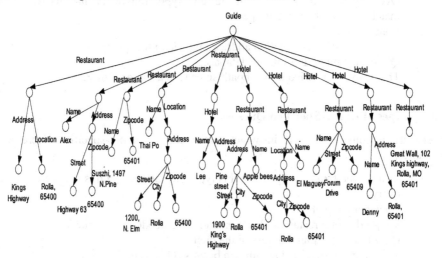

Fig. 1. OEM Database

This is an example of over-specified query in the 'Select', 'From', and 'Where' clause with respect to the path guide.hotel.restaurant in the OEM database because the labels 'street', 'address' and 'name' are not present in the database path. Similarly, we can have queries that are under-specified in Select, From and Where clause.

2.2   Types of Over-Specified Queries

There are several ways in which paths can be over- and under-specified. Here, we present some examples to illustrate.

1) Over-specified as a prefix: In this type, the query has its prefix matching with the database path.
Consider the path
P = guide.hotel.restaurant.address.zipcode in the query, and
Q = guide.hotel.restaurant.address in the database
This is over-specified as a prefix since Q is a prefix of P.

2) Over-specified as a suffix: In this type, the query has its suffix matching with the database path.
Consider the path
P = guide.hotel.restaurant.address.zipcode in the query, and
Q = hotel.restaurant.address.zipcode in the database.
This is over-specified as a suffix since Q is a suffix of P.

3) Over-specified as an infix: In this type, the query has its infix matching with the database path.
Consider the path
P = city.guide.hotel.restaurant.address.zipcode in the query, and
Q = guide.hotel.restaurant.address in the database.
This is over-specified as an infix, as Q is an infix of P.

4) Over-specified as a sub path: In this type, the query has its subpaths matching with the database path.
Consider the path
P = hotel.restaurant.location.address.zipcode in the query, and
Q = restaurant.address in the database.
This is over-specified as a subpath since Q is a sub path of P.

2.3   Types of Under-Specified Queries

There are various ways that in which paths can be under-specified. Here are examples:

1) Under-specified as subpath: In this type, the database path is the prefix to the query.
Consider the path
P = guide.hotel.restaurant.location.address.zipcode in the database
Q = guide.restaurant.address in the query
This is under-specified as subpath because Q is a subpath of P.

2) Under-specified as suffix: In this type, the database path is the suffix to the query.

Consider the path

P = guide.hotel.restaurant.address.zipcode in the database

Q = restaurant.address.zipcode is the path in the query.

This is under-specified as a suffix, as Q is a suffix of P.

3) Under-specified as infix: In this type, the database path is the infix to the query.

Consider the path

P = guide.restaurant.address.zipcode in the database

Q = restaurant.address path in the query

This is under-specified as an infix, as Q is an infix of P.

3   Data Structure and Functions for CQA

The data structure and functions used for CQA algorithms are explained in this section. In order to evaluate our ideas in an experimental setting, the functions sketched below have been implemented in the form of algorithms in Section 4. The basic data structure consists of graph nodes. Each node is called an object. An object is broadly classified as an atomic or non-atomic (complex). Each node has a name (which is unique and serves as OID) and a value. When the object is atomic, the value is always of type string. For cases where the value type is different (for example, integer or long) we convert all the data types into string. Multiple values are converted and then concatenated to form one string. For example, zipcode may be an integer, address may be a string; we can get a node with both zipcode and address in the value by converting the zipcode to a string data type and concatenating it with the address. When the object is not atomic, this field is empty. The graph is represented by decomposing it into different paths. Each path is implemented using a double-linked list, with forward pointers to children nodes and backward pointers to parent node.

The function Root() returns the root (first node) of the path. The function Child() returns the children of the current node, while the function Parent() returns the parent of the current node. The function Is_atomic(node P, node Q) returns P if P is an atomic node, Q if Q is atomic, and is null otherwise. We use the object oriented concept of function overloading to define another function Is_atomic(node P) with one parameter which returns true if a node is atomic or else it returns null. The function Atomic (path expression P, path expression Q) compares P and Q until atomic node is reached else an exception condition will be revoked. The function Match(path expression P, path expression Q) compares paths P and Q and while they match both descends on the paths. If the paths match but one of them finishes before the other, then the path that is finished early is returned (this indicates that the other one is a prefix of it).

If P = guide.restaurant is the query path and Q =guide.restaurant.address.zipcode is in the OEM database then the function Match(P,Q) returns P . The function Path(path expression P, node Q) creates a new path (i.e., a new link list) starting from the root of P until we reach the node Q. As an example, see Figure 1, if P = guide.hotel.restaurant.address and Q = restaurant then Path(P,Q) will make a new path link list guide.hotel.restaurant. The function Stem(path expression P) is the set of paths in the database that matches a prefix of P; it returns a path which is the stem of the over-specified query as a prefix from Path(P,Q). It is as follows: for P as above, Stem(P) is a function which calls Path(P,address). We create a link list starting from Root(P) and follow its children until we reach the final (atomic) node in the path. The Atomic(P,Q) returns the path expression P or Q which ever is smaller or raises an exception if P and Q both mismatches completely. That is, both P and Q are totally different. For example if P = restaurant.address.zipcode and Q = hotel.name, Atomic(path expression P, path expression Q) raises an exception because 'restaurant' and 'hotel', the root nodes of P and Q, are different, and the further comparison is impossible between the two. On the other hand if P = restaurant.address.zipcode and Q = restaurant.address then Atomic(P,Q) returns Q. If P = restaurant.address and Q = restaurant.address.zipcode then Atomic(P,Q) returns P.

Parse(node P, node Q) function decomposes the atomic node into different variables and compares the values of the variables with the ones given in the query. For example, consider the query condition guide.hotel.restaurant.address = 'Rolla'. If there is a branch in the OEM as guide.hotel.restaurant where restaurant being the atomic node and has the value "Great Wall, 102 Kings Highway, Rolla, MO, 65401 " then the parse function will decompose the value of the node 'restaurant' into different variables on the basis of delimiter "," as variable 1 = 'Great Wall', variable2 = '102 Kings Highway' variable3 = 'Rolla', variable4 = 'MO' and variable5 = '65401'. It then compares the node value 'address' i.e. 'Rolla' with all the variable values and finds the match. Function Term (path expression P), where P is over-specified as a suffix, is the set of paths in the database that matches a suffix of P. The function returns the term of the path P. Function Atomic_object(path expression P) returns the atomic node of the path P.

4   Algorithms to Process CQA

The main algorithm to execute CQA is explained below. Input to the algorithm is the subpaths of the OEM database and the given query. The OEM's paths from the root to leaves populate the array Q[ ] and the query is assigned to P. I iterates from 1 to the number of branches present in the OEM.

For i=1 to i<=no. of branches do
   (1) If Match (P, Q [i]) is not null then query will return the result.
   (2) If Match (P, Q [i]) is null then
      Compare P and Q [i] node-wise from root till we get atomic
      object of either one (Atomic (P, Q [i]) function is used)
       (i) If Atomic (P, Q [i]) returns P then it is under-specified as prefix
         (a) Get finalP=Atomic_object (P) and finalQ=Atomic_object (Q[i])
         (b) While finalP is not equal finalQ do
            Get parentQ=Parent (finalQ)
            temp=concat (to_str (Child(parentQ)))
            finalQ=temp
         (c) Parse (finalQ, finalP) and give the results.
       (ii) If Atomic (P, Q [i]) returns Q [i] then it is over-specified as prefix

(a) Assign finalQ=Atomic_object (Q) and finalP=Atomic_object (P)

(b) Get parentP=Parent (finalP)

(c) While finalQ is not equal to parentP do the next 2 steps
- temp=Parent(parentP)
- parentP=temp

(d) Stem(P,finalQ)

(e) Parse (parentP, finalQ) and returns the results

(iii) If Atomic (P, Q [i]) returns an exception then it is neither under-specified as prefix(i) nor over-specified as prefix(ii)

(a) suffixP=P

(b) rootP=root (P) and rootQ=root(Q)

(c) Perform the next two steps till ((Term (rootP) = Q [i]) or Atomic(suffixP,Q[i])) returns some value (This is over-specified on suffix) If rootP is not equal to rootQ then suffixP=suffixP-rootP
- rootP=nextNode(rootP)

(d) If Match(Term(rootP),Q[i]) is not null

Then Query to get the result

Else If Atomic(suffixP,Q[i]) returns Q[i] (It is over-specified as infix) then perform these steps
- Assign   finalQ=Atomic_object   (Q[i])   and finalP=Atomic_object(P)
- Get parentP=Parent (finalP)
- While finalQ is not equal to parentP do the next 2 steps
  * temp=Parent(parentP)
  * parentP=temp
- Stem(P,finalQ)
- Parse (parentP, finalQ) and returns the results

Else If Atomic(suffixP,Q[i]) returns suffix then Goto (iv)

(iv) (It can be under-specified as suffix or under-specified as infix or over-specified as subpath)

(a) Get finalP=Atomic_object (P) and finalQ=Atomic_object (Q[i])

(b) While finalP is not equal finalQ do

Get parentQ=Parent (finalQ)

temp=concat (to_str (Child(parentQ)))

finalQ=temp

(c) Parse (finalQ, finalP) and give the results.

5   Algorithm Testing

Here, we describe the behavior of the algorithm for different cases. Let 'P' be the query expression, and 'Q' be the path in the OEM database in Figure 1.

1) For Under-Specified Paths as Prefix

> P := guide.restaurant.location.address = '65400'.
> Q := guide.restaurant.location.address.zipcode ='65400'

Match(P, Q) will be null initially, and Atomic(P, Q) will return P because on one to one comparison between P and Q, we reach first P's atomic object. This makes it an under-specified path because the number of nodes in the query is less than that in the database path. In this case, we have finalP = location and finalQ = zipcode. We find parentQ of finalQ. Simultaneously we convert street, city and zipcode into strings and concatenate them. For example, consider one non-atomic node like address which has many atomic nodes like street, zipcode and city and the data types of these nodes may be different like zipcode maybe integer type, where as street and city are of string type. We then can do bottom up traversal by converting street, zipcode and city into strings and concatenate them to form one string for the parent node address. We Parse('address' of P, 'address' of Q) to tokenize into variables and match to generate the results.

2) For Under-Specified as Infix

> P := restaurant.address = 'Rolla, 65401'
> Q := guide.hotel.restaurant.address.zipcode = '65401';

Atomic(P,Q) returns an exception and hence, goes to next step where suffixP = P. First, find rootP = root(P) and rootQ = root(Q) and then continue finding the Term(rootP) which is equal to Q. If it is impossible to find the Term(rootP) then go to the next step. Get finalP = Atomic_object(P) and finalQ = Atomic_object(Q) and start comparing the finalP and the parent of finalQ iteratively. While backtracking on finalQ, we concatenate the text values on these nodes (as we did in case of under-specified as prefix). We parse finalQ using Parse (finalP, finalQ) to tokenize into variables and match to generate the results.

3) For Under-Specified as Suffix

> P := restaurant.address = 'Rolla,65401'
> Q := guide.hotel.restaurant.address = 'Rolla,65401'

Atomic(P,Q) returns an exception and hence goes to next step where suffixP = P. We assign rootP = root(P) and rootQ = root(Q) and continue finding Term(rootP) which is equal to Q. If it is impossible to find the Term(rootP) then go to the next step. Get finalP = Atomic_object(P) and finalQ = Atomic_object(Q) and start comparing the finalP and the parent of finalQ iteratively. This differentiates the under-specified as suffix from under-specified as infix because in case of under-specified as suffix, finalP = finalQ. We parse finalQ using parse (finalP, finalQ) to tokenize the location address into variables and match to generate the results.

4) For Over-Specified as a Prefix

> P := guide.hotel.restaurant.zipcode = '65401'
> Q := guide.hotel.restaurant = 'Great Wall,102...............'

Match(P, Q) will be null initially, and Atomic(P, Q) will return Q because on one to one comparison between P and Q we reach Q's atomic object first. This makes P over-specified path as a prefix since the number of nodes is more in P than in Q. In this case, finalP = zipcode and finalQ = restaurant. We find parentP equal to the parent of zipcode in P; that is a restaurant. This is done until parentP equals finalQ. We find Max(Stem(P)) by using function path(P, finalQ). We parse finalQ using Parse (finalP, finalQ) to tokenize 'Great Wall,102..'' into variables on the basis of delimiters ("," or whitespace) and match to generate the results.

5) For Over-Specified as a Suffix

P := city.guide.restaurant.zipcode = '65401'.
Q := guide.restaurant.zipcode = '65401'.

Match(P, Q) returns null. Atomic(P,Q) returns an exception. We assign suffixP=P, rootP=guide, rootQ = restaurant and remove guide from suffixP. This is done until Term(rootP) = Q or Atomic (suffixP,Q) returns some value. If Match(Term(P),Q) is not null, then we can retrieve results as we find that Term(P) and Q are perfect match because in this case, Term(P) = guide.restaurant.zipcode, which is equal to Q.

6) For Over-Specified as Infix

P := city.guide.restaurant.location.zipcode = ' 65400'
Q := guide.restaurant.location = 'Rolla, 65400'

As said in the algorithm Match(P, Q) returns null. This can be viewed as a combination of over-specified as suffix if we consider P as guide.restaurant.location and over-specified as prefix if we consider restaurant.location.zipcode. So for the first case, P is city.guide.restaurant.location and Q is guide.restaurant.location. We run P and Q to get one set of results. For the second case, P is guide.restaurant.location.zipcode and Q is guide.restaurant.location. We run P and Q to get the next set of results.

7) For Over-Specified as Subpath

P = guide.restaurant.location.address = 'Kings Highway , 65400'
Q = guide.restaurant.address = 'Kings Highway'

For a particular query, if none of the above steps in the algorithm yield any match then the query can be classified as over-specified as a subpath. In this example, the path P will be searched for some important nodes (we assume that OEM can define some nodes which are mandatory to be present in the query before it can be processed). In this example, "restaurant" is one such node. The next step is to match the path from root to the important node. For this example, P will be over-specified as suffix. In this case, the paths P and Q are matched for the leaf node "address". Next step is to parse Q and generate results. By applying the algorithm for over-specified and under-specified paths when and where required, the path that is over-specified as a subpath can be realized.

6   Conclusions

We have introduced some of the basic concepts in cooperative query answering (CQA) in semistructured data environment. We argued that CQA is very relevant for semistructured data, and have shown examples of CQA techniques developed to deal with semistructured data. When multiple partial matches are present, ranking those partial matches [S2] and returning only the best ones would benefit the quality of the answer. Other interesting question is to investigate the conditions under which the CQA system can refuse to entertain a given query. This is because it is not always feasible to return the results in case the query is completely different than the data and it does not make sense to execute such queries.

References

[AQMW]   Abiteoul Serge, Quass Dallan, McHugh Jason, Widom Jennifer, Wiener Janet L., The Lorel Query Language for Semi structured Data, International Journal of Digital Libraries, 1(1), November 1996.

[ASV]   Abiteboul Serge, Segoufin Luc, Vianu Victor, Representing and Querying XML with Incomplete Information. PODS 2001

[BC]   Bonifati A. and Ceri S., Comparative Analysis of Five XML Query Languages, SIGMOD Record, 29(1), March 2000.

[CCF+]   Chamberlin, D., Clark, J., Florescu, D., Robie, J., Siméon, J., Stefanescu, M.: Xquery 1.0: An XML Query Language. W3C Working Draft (20 December 2001)

[CC]   Chu W and Chen Q., A Structured Approach for Cooperative Query Answering, IEEE Transaction on Knowledge and Data Engineering, 1994.

[CK]   Chinenyanga T.T. and Kushmerick, N., Expressive and Efficient Ranked Queries for XML Data, in proceedings of the 4th International Workshop on the Web and Databases (WebDB'01), pp. 1-6, USA, 2001.

[DFFS]   A. Deutsch, M. Fernandez, D. Florescu, A. Levy, D. Suciu, A Query Language for XML, in proceedings of the 8th World Wide Web Conference, Toronto, Canada, May 1999.

[FLM]   D. Florescu, A. Levy, A. Mendelzon. Database Techniques for the World Wide Web: A Survey. SIGMOD Records, Vol 27, No. 3, Sept 1998.

[GGM]   Gaasterland T., Godfrey P. and Minker J., An Overview of Cooperative Answering, Journal of Intelligent Information Systems, 1992.

[GMW]   Goldman R, McHugh J, and Widom J., From Semistructured Data to XML: Migrating the Lore Data Model and Query Language, in proceedings of the 2nd International Workshop on the Web and Databases (WebDB '99), Philadelphia, Pennsylvania, June 1999

[S1]   Schlieder, T. ApproXQL: Design and Implementation of an Approximate Pattern Matching Language for XML. Technical Report B 01-02, Freie Universität Berlin, May 2001.

[S2]   Schlieder, T. Similarity Search in XML Data Using Cost-based Query Transformations, in proceedings of the Fourth International Workshop on the Web and Databases (WebDB'01), *Santa Barbara,* USA, May 2001.

[TW]   Theobald A. and Weikum G., Adding Relevance to XML, in proceedings of 3rd International Workshop on the Web and Databases (WebDB'00), Dallas, USA, May 2000.

Using Internet Glossaries to Determine Interests from Home Pages

Edwin Portscher,[1] James Geller[1] and Richard Scherl[2]

[1] New Jersey Institute of Technology, Newark, New Jersey 07102
[2] Monmouth University, West Long Branch, New Jersey 07764

Abstract. There are millions of home pages on the web. Each page contains valuable data about the page's owner that can be used for marketing purposes. These pages have to be classified according to interests. The traditional Information Retrieval approach requires large training sets that are classified by human experts. Knowledge-based methods, which use handcrafted rules, require a significant investment to develop the rule base. Both these approaches are very time consuming. We are using glossaries, which are freely available on the Internet, to determine interests from home pages. Processing of these glossaries can be automated and requires little human effort and time, compared to the other two approaches. Once the terms have been extracted from these glossaries, they can be used to infer interests from the home pages of web users. This paper describes the system we have developed for classifying home pages by interests. On an experiment of 400 pages, we found that the glossary with the highest number of word matches is the correct interest in 44.75% of the pages. The correct interest is in the top three highest returned interests in 72.25% of the pages, and the correct interest is in the top five returned interest matches in 84.5% of the pages.[1]

1   Introduction

Much work has been published on web page classification in the fields of Information Retrieval and Artificial Intelligence. There are many learning methods for classifying web pages [2,8,9]. One type of learning method is supervised learning, e.g., Nearest Neighbor Learners, Bayesian Learners and Discriminative Classification methods such as SVM. There are also unsupervised and semi-supervised learning methods, where an algorithm determines the similarity between documents. Some of these techniques make use of features specific to web pages [11]. Handcrafted rule-based methods and Inductive Learning Methods for text classification have also been developed [8,12,13]. Some approaches analyze the structure of the web pages and the characteristics of the images in them [6]. There are also knowledge-based, Artificial Intelligence approaches [5] for home page classification.

---

[1] This research was supported by the NJ Commission for Science and Technology.

K. Bauknecht, A Min Tjoa, G. Quirchmayr (Eds.): EC-Web 2003, LNCS 2738, pp. 248-258, 2003.

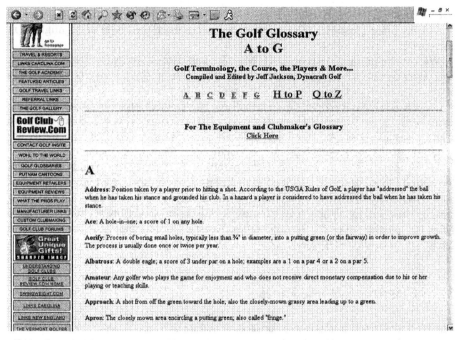

Fig. 1. Example Glossary

Our approach is unique in that we are using glossary information available on the web to categorize web pages. We do so without training sets that would be needed in Information Retrieval and many Machine Learning approaches. We don't need sophisticated Natural Language Processing (NLP) methods or complex knowledge bases as in knowledge-based approaches [12]. We infer an interest by using features specific to web pages, namely the occurrence of terms, which are specific to glossary topics for the particular interest.

2   Extracting Glossaries from the Web

Our classification system uses terms mined from Internet glossaries (for example, Fig. 1) to determine an interest from a home page. These glossaries are freely available on the Internet. There are glossaries on every imaginable topic. They are also very easy to find, a simple Google^{TM} search reveals many results. We have found that glossaries are also easy to process, because they tend to have regular structures. As can be seen from the sample glossary in Fig. 1, the terms that we are interested in are usually in bold or highlighted in some way. This makes it easy to automate the extraction of the glossary terms.

We currently have glossaries on 30 different topics in our system. It took comparatively little time to locate the glossaries on the Web, extract terms from them and manually review the results for errors. For example, to build our glossary for baseball, we searched Google^{TM} for the term "baseball glossary." The first 30 hits of this search returned distinct baseball glossaries. Naturally, there was a good degree of overlap between those glossaries, but some of them contained words rarely found in any of the other glossaries. The glossary terms are usually in bold or highlighted in some way.

We wrote a program to process HTML files and extract words from within HTML tags, such as <b> </b> which mark a bold word. Our program converts the terms to lower case. Any occurring symbols are replaced by blank spaces. We generate one output file per glossary topic. Our baseball file starts out empty; our program puts the terms from the first Internet baseball glossary into the empty text file. Since there are many baseball glossaries, for each baseball glossary after the first, the terms are checked against the baseball file to see whether they have been encountered already. Only if a term is new, it is added to the baseball file. When the program is finished, the output file is manually reviewed to make sure that we have one term per line. We also remove any HTML that may have found its way into the glossary file and run a sorting program to alphabetize all glossary files for easier inspection. We have generated glossary files for 30 topic areas. A list of these topic areas can be seen in the left-most column of Table 1.

3   Classifying Home Pages

The work described in this paper forms one module of a larger system, which has the purpose of extracting demographic information and interest information from home pages of web users. Many home pages follow a structured format, which may be enforced by a portal site. On those pages it is easy to recognize interests of a home page owner, because they are prefixed with a keyword such as "Interests:" However, many other home pages contain interests "hidden" in paragraphs of free text. The purpose of the glossary module is to derive one interest for each free-text input home page. In other words, it classifies web pages by interests.

Our system for categorizing home pages is written in JAVA and is currently set up to use Yahoo Geocities member's home pages as test data. It uses a sophisticated web crawler to crawl linked pages, starting at any home page we specify. The crawler can also run through a Yahoo Geocities member page listing, which lists 20 home pages at a time. When our classifier starts, it first loads all glossary files. Each glossary file is hashed into a different hash table. The web crawler then takes over and visits every page in the member's site. It extracts the words from the HTML page, including words from the Meta tags. These words are then compared against the glossary hash tables in a sliding window sequence from one word to seven words in length. When matches between a word on the web page and a word in the glossary hash table occur, the word or words and the glossary that they occurred in are recorded. At the end of the page the results are tallied and written to a final output file.

The result of the classifier for a given home page consists of a list of pairs *((glossary topic 1, number of word matches 1), (glossary topic 2, number of word matches 2) ....)*. Ideally, the glossary topic with the largest number of word matches should be identical to the topic of the home page that we are classifying.

4   Experimental Results of Home Page Classification

We ran the classifier on 40 pages from each of 10 Geocities topics. After classifying these 400 pages, we found that the glossary with the largest number of word matches was indeed from the same topic as the home page 44.75% of the time. If we consider it a success when the correct topic appears within the top three or top five topics returned by the classifier, then the result percentages become much better.

Table 1. Golf Pages from Yahoo Geocities Golf Topic

	P1	P2	P3	P4	P5	P6	P7	P8	P9	P10
Woodworking	16	15	2	5	83	0	2	8	48	5
Football	128	21	2	10	73	1	10	39	84	4
Soap making	10	0	2	4	0	0	0	1	4	0
Weaving	15	7	0	5	0	1	0	3	13	0
Sewing	31	5	4	5	8	1	4	11	23	1
Scrapbooks	2	2	1	1	13	0	1	0	7	1
Quilting	8	8	0	4	19	2	2	1	47	0
Rubberstamping	2	1	0	4	7	0	0	0	2	3
Baseball	71	30	5	16	39	3	6	29	99	7
Polymer clay	1	1	1	0	1	0	0	0	3	0
Needlecrafts	0	0	0	1	0	0	0	0	0	0
Knitting	4	0	4	1	0	0	5	1	8	1
Jewelry Making	1	5	3	0	1	1	1	2	9	0
Tennis	135	46	9	23	101	8	14	46	148	6
Volleyball	11	11	0	7	14	1	1	6	29	1
Golf	**199**	**110**	**20**	**49**	**291**	**21**	**19**	**96**	**437**	**39**
Archery	54	16	1	5	4	3	7	12	60	3
Fencing	27	7	1	1	12	0	2	17	30	2
Wine	56	38	6	12	166	0	6	28	107	4
Boxing	51	4	0	7	9	1	1	7	21	6
Ceramics	8	6	0	2	62	1	0	0	12	0
Egg Painting	0	0	0	1	0	0	0	0	0	0
Candle Making	0	3	0	0	0	0	1	0	3	0
Real Estate	144	26	31	14	108	5	19	57	109	14
Scuba	0	0	0	0	0	0	0	0	0	0
Mountain biking	15	6	2	3	7	0	2	2	31	1
Caving	91	15	5	15	80	4	9	16	55	4
Auto Racing	7	9	4	7	21	0	3	14	26	0
Hiking	4	3	0	2	3	0	2	1	7	3
Birding	24	15	4	0	56	0	5	7	31	1
Correct Analysis IN*	1	1	3	1	1	1	3	1	1	1

*Correct analysis IN top 1,3,5 results or Wrong

The correct interest is in the top three returned topics 72.25% of the time, and in the top five returned topics 84.5% of the time. If no words of the home page match any glossaries "interest could not be determined" is returned. This result was only returned for a page that contained "site under construction." We consider this as a correct interest analysis. Geocities groups its pages by topic e.g. baseball. However, every once in a while, there is a rogue page, which is stored in a topic area where it does not belong. If a rogue page is from a topic for which we do not have a glossary then a random result will be returned.

Table 2. Golf Pages from Yahoo Geocities Golf Topic

	P11	P12	P13	P14	P15	P16	P17	P18	P19	P20
Woodworking	1	4	4	0	7	0	0	2	0	1
Football	2	4	2	0	13	0	4	2	3	1
Soap making	0	0	0	0	0	0	0	0	0	0
Weaving	0	0	1	0	4	0	2	1	0	0
Sewing	0	1	0	0	1	1	1	0	1	0
Scrapbooks	0	0	1	0	0	0	0	1	0	0
Quilting	4	0	1	1	6	0	0	0	1	0
Rubberstamping	0	1	0	1	1	0	0	1	0	2
Baseball	0	2	8	1	19	1	4	3	7	0
Polymer clay	1	0	0	0	0	0	0	0	0	0
Needlecrafts	0	0	0	0	0	0	0	0	0	0
Knitting	1	1	0	0	1	1	0	0	0	0
Jewelry making	0	0	0	0	0	0	0	0	1	3
Tennis	6	3	8	0	27	1	5	3	8	0
Volleyball	0	0	1	0	10	0	3	0	0	0
Golf	30	8	12	1	83	2	10	6	19	3
Archery	0	0	4	0	9	0	1	1	4	0
Fencing	0	0	1	0	4	0	1	0	1	0
Wine	0	7	11	0	20	0	3	5	5	2
Boxing	0	0	0	0	7	0	2	0	0	0
Ceramics	0	2	0	0	2	0	0	0	0	1
Egg Painting	0	0	0	0	0	0	0	0	0	0
Candle Making	0	0	1	0	0	0	1	1	0	0
Real Estate	6	7	3	2	10	5	6	2	6	4
Scuba	0	0	0	0	0	0	0	0	0	0
Mountain biking	0	1	0	0	4	0	0	0	0	0
Caving	7	3	3	0	10	0	0	1	1	1
Auto Racing	0	1	0	0	3	1	1	0	1	0
Hiking	0	0	0	0	3	0	1	0	0	0
Birding	0	3	1	0	7	1	2	0	2	1
Correct Analysis IN*	1	1	1	5	1	W	1	1	1	3

*Correct analysis IN top 1,3,5 results or Wrong

Tables 1, 2, 3 and 4 show the results of running our system against 40 home pages (P1--P40) from the Golf topic in Yahoo Geocities. In these tables, every number indicates a count of word matches. For example, in Table 1, the first number in the first row indicates that 16 words from the woodworking glossary were found in test page P1. For 32 of these test pages, Golf was the top glossary word match result. For 6 pages, Golf was in the top 3 highest glossary word matches. For 1 page, Golf was in the top 5 results, and one page was not a Golf page at all. This wrong page was accessed due to a bad link, which brought us to a standard Yahoo error message "Sorry, the page you requested was not found." Such error message pages produce the same pattern every time, and in future work we will scan our results for such patterns and, in turn, return an error message. This would improve the accuracy of our system. We did not use this metric when analyzing our results; we considered these pages as wrongly categorized.

Table 3. Golf Pages from Yahoo Geocities Golf Topic

	P21	P22	P23	P24	P25	P26	P27	P28	P29	P30
Woodworking	5	2	38	0	0	10	6	11	2	14
Football	10	2	58	0	4	70	6	16	1	4
Soap making	2	0	18	0	0	7	0	1	0	0
Weaving	3	0	4	0	0	5	1	1	1	2
Sewing	0	5	13	0	1	39	2	3	3	1
Scrapbooks	0	0	6	0	0	0	0	0	0	2
Quilting	1	1	19	0	0	5	4	2	0	1
Rubberstamping	2	0	4	0	0	3	1	0	0	22
Baseball	16	1	58	0	0	38	11	13	4	4
Polymer clay	2	0	1	0	0	3	0	0	0	0
Needlecrafts	0	0	0	0	0	0	0	0	0	0
Knitting	2	0	15	0	0	0	1	3	2	1
Jewelry making	0	0	2	0	0	0	1	0	2	3
Tennis	37	8	121	0	4	110	27	17	9	14
Volleyball	10	1	31	0	1	17	4	1	1	3
Golf	84	20	636	1	19	122	58	80	14	64
Archery	21	1	19	0	1	22	5	3	1	6
Fencing	6	0	12	0	1	12	3	2	1	0
Wine	14	7	63	0	5	66	11	19	3	23
Boxing	7	0	5	0	2	9	0	3	1	1
Ceramics	7	0	0	0	0	1	0	2	0	0
Egg Painting	0	0	0	0	0	0	0	0	1	1
Candle Making	0	0	3	0	0	0	0	0	0	2
Real Estate	18	6	166	2	2	24	11	24	14	12
Scuba	0	0	0	0	0	0	0	0	0	0
Mountain biking	3	0	7	0	1	10	2	2	1	0
Caving	8	3	21	0	2	22	4	8	3	2
Auto Racing	3	0	40	0	0	20	4	5	2	3
Hiking	5	0	6	0	0	5	0	1	0	0
Birding	18	0	3	0	2	13	5	5	3	1
Correct Analysis IN*	1	1	1	3	1	1	1	1	3	1

*Correct analysis IN top 1,3,5 results or Wrong

Page 31 in Table 4 is a David Duval fan page. As one can see in the table, the Golf glossary has 60 word matches, which identifies Golf as the correct home page interest. There are 25 matching words from the Tennis glossary in David Duval's page. Thus, Tennis is a distant second.

Page 11 of Table 2 is shown in Fig. 2. It is the personal home page of a Golf professional. Thirty words from the Golf glossary are found in this home page. The home page does not contain that many words from any other glossary. The second-best match is Caving, and there are only seven words of the Caving glossary in this home page. Thus, the classifier correctly recognizes the topic of this page as Golf.

Table 4. Golf Pages from Yahoo Geocities Golf Topic

	P31	P32	P33	P34	P35	P36	P37	P38	P39	P40
Woodworking	2	5	2	4	3	1	0	14	3	3
Football	11	9	11	0	6	4	4	24	7	8
Soap making	0	3	2	0	0	0	0	1	0	2
Weaving	4	3	2	0	1	0	0	6	0	0
Sewing	2	4	7	1	4	0	2	3	5	2
Scrapbooks	0	1	0	0	0	0	10	0	0	3
Quilting	6	0	2	1	1	0	8	8	0	6
Rubberstamping	0	0	0	0	1	0	0	2	2	2
Baseball	18	13	18	3	5	3	14	27	0	15
Polymer clay	1	3	2	1	2	0	0	3	0	0
Needlecrafts	0	0	0	0	0	0	0	0	0	0
Knitting	1	1	1	0	0	1	0	2	0	1
Jewelry making	1	2	3	0	1	1	0	0	0	0
Tennis	25	27	22	10	8	3	17	42	9	13
Volleyball	1	7	5	2	1	1	1	13	0	3
Golf	60	68	34	19	16	14	38	112	36	47
Archery	8	13	4	2	3	3	4	9	2	12
Fencing	2	1	1	0	2	0	2	11	0	5
Wine	17	13	11	5	9	5	3	49	8	10
Boxing	2	3	4	0	0	0	0	6	0	3
Ceramics	3	0	1	0	0	0	0	3	2	1
Egg Painting	1	0	1	0	0	0	0	0	0	0
Candle Making	1	0	2	0	1	0	0	0	0	0
Real Estate	14	31	27	4	18	4	20	41	7	21
Scuba	0	0	0	0	0	0	0	1	0	0
Mountain biking	11	1	7	1	3	0	0	5	4	2
Caving	5	13	8	3	7	4	3	28	6	16
Auto Racing	3	5	5	2	2	2	3	5	0	4
Hiking	3	0	2	0	1	0	0	1	5	2
Birding	8	2	4	1	1	0	2	8	0	11
Correct Analysis IN*	1	1	1	1	1	1	1	1	1	1

*Correct analysis IN top 1,3,5 results or Wrong

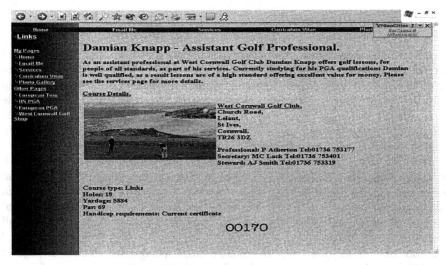

Fig. 2. Example Page P11

Table 5 summarizes the results of running our System with 30 glossaries on 400 pages from 10 topics. Column 2 shows that the glossary with the largest number of word matches was the correct interest for 44.75% of the 400 pages. Column three shows that the correct interest for the page was in the top three returned glossaries in 72.25% of the 400 pages. Column four shows that the correct interest for the page was in the top five highest glossary word matches in 84.5% of the 400 pages. The last column shows the numbers of pages with classifications that were not contained in the top 5 glossary topics returned by our classifier. These results must be considered as wrong.

Table 5. Summary of all Results

	Pages In Top 1	Pages In Top 3	Pages In Top 5	Wrong Pages
Archery	5	14	13	8
Auto Racing	3	15	8	14
Baseball	10	22	5	3
Football	18	11	4	7
Golf	32	6	1	1
Quilting	21	4	7	8
Real Estate	38	2	0	0
Soap Making	11	14	5	10
Tennis	18	17	3	2
Wine	23	5	3	9
Totals of all 400 pages	179	110	49	62
Cumulative Percent	44.75%	72.25%	84.5%	100%

5   Language Independence

In a series of experiments, we have found that several of our glossaries are surprisingly flexible when processing web pages written in European languages other than English. We have been successful in correctly categorizing home pages in Spanish, French, Portuguese, Italian, Swedish, Dutch, and Danish. This is possible due to the fact that many English words are the same in other languages, for example the glossary terms baseball, sangria, champagne, Chablis, and Golf are the same in English, French, German and Italian.

Another reason why were able to classify non-English pages with English glossaries was that we found many pages in different languages that had English words strewn about them. In many cases this was not because the word is the same in that language, but because the page creator decided to use the English word instead of the same word in their native language. For example, a Spanish page about baseball contained: "autor del único *triple play* sin asistencia en nuestras Series Nacionales." We also found home pages that contained a single paragraph, sentence or page in English, while the rest of the site was in a foreign language. This was enough for us to get a correct interest determination. Fig. 3 is a Golf page in Spanish. The interest of the page was correctly determined by our system, with 64 glossary word matches. These results are shown in Table 1, for Page P30.

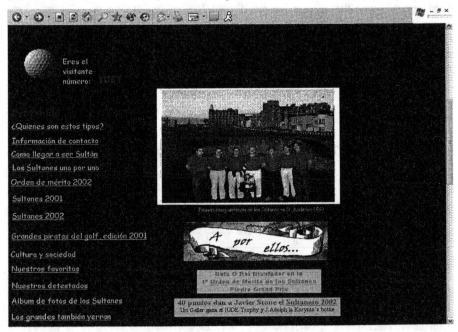

Fig. 3. Sample Foreign Language Page

6   Conclusions and Future Work

In this paper, we have presented a new method for classifying Web pages according to interests. Classic Information Retrieval methods using training sets or Artificial Intelligence methods using knowledge bases are hard to train or build. They require much time and effort. Using free, easily accessible Internet glossaries, we found the correct interest on a small sample set in the top five returned topics 84.5% of the time. In future work, we will analyze links to other pages and use that additional information to improve our answers. There has been successful work in using such links to improve page classification [1,2,4,10]. We also noticed that almost all of the foreign language pages contained links to pages in English, which we will use for improved interest determination for such pages.

Another topic for future research is to determine when a page should legitimately be classified as belonging to two or more interests. For instance, we have encountered pages that express an interest in both football and baseball. How can we distinguish between a person that is truly interested in both and a person that is interested in only one, we may get a false positive, because baseball and football have many words in common?

Many ambiguous words appear in very different glossaries. Thus, "Diamond" could be indicative of an interest in baseball or an interest in jewelry. Clearly, such words have less discriminative power than words that appear only in one glossary. In future work, we will use Information Retrieval methods to reduce the weights of such overlapping words.   We will also experiment with more powerful categorization methods, such as Naïve Bayes classifiers. Most importantly, we are going to add many more glossaries to our system, in order to determine whether classification results stay at an acceptable level.

References

[1]   G. Attardi, A. Gullí, and F. Sebastiani. Automatic Web page categorization by link and context analysis. In C. Hutchison and G. Lanzarone, editors, *Proceedings of THAI-99, 1st European Symposium on Telematics, Hypermedia and Artificial Intelligence*, pages 105-119, Varese, IT, 1999.

[2]   Eric J. Glover, Kostas Tsioutsiouliklis, Steve Lawrence, David M. Pennock, Gary W. Flake. Using Web Structure for Classifying and Describing Web Pages. Proceedings of WWW-02, International Conference on the World Wide Web, 2002.

[3]   B. Gelfand, M. Wulfekuler, and W. F. Punch. *Automated concept extraction from plain text*. In Papers from the AAAI 1998 Workshop on Text Categorization, pages 13--17, Madison, WI, 1998.

[4]   Johannes Furnkranz. Using Links for Classifying Web-pages.   Technical Report OEFAI TR-98-29.   Austrian Research Institute for Artificial Intelligence.

[5]   Hisao Mase. Experiments on Automatic Web Page Categorization for IR System. Technical Report. Department of Computer Science, Stanford University, 1998.

[6]   Arul Prakash Asirvathan, Kranthi Kumar. Ravi. Web Page Classification based on Document Structure. International Institute of Information Technology, 2001.

[7]   John M. Pierre. Practical Issues for Automated Categorization of Web Sites. ECDL 2000 Workshop on the Semantic Web.

[8]   Apte, C., Damerau, F., and Weiss, S., *Automated Learning of Decision Rules for Text Categorization*, ACM Transactions on Information Systems, pp. 233-240, July 1994.

[9]   Heterogeneous Learner for Web Page Classification. H. Yu, K. C.-C. Chang, and J. Han. In *Proceedings of the 2002 IEEE International Conference on Data Mining (ICDM 2002)*, pages 538-545, Maebashi, Japan, December 2002.

[10]   Shyh-Ming Tai, Chen-Zen Yang, Ing-Xian Chen. Improved Automatic Web-Page Classification by Neighbor Text Percolation. Department of Computer Engineering and Science, Yuan Ze University Kaohsiung, Taiwan, November 23, 2002.

[11]   Soumen Chakrabarti. Mining the Web: Discovering Knowledge from Hypertext Data. Morgan Kaufmann Publishers: San Francisco, CA 2003.

[12]   Peter Jackson and Isabelle Moulinier. Natural Language Processing for Online Applications: Text Retrieval, Extraction and Categorization. Amsterdam: John Benjamins Publishing Company, 2002.

[13]   P.J. Hayes and S.P. Weinstein. CONSTRUE/TIS: a system for content-based indexing of a database of news stories. In A. Rappaport and R. Smith, editors, Proceedings of IAAI-90, 2nd Conference on Innovative Applications of Artificial Intelligence, pages 49--66. AAAI Press, Menlo Park, 1990.

Transformation of XML Data
Using an Unranked Tree Transducer

Tadeusz Pankowski

Institute of Control and Information Engineering
Poznan University of Technology, Poland
Tadeusz.Pankowski@put.poznan.pl

Abstract. Transformation of data documents is of special importance
to use XML as the universal data interchange format on the Web. Data
transformation is used in many tasks that require data to be transferred
between existing, independently created Web-oriented applications. To
perform such transformation one can use W3C's XSLT or XQuery. But
these languages are devoted to detailed programming of transformation
procedures. In this paper we show how data transformation can by specify by means of high-level *rule specifications* based on uniform unranked
tree transducers. We show that our approach is both descriptive and
expressive, and we illustrate how it can be used to specify and perform
transformations of XML documents.

1   Introduction

In data exchange, data structured in one system must be restructured and translated into a different form conforming to requirements of the other system. Such
data transformation is used in many tasks that require data to be transferred
between existing, independently created applications. The need of data transformation has become more important recently, as data exchange has expanded
with the proliferation of Web-oriented applications such as Web services, Web
collaboration, E-commerce etc. The widespread interoperability between such
applications is usually performed by means of exchanging data that is encoded
in XML. Such documents carry important information to participants of communication processes, so documents must be interpreted correctly by the requesters
and providers.

In the transformation process, the following three phases can be distinguished [1]: (1) *structure identification* - in this phase we identify the applied
data structuring mechanisms and discover schemas of input and output documents (in this paper we restrict ourselves to XML and DTD); (2) *transformation
specification* - in this phase we specify mappings by means of inter-schema corre-
spondences capturing input and output constraints imposed on the documents;
(3) *performing transformation* - in this phase mapping specifications are translated into operations over the input document that produce an output document
satisfying the constraints and structures of the output schema.

K. Bauknecht, A Min Tjoa, G. Quirchmayr (Eds.): EC-Web 2003, LNCS 2738, pp. 259–269, 2003.

A transformation can be carried out by means of W3C's languages XSLT [2] or XQuery [3]. Typically, XSLT is used to add styling information to an XML source document, by transforming it into another presentation-oriented format such as HTML. However, XSLT is also used to perform XML-to-XML transformations expressing rules for transforming one or more source data trees into one or more result data trees. In constructing a result tree, nodes from the source trees can be filtered and reordered, and arbitrary structures can be added. Data transformation can also be done by means of any XML query language (e.g. XQuery). In such case, mapping specifications are translated into appropriate XQuery queries over the input document. The result of the query is the expected output document, and the result must satisfy the output schema. Both languages are functional with powerful computational capability. However, their operational nature makes them less desirable candidates for high-level *transformation specification* [1].

In this paper we propose a method for specification of XML-to-XML transformations based on tree transducers on unranked trees. The formal framework of the method is that of top-down uniform unranked tree transducers by Martens and Neven [4]. Originally, unranked tree transducers were proposed for type-checking problems for XML queries: statically verifying that every answer to a query conforms to a given output schema. Uniform tree transducers investigated in [4] deals with DTD, and are intended to define tree-to-tree transformation, where the input tree is a regular expression and transformation rules deals with individual symbols. Such transformation is suitable for DTD transformations. However, in the class of applications that we are interested in, we want to transform XML documents, not just their DTD.

The main contributions of this paper are the following:

- we generalize tree transducers to a specification formalism appropriate to transformation specification of a wide class of XML documents – the specification involves XPath expressions;
- we show that transformation rules can be defined by a high-level rule specification formalism, and we show how in systematic and inductive way transformation rules can be applied to the input data tree.

In Section 2 we discussed the problem of representation and processing XML data. The method for specification transformation rules based on unranked tree transducers is proposed in Section 3. An illustrating example how to use the transformation is given in Section 4. Section 5 concludes the paper.

2 Exchange, Representation and Processing of XML Data

An XML document is a textual representation of data and consists of hierarchically nested element structures starting with a root element. The basic component in an XML document is an element. An element consists of a start-tag, the corresponding end-tag and content, i.e., the structure between the tags. With elements we can associate attributes. Because XML documents are tree-structured, a data model for representing them can use conventional terminology for trees. In the XQuery/XPath Data Model proposed by the W3C [5], an XML document is represented by an ordered node-labeled tree (data tree) which includes a concept of node identity.

A node in a data tree conforms to one of the seven node kinds: *root* (or *document*), *element*, *attribute*, *text*, *namespace*, *processing instruction*, and *comment*. Every node has at most one parent, which is either an element node or the root node. Root nodes and element nodes have sequences of children nodes. A tree contains a root plus all nodes that are reachable directly or indirectly from the root. Every node belongs to exactly one tree, and every tree has exactly one root node. In this paper, we restrict our considerations to four types of nodes: root, element, attribute and text nodes. A data tree considered in this paper can be formalized as follows:

Definition 1. *Let Σ and OID be two alphabets of labels and (object) identifiers, respectively. Let $\Sigma = \Sigma_A \cup \Sigma_E$, where Σ_A is a set of attribute labels, and Σ_E is a set of element labels. A data tree conforms to the following syntax, where $oid \in OID$, $a \in \Sigma_A$, $e \in \Sigma_E$, and text denotes a standard string:*

$$\text{data tree} ::= oid(tree, ..., tree),$$
$$\text{tree} ::= e\text{-}tree \mid a\text{-}tree \mid t\text{-}tree,$$
$$e\text{-}tree ::= \langle e, oid \rangle (tree, ..., tree),$$
$$a\text{-}tree ::= \langle a, oid \rangle (string),$$
$$t\text{-}tree ::= \langle oid \rangle (string).$$
□

Each node has its unique identifier, *oid*, and all nodes, except the root node and text nodes, have labels assigned to the incoming edge. Attribute and text nodes have values assigned to them. An example of data tree (there are no attribute nodes in the tree) is given in Fig. 1.

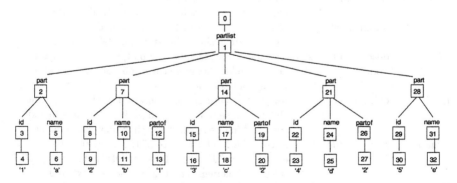

Fig. 1. Data tree describing a flat list of parts

For selecting parts of XML documents represented by a data tree one can use XPath expressions [6]. A path expression locates nodes within a tree, and returns a sequence of distinct nodes. A path expression is always evaluated with respect to a *context*. If E_1/E_2 or $E_1[E_2]$ are path expressions, the *context* for E_2 is a pair (x, S), where: (1) $x \in S$ is called the *context node*; (2) S is the *context set*, i.e., an ordered set of nodes obtained by evaluating E_1 in some context for E_1. For every context (x, S) we can obtain *context size* of S, i.e., the number of nodes in S, and the *context position*, i.e., the position of the context node x in the context set S. Notice that the values of both context position and context size are integers greater than zero (if the result of E_1 is the empty sequence it can not be a context sequence for any expression).

A path expression in XPath consists of one or more steps separated by '/'. Each step selects a sequence of nodes. A step begins at the context node, navigates to those nodes that are reachable from the context node via a predefined *axis*, and selects some subset of the reachable nodes. A step has three parts: an *axis*, a node *test*, and zero or more *predicates*: an *axis* specifies the relationship between the nodes selected by the step and the context node; a *test* specifies the node type and label (name) of the selected nodes; a *predicate* is a further filter for the set of selected nodes.

A predicate consists of a *predicate expression*, enclosed in square brackets. A predicate serves to filter a node set, retaining some nodes and discarding others. For example, in the path expression (qualified step) part[@price="100"], [@price="100"] is the predicate.

In Tab. 1 we describe some axes, their abbreviated forms and examples of use (a node test node() is true for any node) [3, 6].

Table 1. Abbreviated syntax for XPath steps and their meaning

Abbreviated syntax	Meaning	Description and example
.	self::node()	selects the context node; e.g.: ./part is short for self::node()/child::part
..	parent::node()	selects the parent of the context node; e.g.: ../part is short for parent::node()/child::part
//	descendant-or-self:: node()	e.g.: part//part is short for part/descendant-or-self:: node()/child::part and selects all part descendants of the context node
label	child::*label*	selects the *label* element children of the context node; child:: can be omitted because it is the default axis; e.g.: part/name is short for child::part/child::name
@*label*	attribute::*label*	selects the *label* attribute of the context node; e.g.:[@price="100"] is short for [attribute::price="100"]
*	child::*	selects all element children of the context node
@*	attribute::*	selects all the attributes of the context node

The semantics for XPath expressions is given by means of three semantic functions:

$$\mathbb{S} : SExpr \rightarrow [Node \rightarrow 2^{Node}],$$
$$\mathbb{B} : BExpr \rightarrow [Node \times 2^{Node} \rightarrow \{\text{true}, \text{false}\}],$$
$$\mathbb{V} : VExpr \rightarrow [Node \times 2^{Node} \rightarrow String \cup 2^{String}].$$

For a path expression $p \in SExpr$, $\mathbb{S}(p)$ is a function from the set $Node$ of context nodes into a power set of nodes. Similarly, for a predicate expression $b \in BExpr$, $\mathbb{B}(b)$ is a function from the set $Node \times 2^{Node}$ of contexts into Boolean values, and for a value expression $v \in VExpr$, $\mathbb{V}(v)$ is a function from the set of contexts into the union of sets of string values and the power set of string values.

The definition of semantic functions is given in Tab. 2; the predicate $axis(x, y)$, where $axis \in$ {self, child, parent, descendant, descendant-or-self, attribute} means that x is connected with y by means of the $axis$; node tests e, a, $*$, and text() denote, respectively, label of element node, label of attribute node, any element or attribute node, and any text node. The function $label(x)$ returns the label of element or attribute node x, the function $value(x)$ returns the string-value of node x The definition is coherent with that of Wadler [7].

Table 2. Semantics of XPath expressions

$\mathbb{S}(/p)(x)$	$= \mathbb{S}(p)(r)$, where r is the root of the document
$\mathbb{S}(axis :: e)(x)$	$= \{y \mid axis(x, y) \wedge label(y) = e\}$, where
	$axis \in$ {self, child, parent, descendant, descendant-or-self}
$\mathbb{S}(attribute :: a)(x)$	$= \{y \mid attribute(x, y) \wedge label(y) = a \}$
$\mathbb{S}(axis :: *)(x)$	$= \{y \mid axis(x, y) \wedge y$ is an element node$\}$, where
	$axis \in$ {child, descendant, descendant-or-self}
$\mathbb{S}(attribute :: *)(x)$	$= \{y \mid attribute(x, y)\}$
$\mathbb{S}(axis :: text())(x)$	$= \{y \mid axis(x, y) \wedge y$ is a text node$\}$, where
	$axis \in$ {self, child, descendant, descendant-or-self}
$\mathbb{S}(p_1/p_2)(x)$	$= \{z \mid \exists y \in \mathbb{S}(p_1)(x) \wedge z \in \mathbb{S}(p_2)(y)\}$
$\mathbb{S}(p_1\|p_2)(x)$	$= \mathbb{S}(p_1)(x) \cup \mathbb{S}(p_2)(x)$
$\mathbb{S}(p[b])(x)$	$= \{y \mid y \in \mathbb{S}(p)(x) \wedge \mathbb{B}(b)(y, \mathbb{S}(p)(x))\}$
$\mathbb{B}(p)(x, S)$	$= \mathbb{S}(p)(x) \neq \emptyset$
$\mathbb{B}(v_1 = v_2)(x, S)$	$= \mathbb{V}(v_1)(x, S) = \mathbb{V}(v_2)(x, S)$, (coercion and existential
	semantics may be used when needed)
$\mathbb{B}(not\ b)(x, S)$	$= \neg\mathbb{B}(b)(x, S)$
$\mathbb{B}(b_1 or\ b_2)(x, S)$	$= \mathbb{B}(b_1)(x, S) \vee \mathbb{B}(b_2)(x, S)$
$\mathbb{B}(b_1 and\ b_2)(x, S)$	$= \mathbb{B}(b_1)(x, S) \wedge \mathbb{B}(b_2)(x, S)$
$\mathbb{V}(string)(x, S)$	$=$ string
$\mathbb{V}(p)(x, S)$	$= \{value(y) \mid y \in \mathbb{S}(p)(x)\}$
$\mathbb{V}(position())(x, S)$	$=$ the position of x in the ordered set S
$\mathbb{V}(last())(x, S)$	$= size(S)$

3   Transformation of Data Trees

Uniform unranked transducers have been proposed by Martens and Neven [4] to transform input Σ-trees into output Σ-trees, where Σ is an labeling alphabet over which trees are defined. The set, T_Σ, of unranked Σ-trees is the smallest set of strings over Σ and parenthesis, such that if $\sigma \in \Sigma$, and $w \in T_\Sigma^*$, then $\sigma(w) \in T_\Sigma$. There is no a priori bound on the number of children of a node, so Σ-trees are unranked.

In this paper we follow the idea of unranked tree transducers. However, in our approach:

- we are interested the in transformation of *data trees* representing XML-documents;
- transformation rules are defined for *classes of nodes* rather than for individual nodes, thus we will propose a notation for transformation rules specification, which serves as schemas for producing transformation rules.

Now we define the tree transducer used in this paper. For a set Q, we denote by $C_{\Sigma,OID}(Q)$ the set of *tree components*. By a tree component $c \in C_{\Sigma,OID}(Q)$ we understand an expression with the syntax:

$$c ::= oid\langle e, oid'\rangle(q_1, ..., q_n) \mid oid(tree).$$

Definition 2. *Data tree transducer is a tuple*

$$(Q, \Sigma, OID, q_0, R),$$

where Q is a finite set of states, Σ is a labeling alphabet, OID is a set of identifiers, $q_0 \in Q$ is the initial state, and R is a finite set of rules of the form

$$(q, oid) \rightarrow c,$$

where $q \in Q$, $oid \in OID$, and $c \in C_{\Sigma,OID}(Q)$.   □

The transformation defined by $T = (Q, \Sigma, OID, q_0, R)$ on a tree t in state q, denoted by $T^q(t)$, is inductively defined as follows:

1. If $t = oid(t_1, ..., t_N)$, or $t = \langle e, oid\rangle(t_1, ..., t_N)$ and there is a rule
   $(q, oid) \rightarrow oid''\langle e', oid'\rangle(q_1, ..., q_n)$, then

$$T^q(t) = oid''\langle e', oid'\rangle(T^{q_1}(t_1), ..., T^{q_1}(t_N), ..., T^{q_n}(t_1), ..., T^{q_n}(t_N)),$$

   i.e., $T^q(t)$ is obtained from the right-hand side of the rule by replacing every q_i by the sequence $T^{q_i}(t_1), ..., T^{q_i}(t_N)$. Then we say that the transformation $T^{q_i}(t_j)$ denotes the application of a rule with left-hand side equal to (q_i, oid_j) in the context node oid, where oid_j identifies the tree t_j. In the transformation $T^{q_i}(t_j)$ two identifiers are available: $\$q_i = oid_j$, and $\&q_i = oid'$.

2. Otherwise, the rule has the form $(q, oid) \rightarrow oid''(tree)$ and its right-hand side constructs the *tree* according to the given specification, and oid'' will be the parent of the tree.

A set R of rules in a data tree transducer is defined on individual nodes. Now we will define a notation devoted to specification of such transformation rules. There are four kinds of transformation rules:

1. *Initial rule* – maps the root of the input document and its child nodes into the root and child nodes of the output document, it also defines states for further transformations. An initial rule specification is

   $(q_0, /label) \rightarrow new(/)\langle label', new(.)\rangle(q_1, ..., q_n), n \geq 1.$

   The specification invoked in a context node x produces the following set of initial rules:

   $\{(q_0, oid) \rightarrow oid''\langle label', oid'\rangle(q_1, ..., q_n) \mid$
   $oid \in \mathbb{S}(label)(root(t)), oid'' = new(root(t)), oid' = new(oid)\}.$

2. *Intermediate rule* – maps any node except of children of the root into appropriate nodes of the output document, and defines states for further transformations. An intermediate rule is specified by

   $(q, SExpr) \rightarrow new(SExpr')\langle label, new(.)\rangle(q_1, ..., q_n), n \geq 1.$

   The specification invoked in a context node x produces the following set of intermediate rules:

   $\{(q, oid) \rightarrow oid''\langle label, oid'\rangle(q_1, ..., q_n) \mid$
   $oid \in \mathbb{S}(SExpr)(x), oid'' = new(y), y \in \mathbb{S}(SExpr')(oid), oid' = new(oid)\}.$

3. *Copy rule* – copies a subtree of the input tree and includes it into the output tree. Does not define states for further transformations, so every copy rule ends one of transformation branches. A copy rule has specification

   $(q, SExpr) \rightarrow new(SExpr')\langle label, copy(.)\rangle$

   and invoked in a context node x produces the following set of copy rules:

   $\{(q, oid) \rightarrow oid''\langle label, oid'\rangle \mid$
   $oid \in \mathbb{S}(SExpr)(x), oid'' = new(y), y \in \mathbb{S}(SExpr')(oid), oid' = copy(oid)\}.$

4. *Create rule* – creates a tree and includes it into the output tree. Does not define states for further transformations and ends one of transformation branches. A create rule is specified by

   $(q, SExpr) \rightarrow new(SExpr')(tree).$

   The specification invoked in a context node x produces the following set of create rules:

   $\{(q, oid) \rightarrow oid''(tree) \mid$
   $oid \in \mathbb{S}(SExpr)(x), oid'' = new(y), y \in \mathbb{S}(SExpr')(oid)\}.$

The function $new()$ used in rule specifications is a Skolem function. If it is invoked more than once for the same argument it returns a new node identifier only by the first invocation or when it has no arguments. By consecutive invocations it returns the identifier of the node created by the first evaluation with this argument. The function *copy*(.) recursively traverses the subtree identified by its argument and computes *new*() (without arguments) for each node of this subtree. In this way an output image for the input subtree is created. The image inherits labels and values from the input subtree. Within a create rule, the *tree* is created according to its specification.

4   Illustrating Example

Now we show how the tree transducer may be used to construct a hierarchic document of arbitrary depth from the flat data tree from Fig. 1. (This transformation problem was considered in [1]) and [3]. In the input document each part may or may not be part of a larger part; then the id of the larger part is contained in a partof element (see Fig. 1).

We want to convert the flat representation into a hierarchic representation in which part containment is represented by the structure of the document. Each partof element matches exactly one id. Parts having no partof element are not contained in any other part. The DTD of input and output documents are as follows:

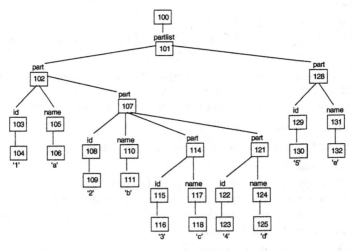

Fig. 2.   The result of the transformation of data tree from Fig. 1 by the transformation rules specified in Tab. 3

DTD of input document:

```
<!DOCTYPE partlist [
  <!ELEMENT partlist (part*)>
  <!ELEMENT part(id, name, partof?)>
  <!ELEMENT id (#PCDATA)>
  <!ELEMENT name (#PCDATA)>
  <!ELEMENT partof (#PCDATA)>
]>
```

DTD of output document:

```
<!DOCTYPE parttree [
  <!ELEMENT parttree (part*)>
  <!ELEMENT part(id, name, part*)>
  <!ELEMENT id (#PCDATA)>
  <!ELEMENT name (#PCDATA)>
]>
```

Data graphs representing some instances of these DTD are given respectively in Fig. 1 and Fig. 2. Specifications of transformation rules are given in Tab. 3.

Application of specifications on the data tree t from Fig. 1 produces the set of transformation rules as is shown in Tab. 4 and in Fig 3.

Table 3. Specifications of transformation rules

$(q_0, /\text{partlist})$	$\rightarrow new(/)\langle\text{parttree}, new(.)\rangle(q_1, q_2)$
$(q_1, ./\text{part}[\text{not partof}])$	$\rightarrow \&q_1\langle\text{part}, new(.)\rangle(q_3, q_4)$
$(q_2, ./\text{part}[\text{partof}])$	$\rightarrow new(../\text{part}[\text{id} = \$q_2/\text{partof}])\langle\text{part}, new(.)\rangle(q_3, q_4)$
$(q_3, ./\text{id})$	$\rightarrow \&q_3\langle\text{id}, copy(.)\rangle$
$(q_4, ./\text{name})$	$\rightarrow \&q_4\langle\text{name}, copy(.)\rangle$

Table 4. Transformation rules produced by the rule specifications from Tab. 3

$(q_0, 1)$	$\rightarrow 100\langle\text{parttree}, 101\rangle(q_1, q_2)$
$(q_1, 2)$	$\rightarrow 101\langle\text{part}, 102\rangle(q_3, q_4)$
$(q_2, 7)$	$\rightarrow 102\langle\text{part}, 107\rangle(q_3, q_4)$
$(q_2, 14)$	$\rightarrow 107\langle\text{part}, 114\rangle(q_3, q_4)$
$(q_2, 21)$	$\rightarrow 107\langle\text{part}, 121\rangle(q_3, q_4)$
$(q_1, 28)$	$\rightarrow 101\langle\text{part}, 128\rangle(q_3, q_4)$
$(q_3, 3)$	$\rightarrow 102\langle\text{id}, 103\rangle(\langle 104\rangle(''1''))$
...	... ...

5   Conclusion

Exchange of information between heterogeneous Web applications requires that both format and structure of data should be transformed frequently. The transformation must preserve meaning of data, so that sender and receiver could interpret it correctly. At present, XML has been accepted as a common format of data for exchanging information. So, the following issues are of special importance: (1) effective transformation of XML data preserving its meaning, and (2) high-level mechanism for specification of XML data transformations. In this

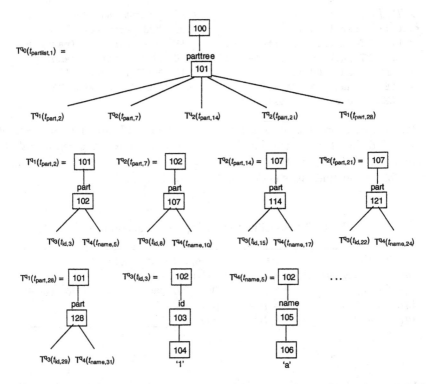

Fig. 3. Transformation of data tree from Fig. 1 by the transducer rules from Tab. 4

paper, we propose a method based on uniform tree transducers to address both of the above problems. The start point of our work are W3C's standards as well as transformation methods for XML data based on tree automata [4, 8, 9, 10]. The proposed method is a part of our project for processing semistructured data and XML [11, 12, 13].

References

[1] Tang, X., Tompa, F. W.: Specifying transformations for structured documents. In Mecca, G., Simeon, J., eds.: Proceedings of the 4th International Workshop on the Web and Databases, WebDB 2001. (2001) 67–72

[2] XSL Transformations (XSLT) 2.0. W3C Working Draft. www.w3.org/TR/xslt20 (2002)

[3] XQuery 1.0: An XML Query Language. W3C Working Draft. www.w3.org/TR/xquery (2002)

[4] Martens, W., Neven, F.: Typecheking top-down uniform unranked tree transducers. In: Database Theory - ICDT 2003. Lecture Notes in Computer Science **2572** (2003) 64–78

[5] XQuery 1.0 and XPath 2.0 Data Model. W3C Working Draft. www.w3.org/TR/query-datamodel (2002)

[6] XML Path Language (XPath) 2.0, W3C Working Draft: (2002) www.w3.org/TR/xpath20.

[7] Wadler, P.: Two semantics for XPath. www.research.avayalabs.com/user/wadler/ (2000)

[8] Vianu, V.: A Web odyssey: from Codd to XML. In: Proceedings of the 20th ACM Symposium on Principles of Database Systems PODS 2001, ACM Press (2001) 1–15

[9] Milo, T., Suciu, D., Vianu, V.: Typechecking for XML transformers. In: Proceedings of the 19th ACM Symposium on Principles of Database Systems PODS 2000, ACM Press (2000) 11–22

[10] Gottlob, G., Koch, C., Pichler, R.: Efficient algorithms for processing XPath queries. In: Proceedings of the 28th Conference on VLDB, Hong Kong, China. (2002) 95–106

[11] Pankowski, T.: PathLog: A query language for schemaless databases of partially labeled objects. Fundamenta Informaticae **49** (2002) 369–395

[12] Pankowski, T.: XML-SQL: An XML query language based on SQL and path tables. Lecture Notes in Computer Science **2490** (2002) 184–209

[13] Pankowski, T.: Querying semistructured data using a rule-oriented XML query language. In: 15th European Conference on Artificial Intelligence ECAI 2002, (F. van Harmelen, ed.). IOS Press, Amsterdam (2002) 302–306

Storing DTD-Conscious XML Data in XEDY

Sourav S. Bhowmick[1], Tay Khim Wee[1], Erwin Leonardi[1], and Sanjay Madria[2]

[1] School of Computer Engineering, Nanyang Technological University Singapore
`assourav@ntu.edu.sg`
[2] Department of Computer Science, University of Missouri-Rolla
Rolla, MO 65409
`madrias@umr.edu`

Abstract. In this paper, we discuss the XEDY system for storing *DTD-conscious* XML data in a standard relational databases management system. For this, we propose a database schema for storing any set of XML documents accompanied by DTDs. We demonstrate that our approach reduces number of join operations while executing queries. User will be able to perform query on the XML data stored in XEDY and also be able to extract the XML data stored in the RDBMS without loss of information. We evaluate the performance of the proposed system in term of insertion and extraction speed and database storage requirement.

1 Introduction

The eXtensible Markup Language (XML) is quickly becoming popular for exchanging and representing data over the Internet. An important question is what is the best way of storing XML documents since the performance of the underlying storage representation has a significant impact on query processing efficiency. Recently, several projects have proposed alternative strategies for storing XML data in a database system. There are basically three alternatives for storing XML data: in semi-structured databases , in object-oriented databases, and in relational systems. This paper presents XEDY (**X**ml **E**nabled **D**atabase **SY**stem), a visual XML data management system built on top of a commercial relational database management system.

Since an XML document is an example of semistructured data, an obvious question is – why not use semistructured database to store this data in lieu of relational DBMS. While this approach will clearly work, we transform the XML data to relational tuples for the following reasons: First, though there has been increasing research in XML data management, development of a full-fledged commercial XML data management system for managing very large volumes of XML data is still in its infancy. On the other hand, twenty years of work invested in relational database technology has made it commercially very successful and ensured simplicity, stability and expressiveness. As relational databases are prevalent in most commercial companies, no additional costs are incurred. Furthermore, RDBMSs are capable of storing and processing large volumes of data (up to terabytes) efficiently. Second, state-of-the-art query optimization

K. Bauknecht, A Min Tjoa, G. Quirchmayr (Eds.): EC-Web 2003, LNCS 2738, pp. 270–280, 2003.

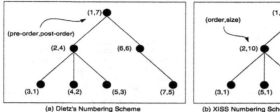 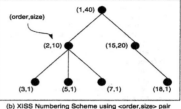

(a) Dietz's Numbering Scheme   (b) XISS Numbering Scheme using <order,size> pair

Fig. 1. Dietz's and XISS Numbering Scheme

and query processing algorithms still rely on relational model. However, algorithms for equivalent efficiency and ease-of-use, but designed for XML, are more difficult to find [11]. In fact, special-purpose XML query processors are not mature enough to process large volumes of data [11]. Third, by using a standard commercial relational database systems, we can exploit the concurrency access and crash recovery features of an RDBMS.

In XEDY, we first generate a relational schema. Second, we parse *DTD-conscious* XML documents and load them into tuples of relational tables in a standard commercial DBMS. Hereafter, in this paper a *DTD-conscious* XML document implies a valid XML document or XML document that satisfies a DTD. XEDY also supports a visual XML-based query interface. Through the interface, DTD structures of stored XML documents are displayed, and users can formulate queries by clicking the relevant data elements and entering conditions. Such queries are specified in a language similar to XQuery [7] and are transformed into SQL queries over the corresponding relational data. The results are formatted as XML documents (if necessary) and returned back to the user. Users will also be able to extract XML documents stored in the database without loss of information. In this paper, we only focus on the storage and extraction of XML data in XEDY. Observe that XEDY creates an illusion of a fully XML-based data management system as the underlying relational system remains hidden from the users.

The rest of this paper is organized as follows. Section 2 discusses the framework for our design of database schema. In Section 3, we present the database schema for storing DTD-conscious XML data. We evaluate the performance of XEDY in term of insertion and extraction speed and database storage requirement in Section 4. We discuss related research in storing XML data in relational environment in Section 5. Finally, the last section concludes the paper.

2 Preliminaries

XML data objects are commonly modeled by a tree structure, where nodes represent elements, attributes and text data, and parent-child node pairs represent nesting between XML data components. To speed up the processing of regular path expression queries, it is important to be able to quickly determine

```
<?xml version="1.0"?>
<addressbook>
    <record>
        <name>Sherlock</name>
        <tel>8273483</tel>
        <email>holmes@barker.org</email>
    </record>
    <record>
        <name>Jane</name>
        <email>jane@domain.com</email>
    </record>
</addressbook>
```

(a) Sample XML Document

```
<!ELEMENT addressbook (record+)>
<!ELEMENT record (name, tel?, email?)>
<!ELEMENT name (#PCDATA)>
<!ELEMENT tel (#PCDATA)>
<!ELEMENT email (#PCDATA)>
```

(b) Sample DTD for the XML Document

Fig. 2. Sample XML document and the DTD

ancestor-descendant relationship between any pair of nodes in the hierarchy of XML data [10]. A suitable *number scheme* of the tree nodes may be used to address this issue. Hence, in this section we address some of the numbering schemes proposed in the research literature [10] for storing tree structured data. In the next section, we will present our own numbering scheme.

2.1 Dietz's Numbering Scheme

Dietz's numbering scheme uses tree traversal order to determine the ancestor-descendant relationship between any pair of tree nodes [8]. According to Dietz: *For two given nodes x and y of a tree T, x is an ancestor of y if and only if x occurs before y in the preorder traversal of T and after y in the postorder traversal.* For example, consider a tree in Figure 1(a) whose nodes are annotated by Dietz's numbering scheme. Each node is labeled with a pair of preorder and postorder numbers. Based on Dietz's scheme, node (1,7) is an ancestor of node (5,3), because node (1,7) comes before node (5,3) in the preorder (i.e., 1<5) and after node (5,3) in the postorder (i.e., 7>3). The ancestor-descendant relationship can be determined in constant time, using this approach, by examining the preorder and postorder numbers of tree nodes. The disadvantage of this approach of number is that it lacks flexibility. All the number of the tree nodes will need to be recomputed when a new node is inserted.

2.2 XISS Numbering Scheme

To get around the problem posed by Dietz's numbering scheme, Li and Moon proposed a new numbering scheme in XISS (XML Indexing and Storage System)[10]. The XISS numbering scheme uses an *extended preorder* and a *size*. The extended preorder will allow additional nodes to be inserted without reordering and the size determines the possible number of descendants.

The XISS numbering scheme associates each node with a pair of number $< order, size >$ and the two conditions that applies to this scheme are as follows: (1) For a tree node y and its parent x, $order(x) < order(y)$ and $order(y) + size(y) <= order(x) + size(x)$. In other words, interval $[order(y), order(y) +$

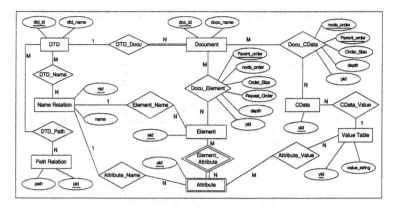

Fig. 3. The XEDY ER Diagram

$size(y)]$ is contained in interval $[order(x), order(x)+size(x)]$. (2) For two sibling nodes x and y, if x is the predecessor of y in preorder traversal, $order(x) + size(x) < order(y)$. An example of the XML tree created by XISS numbering scheme is shown in Figure 1(b).

Compared to Dietz's numbering Scheme, XISS numbering scheme is more flexible and can deal with dynamic up-dates of XML data more efficiently. Since extra spaces can be reserved in the extended preorder to accommodate future insertion, global reordering is not necessary until all the reserved spaces are consumed. On the other hand, Li and Moon did not highlight on how much extra space to allocate. Allocating too little extra space will leads to the ineffectiveness of the numbering scheme and allocating too much extra space may eventually leads to very large numbers being assigned to nodes for very large XML document. Furthermore, if there exists a DTD then it may not be necessary to reserved space for all nodes in the XML tree. Future insertion/deletion in such DTD-conscious XML document is guided by the constraints imposed by the DTD. This lead us to propose a *modified* numbering scheme which we shall discuss in the next section.

3   Database Design of XEDY

In this section, we discuss the design of database schema for storing DTD-conscious XML data in XEDY. We begin our discussion with XEDY-numbering scheme which we will be using in the relational schema design.

3.1   XEDY Numbering Scheme

Our new numbering scheme is an extension of XISS numbering scheme. The proposed numbering scheme will make use of the DTD (Document Type Definition) of the XML documents to generate the appropriate extended preorder

Table 1. Entities, Relationship, and Attributes in XEDY ER Diagram

Entities	
DTD	represents the DTD of XML document
Document	represents the XML document
Element	represents elements in the XML document
Attribute	represents attributes in the XML document
CData	represents the text data contained in the XML document
NameRelation	store all distinct element names and attributes names in XML documents
PathRelation	store all possible distinct paths in the XML DTD
ValueTable	stores all value_string in the XML document
Attributes	
dtd_id	A unique id for each DTD stored in XEDY
dtd_name	DTD name
docu_id	Unique identifier of XML document
docu_name	stores the XML document name
eid	An unique identifier of an element name
aid	An unique identifier of an attribute name
cid	Unique identifier for CData in the XML document
nid	Identifier of a node in the XML tree
name	Stores the names of element or attribute
pid	Unique identifier of a path in DTD
path	The path in a DTD
vid	A unique identifier of the value stored in Value relation
value_string	Store the text data of elements or attributes in the XML document
order	stores the node_order of an Element entity
parent_order	the node_order of the current node's parent
node_order	stores the order of a node generated by XEDY numbering scheme
order_size	calculated from the sum of the order and the size generated by XEDY number scheme
repeat_order	stores the order of the same element name repeating under the same parent
depth	stores the depth of current node in the XML tree

and a size. In order to allocate the additional space meaningfully, the DTD of the XML document will be parsed and used to determine the amount of extra spaces to be reserved. This will result in a numbering scheme that is not only flexible but also meaningful. Specifically, the number of nodes to be inserted depends on the *cardinality* of the element. For instance, for each element with cardinality *optional* (?) in the DTD the maximum number of times this element may appear in the document at any given time is once. Similarly elements with cardinality of *ZeroToMany* (*) or *OneToMany* (+) in the DTD results arbitrary number of insertions of such element in the XML document. For example, consider the XML data in Figure 2. It is evident that the element *addressbook* can have one or more children (*record* elements). Hence, it is necessary to reserve space for future insertion of additional *record* elements. However, we cannot predict the exact amount of additional space for *addressbook*. Now consider the element *record*. This element can have at the most three children (*name*, *tel*, and *email*). Hence, we may reserve space for at the most three nodes for the children of each *record* node. Note that without the existence of DTD it is not possible to guarantee that a *record* element shall always have at the most three children.

3.2 XEDY Schema

We now discuss the database schema for storing DTD-conscious XML data in XEDY. Our schema is designed based on consideration of the following issues: (1) *Generic schema:* The XML documents are modeled in our system by a generic relational schema, which is independent of any particular instance of XML data.

Table 2. The normalized XEDY database schema

DTD (dtd_id, dtd_name)
DTD_Name_Relation (dtd_id, *nid*)
Path_Relation (pid, path)
DTD_Path (dtd_id, *pid*)
CData(cid, *vid*)
Name_Relation (nid, name)
Attribute(aid, *nid*, *vid*)
Element (eid, *nid*)
Value_Table (vid, value_string)
Element_Attri (*eid*, *aid*, node_order, pid)
XML_Docu (docu_id, docu_name, *dtd_id*)
Docu_CData(*docu_id*, *cid*, node_order, parent_order, order_size, node_depth, *pid*)
Docu_Element(*docu_id*, *eid*, node_order, parent_order, order_size, repeat_order, *pid*, node_depth)

(2) *Storage of DTD information:* We store DTD of the documents as it can be used to expedite query processing. (3) *Preservation of document order:* As XML data may be ordered and commercial RDBMS are optimized for unordered relational model, we have implemented a mechanism so that document order is captured in the RDBMS. We achieve this by treating order as a data value. Note that this is particularly important for reconstruction of the XML documents from the tuples as well as for evaluation of order-based functionalities of XQuery [7] (such as BEFORE and AFTER operators, *range* predicates, and numeric literals). (4) *String and numeric data:* It is also necessary to distinguish between string and numeric data in XML data. Currently, for our prototype system we do not distinguish between these two types of data. But our design is flexible enough to be extended to store different types of data. (5) *Lossless extraction of XML document:* Finally, when XML data is stored in relational systems, the original structure of the XML documents may be fragmented in multiple relations. Hence, it is necessary to be able to extract the original document without any loss of information.

Figure 3 depicts the ER diagram of the database. The semantics of the entities and attributes is summarized in Table 1. The database schema is shown in Table 2. The underlined and italics attribute names indicate the primary keys and foreign keys respectively. Observe that the DTD of a set of XML documents is represented by the entities *DTD*, *NameRelation*, and *PathRelation* in Figure 3. The remaining entities represent XML documents.

The *Element* relation in Figure 2 represents the elements in the XML document and is identified by its *eid* and *element_name*. Note that the same *element_name* may exists in different XML documents having different DTDs. The attributes of the relation *Docu_Element*, uniquely identify each element in a specific XML document. Each element will have a different *node_order* generated by the XEDY numbering scheme (extended preorder) and the *order_size* is calculated from the sum of the extended preorder and the size generated by the XEDY numbering scheme. This will save computational cost for queries to determine ancestor-descendent relationships by reducing the number of join operations. The *parent_order* is the *node_order* of the current element's parent and it enables the parent of an element to be determined efficiently with-

Table 3. The de-normalized XEDY database schema

Docu_CData (cid, docu_id, parent_order, node_order, order_size, node_depth, value_string, pid)
Docu_Element (eid, docu_id, nid, parent_order, node_order, order_size, repeat_order, node_depth, pid)
DTD (dtd_id, dtd_name)
DTD_Name_Relation (dtd_id, nid)
Element_Attri (aid, docu_id, eid, nid, value_string, node_order, pid)
Name_Relation (nid, name)
Path_Relation (pid, path, dtd_id)
Xml_Docu (docu_id, docu_name, dtd_id)

Table 4. Ten Samples of XML Documents

S/N	File Name	Filesize	Num. of Element	Num. of Atttributes	Num. of CData	Total Nodes	Max Depth
1	allelements.xml	112 KB	1897	936	1993	4826	3
2	dream.xml	144 KB	3361	0	2895	6256	6
3	r_and_j.xml	216 KB	5081	0	4279	9360	6
4	hamlet.xml	276 KB	6636	0	5574	12210	6
5	a_and_c.xml	308 KB	6347	0	5182	11529	6
6	1998statistics.xml	640 KB	27080	0	25639	52719	6
7	quran.xml	900 KB	6709	0	7449	14158	5
8	nt.xml	1.0 MB	8577	0	8765	17342	5
9	bom.xml	1.47 MB	7656	0	7870	15526	6
10	ot.xml	3.32 MB	25317	0	25963	51280	6

out performing a join. The *pid* attribute in *Docu_Element*, *Docu_CData* and *Element_Attri* relations in Figure 2 stores the identifiers of the paths in DTD (*PathRelation*) required to traverse to this element in the XML document. Storing such identifier of the element will save the need to perform numerous joins for evaluating parent child relationships in a path expression. For example, consider the XML document in Figure 2. From the DTD we can generate a set of paths such as *addressbook.record*, *addressbook.record.name*, *addressbook.record.name.tel*, *addressbook.record.name.email* etc. These paths are stored in the *PathRelation*. Then, the path *addressbook.record[2]* in the XML document is an instance of the path *addressbook.record* and takes us to the second element *record* (stored in *Docu_Element*). The unique identifier of the path *address.record* is stored in the *pid* field of *Docu_Element* table for the element *record*. Since the element is the second record in the document, the *repeat_order* field contains the value "2" for this element. Observe that we maintain the order of XML elements by treating order as a data value of *repeat_order* attribute. Note than in order to retrieve the second child of *addressbook* in a query, we do not need to perform joins to verify the parent-child relationship. We can straight away find it by matching the path identifier of *addressbook.record* in *PathRelation* with the one in the *Docu_Element* table.

Observe that an XML document is fragmented over a number of relations in the normalized database as shown in Figure 3. Consequently, this will involve more number of joins while query processing. To speed up the query processing we now de-normalize the database schema. This will result in lesser number of joins while processing database queries. The tables, *DTD_Path* and *Path_Relation*, were combined together to produce the new table *Path_Relation* (Figure 3). This will result in reduction in number of joins when querying for the path of a particular DTD. The following three tables, *Element*, *Attribute* and *CData* were also combined with the tables, *Docu_Element*, *Element_Attri* and *Docu_CData*, respectively. This will result in minimum number of joins when querying an element, attribute or character data. The table *Value_Table* is eliminated and its field, *value_string* is integrated into the *Docu_CData* table and *Element_Attri* table. This is because the value string is not always duplicated in many XML documents and there is little redundancy incurred in keeping the *value_string* of each *CData* and attribute on its own table. Therefore, it is not worthwhile storing the *value_string* in a separate table and requiring a table join to retrieve the *value_string*. Storing the *value_string* in the tables *Element_Attri* and *Docu_Element* do not create the problem of inconsistency because the values of each character data and attribute applies only to itself. Updating its own value does not require the updating of the value of other character data or attributes. Table 3 depicts the de-normalized XEDY database schema.

4   Experimental Results

We have implemented XEDY entirely in Java 1.4.0. We used Apache's Xerces DOM parser [1] for parsing XML document. We used Wutka's DTDParser [3] for parsing the DTD. MySQL is being used as our prototype RDBMS. The experiments were performed on a Pentium 4, 1.7 GHz with 256 MB RDRAM. We also create appropriate indexes on the relations to expedite query processing. A group of ten XML documents from *Cafe con Leche XML News and Resources* [4] was selected based on their difference in file size, the total number of nodes and the height of the XML documents (Table 4).

Figure 4(a) shows the insertion and extraction time of XML data in normalized (N) and de-normalized(DN) databases. Observe that insertion requires a much longer time compared to extraction. This is because the insertion process requires querying the database for duplicate *element_name* or *value_string* each time before a new node is to be inserted. If a duplicate is found, its primary key will be used as a foreign key in inserting the new node. If no duplicate was found, the *element_name* or *value_string* will be inserted as a new data and its primary key used as a foreign key in inserting the new node. Extraction process only requires querying the database to retrieve the data, it need not check for duplicates and therefore it is faster. From Figure 4(a), it is also not difficult to see that the number of nodes plays a larger role, as compared to its file size, in determining the speed of insertion and extraction. This is due to the increased number of queries that is performed during insertion and extraction.

It is also observed that the insertion time for the de-normalized database schema is much faster, as compared to the normalized database schema. This is due to the way the insertion of XML data is carried out. The normalized database schema has more tables to be inserted. The data on some tables are dependant on other tables. For example, in order to insert the table *Docu_CData*, the other two tables, *CData*, *Value_Table* must be inserted and their primary keys, *cid* and *vid* obtained and inserted as foreign keys in the *Docu_CData* table. This

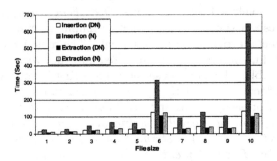

(a) XML Insertion and Extraction Speed Comparison

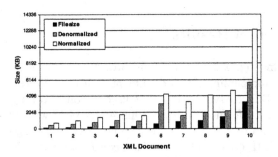

(b) Storage Space Comparison.

Fig. 4. Experimental Results

problem does not exist in the de-normalized database as these three tables were combined into a single table *Docu_CData*. For the normalized database, the insertion of a single XML text data requires two more insertions into the two tables and two more queries to retrieve the primary key of the data inserted, as compared to the de-normalized database. For similar reasons, the extraction time from the de-normalized database is again faster compared to the normalized database.

Figure 4(b) compares the storage space requirement for normalized (N) and de-normalized (DN) databases compared to the XML files. It is observed that the storage space requirement for the de-normalized database is smaller (lesser number of tables and index files) and thus more efficient in database storage space compared to the normalized database. This is due to the greater number of tables in the de-normalized database schema.

5 Related Work

Recently, there has been considerable research effort made by the database research community on storing and querying XML data using relational database systems. Several commercial DBMSs such as Microsoft SQLServer [6], Oracle [5], and IBM's DB2 [4] have supported some features for storing and querying XML documents. In [9], Florescu and Kossman evaluated several alternative mappings for storing XML documents in a relational database system without using DTD. In this approach, XML documents are represented as graph structures and a relational databases is created to store such graph structures as *element* and *values*. Yoshikawa and Amagasa [14] proposed the XRel approach which stores XML data in four tables: *Path, Element, Text*, and *Attribute* tables. This approach stores the information about each node and path information from the root to each node in relational database. Our approach differs from these in the following ways: First we store the DTD as well as the content of XML documents. Second, our mapping technique handles query effectively by reducing the number of join operations. Third, none of these studies consider order of XML elements comprehensively. In fact, only Tatarinov et al. [13] considers storage and querying of ordered XML in relational environment.

Shanmugasundaram et al.[12] proposed an automatic approaches to generate relational schema from XML DTDs. The relations are generated based on the DTD after simplification process. A separate table is used to capture the set-containment relationship between an element and a set of children elements with the same tag. An element can appear only once in its parent is inlined as a column of the table representing its parent. Different DTD may result different relations in the relational database. This approach may generate large number of relations depending on the structure of DTD. XEDY approach differs from this approach in the following ways: First, although we store DTD as well as the content of XML documents, our schema is independent of the structure of DTD. That is, our schema is generic and does not depend on the structure of XML documents. Second, unlike XEDY, this approach does not consider order of XML elements comprehensively.

6 Conclusion

In this paper, we present how DTD-conscious XML data can be stored in XEDY, a visual XML data management system built on top of a commercial relational database management system. This system will parse in the XML document together with its DTD, index the XML data, transform them from XML to relations and stored them into a relational database. User will be able to perform query on the XML data stored and also be able to extract the XML data stored in the RDBMS as XML document without loss of information. Finally, a we evaluate the performance of the proposed system in term of insertion and extraction speed and database storage requirement. As part of future work, we wish to compare the performance of XEDY with other contemporary systems as far as storage and query processing are concerned.

References

[1] Apache Java Parser. http://xml.apache.org/xerces-j/
[2] Cafe con Leche XML News and Resources.
http://www.ibiblio.org/xml/examples/
[3] DTD Parser. http://www.wutka.com/dtdparser.html
[4] IBM DB2 XML Extender.
www4.ibm.com/software/data/db2/extenders/xmlext/.
[5] Oracle XML SQL Utilities. http://ont.oracle.com/tech/xml/oracle_xsu/
[6] Microsoft SQL Server 2000 Books Online, XML and Internet Support.
[7] XQuery 1.0: An XML Query Language.
www.w3.org/TR/2001/WD-xquery-20011220.
[8] PAUL F. DIETZ. Maintaining order in a linked list. *In Proceedings of the Fourteenth Annual ACM Symposium on Theory of Computing*, pp.— 122-127, San Francisco, California, May 1982.
[9] D. FLORESCU, D. KOSSMANN. Storing and Querying XML Data using an RDMBS. *IEEE Data Engineering Bulletin*, 22(3):27-34(1999).
[10] Q. LI, B. MOON. Indexing and Querying XML Data for Regular Path Expressions. *Proceedings of the 27th International Conference on Very Large Databases (VLDB 2001)*, pp. 361-370, Roma, Italy, 2001.
[11] I. MANOLESCU, D. FLORESCU, D. KOSSMANN ET AL. Agora: Living with XML and Relational *Proceedings of the 26th International Conference on Very Large Databases (VLDB 2000)*, Cairo, Egypt, 2000.
[12] J. SHANMUGASUNDARAM, K. TUFTE, C. ZHANG, ET AL. Relational Databases for Querying XML Documents: Limitations and Opportunities. *Proceedings of the 25th International Conference on Very Large Databases (VLDB 1999)*, pp. 302-314, Edinburgh, Scotland, 1999.
[13] I. TATARINOV, S. D. VIGLAS, K. BEYER, J. SHANMUGASUNDARAM ET AL. Storing and Querying Ordered XML Using a Relational Database System. *Proceedings of the SIGMOD 2002*, Madison, Wisconsin, 2002.
[14] M. YOSHIKAWA, T. AMAGASA, T. SHIMURA, S. UEMURA. XRel: a path-based approach to storage and retrieval of XML documents using relational databases. *ACM Transactions on Internet Technology (TOIT), Volume 1, Issue 1*, August 2001.

Efficient Maintenance of XML Views
Using View Correspondence Assertions

Vânia Maria Ponte Vidal[1] and Marco Antonio Casanova[2]

[1] Dept. Computação, Universidade Federal do Ceará
Fortaleza, CE – Brasil
vvidal@lia.ufc.br
[2] Dept. Informática, PUC-Rio
Rio de Janeiro, RJ – Brasil
casanova@fplf.org.br

Abstract. The eXtended Markup Language (XML) has quickly emerged as the universal format for publishing and exchanging data on the Web. As a result, data sources often export XML views over base data. These views may be materialized to achieve faster data access. The main difficulty with this approach is to maintain the consistency of the materialized view with respect to changes of base data. In this paper, we propose an algorithm for the incremental maintenance of XML views. Our algorithm uses the view correspondence assertions for checking the relevance, for the view, of a base update and computes the changes needed for propagating the update to the view.

1 Introduction

Over the last years, the Web has become the largest environment capable of providing access to heterogeneous data sources and XML came to be the standard for the representation and exchange of data over the Web. As a result, data sources often export XML views over base data [3], [6]. The exported view can be either virtual or materialized. Materialized views improve query performance and data availability, but they must be updated in order to reflect changes in the base source.

Basically, there are two strategies for materialized view maintenance: re-materialization and incremental maintenance. In the re-materialization strategy, view data is re-computed at pre-established times. By contrast, in the incremental maintenance strategy, a mechanism periodically modifies view data to reflect updates to local sources. Incremental view maintenance proved be an effective solution [1], [5].

The view maintenance problem has been extensively studied for relational and object-oriented databases [1], [4], [7], [8], [9]. Abiteboul at al [2] proposed an incremental maintenance algorithm for materialized views over semi-structured data, considering the graph-based data model OEM and the query language Lorel. El-Sayed at al [5] proposed an algebraic solution approach based on the XAT XML algebra.

K. Bauknecht, A Min Tjoa, G. Quirchmayr (Eds.): EC-Web 2003, LNCS 2738, pp. 281–291, 2003.
© Springer-Verlag Berlin Heidelberg 2003

In this paper, we propose an algorithm for the incremental maintenance of XML views that uses view correspondence assertions, which define relationships between the view schema and the base data source. We show how to analyze these assertions, at view definition time, to generate information that is used, at run time, to propagate updates to the base data sources to the materialized view. The use of this information brings significant advantage to our approach, when compared to previous approaches to XML view maintenance.

This paper is organized as follows. Section 2 reviews basic concepts and introduces the graphical notation used to represent XML schema types. Section 3 discusses the process of generating view correspondence assertions. Section 4 presents the algorithm for the incremental maintenance of XML views.

2   XML Fundamentals

We adopt a graphical notation [10] to represent the types of a XML schema S. Briefly, the notation uses a tree-structured representation for the types of S, where bold fonts denote the name of the type, "&" denotes references, "@" denotes attributes and "*" denotes multiple occurrences of an element.

Figure 1 shows the types of a XML schema *Bib*, where:

- Tbib is the type of the root element and contains a books element of type Tbooks, an authors element of type Tauthors, and an articles element of type Tarticles;
- Tauthors contains a sequence of zero or more author elements of type Tauthor;
- Tauthor contains the attribute email and the elements name and area. The type ID, specified for the attribute email, allows a unique identification to be associated with each author element;

The attribute author_ref of Tbook contains a reference to an author element of type Tauthor (&Tauthor).

A *link* represents a relationship between XML Types. There is a link from type T_1 to type T_2 iff: (i) T_1 contains an element e whose type is T_2, denoted e $:T_1 \rightarrow T_2$; (ii) T_2 contains an element e whose type is T_1, denoted e $^{-1}:T_1 \rightarrow T_2$; (iii) T_1 contains an element e whose type is a reference $\&T_2$ to T_2, denoted e $\rightarrow:T_1 \rightarrow T_2$; (iv) T_2 contains an element e whose type is a reference $\&T_1$ to T_1, denoted $(e \rightarrow)^{-1}:T_1 \rightarrow T_2$.

We adopt an extension of XPATH that permits navigating through a reference link. The result of a path expression is a sequence of nodes or primitive values.

Let e$\rightarrow:T_1 \rightarrow T_2$ be a reference link. Given an instance $\$e_1$ of T_1, the path expression $\$e_1/e \rightarrow$ returns all instances of T_2 referenced in $\$e_1/e$.

Conversely, given an instance $\$e_1$ of T_1, the path expression $\$e_1/1^{-1}$ returns the instance $\$e_2$ of T_2 such that $\$e_1$ in $\$e_2/1$.

Instances of a type T_1 can be related with instances of a type T_n through the composition of two or more links. Consider links $l_i:T_i \rightarrow T_{i+1}$, for i=1,...,n-1, where T_i are types of an XML schema. Therefore $\delta = l_1/ l_2 /.../ l_{n-1}$ is a path of T_1. Given an instance $\$e$ of T_1, the path expression $\$e/\delta$ selects a set of elements of type T_n. Hence, the type T_δ of the path δ is T_n.

3   Specifying View Correspondence Assertions

In general, we propose to define a view with the help of a *view schema*, as usual, and a set of *view correspondence assertions* [10], instead of the more familiar approach of defining a query on the data sources. These assertions axiomatically specify how view objects are synthesized from data source objects.

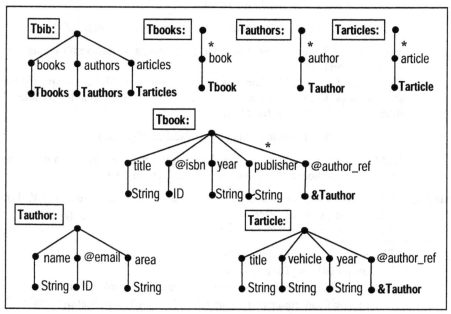

Fig. 1. Graphical representation for the *Bib* XML Schema

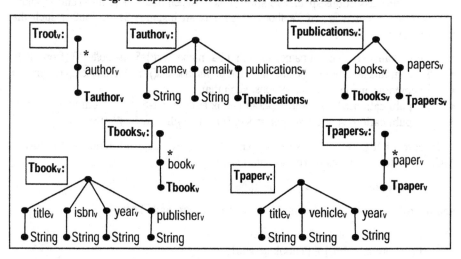

Fig. 2 XML Schema for view V

We exemplify the process, described in [10], for generating the correspondence assertions by matching the schemas V and Bib, represented in Figures 1 and 2. In what follows, let \$V, \$bib be global variables corresponding to the XML documents that represent V and Bib, respectively.

The matching process is top down and consists of two steps:

Step 1: We first match the primary elements of V. For example, the *global collection correspondence assertion* (GCCA) [10]:

$$\Psi_1: [\$V/author_v] \equiv [\$bib/authors/author[\ area = \text{“Database”}]]$$

specifies that \$V/author_v and \$bib/authors/author[area = "Database"] denote the same set of real world objects.

Then, we define *matching correspondence assertions* (MCAs) to specify the criteria for performing the matching of elements in two semantically related collections. For example, the MCA

$$\Psi_2:[Tauthor_v, \{email_v\}] \equiv [Tauthor, \{@email\}]$$

specifies that an author \$a_v in \$V/author_v matches an author \$a in \$bib/authors/author iff \$a_v/email_v/text()=\$a/@email/text().

Step 2: We next specify the correspondence assertions for the sub-elements of V. For example, the *path correspondence assertions* (PCAs) [10], generated by matching the types Tauthor_v and Tauthor:

$\Psi_3: [Tauthor_v/name_v] \equiv [Tauthor/name]$
$\Psi_4: [Tauthor_v/email_v] \equiv [Tauthor/@email]$
$\Psi_5: [Tauthor_v/publications_v/books_v/book_v] \equiv [Tauthor/(Tbook.author\_ref\text{->})^{-1}]$
$\Psi_6: [Tauthor_v/publications_v/papers_v/paper_v] \equiv [Tauthor/(Tarticle.author\_ref\text{->})^{-1}]$

These assertions specify relationships between paths of Tauthor_v and Tauthor.

Given an instance \$a_v of Tauthor_v, if there is an instance \$a of Tauthor such that \$a_v=\$a, then:

- \$a_v contains an element name_v such that \$a_v/name_v/text()=\$a/name/text() (from Ψ_3);
- \$a_v contains an element email_v such that \$a_v/email_v/text()=\$a/@email/text() (from Ψ_4);
- \$a contains an element publications_v such that
- \$a_v/publications_v/books_v/book_v=\$a/(Tbook.author_ref\text{->})^{-1}$ (from Ψ_5)
- \$a_v/publications_v/papers_v/paper_v \equiv \$a/(Tarticle.author_ref\text{->})^{-1}$ (from Ψ_6).

In case of Ψ_5, since Tbook_v is a complex type, we also introduce the following MCA to match instances of Tbook_v with instances of Tbook:

$$\Psi_7: [Tbook_v, \{isbn_v\}] \equiv [Tbook, \{@isbn\}]$$

and the following PCAs, obtained by matching Tbook_v and Tbook:

$\Psi_8: [Tbook_v/title_v] \equiv [Tbook/title]$
$\Psi_9: [Tbook_v /isbn_v] \equiv [Tbook/@isbn]$
$\Psi_{10}: [Tbook_v /year_v] \equiv [Tbook/year]$
$\Psi_{11}: [Tbook_v /publisher_v] \equiv [Tbook/publisher]$

In case of Ψ_6, since Tpaper$_v$ is a complex type, we also introduce the MCA

Ψ_{12}: [Tpaper$_{v,}$ {title$_v$}] $\equiv$ [Tarticle, {title}]

and the following PCAs obtained by matching Tpaper$_v$ and Tarticle:

Ψ_{13}: [Tpaper$_v$/title$_v$] $\equiv$ [Tarticle/title]
Ψ_{14}: [Tpaper$_v$/vehicle$_v$] $\equiv$ [Tarticle/vehicle]
Ψ_{15}: [Tpaper$_v$/year$_v$] $\equiv$ [Tarticle/year].

4   Algorithm for the Incremental Maintenance of XML Views

4.1   Terminology

In this section, we study the maintenance of XML views, defined as follows. Consider V, a view that contains a set of v elements of type Tv, specified by the GCCA

Ψ: [V/v] $\equiv$ [$S/PathExp],

where S is the base source and PathExp= e_1[selExp$_1$]/.../e_n[selExp$_n$], where e_1/.../e_n is a path of the root type of S (Troots), and selExp$_k$, $1 \leq k \leq n$, is a predicate expression [12]. The GCCA Ψ specifies that V/v and S/e_1[selExp$_1$]/.../e_n[selExp$_n$] denote the same set of real world objects. The *sub-elements* of v are specified by the PCA of T$_v$ with Te$_n$ as discussed in Section 3.

Definition 4.1: Let δ_s and δ_p be paths of T$_s$ and T$_p$. We say that δ_s is *semantically related* to δ_p, denoted $\delta_s \equiv \delta_p$, iff there are paths $\delta_{s1},...,\delta_{sn}$, with $\delta_s = \delta_{s1}/.../\delta_{sn}$, and paths $\delta_{p1}, ..., \delta_{pn}$, with $\delta_p = \delta_{p1}/.../\delta_{pn}$, such that

$$[T_s/\delta_{s1}]\equiv[T_p/\delta_{p1}] \text{ and } [T_{si}/\delta_{si+1}]\equiv[T_{pi}/\delta_{pi+1}], 1 \leq i \leq n-1.$$

In the examples of this section, we use *Bib* schema of Figure 1, the view V in Figure 2, and the view correspondence assertions for V, defined in Section 3.

Example 4.1: From PCA Ψ_5:[Tauthor$_v$/publications$_v$/books$_v$/book$_v$] $\equiv$ [Tauthor/(Tbook.author_ref->)$^{-1}$], we have that the path publications$_v$/books$_v$/book$_v$ of Tauthor$_v$ is semantically related to the path (Tbook.author_ref->)$^{-1}$ of Tauthor.

Definition 4.2: Let V be a view specified by the GCCA

$$\Psi: [$V/v]\equiv[$S/e_1[selExp_1] /.../ e_n[selExp_n]].$$

Let $\delta_0 = e_1/.../e_n$ where Tδ_0 = Te$_n$. We say that a path δ of the root type Troots of S *is relevant to* V iff δ satisfies one of the following conditions:
1. δ is a prefix of δ_0,
2. δ is a prefix of δ_0/δ_p, where path δ_p of Tδ_0 is S.R. to the path δ_v of T$_v$ ($\delta_p \equiv \delta_v$)
3. δ is a prefix of δ_p/δ_q, where $\delta_p = e_1/.../e_p$, with p<n, and δ_q is a condition path in selExp$_p$.

Example 4.2: Let $bib/authors/author/(Tbook.author_ref→)^{-1}$ be a path of the root type of the schema Bib (Tbib). From the GCCA

$$\Psi_1:[\$V/author_v]\equiv[\$bib/authors/author[area="Database"]]$$

we have that $\delta_0=\$bib/authors/author$ and $T\delta_0=Tauthor$. Since the path publica-tions$_v$/books$_v$/book$_v$ of Tauthor$_v$ is semantically related to the path $(Tbook.author\_ref→)^{-1}$ of Tauthor (see example 4.1), we have that the path

$$\$bib/authors/author/(Tbook.author\_ref→)^{-1}$$

satisfies condition (2) of Definition 4.2. Thus, the path is relevant to V.

Definition 4.3: Let δ_s and δ_p be paths of T_s and T_p. Suppose that the type $T\delta_s$ of δ_s references the type $T\delta_p$ of δ_p through the link k. Then, we say that δ_s references the path δ_p through k.

Example 4.3: The path $bib/books/book references the path $bib/authors/author through the link   author_ref→. This follows from the fact that Tbook, the type of the path $bib/books/book, references Tauthor, the type of the path $bib/authors/author, through the link author_ref→ .

4.2   The View_Maintainer Algorithm

The View_Maintainer algorithm receives as input the XML source data and an update on base data. As in [2], we describe the algorithm operating on a single update, which can be an insertion, a deletion or a replacement. The insert operation INSERT($target, $child) adds the node $child as a child of $target. The delete operation DELETE($target, $child) removes the node $child, a child of $target. The replace operation removes an existing subtree and adds a new one in its place. We assume that it can be imple-mented as a deletion followed by an insertion.

In outline, the major steps of the View_Maintainer algorithm are:
1.   Obtain all different paths from the root of S to the updated objects that are relevants to V. If no relevant path exists, stop.
2.   For each relevant path δ^* , do
    2.1. Select the updated objects, in δ^*, that are relevant to V. An updated object is *relevant* to V when its new state may cause a change to the state of V.
    2.2. Generate the set of maintenance statements for the relevant objects.
    2.3. Install the maintenance changes in V.

In the following sections we discuss the procedures used in Step 1and 2.

4.3   The Procedure IdentifyRelevantPath

Let $\tau = updateop(\$target, \$child)$ denote an insertion or deletion operation, where $target is a node in $\$S/\delta$ and δ is a path of Troots .

The procedure IdentifyRelevantPaths receives as input a path δ and updated nodes $target and $child and identifies all different paths from the root of S to $child that is relevant to V (see Definition 4.2). Table 1 shows all possible situations that the procedure should verify if a relevant path exists. For each relevant path δ^*, the procedure also obtains the set of all pairs <$t, $c>, where $c is a node in S/δ^* that, as a consequence of the update τ, was deleted or inserted as a child of $t. The set of *updated nodes* in S/δ^*, denoted UpdatedNodes, is also defined in Table 1.

Table 1. Cases of the IdentifyRelevantPath procedure

Case	relevant path (δ^*)	UpdatedNodes
(1) δ/label($child) is relevant to V.	δ / label($child)	{<$target, $child> }
(2) δ references δ_r though k such that δ_r/ k^{-1}/ label($child) is relevant to V.	δ_r / k^{-1}/ label($child)	{<$target, $child> }
(3) δ/ label($child)) references δ_r though *k* such that δ_r / k^{-1} is relevant to V.	δ_r / k^{-1}	{<$t, $child> | $t in $child/*k* }
(4) Exists a path δ_p such that $\delta=\delta_p/\delta_q$ where δ_p references a path δ_r though link k and δ_r/ k^{-1}/ δ_q/ label($child) is relevant to V.	δ_r / k^{-1}/ δ_q/ label($child)	{<$target, $child>}
(5) Exists a path δ_q such that δ/label($child)/$\delta_q$ references a path δ_r though link k and δ_r/k^{-1} is relevant to V.	δ_r / k^{-1}	{<$t, $c> | $c in $child/$\delta_q$ and $t in $c/k}

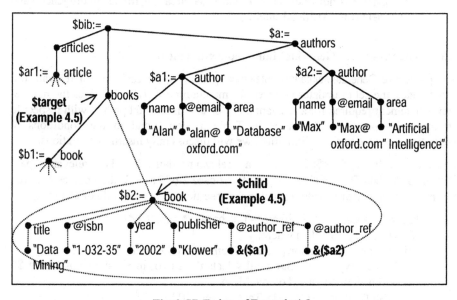

Fig. 3. XML data of Example 4.5

Example 4.5: Suppose that the base update τ=INSERT($target, $child) is applied to the XML data in Figure 3, where $target is a node in $bib/books and $child is the book element b_2. Therefore, the procedure *IdentifyRelevantPath* returns

δ^*= $bib/authors/author/(Tbook.author$_1$_ref $\rightarrow$)$^{-1}$ and
UpdatedNodes={<a_1, b_2>, <a_2, b_2>}.

4.4   The Procedure CheckSelectConditions

The procedure CheckSelectConditions selects the set of pairs <$t, $c> in updatedNodes which are relevant to V. A pair <$t, $c> is relevant to V when the new state of the base source may cause a change to the state of V. By analyzing the CAs of V, we establish, at view definition time, the conditions for efficiently checking the relevance of a given pair of updated nodes in a given relevant path. Table 2 shows the conditions for checking the relevance of a pair <$t, $c> in a relevant path $\delta*$. The cases in Table 2 correspond to the conditions in Definition 4.2 that the relevant path may satisfy.

Example 4.6: Consider the relevant path $bib/authors/author/(Tbook.author_ref$\rightarrow$)$^{-1}$. From the GCCA [$V/author$_v$]$\equiv$[$bib/authors/author[area="Database"]]) we have that δ_0=$bib/authors/author; thus, $bib/authors/author/(Tbook.author_ref$\rightarrow$)$^{-1}$ meets case 2 in Table 2. According to Table 2, a pair of updated nodes <$t, $c> in the relevant path $bib/authors/author/(author_ref$\rightarrow$)$^{-1}$ is relevant to V iff $t/area="Database" or old($t)/area="Database". For the update τ in Example 4.5, where UpdatedNodes={<$a_1,$b_2>,<$a_2,$b_2>}, we have:

1.   <$a_1, $b_2> is relevant to V since $a_1/area="Database" and
2.   <$a_2, $b_2> is not relevant to V, since $a_2/area="Artificial Intelligence" and old($a_2)/area="Artificial Intelligence".

4.5   The Procedure GenerateMaintenanceStatement

The procedure GenerateMaintenanceStatement generates, for each pair of relevant updated nodes, the set of updates required for maintaining V. Table 3 defines the maintenance statement required for a relevant pair <$t, $c> in relevant path $\delta*$ with respect to an insertion operation. The cases in Table 3, correspond to the conditions in Definition 4.2. Due to space limitation, we will discuss only insertion operations.

Example 4.7: Let <$t,$c> be a relevant pair in the relevant path $bib/authors/author/(Tbook.author_ref$\rightarrow$)$^{-1}$. As of case 2 of Table 3, the updates required for the maintenance of V, with respect to the insertion of $c as a child of $t, are:

IF $t/area="Database" and old($t)/area="Database" /* case 2.1 */
{INSERT($target$_v$, $child$_v$) where:
    (i) $target$_v$ =$V/author$_v$[e-mail=$t/email]/publications/books.
    The selExp e-mail=$t/e-mail selects the author in $V/author matching $t, and is defined based on the MCA
    Ψ_2:[Tauthor$_v$, {email$_v$}]$\equiv$[Tauthor, {email}].
    (ii) $child$_v$ is a book$_v$ element generated by call CreateChild("book$_v$", Tbook$_v$, $c, Tbook) which creates, based on the the PCAs of Tbook$_v$ and Tbook, a book$_v$ element corresponding to the book element $c. From the PCAs of Tbook$_v$ and Tbook,   CreateChild("book$_v$", Tbook$_v$, $c, Tbook) returns:
    <book$_v$ ><title$_v$> $c/title/text()</title$_v$>   (from Ψ_8)
    <isbn$_v$> $c/isbn/text() </isbn$_v$>   (from Ψ_9)
    <year$_v$> $c/year/text() </year$_v$>   (from Ψ_{10})
    <publisher$_v$> $c/publisher/text() </publisher$_v$> (from Ψ_{11})

</book$_v$ >}
IF $t/area="Database" and old($t)/area≠"Database" /* case 2.2 */
   {INSERT($V,$child$_v$) where $child$_v$ is an author$_v$ element generated by call
   CreateChild("author$_v$",Tauthor$_v$, $t, Tauthor), which creates, based on the
   the PCAs of Tauthor$_v$ and Tauthor, the author$_v$ element corresponding to the
   author element $t}
IF $t/area≠ "Database" and old($t)/area="Database" /* case 2.3 */
   {DELETE ($V, $childv) where $childv = $V/authorv[e-mail=$t/e-mail]}

Example 4.8: Let τ be the update in Example 4.5. The relevant pair <a_1$, b_2$> in
$bib/authors/author/(Tbook.author_ref→)-1 meets case 2.1 in Example 4.7. The procedure
generates the maintenance statement, INSERT($Target$_v$, $child$_v$) where:

(i) $target$_v$ = $V/author[e-mail="alan@oxford.com"/publications/books
(ii) $child$_v$ = <book$_v$ > <title$_v$> "Data Mining" </title$_v$>
                <isbn$_v$> 1-00305</isbn$_v$> <year$_v$> 2002 </year$_v$>
                <publisher$_v$> Klower </publisher$_v$></book$_v$ >.

The new state of the materialized view V, after the updates, is shown in Figure 4.

5   Conclusions

We proposed an algorithm for the incremental maintenance of XML views using view
correspondence assertions. We showed how to analyze these assertions, at view definition time, to generate information that is used, at run time, to propagate updates to
the base data sources to the materialized view. The use of this information brings significant advantage to our approach, when compared to previous approaches to XML
view maintenance.

Table 2. Checking the relevance of <$t, $c> in the relevant path δ*

Case	Conditions
Case1: δ* is a prefix of δ$_0$, where: (i) δ* = e$_1$/.../e$_p$, p≤n); (ii) $t in S/ e_1$/.../e$_{p-1}$; and (iii) $c in S/ e_1$/.../e$_p$	exists e_1$,...,$e$_{p-2}$, ancestors of $t, where e_k$ in S/e_1$/.../e$_k$, 1≤k≤p-2, such that selExp$_k$(e_k$)=true,1≤k≤p-2, and selExp$_{p-1}$($t)=true and selExp$_p$ ($c)=true.

Case2: δ* is a prefix of δ$_0$ /δ$_p$, where:
(i) δ$_p$ = δ$_{p1}$ .../δ$_{pm}$ is S.R. to the path
  δ$_v$ = δ$_{v1}$/ .../δ$_{vm}$ by the PCAs T$_{δ0}$/δ$_{p1}$ ≡T$_v$ /δ$_{v1}$
  and Tδ$_{pi}$ /δ$_{pi+1}$ ≡ Tδ$_{vi}$ /δ$_{vi+1}$, 1≤i≤m-1;
(ii) δ$_{pm}$ = f$_1$/ .../ f$_t$ / f$_{t+1}$/.../ f$_r$; and
(iii) $t in $S/ δ$_0$/ δ$_{p1}$/.../ δ$_{pm-1}$/ f$_1$ /.../ f$_t$, and
  $c in $S/δ$_0$/ δ$_{p1}$/.../δ$_{pm-1}$/ f$_1$/... f$_t$/ f$_{t+1}$, 1≤ t≤ r
	exists e_1$,...,$e$_n$, ancestors of $t, where
	e_1$ in S/e_1$ and e_k$ in e_{k-1}$/e$_k$, 2≤ k≤n , such that
	selExp$_k$(e_k$)=true, 1≤k≤ n-1, and
	(selExp$_n$(e_n$)=true or selExp$_n$(old($e$_n$)[*]) = true).
	
	[*] old(e_n$)) refers the old state of e_n$

Case3: δ* is a prefix of δ$_p$/δ$_q$ where (i) δ$_p$ = e$_1$/.../ e$_p$, p<n, and (ii)δ$_q$ is a condition path in selExp$_p$	exists e_1$,...,$e$_p$, ancestors of $t, such that e_k$ in S/e_1$/.../e$_k$, 1≤k≤n, and selExp$_k$($e$_k$)=true , 1≤k≤ p-1

Table 3. Maintenance statements for insertions operations (INSERT($t, $c))

Case	Maintenance Statements

Case 1 (as in Table 2)	FOR en in $c / e_{p+1}[selExp_{p+1}]/.../e_n[selExp_n]$ DO
	    INSERT($target_v$, $child_v$) where:
	        $target_v = V and $child_v = CreateChild^{(*)}$ ("v", T_v, e_n, $T_{\delta o}$)
	(*)creates an element v corresponding to e_n

Case 2 (as in Table 2)	Case 2.1: selExp_n(e_n) = true and selExp_n(old(e_n)) = true
	FOR f_r in $c / f_{t+2}/.../ f_r$ DO
	    {INSERT($target_v$, $child_v$) where:
	        $child_v$=CreateChild ("v_m", T_{vm}, f_r, T_{fr}) and
	        $target_v = $V/step_0/ step_1/.../ step_{m-1}$ where
	        (i) $step_0 = v[selExp_v]$ (*);
	        (ii) $step_k$, $1 \le k \le m-1$, is defined as follows:
	            IF δ_{vk} is single-valued {$step_k = \delta_{vk}$} ELSE { $step_k = \delta_{vk}[selExp_{vk}]^{(**)}$; }
	(*)selExp_v is defined based on the MCA of T_v with $T\delta_0$. Given the MCA
	    $[T_v, \{y_1, ..., y_t\}] \equiv [T_{\delta 0}, \{x_1, ..., x_t\}]$, selExp_v=[$y_1$= e_n/x_1 AND ... AND y_t=e_n/x_t].
	(**)Given $[T_{\delta vk}, \{y_1, ..., y_t\}] \equiv [T_{\delta pk} \{x_1, ..., x_t\}]$, the MCA of $T_{\delta vk}$ with $T_{\delta pk}$, and
	    p_k the ancestor of $target s.t p_k in $S/\delta_0/\delta_{p1}/.../\delta_{pk}$, then
	    selExp_{vk} = [y_1= p_k/x_1 AND ... AND y_t= p_k/x_t]

	Case 2.2: selExp_n(e_n) = true and selExp_n(old(e_n)) = false INSERT ($V, $child_v$) where $child_v$=CreateChild ("v", T_v, e_n, $T_{\delta o}$)
	Case 2.3: selExp_n(e_n) = false and selExp_n(old(e_n)) = true DELETE ($V, $child_v$) where $child_v = v[selExp_v]$
Case 3 (as in Table 2)	Case 3.1: selExp_p(e_p) = true and selExp_p(old(e_p)) = false For en in $e_p /e_{p+1}[selExp_{p+1}]/.../e_n[selExp_n]$ do INSERT ($V, $child_v$) where $child_v$=CreateChild ("v", T_v, e_n, $T_{\delta o}$)
	Case 3.2: selExp_p(e_p) = false and selExp_p(old(e_p)) = true For en in $e_p /e_{p+1}[selExp_{p+1}]/.../e_n[selExp_n]$ do DELETE ($V, $child_v$) where $child_v = v[selExp_v]$

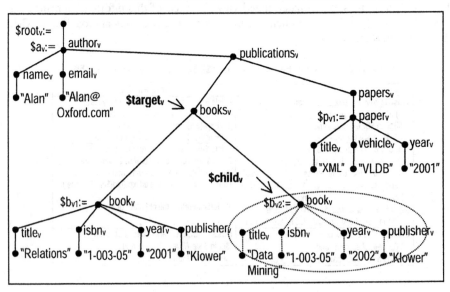

Fig. 4. The new state of the view

References

[1]   Ali, M.A., Fernandes, A.A., Paton, N.W.: Incremental Maintenance for Materialized OQL Views. In Proc. DOLAP (2000) 41–48

[2]   Abiteboul, S., McHugh, J., Rys, M., Vassalos, V., Wiener, J.L.: Incremental Maintenance for Materialized Views over Semistructured Data. In Proceedings of the International Conference on Very Large Databases. New York City (1998) 38-49

[3]   Carey,M.J., Kiernan, J., Shanmugasundaram, J., Shekita, E.J., Subramanian, S.N.: XPERANTO: Middleware for Publishing Object-Relational Data as XML Documents. In *The VLDB Journal*(2000) 646–648

[4]   Ceri, S., Widom, J.: Deriving productions rules for incremental view maintenance. In Proceedings of the International Conference on Very Large Databases (1991) 577-589

[5]   EL-Sayed, M., Wang, L., Ding, L., Rudensteiner, E.: An algebraic approach for Incremental Maintenance of Materialized Xquery Views. In Proceedings of Fourth International Workshop on Web Information and Data Management. McLean, USA (2002)

[6]   Fernandez,M., Morishima, A., Suciu, D., Tan, W.: Publishing Relational Data in XML: the SilkRoute Approach. IEEE Trans on Computers, 44(4). (2001) 1–9

[7]   Gupta, A., Mumick, I.S.: Maintenance of Materialized Views: Problems, Techniques, and Applications. In IEEE Bulletin on Data Engineering, 18(2).(1995)3–18

[8]   Gupta, A., Mumick, I.S., Subrahmanian, V.S.: Maintaining Views Incrementally. In SIGMOD (1993) 157–166

[9]   Kuno, H.A., and Rundensteiner, E.A.: Incremental Maintenance of Materialized Object-Oriented Views in MultiView: Strategies and Performance Evaluation. IEEE Transaction on Data and Knowledge Engineering, 10(5):768–792 (1998)

[10] Vidal, V.M.P., Vilas Boas, R.: A Top-Down Approach for XML Schema Matching. In Proceedings of the 17th Brazilian Symposium on Databases. Gramado, Brazil (2002).

On Verifying
the Internet Open Trading Protocol

Chun Ouyang and Jonathan Billington

Computer Systems Engineering Centre
School of Electrical and Information Engineering
University of South Australia, SA 5095, Australia
Chun.Ouyang@postgrads.unisa.edu.au
Jonathan.Billington@unisa.edu.au

Abstract. The Internet Open Trading Protocol (IOTP) is designed to support a set of electronic transactions that capture common trading activities. The protocol provides reliable trading transaction services that are payment-system independent. To verify IOTP, we use a protocol verification methodology that compares IOTP's service and protocol languages. The service language is generated from the service model specifying only the external behaviour of IOTP, whereas the protocol language is obtained from the protocol model by hiding internal operations of IOTP. Comparing these two languages indicates whether IOTP formally conforms to its service. The initial verification results show that IOTP transactions that are successful, error-free and independent of each other, implement a subset of the service language. We conclude that this subset is a valid implementation of the service and is due to the way IOTP combines messages in some circumstances.

1 Introduction

The *Internet Open Trading Protocol* (IOTP) [7] is being developed by the Internet Engineering Task Force (IETF) to support electronic commerce (e-commerce) over the Internet. The protocol encapsulates different payment systems such as SET [18] and Mondex [12], and provides reliable common transaction services to four trading roles: the Consumer, the Merchant, the Payment Handler and the Delivery Handler. IOTP defines transactions for authentication, deposit, withdrawal, purchase, refund and value exchange. The specification of IOTP, known as Request For Comments 2801 (RFC 2801) [7], is the largest RFC developed by IETF so far, spanning 290 pages. The RFC provides an informal narrative description of IOTP, and is still at an early stage of development as no complete implementation of IOTP yet exists [17, 9].

An important issue in developing a protocol is the verification of its functional correctness. For protocols involving financial transactions, such as IOTP, it is vitally important that they work correctly. We apply a protocol engi-

K. Bauknecht, A Min Tjoa, G. Quirchmayr (Eds.): EC-Web 2003, LNCS 2738, pp. 292–302, 2003.

neering methodology [3] using a formal technique called Coloured Petri Nets[1] (CPNs) [11] to develop models of IOTP at different levels of abstraction. These models constitute formal specifications of IOTP and the service provided to the users of IOTP (i.e., the trading roles), which we refer to as the protocol and service specifications of IOTP, respectively. The verification of IOTP is concerned with proving that the protocol specification provides the requirements stated in its service specification.

As far as we are aware, there is no other work on the verification of IOTP, except our attempts at analysing its functional behaviour. Our work started with the modelling and analysis of just the IOTP Deposit transaction [14]. We then proposed a simplified protocol architecture for IOTP [13]. In [15] we presented a formal specification of the complete set of IOTP transactions. The detailed analysis [15] of transaction termination revealed a lack of synchronization between IOTP protocol entities, and an improved protocol specification has been obtained by removing the detected deficiencies. In parallel with the development of the protocol specification, we have also created a formal service specification for IOTP [16].

This paper extends our previous work [15, 16] by providing the first attempt to verify IOTP against its service. We employ a previously developed protocol verification methodology [5]. Both the service and the protocol languages, which abstractly represent the possible interactions between IOTP protocol entities and trading roles, need to be obtained. The service language is generated from the service model, which specifies the external behaviour of IOTP as seen by its users, whereas the protocol language is derived from the protocol model by hiding internal operations of IOTP. Comparison of these two languages determines whether IOTP formally conforms to its service.

The paper is organised as follows. Section 2 sketches the protocol verification methodology applied to IOTP. Brief introductions to selected parts of the service and protocol definitions of IOTP are given in Section 3 and 4, respectively. Section 5 presents a detailed investigation of the initial verification results for IOTP. Finally, we summarize our contribution and discuss further work in Section 6.

2   Protocol Verification Methodology

Figure 1 shows an abstract model of IOTP operating in a protocol hierarchy. The *IOTP entities* (i.e., the four trading role protocol entities) communicate over the transport medium (e.g., HTTP [8]) to provide the Internet Open Trading Service (IOTS) to *IOTS users* (i.e., the four trading role users). All IOTP entities and the transport medium constitute the *IOTS provider*. *Service primitives* [10] describe interactions between the users and the provider in an implementation

---

[1] CPNs are a state/transition based technique, incorporating concurrency. It has a graphical form with hierarchical constructs, and is suited to the description of distributed systems [4].

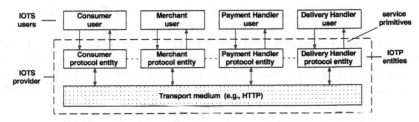

Fig. 1. Abstract model of IOTP and its environment

independent manner. A service specification defines the service primitives and their sequences.

Figure 2 sketches our protocol verification approach for IOTP. There are two parallel paths. The top path is concerned with obtaining the service language. It begins by defining the service provided by IOTP, since no service definition of IOTP is available in RFC 2801 [7]. From the *Service Definition*, a *Service Model* is created using CPNs. In this model, transitions represent service primitive events. The Service CPN Model is used to calculate the *Service State Space* which contains all the possible occurrence sequences of transitions in the Service Model. The Service State Space can be treated as a finite state automaton (FSA) representing the set of global sequences of service primitive occurrences, which we call the Service Language. The Service Language forms the basis against which the protocol is verified.

In the lower path of Fig. 2, the RFC [7] provides the *Protocol Definition* of IOTP that is used to create the *Protocol Model*, also using CPNs. With the Protocol Model, the *Protocol State Space* is calculated and can be used to detect undesired behaviour in the protocol definition. If deficiencies in the protocol model are detected it is modified to remove them. The Protocol State Space of the revised model is interpreted as a FSA that can be reduced by hiding internal operations of IOTP. The *Protocol Language*, which also specifies global primitive sequences, can be generated from the Protocol State Space using automata reduction techniques [2].

Finally, the Service and Protocol Languages are compared using a tool such as FSM [1]. The protocol is a faithful refinement of the service, if the Protocol and Service Languages are equivalent, or if the Protocol Language is an *acceptable* subset of the Service Language.

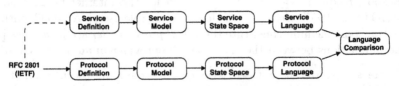

Fig. 2. Steps in our protocol verification methodology

3   Service Definition of IOTP

The Internet Open Trading Protocol (IOTP) provides six reliable transaction services to trading role users. These are *Authentication, Deposit, Withdrawal, Purchase, Refund* and *Value Exchange*, which constitute the Internet Open Trading Service (IOTS). Following the Open System Interconnection (OSI) conventions for defining services [10], the IOTS definition comprises the definition of service primitives and all the possible sequences of primitives. In this section we present a selected part of the IOTS definition that is necessary for understanding our verification results in Sect. 5. A complete definition of IOTS is given in [16].

Each trading transaction service in IOTS is constructed from a set of service modules called *phases*, and service primitives are defined with respect to a certain phase. There are five phases, viz. *Authentication, Offer, Payment, Delivery* and *Cancel*. For example, a Purchase transaction service may consist of an Authentication, an Offer, a Payment and a Delivery phase. The naming conventions needed for primitives is given by *primitive-facility.primitive-type*. The primitive facility identifies a certain feature of the service, such as *Authentication* that allows one trading role (the *Authenticator*) to verify the bona fides of another trading role (the *Authenticatee*). The four primitive types are *request* (req), *indication* (ind), *response* (res) and *confirm* (cnf). Table 1 lists a number of service primitives used in the Authentication, Offer and Payment phases. Note that all trading roles appearing in the primitive description refer to trading role users.

Figure 3 gives two example sequences of primitives in the Offer phase. Each column of the message sequence chart corresponds to a Consumer user (left), a Merchant user (right), or the IOTS provider (middle). Each arrow is labelled by a service primitive. An arrow from the user to the provider represents a primitive (*request* or *response*) being submitted by the user, and an arrow from the

Table 1. Service primitives in Authentication, Offer and Payment phases

Phase	Primitive	Abbr.	Description
Authentication	Authentication.req	areq	Authenticator requests identity information
	Authentication.ind	aind	from Authenticatee via *areq* and *AIND*, and
	Authentication.res	ares	Authenticatee replies with the required
	Authentication.cnf	acnf	information via *ARES* and *acnf*.
	AuthResult.req	arreq	Authenticator notifies Authenticatee of the
	AuthResult.ind	arind	authentication result via *arreq* and *ARIND*.
Offer	TradingOptions.req	toreq	Merchant provides Consumer with available
	TradingOptions.ind	toind	trading options via *toreq* and *TOIND*, and
	TradingOptions.res	tores	*optionally* Consumer replies with his/her
	TradingOptions.cnf	tocnf	trading selection via *TORES* and *tocnf*.
	TradingResult.req	trreq	Merchant informs Consumer about the
	TradingResult.ind	trind	trading result via *trreq* and *TRIND*.
Payment	PayInvoke.req	pireq	Consumer initiates a payment exchange with
	PayInvoke.ind	piind	Payment Handler via *PIREQ* and *piind*.
	PayData.req	pdreq	Payment Handler requests payment-specific
	PayData.ind	pdind	data from Consumer via *pdreq* and *PDIND*,
	PayData.res	pdres	and Consumer replies with the required
	PayData.cnf	pdcnf	payment-specific data via *pdreq* and *PDIND*.
	PayResult.req	prreq	Payment Handler notifies Consumer of result
	PayResult.ind	prind	of payment processing via *prreq* and *PRIND*.

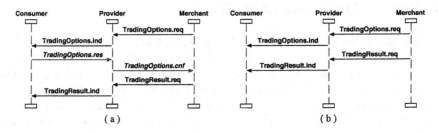

Fig. 3. Primitive sequences in the Offer phase when (a) Merchant asks for Consumer's selection and (b) Merchant does not require the Consumer to reply with its selection

provider to the user represents a primitive (*indication* or *confirm*) being delivered to the user. Fig. 3 indicates the occurrence of *TradingOptions.res* followed by *TradingOptions.cnf* for conveying the Consumer's selection to the Merchant is optional in the Offer phase.

4   Protocol Definition

RFC 2801 [7] provides a definition of IOTP using natural language and diagrams. An introduction to the basic operation of IOTP can be found in [15]. Here we just give a brief introduction to IOTP *document exchanges* and *IOTP messages*, the two concepts to be used in verifying IOTP in Sect. 5. Note that all trading roles appearing in the following description refer to trading role protocol entities.

All six trading transactions are implemented from a set of building blocks called document exchanges. IOTP defines six document exchanges: *Authentication*, *Brand Dependent Offer*, *Brand Independent Offer*, *Payment*, *Delivery*, and *Payment-and-Delivery*. For example, a Purchase transaction comprises an optional Authentication, either a Brand Dependent Offer or a Brand Independent Offer, and finally, a Payment exchange, a Payment followed by a Delivery exchange, or a Payment-and-Delivery exchange.

Transaction information sent between trading roles are encoded in IOTP messages, which are formatted as XML documents [6]. The basic set of IOTP messages designed for trading transactions comprises: *Authentication Request*, *Authentication Response* and *Authentication Status* messages used in an Authentication exchange; *Trading Protocol Options* (TPO), *TPO Selection* and *Offer Response* messages in an Offer exchange; *Payment Request*, *Payment Exchange* and *Payment Response* in a Payment exchange; and *Delivery Request* and *Delivery Response* messages in a Delivery exchange. Apart from these, there are also *Cancel* and *Error* messages for transaction cancellation and error handling, respectively.

5   Verification of the Internet Open Trading Protocol

The CPN service specification [16] and protocol specification [15] of IOTP can be used, respectively, to generate the service language and the protocol language for IOTP. To handle the inherent complexity of IOTP, it is verified incrementally. We start by investigating the basic behaviour of IOTP's six transactions on the assumption that they are successful, error-free and also independent of each other. Taking advantage of the modular construction of both the service and the protocol CPN models, the languages for each of the six transactions can be obtained following the procedure given in Sect. 2. A comparison between the corresponding service and protocol languages determines whether all six transactions conform to the transaction services defined in IOTS. We concentrate on analysing the languages of a Deposit transaction, and briefly discuss the verification results for other transactions.

5.1   Language Comparison for Deposit Transaction

Figure 4 illustrates three FSAs specifying the languages obtained for the verification of a Deposit transaction. In each FSA, the arc labels are the abbreviated service primitive names (see Table 1). Node 0 represents the *initial state*, and nodes drawn with double circles represent *final states*. A primitive sequence leading from the initial state to a final state of a FSA is a sequence *accepted* by that FSA. All the accepted sequences of a FSA constitute the language defined by that FSA. FSA-(a) and FSA-(b) specify the service language and the protocol language for the Deposit transaction, respectively. Comparison of the two languages using FSM [1] shows that the protocol language is a subset of the service language. The primitive sequences, which are in the service but not in the protocol, are represented by FSA-(c).

Service Phases. As mentioned in Sect. 3, each transaction service is provided via a set of phases. A Deposit comprises an optional Authentication, an Offer and a Payment phase. We use FSA-(a) as an example to describe how the three (or two) phases of a Deposit are captured in its service language. In the following the word "subsequence" means the subsequence of primitive occurrences.

- The subsequences defined by nodes (0,8,11-14), (0,8,11,14) and (0,8,10,14) represent the Offer phase at the beginning of the Deposit without Authentication;
- The subsequence defined by nodes (0-5,7) represents the Authentication phase and is followed by the Offer phase subsequences defined by nodes (8,11-14), (8,11,14) and (8,10,14);
- The subsequences defined by nodes (0-6,9,10,14), (0-6,8,11-14), (0-6,8,11,14) and (0-6,8,10,14) represent a small overlap between the Authentication and Offer phases, where the primitives *arind* (in Authentication), *toreq* and *trreq* (both in Offer) occur as interleaving events;

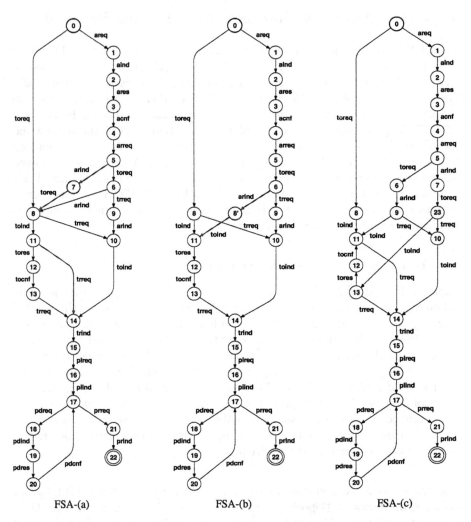

FSA-(a)   FSA-(b)   FSA-(c)

Fig. 4. Three FSAs for the Deposit transaction specifying (a) the service language, (b) the protocol language and (c) the primitive sequences in the service but not in the protocol

- Each subsequence from nodes 15 to 22 represents the Payment phase that completes the Deposit transaction. Subsequences that include nodes (17,18, 21,22,17) represent payment system-specific data exchanges that are only required by a particular payment system (such as SET). This can occur any number of times, catering for various payment systems to be encapsulated by IOTP. From this point of view, we consider IOTP as payment-system independent.

Sequences in the Service but Not in the Protocol. We can derive FSA-(b) from FSA-(a) by: eliminating node 7 and its associated arcs; introducing a new node 8', which duplicates node 8, except that it does not have *trreq* as an output nor *toreq* as an input; and removing the arc labelled *trreq* between nodes 11 and 14 and the arc *arind* between nodes 6 and 8. Closer investigation of each of the missing sequences shows that they cannot be implemented by IOTP due to the restrictions on the procedures of sending IOTP messages given in RFC 2801 [7].

Figure 5 depicts a scenario of how trading role protocol entities (Consumer-PE and Merchant-PE) communicate during an Offer phase when the Merchant User does not require the Consumer User to reply with his/her trading selection. This is implemented by a Brand Independent Offer exchange in IOTP (Sect. 4), where the RFC specifies that the Merchant-PE must send a combined *TPO & Offer Response* message after receiving a *TradingOptions.req* (toreq) followed by a *TradingResult.req* (trreq) from the Merchant User. On receipt of this combined message, the Consumer-PE delivers a *TradingOptions.ind* (toind) and then a *TradingResult.ind* (trind) to the Consumer User. The subsequence defined by nodes (0,8,10,14,15) in both FSA-(a) and FSA-(b) captures this scenario. According to the RFC, the *TPO* and the *Offer Response* messages cannot be sent separately in a Brand Independent Offer exchange. Hence, the subsequence defined by nodes (0,8,11,14,15) in both FSA-(a) and FSA-(c) (capturing the scenario in Fig. 3 (b)) is not implemented by IOTP.

Similarly, the remaining missing subsequences are due to two other combined messages: *Authentication Status & TPO* (in the Authentication and Brand Dependent Offer exchanges) and *Authentication Status & TPO & Offer Response* (in the Authentication and Brand Independent Offer exchanges).

Sequence Calculation. In Fig. 4, nodes 17, 18, 21 and 22 comprise the only cycle of the FSA. By hiding this cycle from each FSA, a limited number of sequences can be calculated for the corresponding language of a Deposit transaction. We can do this for two reasons. Firstly, the subsequences represented by the cycle do not result in any difference between the service and protocol. Secondly, as mentioned before, the subsequences defined by nodes (17,18,21,22,17) represent payment system-specific data exchanges. Hiding these subsequences does

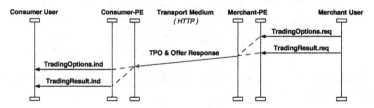

Fig. 5. The Merchant protocol entity sends a combined IOTP message to the Consumer protocol entity to implement the *TadingOptions* service in the Offer phase

not effect the basic functional behaviour of IOTP. These sequences provide the minimum number of sequences for a more abstract view of the Deposit transaction. There are: *10* sequences for the service language (FSA-(a)), *4* sequences for the protocol language (FSA-(b)), and thus *6* sequences in the service but not in the protocol (FSA-(c)). For both FSA-(a) and FSA-(b), the minimum sequence length is *8* for the sequence defined by nodes (0,8,10,14-17,21,22). The maximum sequence length is *16* for the sequence defined by nodes (0-6,8,11,12-17,21,22) in FSA-(a) and by nodes (0-6,8',11,12-17,21,22) in FSA-(b). This indicates that the protocol does preserve the maximum and minimum sequence length specified in the service. Note that FSA-(a) also includes two other sequences, one of length *8* (minimum) and the other of length *16* (maximum).

5.2   Verification Results for Other Transactions

Table 2 lists the statistics of the FSAs representing the service and the protocol languages for three other transactions: Authentication, Purchase and Value Exchange. Each FSA for Purchase has *2* final states, because a Purchase may stop at the end of a Payment phase or a Delivery phase that follows the Payment phase. Due to the current abstraction level in modelling IOTS and IOTP, Withdrawal and Refund transactions are the same as Deposit in terms of transaction procedures, and hence their verification results can be inferred from those for a Deposit transaction. Comparison of the two languages for each transaction shows that only Authentication has identical service and protocol languages. For Purchase or Value Exchange, the protocol language is a subset of the service language. The statistics of the FSA representing the primitive sequences that occur in the service but not in the protocol are given in Table 3.

Analysing the verification results for Purchase and Value Exchange is performed in the same way as for Deposit (Sect. 5.1). A Purchase or a Value Ex-

Table 2. Statistics of IOTS FSA and IOTP FSA for three transactions

Transaction	Language	States	Arcs	Final-states
Authentication	service	7	6	1
	protocol	7	6	1
Purchase	service	46	58	2
	protocol	43	50	2
Value Exchange	service	30	36	1
	protocol	30	34	1

Table 3. Statistics of FSA representing primitive sequences in the service but not in the protocol

Transaction	States	Arcs	Final-states
Purchase	48	61	2
Value Exchange	31	37	1

change starts with an optional Authentication followed by an Offer phase, which is the same as the beginning of a Deposit. Hence, the three combined IOTP messages are also used in Purchase and Value Exchange. A Purchase transaction may also involve a Payment-and-Delivery exchange, which introduces two more combined IOTP messages: *Payment Request & Delivery Request* and *Payment Response & Delivery Response*. Again, these two combined IOTP messages prevent some subsequences of primitives (associated with the Payment and Delivery phases) that occur in the service, from occurring in the protocol.

6   Conclusions

We have presented some initial results of verifying IOTP, with respect to a set of *simple* transactions that are successful, error-free and independent of each other. We have performed a thorough investigation of the verification results for these transactions, and have presented them in detail for the Deposit transaction. Our investigations have shown: 1) the service and protocol languages of the Authentication transaction are equivalent; and 2) for all other transactions, the protocol language is a (proper) subset of the service language, due to IOTP combining messages. We believe that the subset of sequences implemented by the non-Authentication transactions is an *acceptable* refinement of the service, because the subset just eliminates some possible interleavings of primitive events. Further work is required to determine the minimal subset of sequences that would be an acceptable implementation of the service.

The verification of successful and error-free IOTP transactions is the first step in verifying IOTP. In the future, we shall take into account transaction cancellation and error handling procedures, including message retransmissions.

References

[1] AT&T. FSM Library. URL: http://www.research.att.com/sw/tools/fsm.

[2] W. A. Barret and J. D. Couch. *Compiler Construction: Theory and Practice*. Science Research Associates, 1979.

[3] J. Billington. Formal Specification of Protocols: Protocol Engineering. In *Encyclopedia of Microcomputers*, pages 299–314. Marcel Dekker, New York, 1991.

[4] J. Billington, M. Diaz, and G. Rozenberg, editors. *Application of Petri Nets to Communication Networks: Advances in Petri Nets*, volume 1605 of *Lecture Notes in Computer Science*. Springer-Verlag, Berlin, 1999.

[5] J. Billington, M. C. Wilbur-Ham, and M. Y. Bearman. Automated Protocol Verification. In *Protocol Specification, Testing, and Verification, V*, pages 59–70. Elsevier Science Publishers, 1986.

[6] T. Bray, J. Paoli, C. M. Sperberg-McQueen, and E. Maler. *Extensible Markup Language (XML) 1.0 (Second Edition)*. W3C Recommendation, October 2000.

[7] D. Burdett. *Internet Open Trading Protocol - IOTP Version 1.0*. IETF Trade Working Group, April 2000. URL: http://www.ietf.org/rfc/rfc2801.

[8] D. E. Eastlake and C. Smith. *Internet Open Trading Protocol – HTTP Supplement*. IETF Trade Working Group, Sept. 2000. URL: http://www.ietf.org/rfc/rfc2935.

[9] InterPay I-OTP. URL: ftp://ftp.pothole.com/pub/ietf-trade/IETF-London/ InterPay2001London.ppt.

[10] ITU. *Information Technology – Open Systems Interconnection – Basic Reference Model: Conventions for the Definition of OSI Services.* ITU-T Recommendation X.210 | ISO/IEC 10731, November 1993.

[11] K. Jensen. *Coloured Petri Nets. Basic Concepts, Analysis Methods and Practical Use. Vol 1-3.* Monographs in Theoretical Computer Science. Springer-Verlag, 1997.

[12] Mondex. URL: http://www.mondexusa.com/.

[13] C. Ouyang, L. M. Kristensen, and J. Billington. An Improved Architectural Specification of the Internet Open Trading Protocol. In *Proceedings of 3rd Workshop and Tutorial on Practical Use of Coloured Petri Nets and the CPN Tools*, pages 119–137. DAIMI PB-554, University of Aarhus, ISSN 0105-8517, 2001.

[14] C. Ouyang, L. M. Kristensen, and J. Billington. Towards Modelling and Analysis of the Internet Open Trading Protocol Transactions using Coloured Petri Nets. In *Proc of 11th Annual International Symposium of the International Council on System Engineering*, 2001. 8 pages.

[15] C. Ouyang, L. M. Kristensen, and J. Billington. A Formal and Executable Specification of the Internet Open Trading Protocol. In *Proceedings of 3rd International Conference on Electronic Commerce and Web Technologies*, volume 2455 of *Lecture Notes in Computer Science*, pages 377–387. Springer-Verlag, 2002.

[16] C. Ouyang, L. M. Kristensen, and J. Billington. A Formal Service Specification of the Internet Open Trading Protocol. In *Proceedings of 23rd International Conference on Application and Theory of Petri Nets*, volume 2360 of *Lecture Notes in Computer Science*, pages 352–373. Springer-Verlag, 2002.

[17] Hitachi SMILEs. URL: http://www.hitachi.co.jp/Div/nfs/whats_new/ smiles.html.

[18] Visa and MasterCard. *SET Secure Electronic Transaction Specification. Version 1.0. Vol 1-3*, May 1997. URL: http://www.setco.org/set_specifications.html.

Strategies for E-commerce Applications in Tourism

Jürgen Palkoska, Franz Pühretmair, Roland R. Wagner and Wolfram Wöß

Institute for Applied Knowledge Processing (FAW)
Johannes Kepler University Linz, Austria
{jpalkoska,fpuehretmair,rwagner,wwoess}@faw.uni-linz.ac.at

Abstract. Tourism industry has more and more realized the potential of Web-based tourism information systems (TIS) to increase the competitiveness by providing individual and specialized information about tourism objects. This lead to a broad spectrum of tourism information systems distributed over various Web sites. But the described situation is not really satisfying for users of such systems, the tourists, which require flexible and easy-to-use search functionalities and adequate user interfaces. To fulfill the tourists request for an extensive data collection on the one hand and to provide adequate search functionalities on the other hand, it is necessary to make accumulated data from different sources accessible. The integration of distributed data sources has great impact on the quality of tourism information systems and follows the trend not to implement further systems, but to extend and improve existing systems. Beside data integration, in this paper flexible electronic data interchange mechanisms, advanced search functionalities and powerful visualization possibilities are identified as the most important strategies to improve and enhance near future tourism information systems.

1 Introduction

During the last years the introduction of World Wide Web (WWW) based applications has been very successfully especially in the field of tourism electronic commerce and still the turnovers are increasing rapidly. Until now, many Web-based tourism information and reservation systems have been developed. To fulfill the tourists' request for an extensive data collection on the one hand and to provide adequate search functionalities on the other hand, it is inevitable to make accumulated data from different sources accessible. There are a number of approaches that have been investigated so far to realize data access to heterogeneous data sources, for example, IRODB [4], XML-KM [5] and InTouriSME [1]. A further approach is the reference model RMSIG [6], [7], which enables uniform access to and interaction between components of an electronic market based on different specific models.

In general, data access to heterogeneous tourism information systems (TIS) is possible in a twofold way: Firstly, as business-to-consumer (B2C) communication between a potential tourist and a tourism information system. Secondly, as business-

K. Bauknecht, A Min Tjoa, G. Quirchmayr (Eds.): EC-Web 2003, LNCS 2738, pp. 303-314, 2003.

to-business (B2B) communication between various tourism information systems [16]. To enable uniform data access to heterogeneous TIS in the field of B2C and especially in the field of B2B several problems have to be considered [2], [16]. The main problem is the establishment of *adequate* data interchange facilities between heterogeneous TIS server applications as well as between client and server applications. For this, an adapter concept is introduced, which allows uniform and homogenous electronic data interchange (EDI) between a Web-based client application and several distributed heterogeneous TIS. Moreover, EDI between different TIS server applications is supported.

Besides transparent data access, vague query facilities are also an important topic for modern TIS. If a tourist looks for instance for a hotel room in the city of *Salzburg*, but all rooms are booked up, he would be happy to get at least a room in a neighbor city. Unfortunately, relational databases do not support vague query results and so we need advanced retrieving techniques in order to provide *best match searches*. The best solution would be to realize modules that can easily be added to existing database applications to provide semantic based similarity search functionality.

Furthermore, customized presentation mechanisms have to be provided by modern TIS, allowing adaptation of destination information with respect to presentation aspects in terms of layout properties. Another important topic for TIS is the design of Tourist maps. The growing capability of the Internet has created a demand for applications that use geographic information. Maps are easily readable pictures of a place that explain the location and show where certain things are. Maps also present the characteristics and features of a place, which make it unique and different from other places and illustrate distances between places or buildings. Tourist maps extended with powerful geographic search facilities and embedded interactivity support the tourists decision making process in a powerful and innovative way.

The paper is organized as follows: Section 2 gives an overview of the TIS-QL approach which enables data access to heterogeneous TIS based on a standardized interface. In section 3 we discuss advanced search functionalities, comprising vague queries, phonetic search and geographic search methods. Section 4 describes advanced visualization technologies. Finally, Section 5 gives the conclusion.

2   Tourism Information System Query Language (TIS-QL)

To fulfill the tourists request for an extensive data collection on the one hand and to provide adequate search functionalities on the other hand, it is necessary to make accumulated data from different sources accessible. For this, adequate data interchange facilities are a prerequisite. Normally, existing EDI solutions use standardized messages based on application depending guidelines for the data interchange specification. Updates of such messages entail the adaptation of each participating application. This is the main reason, why standards which are based on structured messages require a long-term specification process. Especially for applications in eTourism which are characterized by frequent updates and extensions, this inflexibility is not appropriate.

In contrast to existing EDI solutions the introduced tourism information system query language (TIS-QL) is a *query language* which is designed for tourism information systems. A primary goal of TIS-QL is not to provide a further communication and message standard, but to enable flexible specified queries with the purpose to exchange data between a client and a server.

TIS-QL is based on an adapter concept allowing uniform and homogenous data interchange between a Web-based client application and several distributed heterogeneous tourism information systems. In addition, data interchange between various TIS server applications is supported. The key advantage of this concept is that both the client adapter and the server adapter are designed as add-on modules and consequently their installation causes only low adaptation effort regarding existing applications (Figure 1).

The structural order of data fields or attributes is not relevant to specify a correct TIS-QL statement. It is sufficient to specify a valid query statement corresponding to the language rules and the underlying general data model for tourism information systems [3].

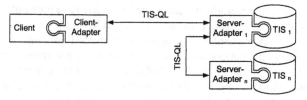

Fig. 1. TIS-QL communication possibilities

TIS-QL supports interchange of two kinds of information:

- plain tourism data, e.g., hotels, sightseeing, sports facilities, camping sites and
- common (meta) information about tourism information systems, e.g., national languages or currency information.

Meta information is important for both B2C and B2B communication. For example, in the case of B2C communication a user needs information about the national languages supported by a TIS or information about attributes used to describe a special tourism object, e.g., a camping site. In the case of B2B communication data interchange is only useful and possible, if both systems support a subset of equal national languages or a subset of equal attributes of camping sites. To establish such a TIS-QL based connection a client and a server adapter are required.

2.1   Client Adapter

The client adapter is responsible for the availability of a uniform user interface presented to a user. For this, the client adapter initiates the communication process, temporarily stores the query results and transfers this result to the encapsulated client application (Figure 2). Updates of the communication specification only affect the client adapter – the client application itself remains unchanged.

The client adapter offers the advantage to tourists to communicate with all those TIS supporting the adapter concept. Because tourists have access to various TIS via a generic and uniform user interface provided by the client adapter, they do not have to cope with differences in information presentation and interaction with TI systems.

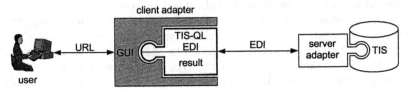

Fig. 2. Client adapter components

2.2   Server Adapter

Analogous to the client adapter, the server adapter transforms data from the uniform TIS-QL interface into a form which corresponds to the data structures of the TIS database [3]. Hence, a server adapter has to be individually implemented for a specific TIS. The TIS itself is independent of B2B or B2C communication specification changes. Since the sever adapter is designed as advanced data interface, the tourism information system remains encapsulated and has not to be adapted. The main task of the server adapter is to transform the TIS-QL communication and the resulting data flow into a form which is appropriate for the database or file system of the TIS. The extension of TI systems with advanced search functionalities is discussed in the next section.

3   Advanced Search Functionalities

Web-based TIS offer tourists an enormous quantity of information and data. But this amount of information is useless if the application does not offer adequate search functionalities, which support the tourist in finding the most relevant data for each request. In this context several problems can be identified. For instance in many cases the tourist has only vague or ambiguous input information. Furthermore, most of the existing TIS support only conventional search functionalities and return only exact hits. Therefore the result set provided by the TIS can be empty, incomplete or not satisfying, although the search criteria are exactly defined by the tourist. Hence novel TIS have to provide advanced search functionalities, in order to satisfy the needs of information providers as well as those of tourists. To cope with the mentioned problems three complementary concepts have been developed in order to enhance the search process. In the following these query mechanisms are described in detail.

3.1   Vague Queries

Relational databases represent the de facto standard in many application areas. They provide standardized query languages (e.g. SQL) for retrieving records and modifying data. However, this type of databases is mainly designed for crisp query processing. With new evolving types of information systems like E-Commerce applications the crisp query feature of relational databases can lead to drawbacks. TIS represent a typical example for an application area, where intelligent query mechanisms are desired, in order to support the customers in searching for proper holiday arrangements. If a tourist looks for instance for a hotel room in the city of "Salzburg", but all rooms are booked up, he would be happy to get at least a room in a neighbor city of "Salzburg".

Since conventional relational databases do not support vague query results, many of today's TIS lack for advanced query techniques. The ability of database systems to carry out phonetic string searches and to search within fuzzy numeric domains is often not sufficient. VQS (Vague Query System) is an example for a concept, that provides the capability to enhance database systems with vague query facilities [9]. It provides semantic search mechanisms in order to regard the meaning of the database objects and to allow the search for similar objects. The main features of VQS can be summarized as follows:

- Semantic based similarity searches: In the case of failing to find an exact match, the system is able to provide at least objects lying semantically close to the query. Retrieving the best match is realized by regarding semantic meta-information of the query-attributes.
- Integration into existing database systems: Applying VQS does not require special database management systems (DBMS). It is possible to work on-top of existing database systems and therefore on top of existing TIS.
- Application area independence: Adding the system to existing applications does not require the structure of the underlying databases to be changed.
- Transparent query facilities: The query-language of VQS is very similar to SQL.

In order to represent the semantics of abstract database attributes VQS uses numeric coordinates in a feature space. For this purpose so-called *NCR-Tables* (*Numeric-Coordinate-Representation-Tables*) have been introduced that define the numeric feature space [9]. The attribute itself is the key of the NCR-Table (*NCR-Key*). Furthermore, NCR-Tables contain several numeric *NCR-Columns*, which represent the dimensions of the feature space. NCR-Tables can be mapped to corresponding attributes of existing database relations. In this way NCR-Tables represent the semantic meaning of the attributes. Structure and content of NCR-Tables have to be defined by Domain Experts on the basis of the specific requirements of the application.

VQS represents similarity of attribute values as the Euclidean distance between the coordinates stored in the associated NCR-Tables. If a query spans more than one attribute, the system has to find the record, of which the semantic definition is the nearest according to all criteria. A special capability of VQS is to build a "combined" semantic distance over all query conditions. The result of this computation is one single number. It is called *Total Distance (TD)* and lies within the interval [0;1]. A Total Distance of *0* indicates an exact match, *1* says that no relevant semantic correspondence exists between the query and the regarded record. In order to stress particular query conditions VQS allows to define individual weights for the single criteria.

In order to give information about the relevance of the vague query result to the user, VQS provides a ranked list of all retrieved records together with an additional attribute *TD*. The user can judge about the single records' relevance for his needs by means of the *TD*-values.

VQS provides a specialized query language *VQL* (*Vague Query Language*), which is close to the SQL-syntax. Since the user does not need to be concerned about the semantics behind the attributes, VQL is very useful for carrying out ad hoc queries. A formal definition of the query language can be found in [9].

The search for a short holiday arrangement in the city of Salzburg, beginning on Jul-31-2003 and ending on Aug-03-2003, could for instance result in the following VQL-statement (dates are represented in an internal format):

```
SELECT FROM Short_Holidays WHERE
City IS 'Salzburg' AND
FROM_DAY IS 212 AND
DURATION IS 4
INTO ResultTable1;
```

The result of the advanced query is presented to the user by means of a ranked list together with information about the Total Distance.

Table 1. Ranked Result Set of the Exemplary VQL-Query

ResultTable1	ID	Hotel	TD
	6	Harriot	0.043
	1	Royal	0.075
	3	Imperial	0.157
	4	Rose	0.249
	2	Kingston	0.333
	5	CityView	0.667

3.2 Geographic Search

Ordinary attribute queries used in common TIS list records that fulfill specific criteria. With such queries it is often fairly not possible to explain what the tourist is searching for. Tourists have problems to find what they are looking for, especially in reference to the geographic position of the tourism object and its surroundings. For example tourists that intend to find the optimal location to stay or to spend their holiday and their decision making is influenced by the location of tourism objects (like surrounding nightlife objects or nearby skiing slopes), attribute queries will not deliver what the tourist expects. The solution to support the needs of this user group is a geographic search for tourism objects. The spatial equivalent of "find" is "locate" and its representation is a set of tourism objects in geographic context represented on maps. Current TIS often have backlogs in offering such GIS functionalities.

The power of GIS proceeds not only from the richness of maps and their symbology, but also from the capacity of doing spatial analysis operations, which offer the user the possibility to perform geographic queries. A geographic search capability [10] lets the tourist quickly search the database using geographic criteria. A geographic search for tourism objects is a mixed query which combines alphanumeric tourism attributes and geographic criteria to search for "What is where?".

- **"What"**: attributes of tourism objects
- **"Where"**: in geographic space

Some spatial analysis operations are needed to offer proximity search operations to tourists. These operations are:

- **Nearness:** to search for the nearest tourism object in reference to a given point or a reference object.
- **Distance:** to find elements located within a specified distance to a given point or reference object.
- **Region:** to search for objects located within a geographic region

A geographic search for tourism objects can be divided into three different search scenarios [12].

- First, the object related search, which offers results to queries like "Which is the nearest hotel to the "Vienna opera house"" or "Show all hotels which are located within a distance of 500 meters to the "Schönbrunn castle"".
- Second, the area-based search, which supports queries like "All hotels in "St. Anton"" or "All sights in a specific geographic region".
- Third, the combination of object driven and area-based search, enlarged with additional tourism object criterions like hotel category and/or availability. This leads to complex geographic queries that allow to ask for a set of tourism objects that fulfill specific object criteria within a geographic region like "All 3-star hotels within a distance of 500 m to the selected location" or "Which is the nearest 5-star hotel to the "Spanish riding school" in Vienna, which has one vacant double room from 17th of May 2003 to 24th of May 2003".

The geographic search facility is an enormous improvement for tourists searching for objects in geographic context and means a reduction of the search granularity from the size of a city to a few meters. Existing Internet solutions for such scenarios are rare, but very needful, especially for tourists.

3.3   Phonetic Search

Detecting phonetic similarities is no problem for humans, but it is still a problem for software systems. In the context of tourism information systems phonetic similarities are very helpful when searching for accommodations or regions, etc. But in this case a simple dictionary based approach is not appropriate, because of the large amount of data and frequent updates within tourism information systems. Improved phonetic string search algorithms are based on substitution rules, which replace similar sounding input strings with an identical standard string.

Soundex, one of the first phonetic search algorithms has been developed by Donald E. Knuth [8]. The Soundex code consists of the firsts letter of the word, followed by three digits.

All vowels are deleted by the Soundex algorithm. If two or more adjacent letters, which are not separated by a vowel, have the same numeric value, only one value is used. This also applies, if the first and the second letter in name have the same value, the second letter would not be used to generate a digit. If the word consists of less then tree consonants which could be converted, the code is filled up with zeros. The result of this algorithm is not very precise, but it is quite efficient. The character replacement for the village names "Fehring", "Frankenmarkt" and "Frauenstein" results for each example in the same Soundex-Code "F652".

Similar to the Soundex algorithm, the *Metaphone algorithm* [13] also performs a transformation into a phonetic code. But in addition to the Soundex algorithm also character groups (dipthongs) based on the English language are considered. Vowels are considered only at the beginning of a word. Due to a higher complexity of the phonetic rule concept the resulting phonetic code of this algorithm is more precise. However, it is a serious drawback that this algorithm is restricted to the English language. Therefore similar algorithms for other languages have been developed. A representative example is a phonetic algorithm for German language applications, which calculates a phonetic code as the result of character replacement [11]. The used substitution rules are based on the German language. For example, the characters "F" and "W" as well as the strings "PH" and "PF" are each transformed into the phonetic code "F".

The new approach is not based on only one specific algorithm, but it combines the advantages of several different algorithms. Within tourism information systems it is important to use phonetic search algorithms for names of cities, regions and accommodations. In many cases such names are quite long and then only parts of those names are used as a search criteria by the tourists. In spite of using a phonetic search algorithm, the result set is not satisfying in this case. To cope with this problem a name is divided into single words. For example, "New York" is divided into "New" and "York". Afterwards, stop words (pronoun, verb, adjective, copula) are deleted. Finally, for each word a phonetic code is calculated and stored in a special database table. During the search process, this phonetic code is compared with the phonetic code which results from a search criterion specified by a tourist.

4   Visualization Technology

In this section concepts for a proper visualization of tourism information are discussed. For this purpose multi-layout mechanisms are introduced, allowing information providers to adapt the layout of their Internet presentation to their specialized needs.

Furthermore the concept of *Touristic Maps* is discussed. Touristic maps in SVG are a powerful, user-friendly and interactive access to tourism data with great benefits for tourists in decision making. The flexibility of the presented concepts and its implied technologies significantly improve the tourists decision making process and offer substantial advantages for TIS.

4.1   Multi-layout

From the information providers' point of view, TIS have to offer an individual Internet presentation, no matter if a hotel, a city, a region or a whole country should be represented. Therefore several *layout aspects* have to be subject to customization.

Tiscover [14] is an example for a TIS, that provides a standard layout for each tourism object type, ensuring a consistent presentation and navigation through the system. This standard layout associates each tourism object by default. To cope with the requirement of an individual presentation, however, a specialized application called *Layout Assistant* allows the information providers to customize the standard layout, e.g., according to their corporate identity. The type and degree of customization can be parameterized through a set of *layout guidelines*. The tourism information provider is free in changing, e.g., header and side bars, background image, colors of texts and background color. The Web pages' superstructure, the position of the elements, and the font of texts cannot be changed and the text style can only be changed according to predefined parameters. Several different layouts can be defined for the same tourism object, e.g., allowing different presentations in winter and summer. Figure 3 shows an example of a standard layout and the corresponding customized layout of a tourism object in the city of Salzburg.

What layout is represented to the user can be decided on the basis of the referred URL (Uniform Resource Locator). Due to the strict separation between content, stored within the database, and presentation, which is achieved using Java Server Page technology, changes in content are immediately reflected in every layout at the time the Web page is accessed by a tourist.

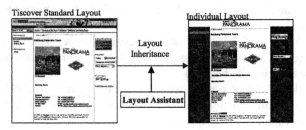

Fig. 3. Inheritance of layout

4.2   Dynamically Generated Interactive Tourist Maps

When starting from the user needs, there is the need to present tourism objects in geographic context on interactive tourist maps. Tourist maps give tourists the ability to see where objects are, how they can be reached and which objects are located nearby. Furthermore maps show the characteristics and features of a place that make it unique and different from other places and illustrate distances between places or buildings.

Maps are models of the real world, each piece of information in a map is located on themed layers which can be used together. To make maps usable for tourism applications, traditional layers like roads, buildings, watercourses, vegetation, etc. have to be extended with tourism layers like hotels, restaurants, sights, culture and sports objects, etc. Maps give tourists visual decision support when planning their vacations.

To meet the tourists interests, the information must be disseminated through an interactive session. Tourists need the possibility to interact with the map, to select features to be displayed while ignoring unwanted data or to use the map as a starting point for further navigation or online-booking. In principal there are two different interaction activities: navigation capabilities and geographic search.

Because the map representation is limited to a small Browser window where the map is presented the user must be supported with navigation capabilities to navigate through the map. These navigation capabilities are:

- Zoom in / out
- Scroll to the east, south, west, north or their combinations northeast, southeast, southwest and northwest
- Pan to define a new map center
- Bring the map back to full extent

As explained in the geographic search section of this paper the geographic search is to identify tourism objects in geographic context (location, nearness, distance or region). The result of both navigation and geographic search is a tourist map that enables the tourist to do visual decision making. To be a useful help, tourist maps must contain some basic information as presented in [15]:

- Meaningful object symbols representing the type of a tourism object (e.g.: hotel, sight, restaurant, etc.)
- Alphanumerical text that describes the object (e.g., name and category of a hotel)
- Coloring of the hotel symbol to visualize its availability, if the query is based on a time period (e.g.: green if there are rooms available and red if the hotel is fully booked)
- Link the object symbol with the objects homepage (URL) to get more detailed information on the object and to offer the ability for online reservation.

To be really useful for tourists decision making, maps must contain the most up-to-date information available. This can be achieved when data integrated into a tourist map is pulled directly from the according database. Changes in the GIS and tourism data must be immediately reflected on the next map creation.

5   Conclusion and Future Work

We described strategies for E-Commerce applications in tourism that help information providers to increase their competitiveness. Furthermore we showed the drawbacks of existing TIS and introduced features that have to be provided by modern TIS.

Data access to different heterogeneous data sources is an important competition factor for the participants of electronic markets. Especially in the field of tourism information systems, the tourists' request for an extensive data collection and adequate search functionalities more and more increases the necessity of co-operations between tourism information systems. Hence, data access to heterogeneous TIS is required in the field of B2C as well as B2B to be able to provide accumulated data of different sources. Supporting both communication types the presented approach is based on a uniform client/server and server/server communication using TIS-QL and the introduced adapter concept. In order to evaluate the client and server adapter concept and to have a detailed look on performance and usability features, prototypes for the Austrian tourism information system Tiscover have been implemented.

Moreover, tourism industry now realized the potential to increase data quality by providing individual and specialized information about tourism objects. For this, appropriate search as well as presentation features are required. This paper explains advanced query mechanisms developed to enhance TIS search functionalities which significantly improve the search process and give tourists the possibility to find the best matching result as easy and as fast as possible.

The advantage of individual information presentation is twofold. It increases the quality of information and on the same time it keeps the information providers individuality. In order to cope with these demands, concepts for individualized multi-layout presentation abilities and interactive presentation of tourism objects on dynamically generated interactive tourist maps, enabled by SVG (Scalable Vector Graphics), the new two-dimension graphics standard to present vector graphics in the Internet, are presented.

Together, the presented approaches offer trend-setting abilities for today's tourism information systems, each of them offer tourism information providers the ability to increase the quality of presented information, help tourists to find what they are looking for and present it in an individual, easy readable and meaningful way. Multi-layout and phonetic search already present their power in the current version of the Tiscover system. The other concepts are realized in the form of operative prototypes and are also planned to improve Tiscover.

References

[1] Antich, A., Merino, M.: MDS structure inside CAP Database. Deliverable of InTouriSME – Building an Internet–based Tourism Constituency for SMEs in the Less Favored Regions of Europe, EU–Project 21349, Deliverable D.5.1.2.5.2 V2.0 (1999)

[2] Dunzendorfer, A., Küng, J., Wagner, R.: Data Access to Heterogeneous Tourism Information Systems. Proceedings of the 5th Information and Communication Technologies in Tourism (ENTER) 1998, Istanbul. Springer Computer Science (1998)

[3] Dunzendorfer, A., Küng, J., Wagner, R.: A General Datamodel for Tourism Information Systems, Proceedings of the 6th Information and Communication Technologies in Tourism (ENTER) 1999, Innsbruck. Springer Computer Science (1999)

314   Jürgen Palkoska et al.

[4]   Gardarin, G., Gannouni, S., Finance, B., Fankhauser, P., Klas, W., Pastre, D., Legoff, R., Ramfos, A.: IRO–DB – A Distributed System Federating Object and Relational Databases. In: Bukhres O. and Elmargarmid A.K. (eds.) Object–Oriented Multidatabase Systems. Prentice Hall (1994)

[5]   Gardarin, G., Huck, G., Bezares, J., Muñoz, J., Pühretmair, F., Busse, R., Muñoz, J., Iglesias, J., Niño, M.: General Architecture Specification, Project: XML–KM, XML–based Mediator for Knowledge Extraction and Brokering. EU–Project IST 12030, Deliverable D11 V2.3, e–XMLmedia, GMD, IBERMATICA, SITESA (2001)

[6]   Höpken W.: Modeling of an Electronic Tourism Market. Proceedings of the 6th Information and Communication Technologies in Tourism (ENTER) 1999, Innsbruck. Springer Computer Science (1999)

[7]   Höpken W.: Reference Model Of An Electronic Tourism Market. Proceedings of the 7th Information and Communication Technologies in Tourism (ENTER) 2000, Barcelona. Springer Computer Science (2000)

[8]   Knuth, D. E.: The Art of Computer Programming. Vol. 3, Addison-Wesley, (1973)

[9]   Küng, J., Palkoska J., "VQS - A Vague Query System Prototype", Proceedings of the Eighth International Workshop on Database and Expert Systems Applications, DEXA 97, pp. 614-618, IEEE Computer Society Press, Toulouse, France (1997)

[10]   Larson, R., Geographic Information Retrieval and Spatial Browsing, University of California, Berkeley, USA (1996)

[11]   Michael, J.: Doppelgänger gesucht, Ein Programm für kontextsensitive phonetische Textumwandlung. c't 25/1999, p. 252, Germany (1999)

[12]   Palkoska, J., Pühretmair, F., Tjoa, A M., Wagner, R., Wöß, W.: Advanced Query Mechanisms in Tourism Information Systems. Proceedings of the 9th International Conference on Information and Communication Technologies in Tourism, (ENTER 2002), pp. 438-447, ISBN 3-211-83780-9, Springer Verlag, Innsbruck, Austria (2002)

[13]   Philips, L.: Hanging on the Metaphone. In: Computer Language, Vol. 7 No. 12, pp. 39 – 43, http://webbtide.com.au/metaphone.html (1999)

[14]   Pröll, B., Retschitzegger, W., "Discovering Next-Generation Tourism Information Systems - A Tour on TIScover", *Journal of Travel Research*, Sage Publications Inc., 39(2), November 2000

[15]   Pühretmair, F., Wöß, W., XML-based Integration of GIS and Heterogeneous Tourism Information. Proceedings of the 13th Conference on Advanced Information Systems Engineering (CAiSE'01), pp.346-358, ISBN 3-540-42215-3, Springer Verlag, Interlaken, Switzerland (2001)

[16]   Wöß, W., Dunzendorfer, A.: Configurable EDI for Heterogeneous Tourism Information Systems Based on XML. Proceedings of the 8th Information and Communication Technologies in Tourism (ENTER) 2001, Montreal. Springer Computer Science (2001)

Analysis and Design of e-Commerce Applications on the Web: A Case Study of OO Techniques and Notations

Mohamed T Ibrahim[1], Maliheh Hamdollah[1] and Patrick T. R. O'Brien[2]

[1] The University of Greenwich, London UK   [2] The OU, IBM UK & The Open University.

m.t.ibrahim@greenwich.ac.uk, hm019@greenwich.ac.uk

Abstract.

This paper reports on a study and comparison of two techniques and notations suitable for the analysis and design of Web-based electronic commerce (e-commerce) applications. Some of the challenges facing developers of Web-based e-commerce applications are identified, examined and discussed. Individually these challenges are not unique but their combination and severity make the development of applications for the WWW a rather difficult software-engineering problem. Techniques and notations devised to address some of these challenges are identified from the literature. The Technique for Analysing and Specifying Transactional Internet Sites of Beaudet et al. (1998) and the Object-Oriented Hypermedia Design Method (OOHDM) of Schwabe and Rossi (1998) were selected to analyse and design a typical e-commerce application. The results of this study are then used to evaluate the suitability of the two approaches for the development of Web-based applications. The paper concludes that the Beaudet et al. approach is more suited to rapid development projects and OOHDM to situations where comprehensiveness of specification is more important than speed. Both approaches need to be supplemented by additional techniques and supporting notations, particularly in the area of physical design.

1. Introduction

The Internet and World Wide Web (WWW) are increasingly being used for commercial purposes. A survey of 500 corporate executives conducted in the USA in 1997 by Feher and Towell (1997) indicated that 85% of respondents were already using the Internet. Significant growth was anticipated in its use for EDI, commerce and banking. KPMG Management Consulting (1998) conducted a pan-European survey of 500 companies in July 1998, which showed that 50% thought electronic commerce (e-commerce) to be vital to global competitiveness. Dramatic growth in Internet marketing and transactions was expected over the next five years. Internet transactions as a percentage of total sales were expected to grow from 1% to around 10% in three years and to reach 16% within five.

Many practitioners' opinions, e.g. as described above, led us to seek answers to the following questions: (i) What are the nature, characteristics and software engineering

K. Bauknecht, A Min Tjoa, G. Quirchmayr (Eds.): EC-Web 2003, LNCS 2738, pp. 315-327, 2003.

challenges of e-commerce applications on the WWW? (ii) Are they unique to Web-based development? (iii) Do techniques and notations exist which are designed specifically for the development of Web-based applications? (iv) If so, are these techniques and notations suitable for their purpose?

1.1 Structure of this paper

Part of the literature survey was aimed at providing information to answer at least Questions 1 and 2 above, and possibly provide empirical data for the resolution of Question 3. Further data was gathered from practitioners with experience of Web-application development. The data gained from these two steps was used to derive a set of criteria for evaluating the suitability of techniques and notations for Web-application development. A case study application development was then conducted using techniques and notations identified in the earlier research. The experiences of the case study were used to evaluate the techniques and notations against the evaluation criteria.

Section 2 reviews some related literature. Section 3 introduces the two selected techniques under study. We describe in section 4 the evaluation methods used and explain why they were chosen. Section 5 describes a case study using two different sets of techniques and notations for analysis and design of Web-based applications. We then give results of evaluating the two approaches to analysis and design chosen for the case study in section 6. Conclusions and further work are found in section 7.

1.2 Related work

Artz (1996), Treese and Stewart (1998), Riggins and Rhee (1998) and Papazoglou and Tsalgatidou (1999) provide wider definitions, which incorporate the replacement and extension of Electronic Data Interchange (EDI) by extranets (business-to-business applications of Internet technology). Internet e-commerce is distinct from EDI in that it uses shared public networks, rather than specialised networks or Valued Added Networks (VANs) and enables spontaneous business transactions, without prior agreement of the parties. They also see e-commerce as having the potential to support the complete external business process, including the information stage (electronic marketing, networking), the negotiation stage (electronic markets), the fulfilment stage (order process, electronic payment) and the satisfaction stage (after sales support). Riggins and Rhee (1998) identify three classes of e-commerce applications: business-to-consumer, business-to-business and intra-organisational (collaborative use, e.g. virtual development teams).

1.3 The Application Domain & Technology Challenges

Treese and Stewart (1998) identify a general-purpose value chain for current Internet Commerce applications.

Internet e-commerce applications may cover some, or all, of the functions in the diagram: **Attract**: Potential customers must be attracted to the site by various forms of advertising and it must make a favourable enough impression to make them want to stay once they get there. **Interact**: The site provides information about the

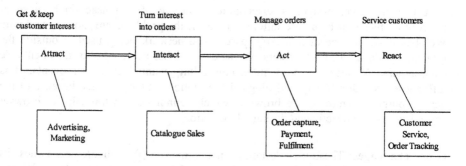

Figure 1: the Commerce Value Chain {reproduced from Trees and Stewart, (1998)}

organisation, its services and goods. More sophisticated applications provide content tailored to the customer based on previously collected user preferences. **Act:** This involves functions such as order processing, payment processing (e.g. credit card payment) and fulfilment handling, which is often provided by links to the organisation's existing back-office systems. **React:** includes the provision of on-line access to order progression information, i.e. the customer can query the order status, or submit messages to support staff (e.g. through an email link from the Web page). There are, to the best of our knowledge, several challenges facing enterprises developing and using the web for e-commerce. We only describe some of what we believe are the most important ones. Space limitations prevented the authors from discussing all of these challenges in detail but we list these challenges at the end of this section.

Security

One of the most commonly cited challenges for e-commerce applications on the Web (and the Internet in general) is that of security. This is a huge subject in its own right and cannot be done justice in the confines of a paper focused on techniques for analysis and design. Because of its importance to the future success of e-commerce on the Web it has attracted a good deal of attention and there is a large body of literature on the subject.

Maintenance

Brereton et al. (1998) argue that the use of hypertext is approaching similar levels of complexity to software and becoming a maintenance burden for many organizations. As the scale and scope of its use grows, maintenance of hypertext documents (e.g. HTML) may be as important to organizations' economic success as software maintenance.

Transactions

Treese and Stewart (1998) describe a typical set of activities involved in an Internet commerce sale, which might need to be grouped into a single transaction: Debit purchaser's account; Credit seller's account; Record sale for business records; Transmit order to fulfilment centre; Issue receipt to purchaser.

Any client-server system is susceptible to failure of a transaction because of network problems or hardware failure. However, the problems are more severe with Web-based systems because a large part of the network being used is outside the influence of the application owners and the designer has less control of the client side environment. A particular problem is controlling unanticipated user events. It is difficult to prevent arbitrary and illogical user actions at the interface because of the general-purpose nature of the browser, which cannot be constrained; i.e. browser controls cannot be deactivated during a transaction.

Other challenges: These include but are not limited to (i) Technological issues (ii) Changing Deadlines (iii) Knowledge Barriers and (iv) User interface design. Space limitation on the paper meant that these can be discussed here.

3.1 Techniques and Notations for Analysis and Logical Design

Object-Oriented Hypermedia Design Method (OOHDM)

OOHDM has four steps: Conceptual Design, Navigational Design, Abstract Interface Design and Implementation, which can be combined into iterative and incremental development processes. There are four key concepts: Navigational objects are views of conceptual objects; Abstractions are used to organise the navigation space; Interface issues are separated from navigational issues; Some design decisions should be postponed until implementation.

Beaudet et al.

Beaudet et al. (1998) describe a technique and notations used successfully on a number of Internet application development projects, in conjunction with standard object modelling approaches. Their technique addresses problems with the development of transactional Internet sites, particularly the definition of the connection between the user interface and the host system, navigation within the site, transactions and dialogue between user and system. The authors have found that existing specification methods do not cover all aspects of the requirement of a transactional Internet application, or allow for validation, scalability and timely execution.

4. Evaluation Method

Introduction

The objective of this paper was to answer the three questions posed in Section 1. The information provided by the literature survey (Section 2) and Web-application developers (Section 3) established the nature, characteristics and software engineering challenges of e-commerce applications on the WWW (Question 1). This information suggests that the software engineering problems themselves are not unique but the compound effect can make Web-application development a challenging undertaking. Fortunately, the answer to Question 2 is that techniques and notations formulated specifically for Web application analysis and design, do exist. As mentioned above, three such approaches were identified. This section describes the methods selected to answer question 3.

Evaluation Criteria

In Sections 2 and 3, the following categories of problems were identified: (1) Security, (2) Maintenance, (3) Technical Limitations, (4) User Interface (UI) Design, (5) Transactions, (6) Tool Support, (7) Changing Deadlines and (8) Knowledge Barriers. It is impossible to address all of these problems adequately in the limited space available for this paper. The choice of analysis and design techniques to be used on a project will not solve the problems of Tool Support identified in the literature. Table 1 shows the relationship between the categories of software-engineering problem and the evaluation criteria derived from them.

Table 1 Development Problems and Derived Evaluation Criteria

PROBLEM	DERIVED EVALUATION CRITERIA
Maintenance	Must illustrate structure of Web application including navigation; Must be comprehensive: cover all aspects of the design; Must be easily understood by maintenance personnel who were not part of the original development team.
Technical Limitations	Techniques and notations cannot in themselves address the limitations of existing technology. However they can help the developer by: Facilitating implementation of the design in the technical environment; Providing implementation neutral, portable designs, so that it is possible to incorporate new technological advances easily, without the need to rewrite the design; Support for modular design; Allowing for the specification of sequence and state of data over time.
User Interface Design	Expression of navigational structure; Capture detail of the components of the UI design; Expression of UI dialogue; Expression of function/behaviour of the system.
Transactions	Expression of system function; Specification of transactions; Specification of sequence.
Challenging Deadlines	It must be possible to produce analysis and design documentation quickly with the techniques and notations. This suggests the following characteristics: Simplicity; Small number of models; Ease of transformation between models/notations.
Knowledge Barriers	Easy to understand and apply for inexperienced staff; Easy to integrate with existing development methods.

Several of the criteria in Table 1 are common to more than one problem category. The matrix in Table 2 shows the interrelationship between problems and the evaluation criteria derived from them.

Table 2 Initial Evaluation of the Approaches

Criterion	Conallen	Schwabe & Rossi	Beaudet et al.
Expression of application structure	High	High	Medium
Navigation modelling	Medium	High	High
Comprehensiveness	Low	High	High
Ease of application	Medium	Low	High

Criterion	Conallen	Schwabe & Rossi	Beaudet et al.
Ease of understanding	Medium	Low	High
Implementation neutrality & portability	None	High	High
Support for modular design	Medium	Medium	Medium
Modelling of UI	Medium	High	High
Expression of system function & behaviour	None	Medium	High
Specification of transactions	None	Low	High
Small number of models	High	Low	High
Ease of transformation between notations	Not applicable	Low	Medium

The Bookstore Case Study

The Case Study was based on a retail bookstore, a typical business-to-consumer e-commerce application currently found on the WWW. Examples of such applications are Amazon.co.uk and the Internet bookshop at W H Smith Online. A generic statement of requirements was built by recording the experience of shopping at these sites. The requirement was for a simple retail site that enabled the user to browse a catalogue of books, add selected books to a shopping basket and finally purchase them online by credit card. It was assumed that in most retail organisations implementing a Web-based application of this kind, functions such as order fulfilment, credit card payment validation and accounting would be supported by existing systems. Therefore, the Web-based application would not be required to provide this functionality itself but would need to interface to existing corporate systems.

Development Process for the Case Study

Development process or lifecycle, as Rumbaugh (1995) points out, is a fundamental aspect of a method. Without some idea of process it would be impossible to apply techniques and notations effectively to a development project. Grimm and Dorballa (1998), Treese and Stewart (1998), Conallen (1998), Booch et al. (1998), Beaudet et al. (1998), Schwabe and Rossi (1998) and Schneider and Winters (1998) all recommend an iterative and evolutionary development process.

The two techniques and notations to be evaluated both start with the construction of an object model using an OO method. In OOHDM (Schwabe and Rossi (1998)) the first stage of the method is to produce the Conceptual Design using UML notations. The first step in the analysis and design of this work was to produce a common conceptual model from the statement of requirement, using UML techniques and notations. This was then used as the starting point for the application of the two approaches under consideration, following the spiral model adapted from Harmon and Watson (1998).

Conceptual Model

The construction of the Conceptual Model started by deriving an overall System Use Case Diagram from the Statement of Requirement. We followed the approach described in Schneider and winters (1998) for building the Use Case Model by first identifying the Actors, then establishing use cases for each actor based on their functional requirements of the system. The use case model is not shown here but will be made available in a fuller version of the paper (email the first author fro a copy.)The Physical Class Diagram showing key operations and handler classes is shown in Figure 2. For the sake of clarity, operations for creating instances of classes, setting and retrieving their attributes are not shown.

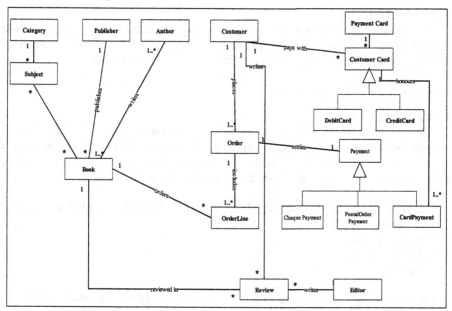

Figure 2:Conceptual Model: Analysis Class Diagram

Beaudet et al. Approach

Navigation Section

The Navigation Section comprises a set of diagrams using an adapted flow chart notation. It demonstrates the navigation paths between interface items (screens) and the transactions associated with them. The approach does not include a top or system level diagram, so it could be difficult to work out how to partition the dialogue into component logic flows.

Interface Section

The notation can be used to produce an implementation independent design. However, it requires discipline to avoid including elements specific to the target environment. For instance, it was assumed that all the screen types were HTML, when XML or Java Applets might equally have been used.

Transactions Section

The Transactions Section comprises a transaction description for each interface item in the Interface Section. The notation used is a table in a similar layout to that used in the Interface Section. An entry is included for each data item crossing the system boundary describing its type, format and value. There seemed to be no obvious way to describe the processing involved in the transactions, beyond the single box in the table labelled description. Also, no specific notation is provided to indicate the presence of repeating groups of information as might result from running a query against a database.

Build and Test

The Beaudet et al approach does not provide any additional techniques or notations to cover the physical design and implementation processes. The approach is intended to supplement rather than replace conventional development methods.

Development Using OOHDM

Navigational Design

An example of the definition for the Book Node in the Catalogue View is reproduced in Figure 3. This shows that the Anchor object toAuthor allows the user to navigate to the Author object associated with the book by means of the *writes* relationship in the Class Model from the Conceptual Schema.

NODE Book   [FROM Book: Bk] [INHERITS FROM Author, Publisher, Review]
title: String
our price: Money
list price: Money
pages: Integer
...
publisher: String [SELECT name] [FROM Publisher: Pub WHERE Pub publishes Bk]
toAuthor: Anchor (writes)
toShoppingBasket: Anchor (added to)
END

Figure 3: Part of OOHDM Navigational Class Schema Node Definition

Abstract Interface Design

The notation did not appear to offer any way to indicate whether an attribute of an ADV was an input or an output field. The ADV diagrams show the static aspects of the interface objects. Dynamic aspects are captured using state charts where required. The *Checkout* Use Case is central to the commercial requirements of the case study application as it enables the customer to place an order for the items in his/her shopping basket and pay for them using a credit card. Therefore a state chart for the ADV Order Diagram is produced, which provides the interface to the *Checkout* Use Case.

Implementation

The final phase of OOHDM is Implementation. Schwabe and Rossi (1998) point out that the models produced in the previous phases of the method are intentionally independent of any implementation platform. In common with many development methods, OOHDM does not provide techniques or notations for implementation. Some guidance is given on implementing Conceptual and Navigation objects in relational databases, as well as implementing contexts and interfaces. However, the method alone cannot be used to express the physical design or to show how it was transformed from the previous "logical" design models. It was not possible, therefore, to complete the case study design using OOHDM.

Prototype Implementation

Single Prototype Implementation

It was not possible to express the physical design of the prototype using either of the approaches under evaluation. Consequently A single prototype was developed using both sets of documentation as a guide. The purpose of doing this was to provide some indication of how easily the logical designs produced using the approaches under consideration could be transformed into the implementation environment.

Implementation of the Web Site

The main structure of the Web application was implemented as a set of interconnected HTML pages using the NetObjects Fusion Web site-authoring tool. This product provides visual tools for building a hierarchy of HTML pages and for creating the page content, without the need to write HTML code. The resultant layout is then converted to HTML. It was found that it was relatively easy to transform the Beaudet et al. Navigation Structures and Interface Components directly into a physical implementation using this tool.

Dynamic Elements of the Application

Finally, the dynamic components would be linked into the static Web pages using standard HTML forms and hyperlinks. Unfortunately, although the queries and forms to provide this functionality worked perfectly in Access, the ASP components generated by the tool did not. After many fruitless hours spent trying to debug the generated code, it was decided that the law of diminishing returns had come into play. The prototyping exercise had served its purpose of exploring the ease with which the design documentation could be converted into a physical implementation and there was nothing further to be gained by expending more time on it.

6. Evaluation of Results

6.1 Beaudet et al.

Expression of Application Structure

The Beaudet et al. (1998) approach is intended to be used in conjunction with a conventional development method. Thus it might be argued that where there are gaps in its coverage, they would be filled by appropriate techniques or notations from the development method being used. For instance there is no technique or notation to model underlying data structures, so it would be necessary to use a Class Model or Entity Relationship Diagram to address this part of the analysis and design.

Navigation Modelling

The Navigation Section of the Beaudet et al. (1998) approach provides a very good expression of the navigational design. The notation expresses the various navigation paths available from each screen and the conditions attached to their navigation. However, it would be easier to conceptualise the application's navigation structure if there were a system or subsystem wide diagram to provide an overview for the entire application, or at least for substantial parts of it.

Comprehensiveness

The Beaudet et al. approach is not intended to cover all aspects of an application's design, so it can not be fully comprehensive. It provides good coverage of the external design of a Web-based system, primarily at a logical level. Support for physical design as discussed in Section 6 is weak.

Ease of Application and Understanding

It was found that the Beaudet et al techniques and notations extremely easy to use. The navigation section uses a modified flowcharting notation, with three basic symbols. These symbols are used to represent different semantics to the normal flowcharting convention; for example the diamond is used to represent a transaction rather than a decision, which might cause some initial confusion.

Expression of System Function and Behaviour

The Beaudet et al. approach does not cover the complete system function as noted in section 5. Coverage of the external function and behaviour of the system is generally good. However, the notations would need to be supplemented by text or other notations to provide a full explanation of the processing logic involved in the system transactions. For critical transactions, such as those involving the placement of an order or credit card payment, some additional notation such as a state transition diagram would be required to capture the full behavioural requirements.

6.2 OOHDM

Expression of Application Structure

OOHDM does set out to cover the full design space for a Web application. The Conceptual Model that is produced by following the method models the underlying data objects and their behaviour. The Navigation Design and the Abstract Interface Design look at various aspects of the UI design. The Implementation Stage, as the name suggests, deals with the implementation of the design in the target environment. However, the method on its own fails to provide full coverage of the application structure. It would be necessary to supplement OOHDM with other techniques and notations to express the structure of the application fully.

Navigation Modelling

The required navigation of the application is expressed comprehensively through the two models of the Navigation Design. Separate views are provided for each user profile. However, no techniques are provided to assist the practitioner in identifying and developing the User Profiles and views. Also there is no attempt to identify the elements which are common to all views. The practitioner could end up with a large number of separate navigational views, which would have to be synthesised somehow into a single application.

Comprehensiveness

OOHDM could not be used on its own to analyse and design a Web-based application. As noted previously, it does not provide techniques or notations for physical design and does not help the practitioner in identifying the different User Profiles, which are modelled in Navigation Design. There are a few other minor omissions. For instance, in the Abstract Interface Design, there is no way to specify whether a data item is input or output. Similarly, there was no obvious means to specify error handling.

Ease of Application and Understanding

It was found that the Navigational Context Schema and the Abstract Interface Design notations difficult to use. In the case of the Navigational Context Schema in particular, it seemed that the adherence to the Object-Oriented paradigm had been made at the expense of ease of use. It was difficult to understand the concepts behind the notation and what value it added in preference to more conventional techniques, such as flow-charting. I think that this would also compromise the utility of the notations as a means of communication, both with other development staff and certainly with users. It would also make the method difficult to use for inexperienced developers.

Expression of System Function and Behaviour

The system behaviour and function is specified through the operations of the classes defined in the conceptual model and the use of state charts in the Abstract Interface Design. Operations describe the processing associated with individual classes and the state charts specify sequence and dynamic behaviour. These features address processing and behaviour of system components, rather than system functions as a whole. There is no mechanism to show how the objects co-operate to deliver the transactions of the system. In order to convey this transactional view, it would be necessary to use additional techniques and notations such as UML Sequence or Collaboration diagrams.

Number of Models

OOHDM involves the production of the conceptual model, a navigational class schema and navigational context schema for each user profile and each context within each profile. In addition there is an ADV for each ADO in the navigational class schema and possibly a state chart as well. For a complex system, this could result in a large number of models to articulate the logical design. This suggests that the method does not lend itself to rapid development of a specification.

Choice of Approach

There is no obvious choice between these two approaches. OOHDM provides a comprehensive specification involving a large number of models but is not easy to use. On the other hand, the Beaudet et al. (1998) approach is less comprehensive but easier to understand and apply. Neither covers the full design space and therefore it would be necessary to supplement both with other techniques and notations. OOHDM adheres strongly to the OO paradigm, whereas the Beaudet et al. approach is largely structured or procedural in nature.

The Beaudet et al. approach is simpler and could consequently be easier for inexperienced developers to learn and apply. It has fewer models, so this should make it quicker to use but it would be necessary to supplement it with some other development techniques to gain full coverage of analysis and design. To conclude, the Beaudet et al. approach might be preferable where time pressures are great and OOHDM, where comprehensiveness of specification is more important than speed of development.

7. Conclusions and Future work

Questions 1 and 2 above were answered by means of a literature survey and primary data collected from experienced Web-application developers. Web-application development presents a number of challenges, which although severe are not unique to the medium. Three separate sets of techniques and notations designed for Web-application development were identified from the literature. The remaining approaches of Beaudet et al (1998) and the OOHDM method of Schwabe and Rossi (1998) were evaluated against criteria derived from the literature survey and the primary data collected to answer Question 1. The data for the evaluation was obtained through the conduct of a case study development project resulting in the production of a prototype e-commerce Web-application. The results of the evaluation answered Question 3. The approaches of Beaudet et al. (1998) and Schwabe and Rossi (1998) are suitable for Web-application development up to a point but neither provides full coverage of the development lifecycle. Further techniques and notations are required to complete physical design of the application.

References
Booch, G., Rumbaugh, J. and Jacobson, I., (1998), *The Unified Modelling Language User Guide*, Addison-Wesley Longman, Reading, Mass.
Harmon, P. and Watson, M. (1998), *Understanding UML: The Developers Guide: with a Web-Based Application in Java*, Morgan Kaufmann Publishers, San Francisco, CA.
Jacobson, I., Christerson, M., Jonsson, P. and Oevergaard, G. (1992), *Object Oriented Software Engineering: A Use Case Driven Approach*, Addison-Wesley, Reading, M.A.
Rumbaugh, J., Blaha, M., Premerlani, W., Eddy, F. and Lorensen, W. (1991), *Object Oriented Modelling and Design*, Prentice Hall International, Englewood Cliffs, N.J.
Schneider, G. and Winters, J.P. (1998), *Applying Use Cases: A Practical Guide*, Addison Wesley Longman, Reading, Mass.

Treese W.G. and Stewart L.C. (1998), *Designing Systems for Internet Commerce,* Addison Wesley Longman, Reading, MA.

Artz, J.M. (1996), 'A Top-Down Methodology for Building Corporate Web Applications', *Internet Research: Electronic Networking Applications and Policy*, Vol. 6, No.2/3, pp. 64-74

Beaudet, P.J., Modir Massihai, S. and Pinto, J.A. (1998), A Technique for Analyzing and Specifying Transactional Internet Sites, *Research Disclosure*, Vol. 41, No. 414 (Oct)

Brereton, P., Budgeon, D. and Hamilton, G. (1998), 'Hypertext: The Next Maintenance Mountain', *IEEE Computer*, Vol. 31, No. 12, pp. 49-55.

Feher, A. and Towell, E. (1997), 'Business Use of the Internet', *Internet Research: Electronic Networking Applications and Policy*, Vol. 7, No. 3, pp 195-200.

Kochikar, V. P. (1998), 'The Object-Powered Web', *IEEE Software*, May/June, 1998, pp. 57-62.

Nambisan, S. and Wang, Y-M. (1999), 'Roadblocks to Web Technology Adoption', *Communications of the ACM*, Vol. 42, No. 1, pp. 98-101.

Nielsen, J. (1999), 'User Interface Directions for the Web', *Communications of the ACM*, Vol. 42, No. 1, pp. 65-72.

Riggins, F.J. and Rhee, H-S. (1998), 'Toward a Unified View of Electronic Commerce', *Communications of the ACM*, Vol. 41, No. 10, pp. 88-95

Schwabe, D. and Rossi, G. (1998), 'An Object-Oriented Approach to Web-Based Application Design', *Theory and Practice of Object Systems*, Vol. 4, No. 4, pp. 207-225.

Wan, H. A. and Chung, C-W. (1998), 'Web Page Design and Network Analysis', *Internet Research: Electronic Networking Applications and Policy*, Vol. 8, No. 2, pp. 115-122.

Mace, S., Flohr, U., Dobson, R. and Graham, T. (1998), 'Weaving a Better Web', BYTE, Vol. 23, No. 3, March 1998, pp. 58-68.

Grimm, B. and Dorbala, S., (1998), *Successful Deployment of Electronic Commerce Applications: Process is Key*, developer.com, Tech Focus, April, 1998.

Booch, G. (1998), *Java*, Rational Software Corporation Web Site, http://www.rational.com/support/techpapers/java.html, 17/04/98.

Conallen, J. (1998), *Modelling Web Application Design with UML*, White Paper on Rational Software Web site, dated 6 June 1998, http://www.rational.com/uml/resources/whitepapers.

InterForum White Paper (1999a), *Electronic Commerce – the Challenge for UK Business*, http://WWW.interforum.org/whit3.htm accessed 21 Feb 1999.

InterForum (1999b), *Frequently Asked Questions About E-Commerce*, http://www.enterprisenetwork.co.uk/clubs...et/entnet/topical/c--eco-ifo-faq-d.fhtml, accessed 21 Feb 1999.

Internetbookshop at WH Smith Online, http://www.bookshop.co.uk/

Merkow, M. (1999), *cXML: A New Taxonomy for E-Commerce*, internet.com LLC, http://www.webreference.com/ecommerce/mm/column21/index.html, created 25 Feb 1999.

Microsoft Developers' Network (MSDN) (1999), http://www.msdn.microsoft.com/workshop/server/asp.

Nielsen, J. (1996), *Top Ten Mistakes in Web Design*, useit.com Alertbox, May 1996, http://www.useit.com/alertbox/9605.html.

Web Metrics for Retailers*

Maximilian Teltzrow and Oliver Günther

Institute of Information Systems, Humboldt-Universität zu Berlin
Spandauer Str. 1, 10178 Berlin, Germany
{guenther,teltzrow}@wiwi.hu-berlin.de
http://www.wiwi.hu-berlin.de/iwi

Abstract. In this study, we first propose a set of web usage metrics for *multi-channel* retailers. We then apply these metrics to data originating from a retailer who operates both an e-shop and a number of traditional stores. We focus in particular on the analysis of k-Means session clusters exhibiting an interest in offline purchases. Web usage metrics measuring the success of Web sites have been proposed before. In the domain of Web merchandizing, success is measured eventually by the number of purchases accomplished. Basic statistics such as conversion and traffic have been proposed to quantify this notion of success. However, when it comes to retailers with *multiple* distribution channels, there is a definite lack of standard metrics based on web log and transaction data. This paper tries to remedy this void.

1   Introduction

In contrast to Internet-only retailers, distribution of products across multiple sales channels - often referred to as multi-channel retailing - is the norm today and has become a distinct business model [1]. Multi-channel retailers were able to increase their online market share steadily to 67% in 2001 from 52% in 1999 – in contrast to Internet-only retailers, who lost market share correspondingly [2].

Though retail sites experience significant traffic growth, conversion of online visitors to paying customers remains low: for US retailers conversion increased to 3.1% in 2001 up from 2.2% in 2000. In 2001, online retail sales accounted for only 2.4% (1.7%) of the US (EU) retail market [2].

A primary reason for low conversion rates seems to be privacy concerns: a summary of recent surveys indicates that the percentage of non-online shoppers who were not purchasing online because of privacy reasons varies between 64% and 68% [3] and the number of online shoppers who would buy more if they were not worried about privacy/security issues varies between 20% and 37% [3]. Moreover, 49% of

---

*   This research was supported by the Deutsche Forschungsgemeinschaft, Berlin-Brandenburg Graduate School in Distributed Information Systems (DFG grant no. GRK 316/2)

K. Bauknecht, A Min Tjoa, G. Quirchmayr (Eds.): EC-Web 2003, LNCS 2738, pp. 328-338, 2003.

European online consumers want to see or touch a product before they buy it and 57% move offline to purchase simply because of hedonistic reasons [4].

The cited surveys demonstrate that many consumers still rely on offline stores for the actual product purchase whereas the Internet becomes more important for information collection about retail products. Thus, online sales figures do not appear to be sufficient as the only success metric for a retailer's web performance. The development of web usage metrics measuring the Internet's contribution to the overall sales performance of a multi-channel company is a challenging task. Thus, the question arises: Are there quantifiable cross-channel effects justifying significant investments in current and future Internet projects?

Surveys suggest that the Internet has a distinctive influence on offline sales. According to a recent report, up to 71% of online shoppers research products online and buy them offline [5]. In 2002, 64.7% of Internet purchasers said they sometimes or often browse in traditional retail locations and then buy online – up from 50.3 percent in 2001 [5].

In order to measure cross-channel effects, marketing typically uses research methods based on questionnaires, interviews or focus groups. However, survey-based research might lack precision as it is difficult to reach a representative sample, it can incur high costs and the method of data collection can bias the respondents' statements. In contrast, our approach focuses on the evaluation of user and usage data derived from anonymized purchase and web log data.

Our research contribution is threefold: First, we formalize and enhance existing classifications for web usage metrics in marketing research that focus on online customer behavior. Moreover, we suggest data requirements to calculate the proposed metrics. Specifically, we refer to a report that uses the customer life cycle [6] as a guideline for its metrics classification [7]. Second, we propose new metrics that quantify the influence of the Internet sales channel on store sales – which has been missed by existing metrics classifications. Third, we apply our metric definitions to actual web log data and transaction data from a retailer with multiple distribution channels. In particular, we pick one web usage metric – session clusters exhibiting high affinity towards offline sales – and discuss the results in detail.

Our research should support web analysts to optimize the navigational paths of web pages in order to improve browse-to-buy ratios and retention rates. It should also be of interest to IT researchers as it highlights implications from consumer behavior theory pointing towards micro segmentation and customer profiling, thus representing a first step towards personalization [8].

2   Related Work

Related work comes from both marketing and IT research. Metrics for e-commerce measuring the long-term impact of the Internet on traditional business structures have been proposed in survey-based research before [9].

In contrast, we will focus on web usage analysis measuring the sales performance of web sites [7, 10, 11]. We believe that metrics based on web usage and transaction data can provide retail managers with a fast and efficient analysis of the company's web performance. However, though some authors have addressed multi-channel retailing in conceptual frameworks [1, 9], none of the authors has defined and tested web usage metrics specifically measuring the potential synergies arising from the integration of e-commerce with traditional sales channels.

A comprehensive classification of web usage metrics for online retailers has been proposed by Cutler and Sterne [7]. The report enhances the categorization of basic web log statistics such as *hits*, *visits* and *click-through rates* by incorporating the marketing model of the customer life cycle [6]. The model is helpful for the classification of the proposed metrics as it differentiates several phases of the customer's decision-making process in an online store [11]. However, the report lacks a clear formalization of the proposed metrics.

Furthermore, web metrics classifications in marketing often lack crucial technical clarifications. The proposed metrics often depend on the availability of specific data formats and cannot be calculated without adequate collection and storage methods. Few of the proposed web usage metrics have been applied in a case study.

A more general shortcoming of most metrics systems proposed so far is the lack of adaptability of web metrics to the different goals of different web sites. For example, an information site might require a different set of metrics than an e-shop. In this research, however, we specifically focus on metrics for retailers with multiple distribution channels.

We do not regard customer typologies characterized by their browsing strategies, which has been addressed before [12, 13].

3   Life Cycle Metrics

In Table 1, we present a selection of customer-specific and behavior-oriented web usage metrics proposed by Cutler and Sterne [7]. We adapted the customer life cycle to organize the metrics as it reflects our abstract view on the business process and supports our analysis of multi-channel affinity.

The metrics describe the points in the customer life cycle where a company

- claims someone's attention (*acquisition*)
- turns visitors into paying customers (*conversion*)
- keeps customers recurring (*retention*)
- turns customers into company advocates (*loyalty*)

In contrast, *abandonment*, *attrition* and *churn* measure at which point of the customer life cycle consumers leave the site or cease buying from the company.

We enhanced the textual description of the proposed metrics with short definitions and explanations in order to facilitate a reliable and precise calculation.

Furthermore, an overview of required data and collection methods for the proposed metrics is included in the last columns of Tables 1 and 2. For the metric *reach*, marketing data about the number of Internet users and the overall size of the target market is required. Metrics such as *abandonment* and *conversion* depend on the availability of methods to re-identify users. *Attrition* or *retention* require transaction data such as a customer ID and the number of purchased products. Thus, user registration or at least cookie identifiers are necessary for many of the proposed metrics. However, not all companies offer such features on their site, which is often due to privacy reasons. In the absence of cookie identifiers, session IDs may be used alternatively to calculate metrics with an acceptable level of accuracy [14]. If session IDs could substitute cookies, it is indicated by brackets. However, metric results may be incomparable between companies if input formats differ.

Some of the metrics defined in Table 1 could be modified according to the specific business goals and the data available. For example, metrics such as *retention* and *conversion* are not necessarily purchase-related.

Table 1. Metrics for E-Business (according to Cutler and Sterne [7])

Category	Metric	Definition	Requirement[1]
Life Cycle Metrics	Reach (Z)	Ratio of individuals (i) from the whole population (W) that are potential site users (P)	Mktg
	Acquisition (A)	Ratio of potential site users (P) that become (unique) site users (U) in a time period (t)	Cookies (SID)
	Conversion (C)	Ratio of visitors (U) who have been converted to customers (K) in a time period (t)	Cookies (SID)
	Retention (R)	Ratio of customers (K) who made purchases (p) repeatedly in a time period (t)	TA
	Loyalty (L)	Ratio of customers (K) who are intellectually or emotionally binded to a company (index of multiple variables)	Cookies, TA
Life Cycle Interruption Metrics	Abandonment (O)	Ratio of visitors who commence but do not complete a specific task (T) in a time period (t); e.g. abandoned carts	Cookies (SID)
	Attrition (G)	Ratio of customers (K) who have ceased buying from the e-shop in a time period (t)	TA
	Churn (H)	Attrited Customers per total number of old and new customers at the end of a time period (t_n)	TA

[1]Mktg: Marketing Data, TA: Transaction Data, SID: Session ID

4   Cross-Channel Metrics

Table 2 proposes a list of metrics for the quantitative analysis of the Internet's impact on store sales. They supplement the metrics in Table 1 as they indicate visitors' affinity towards offline stores in different phases of the buying process.

The first five metrics focus on converted customers' delivery and payment preferences giving valuable insights about the online users' affinity towards offline stores. The proposed metrics depend on the availability of transaction data and the company's ability to combine online purchases and offline pick-up, payment or service. Though the market research company Jupiter found that most customers would prefer online orders and in-store pick-ups, not all retailers with an e-shop offer such flexibility [15]. Online consumers would be interested in an in-store pickup service because it eliminates shipping and handling costs and provides instant gratification by eliminating the lag time of shipping. The study found that three times as many online consumers would prefer to pick up an order in a local store than meet a retailer's minimum order threshold for free shipping [15].

Furthermore, the correlation between online customers per zip code area and the distance to the next store could indicate if the existence of offline stores influences the purchase decision of online buyers. The results need to be normalized with the population density per zip code area.

Visits on specific site concepts such as a store locator, information pages about offline services, pages referring to offline campaigns or pages for offline inventory searches also give insight about users' multi-channel affinity.

We will in detail focus on the evaluation of session clusters exhibiting a general interest in offline information.

Table 2. Multi-Channel Metrics

Category	Metric	Definition	Requirement[1]
Multi-Channel Metrics	Offline Payers (PY_{off})	Ratio of online transactions where customers prefer in-store payment (y_{st}) in a time period (t)	TA
	Payment Migration (Mi_{py})	Ratio of repeat customers' online transactions where customers switch from offline payment (p_{off}) to online (p_{on}) in (t)	TA
	Deliveries to Stores (D_{off})	Number of online transactions where customers prefer personal in-store pickup of orders (d_{st}) in (t)	TA
	Delivery Migration (Mi_{dl})	Ratio of repeat customers' online transactions where customers switch from picking up orders personally at a store (d_{st}) to direct delivery (d_{di}) in (t)	TA
	Returns to Stores (Sv_{off})	Ratio of online transactions where customers return products to local store	TA
	Customer/ Store-Distance Correlation (ρ)	Correlation between the number of online customers per zip code area (K_{zip}) and the distance to the next shop (l_{min}) in (t); normalized with population density	TA, Mktg
	Store Locator Visits (SV)	Ratio of unique user sessions (visits) (V) that accessed the shop locator on a web site in (t)	Cookies, (SID)
	Store Locator Exits (SLE)	Ratio of unique user sessions (visits) (V) that ended with a visit on the store locator in (t)	Cookies, (SID)
	Multi-channel Clusters (XL_{mc})	Clusters of visits (V) exhibiting interest in pages related to offline information (C_{mc}) in (t)	Cookies, (SID)

[1]Mktg: Marketing Data, TA: Transaction Data, SID: Session ID

5   Evaluation

To investigate the utility of our metrics proposal, we looked at data from a retailer who operates an e-shop and a network of more than 5000 retail shops in over 10 European countries. The company sells a variety of consumer electronic products both online and offline. The online retailer offers various transaction options for *payment, delivery* and *returns*. They can be selected in almost any combination both online and offline.

The store has recorded about 300,000 visits in a month with an average of ten page impressions per visit. In detail, we investigated transaction information of 13653 customers who bought online over a period of a couple of months in 2001 and 2002. Furthermore, we looked in detail at a sample of the company's web logs from two days in 2002. In the absence of cookie identifiers, sessions were determined by the use of session IDs, which were available in the log file. For sessionizing, standard web evaluation parameters have been used: the session scripts use a typical inactivity time limit of 30 minutes indicating the end of a user's visit. Visits of robots, archivers and administration services, which are identified by their IP addresses, were sorted out. After cleaning and preprocessing, the server log contained 16,383 unique user sessions.

For incorporating domain knowledge in the log analysis, we built a concept hierarchy of business terms as a model of the business purpose underlying the web site as depicted in Table 3. We adapted the phases of the customer buying process [11], which allows us to deal with terms that directly reflect our abstract view on the business process. We differentiated several phases of the customer's purchase experience, which include *acquisition, information, transaction* and *purchase*.

After removing irrelevant records such as requests of graphics or JavaScript files from the raw data, we mapped each of the 760,535 page requests stored in the web log onto concepts from the hierarchy. This procedure provides two main benefits: first, the data are much easier to interpret by the analyst in a highly interactive analysis approach. Second, through the aggregation of granular data into more general concepts, statistical analysis could be done on a more general level, e.g. on product group rather than on a product level.

We differentiated in detail the concepts acquisition (home), information catalogue (infcat), information product (infprod), service, transaction (transact) and offline information (offinf). All web pages that are semantically related to the initial acquisition of a visitor (e.g. the home page) have been mapped onto the home concept. The information node consists of the child catalogue information, where product information is a child of catalogue information. The service concept is related to general company information, registration, games and other trust-building information. Finally, transaction represents the concept of a customer entering the order process. It consists of several steps such as check-out, fulfillment, input of customer data and payment. The multi-channel (offline) concept is the most important one in our analysis as it includes all pages related to any offline information. Pages belonging to the store locator, information about offline services or specific offline referrers have been mapped onto this concept. The proposed taxonomy concepts could be used for similar taxonomies on other large retail sites.

Table 3. Site Taxonomy

6   Metrics Results

The results of the metrics analysis in Table 4 refer to a time frame of 8 months. For the calculation of the proposed metrics, the following assumptions have been made: *reach* (Z) has been calculated as the number of Internet users divided by the population in the site's target market. *acquisition* (A) has been calculated based on the number of unique user sessions within the time frame divided by the number of potential site users. However, due to the absence of cookie identifiers, we assumed that each session originated from a different user, which must not be true. *conversion* (C) has been calculated as the number of buyers divided by the number of sessions. Some of the proposed metrics cannot be calculated due to the short time frame of the data set. *Attrition, churn* and *loyalty* depend on the availability of data from a longer time period before reasonable results can be deducted.

Table 4. Metrics Results

Category	Results	Category	Results
Life Cycle Metrics	$Z = 37\%$ $A = 8\%$ $C = 0.56\%$ $R = 10\%$ $L = $ n.a.	Multi-Channel Metrics	$PY_{off} = 71\%$ $Mi_{py} = 10\%$ $D_{off} = 71\%$ $Mi_{dl} = 15\%$ $S = 87\%$ $\rho = -0.3$, p<0.001 $SV = 13\%$ $SLE = 6\%$
Life Cycle Interruption Metrics	$O = 95.3\%$ $G = $ n.a. $H = $ n.a.		

The evaluation of online customers' payment, delivery and return preferences suggests a strong interest in offline stores for the completion of transactions. Most of the online customers prefer order payment and pick-up at a store. The migration metrics indicate a small group of repeat customers who switched to online payment after their first in-store purchase. 13% of all users visit the store locator and 6% leave the site after locating a store, which could be interpreted as an alternative conversion metric in the customer buying process.

Furthermore, it has been found that a significant correlation exists between the number of customers per zip code and the distance to the next shop. The results have been normalized with the population density. It seems that the probability to purchase online increases with the vicinity of a store. This unexpected finding supports a retailer's multi-channel strategy. It could be also used to determine locations for new store openings. A detailed description of the calculation procedure and premises for this metric are addressed in future work.

7   Session Clustering

Our further analysis focuses on the analysis of a specific metric - session clusters exhibiting an affinity for the use of offline channels - based on web log data from the multi-channel retailer.

Web log clustering has become a promising approach to group online visitors according to their interests exhibited by their browsing behavior [16-18]. A number of clustering approaches for web server logs have been proposed to generate a model of user actions. Shahabi et al. [16] described a clustering procedure for user sessions based on k-Means. Fu et al. [17] suggested a hierarchical clustering technique based on page URLs which are organized into a concept hierarchy. Heer and Chi [18] proposed a technique that utilizes a number of information sources to create a model of user profiles, which can then be grouped using standard clustering algorithms.

We used k-Means cluster analysis as an efficient and scaleable method to assign sessions to a fixed number of clusters whose characteristics were not yet known but were based on a set of specific site concepts (variables). Let

$$S = \sum_{i=1}^{n} s_i$$

be the number of unique user sessions (cases) (s) , where s_i represents the number of sessions initiated by individual i, and

$$C = \sum_{p=1}^{n} c_p$$

be the number of site concepts (variables) (c), where c_p denotes the matching pages (p). If x_{sc} denotes the value of case s in variable c and $\overline{x}_{kc}$ the mean (centre) of cluster k in variable c, then the function to minimize is:

$$SQ_{in}(k) = \sum_{k} \sum_{s \in k} \sum_{c} (x_{sc} - \overline{x}_{kc})^2 \longrightarrow \min$$

According to our notation of variables, a multi-channel cluster (K_{mc}) would match the following expression:

$$K_{mc} = \begin{cases} home\,[0;\infty],\, infcat\,[0;\infty],\, infprod\,[0;\infty], \\ transact\,[0;\infty],\, service\,[0;\infty],\, offinfo\,[1;\infty] \end{cases}$$

A multi-channel cluster is defined by the inclusion of the offline information variable. However, we did not regard a user session's sequential order of clicks as described in Spiliopoulou et al. [12].

We used the cases with the largest distances to each other as starting points for the initial cluster partition.

8   Cluster Results

We first clustered user sessions based on original session vectors. However, due to some outliers with very high numbers of clicks, the session clusters were unsatisfactory and the sessions clustered only around the semantically related variables *infcat* and *infprod*. For much higher cluster numbers (>15), the clustering algorithm returned more differentiated results. As we wanted to find out if a customer visited a concept at least once, we dichotomized the data, coding it 0-1. Furthermore, we reduced the noise level by eliminating uninteresting paths of single clicks to the home page [18]. 987 sessions matched this pattern and were sorted out.

After dichotomizing and deleting uninteresting sessions, we reran the cluster analysis until we found a session cluster that included the variable *transact*. The variables were highly significant with an error probability of $p<0.0001$. A nine cluster solution finally returned a small group of sessions (cluster 5) that access the *transact* concept (Table 5). It appears that potential buyers are exploring all aspects of a site except offline information. Though it is the smallest group (415), their online behavior is most interesting for recommendation and personalization efforts and should be explored in more detail. The largest group (cluster 3) tends to visit product information only and reaches the site most likely from referring sites. However, its transaction probability is low. The site could use this information to reevaluate its online marketing strategy. The second largest group (cluster 1) leaves the site after exploring the *home* and *infcat* concept. This could be an indicator for the company to improve the attractiveness of its category pages. Finally, we found a large group of sessions (1268) that focuses mainly on offline information (cluster 2). This group of "offline prospects" seems to use the site to find the next store or collect information about offline services. The variable *offinfo* was also included in clusters 7 and 8. The users in these groups tend to be "true multi-channel users" combining the convenience of online information collection and offline shopping.

Table 5. Final Cluster Solution (Valid: 15396, Missing: 0)

Cluster No	1	2	3	4	5	6	7	8	9
HOME	1	0	0	1	1	0	1	1	0
INFCAT	1	0	0	1	1	1	0	1	0
INFPROD	0	0	1	1	1	1	0	0	0
OFFINFO	0	1	0	1	0	0	1	1	0
SERVICE	0	0	0	0	1	1	0	0	1
TRANSACT	0	0	0	0	1	0	0	0	0
CASES	3856	1268	4620	1154	415	301	898	378	2509

9   Conclusion

We enhanced an existing web metrics classification and proposed new metrics for retailers with e-shop and stores. Thus, companies can measure the influence of their e-stores on traditional stores more objectively. We added metrics requirements and indicated that companies need to apply specific data collection methods in order to calculate the proposed metrics.

We developed a site taxonomy for a multi-channel retailer and applied k-Means clustering on a sample of user sessions. We found session clusters exhibiting a distinctive interest in offline information, indicating a group of site visitors that uses traditional channels for purchases. In contrast, visitors focusing on most site concepts except offline information tend to have a high transaction probability. Thus, our research provides a first approach for measuring the interrelation between online and offline sales channels based on transaction, web log and external data and represents a contribution towards user segmentation and personalization.

References

[1]   Steinfield, C.: Understanding Click and Mortar E-Commerce Approaches: A Conceptual Framework and Research Agenda. Journal of Interactive Advertising, Vol. 2(2). (2002)
[2]   BCG, Shop.Org: The State of Retailing Online 5.0. Press Release, (2002)
[3]   Teltzrow, M., Kobsa, A.: Impacts of User Privacy Preferences on Personalized Systems - a Comparative Study. In: CHI-2003 Workshop "Designing Personalized User Experiences for eCommerce: Theory, Methods, and Research" (2003). Fort Lauderdale, FL
[4]   Omwando, H.: Choosing the Right Retail Channel Strategy. Tech Strategy Report, Forrester Research, (August 2002)
[5]   Doyle, J.I.: UCLA Internet Report. University of California, LA, http://ccp.ucla.edu/pdf/UCLA-Internet-Report-Year-Three.pdf.   (February 2003)
[6]   Howard, J.A., Sheth, J.N.: The Theory of Buying Behavior. John Wiley & Sons Inc., New York (1969)
[7]   Cutler, M., Sterne, J.: E-Metrics - Business Metrics for the New Economy. Technical Report, Netgenesis Corp., http://www.netgencom/emetrics. (2000)
[8]   Kobsa, A., Koenemann, J., Pohl, W.: Personalized Hypermedia Presentation Techniques for Improving Customer Relationships. The Knowledge Engineering Review, Vol. 16(2). (2001) (111-155)
[9]   Straub, D., Hoffman, D., Weber, B., and Steinfield, C.: Measuring E-Commerce in Net-Enabled Organizations: An Introduction to the Special Issue. Information Systems Research, Vol. 13(2). (2002) (115-124)
[10]   Novak, T.P., Hoffman, D.L.: New Metrics for New Media: Toward the Development of Web Measurement Standards. World Wide Web Journal, Vol. 2(1). (1997) (213-246)

[11] Gomory, S., Hoch, R., Lee, J., Podlaseck, M., Schonberg, E.: Analysis and Visualization of Metrics for Online Merchandizing. In: WebKDD, Springer, (1999). San Diego, CA

[12] Spiliopoulou, M., Pohle, C., Teltzrow, M.: Modelling Web Site Usage with Sequences of Goal-Oriented Tasks. In: Multikonferenz Wirtschaftsinformatik, Physika-Verlag, (2002). Nürnberg, Germany

[13] Moe, W.: Buying, Searching, or Browsing: Differentiating between Online Shoppers in-Store Navigational Clickstream. Journal of Consumer Psychology, Vol. 13(1&2). (2001)

[14] Berendt, B., Mobasher, B., Spiliopoulou, M., Wiltshire, J.: Measuring the Accuracy of Sessionizers for Web Usage Analysis. In: Proceedings of the Workshop on Web Mining at SIAM Data Mining Conference 2001 (2001). Chicago, IL, (7-14)

[15] Swerdlow, F.S., Deeks, J., Cassar, K.: In-Store Pickup Implement Last Mile Policies to Optimize Technology Investments. Vol. 10, Jupiter Research, (November 2002)

[16] Shahabi, C., Zarkesh, A.M., Adibi, J., Shah, V.: Knowledge Discovery from User's Web-Page Navigation. In: 7th IEEE International Conference On Research Issues in Data Engineering (1997), (20-29)

[17] Fu, Y., Sandhu, K., Shih, M., Asho: Generalization-Based Approach to Clustering of Web Usage Sessions. In: WebKDD 1999 (1999). San Diego, CA, (21-38)

[18] Heer, J., Chi, E.H.: Separating the Swarm: Categorization Methods for User Access Sessions on the Web. In: ACM CHI 2002 Conference on Human Factors in Computing Systems, ACM Press, (2002). Minneapolis, MN

Metamodeling-Based Semantic Web Languages

Wenming Wu and Yisheng Dong

Department of Computer Science and Engineering, Southeast University, 210096
wwmm@seu.edu.cn

Abstract. RDF Schema and Web Ontology Language (OWL) have nonstandard metamodeling architecture. As a result, these languages are difficulty to read and implement. Thus it is significative to make the OWL meta-model simpler. This paper introduces a modified RDF Schema (M-RDFS) as a metamodeling basis for OWL; it also describes how to overcome some problems of the original RDF Schema. Based on this metamodeling architecture, the M-RDFS will be a meta-language for OWL, thus it will not directly define specific ontologies. This paper introduces a conventional metamodeling architecture for semantic web languages. This method makes the modified RDF Schema easier to read and formalize, and it offers a firm semantic basis for OWL.

1   Introduction

According to Tim Berners-Lee [1], the Web will evolve toward the Semantic Web. Semantic Web is an important effort towards Web intelligence. Semantic Web is not a separate Web but an extension of the current Web where information is given well-defined meaning, better enabling computers and people to work in cooperation [2].

Ontologies will play a crucial role in the Semantic Web [3][4] since ontologies can provide shared domain models, which are understandable to both human and computers. An ontology is a formal, explicit specification of the shared conceptualization [5].

Currently, main work of the Semantic Web focus on OWL [6], which can formally describe the semantics of classes and properties used in web documents. OWL will provide a web-based ontology language. Further extensions will provide rule languages and finally a full-fledged machine processable Semantic Web [7].

Resource Description Framework (RDF)[8] and RDF Schema[9] are supposed to be the foundation of the Semantic Web since the OWL is layered on top of them. However, recent research has shown that RDF Schema has nonstandard metamodeling architecture [10][11]. As a result, RDF Schema is very difficult to be read and formalized [11][12] for some reasons, and OWL will suffer from the same problems. Furthermore, since OWL-Lite[6] is a light version of OWL. If RDF Schema still acts a light weight ontology language, its role is embarrassed.

In response to the problems, this paper modifies the original RDF Schema. Inspired by MOF [13], it also introduces conventional metamodeling architecture for Semantic

K. Bauknecht, A Min Tjoa, G. Quirchmayr (Eds.): EC-Web 2003, LNCS 2738, pp. 339-347, 2003.

Web languages. This paper proposes M-RDFS as a metamodeling basis for OWL. Thus, M-RDFS offers a firm semantic basis for OWL. Based on this metamodeling architecture, the responsibility of M-RDFS is to define the language layer. M-RDFS will not directly define specific domain ontologies, but be a meta-language for OWL. This architecture is layered clearly.

The rest of this paper is organized as follows. Section 2 presents some problems of RDF Schema. Section 3 demonstrates how to solve the problems, it also proposes M-RDFS as a metamodeling basis for OWL, and details the metamodeling architecture and the responsibility of each layer. Section 4 discusses the advantages and drawbacks of the metamodeling architecture. We also talk about related works. Section 5 provides conclusions.

2   The Problems of RDF Schema

Basically, RDF Schema defines a simple modeling language on top of RDF. It introduces classes, is-a relationships between classes (*rdfs:subClassOf*) and properties (*rdfs:subPropertyOf*), instance-of relationships (*rdf:type*), and domain and range constraints for properties as modeling primitives. With these primitives we can build an ontology for a specific domain. So, RDF Schema can be viewed as a light-weight web ontology language. Figure 1 illustrates the subclass-of and instance-of hierarchy of the core primitives of RDF Schema.

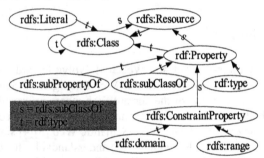

Fig. 1. Basic Class Hierarchy for the RDF Schema

However, the RDF Schema specification is difficult to read and formalize for some problems. Though the development of the RDF Model Theory by the W3C RDF Core Working Group has improved matters considerably, there are three problems as follows:

- Russell's paradox: RDF Schema has several objects that are meta-classes, including the class of all objects, *rdfs:Resource*, and the class of all classes, *rdfs:Class*. However, *rdfs:Resource* is a super class of *rdfs:Class*, meanwhile, *rdfs:Resource* is an instance (*rdf:type*) of *rdfs:Class*. This means a super set *rdfs:Resource* is a member of the subset *rdfs:Class*. These violate the principles of the set theory, i.e., that set membership should be a well-defined relationship.

These problems [10] lead to Russell's paradox. The paradox arises within naive set theory by considering the set of all sets that are not members of themselves. Such a set appears to be a member of itself if and only if it is not a member of itself, hence the paradox.

- Self-Instantiation and referencing [14]: For example, in RDF Schema the *rdfs:Class* is an instance of itself which make it difficult for object oriented developed to accept that a construct is a class and an object at the same time.

- Layer mistake for classes and properties: In RDF Schema, the user can define specific class, which will be treated at the same level as a class describing the language itself. For example, if the user creates a resource *Person* as an instance of *rdfs:Class* and a subclass of *rdfs:Resource*, we end up with the *Person* and the rdfs:Class at the same modeling level while the first is a user defined class and the later is an RDFS defined class. Similarly, the properties *rdfs:subClassOf*, *rdf:type*, *rdfs:domain*, and *rdfs:range* are defined both the RDF Schema primitives and specific ontology. That is, the RDF Schema plays dual roles. This leads to layer mistake due to RDF Schema as a language which does not distinguish the language layer and specific ontology layer.

Above problems of RDF Schema lead to the unclear semantics and make it very difficult to understand and formalize. Though RDF Schema makes itself compact, it overspends. Furthermore, OWL layered on top of RDF Schema as a simple same-syntax semantic extension has the same problems.

3   The Metamodeling Architecture

3.1   M-RDFS

For solving the above problems, it modifies the RDF Schema and introduces M-RDFS. Figure 2 demonstrates the change from RDF Schema to M-RDFS.

First, we introduce a new primitive *owl:Resource*. Figure 2 shows that *rdfs:Class* is *rdfs:subClassOf rdfs:Resource*; *owl:Resource* is *rdf:type rdfs:Class*; and *owl:Class* is *rdf:type* of *rdfs:Class*. Thus, in M-RDFS, *rdfs:Resource* is no longer an instance of *rdfs:Class*, and *rdfs:Class* is no longer an instance of itself. So, we will not worry about the Russell's paradox and Self-Instantiation and referencing problem.

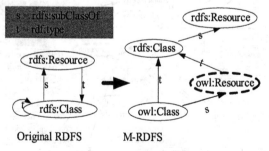

Original RDF   M-RDFS

Fig. 2. From RDF Schema to M-RDFS

Furthermore, M-RDFS is a meta-language of OWL in this paper. We restrict all primitives of M-RDFS to define the OWL language and itself, not specific ontologies. Hence, M-RDFS will not play dual roles. So it simply solves the "layer mistake" problem.

3.2   The Four Layer Metamodeling Architecture

Inspired by MOF and Case Data Interchange Format [15] (CDIF) which are conventional metamodeling architecture, we define a four-layer metamodeling architecture similar to MOF's. This kind architecture is a proven infrastructure for defining the precise semantics required by complex models.

Table 1 illustrates alignment between this metamodeling architecture with M-RDFS and the MOF metamodeling architecture.

Table 1. Alignment between M-RDFS and MOF Metamodeling Architecture

M-RDFS Metamodeling Architecture	MOF Metamodeling Architecture
Meta-language Layer (M-RDFS)	Meta-meta-model (MOF Layer)
Language Layer (OWL)	Meta-model (OA&DF Layer)
Ontology Layer (Domain Ontology)	Model (User Object Model)
Ontology Instance Layer (Ontology Instance)	User Objects (user data)

The functions of these layers are summarized as follows:

- Meta-language Layer (M-RDFS): It is the infrastructure for metamodeling architecture. Its responsibility is to define the Language Layer. Examples of modeling primitives in this layer are: *rdfs:Class, rdfs:Resource, rdf:Property, rdf:type, rdfs:domain, rdfs:range, rdfs:subClassOf, rdfs:subPropertyOf.*
- Language Layer (OWL): It is an instance of the Meta-language Layer. It defines a language for specifying ontologies.   Examples of modeling primitives in this layer are: *owl:Class, owl:Resource, owl:Property, owl:type, owl:domain, owl:range, owl:subClassOf, owl:subPropertyOf, owl:intersectOf,* etc.

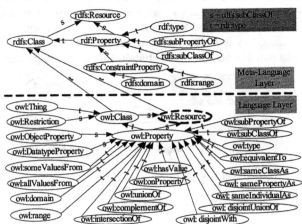

Fig. 3. Directed Labeled Graph of OWL with M-RDFS as meta-language layer

Figure 3 illustrates the relation between M-RDFS and OWL. In this architecture, M-RDFS will form the basis for the metamodeling architecture. Its responsibility is to define a language layer, while RDF Schema is originally a light-weight ontology language. That is, M-RDFS will be a meta-language and can not directly define specific ontologies. The language layer OWL will be completely responsible for defining specific ontologies.

- Ontology Layer: The Ontology Layer is an instance of Language Layer. An ontology describes a specific domain knowledge. For example, in an ontology for *person* we define the concepts *Professor*, *Student* and *PhDStudent*, which are instances of *owl:Class*, and *directedBy* is an instance of *owl:Property*.
- Instance Layer: It is an instance of Ontology Layer. Its primary responsibility is to define a specific in terms of the ontology defines in the Ontology Layer. Examples in this layer are *John*, *Peter*, and {*John, directedBy, Peter*}.

Figure 4 demonstrates an example in new OWL language as follows:

```
<!-- define a simple ontology -->
<owl:Class owl:ID="Person">
</owl:Class>
<owl:Class owl:ID="Student">
    <owl:subClassOf owl:Resource="#Person"/>
</owl:Class>
<owl:Class owl:ID="PhDStudent">
  <owl:subClassOf owl:Resource="#Student"/>
</owl:Class>
<owl:Class owl:ID="Professor"/>
<owl:Property: owl:ID="directedBy"/>
<!-- a instance of the ontology-->
< PhDStudent owl:ID="John"/>
< Professor owl:ID="Peter"/>
<owl:Description owl:about ="#John">
  <directedBy owl:Resource="#Peter">
</owl:Description >
```

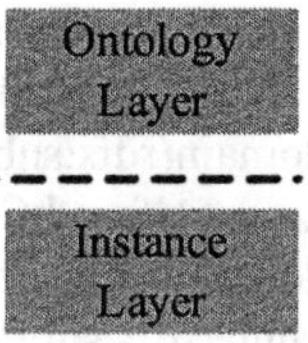

Ontology Layer

Instance Layer

Fig. 4. A revised version of ontology

3.3   The Semantics of M-RDFS and OWL

In this section we descirbes the semantics of M-RDFS and OWL. The purpose of this is to define clearly the consequences and allowed inferences from constructs in these languages. Here, we use L_{base} [16] which is expressive enough to state the content of all M-RDFS and OWL. L_{base} has a pre-defined model-theoretic semantics. L_{base} is intended to provide a framework for specifying the semantics of all of these languages in a uniform and coherent way. The strategy is to translate the various languages into a common 'base' language thereby providing them with a single coherent model theory [16]. Then, the semantics of languages L_i is defined by specifying how expressions in the L_i map into equivalent expressions in L_{base}, and by providing axioms written in L_{base} which constrain the intended meanings of the languages special vocabulary.

The intended result is that the model theory of L_{base} is the model theory of these languages, even though the languages themselves are different. This makes it possible to use a single inference mechanism to work on these different languages. This also allows the meanings of expressions in different languages to be compared and combined, which is very difficult when they all have distinct model theories.

We give in the following table a sketch of the axiomatic equivalent for basic M-RDFS and OWL, in the form of a translation from N-triples.

Table 2. Basic L_{base} axioms for M-RDFS and OWL

rdf:type(?x,?y) iff ?x(?y)
?x(?y) implies rdfs:Class(?x)
?x(?y,?z) implies rdf:Property(?x)
rdfs:domain(?x,?y) iff (forall (?z1, ?z2)(?x(?z1,?z2) implies ?y(?z1))
rdfs:range(?x,?y) iff (forall (?z1, ?z2)(?x(?z1,?z2) implies ?y(?z2))
rdfs:subClassOf(?x,?y) iff (forall (?z)(?x(?z) implies ?y(?z))
rdfs:subPropertyOf(?x,?y) iff (forall (?z1 ?z2)(?x(?z1,?z2) implies ?y(?z1,?z2))
rdfs:domain(rdfs:domain, rdf:Property)
rdfs:domain(rdfs:range, rdf:Property)
rdfs:range(rdfs:domain, rdfs:Class)
rdfs:range(rdfs:range, rdfs:Class)
rdfs:subClassOf(rdfs:Class, rdfs:Resource)
rdf:type(owl:Resource, rdfs:Class)
rdf:type(owl:Class, rdfs:Class)
rdf:type(rdfs:subClassOf, rdf:Property)
rdf:type(rdfs:subPropertyOf, rdf:Property)
rdf:type(rdf:type, rdf:Property)
rdfs:domain(rdfs:subClassOf, rdfs:Class)
rdfs:range(rdfs:subClassOf, rdfs:Class)
rdfs:domain(rdfs:subPropertyOf, rdf:Property)
rdfs:range(rdfs:subPropertyOf, rdf:Property)
rdfs:range(rdf:type, rdfs:Class)
rdf:type(owl:thing, owl:Class)
rdf:type(owl:sameClassAs, owl:Property)
rdf:type(owl:samePropertyAs, owl:Property)
rdf:type(owl:sameIndividualAs, owl:Property)
rdf:type(owl:subPropertyOf, owl:Property)
rdf:type(owl:subClassOf, owl:Property)
rdf:type(owl:equivalentTo, owl:Property)
rdf:type(owl:disjiontWith, owl:Property)
rdf:type(owl:unionOf, owl:Property)
rdf:type(owl:complementOf, owl:Property)
rdf:type(owl:intersectionOf, owl:Property)
rdf:type(owl:domain, owl:Property)
rdf:type(owl:range, owl:Property)
rdf:type(owl:Restriction, owl:Class)

4   Discussions and Related Work

This paper presents some problems of the original RDF Schema. Briefly, though the original RDF Schema is compact, it can not provide clear semantics and this makes it impossible formalized. If OWL is directly extended by the original RDF Schema, it will suffer from the same problems. For solving these problems, we introduce M-RDFS. It also proposes a metamodeling architecture where M-RDFS is defined as meta-language layer. This architecture is an infrastructure for defining the precise semantics required by complex models. There are several advantages associated with this approach:

M-RDFS provides core constructs by recursively applying them to successive language layer. This approach can easily distinguish the meta-language layer and language layer and ontology layer. It will not lead to Russell's paradox.

M-RDFS has clear formalized semantics, and it provides an architectural basis for defining OWL.

The architecture provides a basis for aligning the metamodeling architecture with other standards based on four-layer metamodeling architecture, e.g., the OMG OA&DF, MOF and CDIF. So, it is easy to understand and use.

The architecture is clearly layered. The layered method provides explicit separation between different levels of abstraction. M-RDFS provides a flexible mechanism to tailor and extend language layer. The responsibility of each layer is clear, thus it will not lead to layer mistake and self instantiation and referring problems.

However, the drawbacks of this architecture are obvious: it does not completely accord with W3C specification; it will require some existing tools and applications reworking.

Recently, some related works also concern RDF Schema and OWL. Peter Patel-Schneider [7][17]presented some problems that occur when naively building OWL on top of RDF and RDF Schema, and described some possible strategies to overcome the problems. Cranefield[18][19] proposed UML as a Web ontology language and discussed relationships between UML and Semantic Web. However, these works did not response to the problem of the metamodeling architecture of RDF Schema and OWL. O-Telos-RDF[20] described the formalization of an RDF(S) variant, which provides enhanced functionalities for meta-modeling and reified statements. This formalization is based very closely on the formalization of the modeling language O-Telos, which is based on a semantic network model. The proposed approach has an advantage over O-Telos-RDF, because the proposed approach used a model theoretic semantic (L_{base}) to interpret data model which could be more formal than semantic network model. Pan [10] firstly proposed a fixed layer modeling architecture called RDFS(FA), which used a model theoretic semantic to interpret data model. However, RDFS(FA) described a portion of the RDF Schema specification. We describe almost all elements of the M-RDFS and OWL. Further, the RDFS(FA) modeling architecture is relatively verbose, and the proposed approach is compact, simple. Thus, the proposed approach can easily distinguish the meta-language layer, language layer, ontology layer and instance layer.

5   Conclusions

This paper introduces M-RDFS to solve some problems of the original RDF Schema. It also proposes a metamodeling architecture where M-RDFS as a meta-language for OWL. So, M-RDFS will not directly define specific domain ontologies, but be a meta-language. Its primary responsibility is to define the language layer OWL. Only OWL can define specific ontologies. It provides a clear layered architecture, which makes M-RDFS much easier to read and formalize, and it offers a firm semantic basis for OWL. A fly in the ointment, this approach loses a bit of RDF Schema and OWL compatibility.

The future work is to develop tools for supporting the architecture, such as a tool which transforms ontologies in the original RDF Schema format to the pure OWL format.

References

[1]   T. B. Lee. Weaving the Web. Harper, San Francisco, 1999.

[2]   T. B. Lee, J. Hendler, O. Lassila. The Semantic Web. Scientific American. May, 2001.

[3]   D. Fensel, I. Horrocks. OIL: An Ontology Infrastructure for the Semantic Web. IEEE Intelligent Systems Vol. 16, No. 2, March/April 2001.

[4]   S. Decker, et al: The Semantic Web: the respective roles of XML and RDF. IEEE Internet Computing vol. 4 (5) Sept./Oct. 2000 pp. 63-74

[5]   T.R.Gruber. A translation approach to portable ontologies. Knowledge Acquisition, 5(2): 199-220,1993.

[6]   M. Dean, D. Connolly. OWL Web Ontology Language 1.0 Reference, W3C Working Draft, http://www.w3.org/TR/2002/WD-owl-ref-20020729/.29 July, 2002.

[7]   P. F.Patel-Schneider, D. Fensel. Layering the Semantic Web: Problems and Directions. Proceedings of the first International Semantic Web Conference 2002 (ISWC 2002), Sardinia, Italia. June 9-12, 2002.

[8]   R. Lassila, Swick. Resource Description Framework (RDF) Model and Syntax Specification. W3C Recommendation, http://www.w3.org/TR/REC-rdf-syntax. 22 February, 1999.

[9]   D. Brickley, R. Guha. Resource Description Framework (RDF) Schema Specification, http://www.w3.org/TR/2000/CR-rdf-schema-20000327.   27 March 2000.

[10]   J. Pan and I. Horrocks. (2001). Metamodeling architecture of web ontology languages. Presented at First Semantic Web Working Symposium (SWWS'01). 2001.

[11]   W. Nejdl, M. Wolpers, and C. Capella. The RDF Schema Specification Revisited. In Modelle und Modellierungssprachen in Informatik und Wirtschaftsinformatik, Modellierung 2000. Apr, 2000.

[12]   D. Broekstra et al., 2001. Enabling Knowledge Representation on the Web by extending the RDF Schema. 10th International WWW Conference, Hong Kong 2001

[13]   MOF-Parters. Meta Object Facility version 1.1, July, 1997.

[14]   S. Yacoub. Bootstrapping Semantic Web Languages using a UML Meta-Modeling Approach. http://www.hpl.hp.com/techreports/2002/HPL-2002-200.pdf, July 26, 2002

[15]   CDIF Framework for Modeling and Extensibility, EIA/IS-107. Nov, 1993.

[16]   R.V.Guha, P. Hayes. Lbase: Semantics for Languages of the Semantic Web, January 2003, http://www.w3.org/TR/lbase/.

[17]   P. F.Patel-Schneider. Two Proposals for Semantic Web Ontology Language. 2002 International Workshop on Description Logics - DL2002, Toulouse, France. Apr, 2002.

[18]   S. Cranefield and M. Purvis. UML as an ontology modelling language. In IJCAI-99 Workshop on Intelligent Information Integration, 1999.

[19]   S. Cranefield. Networked Knowledge Representation and Exchange using UML and RDF. In Journal of Digital Information, volume 1 issue 8. Journal of Digital Information, Feb, 2001.

[20]   W. Nejdl, H. Dhraief, and M. Wolpers. O-telos-rdf: A resource description format with enhanced meta-modeling functionalities based on o-telos. In Workshop on Knowledge Markup and Semantic Annotation at the First International Conference on Knowledge Capture (K-CAP'2001), Victoria, BC, Canada, October 2001.

Designing Web Menu for Configurable Goods

Takayuki Shiga, Mizuho Iwaihara, and Yahiko Kambayashi

Department of Social Informatics, Kyoto University
Sakyo-Ku, Kyoto, 606-8501 Japan
{tshiga,iwaihara,yahiko}@db.soc.i.kyoto-u.ac.jp

Abstract. Configurable goods are becoming a popular style for e-commerce web shopping sites in which buyers can configure a product of their needs from menus listing components. In this paper, we propose a sophisticated system support for designing web menu for configurable goods. We discuss evaluating correlations between component classes of configurable goods. Such correlations can be used to design web menus which cause less trial errors and give an aggregated view of product constraints. Choosing a proper quantitative measure for correlation is an important issue here. We compare a number of statistical and mining methods by experiments and show that Cramer's coefficient is most suitable for this problem. Then we show an algorithm which generates a tree structure for web menus such that closely correlated component classes are clustered, and hence users can easily select components.

1 Introduction

In the rapidly growing e-commerce applications, configurable goods are becoming a popular style for web shopping sites in which buyers can configure a product of their needs from menus listing parts. Personal computer is a typical example of configurable goods, and applications are expanding to various domains such as new cars, housing, and travel packs. Current web sites for configurable goods offer typical models to buyers and a buyer picks up one model and customize it to match his/her needs. Interactions with a configuring system are carried out to check whether configured products satisfy constraints. One important issue here is that a poor designed web menu causes a large number of trial errors in constraint checking. Another issue is that designing a proper web menu requires knowledge of experts, and it is costly. Thus a more sophisticated system support for designing web menu for configurable goods is required.

The web menu proposed in [7] can be used to compare goods having multiple attributes. However, it is restricted to non-configurable goods such as old cars, where buyers cannot change configuration. Since typical configurable goods offer more than 1 billion combinations of components, examining all the combinations is impractical. One popular approach is that let the user describe his/her preference on components, and then the system solves a constraint satisfaction problem under the preference [6]. However, describing preference is not a trivial task, requiring knowledge on available components, and requiring search on components anyway.

K. Bauknecht, A Min Tjoa, G. Quirchmayr (Eds.): EC-Web 2003, LNCS 2738, pp. 348–358, 2003.

In this paper, we propose evaluating correlations between components of configurable goods. By using such correlations, we can design web menus which cause less trial errors and give an aggregated view of product constraints.

Choosing proper statistical correlations is an important factor here, and we compare a number of statistical and mining methods by experiments. In the data mining field, frequently occurring association rules can be discovered by the support-confidence framework[1][2]. However, this framework is not suitable for evaluating correlation between two sets, and Brin et al. proposed evaluating correlations by chi-squared value [3][8]. In this paper, we discuss what statistical measure is appropriate for evaluating correlations between component classes of configurable goods. We show through experiments that Cramer's coefficient is most suitable among four different measures. Then we show an algorithm which utilizes correlations and generates tree structures of web menus.

Our approach is unique among existing studies on configuration[9] in the sense that we focus on summarizing product dependencies by a statistical measure, so that users can figure out in what degree component classes are related. To the best of the authors' knowledge, our work of utilizing correlation for designing web menu is the first in the configuration field.

This paper is organized as follows. In Section 2, we discuss measures for evaluating correlations between component classes. In Section 3, we take an example of PCs and show experiments for evaluating correlations. In Section 4, we show an algorithm for generating tree-structured web menus utilizing correlations of component classes. In Section 5, we verify that the proposed algorithm actually generates web menus which reduce cost for selecting components. Section 6 concludes this paper.

2   Evaluating Correlations between Component Classes of Configurable Goods

2.1   Characterization of Constraints of Configurable Goods

We model configurable goods as follows. A *component class* contains a set of components. A *constraint* is a logic formula defined on attributes of component classes. When a buyer selects a component from each class and configures a product, all the constraints associated to the selected components must be satisfied. A *relationship* exists on a set of component classes if there is a constraint on those classes. Namely, we use the term "relationship" as an aggregated pattern of constraints. Relationships provide users useful information on how component classes are related. However, relationships obtained by just aggregating existing constraint patterns are too simple and not useful for selecting components. We need a statistical measure of *correlations* between component classes. In the following, we show examples of constraints on component classes from the domain of configurable PCs.

- If CPU is Pentium and Socket is 478, then Motherboard can be selected from Sokect478 or FSB533.
- If Matrox P128MB is selected as Graphic Card, then Windows95 cannot be selected.
- If Motherboard has onboard sound, then SoundCard is not necessary.
- The total memory capacity cannot exceed the limit of Motherboard.

These constraints have the following properties:

- Constraints can be represented as equalities/inequalities on class and attribute variables, and Boolean combinations of those predicates[4][5].
- Those Boolean combinations can be arbitrary, including negative correlations such as "if $x = a$, then $y \neq b$".
- Constraints are heterogeneous in the way that some constraints are applicable to only a few components while other constraints are applicable to most of the components in a class.

Given such a set of constraints on component classes, we are interested in statistics which represents how a component is dependent to other components. Such a statistics should be useful information for buyers to navigate through component classes and choose components, or for web e-commerce site programmers to design web menus by which buyers can easily configure their own combination of components. In the following, we discuss candidates for measure of correlations between component classes.

2.2   Association Rules

First, we look at association rules which are well-known in the datamining field [1]. Given an item set $I = \{i_1, i_2, ..., i_k\}$, a collection $B = \{b_1, b_2, ..., b_n\}$ of subsets $b_i \subset I$ is called a basket data. An association rule is intended to capture a certain dependence among items in B. We say that $X \Rightarrow Y$ holds if (i) X and Y occur together in at least s% of the n baskets (*support*), and (ii) of all the baskets containing X, at least c% of the baskets contain Y (*confidence*). A typical application of association rules is market basket analysis, such that finding rules such like "when people buy coffee, it is likely that they also buy sugar." The confidence statistic ensures that the statement is true enough. On the other hand, the support statistic ensures that the statement is significant enough. The support-confidence framework finds frequently occurring association patterns.

Several limitations of the support-confidence framework have been reported in the literature. The first is that the framework does not capture negative association rules, such as "when people buy coffee, it is likely that they do not buy tea." The set of people who do not buy tea is the complement of the set of people who buy tea, and we need to know the total set of people to express such negative association rules. However, the support-confidence framework counts only positive occurrences of basket patterns. When ignored negative association rules are more dominant than positive ones, finding only positive association rules can produce wrong conclusion.

2.3 Chi-Squared Test

To overcome the above-mentioned shortfalls of the support-confidence framework, Brin et al.[3] proposed measuring significance of associations through the chi-squared test for correlation. The key idea is to use correlation statistic instead of the minimum confidence.

The chi-squared test is based on the chi-square distribution. We describe the chi-squired test in the following. Assume that variable A's (respectively, B's) values can be classified into k (resp.m) categories. The contingency table is formed by putting variable A across the rows and B across the columns, then filling in the number of instances in the population where a category of both variables A and B are satisfied. The contingency table has $k \times m$ cells. Let O_{ij} be the observed frequency of the cell for the ith category of variable A and jth category of variable B. Let $n_{i.}$ (resp. $n_{.j}$) be the sum of the cells of the ith category of A (resp. B). The expected value of the cell for A's ith category and B's jth category is obtained by $E_{ij} = n_{i.}n_{.j}/n$. Let χ_0^2 be the sum of $(O_{ij} - E_{ij})^2/E_{ij}$ for each i and j. Namely,

$$\chi_0^2 = \sum_{i=1}^{k}\sum_{j=1}^{m}(O_{ij} - E_{ij})^2/E_{ij},$$

then this is a normalized deviation from expectation.

Now consider applying the chi-squared test to a relationship between component classes. If χ^2 value is close to 0, then two classes are mostly independent and the constraints are likely to be satisfied for arbitrary combinations of components from those classes. Such a situation happens when a condition is set on a small fraction of components as an exceptional case, but the majority is free from constraints. On the other hand, if χ^2 value is large, it indicates that the two classes have some correlation and the user needs to select a pair of components from those classes. Otherwise, the user has a larger possibility of facing an constraint error.

2.4 Cramer's Coefficient

The chi-squared test has a problem when it is used as a measure for correlation of relationships, because the χ^2 value is influenced by the total number of categories, and comparing χ^2 values of different relationships for correlation is not possible. Cramer's coefficient is a measure of association that normalizes the χ^2 value by the following formula:

$$V = \sqrt{\frac{\chi^2}{N(min(k,m) - 1)}},$$

where, N is the cardinality of items. Cramer's coefficient ranges from 0 to 1. A Cramer's coefficient of 0 indicates that the calculated chi-square is 0, i.e. the observed frequencies are all equal to the expected frequencies. This means that there is perfect independence between the two variables. A Cramer's coefficient of 1 indicates that the calculated chi-square is the highest possible value, which indicates a perfect relationship between two variables.

2.5   Join Coefficient

Yet another candidate for the measure of relationships of component classes is the join coefficient. The join coefficient is used to evaluate cost of a join operation in relational database systems. For a join operation of two relations, its result size (number of tuples) ranges from 0 to the size of Cartesian product of those relations. As a measure of correlation between two component classes, the join coefficient can be formalized as follows. Let R_1 be the binary relation holding pairs of categories of A and B satisfying the constraints. Let $| R_1 |$ be the number of tuples of R_1. The join coefficient θ_{AB} is defined as:

$$\theta_{AB} = \frac{| R_1 |}{| \pi_A(R_1) | \cdot | \pi_B(R_1) |},$$

where π_A is the projection operator onto attribute A. The join coefficient θ_{AB} ranges from 0 to 1. If θ_{AB} is equal to 1, then categories of A and B are perfectly independent, and a θ_{AB} value far less than 1 means two variables are more dependent. Although the join coefficient can capture how close to perfect independence, it only counts instances and does not care how two categories are associated by those tuples. Therefore it is predictable that the join coefficient is not a good measure when relationships are close to a perfect correlation.

3   Experiments on Evaluating Correlations

3.1   Objectives of Experiments

In this section, we compare correlations by means of chi-squared value, Cramer's coefficient, support-confidence and join coefficient on the same pairs of component classes, and determine what measure is the best for evaluating correlation between component classes.

Since the support-confidence framework cannot directly be used for measuring correlations, we use percentage of component pairs satisfying minimum support and confidence.

Component instances and constraints are collected from PC sale web sites GIGABYTE[1], PC-kobo[2] and DOS/V Paradise[3].

Results are shown in Table 1. The *sup*-value is the percentage of component pairs such that support-value is more than 20% and confidence-value is more than 80%. Class-1 and 2 are component classes, and Attribute-1 and 2 are attributes

---

[1] Gigabyte http://www.gigabyte.com/
[2] PC-kobo http://www.pc-koubou.jp/
[3] DOS/V Paradise http://www.dospara.co.jp/

Table 1. Correlations for each pair of attributes of component classes

Pair No.	Class-1	Class-2	Attribute-1	Attribute-2	χ^2	V	sup	θ
1			Socket	Socket	2346	1.000	0.222	0.338
2	CPU	Mother	FSB	FSB	1497.26	0.647	0.078	0.338
3			Socket	FSB	1253.40	0.727	0.104	0.338
4			FSB	Socket	1191.92	0.711	0.125	0.338
5			Memory Type	Memory Type	328	1.000	0.194	0.348
6	Memory	Mother	Memory Type	FSB	36.24	0.332	0.000	0.348
7			Capacity	Memory Type	25.73	0.280	0.056	0.525
8	Case	Mother	Size(Type)	Size(Type)	1014	1.000	0.194	0.525
9			Size(Type)	Memory Type	10.91	0.104	0.056	0.525
10	CPU	Memory	FSB	Memory Type	10.45	0.162	0.172	0.259

χ^2: chi-squared value, V: Cramer's coefficient,
sup: support-confidence, θ: join coefficient

of Class-1 and 2, respectively. For example, CPU is a component class having attributes Socket and FSB, while Mother is another component class having attributes Socket and FSB.

We calculate correlations for each pair of attributes of component classes. For example, in Pair No.1, we divide the components in CPU into categories by the values of Socket, and also divide the components in Mother by the values of Socket, then compute correlations between those categories.

3.2 Discussion

Results show that the correlation between Socket values of CPU and Socket values of motherboard (No.1) is strongest in the correlations between CPU and motherboard, by all the measures except the join coefficient. This result conforms to the fact that CPU and motherboard are categorized according to an industry standard for Socket and all the combinations must follow this standard. The same observation applies to the results from No.5 to No.9.

Unlike the other three measures, the chi-squared measure is not normalized to ranges from 0 to 1. Hence its maximum values are influenced by the cardinality of categories. Thus we cannot use the chi-squared measure for comparing different pairs of component classes.

As for the support-confidence, it is difficult to set a proper value for minimum support, resulting in an apparently wrong result such as No.6 of value 0, although it is obvious that this pair is not perfectly ndependent. Moreover, the support-confidence value of No.1 is higher than that of No.5, but it is not acceptable because both relationships are perfect correlations, and the values should be same and the highest.

As for the join coefficient, the values from No.1 to No.4 and the values from No.5 to No.9 were the same, contradicting the fact that there are apparently differences of correlations between those pairs. This can be explained by the property of join coefficient such that it only counts satisfying instances of relationships and does not reflect deviation from perfect dependence/independence.

Overall, Cramer's coefficient is the only measure which did not exhibit any fault, and we conclude that it is the best measure among the four for evaluating correlations between component classes.

4   Generation of Web Interface Structure

In this section, we discuss generating user interface structures for configurable goods. By utilizing correlation between component classes, we can provide users with informative visualization of how component classes are related. Fig.1 shows component classes of correlations of configurable PCs, where edges are labelled by Cramer's coefficient. Web interfaces for configurable need to incorporate the following factors besides basic search functions:

- Buyer's preference on components and component classes.
- Reduction of violations of combination constraints.
- Visualization of correlations between component classes.

One of the most basic tasks of users for configuring a product is browsing components in a component class and selecting appropriate components. This component selection on a component class can be realized by a pull-down menu or an icon table. By combining such *component selection menus* as a building block, a web menu can be constructed. Placement of component selection menus on one screen can be modelled as a rooted tree, where each node corresponds to one menu, and the screen is divided according to the tree structure. For web

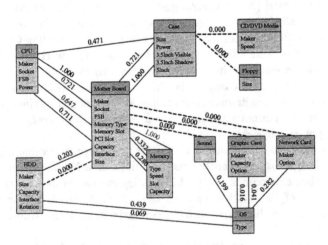

Fig. 1. Graph structure in configurable PCs

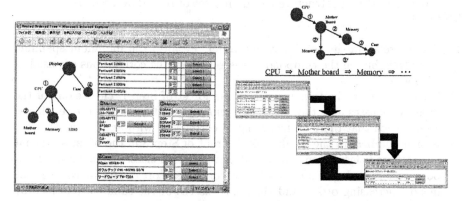

Fig. 2. Rooted ordered trees   **Fig. 3.** Screen transition graph

menus comprising of multiple screens, we use a *screen transition graph*, where each node corresponds to one screen, and each screen has a tree-structured menu. An example of a tree-structured web menu and a screen transition graph are shown in Fig.2 and Fig.3, respectively.

Although the above modelling of web menus for configurable goods are popular and widely used, finding proper tree structures remains as an important problem.

We use *rooted ordered trees* as a more sophisticated model of web menu structures. A rooted ordered tree has a root, and children sharing a common parent node are numbered, forming a total order from the smallest sibling to the largest sibling. We use this tree structure for placing component selection menus on the screen, in the way that the root is placed at the most conspicuous position, such as top-left of the screen, and then the tree grows going away from the root. Sibling nodes are grouped in one area, and the sibling order is used in the way that the smallest sibling comes to the most conspicuous position in the area.

There are a number of methods for arranging a rooted ordered tree onto a web screen. However, we do not determine any particular method; optimum one will depend on component classes and users' environments. We rather focus on finding proper trees as a generic structure, where actual generation of web menus shall be determined at runtime for a particular environment. In the following, we show an algorithm which generates rooted ordered trees for web menus, in which correlations and user's preference are considered.

Algorithm for generating rooted ordered trees for web menu

Input: Component classes, correlations by Cramer's coefficient, cardinality of components, a set of *preferred component classes* such that the user prefers to start selection from those classes.

Output: A web menu structure based on a set of rooted ordered trees.
Method:

1. Sort correlations in non-increasing order. Perform the minimum spanning tree algorithm on the component classes, where the correlations are used as edge weight.
2. For each tree in the minimum spanning forest of Step 1, choose one of the preferred classes as a root. If there is no preferred class in the tree, choose a node such that there is the strongest correlation with another node.
3. Assign numbers to the children of the root of Step 3 in the order such that (1) preferred classes come first, and non-preferred classes come next, (2) for both preferred classes and non-preferred classes, sort classes by correlations in non-increasing order, and then sort classes of the same correlations by component cardinalities in non-decreasing order. The last sorting is intended to let the user select from classes having fewer components.
4. Recursively apply Steps 2 and 3 to each subtree of the root.
5. For the trees obtained in Steps 1-4, sort them by the number of preferred classes in non-increasing order.

Note that we can use a lower threshold for pruning edges of weak correlations.

5   Using Correlations for Determining Selection Order

The algorithm we presented in Section 4 generates tree structures such that component classes having strong correlations are closely clustered. This strategy is based on the idea that classes having stronger correlations are likely to have more restrictive constraints, so that selecting components from those classes together will reduce the chance of encountering combination errors. On the contrary, component classes having weak correlations should have less restrictive constraints, and combinations between those classes are relatively freely chosen. In this section, we evaluate this strategy through comparison of search costs under different selection orders.

We assume the following: (success case) the user chooses a desired component from each component class in a successful case, where the probability of selecting a component is uniform, and (failure case) if there is no desired component, the user backtracks the tree and try again, and finish the search when there is no more components.

We again use extracted components and constraints of configurable PCs. We picked up component classes CPU, motherboard, memory, where we label those classes as "A", "B", and "C", respectively. There are six different orderings for those classes. We compute costs of success and failure searches for the six orderings.

Next, each correlation (chi-squared value: χ^2, Cramer's coefficient: V, and the join coefficient: θ) between the three component classes is calculated. Results are shown in Fig.4.

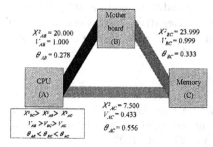

Order	Success	Failure	Total	Avg.
①A→B→C	198	1256	1454	6.73
②A→C→B	260	2352	2612	12.09
③B→A→C	200	1256	1456	6.74
④B→C→A	200	1280	1480	6.85
⑤C→A→B	260	2352	2612	12.09
⑥C→B→A	200	1280	1480	6.85

Cost order : ① < ③ < ④ = ⑥ < ② = ⑤

Fig. 4. Correlations among three component classes

Fig. 5. Searching cost in detail among three component classes

The cost is calculated as the number of components visited. For details, if we search the combination (Pentium4 2.2GHz(A1) - 8IRX(B1) - DDR SDRAM 128MB(C1)), the search successes because there is a path connecting three nodes. In the order ①, because we must choose A1 from six items in A, the first cost is decided as 6. Because there are three paths which connect A1 to items in B and one of the paths is connected B1, the second cost is 3. Finally, in a similar way, because there are two branches which connect B1 to items in C and one of the paths is connected C1, the final cost is 2. When all of the values are summed, the cost in this order is 11 (= 6+3+2).

Here, when there is a path connecting the indicated nodes, we call the search success, and when there is no path, we call the search failure. There are 216 searches in all, where 90 searches are success, and the rest are failure searches. Table 5 shows the costs for each ordering of component classes. "Total" is the sum of success and failure search costs, and "Avg." is the average cost per search.

Now we examine selection orders obtained from correlations between component classes are actually giving lower search costs. Table 5 shows the ranking of the six selection orders by average costs. This ranking exactly corresponds to the ranking obtained from Cramer's coefficient and the join coefficient. This result supports our idea of using Cramer's coefficient for web menu generation. On the contrary, the ranking by chi-squared value does not correspond to the cost ranking. As before, this can be explained by the fact that chi-squared value is influenced by the cardinality of components, and may not be used for comparing correlations of different pairs of component classes.

6   Conclusion

In this paper, we proposed a method for evaluating correlations between component classes of configurable goods. We showed that Cramer's coefficient was the most effective measure for evaluating correlations. The measure can be used for designing web menus where related component classes are clustered in a menu, so that users can easily figure out how component classes are related, and can configure products efficiently. Although Cramer's coefficient can capture negative correlations, we have not explored this direction. Negative correlations are useful for handling negative preferences, such as a user specifies undesired components.

References

[1] R. Agrawal, T. Imielinski, and A. Swami, "Mining Association Rules between Sets of Items in Large Databases", *Proc. of the ACM SIGMOD Int'l Conf. on Management of Data*, ACM SIGMOD'93, pp. 207–216, 1993.

[2] R. Agrawal and R. Srikant, "Fast Algorithms for Mining Association Rules", *Proc. of the 20th VLDB Conference*, pp. 487–499, 1994.

[3] S. Brin, R. Motwani, and C. Silverstein, "Beyond Market Baskets: Generalizing Association Rules to Correlations", *Proc. of the ACM SIGMOD Int'l Conf. on Management of Data*, ACM SIGMOD'97, pp. 265–276, 1997.

[4] M. Iwaihara, "Supporting Dynamic Constraints for Commerce Negotiations, *IEEE Press*", 2nd Int. Workshop in Advanced Issues of E-Commerce and Web-Information Systems(WECWIS), pp. 12–20, 2000.

[5] M. Kozawa, M. Iwaihara and Y. Kambayashi, "Constraint Search for Comparing Multiple-Incentive Merchandises", *Proc. 3rd International Conference on Electronic Commerce and Web Technologies* (EC-Web), LNCS 2455, pp. 152–161, 2002.

[6] U. Junker, "Preference Programming for Configuration", *Proc. IJCAI'01 - Configuration Workshop*, Seattle, 2001.

[7] J. Lee, P. Wang, and H. S. Lee, "A Visual One-Page Catalog Interface for Analytical Product Selection," *Proc. 2nd Int. Conf. Electronic Commerce and Web Technologies* (EC-Web), LNCS 2115, pp. 240–249, 2001.

[8] S. Morishita, and A. Nakaya, "Parallel branch-and-bound graph search for correlated association rules", *Proc. of ACM SIGKDD Workshop on Large-Scale Parallel KDD Systems*, ACM SIGKDD, pp. 265–276, 1999.

[9] D. Sabin and R. Weigel, "Product Configuration Frameworks - A Survey," *IEEE Intelligent Systems*, 13(4), pp. 32–85, 1998.

Customizing Business Processes in Web Applications

Gustavo Rossi*, Hans Albrecht Schmid**, and Fernando Lyardet***

*LIFIA-Universidad Nacional de La Plata, Argentina
gustavo@sol.info.unlp.edu.ar
**University of Applied Sciences, Konstanz, Germany.
schmidha@fh-konstanz.de
*** Technical University of Darmstadt
fernando@tk.informatik.tu-darmstadt.de

Abstract In this paper we discuss several issues related to the introduction of business processes in the life cycle of Web based E-commerce applications. We first argue that business processes have been so far neglected by modeling and design methodologies treating them as by-products of conceptual and navigational design artifacts, and as a consequence introducing different design and usability problems in the final products. We introduce a novel approach in which processes and activities are treated as first class citizens during application modeling and design. In the core of the paper we analyze the problem of customizing business processes to different user profiles or individuals. We show that using our approach we obtain modular and evolvable solutions.

1. Introduction

With the introduction of new technological advances brought by the World Wide Web, the Internet is being used as a platform for the implementation of complex business applications. Even the most simple e-commerce application includes some kind of embedded business process that must be correctly executed to guarantee the success of the application. The growing trend on automating business tasks by making the underlying applications interoperable using the Internet, brings new problems to software designers. However while there has been a considerable amount of work related with the specification and implementation of business processes in the context of conventional workflow-like applications [7], or with the use of the Internet platform for supporting complex interactions between distributed processes (e.g. using Web Services) [1], the interplays between processes and the usual navigational paradigm of Web applications remains barely unexplored. Moreover, mature Web design methods like OOHDM [9] or WebML [2] either neglect processes or just treat them as by-products of the navigational specification thus introducing design and usability problems.

In [8], we introduced a novel approach for designing business processes in Web Applications by extending the OOHDM design framework with processes and activities both in the conceptual and navigational models. This approach is built on sound software engineering principles: it treats business processes and activities as

K. Bauknecht, A Min Tjoa, G. Quirchmayr (Eds.): EC-Web 2003, LNCS 2738, pp. 359-368, 2003.

first class citizens in the development life cycle; by further decoupling activities from the processes in which they are executed, and by clearly separating process control flow from the navigational behavior of the overall application, our approach improves activities reuse and helps to get rid of inconsistent states and incorrect execution behaviors.   This kind of behaviors arises as the result of the interplay between navigation (the usual way of exploring the Web) and the execution of the business process. Objectifying processes and clearly indicating the effect of navigation in the state of process objects is one of the key strategies of our approach. In this paper we elaborate our previous ideas and discuss the problem of customizing business processes.

The structure of the paper is as follows: we first summarize our approach for introducing business processes in OOHDM emphasizing the interplays among processes and navigation. We next present our approach to customize processes to different user profiles or individuals and then present some concluding remarks and further work.

2. Modeling and Designing Business Processes in Web Applications

Introducing business processes in software applications is a difficult task, and it is widely recognized that the different components of a business process should be treated as first-class objects. For example, in [7] the authors introduce components for processes, synchronization features, histories, etc., in the context of a general architecture for workflow applications. We have put our focus in the integration of typical concepts of business process execution with the usual navigational semantics of the WWW. For achieving this objective, instead of defining a new approach from scratch, we decided to enrich OOHDM, a state-of-the-art design method for "conventional" Web applications design, with process features. The result has been appealing as we could use the standard mechanisms for extending the OOHDM framework (namely adding new meta-classes and refining existing behaviors).

OOHDM (as other Web design methods like [2]) focuses on three different design concerns: conceptual or application modeling, navigation design and interface design (we ignore interface issues in this paper). During conceptual modeling, domain classes and application functionality are described using UML [3] primitives.

We partition the conceptual model in two types of classes (described using UML stereotypes): entities and processes. While entities model usual business objects, processes represent set of activities that must be performed to achieve a goal. A process is a composite [4] of activities, which encapsulate their own state (active, suspended, etc); control flow is further decoupled from activities and represented in the corresponding process.

In Figure 1 we show the OOHDM conceptual schema of a simple CD store. At the bottom of Figure 1, we show entities like CD, or ShoppingCart, and at the top of Figure 1, process and activity classes. The conceptual model shows that a business process like CheckOut is typically composed of several activities like the Login Act, ConfirmItems Act, ShippingAddress Act, DeliveryOptions Act, ConfirmAll Act, and PaymentOptionsAct. This is represented by an aggregation relationship in the conceptual schema. Control flow between activities can be represented using UML activity diagrams (we omit them in this paper for the sake of conciseness). The main consequences of treating activities as first class objects are that we are able to reuse the same activity class in different business processes, and that we can implement different flow of activities for the same process, for example to customize it to different users (as shown in Section 3).

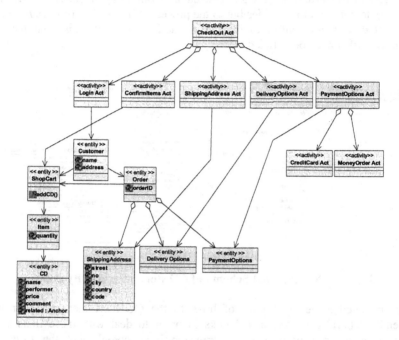

Figure 1: Conceptual Schema of CD store with processes

In OOHDM, the navigational model describes the objects that the user will perceive (i.e. the nodes), and the navigation topology (links and indexes); node classes represent a view of conceptual classes, while links represent the hypermedia counterpart of application relationships. OOHDM structures the navigational space into navigational contexts. A context usually represents a set of nodes in a particular task the user is performing. For example a customer can search and access CDs of a particular group, CDs in a musical gender, or CDs in a period of time, etc. Each time he accesses a particular CD of one of these sets, we may provide him with context-related features such as going to the next or previous CD in this set. We can also allow or prevent the user from performing certain actions according to the actual context.

We have slightly extended the OOHDM meta-model by defining activity nodes (the process counterpart of nodes) as shown in Figure 2.

In the navigational model, activity nodes, like LoginAct Node and ShippingAddressAct Node (Figure 2 right) play the same role as navigational nodes. They describe, in an abstract way, the visible attributes, anchors and operations with which the user will interact during process execution. The interface of an activity node (for example a Web page) will contain buttons like "cancel" or "next" that control the input processing of an activity and the control flow to a subsequent activity. Activity nodes like LoginAct Node are shown in the context of the corresponding process node to which they belong (a composite in OOHDM), like the CheckOutAct Node. This is indicated by drawing the activity nodes within the box of the process in which they are actually executed. Incoming links (like "resume" from CD node) do not point to activities but to the process node; when a process node must be activated, it gives control to the current activity (e.g. the one that has been suspended or that must be initiated).

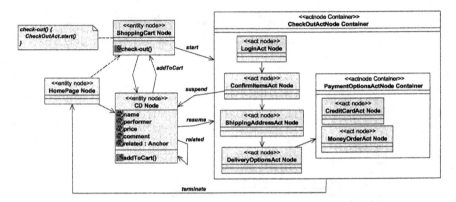

Figure 2:Navigational Schema of CD store with activity nodes

We have added some new types of links to the OOHDM meta-model, namely "suspend", "abort" and "terminate" links in order to deal with those links whose source node is an activity node. Suspension links complement the usual link navigational semantics by triggering a message to suspend the activity that corresponds to the source node. In our example, when the user navigates from the ConfirmItems activity node to the CD node (following the "suspend" link), the process is suspended (and will be later resumed in the corresponding state). Abortion and termination links are similar to the suspend link.

The use of activity nodes and associated links help to overcome the usability problems occurring when implementing business processes in the Web by emulating them as navigation sequences. In our approach, when an activity is left, it is suspended, aborted or terminated and the corresponding process is aware of this change of state. This awareness is achieved as the outgoing links trigger the change of state in the corresponding activity/process.

When the process is resumed it can then be started in the corresponding activity because, as previously mentioned, when a process node is started/resumed it gives control to the corresponding child activity; at the same time, as activities are modeled as first class objects, they can store their state and be re-initiated safely.

A further problem arises when leaving a process using a navigation link. For example in the checkout process, we can navigate to a CD page from the ConfirmItems activity as shown in Figure 2. Should the user be allowed to add the CD to the shopping cart again, while the checkout process is suspended, and if so what would be the semantics of this action? We may not want to allow this operation since the checkout process may already have created the order with the items currently in the shopping cart. Therefore, an item added during navigation would not be taken into account when the checkout process is resumed, thus confusing the customer. More generally, when a business process is suspended, a user should not perform operations that modify the state of resources being used by the process.

A good solution is to remove the action: "add to cart" from a CD node, when we access the CD after leaving the checkout process. We can achieve this objective easily by combining processes with OOHDM navigational contexts. In our approach, every process defines a navigational context: this means that when a user suspends a process, navigation occurs in the navigational context of this process. The navigational context of a process specifies, in the same way as a usual navigational context, which restrictions or additions apply to a node when it is accessed in the context of this process. In this way, we can make a "fine-tuning" of the features of nodes when accessed in the context of a business process or even from a particular activity in the process.

3. Customizing Processes

Customization has become hype in areas such as electronic commerce; we can find hundreds of applications that claim to be fully customizable to different user profiles or individuals. There are many different customization patterns: for example we may personalize the links allowing different users to explore different pages such as in Amazon recommendations; we can adapt the contents and/or the structure of a page to let different users access individualized contents, as in my.yahoo.com, etc.

Regarding business processes, we may also have many alternatives: for example in the checkout process of www.amazon.com, a new customer has to follow the previously mentioned step by step procedure (one page for each activity), while a registered customer just confirms all data in one page as shown in Figure 3; a customer can also sign for what is called "one-click" check-out in which the process is "automatic", etc.

A more elaborated customization policy may provide special offers for holders of a particular credit card; in this case we may need to "expand" the normal process control flow to add a new activity to let the user select from a number of offers. Notice that many of these customized behaviors may require modifying the application code, e.g. the process classes; thus, the way in which we design processes and activities is critical to achieve modular and painless software evolution. For the sake of conciseness we will only focus customization to the user profile, i.e. personalization, ignoring other customization criteria such as date, time, actual network connection, etc. However, the principles exposed here are easily applied to the most general customization case.

Figure 3: One page checkout in Amazon for registered users

We have claimed elsewhere [10] that customization should be addressed using a design more than an implementation view. This means that once we understand *what* we want to personalize, we have to express this personalization feature using the corresponding design primitives, before deciding *how* it will be implemented. Treating processes and activities as first class objects, and modeling them in the context of the OOHDM framework allow us to apply most of the design rules defined in [10] for achieving seamless process customization.

The simpler example of process customization consists in providing different navigation/interface functionality for the same process or activity to customize it to different user roles. For example when an Amazon employee performs the checkout process he may be provided with different navigational options that a regular user can not see; in OOHDM this is achieved by defining different navigational schema, providing different linking topologies, one for each user role as shown in the simplified diagram of Figure 6. Both navigational views in Figure 4 share the same conceptual model (e.g. the one in Figure 1). However, while performing checkout the customer can navigate to the CDs in the cart while the employee can also access information about benefits related with the products he is buying. Notice that this "pure" navigational customization is transparent for process and activity classes.

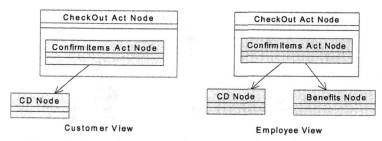

Figure 4: Customizing processes using OOHDM views

We may want to provide a simplified checkout interface for registered users like the one in Figure 3. Again, the OOHDM viewing mechanism allows specifying the ExpressCheckOut activity node containing all the information provided by the former simpler activities as shown in Figure 5.

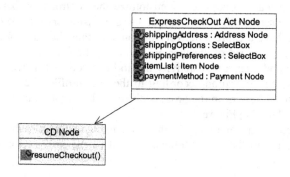

Figure 5: Modeling an express checkout activity node

This activity provides an interface in the spirit of OOHDM composite nodes. Each component node, e.g. item List or shipping address, replaces the corresponding activity in Figure 2. Notice that each of these attributes belongs to a type (e.g. Item Node), which is itself a full-fledge node class. There is no need to define an "internal" control flow; however, if this activity is left following an anchor, the semantics of suspension and resumption remain as discussed before, as well as the notion of navigational process context.

However there is a subtlety in this example regarding the process state and the control flow: when the checkout process is started it has to check whether it is dealing with a registered user to define the corresponding activity view.

An elegant solution to this problem consists in delegating the decision about which activity must me started, to a user profile object; the profile object then returns the corresponding (activity) view as shown in Figure 6. The process object will then be ready to receive the "done" message to finish processing, for example defining its current state as being in the ConfirmAll activity

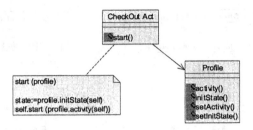

Figure 6: Customizing different views of the same process

In Figure 6 the start method in CheckOut asks the profile to return the initial state and then starts the corresponding activity, also provided by the profile object. Notice that class Profile also contains methods for defining states and activities; in this way we avoid having to sub-class Profile for different user profiles.

Finally, we might want to completely customize the control flow between activities according to the user profile. For example certain customers that paid a special fee when registering have a express delivery option, and thus they do not have to choose one of the options; or a set of cheaper products may be offered to customers paying with a Visa card and thus, a new activity has to be introduced. If we want to achieve complete process customization according to the user profile, the best solution is to decouple the control flow from the process object and delegate it to the corresponding profile object as shown in Figure 7.

In the micro-arquitecture of Figure 7, the behavior for deciding which is the "next" activity is delegated to the profile object as well as the information on the current state.

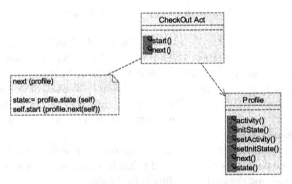

Figure 7: Decoupling process control flow for achieving customization

A generic architecture for achieving more complex customization policies such as those related with network connection, interface appliances, etc., is described in [5]. It further decouples those policies from the application code (in particular from the process objects) in order to separate the different concerns involved in the problem: the customization rules, the process (and domain) objects and the profile. Our approach can be easily used in the context of this architecture just by further separating the rules that guide processes to a separate component.

4. Concluding Remarks

In this paper we have elaborated our approach for introducing business processes in Web applications to show how to customize business processes. We have shown that treating processes as first class citizens allows us to model different customization strategies: for example we can adapt a business process either to an individual or to different user profiles in a seamless way, i.e. without having to deal with messy code. For the sake of space we have not discussed other possible customization examples. For example it is not difficult to adapt the process control flow to the context in which the process is being executed by combining the idea of navigational context with the requirements posed by customization.

We have used the proposed design method successfully for a number of Web applications, both in student projects and in cooperation with software houses in real world projects. Some of these applications are a customer relation management system for small and medium sized shops and companies, which embodies different business processes, a cooperative travel agency where users can share traveling opportunities, and several Web shops. We are currently working on defining a software arquitecture to implement business processes in Web applications by extending the Model-View Controller paradigm [6] with a new layer: the process layer. In this way we can overcome the well-known disadvantages of the MVC when used in applications with complex logic. In the same direction we are studying how to improve our notation by including some advanced UML features such as stereotypes and constraints. We are finally studying how to extend the OOHDM meta-model to include features related with workflow applications in which different users can collaborative participate in the execution of the same business process.

References

1.Business Process Specification Schema, www.ebxml.org
2. Ceri, S., Fraternali, P: Web Modeling Language (WebML): a modeling language for designing Web sites. Proceedings of the 9th. International World Wide Web Conference, Elsevier 2000, pp 137-157.
3. Conallen, J., Building Web Applications with UML. Addison Wesley 2000.
4. Gamma, E., Helm, R., Johnson, R., Vlissides, J.: Design Patterns. Elements of reusable object-oriented software. Addison Wesley 1995.
5. Kappel G., Retschitzegger W.. Modeling Ubiquitous Web Applications: The WUML approach. International Workshop on Data Semantics in Web Information Systems (DASWIS-2001), Springer Verlag LNCS, 2001.
6. Krasner, G. Pope, S.: A cookbook for Using Model-View-Controller interface paradigm in Smalltalk 80. Journal of Object Oriented Programming, August/September 1988, 26-49

7. Manolescu, D. and Johnson, R. A micro-workflow component for federated workflow. OOPSLA Workshop on O-O Workflow, available at http://micro-workflow.com

8. Schmid H. A., Rossi, G.: "Modelling and Designing Business Processes in Web Applications" in Proceedings of EC-Web 2002, the International Workshop on E-Commerce and the WWW, Springer Verlag LNCS, 2002.

9. Schwabe, D., Rossi, G.: "An object-oriented approach to web-based application design". Theory and Practice of Object Systems (TAPOS), Special Issue on the Internet, v. 4#4, pp.207-225, October, 1998.

10. Schwabe, D, Rossi, G, Guimaraes, R: Cohesive Design of Personalized Web Applications. IEEE Internet Computing, pp 34-43, March 2002

Characterizing Crawler Behavior
from Web Server Access Logs

Marios Dikaiakos[1], Athena Stassopoulou[2], and Loizos Papageorgiou[1]

[1] Department of Computer Science, University of Cyprus
PO Box 20537, Nicosia, Cyprus
{mdd,loipap}@ucy.ac.cy
http://www.cs.ucy.ac.cy/mdd
[2] Dept. of Computer Science, Intercollege
P.O. Box 24005, Nicosia, Cyprus
stassopoulou@cytanet.com.cy

Abstract. In this paper, we present a study of crawler behavior based on Web-server access logs. To this end, we use logs from five different academic sites in three countries. Based on these logs, we analyze the activity of different crawlers that belong to five Search Engines: Google, AltaVista, Inktomi, FastSearch and CiteSeer. We compare crawler behavior to the characteristics of the general World-Wide Web traffic, and to general characterization studies based on Web-server access logs. We analyze crawler requests to derive insights into the behavior and strategy of crawlers. Our results and observations provide useful insights into crawler behavior and serve as basis of our ongoing work on the automatic detection of WWW robots.

1 Introduction

Log analysis and World-Wide Web characterization have been the target of intensive research in recent years [7, 6, 2, 3]. Web characterization results have provided significant insights into Web usage, performance analysis, infrastructure design, etc. Machine learning and data mining techniques have been applied to process logs in order to mine user profiles, communities of pages, patterns of use, and guide the improvement of Web design, etc. [8]. So far, however, most studies have focused on general Web traffic. Very little emphasis has been put on the characterization of automated Web clients like robots or crawlers, and the contribution thereof to WWW workloads. *Web crawlers* are programs that traverse the hypertext structure of the Web starting from a "seed" list of hyperdocuments and recursively retrieving all documents accessible from that list [1]. The number and the variety of active robots operating on the Internet increases continuously, resulting to a noticeable impact on WWW traffic and Web-server activity.

In this paper, we seek to characterize the activity of Web crawlers, gain an insight into their behavior, and identify common characteristics of different crawlers. Investigating and understanding crawler activity is important as it

K. Bauknecht, A Min Tjoa, G. Quirchmayr (Eds.): EC-Web 2003, LNCS 2738, pp. 369–378, 2003.
© Springer-Verlag Berlin Heidelberg 2003

Table 1. Summary of access log characteristics

Log Acronym Log Origin Country Code	CS-UCY CS, UCY CY	CC-UCY CC, UCY CY	ICS-FORTH ICS, FORTH GR	SL-NTUA SOFTLAB, NTUA GR	CSE-TOR CSE, U. of Toronto CA
Log Duration (days)	176	114	45	58	42
Starting Date	11/9/01	15/1/02	11/3/02	1/1/02	13/2/02
Ending Date	6/3/02	9/3/02	25/4/02	27/2/02	27/3/02
Log Size (MB)	184.8	150.7	81.8	525.9	243.7
Total Requests	1,767,101	1,467,266	786,300	2,724,074	2,565,214
Distinct URL's Requested	69,918	47,751	58,225	102,088	48,229
Avg Requests/Day	10,040.35	12,850.46	17,473.33	46,966.8	61,076.52
Bytes Transferred (MB)	23,618.53	18,946.92	8,021.12	745,387.42	36,234.55
Avg Bytes/Day (MB)	134.20	166.20	178.25	12,851.51	862.73

enables researchers to:(i) estimate the impact of robots on the workload and performance of Web servers; (ii) investigate the contribution of crawlers in WWW traffic; (iii) discover and compare the strategies employed by different crawlers to reap resources from the Web and (iv) model the activity of robots to produce synthetic crawler workloads for simulation studies. Finally, characterization is the basis for the automatic detection of robots. For the purposes of our study, we concentrate on the characterization of five different crawlers, four of which belong to well-known search engines: *Google* (http://www.google.com), *AltaVista* (http://www.altavista.com), *Inktomi* (http://www.inktomi.com), and *FastSearch* (http://www.fastsearch.com). The fifth crawler belongs to *CiteSeer*, also known as "ResearchIndex," the Digital Library and Citation Index of NEC Research Institute (http://www.citeseer.nj.nec.com).

We employ and analyze access logs from five different academic sites in three countries: (a) The University of Cyprus; one set from the departmental Web server of the Computer Science Department (log acronym *CS-UCY*) and one set from the main University Web server (*CC-UCY*); (b) The Institute of Computer Science, Foundation of Research and Technology, Hellas in Greece (*ICS-FORTH*); (c) The Software Engineering Laboratory server at the National Technical University of Athens, Greece (*SL-NTUA*); (d) The departmental server of Computer Science and Engineering at the University of Toronto, Canada (*CSE-TOR*). These logs were given to us under a non-disclosure agreement in order to protect the privacy of end-users accessing the respective sites. The logs capture a period spanning from the fall of 2001 to the winter of 2002; log durations range from 42 to 176 days. Overall, these logs capture a total of 9,3 million HTTP requests for 326,211 distinct URL's, and a total of 812 GB of transferred data. In Table 1 we present an overview of the log-suite employed in this paper. To process the access-logs, we designed and developed ALAN (A Log ANalyzer). ALAN is a library written in JAVA that provides classes and methods for pre-processing and filtering access-logs, identifying the IP addresses of known crawlers. ALAN produces output compatible to Matlab.

The characterization of our logs is given in Section 2 and a summary of our conlucions in Section 3. An extended presentation of our analysis is given in [5].

Table 2. Contribution of selected crawlers to Web-server activity

Log Acronym	CS-UCY	CC-UCY	ICS-FORTH	SL-NTUA	CSE-TOR
% of total requests	10.32 %	9.48 %	12.67 %	4.02 %	10.18 %
% of bytes	5.72 %	5.11 %	4.33 %	0.08 %	5.84 %

Table 3. Percentage of HTTP responses to selected crawlers over all logs

Response Codes	2xx	304	3xx (except 304)	4xx
All clients	72.26%	16.47 %	1.98%	9.29%
Google	41.86%	42.21%	3.31%	16%
Inktomi	33.73%	33.14%	7.4%	25.7%
AltaVista	80.18%	0%	0.53%	19.28%
Fastsearch	52.58%	33.17%	2.25%	11.99%
CiteSeer	59.59%	1.09%	4.21%	35.10%

2   Characterizing Crawler Behavior

Considering all crawlers and logs, we end up with a total of 792,285 crawler-induced requests generating a traffic of 5GB of data; individual crawlers generate HTTP traffic of 1.1 to 33.52 MB/day on each Web server examined. Collectively, the activity of the five crawlers represents the 8.51% of the total number of requests included in our logs and the 0.65% of the bytes transferred. The impact of the five crawlers on each individual Web server is presented in Table 2. From this table we can see that in four out of the five sites, the five crawlers are responsible for the 9.48-12.67% of the total incoming requests and for the 4.33-5.84% of outgoing traffic, which represent a sizable proportion of the overall HTTP activity in these particular servers. Crawler contribution to the outgoing traffic in the fifth site (SL-NTUA) is negligible; this is because the SL-NTUA server hosts very large and very popular multimedia files, which are of no interest to crawlers.

2.1   HTTP-Traffic Characteristics

An analysis of general HTTP traffic captured by our logs discovers trends similar to those published in the literature [2, 7]. These trends change, however, if we focus on traffic stemming from the five crawlers of our study. Almost 100% of all HTTP requests are GET's. The percentage of different response codes for the five crawlers examined, averaged over all five logs of our log-suite, are presented in Table 3: crawlers implementing caching, such as Google, Inktomi, and FastSearch, issue cache-validation commands at a rate much higher than the rate observed in the general population of WWW clients: 42.21%, 33.14% and 33.17% versus 16.47%. From Table 3 we can observe also that responses to crawler requests exhibit a proportion of 4xx error codes higher than the observed rate for all clients. Most of the error codes are due to unavailable resources "404 Not found." The higher rate of 4xx codes can be explained by the fact that human users are able to recognize, memorize and avoid erroneous links, unavailable resources, temporarily unavailable sites etc. It is the (rational) behavior and choices of those users that determine the all-clients characterization. A crawler should try to minimize the number of HTTP requests that lead to 4xx replies, as these represent a mere overhead in its operation.

2.2 Resource Referencing Behavior

Classification of Requested URL Resources by File Type For most Web sites, the resources that receive the overwhelming majority of requests are text (text/plain, text/html) and image files (image/jpeg, image/gif, etc.) [7, 2]. The remaining content types constitute a relatively small portion of requested URL resources (postscript and PDF, audio and video, scripts, applets). However, the mixture of content types requested may vary dramatically from site to site according to the site's design and the profile of its user base. In our log-suite, over 90% of all requests in four out of the five logs target text or image resources.

The situation is different if we focus on requests arising from the five crawlers studied. Text-file requests represent the 71.67-97.22% of total requests, whereas requests for image resources are practically non-existent. Finally, crawlers such as Google and NEC's CiteSeer, which try to index other than textual documents where available (e.g., postscript, pdf, compressed files), pursue the retrieval of the corresponding URL resources more aggressively than the general population of WWW clients.

Distinct Requests When studying the patterns of URL requests arriving at a particular Web server, it is interesting to estimate the percentage of *separate* (distinct) resources requested over the *total* number of requested resources [2]. Taking into account requests from all clients captured in our log suite, gives a small percentage of distinct requests between 1.88-7.4%. This observation agrees with prior Web characterization studies (e.g., [2]). Nevertheless, it changes drastically if we focus on requests arriving from IP addresses that belong to individual crawlers: percentages increase by an order of magnitude and up to 100%. This is because the percentage of distinct over total requests coming from a crawler depends on the (typically limited) number of visits this particular crawler pays to the Web site at hand, within the time frame captured by the access log under study. For instance, in the period captured by the ICS-FORTH log, CiteSeer visits ICS's Web site only once and the corresponding percentage is 100%.

Resource Popularity and Concentration of Requests *Popularity* of a URL resource is measured as the proportion of requests accessing the resource over the total number of requests reaching its Web site. A large number of Web characterization studies showed that resource popularity follows a *Zipf*-like distribution [7]. To test if a distribution is Zipf-like, we produce a log-log plot of the number of requests for each resource versus the resource's popularity rank.

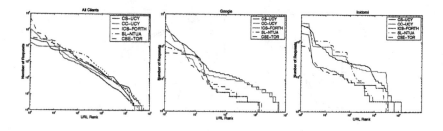

Fig. 1. Resource popularity (All clients, Google, Inktomi)

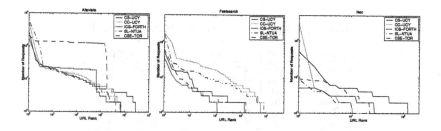

Fig. 2. Resource popularity (AltaVista, FastSearch, NEC's CiteSeer)

Resources are placed on the horizontal axis in decreasing order of rank; if the distribution is Zipf-like, the graph should appear linear with a slope of -0.5 to -1. Figures 1 and 2 present popularity plots for the distinct resources in our logs versus the rank of these resources.

We calculate the popularity of Web resources based on *crawler requests only* and plot our findings in the diagrams of Figures 1 and 2. Statistical observations for the case of crawler-logs are harder as the total number of requests issued by each crawler during our period of observation is small, i.e., one to two orders of magnitude smaller than the total number of requests coming from all clients. These "crawler" plots, however, provide some insights into crawler referencing patterns: many of the popularity diagrams display a step-wise shape with URL resources clustered into smaller subsets of equal popularity. In other words, the frequency of visits of a crawler on a particular Web site varies for different subsets of resources within the site.

Popularity studies for WWW access show that URL requests are highly concentrated around a small set of resources. The *concentration* of requests can be expressed by sorting the list of distinct URL resources requested into decreasing order of rank, and then plotting the cumulative frequency of requests versus the *fraction* of the total URL resources requested. Previous Web characterization studies have shown that resource-popularity is highly concentrated [7]. Our logs exhibit a high concentration of references on a small subset of unique resources: 10% of separate (distinct) URL resources attract a 75-90% of all requests. Fo-

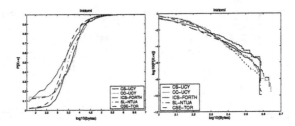

Fig. 3. Size distribution for successful responses: cumulative histogram and heavy tail of Google

Table 4. Average size of HTTP responses (in KB)

Log acronym	CS-UCY	CC-UCY	ICS-FORTH	SL-NTUA	CSE-TOR
All clients	13.69	13.22	10.45	280.20	14.46
Google	30.34	13.45	19.83	7.17	38.67
Inktomi	4.31	3.31	1	6.91	3.12
AltaVista	3.02	9.24	2.85	5.12	6.62
FastSearch	1.67	6.30	3.83	6.45	28.89
CiteSeer	32.37	7.49	51.75	17.12	115.82

cusing on crawler-induced requests, however, it becomes apparent that crawler-references are *not* highly concentrated around a small set of URL resources. For instance, in the vast majority of cases, 50% of the most popular resources attract between 60-80% of all crawler-induced requests. This behavior is expected since crawlers typically try to reach as many resources as possible when visiting a particular Web site.

2.3   Size Distributions

Several Web characterization studies have explored the size distribution of URL resources and HTTP messages and showed that average resource sizes are relatively small with an average size of 4 to 8 KB for HTML and 14 KB for images, and a wide variability [4, 7]. Resource-size distribution is typically captured by a hybrid model that describes the body of the distribution with a *lognormal* and the tail with a *heavy tailed (Pareto)* distribution [4, 7]. Analyzing our log-suite reveals that the mean size of an HTTP response across all logs and for all clients is 91.53 KB. The average response size for all clients is very high if compared to observations of other studies because of the very large files downloaded from the SL-NTUA server; omitting the SL-NTUA logs results to a drop of the mean size to 13.5 KB.

If we concentrate on crawler traffic only, we get a mean HTTP-response size of 7.03 KB. Evidently, there is a high variability in actual response sizes to the same crawler across different logs, as it can be seen from Table 4. Further evidence for the response-size variability can be derived if we compare the mean to the median values of HTTP responses. For instance, looking at the ICS-FORTH logs, the mean transfer size of HTTP responses that carry HTML resources is 5.53 KB, whereas the median is 0.19 KB. The respective values for image resources are 6.43 KB and 1.19 KB respectively. Similar observations hold for other types of URL resources and other logs. From Table 4 we can also notice that different crawlers exhibit widely different average response sizes. This is attributed to the fact that, in contrast to Inktomi and AltaVista, Google and CiteSeer download postscript, pdf, and image resources, which have larger average sizes.

In our study, a significant portion of the HTTP traffic corresponds to messages carrying no content and having a very small size. For instance, over 40% of Google messages have 3xx and 4xx codes. Therefore, it is interesting to study the size distribution of successful messages with a 200 OK code; this will provide insights on the size and type of content *downloaded* by users and crawlers. In Figure 3 we present diagrams with the body and the tail distribution of the sizes of successful responses to Inktomi (similar plots for the remaining crawlers are given in [5]). From these diagrams we observe that high variability is also present in the sizes of successful HTTP responses.

2.4   Temporal Behavior

Distribution of Inter-arrival Times Earlier studies have shown that general HTTP traffic is bursty and highly variable, and inter-arrival times of HTTP requests are heavy tailed [7, 4]. To investigate the inter-arrival-time distribution of crawler requests, we process our logs to measure and extract all time-intervals between successive HTTP requests issued by a particular crawler. A crawler employs multiple fetchers to crawl a site and different fetchers may reside on different IP addresses. Therefore, we take into consideration requests coming from all IP addresses identified with that crawler and study the statistical characteristics of the union of all corresponding time-intervals.

In Figure 4, we present logarithmic diagrams of the empirical density of inter-arrival times of HTTP requests from Google, AltaVista and Inktomi on CS-UCY. From these diagrams we can see that the time between subsequent HTTP requests is highly non-uniform and heavy-tailed. The observed distributions reflect the presence of multiple underlying distributions representing the behavior of fetcher-processes residing at different IP hosts of the same crawler. This effect is more pronounced for Google and Inktomi, which use a very high number of different IP hosts, than for AltaVista. Furthermore, the inter-arrival-time distribution of requests coming from an individual IP host is the combination of two underlying distributions: the first distribution represents the inter-arrival times of HTTP requests generated by the fetcher-process(es) of this IP host within one "crawling-session." The second represents the times between subsequent crawling-sessions. Shorter inter-arrival times are observed within a crawling-session whereas longer intervals correspond to periods of "silence," or crawler inactivity.

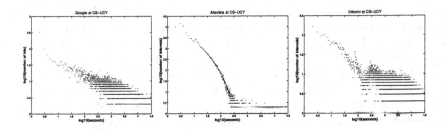

Fig. 4. Distribution of inter-arrival times for Google, AltaVista and Inktomi on CS-UCY

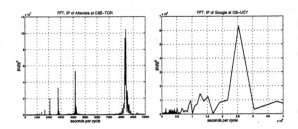

Fig. 5. Power spectral density of an AltaVista and Google IP address hitting CSE-TOR

Crawler Periodicity An interesting point that arises when investigating a crawler's activity is whether they exhibit a periodic behavior. By plotting the time activity (i.e. the active and inactive periods of time) of a crawler's processes that issue requests to a server, we have observed that several of them seem to exhibit, at least partially, a periodic pattern. We investigated further this observation and verified the periodicity for several IP addresses belonging to crawlers and estimated their time cycles.

For this task, we use the Fast Fourier Transform (FFT). The FFT maps a function in the time field to a, complex in general, function in the frequency field. The idea is that by observing peaks of magnitude in the frequency field we can easily conclude that time activity has periodicity. The frequency coordinate of each possible peak is inversely proportional to the time cycle of the periodicity. Since we are not interested in the phase of the frequency plot, we will illustrate the spectral density function that is the square of the magnitude of the FFT. Before implementing the FFT, we pre-process the requests issued from a certain IP address belonging to a crawler. Time is assumed to be sliced; we use a 10 sec time interval (granularity). Ideally, the granularity should be as small as possible, but we tried to keep the number of resulting points relatively small for a faster FFT computation. We count the requests issued from the IP of interest in each time interval. Because our focus at this stage is on the presence of some periodic action, we assign the value of one to the intervals that have at least one hit and the value of zero to the ones with zero hits. Consequently, we produce an ON-OFF signal that represents the crawler's time activity for the selected granularity. This signal is passed as input to the FFT function. The resulting diagrams reveal periodic behavior for several crawlers' IP addresses and in some cases this phenomenon is rather intense.

In Figure 5, we present two examples. We plot the power spectral density function with respect to the inverse frequency (time) of the activity of an IP belonging to Altavista and hitting CSE-TOR, and of a Google IP hitting CS-UCY. FFT specifies the main periods observed on that signal. We observe a periodic behavior which corresponds to the peak of around 8400 sec in the left diagram of Figure 5, and a dominating period of about 2.5×10^6 seconds in the right diagram.

3 Conclusions

Our analysis produced a number of insights regarding crawler traffic and crawling characteristics. In particular: (a) Crawler-induced HTTP messages carry *GET* requests at a much higher percentage than the general population of Web clients. Crawlers that implement caching and employ conditional *GET*'s, receive *304* replies at a rate significantly higher than "average" Web clients. Therefore, caching at the crawler-side can reduce significantly the crawler-induced traffic on the World-Wide Web. (b) Crawler requests result to a percentage of HTTP replies carrying error codes (with *4xx* numbers) at a rate higher than what is observed for the general Web-client population. Therefore, there is room for improvement in crawler design, so that crawlers avoid following broken or erroneous links. (c) As expected, a crawler seeks text and HTML resources at a rate much higher than the general population of Web clients. Crawler interest for images is minimal. Crawlers that belong to Search Engines which index non-textual formats (postscript, PDF, etc.), however, fetch this type of resources more aggressively than the general Web-client population. (d) In contrast to observations for "concentration" of HTTP requests, crawler-induced requests are not highly concentrated to a small subset of Web-site resources. Furthermore, crawler visits at a Web site do not result to "Zipf-like" popularity plots. It seems that crawlers classify resources into subsets; each subset is being visited by a crawler with a different frequency. (f) HTTP replies to crawler requests exhibit a high variability in size; the same remark holds for successful responses to crawler requests that carry Web resources back to a crawler. The size of these messages can be modeled as a heavy-tailed, Pareto distribution. Average and median size of crawler-induced HTTP responses are much smaller than those for the general Web-client population. (g) Inter-arrival times of crawler requests are highly variable and exhibit characteristics of heavy-tailed distribution. Periodicity properties can be investigated with Fourier transforms, which help us identify the time-periods of crawler visits upon a Web site.

Acknowledgments

The authors wish to thank professors A. Bilas of the University of Toronto, V. Markatos of the University of Crete, M. Skordalakis of the National Technical University of Athens, and the University of Cyprus Computer Center for providing access to their Web server logs. This work was supported in part by the Research Promotion Foundation of Cyprus, under the PENEK 23/2000 project, and by the Planning Bureau of the Republic of Cyprus, through the WebC-MINE grant for Scientific Collaboration between Cyprus and Greece.

References

[1] A. Arasu, J. Cho, H. Garcia-Molina, A. Paepcke, and S. Raghavan. Searching the Web. *ACM Transactions on Internet Technology*, 1(1):2–43, 2001.

[2] M. Arlitt and T. Jin. Workload Characterization of the 1998 World Cup Web Site. Technical Report HPL-1999-35R1, Hewlett-Packard Laboratories, September 1999.

[3] P. Barford, A. Bestavros, A. Bradley, and M. Crovella. Changes in Web client access patterns: Characteristics and caching implications. *World Wide Web (special issue on Characterization and Performance Evaluation)*, 1999.

[4] M. Crovella. Performance Characteristics of the World-Wide Web. In C. L. G. Haring and M. Reiser, editors, *Performance Evaluation: Origins and Directions*, pages 219–233. Springer, 1999.

[5] M. Dikaiakos, A. Stassopoulou, and L. Papageorgiou. Characterizing Crawler Behavior from Web Server Access Logs. Technical Report TR-2002-4, Department of Computer Science, University of Cyprus, November 2002.

[6] A. Feldmann. Characteristics of TCP Connection Arrivals. In K. Park and W. Willinger, editors, *Self-Similar Network Traffic and Performance Evaluation*. John Wiley, 2000.

[7] B. Krishnamurthy and J. Rexford. *Web Protocols and Practice*. Addison-Wesley, 2001.

[8] G. Paliouras, C. Papatheodorou, V. Karkaletsis, and C. Spyropoulos. Clustering the Users of Large Web Sites into Communities. In *Proceedings of the International Conference on Maching Learning (ICML)*, pages 719–726, 2000.

Enterprise Model Integration

Harald Kühn[1], Franz Bayer[1], Stefan Junginger[2], and Dimitris Karagiannis[3]

[1] BOC Information Systems GmbH
Rabensteig 2, 1010 Vienna, Austria
{harald.kuehn, franz.bayer}@boc-eu.com
[2] BOC Information Technologies Consulting GmbH
Voßstr. 22, 10117 Berlin, Germany
stefan.junginger@boc-de.com
[3] University of Vienna, Department of Knowledge Engineering
1210 Vienna, Austria
dk@dke.univie.ac.at

Abstract. Due to rapid changing business requirements the complexity in developing enterprise-spanning applications is continually growing. A vital field of delivering technical concepts and technologies for integrating heterogeneous applications and components to support inter-organisational business processes is the area of Enterprise Application Integration (EAI). A common characteristic of all EAI approaches is their focus on technical and runtime aspects of integration. From our project experiences in developing large B2B applications, it is necessary to integrate applications on the business and conceptual level as well. Because of the diversity of models and modelling languages for developing enterprise applications, we propose the *Enterprise Model Integration (EMI)* approach. In this paper we describe basic concepts of EMI, a pattern system for metamodel integration, and a case study applying EMI for developing B2B applications. The EMI approach is compatible with the MDA infrastructure and implemented within the meta model management tool ADONIS.

1   Introduction

Due to rapid changing business requirements such as faster time to market, shorter product lifecycles, increased interdependencies between business partners, and tighter integration of their underlying information systems, the complexity in developing enterprise-spanning applications is continually growing. Amongst others, a vital field of delivering technical concepts and technologies for integrating heterogeneous applications and components to support inter-organisational business processes is the area of *Enterprise Application Integration (EAI)*. The main idea of EAI is to provide technical solutions to integrate workflows and heterogeneous parts of enterprise applications in a continuous business application [5, 19, 22]. For technical integration differ-

K. Bauknecht, A Min Tjoa, G. Quirchmayr (Eds.): EC-Web 2003, LNCS 2738, pp. 379–392, 2003.
© Springer-Verlag Berlin Heidelberg 2003

ent approaches have been helpful, e.g. *data-oriented-, application interface-oriented-, method-oriented-, portal-oriented- and process-oriented application integration approach* [8]. A common characteristic of all EAI approaches is their *focus on technical and runtime aspects of integration*, i.e. on the level of target systems and execution environments (see fig. 1).

Our project experiences in developing large B2B applications indicated that it is necessary to *integrate applications on the business and conceptual level* as well as using models such as business models, business process models, product models, interaction models, (abstract) interface models etc. [14, 15]. Today, target systems such as workflow management systems (WMS), ERP systems, J2EE systems, groupware and messaging systems or company-specific software systems, mainly use proprietary model representations to describe aspects such as business logic, business rules, control and information flow, security aspects etc.

Standardisation organisations such as the World Wide Web Consortium (W3C), the Object Management Group (OMG) or the Workflow Management Coalition (WfMC) have reached to establish *standardisations on an execution level* such as W3C's HTTP-protocol or the XML data meta language, OMG's Common Object Request Broker Architecture (CORBA) or WfMC's interface 4 for process interoperability [18, 23, 24]. *Standardisations on modelling level* still can rarely be found, almost the only, but prominent, example is the UML for modelling object-oriented systems [17]. In addition, the OMG community started to establish a relatively new vision with the Meta Object Facility (MOF) and the Model Driven Architecture (MDA) to improve productivity in software development, applying object-orientation, metalevel concepts and modeling [2, 16].

Because of the diversity of models and modelling languages for developing enterprise applications, we propose the *Enterprise Model Integration (EMI) approach*. This approach is based on object-oriented metamodelling concepts to describe context-specific, integrated modelling languages. These modelling languages are used in enterprise application development projects integrating heterogeneous target systems. The EMI approach is compatible to the MDA infrastructure and is implemented within the meta model management tool ADONIS [9].

The remainder of the paper is organised as follows. Chapter 2 gives an introduction in model integration concepts. In chapter 3 a pattern system for metamodel integration patterns is presented and three concrete metamodel integration patterns are described. Chapter 4 describes a real life case study applying EMI developing a B2B application for direct sales companies based on heterogeneous and web-based technologies. Chapter 5 gives a summary and outlook to future developments and research directions.

2   Model Integration Concepts

Under *Enterprise Model Integration (EMI)* we subsume all tasks and concepts necessary for the integration of metamodels of modelling languages describing different aspects of a company. The following sections describe some basic concepts of EMI.

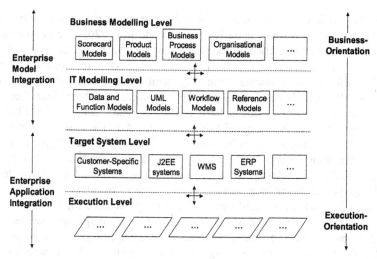

Fig. 1. From EMI to EAI

2.1   Object-Oriented Metamodelling

According to Falkenberg et al. [6], we define a model as "a purposely abstracted, clear, precise and unambiguous conception. A model denotation is a precise and un-ambiguous representation of a model, in some appropriate formal or semi-formal language". The language for representing a model is described by its metamodel, i.e. the metamodel is a model of its corresponding modelling language [3, 12]. Applying language theory for levelling languages, the result is a hierarchy of models, meta-models etc. [21]. This paper focuses on the metamodel level. In the following the terms "modelling language" and "metamodel" will be used synonymously.

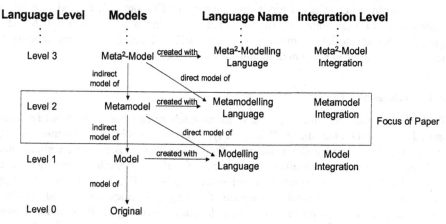

Fig. 2. Model Integration Levels

To enable the integration of models describing an enterprise, a necessary prerequisite is the integration of their underlying metamodels [13, 20]. For describing metamodels, we use an object-oriented metamodelling approach. The concepts of a modelling language are described by elements such as classes, relationships, attributes, and behaviour. These elements form a generalisation/specialisation hierarchy in which subordinated classes inherit common structure and behaviour from higher classes. Using view mechanisms, subsets of classes, relationships and attributes from the class hierarchy can be assigned to model types. A model type represents a concrete modelling language, e.g. a business process modelling language, a modelling language describing organisational structures or an information system modelling language. Linking and relating the model types, they form a set of interrelated modelling languages to describe a certain domain under consideration. For a detailed description of our object-oriented metamodelling approach see e.g. [9, 11].

For the integration of metamodels, we distinguish three major approaches: vertical, horizontal, and hybrid metamodel integration. These approaches will be briefly explained in the following sections using the levels described in fig. 1, which represent different views in metamodel integration.

2.2   Vertical Integration

Vertical integration of metamodels is a typical top-down or bottom-up integration approach (inter-level integration). Taking business goals and business strategies as starting points for application development, the top-down approach of EMI showed to be helpful. Metamodels from the business modelling level are integrated and refined with metamodels from the IT modelling level, e.g. business process metamodels are integrated with metamodels for data and function modelling. The metamodels of the IT modelling level themselves will be integrated and refined with metamodels of the target system level, e.g. metamodels for logical data modelling will be integrated with metamodels describing business objects of a concrete ERP system.

In re-engineering oriented modelling approaches (bottom-up), the existing target systems and IT modelling metamodels serve as starting points, which will be integrated with metamodels from the business modelling level, e.g. to bring models of legacy applications in relation to models of the business strategy.

2.3   Horizontal Integration

In the *horizontal integration approach*, metamodels of same level of detail are integrated (intra-level integration). This is the typical case when business partners, which form a supply or service chain, integrate their business processes, their applications, and their IT systems. Therefore, the metamodels of the modelling languages used have to be aligned and integrated on each modelling level. E.g. if one business partner uses a business process modelling language focusing on business events and the other partner uses a business process modelling language focusing on information flows, the concepts of event and information flow have to be integrated. A possible integration is that events can produce and consume information objects to represent the information flow.

2.4   Hybrid Integration

The *hybrid integration approach* is adequate if the horizontal and vertical integration directions are mixed and/or the modelling levels of the metamodels to be integrated differ noticeably. Hybrid integration can be useful for integrating metamodels of business partners which model their processes, systems etc. on different abstraction levels. Another example is the integration of metamodels of Balanced Scorecard approaches [10] with metamodels for data modelling to provide a starting point to gain quantitative data from runtime and data warehouse systems in the context of measuring mid-term and long-term business goals.

3   Metamodel Integration Patterns

To facilitate metamodel integration and to reuse experiences from former metamodel integration projects, we propose to use *metamodel integration patterns*. Some important patterns will be described in the following sections.

3.1   Patterns: Templates and Systems

The reuse of expert knowledge and experiences is of high interest in all areas of human work. Major advantages are savings in time and cost and improved quality of problem solutions. A possibility to make expert experiences explicit and reusable are so called *"patterns"*. The basic idea of patterns comes from the architect Christopher Alexander, which captured and reused design experiences in architecture and civil engineering by using a pattern language [1]. The community of object-oriented software development adapted this idea for capturing software design experience in so called "design patterns" [4, 7].

We adapt the pattern idea of the before-mentioned authors to capture experiences in the area of metamodel integration. To describe a pattern, we use a *pattern template* consisting of five elements:

- *Name:* the name of the metamodel integration pattern.
- *Context:* a description of the situation an integration problem occurs.
- *Problem:* a description of the integration problem which has to be solved.
- *Solution:* a set of guidelines, instructions and rules to solve the problem.
- *Example:* a description of a typical application of the integration pattern.

A set of patterns describing a family of problem solutions for a given domain is called *a pattern system*. A pattern system consists of pattern descriptions and relationships between the patterns, describing their interdependencies. The following section presents our proposal of a pattern system for metamodel integration. Pattern structures will be described by UML class diagrams.

3.2   A Pattern System of Metamodel Integration Patterns

Our pattern system proposal for metamodel integration patterns consists of six patterns. These patterns are classified into loose integration patterns, intermediate integration patterns, and strong integration patterns. All patterns are applicable within the integration approaches explained in chapter 2. *Loose integration patterns* are used for metamodels which are largely complementary. Each of the metamodels can exist without depending on the existence of the other metamodel. *Intermediate integration patterns* are used to reuse parts of a source metamodel to build a new metamodel or to aggregate parts into an existing one. Some parts of the new metamodel can exist without depending on the source metamodel, other parts can not exist independently. *Strong integration patterns* are used to build a new metamodel completely depending on a source metamodel. The new metamodel can not exist independently of the source metamodel.

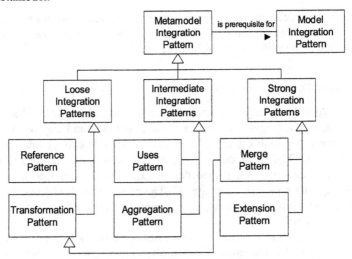

Fig. 3. Pattern System for Metamodel Integration

The *reference pattern* can be compared to a hyperlink which references parts of another metamodel. Applying the reference pattern results in navigation paths from one metamodel to another independent metamodel. The *transformation pattern* provides rules to transform parts of source metamodels to concepts provided by a target metamodel. This pattern can be used e.g. for describing transformation rules between Platform Independent Models (PIM) and Platform Specific Models (PSM) in the MDA infrastructure [16]. The *uses pattern* enables the usage of a part of a source metamodel in a target metamodel without redefining the part in the target metamodel. The *aggregation pattern* aggregates one or more parts from one or more source metamodels in a new concept in a target metamodel. The *merge pattern* takes one or more parts from one or more source metamodels and merges them into a new concept in a target metamodel. The *extension pattern* enlarges a part of a metamodel with new concepts to broaden the expressiveness of the metamodel.

The following sections will describe the reference, transformation, and merge pattern in more detail.

3.3   Reference Pattern

Name: Reference Pattern

Context: Two or more metamodels are complementary. The integration should support loose coupling and navigation between the complementary parts.

Problem: The integration of two or more metamodels should not change the original metamodels. Each metamodel should be independent from each other to enable the further development and improvement of each metamodel without influencing the other metamodels.

Solution: A reference link connects exactly one part of the source metamodel with one part of the target metamodel. A reference link has at least one reference domain which describes the possible source and target parts to connect.

Example: Integration of a business process metamodel with a use case metamodel to refine activities of business processes to use cases.

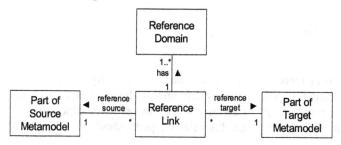

Fig. 4. Reference Pattern

3.4   Transformation Pattern

Name: Transformation Pattern

Context: Two or more metamodels are complementary. The integration should support loose coupling, but parts of the target metamodel are generated from parts of the source metamodels.

Problem: The integration of two or more source metamodels should not change these metamodels. Each source metamodel should be independent from other source metamodels and from the target metamodel, but the target metamodel depends on the source metamodels. Each source metamodel should be developed and improved independently, but the target metamodel should be changed accordingly, if necessary.

Solution: A transformation rule generates exactly one part of the target metamodel from one or more parts of the source metamodels. The transformation rule consists of at least one transformation action and none, one or more transformation constraints. The transformation constraints determine the behaviour of the transformation actions.

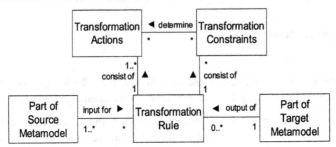

Fig. 5. Transformation Pattern

Example: Activities in business processes are executed by resources such as human or technology-based actors. The business process metamodel contains an assignment rule to relate the relevant parts of the resource metamodel with the business process metamodel. The assignment rule is automatically updated by a transformation rule after changing the resource metamodel.

3.5   Merge Pattern

Name: Merge Pattern

Context: Two or more metamodels are used concurrently. They describe modelling languages ranging from nearly equivalent up to orthogonal expressiveness. To reduce the effort in maintaining the metamodels or to use their expressiveness within an integrated modelling language, the relevant parts should be merged into a single metamodel.

Problem: By integrating different parts of source metamodels into one part of the target metamodel, no syntactic, semantic or notational expressiveness should be lost or misinterpreted. The source metamodels should not be changed.

Solution: The merge pattern is a specialisation of the transformation pattern. A merge rule generates exactly one part of the target metamodel from one or more parts of the source metamodels. The merge rule consists of at least one merge action and none, one or more merge constraints. Three types of merge constraints can be distinguished, which determine the behaviour of the merging: syntactic, semantic, and notational constraints.

Example: A data modelling language and a business process modelling language should be merged to enable data flow modelling. The resulting language should still have the former properties of data and process modelling.

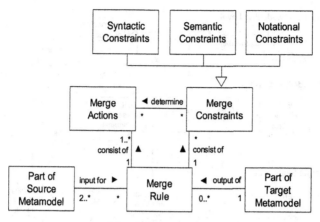

Fig. 6. Merge Pattern

4   Case Study: Development of a Direct Sales B2B Application

Case Study Description

Companies in the direct sales business use Internet technologies either to reduce their costs of administration or to establish new strategies for their world wide sales network. Usually, regional sales partners of world wide acting sales companies established different business processes and information systems over the years. The main reasons are legal requirements, varying regulations in different markets, diversified product bundles, and logistical constraints. If such a company decides to develop a new standardised sales application based on ERP, a large set of notations and application scenarios have to be integrated in a common metamodel.

The following case study presents the realisation of *a B2B application of a direct sales company* developed on an Internet technology based ERP system. Modelling the business details of the considered sales processes in different countries requires a modelling language designed for the use of business experts. The language for modelling the customer-specific requirements of the processes to be implemented from the IT point of view is the proprietary modelling language of the ERP system. This modelling language is EPC (event driven process chains), in which the reference processes of the ERP system are described. Based on a first compliance check if the functionality of the ERP system will be sufficient to implement all requirements, it was decided to enhance the functionalities with customer-specific application components. UML use case and class diagrams were integrated into the metamodel to be used to analyse and design the particular domain object model and the additional application components. Fig. 7 shows an overview of the different metamodels which have to be integrated and merged. The following sections describe the integration in more detail using the levels of fig. 1.

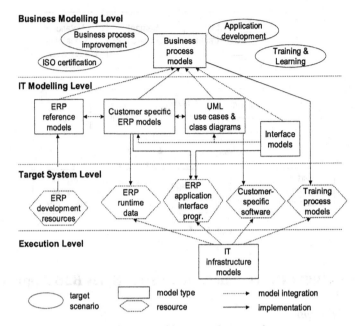

Fig. 7. EMI architecture of case study

Applying EMI on Business Level

In the past, the subsidiaries of the direct sales company modelled business processes in each country with different modelling languages and for different target scenarios such as ISO certification, business process improvement, and legacy systems documentation. The result of applying the EMI approach with *horizontal integration* and using *transformation and merge patterns* was a new metamodel on the business level which integrated all modelling languages and requirements of the before-mentioned application scenarios. The new metamodel supports requirements definition, modelling concepts for quality management, business process-based training&learning, and mechanisms for managing quantitative aspects of the business processes such as cycle times, workloads etc.

Applying EMI on IT Level

After deciding to use ERP technology for implementing the new direct sales application, ERP experts developed a compliance check to match business requirements with system functionality. The compliance check is based on business process details and the ERP reference models. For this reason the underlying modelling languages had to be *integrated vertically*. By applying the *reference pattern* using references from business activities to EPC functions and their application context, the business process metamodel and the EPC metamodel were integrated. Each function of an EPC represents a set of calls and transactions in the ERP system. The extended metamodel supports detailed compliance checks, documentation of customising know-how, and the definition of the ERP system requirements. Applying the compliance checks, i.e.

comparing the as-is functionality and the to-be requirements, it was identified that the ERP system lacks components needed for the direct sales specific commission system. The company decided to develop these components with its own development staff using an object-oriented development environment. Therefore, UML use case and class diagrams were integrated in the metamodel by using *reference patterns*. Additionally, a new model type was designed for modelling the interfaces between the ERP application components, new commission components, and existing legacy systems. The *horizontal integration* of this model type on the IT level implied interdependencies to EPCs and use cases. The main advantages of this integration are the comprehensive requirements definition, the documentation of business process details, and the corresponding conversion in system functionalities.

Applying EMI on Execution Level

At the early beginning of the project the IT strategy and the corresponding IT infrastructure were set up. Administrative processes specify the way releases are uploaded in the production environment. These processes and the responsible actors are linked with the corresponding environment in the IT infrastructure model. Additionally, the infrastructure model is used to manage the complexity of IT operations. As shown in fig. 7 the infrastructure model was *integrated vertically* by using the *reference pattern*.

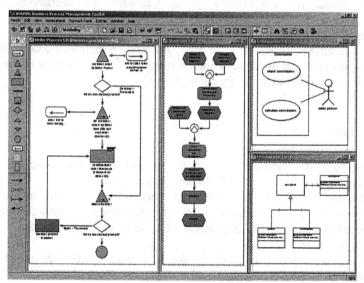

Fig. 8. Integrated Modelling Languages of the Case Study

Realisation within the Meta Model Management Tool ADONIS

The target metamodel was realised within the meta model management tool ADONIS. In fig. 8 instances of the model types "business process model", "EPC", "use case diagram" and "class diagram" are modelled and linked according to the integrated metamodel.

5   Summary and Outlook

Enterprise Model Integration (EMI) has shown to be a valuable aid in B2B application development projects. The diversity of modelling languages, programming languages, target systems, development methodologies, and standardisations, led us to a flexible metamodel integration approach using object-oriented metamodelling concepts and technologies. The major advantages from our experiences using EMI are considerable savings in time and costs in application development, increased quality of delivered solutions, and enhanced acceptance because of directly mapping the domain under consideration. The usage of metamodel integration patterns helped us to standardise the procedures of metamodel integration. This was especially helpful in handling situations where the steps to follow integrating heterogeneous metamodels were not always obvious for the metamodeller. E.g. integrating similar metamodels and how to select the necessary parts of each metamodel to have a minimal, but complete, metamodel.

We are currently working on concepts and mechanisms to integrate on model level (level 1 in fig. 2). There, we expect increased usage of best practices and reference models to reduce modelling effort and to improve optimisation and benchmarking.

Another trend in enterprise modelling we expect is the combination of different modelling paradigms such as prescriptive, descriptive and decision-oriented approaches to an integrated modelling approach. An example is the integration of Balanced Scorecard languages with IT oriented languages.

Modelling always means effort in time and costs. Nevertheless, to handle complexity in business and application engineering, we see models moving from some kind of "luxury article" to an "everyday necessity".

References

[1]   Alexander, C.; Ishikawa, S.; Silverstein, M.: A Pattern Language: Towns, Buildings, Construction. Oxford University Press, 1977.

[2]   Atkinson, C.; Kühne, T.: The Role of Metamodeling in MDA. In: Bezivin, J.; France, R. (Eds.): Proceedings of the International Workshop in Software Model Engineering (in conjunction with the UML'2002), Dresden, Germany, October 2002.

[3]   Brinkkemper, S.; Lyytinen, K.; Welke, R. J. (Eds.): Method Engineering. Principles of method construction and tool support. Proceedings of the IFIP TC8, WG8.1/8.2 Working Conference on Method Engineering, Atlanta, USA, August 1996. Chapman & Hall, 1996.

[4]   Buschmann, F.; Meunier, R.; Rohnert, H.; Sommerlad, P.; Stal, M.: Pattern-Oriented Software Architecture – A System of Patterns. John Wiley & Sons, 1996.

[5]   ebXML: ebXML Homepage. http://www.ebxml.org, access 2003-03-08.

[6]   Falkenberg, E. D.; Hesse, W.; Lindgreen, P.; Nilsson, B. E.; Oei, J. L. H.; Rolland, C.; Stamper, R. K.; van Assche, F. J. M.; Verrijn-Stuart, A. A.; Voss, K.: The FRISCO Report: A Framework of Information Systems Concepts. International Federation of Information Processing, WG 8.1 Task Group FRISCO, 1996.

[7]   Gamma, E.; Helm, R.; Johnson, G.; Vlissides, J.: Design Patterns – Elements of Reusable Object-Oriented Software. Addison-Wesley, 1994.

[8]   Johannesson, P.; Wangler, B.; Jayaweera, P.: Application and Process Integration – Concepts, Issues, and Research Directions. In: Brinkkemper, S.; Lindencrona, E.; Solvberg, A. (Eds.): Information Systems Engineering Symposium CAiSE 2000, Springer-Verlag, 2000.

[9]   Junginger, S.; Kühn, H.; Strobl, R.; Karagiannis, D.: Ein Geschäftsprozessmanagement-Werkzeug der nächsten Generation – ADONIS: Konzeption und Anwendungen. In: WIRTSCHAFTSINFORMATIK, Vol. 42, Nr. 5, Vieweg-Verlag, 2000, pp. 392-401.

[10] Kaplan, R. S.; Norton, D. P.: The Balanced Scorecard: Translating Strategy into Action. Harvard Business School Pr., 1996.

[11] Karagiannis, D.; Kühn, H.: Metamodelling Platforms. Invited Paper. In: Bauknecht, K.; Min Tjoa, A.; Quirchmayer, G. (Eds.): Proceedings of the 3rd International Conference EC-Web 2002 – Dexa 2002, Aix-en-Provence, France, September 2002, LNCS 2455, Springer-Verlag, p. 182, (full version: http://www.dke.univie.ac.at/mmp).

[12] Kelly, S.; Lyytinen, K.; Rossi, M.: MetaEdit+ - A Fully Configurable Multi-User and Multi-Tool CASE and CAME Environment. In: Constantopoulos, P.; Mylopoulos, J.; Vassiliou, Y. (Hrsg.): Advanced Information System Engineering. Proceedings of 8th International Conference, CAiSE'96, Heraklion, Crete, Greece, May 1996, LNCS 1080, Springer-Verlag, 1996, pp. 1-21.

[13] Kronlöf, K. (Ed.): Method Integration – Concepts and Case Studies. John Wiley & Sons, 1993.

[14] Kühn, H.; Junginger, S.; Bayer, F.: How Business Models Influence the Development of E-Business Applications. In: Stanford-Smith, B.; Kidd, P. T. (Eds.): Proceedings of the eBusiness and eWork 2000, Madrid, Spain, October 2000, IOS Press, pp. 1024-1030.

[15] Kühn, H.; Junginger, S.; Bayer, F.; Petzmann, A.: Managing Complexity in E-Business. In: Baake, U. F.; Herbst, J.; Schwarz, S. (Eds.): Proceedings of the 8th European Concurrent Engineering Conference 2001 (ECEC'2001), Valencia, Spain, April 2001, SCS, pp. 6-11.

[16] OMG Object Management Group: Model Driven Architecture (MDA). Document number ormsc/2001-07-01. http://www.omg.org/cgi-bin/doc?ormsc/01-07-01.pdf, access 2003-03-08.

[17] OMG Object Management Group: OMG Unified Modeling Language Specification, Version 1.4. September 2001. http://www.omg.org/cgi-bin/doc?formal/01-09-67.pdf, access 2003-03-08.

[18] OMG Object Management Group: Meta Object Facility (MOF) Specification, Version 1.4. April 2002. http://www.omg.org/cgi-bin/?formal/02-04-03.pdf, access 2003-03-08.

[19] RosettaNet: RosettaNet Homepage. http://www.rosettanet, access 2003-03-08.

[20] Sprinkle, J. M.; Karsai, G.; Ledeczi, A.; Nordstrom, G.: The New Metamodeling Generation. In: Proceedings of the 8th Annual IEEE International Conference and Workshop on the Engineering of Computer-Based Systems, Washington, D. C., April 2001.

[21] Strahringer, S.: Metamodellierung als Instrument des Methodenvergleichs. Eine Evaluierung am Beispiel objektorientierter Analysemethoden. Shaker-Verlag, 1996.

[22] Vernadat, F.: Enterprise Modeling and Integration – Principles and Applications. Kluwer Academic Publishers, 1996.

[23] WfMC Workflow Management Coalition: Workflow Process Definition Interface – XML Process Definition Language. WFMC-TC-1025. http://www.wfmc.org, access 2003-03-08.

[24] W3C World Wide Web Consortium: W3C Homepage. http://www.w3c.org, access 2003-03-08.

Matching Algorithms for Composing Business Process Solutions with Web Services

Juhnyoung Lee

IBM T. J. Watson Research Center
Yorktown Heights, New York 10598, USA
jyl@us.ibm.com

Abstract. The automation of process integration with Web service technologies requires the automation of discovery and composition of Web services. This paper addresses these two problems in the Web service-based business process integration: the discovery of Web services based on the capabilities and properties of published services, and the composition of business processes based on the business requirements of submitted requests. The proposed solution comprises multiple matching algorithms, a micro-level matching algorithm, which matches the capabilities of services with activities in a process request, and macro-level matching algorithms, which are used to compose a business process by identifying services that satisfy the business requirements and constraints of the request. The solution from the macro-level matching algorithms is optimal in terms of meeting a certain business objective, e.g., minimizing the cost or execution time, or maximizing the total utility value of business properties of interest.

1   Introduction

A *business process* refers to a process in which work is organized, coordinated, and focused to produce a valuable product or service. Business processes comprise both internal and external business partners and drive their collaboration to accomplish shared business goals by enabling highly fluid process networks. A *business process solution* consists of a model of the underlying business process (referred to as a *process model* or a *flow model*) and a set of (flow-independent) business logic modules. The abstractions of the elementary pieces of work in a flow model are called *activities*; the concrete realizations of these abstractions at process execution time are referred to as *activity implementations*. The prevalent technique for creating business process solutions follows a manual and tedious approach involving assimilation of varied process design and vendor specifications and writing vast amount of code that produces a tight inflexible coupling between processes.

Web services provide a set of technologies for creating business process solutions in an efficient, standard way. The promise of Web services is to enable a distributed environment in which any number of applications, or application components, can

K. Bauknecht, A Min Tjoa, G. Quirchmayr (Eds.): EC-Web 2003, LNCS 2738, pp. 393-402, 2003.

interoperate seamlessly within an organization or between companies in a platform-neutral, language-neutral fashion. From the perspective of business process solutions, a Web service could represent an activity within a business process, or a composite business process comprising a number of steps [8].

Building a business process solution by using Web services involves specifying the potential execution order of operations from a collection of Web services, the data shared among the Web services, which business partners are involved and how they are involved in the business process, and joint exception handling for collections of Web services. A basis for these specification tasks is the discovery, composition, and interoperation of Web services, which are primary pillars of automatic process integration and management solutions. In this paper, we address the following two problems of the Web service-based business process automation: the location of services based on the capabilities of published services, and the composition of business processes based on the business requirements of submitted process requests. This paper discusses solutions to these problems, and, especially, focuses on the following aspects: the specification of the capabilities of services and the requirements of requests, and the algorithms for matching published services and submitted process requests in terms of service capabilities and requested business requirements.

The rest of this paper is structured as follows: Section 2 summarizes the previous work on the problems of interest, discusses their limitations, and explains how the work presented in this paper addresses them. Section 3 presents a matching algorithm for locating services based on service capabilities and properties. Section 4 presents matching algorithms that are designed to satisfy the business requirements and provide optimal solutions in terms of meeting certain business objectives. In Section 5, conclusions are drawn.

2   Related Work

Recently, there have been active studies related to the Web service-based process automation in both academia and industry. Industrial effort for the business process automation is centered around the Business Process Execution Language for Web Services (BPEL4WS), which is an XML-based workflow definition language that allows companies to describe business processes that can both consume and provide Web services [15]. Along with complementary specifications, WS-Coordination [16] and WS-Transaction [17], BPEL4WS provides a basis for a business process automation framework, and is viewed to become the basis of a Web service standard for composition. With the BPEL4WS specification, vendors such as IBM provide workflow engines (e.g., BPWS4J [14]) on which business processes written in BPEL4WS can be executed. Running on Web application servers such as Apache Tomcat, the workflow engines support the coordinated invocation, from within the process, of Web services.

The focus of BPEL4WS is limited to the specification of flow models and the coordinated invocation of Web services via the workflow engine. The BPEL4WS specification does not directly address the discovery of services and the composition of business processes fulfilling various business objectives. Instead, it assumes that these tasks are executed separately, and that the business manager who creates a BPEL4WS document has the information on the selected Web services before creating the process document. Also, BPEL4WS is limited in specifying business requirements and preferences that can be critical in selecting services in real-world applications.

We claim that for automating business processes and, hence, for supporting "real-time enterprises," the discovery and composition of services should be seamlessly integrated with the capabilities BPEL4WS provides, i.e., the flow model specification and the coordinated invocation of services. If this integration is achieved, a business manager can create a business process model without knowing upfront specific Web services that will be used for implementing activities of the process. Instead, s/he only needs to specify business requirements and preferences for the process along with the flow model in the process document. Then, a set of services, which matches the specified requirements and optimizes certain selected business objectives, will be automatically identified and specified in the final version of the process document, which will be passed to the workflow engine for the execution of the process.

In [7], we discussed issues involved with the specification of business requirements and objectives in process request documents: what are the types of requirements that need to be specified in request documents, how can BPEL4WS be used and extended for specifying the requirements, and how can the specified requirements be used in the discovery of services and the composition of processes? Also, we discussed a related topic, i.e., how to specify the capabilities of Web services using an existing Web service standard, most notably UDDI (Universal Description Discovery and Integration), an XML-based standard, which provides a registry of businesses and Web services [18]. There are some studies, mostly from academia, done for the specification of service capabilities and process requests by using semantic knowledge-based markup languages, notably, DAML-S [2]. It is a service description language, providing a semantic view of Web services including the abstract description of the service capabilities. Based on the semantic representation of services and requests, several algorithms for matching published Web services and submitted service requests were proposed [3, 10, 11]. In [7], we proposed to specify the business requirements and preferences in an extended format of the business process specification standard, i.e., BPEL4WS, instead of depending on DAML-S. We believe that it will facilitate the seamless integration of service discovery and workflow specification, which have been traditionally studied separately.

For matching published services and submitted process requests in terms of service capabilities and requested business requirements, in this paper, we propose a system of multiple matching algorithms, a *micro-level matching* algorithm, which matches the capabilities and attributes of published services with activities in a process request, and *macro-level matching* algorithms, which are used to compose a business process by selecting one service for each activity among the candidate services selected by the micro-level algorithm. The output from the macro-level matching algorithms satisfies the business requirements and constraints of the submitted request, and provides optimal solutions in terms of meeting a certain business objective, e.g., minimizing the cost or execution time, or maximizing the total utility values of business-related properties of interest.

Some previous work envisioned the task of business process composition as an AI-inspired planning problem [3, 12]. They represent a Web service by a rule that expresses the service capable of producing a particular output, given a certain input. Then, a rule-based expert system is used to automatically determine whether a desired composite process can be realized using existing services, and construct a plan that instantiates the process. We believe that this is an interesting approach in its own right, but we do not discuss this approach further in this paper.

3   Service Discovery with Micro-level Matching

For the location of services for business activities based on service capabilities and attributes, we adopt an intuitive matching algorithm that uses semantic knowledge as well as other information retrieval filters. This algorithm returns a (pre-specified) number of services that sufficiently match with an activity in the request. It is based on the previous work in [3, 10] which allows service providers to advertise their services in DAML-S service profile markup, and match submitted requests again in DAML-S profile markup with appropriate services. Unlike this previous work, our work does not depend on DAML-S profile, but utilizes the specification of service capabilities and request requirements directly stored in UDDI records and BPEL4WS documents, respectively. This algorithm is referred to as a micro-level matching algorithm, because it mostly deals with a single atomic process of a request.

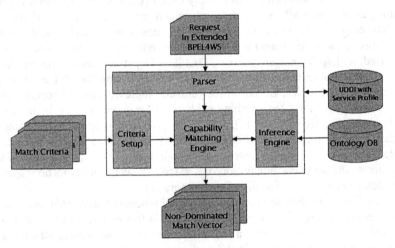

Fig.1. Micro-level matching algorithm

Fig. 1 depicts the architecture of the micro-level matching algorithm. The Parser module is capable of parsing an input BPEL4WS document and creates objects storing business requirements specified in the documents. The Inference Engine module parses and reasons with ontologies that provide the working model of entities and interactions in knowledge domains of interest, specified in the DAML+OIL language [5, 6]. The Capability Matching Engine interacts with the Inference Engine and the

UDDI augmented by the service profiles that specify the capabilities and attributes of services. The engine generates a pre-selected number of non-dominated services matched with the target attributes in the input request. The output is stored in the Non-Dominated Match Vector. The matching process is customized by the specification of Match Criteria that is parsed by the Criteria Setup module. The Capability Matching Engine generates a Non-Dominated Match Vector for each Match Criteria.

The Capability Matching Engine is based on the semantic matching algorithms outlined in [3, 10]. While the matching algorithm presented in [10] is constrained to match only input and output messages of Web services, the algorithm proposed in [3] generalized the previous algorithm to match for any attribute of services and requests by parameterizing the match criteria such as quality, service categories as well as input and output messages. Fig 2 outlines the main control loop of the matching algorithm which is based on the work in [3]. The *degree of match* is a measure of the semantic distance between the conceptual meanings of the service attributes [3, 10]. Each attribute has a lexical concept attached to it that is defined in the Ontology Database available to the Inference Engine. We use three different degrees of matches based on specialization relationship as defined in [10]. As given in the degreeOf-Match module of Fig. 2, the degrees of match are preferentially ordered based on the semantic distance that the degree represents: an EXACT match between concepts is preferred to a PLUG_IN match, and a PLUG_IN match is preferred over a SUBSUMES match [10].

```
matchAttribute(request, service, matchCriteria) {
    for each criteria in matchCriteria do {
        requestAttributes = request(attributeCriteria);
        serviceAttributes = service(attributeCriteria);
        for each requestAttribute in requestAttributes do {
            for each serviceAttribute in serviceAttributes do {
                degreeMatch = degreeOfMatch(requestAttribute, serviceAttribute);
                if (degreeMatch < matchLimit)
                    return fail;
                if (degreeMatch < globalDegreeMatch)
                    globalDegreeMatch = degreeMatch;
            }
        }
    }
    return success;
}

degreeOfMatch(requestAttribute, serviceAttribute) {
    if (requestAttribute == serviceAttribute) return EXACT;
    if (requestAttribute subclassOf serviceAttribute) return EXACT;
    if (serviceAttribute subsumes requestAttribute) return PLUG_IN;
    if (requestAttribute subsumes serviceAttribute) return SUBSUMES;
    else return FAIL;
}
```

Fig.2. Capability matching algorithm

As briefly mentioned above, the matching process is customized by the Match Criteria component, which specifies a set of target attributes for match and their least preferred degree of match, i.e., matchLimit. For example, the user may specify the matchLimit of the output message as EXACT, while that of the input message as SUBSUMES. Any match on an attribute whose degree falls below matchLimit is considered a fail.

4   Process Composition with Macro-level Matching

The micro-matching algorithm works with other matching algorithms, macro-level matching algorithms, which are used to compose a business process by selecting one service for each activity in the request. The output from the macro-level matching algorithms satisfies the business requirements of the submitted request, and provides optimal solutions in terms of meeting a certain objective, e.g., minimizing the cost or execution time, or maximizing a certain quality measure. In this paper, we model the macro-level matching problem as a variation of the *multiple-choice knapsack problem* [9], and design a configurable, generic optimization engine, which can be repeatedly run with variations of configuration criteria in search for a business process solution best fit the need.

As an alternative approach, we model the macro-level matching problem as a *multi-attribute decision making problem*. This model is particularly useful when it is not sufficient to provide an optimal solution for a single measure, but requires maximizing the total utility value of multiple business measures of interest. Our algorithm is based on *multi-attribute decision analysis*, which computes the scores of the candidate service combinations by considering their attributes values and capabilities, ranks the candidates by score, and selects services among the top-rankers. In this paper, we will not discuss this multi-attribute decision analysis approach any further. The details of this work can be found in [7].

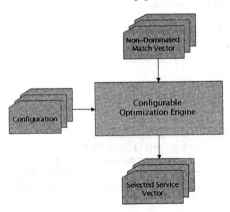

Fig. 3. Macro-level matching algorithm

Fig. 3 displays the architecture of the macro-level matching algorithm. The input to the matching algorithm is a set of Non-Dominated Match Vectors, one vector for each atomic activity in the request, which were generated by the micro-level matching algorithm. The output of the optimization engine is a set of services selected from the input, one service from each Non-Dominated Match Vector. The match engine can be customized for different business objectives and constraints as specified in another input to the engine, the Configuration.

We model the macro-level matching problem as a variation of the multiple-choice knapsack problem [9]. The "multiple-choice" term in this problem designation refers to the requirement of selecting exactly one service from each candidate list, i.e., each Non-Dominated Match Vector. For a specific example, consider the following problem:

We are given a set of m business activities in our business process request, a_1, ...,a_m such that activity, a_i, contains n_i candidates of Web services from the micro-level matching step. The j-th candidate for activity a_i has cost c_{ij}, and execution time t_{ij}. Given the total execution time limit T for this business process, the goal of this macro-level matching algorithm is to compose an implementation plan for this business process by selecting one and only one Web service candidate from each candidate list such that the overall cost is minimized without exceeding our total execution time limit.

If we use indicator variable x_{ij} to indicate whether the j-th service from the candidate list for activity a_i was selected, we can formalize the problem with the following equations:

minimize
$$C = \sum_{i=1}^{m} \sum_{j=1}^{ni} c_{ij} x_{ij} \tag{1}$$

subject to
$$\sum_{i=1}^{m} \sum_{j=1}^{ni} t_{ij} x_{ij} \leq T \tag{2}$$

$$\sum_{j=1}^{ni} x_{ij} = 1, i = 1,...,m \tag{3}$$

$$x_{ij} \in \{0,1\}, \forall i, j. \tag{4}$$

The multiple-choice knapsack problem is known to be NP-hard [9]. It is possible to exactly solve the above problems using branch-and-bound algorithms, but because the worst-case running time of these algorithms is exponential in both the number of activities and the number of candidates on each list, branch-and-bound algorithms are often too slow to be useful. An alternative approach is to use dynamic programming techniques, and there are a number of algorithms known in this direction [9]. By using off-the-shelf software packages of optimization algorithms such as IBM's OSL [13], the given problem can be implemented in a straightforward manner.

With this model in place, we can vary the problem with different objective functions and constraints. The variation of the problem can be implemented by using the Configuration component in Fig. 3. For example, some processes may need to be optimized for execution time, while other measures such as cost will be treated as a constraint. In this case, the problem can be re-formulated as follows:

We are given a set of m business activities, a_1, ...,a_m such that activity, a_i, contains n_i candidates of Web services. The j-th candidate for activity a_i has cost c_{ij}, and execution time t_{ij}. Given the total cost budget C for this business process, the goal of this algorithm is to compose an implementation plan for this business process by selecting one and only one Web service candidate from each candidate list such that the overall execution time is minimized without exceeding our total execution time limit.

If we use indicator variable x_{ij} to indicate whether the j-th service from the candidate list for activity a_i was selected, we can formalize the problem with the following equations:

minimize $$T = \sum_{i=1}^{m} \sum_{j=1}^{ni} t_{ij} x_{ij} \tag{5}$$

subject to $$\sum_{i=1}^{m} \sum_{j=1}^{ni} c_{ij} x_{ij} \leq C \tag{6}$$

$$\sum_{j=1}^{ni} x_{ij} = 1, i = 1,...,m \tag{7}$$

$$x_{ij} \in \{0,1\}, \forall i, j. \tag{8}$$

Yet another variation of this problem is an optimization on an interesting metric such as the degree of match described in the previous section. For example, the problem can be formulated as follows:

We are given a set of m business activities, $a_1, ...,a_m$ such that activity, a_i, contains n_i candidates of Web services. The j-th candidate for activity a_i has combined degree of match d_{ij}, cost c_{ij}, and execution time t_{ij}. Given the total cost budget C and the total execution time limit T for this business process, the goal of this algorithm is to compose an implementation plan for this business process by selecting one and only one Web service candidate from each candidate list such that our overall degree of match is maximized without exceeding our total cost budget and the total execution time limit.

If we use indicator variable x_{ij} to indicate whether the j-th service from the candidate list for activity a_i was selected, we can formalize the problem with the following equations:

maximize $$D = \sum_{i=1}^{m} \sum_{j=1}^{ni} d_{ij} x_{ij} \tag{9}$$

subject to $$\sum_{i=1}^{m} \sum_{j=1}^{ni} c_{ij} x_{ij} \leq C \tag{10}$$

$$\sum_{i=1}^{m} \sum_{j=1}^{ni} t_{ij} x_{ij} \leq T \tag{11}$$

$$\sum_{j=1}^{ni} x_{ij} = 1, i = 1,...,m \tag{12}$$

$$x_{ij} \in \{0,1\}, \forall i, j. \tag{13}$$

Sometimes in a business process, the degree of match of an activity can be more important than those of other activities. In such a case, the variant importance of degree of match of different activities can be reflected in the model by the assignment of weight w_i for each a_i. Then the objective model is slightly modified as follows:

maximize $$D = \sum_{i=1}^{m} w_i \sum_{j=1}^{ni} d_{ij}x_{ij}$$ (9)'

In addition to varied business objectives, the optimization problem of matching can be subject to *business rules* such as:

- The minimum number of service providers participating in a business process should be set to avoid depending too heavily on just a few partners,
- The maximum number of service providers should be limited to a certain number to control the administrative overhead of managing providers,
- The number of services granted to a service provider should be limited to a certain number, and
- At least one (or some fixed number of) minority provider(s) need to be chosen.

These business rules can be expressed in linear inequalities with binary variables, and added as constraints to the multiple-choice knapsack problem model in a straight-forward manner. The problem can be solved in the same manner for identifying the service set satisfying the given business objective and fulfilling the constraints of the given business rules.

5   Concluding Remarks

In this paper, we addressed two primary problems of the Web service-based business process automation: the location of services on the basis of the capabilities of published services, and the composition of business processes on the basis of the business requirements of submitted process requests. We proposed a solution, which comprises multiple matching algorithms, a micro-level matching algorithm and a macro-level matching algorithm. The first algorithm reasons with semantic information of services and returns services that sufficiently match with an activity in the request. The second algorithm solves a variation of the multiple-choice knapsack problem that models the macro-level matching problem for optimizing a business objective and fulfilling other business constraints.

References

[1]   R. T. Clemen, Making Hard Decisions: an Introduction to Decision Analysis, Wadsworth Publishing Company, Belmont, CA, 1996.
[2]   DAML-S Coalition, "DAML-S: Web Service Description for the Semantic Web," Proceedings of the 1st International Semantic Web Conference, June 2002.
[3]   P. Doshi, R. Goodwin, R. Akkiraju, S. Roeder, "A Flexible Parameterized Semantic Matching Engine," IBM Research Report, 2002.

[4]   W. Edwards, "How to Use Multi-Attribute Utility Measurement for Social Decision Making," IEEE Transactions on Systems, Man, and Cybernetics SMC, vol. 7:326-340, 1977.

[5]   D. Fensel, I. Horrocks, F. van Harmelen, D. L. McGuinness, and P. F. Pate, "OIL: An Ontology Infrastructure for the Semantic Web," IEEE Intelligent Systems, Vol. 16, No. 2, 2001.

[6]   J. Hendler, and D. L. McGuinness, "DARPA Agent Markup Language," IEEE Intelligent Systems, Vol. 15, No. 6, 2001.

[7]   J. Lee, and M. S. Park, "Integration and Composition of Web Service-based Business Processes," To appear in the Internaltional Journal of Computer Information Systems.

[8]   F. Leymann, D. Roller, and M. T. Schmidt, "Web Services and Business Process Management," IBM Systems Journal, Vol. 41, No. 2, 2002.

[9]   S. Martello, and P. Toth, Knapsack Problems, Chichester, New York, John Wiley & Sons, 1990.

[10]   M. Paolucci, T. Kawamura, T. R. Payne, and K. Sycara, "Semantic Matching of Web Services Capabilities," Proceedings of the 1st International Semantic Web Conference, June 2002.

[11]   M. Paolucci, T. Kawamura, T. R. Payne, and K. Sycara, "Importing the Semantic Web in UDDI," Workshop on Web Services, e-Business, and the Semantic Web: Foundations, Models, Architecture, Engineering and Applications, Toronto, Ontario, Canada, May 2002.

[12]   S. R. Ponnekanti, and A. Fox, "SWORD: A Developer Toolkit for Web Service Composition," Proceedings of the 11th World Wide Web Conference, Honolulu, Hawaii, May 7-11, 2002

[13]   IBM Optimization Solutions and Library,
       http://www-3.ibm.com/software/data/bi/osl/index.html.

[14]   "BPWS4J," IBM Corporation, http://alphaworks.ibm.com/tech/bpws4j, August 2002.

[15]   "Business Process Execution Language for Web Services, Version 1.0," BEA Systems, IBM Corporation, and Microsoft Corporation, Inc.,
       http://www.ibm.com/developerworks/library/ws-bpel/, July 2002.

[16]   "Web Services Coordination (WS-Coordination)," BEA Systems, IBM Corporation, and Microsoft Corporation, Inc.,
       http://www.ibm.com/developerworks/library/ws-coor/, August 2002.

[17]   "Web Services Transaction (WS-Transaction)," BEA Systems, IBM Corporation, and Microsoft Corporation, Inc.,
       http://www.ibm.com/developerworks/library/ws-transpec/, August 2002.

[18]   "UDDI Version 3 Published Specification,"
       http://www.uddi.org/pubs/uddi-v3.00-published-20020719.htm.

Dynamic Modelling of Strategic Supply Chains

Antonia Albani, Alexander Keiblinger,
Klaus Turowski, and Christian Winnewisser

Chair of Business Information Systems (Wirtschaftsinformatik II)
University of Augsburg
Universtitätsstraße 16, 86159 Augsburg, Germany
{antonia.albani,alexander.keiblinger,klaus.turowski,
christian.winnewisser}@wiwi.uni-augsburg.de

Abstract. The high level of complexity connected with the modelling of supplier networks often diminishes the practical impact of supply chain management approaches. Furthermore, many of those approaches primarily focus on operative tasks. This paper proposes a concept for the dynamic modelling of supply chains. In addition, the business domain of strategic supply chain management is introduced, extending the traditional frame of reference in strategic sourcing from a supplier-centric to a supply-chain-scope. Concluding, a business component model for the domain of strategic supply chain development is laid out to illustrate the feasibility of the proposed concept.

1   Introduction

The supply chain is one of the most analysed objects of reference in research centred around inter organisational systems (IOS), virtual enterprises and value networks, especially with respect to the perceived business value. However, failed initiatives, primarily in the field of supply chain management, have spurred concern about the practicability of present approaches and theories and have shown the need for further refinement and adaptation. According to [11], one of the most important reasons for failure can be found in the high degree of complexity that is connected with the identification of supply chain entities and the modelling of the supply chain structure, as well as the high coordination effort. In addition, many research efforts in supply chain management have been based on the more operative interpretation of [8, S. 22-38, 9, S. 16-22], primarily focusing on the optimisation of forecast and planning accuracy, and the optimisation of material flows over the whole supply chain, whereas more strategic tasks such as long term supplier development have not been widely discussed in a network perspective yet.

Therefore, this paper introduces the concept of strategic supply chain development, which extends the traditional frame of reference in strategic sourcing from a supplier-centric to a supply-chain-scope. To address the complexity issues in supply chain modelling, the proposed concept includes an outline for the dynamic modelling of

K. Bauknecht, A Min Tjoa, G. Quirchmayr (Eds.): EC-Web 2003, LNCS 2738, pp. 403-413, 2003.

strategic supply-chains. The respective business domain will be described in section 2. In section 3, the concept of dynamic supply chain modelling will be detailed further and challenges of the technological development will be discussed. Based on these findings, a business component model for the domain of strategic supply chain development will be outlined in section 4.

2   From Strategic Sourcing to Strategic Supply Chain Development

The relevance of the purchasing function in the enterprise has increased steadily over the past two decades. Till the 70ies, purchasing was widely considered an operative task with no apparent influence on long term planning and strategy development [13]. This narrow view was broadened by research that documented the positive influence that a targeted supplier collaboration and qualification could bring to a company's strategic options [2]. In the 80ies, trends such as the globalisation, the focus on core competencies in the value chain with connected in-sourcing and out-sourcing decisions, as well as new concepts in manufacturing spurred the recognition of the eminent importance of the development and management of supplier relationships for gaining competitive advantages. As a result, purchasing gradually gained strategic relevance on top of its operative tasks [10].

Based on these developments, purchasing has become a core function in the 90ies. Current empiric research shows a significant correlation between the establishment of a strategic purchasing function and the financial success of an enterprise, independent from the industry surveyed [3, S. 513]. One of the most important factors in this connection is the buyer-supplier-relationship. At many of the surveyed companies, a close cooperation between buyer and supplier in areas such as long-term planning, product development and coordination of production processes led to process improvements and resulting cost reductions that were shared between buyer and suppliers [3, S. 516].

In practice, supplier development is widely limited to suppliers in tier-1. With respect to the above demonstrated, superior importance of supplier development we postulate the extension of the traditional frame of reference in strategic sourcing from a supplier-centric to a supply-chain-scope, i.e., the further development of the strategic supplier development to a strategic supply chain development. This re-focuses the object of reference in the field of strategic sourcing by analysing supplier networks instead of single suppliers. Embedded in this paradigm shift is the concept of the value network that has been comprehensively described, e.g., [12, 19].

The main reason for the lack of practical implementation of strategic supply chain development can be found in the high degree of complexity that is connected with the identification of supply chain entities and the modelling of the supply chain structure, as well as the high coordination effort, as described by [11].

2.1   Relation to Supply Chain Management

Many research efforts to supply chain management refer to [8, S. 22-38, 9, S. 16-22], who give a rather operative interpretation. According to their work, main tasks include the optimisation of forecast and planning accuracy, and the optimisation of material flows over the whole supply chain. The main aim is the minimisation of inventory and lead time, which is also partially mirrored by many current initiatives based on the Supply Chain Council's SCOR-model. Therefore, primarily the tasks of the operative purchasing function are put in a network context.

The concept of strategic supply chain development as introduced in this paper is based on the tasks of the strategic purchasing function and extends the frame of reference in strategic sourcing from a supplier-centric to a supply-chain-scope. It should not go unnoticed that [4] refer to current research that give an extended interpretation of supply chain management and partly consider supplier relationships as well. According to this broad definition, strategic sourcing could be regarded as part of supply chain management as well. However, the tasks of strategic purchasing are generally not discussed in a network context.

Independent from this discussion, the problems described by [11] and the resulting hurdles for a practical implementation of the concept of strategic supply chain management remain imminent.

2.2   Description of the Functional Tasks
of Strategic Supply Chain Development

The functional tasks of strategic supply chain development are defined next. Those tasks will be derived from the main tasks of strategic sourcing. The most evident changes are expected for functions with cross-company focus. The functional tasks of strategic supply chain development have been illustrated in a function decomposition diagram (Figure 1). Processes and tasks that will be automated have been shaded. Following, only selected tasks will be described, focusing on changes to current tasks of strategic purchasing.

Task „Model strategic supply chain": The process "supplier selection" from strategic purchasing undergoes the most evident changes in the shift to a supply chain centric perspective. The expansion of the traditional frame of reference in strategic sourcing requires more information than merely data on existing and potential suppliers in tier-1. Instead, the supply chains connected with those suppliers have to be identified and evaluated, e.g., by comparing alternative supply chains in the production network. As a consequence, the task "supplier selection" is only part of the process that leads to the modelling of strategic supply chains.

According to the assumptions described above, the rating of supply chains requires the evaluation of networks instead of single suppliers. There has been preparatory work on evaluation methods for business networks (e.g., [17, 15]) on which we have based initial methods for the described application. However, there is need for further research, especially in the area of aggregation of incomplete information. For the time being, the problem has been tackled by identifying strategic, "mission critical" suppliers through a multi-dimensional mix of evaluation criteria (e.g., in the area of volume, quality, service levels, processes) and by aggregating the evaluation results for these suppliers as representatives for the whole supply chain.

In the first round of implementation, the selection of suppliers will not be automated by the application. Strategic supply chain development deals with long-term supplier relationships. An automation of respective fundamental contract negations seems neither feasible nor desirable in the short term. In fact, the results from automated supply chain identification and evaluation should be used as decision support for supplier selection.

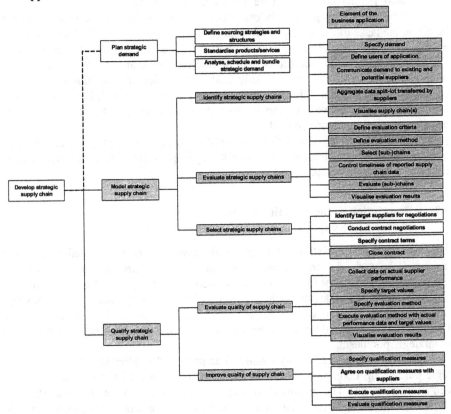

Fig. 1. Functional decomposition diagram for the supply chain development

Task „Qualify strategic supply chain": In addition to the selection of suitable supply chains and composition of alternative supply chains, the performance improvement of strategic important supply chains is one of the major goals of strategic supply chain development. Main prerequisite is the constant evaluation of the actual performance of selected supply chains by defined benchmarks. The application supports respective evaluation methods and enables the user to identify imminent problems in the supply chain and to initiate appropriate measures for qualification of supply chain partners.

This is important because of the long-term character of strategic supply chain relationships. As a result of the long-term perspective, qualification measures – e.g., along the dimensions product, processes and management abilities – require deployment of resources on the buyer side as well. Because of this effort, problems in the supply chain should be identified proactively and qualification measures should be tracked.

Task *"Plan strategic demand"*: Strategic planning, i.e., analysing, scheduling and grouping of long-term demand, primarily affects intra-company processes that will not change significantly by switching to a supply chain perspective in strategic purchasing and therefore will not be included in the first stage of the application.

3   Concept and Technological Issues in Self-Modelling Supply Chains

The concept of the supply chain as a dynamic, self-modelling network constitutes the basis for the identification of strategic supply chains, as described in section 2, for the domain of strategic supply chain development. Based on a sample supply chain, as shown in Fig. 2, the concept and the technological issues for developing self-modelling supply chains will be explained and illustrated in this section.

Fig. 2 on the left shows the complete network of existing and alternative supply chains for a specific demand, with the currently active supplier (supplier 1-2) being highlighted. In order to be able to visualise and evaluate the network at a particular date in a structured way, a specific strategic demand is communicated from the producer to existing and selected alternative suppliers in tier-1. Subsequently, the suppliers in tier-1 report the demand to their own respective suppliers. E.g., for supplier 1-2, these are the suppliers 2-2, 2-3 and 2-4 in tier-2. In the following, these suppliers report the demand to their related suppliers in tier-3, which split-lot transfer the requested information. The requestors aggregate the received information with the own information and send it back to the supplier 1-2 in tier-1. Having aggregated the information of all suppliers, the supplier 1-2 adds its own information before split-lot transferring it to the producer.

With the suppliers' data locally available, the producer can visualise the selected sub-chain as a network, in which each participant of the sub-chain constitutes a network hub. Based on that data, the producer is able to evaluate the performance of the selected sub-chain by self defined benchmarks. In order to optimise sub-chains, alternative supply chains can be visualised and modelled by applying the same concept as described above. Fig. 2 on the right highlights an alternative virtual supply chain. In the event of this alternative supply chain being the best performing sub-chain in the network, the existing supply chain can be modified, substituting supplier 1-2 in tier-1 with the new supplier 1-1, while keeping supplier 2-2 in tier-2 and supplier 3-1 in tier-3.

For the development of self-modelling supply chains different technological issues, e.g., distributed systems, asynchronous communication, consistency of data and synchronisation need to be discussed, since the concept described above poses multiple technological challenges which have implications on the system design. These challenges will be described first. Later rationales for the chosen technologies in the domain model of strategic supply chain development will be given.

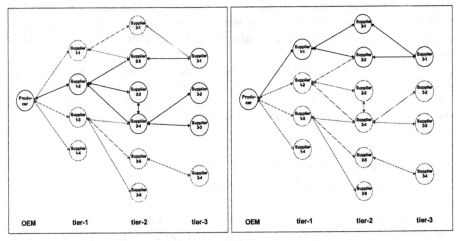

Fig. 2. Left: Supplier network   Right: Alternative supply chain

Distributed Systems: As defined by [16], the network of independent systems that constitute strategic supply chains appears to the user of a single node inside that network as a single system and therefore represents a distributed system. It is an open peer group of loosely coupled systems. There are no server or directory infrastructures and apart from the fact, that every node implements such functions for its own view of the network, no hierarchy exists. Therefore there is no single point of failure in the system.

Asynchronous Communication: To enable such loosely coupled networks, messaging can be used as transport constituting communication channels. Messaging systems encapsulate sending and receiving of messages and allow multiple transport mechanisms, e.g. SOAP/XML, JMS or even SMTP. By using the concept of conversations [7], based on messaging, pre-programmed patterns (conversational policies inside conversational contexts) can be implemented for flexible transactions of information between nodes. Conversation policies are used in the agent community for coupling internal states of agents but are used in this context to couple business process. Conversation policies are machine readable patterns of message exchange in a conversation between systems and are composed of a message schema, sequence and timing information.

    To support the direct conversation with suppliers in the different tiers of the network or with filtered groups of them, unicast and multicast methods of addressing peers or groups of peers are needed. For the discovery of new potential suppliers, the mechanism of broadcast messages is needed as well. The client-server paradigm, using synchronous invoke/return schemes would create unnecessary dependencies between systems and could lead to deadlock situations. A higher level of robustness can be achieved by applying peer-to-peer approaches and using conversation.

Consistency of Data: With loosely coupled information systems the problem of data consistency arises. Mechanisms need to be implemented in order to guarantee that at some specific point in time the data used to generate virtual supply chains is accurate.

Synchronisation: The update of information and the synchronisation between systems are typical problems in peer-to-peer scenarios and have to be considered for the specific application domain.

In the following it is shown how those technical issues have been addressed in the business application of strategic supply chain development.

There are different configurations of systems in the network of strategic supply chain, ranging from a very simple configuration where business data is entered manually to an integrated solution, e.g. coupled with an enterprise integration system, the software composing the functionality of nodes has to be scalable to the demands of the company participating in the network. As a possible solution to build distributed networks, business component technologies [18] are suggested. The underlying idea of business components combines components from different vendors to an application which is individual to each customer. This principle of modular black-box design has been used in this system design and will be exemplified in section 4.

For the issues of asynchronous communication, consistency of data and synchronisation, communication channels that support the message exchange between business components, and therefore between communication components of each participating node of the strategic supply chain network, are proposed. They act as a coordination instance and decrease the coupling between components. Potential technologies are software busses, event channels or tuple spaces [6, 16]. Tuple spaces support the data driven communication according to the pull-principle where an interested party has to request data, filtered by specific restrictions configured by the requesting party. Tuple spaces act as message buffer, allowing asynchronous communication by storing messages until they are explicitly deleted or fetched. Therefore they decouple sender and receiver of messages in a temporal manner. Tuple spaces are special associative memories where data is not chosen by keys but by patterns of the message content.

If a network node has identified a suitable supply chain it may request information about changes in the respective supply chain. To support this, the *Publisher Subscriber Pattern* [5] has been combined with tuple spaces on a conception level. A subscriber gets an event if data changes within tuples of interest. This allows network participants to shape virtual supply chains out of the crowds of service and product suppliers participating in the network. Such extensions to tuple spaces complement them and create an integral solution for a data driven and reactive network for the exchange of strategic supply chain data.

Having discussed tuple-spaces and business components as possible solutions for the development of self-modelling, distributed supply chains, in the next section an optimised business component model for the domain of strategic supply chain development is presented. The deployment of different business components on different network hubs is explained and the communication between those distributed business components is illustrated.

4   Business Component Model for the Business Domain of Strategic Supply Chain Development

To illustrate the feasibility of the concepts described above, a business component model for the domain of strategic supply chain development has been derived, based on the Business Component Modelling (BCM) process [1]. The business component model is shown in Fig. 3, in accordance with the notation of Unified Modelling Language [14], with all component services listed and with the dependencies between the individual business components represented by arrows.

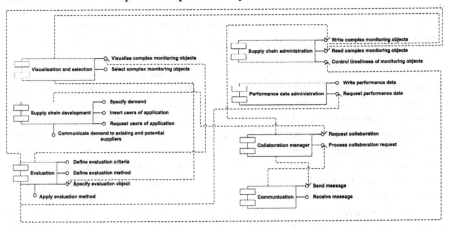

Fig. 3. Business component model

The model consists of seven components which provide services performing certain business tasks of the specified domain. The component *supply chain development* offers services for the specification of the demand and for the definition of application users. The *supply chain administration* is responsible for aggregating and managing the data received from the suppliers, whereas the *visualisation and selection* component visualises the virtual supply chains and allows selection of sub-chains in order to evaluate them. Services for the definition of evaluation criteria and methods and for rating supply chains are provided by the *evaluation* component. The performance data, resulting from evaluating supply chains, is administrated by the *performance data administration* component. Since the components are located on different network hubs, two additional components are needed for inter-component communication, namely the *communication manager* and the *communication* component. In order to illustrate the deployment of those components and the communication between them a deployment and a sequence diagram are introduced next.

Fig. 4 shows the deployment of business component instances on different network hubs. For the domain of supply chain management different systems use the specified components, namely the producer system and all suppliers systems. The producer holds all components belonging to the strategic supply chain development system including the supply chain development and the evaluation components. Whereas the suppliers utilise only those components necessary for recording and sending the own data to the producer and for acquiring the data received from their own suppliers.

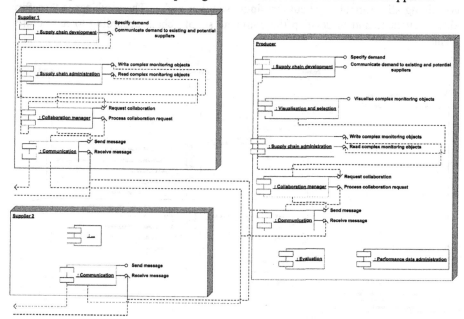

Fig. 4. Instantiation and deployment diagram

The dependencies and services calls are presented by arrows. For a more coherent display not all component services and dependencies are shown. The dependencies and the dataflow are given by means of an example and are illustrated in Fig. 5.

Example: Using the services of the supply chain development component a producer is able to specify the demand and to communicate the demand to all suppliers in tier-n. Triggered by that request, the supply chain development component accesses the service *request collaboration* of the collaboration manager component which uses the *send message* service of the communication component in order to send the demand to the suppliers in tier-1. The service requests of the different components are visualised in Fig. 5 by arrows. The communication components of the suppliers in tier-1 receive the message sent by the producer and forward the request to their collaboration managers accessing the *process collaboration request* service. Each collaboration manager uses the *communicate demand to existing and potential suppliers* service of the supply chain development component to forward the demand to existing and potential suppliers. The collaboration manager and the communication components are responsible for communication between the systems.

Supplier 1, having received the information data from supplier 3, stores the data using the service *write complex monitoring objects* in its own system. This information together with information about all the suppliers is sent back to the producer. At any time the producer receives the aggregated information from its suppliers in tier-1 and their relative suppliers. This information is given to the supply chain administration component in form of a complex monitoring object. Each user can then request to *visualise the complex monitoring object*. The complete supply chain is presented containing all information about the single supplier nodes. The producer is therefore able to evaluate and to develop the complete supply chain according to its requirements.

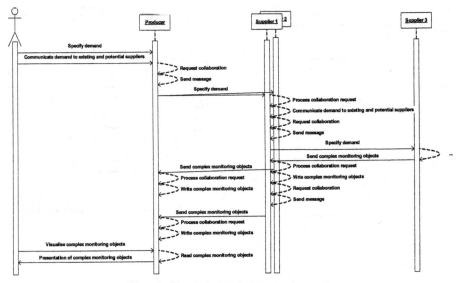

Fig. 5. Sequence diagram

5   Conclusion

In today's economy, formerly closely-linked value chains are more and more transforming into flexible networks, thus significantly changing the buyer/producer - supplier relationship. As laid out in this article, those points hold especially true for the field of strategic purchasing, where an extension from a chain to a network perspective is desirable - however, complexity issues connected with the modelling of supplier-networks have to be overcome. Having identified the need for managing the complexity of supplier network modelling and for extending the frame of reference of strategic purchasing, the concepts of dynamic supply chain modelling and strategic supply chain development have been introduced. Conceptual and technological issues have been discussed and a business component model for strategic supply chain development, addressing the identified issues and proposing a concept and methodology to overcome them, has been identified. As pointed out in the article, further research has to be conducted in the area of network evaluation as well as for the assessment of the practicability of the proposed approach during the further prototypical implementation of the derived business component model for strategic supply chain development.

References

[1]   A. Albani, A. Keiblinger, K. Turowski and C. Winnewisser, Domain based identification and modelling of business component applications, In Proceedings of the 7th East-European Conference on Advances in Databases and Information Systems, Dresden, Germany, September 2003.

[2]   D. Ammer, *Materials Management*, Homewood, 1968.

[3]   A. S. Carr and J. N. Pearson, *Strategically managed buyer - supplier relationships and performance outcomes*, Journal of Operations Management, 17 (1999), pp. 497 - 519.

[4]   A. S. Carr, Smelzer, L.R., *The relationship of strategic purchasing to supply chain management*, European Journal of Purchasing & Supply Management, 5 (1999), pp. 43 - 51.

[5]   E. Gamma, R. Helm, R. Johnson and J. Vlissides, *Design patterns: elements of reusable object-oriented software*, Addison-Wesley, Reading, Mass., 1995.

[6]   D. Gelernter, *Multiple tuple spaces in Linda*, Proc. of PARLE '89, Springer Verlag (1989), pp. 20-27.

[7]   J. E. Hanson, P. Nandi and S. Kumaran, Conversation support for Business Process Integration, Proceedings 6th IEEE International Enterprise Distributed Object Computing Conference (EDOC-2002), IEEE Press2002, pp. 65-74.

[8]   J. B. Houlihan, *International Supply Chain Management*, International Journal of Physical Distribution and Logistics Management, 15 (1985), pp. 22-38.

[9]   T. Jones and D. Riley, *Using Inventory for Competitive Advantage through Supply Chain Management*, International Journal of Physical Distribution and Logistics Management, 5 (1985), pp. 16-22.

[10]   L. Kaufmann, Purchasing and Supply Management - A Conceptual Framework, Handbuch Industrielles Beschaffungsmanagement, Hahn, D, Kaufmann, L. (Hrsg.), Wiesbaden, 2002, pp. 3 - 33.

[11]   D. M. Lambert and M. C. Cooper, *Issues in Supply Chain Management*, Industrial Marketing Management, 29 (2000), pp. 65-83.

[12]   T. W. Malone and R. J. Lautbacher, *The Dawn of the E-Lance Economy*, Harvard Business Review (1998), pp. 145 - 152.

[13]   R. McIvor, P. Humphreys and E. McAleer, *The Evolution of the Purchasing Function*, Journal of Strategic Change, Vol. 6 (1997), pp. 165 - 179.

[14]   OMG, OMG Unified Modelling Language Spezification Version 1.4, 2001.

[15]   M. Sawhney and J. Zabin, The Seven Steps to Nirvana: Strategic Insights into eBusiness Transformation, New York, 2001.

[16]   A. S. Tanenbaum, *Distributed Operating Systems*, Prentice Hall, 1995.

[17]   D. Tapscott, D. Ticoll and A. Lowy, *Digital Capital: Harnessing the Power of Business Webs*, Boston, 2000.

[18]   K. Turowski, ed., *Standardized Specification of Business Components*, Gesellschaft für Informatik, Working Group 5.10.3 - Component Oriented Business Application Systems, Augsburg, 2002.

[19]   H.-J. Warnecke, Vom Fraktal zum Produktionsnetzwerk. Unternehmenskooperationen erfolgreich gestalten, Berlin, 1999.

Group Typical Preference Extraction Using Collaborative Filtering Profile

Su-Jeong Ko

Department of Computer Science
University of Illinois at Urbana-Champaign
1304 West Springfield Ave. 1213 Digital Computer Laboratory
Urbana, Illinois 61801 USA
{sujeongko@yahoo.co.kr}

Abstract. This paper proposes the association word mining method. Using this method, the profile of the collaborative user is created, and based on this profile, users are grouped according to the vector space model and Kmeans algorithm. Consequently, the existing collaborative filtering system's problems of sparsity and of recommendations based on the degree of correlation of user preferences are eliminated. Moreover, to address the said system's shortcoming whereby items are recommended according to the degree of correlation of the two most similar users within a group, entropy is used. Thus, the typical preference of the group is extracted. Since user preferences cannot be automatically regarded as accurate data, users within the group who have entropies beyond the threshold are selected as typical users. The typical preference can be extracted by assigning typical user preferences in the form of weights. The method enables dynamic recommendation because it decreases the inaccuracy of recommendations based on unproven user preferences.

1   Introduction

Collaborative filtering systems[6, 8, 14] incur the following problems. First, because there is less probability that two users will prefer the same items, this method has a sparsity problem whereby an accurate recommendation cannot be made. Secondly, although the preference correlation of two users may not be very high, their preferences can serve as useful data for preference prediction. The preference information of the two users cannot be used to give a recommendation, however, because their degree of mutual correlation is low[9]. Thirdly, the degree of correlation is computed between only two users. Suppose that the degree of correlation of two users allows for a recommendation. If one user carelessly evaluates an item, an unexpected item will be recommended to the other user[3]. Studies have been conducted to address the problem of sparsity in such a case. One such study explores a method that uses one of EM algorithm[14], Kmeans algorithm[2,10], entropy

K. Bauknecht, A Min Tjoa, G. Quirchmayr (Eds.): EC-Web 2003, LNCS 2738, pp. 414-423, 2003.

weighting and SVD, which groups users using the feature selection of a group[5, 12]. This method does not find similar users by grouping users who have similar item preferences, but applies the item preferences of similar users to all the users within a group. It can thus address the problem of sparsity[12]. The method has another shortcoming, though, in that a recommendation is made depending on the correlation match between only two users and cannot be made when there is a low degree of preference correlation[15]. This paper proposes the association word mining method, which reflects not only the preference rating of items but also information on them. Using this method, the profile of the collaborative user is created, and based on this profile, users are grouped according to the vector space model and Kmeans algorithm. Moreover, to address the said system's shortcoming whereby items are recommended according to the degree of correlation of the two most similar users within a group, entropy is used. Thus, the typical preference of the group is extracted. The typical preference can be extracted by assigning typical user preferences in the form of weights. The method reduces the time for retrieving the most similar users within the group. The proposed method has been evaluated against the database that stores user preferences entered on the Web, and has been proven to have a higher efficiency than existing methods.

2   Generating the Weighted User Profile

This paper generates a content based user profile and a collaborative user profile to rate preference automatically based on a collaborative user profile. The collaborative user profile is generated based on {user-item} matrix. For the generation of collaborative user profile, the feature extraction should be done first. This paper uses web documents as item.

2.1   Feature Extraction for Item

In this paper, to express the characteristics of the documents as either a bag-of-words or a bag-of-associated-words[5], it is a necessary preprocess the document by analyzing its morphology. The system used in the morphological analysis is identical to the user-focused intelligent information retrieval system. The Apriori algorithm[1] is used to mine related data from the words extracted from morphological analysis. The associated word mining algorithm, Apriori, is used to find the associative rules of items out of the set of transactions. The mined data, or the set of associated words from each document, are represented as a related-word-vector model. As a result, document $\{d_j\}$ is represented as Equation (1) in the form of a related-word-vector model.

$$d_j=\{(AW1r:w_{11}\&w_{12}...\&w_{1(r-1)}=>w_{1r}),(AW2r:w_{21}\&w_{22}...\&w_{2(r-1)}=>w_{2r}),...,(AWkr:w_{k1}\&w_{k2}...\&w_{k(r-1)}=>w_{kr}),...,(AWpr:w_{p1}\&w_{p2}...\&w_{p(r-1)}=>w_{pr})\} \quad (1)$$

In Equation (1) $(w_{11}\&w_{12}...\&w_{1(r-1)}\&w_{1r})$ represents related words, $\{w_{11}, w_{12}, w_{1(r-1)}, w_{1r}\}$ the structure of the related words, r the number of words that compose the related words, and p the number of related words that represent the text. The '&' shows that the words on each side are related. For the best results in extracting the related words, the data must have a confidence of over 85 and a support of less than 20[11].

2.2   Collaborative User Profile

The collaborative filtering system based on web documents recommends a document to users according to {user-item} matrix. The user in collaborative filtering systems doesn't rate preference on all documents. Therefore, the missing value is occurred in {user-item} matrix. The missing value causes the sparsity of {user-item} matrix. In this section, the collaborative user profile generation is mentioned to reduce the sparsity of {user-item} matrix caused by the missing value.

If we define m items which are composed of p feature vectors and a group of n users, user group is expressed as $U=\{cu_{ij}\}(i=1,2,...,n)$, document group is expressed as $I=\{d_{j}\}(j=1,2,...,m)$. And $R=\{r_{ij}\}(i=1,2,...,n \; j=1,2,...,m)$ is a matrix of {user-item}. The element in matrix r_{ij} means user cu_i's preference to document d_j. Collaborative filtering system uses an information that user rates the preference for web pages. Preference levels are represented on a scale of 0~1.0 in increments of 0.2, a total of 6 degrees, only when the value is higher than 0.5 is the user classified as showing interest. The web documents used in this paper are computer-related documents gleaned by an http down loader. The features of web documents are extracted by association word mining described in section 2.1.

The profile of collaborative filtering user cu_i is generated based on the document features extracted from collaborative filtering user's preference rating. In case a collaborative user rates preference low, the weight of rated document is given low. In case a collaborative user rates preference high, the weight of rated document is given high. Therefore, the preference of association words expressed in features is indicated various values according to the weight. As a collaborative user defines the preference rating r_{ij} on the document d_j, the weight of each association word that is extracted from document d_j is defined as r_{ij}. The weighted association words are defined as $AWTkrj$. Equation (2) is the equation that defines the initial weight $AWTkrj$, which are structural elements, to generate the user cu_i's profile. The initial weight $AWTkrj$ of association words is defined as the initial preference, the elements of {user-item} matrix. The preference that user rates directly is the most correct and important data for automatic preference rating.

$$AWTkrj = Preference\,(\,AWkrj\,) = r_{ij} \; (\text{user:}cu_i, 1 \leq k \leq p, 1 \leq j \leq m) \qquad (2)$$

Equation (3) is to define all association words as $AWRj'$ lining extracted association words from all documents rated by user.

$$AWRj' : AW1r1...= AWkrj ...= AWprm \qquad (1 \leq j' \leq p', 1 \leq k \leq p, 1 \leq j \leq m) \qquad (3)$$

Equation (4) is the equation to change a weight according to the frequency of the extracted association word from all documents rated by user, after giving initial weight to association word $AWTkrj$ by Equation (2). Equation (4) defines the weight of $AWRj'$, and the weight of association words $AWRj'$ is defined as $AWRTj'$. The weight of association words $AWRTj'$ is supposed to multiply the weight whenever a collaborative user cu_i finds a association word by searching into the association word set extracted from all rated documents.

$$AWRTj' = \prod_{j=1}^{m} \prod_{k=1}^{p} AWTkrj \mid (AWRj' = AWkrj) \quad \text{(user:cui, } 1{\leq}j'{\leq}p') \tag{4}$$

In Equation (4), p' means the number of non-repeated association words among association word set extracted from documents rated by user cu_i, m means the number of all rated documents.

By definition in Equation (4), the repeated association words out of association word set, which user cu_i' rates preference, are calculated by the Equation (4) and the final weight $AWRTj'$ is given to association word $AWRj'$. By Equation (4), the profile of collaborative user cu_i is defined as CU_i like in Equation (5). Equation (5) tells the method on how to give weight $AWRTj'$ to non-repeated association words $AWRj'$ out of association word set, which are extracted from the rated documents by collaborative user cu_i.

$$CU_i = \{AWRT1 \bullet AWR1, AWRT2 \bullet AWR2, \ldots, AWRTj' \bullet AWRTj', \ldots, AWRTp' \bullet AWRp'\}$$
$$\text{(user:}cu_i, 1{\leq}j'{\leq}p') \tag{5}$$

In Equation (5), p' is the number of non-repeated association words among association word set that user cu_i extracts from rated documents.

3   Collaborative User Clustering and Group Typical Preference Extraction

We describe the method for clustering users into group and extracting group typical preference based on collaborative user profile in Chapter 2. In order to cluster users, we compute similarity between users by using vector space model and cluster users into group by using Kmeans algorithm based on the results.

3.1   Collaborative User Clustering Using the Vector Space Model and Kmeans Algorithm

To determine similarities between users, this paper uses the vector space model, which is widely used in the information retrieval field when grouping users that show similar inclinations. Moreover, this paper uses Kmeans algorithm to group users. In the vector space model, all information - such as stored text and natural information requests - is represented as a set of words and a vector[2]. According to the vector space model, the collaborative user profile CU_i of the collaborative user cu_i in Equation (5) is defined as a vector in the dimension p'.

When computing similarities between users according to the vector space model using the collaborative user profile in Equation (5), the vector length normalization process in Equation (6) is required[17]. When there are many association words in the form of profiles, the vector length normalization process sets the length of the collaborative user vector at 1 in order to solve the imbalance problem through the influence of the word count. This process divides the weight of each word by the square root of the sum of the square of the weight.

$$w_1 = \frac{AWRT\ 1}{\sqrt{\sum_{i=1}^{p'} AWRTi^{\ 2}}} \qquad w_n = \frac{AWRTn}{\sqrt{\sum_{i=1}^{p'} AWRTi^{\ 2}}} \tag{6}$$

In Equation (6), n is the total count of words in one document. $AWRTi$ is the weight of each association word, and w_i is the adjusted weight of each association word. According to this principle, the vector similarity between two collaborative users, CU_i and CU_j, is obtained in Equation (7).

$$Sim(CU_i, CU_j) = \sum_{AWRj'} w_{j'i} \times w_{j'j} \tag{7}$$

$AWRj'$ in Equation (2) is the common association word that appears in the profiles of collaborative users CU_i and CU_j. $w_{j'i}$ is the weight of the association word $AWRj'$ contained in the profile of the collaborative user CU_i, and $w_{j'j}$ is the weight of the association word $AWRj'$ contained in the profile of the collaborative user CU_j. Kmeans algorithm[2] groups users according to similarities between collaborative users, as computed using Equation (7). Kmeans clustering algorithm is the simplified form of the Maximum-Likelihood(ML) method in data classification and does not guarantee absolute convergence. Moreover, it has a shortcoming in that the number of groups must first be determined for the algorithm to perform well, and the convergence of clustering results differs depending on the group center's initial value. The algorithm has been efficiently applied, however, to user grouping because of its simplicity[2]. Three steps are required to group users using Kmeans algorithm. In the first step, the number of K clusters and centers are initialized. In the second step, based on similarities between collaborative users, the user group is obtained and the collaborative user is assigned to a group. In the third step, to distinguish users whose group has been determined, if the similarity average changes under the threshold, the process is completed. This paper sets the threshold at 0.01. Otherwise, the process is repeated from second step for users who are closest to the average.

3.2   Extracting Group Typical Preference

This chapter predicts the typical preference of users within a group using the distribution of user preferences. The distribution of user preferences for items is very significant in the collaborative filtering system. The typical preference of users within a group must be based on the more carefully chosen preferences of the users. Carefully chosen user preferences are more accurate than identical preferences because users cannot have identical tastes for all items in which they are interested. The entropy is used to predict the typical preference of users within a group. The process of dynamic recommendation by predicting the typical preference of a group using entropy is shown in Fig. 1.

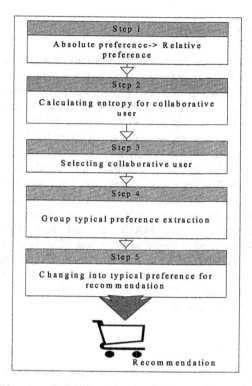

Fig. 1. Flowchart for extracting group typical preference using entropy

In Step 1, the absolute user preference is converted into the relative preference. When the entropy of a collaborative user is computed based on the absolute preference, accurate values cannot be computed because the computation is greatly influenced by the absolute value of the preference rather than the preference distribution. In Step 2, the entropy of the collaborative user is obtained based on the relative preference converted. In Step 3, to predict the typical preference of the group, users with high numerical values are extracted. In this step, the threshold for the entropy of the collaborative users is set, users beyond the threshold are extracted, and users with low entropy are excluded. Step 4 predicts the typical preference of the group. The typical preference is predicted by multiplying the users' absolute preferences with their entropy weighting. Step 4 predicts the typical preference of the group. The typical preference is predicted by multiplying the users' absolute preferences with their entropy weighting. The entropy of a collaborative user must be lowered to a decimal fraction so that it may be applied as a weight. When an entropy value over 1 is used, the predicted typical preference turns out the same and the predicted typical preference cannot be used for recommendation. Step 5 converts the typical preference in Step 4 into the typical preference that may be used for recommendation. The typical preference from Step 4 is not the value 0, 0.2, 0.4, 0.6, 0.8 or 1 used in the collaborative filtering matrix. Thus, the process of converting the typical preference predicted in Step 4 into the preference that may be used for actual recommendation is required.

4   Performance Evaluation

The database for collaborative filter recommendations was created from the data of 200 users and 1600 web documents. Users evaluated a minimum of 10 of the 1600 web documents. The database for content_based filter recommendations was created from 1600 web documents. These 1600 web documents were collected from computer related URLs by an http downloader, then hand-classified into 8 areas of computer information. The 8 areas were classified under the labels of the following classes: {Games, Graphics, News and media, Semiconductors, Security, Internet, Electronic publishing, and Hardware}. The basis for this classification comes from search engines such as AltaVista and Yahoo that have statistically analyzed and classified computer related web documents. Of the 200 users, 100 were used as the training group, and the remaining users were used as the test group.

In this paper, mean absolute error(MAE) and rank score measure(RSM), both suggested by paper[4] are used to gauge performance. MAE is used to evaluate single item recommendation systems. RSM is used to evaluate the performance of systems that recommend items from ranked lists. The accuracy of the MAE, expressed as Equation (8), is determined by the absolute value of the difference between the predicted value and real value of user evaluation.

$$S_a = \frac{1}{m_a} \sum_{j \in P_a} |P_{a,j} - V_{a,j}| \tag{8}$$

In Equation (8), p_{aj} is the predicted preference, v_{aj} the real preference, and m_a the number of items that have been evaluated by the new user.

The RSM of an item in a ranked list is determined by user evaluation or user visits. RSM is measured under the premise that the probability of choosing an item lower in the list decreases exponentially. Suppose that each item is put in a decreasing order of value j, based on the weight of user preference. Equation (9) calculates the expected utility of user U_a's RSM on the ranked item list.

$$R_a = \sum_j \frac{\max(V_{a,j} - d, 0)}{2^{(j-1)/(\alpha-1)}} \tag{9}$$

In Equation (9), d is the mid-average value of the item, and α is its the halflife. The halflife is the number of items in a list that has a 50/50 chance of either review or visit. In the evaluation phase of this paper the halflife value of 5 shall be used. In Equation (10), the RSM is used to measure the accuracy of predictions about the new user.

$$R = 100 \times \frac{\sum_u R_u}{\sum_u R_u^{max}} \tag{10}$$

In Equation (10), if the user has evaluated or visited an item that ranks highly in a ranked list, R_u^{max} is the maximum expected utility of the RSM.

For evaluation, this paper uses all of the following methods: The proposed method using typical preference (R_P_R), the method of recommendation using Kmeans user clustering(K_C_R)[10], the method of recommendation using feature of group(E_S_R)[12].

Fig. 2 shows the MAE of R_P_R , K_C_R , E_S_R based on Equation (9) and Equation (10).

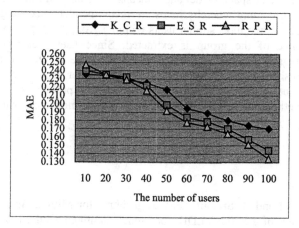

Fig. 2. MAE varying at the number of users

In Fig. 2, as the number of users increases, the performance of the R_P_R increases, whereas K_C_R and E_S_R show no notable change in performance. In terms of accuracy of prediction, it is evident that method R_P_R is more superior to others. On the other side, in case that the number of users is small, the performance of R_P_R decreases a little. We must study this problem in the future.

Fig. 3 shows the time required for recommendation by changing the number of clustered users. In Fig. 3, although the number of users increases, R_P_R is more superior to others.

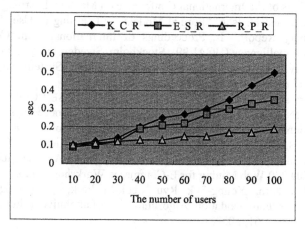

Fig. 3. The time required for recommendation by changing the number of clustered users

5   Conclusion

This paper proposed the association word mining method, which reflects not only the preference rating of items but also information on them. Using this method, the profile of the collaborative user is created, and based on this profile, users are grouped according to the vector space model and Kmeans algorithm. Moreover, to address the said system's shortcoming whereby items are recommended according to the degree of correlation of the two most similar users within a group, entropy is used. Thus, the typical preference of the group is extracted. Since user preferences cannot be automatically regarded as accurate data, users within the group who have entropies beyond the threshold are selected as typical users. After this selection, the typical preference can be extracted by assigning typical user preferences in the form of weights. The method reduced the time for retrieving the most similar users within the group.

References

[1]   R. Agrawal and R. Srikant, "Fast Algorithms for Mining Association Rules," Proceedings of the 20th VLDB Conference, Santiago, Chile, 1994.

[2]   K. Alsabti, S. Ranka, and V. Singh, "An Efficient K-Means Clustering Algorithm," http://www.cise.ufl.edu/ranka/, 1997.

[3]   C. Basu, H. Hirsh, and W. W. Cohen, "Recommendation as classification:Using social and content-based information in recommendation," In proceedings of the Fifteenth National Conference on Artificial Intelligence, pp. 714-720, Madison, WI, 1998.

[4]   John. S. Breese and C. Kadie, "Empirical Analysis of Predictive Algorithms for Collaborative Filtering," Proceedings of the Conference on Uncertainty in Artificial Intelligence, Madison, WI, 1998.

[5]   D. Billsus and M. J. Pazzani, "Learning collaborative information filters," In proceedings of the International Conference on Machine Learning, 1998.

[6]   J. Delgado and N. Ishii, "Formal Models for Learning of User Preferences, a Preliminary Report," In Proceedings of International Joint Conference on Artificial Intelligence (IJCAI-99), Stockholm, Sweden, July, 1999.

[7]   Inha University, "Intelligent Information Retrieval System centering User", Technical research report, 1997.

[8]   A. Kohrs and B. Merialdo, "USING CATEGORY-BASED COLLABORATIVE FILTERING IN THE ACTIVE WEBMUSEUM," Proceedings of the IEEE International Conference on Multimedia and Expo - Vol. 1 , 2000.

[9]   Sarwar, B. M., Karypis, G., Konstan, J. A., and Riedl, J., "Application of Dimensionality Reduction in Recommender System-A Case Study," In ACM WebKDD 200 Web Mining for E-Commerce Workshop, 2000.

[10]   Taek-Hun Kim, Young-Suk Ryu, Seok-In Park, Sung-Bong Yang, "An Improved Recommendation Algorithm in Collaborative Filtering," EC-Web 2002, pp. 254-261, 2002.

[11] S. J. Ko and J. H. Lee, "Feature Selection using Association Word Mining for Classification," In Proceedings of the Conference on DEXA2001, LNCS2113, pp. 211-220, 2001.

[12] Y. S. Lee and S. W. Lee, "Group Feature Selection using Entropy Weight and SVD," Transaction of KISS(B), Vol. 29, No. 4, 2002.

[13] W. S. Lee, "Collaborative learning for recommender systems," In Proceedings of the Conference on Machine Learning, 1997.

[14] G. J. McLachlan and T. Krishnan, The EM Algorithm and Extensions, New York: John Wiley and Sons, 1997.

[15] M. Pazzani, D. Billsus, Learning and Revising User Profiles: The Identification of Interesting Web Sites, Machine Learning, Kluwer Academic Publishers, pp. 313-331, 1997.

[16] Badrul Sarwar, George Karypis, Josephp Konstan, and John Ridedl, "Analysis of Recommendation Algorithms for E-Commerce," Proc. Of The ACM E-Commerce 2000, 2000.

[17] G. Salton and M. J. McGill, *Introduction to Modern Information Retrieval*, McGraw-Hill, 1983.

Exploiting Similarity Measures
in Multi-criteria Based Recommendations

Nikos Karacapilidis and Lefteris Hatzieleftheriou

MIS Lab, MEAD, University of Patras
26500 Rio Patras, Greece
nikos@mech.upatras.gr

Abstract. The need for developing efficient and effective recommender systems has lately become fundamental, basically due to the vast amount of on-line information and the increasing popularity of Internet applications. Such systems are based on various recommendation techniques, which aim at guiding users to survey objects that appear as interesting or useful to them. By exploiting the concept of fuzzy similarity measures, this paper presents a recommendation framework that builds on the strengths of knowledge-based and collaborative filtering techniques. Following a multi-criteria approach, the proposed framework is able to provide users with a ranked list of alternatives, while it also permits them to submit their evaluations on the existing objects of the database. Much attention is given to the extent in which the user evaluation may affect the values of the stored objects. The applicability of our approach is demonstrated through a web-based tool that provides recommendations about visiting different cities of a country.

1 Introduction

The development of recommender systems receives increasing interest in the last few years. This is basically due to the overwhelming volume of information available online and the growing attractiveness of applications deployed on the Internet. Such systems are based on various techniques, which aim at guiding users to survey objects that appear as interesting or useful to them in a personalized way. These techniques can be explicit or implicit. The former require the users to precisely specify their profile (interests, preferences etc.), which is then captured in a limited manner, while they are rather "passive", in that they do not adapt to the evolving users' behavior. On the other hand, implicit techniques try to infer the users' preferences from their history, they are "active" and may encapsulate learning algorithms that follow one's changing behavior over time.

According to their background data (information that the system possess before getting into the recommendation process), input data (information given by the users in order to generate recommendations) and the recommendation algorithm followed, recommendation techniques can be classified into five basic categories [1], namely

K. Bauknecht, A Min Tjoa, G. Quirchmayr (Eds.): EC-Web 2003, LNCS 2738, pp. 424–434, 2003.

collaborative, content-based, demographic, utility-based and knowledge-based. Generally speaking, each of the above categories has some pros and cons. For instance, the major shortcoming of the Collaborative Filtering (CF) technique, which is widely used due to the fact that the system becomes adaptive and has sufficient implicit feedback, is that it cannot efficiently handle the "ramp-up" problem (it can occur as a "new user" or "new item" problem) [6, 7]. Another drawback of systems having adopted CF is that the quality of the system's recommendations is dependant on large historical data sets. Knowledge-based (KB) techniques have been also used extensively; they do not create ramp-up problems, are sensitive to changes of preference, can include non-product features and, finally, can map the user needs to products. However, they have two major weaknesses: their suggestion ability is static (does not learn), while the underlying knowledge must be efficiently engineered.

Building on the above techniques, a variety of recommender systems and models has been implemented during the last few years. For instance, Entrée [1] exploits KB techniques to provide recommendations for restaurants in Chicago. It has an extensive and well-constructed database, supports second level of recommendation, does not create the "ramp-up" problem, while it is static due to the absence of user evaluation ability. Movielens (http://www.movielens.umn.edu) builds on CF and demographic techniques to provide ratings for films. It has a huge database, can give multi-criteria recommendations, but it suffers in the presence of noisy data inputs. PTV [5] uses content-based and CF techniques to provide TV-shows recommendations. It integrates WAP technologies, while it cannot handle the "ramp-up" and noisy data problems. Furthermore, as in Movielens, its data set is sparse. Kurapati et al. [8] have presented an integrated approach (which combines implicit view history, explicit TV viewing preferences, feedback information on specific shows and Bayesian classifier method) to provide recommendations for TV-shows. Their approach is actually a step beyond PTV, with potentially better results, while it suffers from the "gray-sheep" problem and "missing data". The Wasabi Personal Shopper [3] provides a conversational interface to a database, based on the principles of case-based reasoning, to provide recommendations on wines. It combines CF and KB techniques to overcome their weaknesses, while it suffers from noisy data and does not exploit similarity measures capabilities.

An important issue to be taken into account in the development of recommender systems concerns the evaluation provided by the users and the influence that this has in the classification of the stored objects. Similarities of user profiles should be considered in parallel with their contributions (evaluations), in that there is a need of smoothing out points of disagreements. The appropriate clustering of users (appearing as a problem in CF) through an efficient management of their profiles, can be a remedy to this problem. In the majority of cases, another main issue is related to the desired multi-criteria based management of recommendations and evaluations of the stored objects. A third issue concerns the robustness of the recommendation algorithm used, in that it has to appropriately deal with noisy data (e.g., inputs from malicious users attempting to credit or discredit the values of the stored objects).

The work described in this paper concerns a hybrid recommendation framework that, by building on the strengths and overcoming the weaknesses of CF and KB techniques, attempts to solve the above issues. In the sequel, Section 2 presents in detail the proposed approach, while Section 3 demonstrates its application through a web-based recommender tool. Section 4 comments on the robustness of our approach and outlines experiments carried out in order to specify certain parameters of the framework. Finally, Section 5 concludes with final remarks and directions for future work.

2   The Recommendation Framework

Based on a KB technique, the proposed approach (see Fig. 1) exploits the concept of fuzzy similarity measures in order to make its suggestions more accurate. Feature selection and knowledge construction is performed through a web mining process. CF is performed through a questionnaire that enhances the system ability of categorizing a user and criticizing his evaluation. Evaluation submitted by the users goes also through a filtering process before the system takes it into account. In such a way, the proposed approach overcomes the static ability suggestion problem and gives a dynamic nature to the recommendations provided. Furthermore, our framework is based on a multi-criteria approach, thus providing the ability of making multi-level recommendations across a set of objects' attributes (second level of evaluation according to the best performance of the retrieved objects to each object's feature).

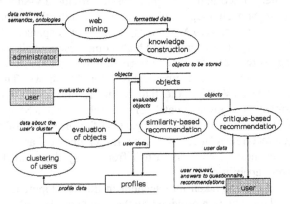

Fig. 1. The data flow diagram of the recommender tool

2.1   Knowledge Construction

Background data are gathered through appropriate text mining and knowledge construction processes [4, 9]. These concern the selection of objects and their associated features to be stored in the database. Although important, the description of these processes goes out of the scope of this paper. We only mention here that for the application described in the next section we have performed web mining, while we have experimented with diverse feature selection and knowledge construction techniques proposed in the literature [12], such as document frequency, information gain, mutual information, term strength, and association word mining through the Apriori algorithm. In addition, the knowledge construction process (see Fig. 1) applies Bayesian classification on the mined data and maintains a knowledge base of related words.

2.2   Recommendation Process

Recommendation provided by the system can be based on either a critique on certain features of the stored objects (critique-based recommendation, see Fig. 1) or the similarity between an object already known to the user and the rest objects that are stored in the database (similarity-based recommendation, see Fig. 1).

Critique-Based Recommendation. The user is asked to determine how much is interested in or attracted by a set of features F_i that characterize each object O_j. The choices offered to the user are in the set {minimal interest, less interest, neutral, much interest, extensive interest} (each choice is associated to a value in the interval [0.2 … 1.0]; however, alternative ratings, following different granularity levels, may be also applied). The user is also able to choose the number N of the recommendations to be returned by the system. Getting input from the above critique, the system creates a fuzzy set A. This set is associated with the specific user and is stored in the database along with the user's ID (to be exploited later, during the evaluation filtering process).

Each object stored in the database corresponds to a fuzzy set B, which is compared to the fuzzy set A that has just been created by the user (B is structured according to the scores stored for each of the associated object's features). For this comparison, our model uses a similarity measure $Q_{A,B}$ that is based on the difference of grades of membership and the volume of the two fuzzy sets. The $Q_{A,B}$ similarity measure was selected among various fuzzy sets similarity measures [11], after evaluating their properties. $Q_{A,B}$ was the only one which was a proximity measure. In fuzzy sets theory, a similarity measure is called a proximity measure when it stands: $Q_{A,B} = Q_{A^\wedge, B^\wedge}$ where $A^\wedge$ and $B^\wedge$ are the supplements of A and B, respectively. Using this proximity measure, we can efficiently consider the influence of both high and low similarity. It is:

$$Q_{A,B} = \{\sum_{i=1}^{n}[1 - abs(A(i) - B(i))]\} / n \qquad (1)$$

where $A(i)$ and $B(i)$ the score of feature i given by the user and stored in the database, respectively, and n the total number of features for an object. The results of this process are temporarily stored in a table containing the score (similarity) of each stored object against the user's preferences. In the sequel, using the MadSelect algorithm [2], the best N objects and their associated scores are retrieved. In other words, the model provides the N most similar objects to the description given by the user. The proposed model also provides a second level recommendation, which classifies the N retrieved best objects according to each object's discrete feature. As a result, the user is informed about which of the N objects performs better according to each feature and may get motivated for further contemplation.

Similarity-Based Recommendation. According to this mode, a user is able to choose (among the stored objects) one that he has tested before (an object that was proved to be interesting or useful to him) and request a number N of recommendations that are as similar as possible to this object. As in the previous mode, the similarity between the associated fuzzy sets is explored. The similarity measure used is the one shown in (1), while the results are given in the way described above. The only difference is that the system excludes the selected object from the recommendations to be provided.

2.3   Evaluation Process

In order to better categorize a user (*clustering of users*, see Fig. 1), the proposed framework uses a multiple-choice questionnaire. The answers given are exploited by the proposed framework during the evaluation process. More specifically, these answers are critical in deciding the extent in which an evaluation will be taken into account, that is, the extent in which the values given to the stored objects will be affected. Each answer i to a question j is associated with a score $s_{i,j}$, while the overall score S_u assigned to a user u is:

$$S_u = m \sum_{i=1}^{n} s_{i,j} \tag{2}$$

where n is the number of questions and m a small number, which can be appropriately selected upon the recommendation context. The questions provided must be carefully chosen and are also dependant on the context of the recommendation. In any case though, they should attempt to capture one's status and expertise. Web-mining techniques, similar to those used for the knowledge construction process, may be of much help here.

User Evaluation. To evaluate a stored object a user is asked to assign one of the {Very Bad, Bad, Average, Good, Very Good} values to each of its features (these values are also associated to a number from the interval [0.2 ... 1.0]; alternative ratings may be also considered here). Based on the values assigned, the system codifies the evaluation of a user u for an object o_i by creating a fuzzy set $E_u(o_i)$. Following that, the user evaluation goes through a two-level filtering process. At the first level, the proposed model compares the users evaluations with the fuzzy set of the object that is stored in the database. For this comparison, the system uses a similarity measure that is based on the maximum difference of the two fuzzy sets. This measure is defined as:

$$L_{E,B} = 1 - \max(abs(E_u(o_i) - B(o_i))) \tag{3}$$

where $E_u(o_i)$ is the user's evaluations fuzzy set and $B(o_i)$ is the stored fuzzy set. If $L_{E,B} \leq e$, where e is a small value that is different for each application, the user's evaluation must be filtered. When the system is calculating $L_{E,B}$, it keeps track of the feature that actually influences $L_{E,B}$. In such a case ($L_{E,B} \leq e$), this feature is ignored and the process is repeated until $L_{E,B} > e$.

The second level of the filtering process aims at discarding (parts of) evaluations submitted by users belonging to a certain group. As mentioned in Section 2.2, each time a user requests a recommendation, his preferences (critique) is stored in the database along with the user's ID (*profiles*, see Fig. 1). User's preferences are exploited to classify a user into a cluster. In the general case, each such cluster corresponds to a group of users that give much credit to a certain feature of the objects. For instance, a user belongs to the *feature(i)-driven* cluster if he has requested an object by making the following selections for its features:

Feature	Selection	Value
i	much interest ∨ extensive interest	≥ 0.8
j (j ≠ i)	minimal interest ∨ less interest ∨ neutral interest	≤ 0.6

Users belonging to the *feature(i)-driven* are not then allowed to evaluate an object's features with the following values (our framework actually discards the corresponding parts of their evaluation):

Feature	Evaluation	Value
i	Very Bad	≤ 0.2
j (j ≠ i)	Very Good	> 0.8

We can define one cluster for each feature, even though it is more rational to define a cluster only for some of the features. The purpose of this second filtering level is to determine whether a user is focused on a single feature, since it is common for this kind of users to give overestimated (or underestimated) evaluations. In case that a user cannot be classified in one of the abovementioned clusters, he is considered as *neutral* and his evaluation does not go through this second filtering level.

The filtered evaluation is used to change the values assigned to the features of the corresponding object in the database, according to the formula:

$$v'_{db}(o_i, f_j) = (1 - mS_u)\, v_{db}(o_i, f_j) + (mS_u)\, v_{ev,u}(o_i, f_j) \tag{4}$$

where, $v_{db}(o_i, f_j)$ and $v'_{db}(o_i, f_j)$ are the values of the feature j for the object i stored in the database before and after the evaluation is taken into account, respectively, and $v_{ev,u}(o_i, f_j)$ is the related value assigned during the evaluation of user u (S_u is calculated through equation (2)).

3   CityGuide: A Recommender Tool

This section discusses briefly the application of the previously described framework to a web-based recommender tool, namely CityGuide, which provides recommendations about visiting different cities. In the examples given below, web mining techniques have been applied to construct a knowledge base with information about a set of features holding for 36 cities in Italy. The two modes of the recommendation process are shown in Fig. 2a. The user may either declare his interest towards a set of features (costs, sightseeing, tourism growth, summer and winter activities) or ask for cities which are similar to one that is familiar to him. The desired number of responses from the system is also specified. The results of the above request (for the first mode of the recommendation process) are given in Fig. 2b. The left part of the table contains the recommendations provided together with the associated scores, while the right one informs the user about which of the retrieved results performs better at each evaluation criterion (feature).

The user interface for the evaluation purposes is illustrated in Fig. 3. As shown, there is a set of multiple choice questions the user may go through (left part), while one may select a city and rate its features (middle and right parts). After the submission of a user's evaluation, the tool calculates the new values for the selected object, as described in the previous section.

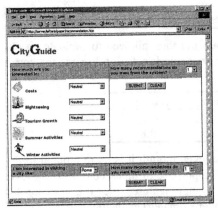

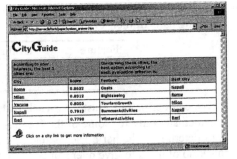

a. The two modes of
the recommendation process

b. Recommendations provided by
the system

Fig. 2. CityGuide: Screenshots related to the recommendation process

Fig. 3. CityGuide: Evaluation provided by the users

4   Discussion

To test the performance of our framework, we used the *robustness* measure (proposed in [10]). This measure actually calculates the power of the algorithms used in a recommendation framework to make good predictions in the presence of noisy data. Robustness of a prediction $p_{u,j}$ (of a user u for an object j) has been defined as:

$$Robust(u, j, c) = 1 - \max_{T \in A:C(T) \leq c} NAE(u, j, T) \qquad (5)$$

where c is the attack's cost, T is an attack scenario (A is the set of all possible attacks, where a cost function $C : A \rightarrow \mathscr{R}$ is defined) and NAE is the normalized absolute error given by:

$$NAE(u, j, T) = \frac{abs(p_{u,j} - p_{u,j}^T)}{\max\{abs(p_{u,j} - R_{max}), abs(p_{u,j} - R_{min})\}} \qquad (6)$$

where $p_{u,j}$, $p_{u,j}^T$ are the system's pre-attack and post-attack T predictions on an object j for a user u, assuming that the set of vote values is bounded above and below by R_{max} and R_{min}, respectively.

Scenario 1: Random Attack. In such an attack, the goal of a user is to reduce the overall performance of the system. As stated in [10], focus is not on particular users or products; rather, it is to target all users and items equally in an attempt to compromise the general integrity of the system. In this attack type, a number N of random attack profiles is generated. The results obtained from the above experiments are shown in the left graph of Fig. 4, where robustness is plotted against the number of attack profiles (note that such an attack concerns a particular object in the database). The alternative curves shown correspond to three different values of the variable m. The minimum robustness value obtained for $m=0.05$ was 0.87 (note that robustness degrades rapidly for the other two values examined); this observation led us to the conclusion that this value of m seems appropriate for the context of CityGuide, since the associated minimum robustness value indicates that this kind of attack cannot be successful. Furthermore, we observed that the increase of the number of attack profiles does not necessarily decrease robustness (so it was not necessary to continue the experiment for a greater number of attack profiles). This is mainly due to the fact that the attack profiles were randomly constructed.

Scenario 2: Focused Product Push/Nuke Attack. In these attacks, a malicious user is attempting to force the predicted rating of a particular object to a target rating. To experiment with this attack type, a number N of attack profiles has been used to discredit a certain object. Once again, the results obtained for three different values of m are illustrated in the right graph of Fig. 4. In the case of $m=0.05$, the minimum robustness value was 0.929. It should be noted here that this value is greater than the one at the random attack scenario, while experiments with the Movielens and PTV databases (described in [10]) have concluded the opposite. This is due to the filtering performed during the evaluation process, which is designed to pay much attention into malicious attacks.

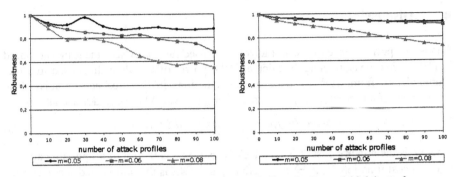

Fig. 4. Robustness degradation in a random (left) and a focused (right) attack

As noted above (as well as in Section 2), the selection of the value of the variable *m* is crucial and should take into account the context under consideration. This variable is actually a metric of how much the system takes into account the evaluation provided by the users and affects the robustness of the recommendation algorithms. Its value for CityGuide is 0.05. To select this value, and further to the experiments described above, we carried out a set of calculations concerning the number of evaluations required to increase (decrease) the value of an object's feature by 0.2 and 0.4 (these values correspond to a scalar change of the rating of a feature's value by one and two levels, respectively). The results of these experiments, with respect to three different user categories (namely, well-experienced, non-experienced and average users) are shown in Fig. 5. From all the above experiments, it was concluded that the value of 0.05 was the appropriate one for the CityGuide case (in both cases, and speaking about average users, a number of about 50 evaluations could produce the required changes in the features of the objects). Similar experiments have been conducted in order to decide the value of *e* (see Section 2). In the case of CityGuide, it is *e*=0.2. Generally speaking, increase of *e* leads to an increase of the framework's robustness, while the extent in which the values of the objects' features are affected is decreased.

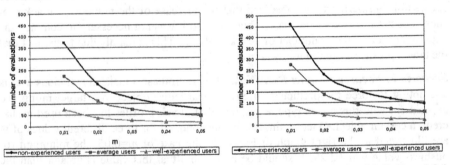

Fig. 5. Evaluations required to change the value of an object's feature by 0.2 (left) and 0.4 (right) for three different user categories

Another important issue in a recommendation framework concerns the selection of the similarity measure to be used for set-valued attributes. For instance, both Entrée [1] and Wasabi [3] use the following measure:

$$sim(A_i, B_i) = abs(a_i \cap b_i) / abs(a_i) \tag{7}$$

As argued in [1, 3], metrics of this type present some difficulty in case retrieval. Having performed a set of experiments concerning eight different similarity measures for our framework (including the one used in [1, 3]), we concluded that the one finally used ($Q_{A,B}$ – see section 2) is more efficient, in that it is the only proximity measure, while it better reflects changes of users' profiles and interests.

5   Conclusion

Building on the strengths of collaborative filtering and knowledge-based techniques, this paper presents a hybrid approach to build a recommender system. The proposed framework handles efficiently issues such as the evaluation provided by the users and the influence that this has in the classification of the stored objects, the multi-criteria based management of recommendations and evaluations of these objects, and the robustness of the recommendation algorithm used. CityGuide, which is an application of this approach, has been thoroughly tested for a period of 4 months from a set of 54 users with diverse experience in travelling to the cities stored in the database. The evaluation feedback is very promising, in that users have argued in favour of the framework's rationality and recommendations provided. Further work directions comprise investigations on the engineering of the various parameters of the framework (association of them with the mining process and the context considered each time) and on the possibility of integration of other recommendation techniques.

References

[1]   Burke, R.: Hybrid Recommender Systems: Survey and Experiments. User Modeling and User-Adapted Interaction 12 (2002) 331-370.
[2]   Burke, R.: Ranking algorithms for costly similarity measures. In: Aha, D., Watson, I., Yang, Q. (eds.): Case-Based Reasoning Research and Development (Proc. of the 4th Intern. Conference on Case-Based Reasoning). Springer-Verlag, New York (2001) 105-117.
[3]   Burke, R.: The Wasabi Personal Shopper: A Case-Based Recommender System. In: Proceedings of the 11th Innovative Applications of Artificial Intelligence Conference on Artificial Intelligence (IAAI-99), Orlando, Florida, AAAI Press (1999) 844-849.
[4]   Cho, Y., Kim J., Kim, S.: A personalized recommender system based on web usage mining and decision tree induction. Expert Systems with Applications 23 (2002) 329-342.

[5]   Cotter P. and Smyth B.: PTV Intelligent Personalised TV Guides. In: Proceedings of the 12th Conference on Innovative Applications of Artificial Intelligence (IAAI 2000), Austin Texas, AAAI Press (2000) 957-964.

[6]   Kim, T.H., Ryu, Y.S., Park, S.I., Yang, S.B.: An Improved Recommendation Algorithm in Collaborative Filtering. In: Bauknecht, K., Tjoa, A.M., Quirchmayr, G. (eds.): Proc. of EC-Web 2002, LNCS, Vol. 2455. Springer-Verlag, Berlin (2002) 254-261.

[7]   Konstan, J., Miller, B., Maltz, D., Herlocker, J., Gordon, L., Riedl, J.: GroupLens: Applying Collaborative Filtering to Usenet News. Communications of the ACM 40 (1997) 77-87.

[8]   Kurapati, K., Gutta, S., Schaffer, D., Martino, J., Zimmerman, J.: A multi-Agent TV Recommender. In: Proceedings of the UM 2001 Workshop on Personalization in Future TV. Sonthofen, Germany (2001).

[9]   Nahm, U., Mooney, R.: Text Mining with Information Extraction. In Proc. of Spring Symposium on Mining Answers from Texts and Knowledge Bases, Stanford, CA (2002) 60-68.

[10]   O'Mahony M, Hurley N., and Silvestre C.: Promoting Recommendations: An attack on Collaborative Filtering: In: Proceedings of DEXA 2002, Lecture Notes in Computer Science, Vol. 2453, Springer-Verlag, Berlin (2002) 494-503.

[11]   Wang, W.J.: New similarity measures on fuzzy sets and on elements, Fuzzy Sets and Systems 85 (1997) 305-309.

[12]   Yang, Y., Pedersen, J.O.: A Comparative Study on Feature Selection in Text Categorization. In: Proceedings of the 14th Intern. Conference on Machine Learning (1997) 412-420.

Brokering Services in Cooperative Distributed Systems: *Privacy-Based Model*

Abdulmutalib Masaud-Wahaishi[1], Hamada Ghenniwa[1]and Weiming Shen[2]

[1] Cooperative Distributed Systems Engineering Group
Department of Electrical & Computer Engineering
The University of Western Ontario
1201 Western Road
London, ON. N6G 1H1, Canada
Email: amasaud@engga.uwo.ca , hghenniwa@eng.uwo.ca

[2] Integrated Manufacturing Technologies Institute, National Research Council Canada
London, Ontario, Canada.
Email: weiming.shen@nrc.ca

Abstract. With the huge explosion of the Internet and the increasing demand on service and data network supply, many rapidly growing research avenues and industries are being created and revolutionized, such as electronic business. An important aspect of cooperative distributed systems is the ability of its entities to exercise some degree of authority in sharing their capabilities. This paper presents novel agent-based architecture for capability-based integration, or brokering services. The proposed architecture is based on several design principles that deal with transparency, heterogeneity and autonomy as well as the privacy issues. Here, privacy has been treated in terms of three attributes: the entity's identity, capability and preferences. A brokering service is modeled as an agent with a specific architecture and interaction protocol that are appropriate to meet the required privacy degree. The proposed architecture has been implemented for distributed information gathering application using a FIPA-complaint platform (JADE).

1. Introduction

Cooperative distributed systems (CDS) consist of entities that are able to exercise some degree of authority in sharing their capabilities. These entities might need to locate and interact with other entities to accomplish specific. This is known as capability-dependency problem [9]. In open environments, such as the World Wide Web, users and service providers are concerned about their privacy from different perspectives and they might wish to protect their identities and capabilities form being used, identified or to whom it might be revealed. The objective of the work presented in this paper is to develop an agent-based model for capability-based integration (*brokering services*) as an intermediary layer with the ability to support several degrees of privacy.

K. Bauknecht, A Min Tjoa, G. Quirchmayr (Eds.): EC-Web 2003, LNCS 2738, pp. 435–444, 2003.

The rest of this paper is organized as follows: Section 2 discusses several attempts related to the work presented here. Section 3 describes our view of modeling cooperative distributed systems based on the Coordinated Intelligent Rational (CIR) agent model, then introduces the proposed brokering architecture. Section 4 describes the current implementation. Section 5 provides a discussion and a summary of the main contribution of the work.

2. Related Work

Several integration solutions in cooperative distributed systems were proposed in various application domains and disciplines. In distributed databases the focus was on integrating different database contents, such as in Global and federated [20]. Many efforts toward agent-based integration solutions rely on the concept of mediator [22]. Examples of mediator-based systems are TSIMMIS [6] , and OBSERVER [12]. In the brokering-based architecture a special agent acts as a *broker* that identifies both the preferences and capabilities of the participants, and routes both requests and replies appropriately. Examples of broker-based systems include MACRON [5], NZDIS [19], SHADE and COINS [16]. In the matchmaking-based approaches an intermediary entity identifies the relevant provider(s) for the requester, which then choose and contact the appropriate provider directly. Examples of matchmaker-based systems include InfoSleuth [2], RETSINA [21], and IMPACT [1]. The facilitator-based integration [8] extends the functionality of the mediator with automatic resource identification and data conversion. FIPA agent software integration specification [5] provides a mechanism and interaction description for software resources that are shared and dynamically controlled in an agent community. BCKOA (Business-Centric Knowledge-Oriented Architecture) framework proposed integration architecture for CDSs [10]. The work in this paper is based on the coordination and cooperation services proposed in BCKOA framework. However, none of the above mentioned approaches treated privacy as an architectural element.

Many solutions were proposed to tackle different privacy challenges encountered in various application domains. The work in [13] investigated network-based approaches for assuring anonymity and privacy over networks. In [11] Goldberg gives an overview of the existing and potential Privacy Enhancing Technologies (PET) for the Internet based on the implementation techniques and functionalities. The Privacy Incorporate Software Agent (PISA) [18] targets the creation of privacy enhancing technologies for next generation electronic business applications. The Platform for Privacy Preferences (P3P) [3], is an industry standard that enables web sites to express their privacy practices in a standardized format. The work in [4] adopted an agent-based integration with different roles of middle agents based on the initial status of the preferences and capabilities of the participants. The objective of the work presented here is to develop brokering services that deal with various degrees of privacy as related to the identity and capabilities of the participant entities (requesters and providers) of a cooperative distributed system.

3. Agent-based Architecture for Cooperative Distributed Systems

Agent-orientation is a very promising design paradigm for integration in CDS environments and provides the next step in the evolution of computational modeling, programming methodologies, and software engineering paradigms. In our view, an agent can be described as an individual collection of primitive components that provide a focused and cohesive set of capabilities. Figure [9] depicts the CIR-agent model. The basic components include knowledge, problem-solving, interaction, and communication components, as shown in Figure 1(b). A particular pattern of components is required to constitute an agent. No specific assumptions need to be made on the detailed design of the agent components. Therefore, the internal structure of the components can be designed and implemented using object oriented or another technology, provided that the developer conceptualizes the specified architecture of the agent as described in Figure 1.

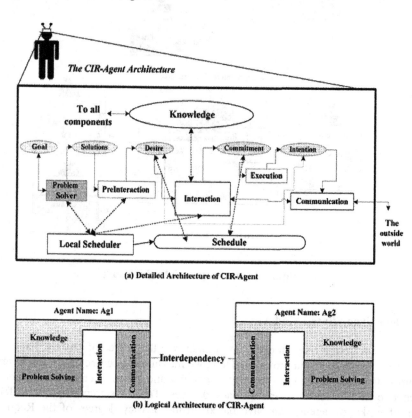

(a) Detailed Architecture of CIR-Agent

(b) Logical Architecture of CIR-Agent

Figure 1 The CIR Agent Architecture

To deal with the capability interdependency problem, agents can solicit assistance from each other. In this context an agent's role can be categorized as service-request or a service-provider. In point-to-point interaction configuration, shown in Figure

2(a), agents should be responsible to identify and interact with the appropriate agents to achieve its goals. However, this configuration is both inflexible and computationally expensive. Alternatively, a layered architecture, shown in Figure 2(b), is proposed with a brokering layer to enable collaboration between different participant agents. The separation of layers in this architecture corresponds to an appropriate separation of responsibilities in the development of the applications in an open, heterogeneous environment.

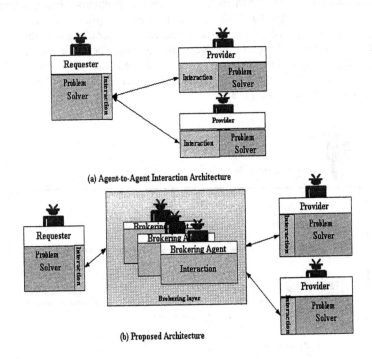

(a) Agent-to-Agent Interaction Architecture

(b) Proposed Architecture

Figure 2 The Proposed Architecture

3.1 The Privacy-Based Model

An important design issue in open environments is the degree of privacy that can be provided to requesters and providers. Here, we measure the degree of privacy in terms of three attributes: the entity's identity, capability and goals. Therefore, an agent can categorize its role under several privacy degrees. Table 1 summarizes the different roles of brokering agents can have based on the privacy degrees of the Requester (RA) and Provider (PA) agents. A detailed description for each role and the associated interaction protocol is presented below.

Table 1. Brokering layer roles catogrized by the privacy concern of the requsters and providers agents

Brokering layer's Knowledge					The Broking layer Interaction protocol	
Brokering Agent name	g(RA)	I(RA)	I(PA)	C(PA)	With Requesters	With Providers
Broker	Known	Known	Known	Known	Receive request Deliver result	Search for relevant agents Negotiate Obtain result
Advertiser	Known	Known	Known	Not Known	Receive request Deliver result	Advertise request to known PA
Anonymizer	Known	Known	Known	Not Known	Receive request Deliver result	PA check for requests PA to reply back with results
Mediator	Known	Not Known	The Identities and capabilities of the provider agents can be either on of the status shown in cases (1,2, or 3)		Receive request RA retrieve result	The brokering layer's interaction protocols with providers agents will follow the same interaction protocol depicted in any selected case shown in (1,2, or 3)
Broadcaster	Not Known	Known			Advertise services to known RA	
Bulletinboard	Not Known	Not Known			RA to check for services.	

The Broker agent protects the privacy of both requesters and providers. Neither the requester nor a provider knows the other in any particular transaction. However, agents need to benefit from the services supported by the broker agent are required to reveal their identities, goals and capabilities to the broker. The interaction pattern for this degree of privacy is shown in Figure 3. The broker's functionality will be typically as follow: formulate the request; contacts (a set of) the relevant providers, and forwards, controls appropriate transaction to achieve a better deal that fulfills the requester's goal; and returns the result of the services to the requester agent. It is essential that both the requester and service provider agents be aware of the broker identity as well as its capability.

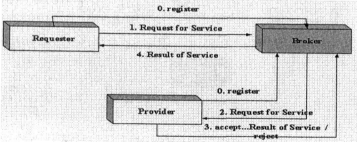

Figure 3 The Interaction Pattern for the Broker Agent

The Advertiser performs services for providers that wish to hide their capabilities. The advertiser's interaction protocol with providers is similar to the broker agent, except with it formulates the requests and broadcasting them to each registered provider with unknown capability. Figure 4 shows the interaction pattern for the advertiser agent with provider and requester agents.

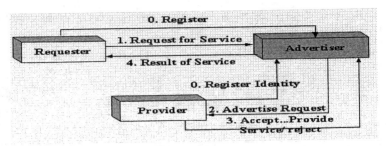

Figure 4 The Interaction Pattern for the Advertiser Agent.

The Anonymizer agent protects both the identity and the capability of provider agents. As shown in Figure 5, The anonymizer maintains a repository of service's requests along with the required preferences, which can be used by the Providers to determine the requests that can be served. Note that providers should be able to link the result of the service to the requester.

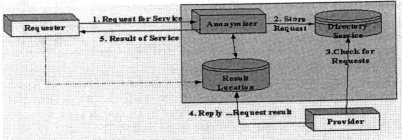

Figure 5 The Interaction Pattern for the Anonymizer Agent.

The Mediator agent protects the identity of a requester, dynamically identifies service providers, and acts on behalf of the requesters to fulfill their goal(s). The interaction pattern with provider agents is shown in Figure 6.

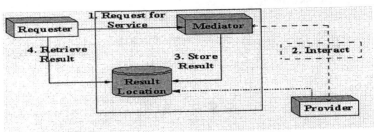

Figure 6 The Interaction Pattern for Mediator Agent.

The Broadcaster agent controls a set of stored services from various providers and deals with requesters that prefer to hide their goals. The broadcaster forwards advertised services to registered requesters with unknown preferences. The broadcaster sends the notifications along with the related parameters required for providing the service. As shown in Figure 7, the requesters check the service's repository for further information or to browse other services that have been previously posted. Additionally, the broadcaster's architecture will vary significantly to include the interaction pattern with providers of different degree of privacy as previously mentioned.

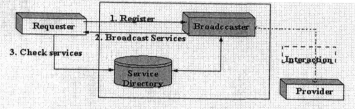

Figure 7 The Interaction Pattern for Broadcaster Agent

The Bulletinboard agent's functionality is similar to the anonymizer, but with requester and provider behaviors reversed. As shown in Figure 8, requesters might post their requests on the Bulletinboard's service repository, or check for services that would be of an interest. Here, it is the requester's responsibility to check for the availability of the service's result and hence retrieve it. Also, the requester should be able to identify, through the brokering layer, the service and the result repository.

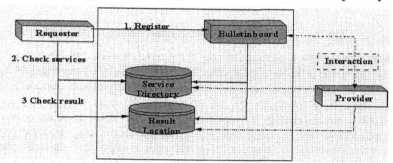

Figure 8 The Interaction Pattern for Bulletinboard Agent

4. Design and Implementation

The different brokering layer agent's architecture is based on the CIR-agent model and is being implemented in Java based on JADE platform [13]. Different brokering agents are available to domain-specific agents that might play the role of a service provider or a requester. Initially, domain-specific agents register with the brokering layer. The registration-agent identifies the brokering agent type that is relevant to the required privacy degree of of the domain-specific agent. All agents are implemented in terms of knowledge and capabilities. The agent's knowledge contains the information about the environment as well as the agent self-model, others agents' model, goals, and the local history of the world. The capabilities of an agent include communication, reasoning and domain action components. The communication capability allows the agents to exchange messages with the other elements of the

environment, including users, agents and objects. The implementation of this
component takes advantage of the existing Agent Message System of the Jade

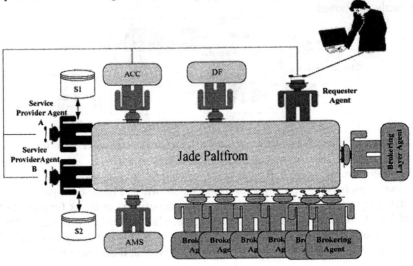

Figure 9 The Prototype Architecture using JADE platform

platform. The agent's reasoning includes the problem solver, and interaction devices
such as: assignment, knowledge update. The problem solver component varies from
one brokering agent to another. They comprise search algorithms modules, mapping
requests to service instances, delegation modules, or modules that are related to
maintaining simple directory services. For example, the broker agent's problem solver
is implemented by making use of the existing Jade behavior classes:
FipaContractNetIntitiatorBehavior. Domain agents play the role of providers,
however, the problem solver component is also concerned with answering requests
that relate to accessing its own available information and service's resources, and it
gives the agent the ability to reason about its own capability to achieve a specific goal.
The problem solver component of the provider provides access to relational databases
via the Java Database Connectivity (JDBC) and Microsoft's Open Database
Connectivity (ODBC) [17]. The requester agent's problem solver identifies the
possible class of goals, and assists in soliciting requests from the brokering layer as
well. The brokering layer agent's problem solver provides basic registration services
and can be viewed as a *matchmaking* facility across the layer.

5. Discussion and Conclusion

The proposed approach for brokering service is novel in the sense that it treats the
privacy as an architectural design issue. Unlike, the work in [4] our proposed model
provides brokering services with a range of privacy degrees. This approach allows
participants (service requesters or providers) to cooperate without revealing their
preferences or capabilities. In another approach [15], it is presumed that capabilities

and preferences come to be known by all participants in the society, which leads to a chaotic environment where agents might violate any privacy requirements.

The proposed multi-layer architecture minimizes the architecture complexity encountered in direct-interaction architectures (where interaction between agents often take a more complex processes for encompassing series of message exchange and forming a single point of failure), and makes it less vulnerable to failures. The separation of responsibilities allows developers and programmers to focus on solving their particular application's problems in a manner and semantics most suitable to the local perspective. In addition, the architecture has trim down the negotiation mechanisms from the domain service application to specialized entities within the layer. Based on The CIR model architecture, agents are modeled as autonomous agents that consider their goals, make decisions about how to achieve those goals, and act on these decisions. The problem solver components of these autonomous agents are viewed and designed as goal-driven behaviors. This supports the heterogeneity aspect, and hence satisfying the transparency feature by hiding the agent structure so that agents can only communicate with each other at the "goal-level".

Different application domains can benefit from the proposed model, such as intelligent cooperative information systems, and agent-based electronic business. In cooperative information system, the proposed brokering services can help users to locate and retrieve information from distributed resources in an open environment. The opportunity for exploiting the proposed system in *e*-business applications are enormous. For example, it can provide facilities for locating information on Web sources or other agents that are required to solve a common problem by name (white pages), by capabilities (yellow pages), and content-based routing. The model presented in this paper has the ability to maintain, update, and access distributed directory services (listing products and business services).

References

[1] Arisha K. Eiter T., Kraus S., Ozcan F., Ross R, and Subrahmanian V.S. IMPACT: The Interactive Maryland Platform for Agents Collaborating Together, IEEE Intelligent Systems (1998).

[2] Bayardo R. et. al.: Infosleuth: Agent-Based Semantic Integration of Information in Open and Dynamic Environments," MCC Technical report MCC-INSL-0088-96, October 1996.

[3] Cranor L, et al.: The platform for privacy preferences 1.0 (P3P1.0) specification. W3C Recommendations, see www.w3.org/TR/P3P/, April 2002.

[4] Decker K., Sycara K., and Williamson M.," Middle-agents for the internet" In IJCAI97 International Joint Conference on Artificial Intelligence, Nagoya, Japan, 1997.

[5] Decker, k., Lesser V., Nagendra Prasad M. and Wagner T.: MACRON: An architecture for Multi-agent Cooperative Information Gathering (1995), Proceedings of the CIKM '95 Workshop on Intelligent Information Agents.

[6] FIPA Agent Software Integration Specification; see - www.fipa.org/specs/fipa00079/XC00079B.html

[7] Garcia-Molina H., at al. "Integrating and Accessing Heterogeneous Information Sources in TSIMMIS". In Proceedings of the AAAI Symposium on Information Gathering, pp. 61-64, Stanford, California, 1995.

[8] Genesereth M, "Infomaster: An Information Integration System," in proceedings of 1997 ACM SIGMOD Conference, 1997.

[9] Ghenniwa H. and Kamel M., ``Interaction Devices for Coordinating Cooperative Distributed Systems", Journal of Intelligent Automation and Soft Computing, 2000.

[10] Ghenniwa H. and Shen W., "Service-Oriented eMarketplace: An Agent-based Model", accepted in Production Planning & Control Journal, 2002.

[11] Goldberg I., D. Wagner, Eric. Brewer. "Privacy-enhancing technologies for the Internet" In Proceedings of IEEE COMPCON 97, pages 103-109, 1997.

[12] Gruber T., "A Translation Approach to Portable Ontology Specifications", Knowledge Acquisition, Vol. 5, No. 2, p.199-220, 1993.

[13] JADE – Java Agent Development Environment see http://sharon.cselt.it

[14] Korba L. and Song R. "Investigating of Network-Based Approaches for Privacy". NRC Report: ERB-1091, NRC No.: 44900, Nov. 2001.

[15] Kuokka D. and Harada L. On using KQML for Matchmaking. In proc. ICMAS-95.AAAI Press, June 1995.

[16] Kuokka D. and L. Harada. Information Gathering from Heterogeneous, Distributed Environments. Conference on Information and knowledge Management. MIT Press, 1995.

[17] Open database connectivity - http://www.java.sun.

[18] PISA – the Privacy Incorporated Software Agent; see <http://www.cbpweb.nl/bis/top-1-1-9.html>.

[19] Purvis, M. et al. The NZDIS Project: an Agent-Based Distributed Information Systems Architecture. Proceedings of the 33rd Hawaii International Conference on System Sciences – 2000.

[20] Sheth A., and Larson J, ``Federated Database Systems for Managing Distributed, Heterogeneous, and Autonomous Database", ACM Computing Surveys, vol.22, no.3, pp. 183-235, 1990

[21] Sycara k. et al. "The RETSINA MAS Infrastructure", Tech. Report CMU-RI-TR-01-05, Robotics Institute, Carnegie Mellon University, March, 2001.

[22] Wiederhold G., "Mediators in the Architecture of Future Information Systems," IEEE Computer, 25:3, pp. 38-49, 1992.

Enterprise Application Integration – Future Revisited?

Gerald Quirchmayr[1,2] and A Min Tjoa[3]

[1] University of Vienna
Institute for Computer Science and Business Informatics
Liebiggasse 4, A-1010 Vienna, Austria
Gerald.Quirchmayr@univie.ac.at
[2] University of South Australia
School of Computer and Information Science
Mawson Lakes, SA-5095, Australia
Gerald.Quirchmayr @unisa.edu.au
[3] Vienna University of Technology
Institute of Software Technology
Resselgasse 3/188, 1040 Vienna, Austria
Tjoa@ifs.tuwien.ac.at

Abstract. In this paper we reflect on enterprise application integration and try to give appreciation of its benefits for the development of future work environments, especially mobile applications. We look at requirements for and opportunities provided by integration concepts and draw conclusions about what integrated environments and enterprise resource planning systems can contribute in terms of serving as a sound and future proof basis for mobile and ubiquitous use of technology. Some of the research issues identified are, not astonishing at all, pointing back to open questions already encountered in database and artificial intelligence projects in past decades. Thanks to the advances of information technology some answers can now be given.

1   EAI – Requirement for Successful Present and Future Systems

EAI proposals and solutions have now been discussed for several decades. Approaches developed by research and practice have lead to varying levels of success. Systems based on standardized processes have, in spite of all the criticism they have recently received, been the most successful products provided by industry. Customization and the related necessary efforts will for a long time remain the focus of discussion among users, system administrators, consultants and developers. Standards, as decades of development have shown, introduce additional freedom, but they also take away several possibilities, primarily restricting the individualization and adaptability of solutions. However, in order to meet the requirements of interoperability, compatibility, interface definition and ultimately virtual enterprises, standards will have to be

K. Bauknecht, A Min Tjoa, G. Quirchmayr (Eds.): EC-Web 2003, LNCS 2738, pp. 445–450, 2003.

adhered to. Some of them, such as ODETTE and ANSI X.12 have been around for a long time and have inspired more ambitious developments, such as UN/EDIFACT and ebXML (for details see [UN/EDIFACT] and [ebXML].

The present focus of industry and research is on functional and terminological integration. The leading examples are the many ontology-related projects (as example of one major project see [Bozsak et al. 2002]) and integrated information systems platforms which will together form the basis for scalable integration mechanisms of the future (see [SAP 2003], [ORACLE 2003] and [IBM 2003]).

The development which has so successfully started with functional integration, data -, object – and component directories will now lead us back to research problems encountered by database and expert systems researchers when trying to develop schema integration concepts and modeling relationships in semantic networks. The major difference is the power of today's hard- and software which allows us to try methods and concepts that had to be shelved as impractical in earlier developments. The efficient integration on different levels, typically processes, functions, data, protocols or the comparatively simple issue of formats, remains a core research question. Though some of the hopes raised by EAI can already be regarded as overstated, the already existing benefits and the ones to come result in major improvements for information systems. For an early critical view of e-commerce the reader is referred to [Milosevic and Bond 1995].

2   New Generations of Mobile Systems: Fascinating Technology, Developing Opportunities, but Where Is the User Acceptance?

Mobil systems today are more of a necessity than ever before. Being able to communicate and access information via mobile phones, smart phones and laptops connected to a WLAN (linked via Bluetooth or GPRS cards), has become standard business practice. Given the boom of the late 1990's it was a considerable shock for communication service providers to see the latest technologies, such as UMTS, see a very slow uptake. Some of the limiting factors identified so far are cost, the lack of choice in end user devices, and ultimately the lack of end user applications. A closer look at the issue reveals that some of the problems are more fundamental. The level of integration still is far too low for application providers to allow them to become active with a reasonable and justifiable effort. The second major issue is that business processes are far from being able to make full use of the technology. One consequence of the bursting e-commerce bubble is that management today is more careful, sometimes even regards technology as suspicious, if not dangerous. The pressure to cut cost and to delay investments adds to a rather bleak perspective.

What at first glance only looks like a developing catastrophe actually is a unique opportunity too. Because of the slow pace of the introduction of new technology at this stage, information systems planning gets back some desperately needed breathing space. When dealing with the Y2K problem, the introduction of the Euro and major mergers in all sectors, there hardly was time to deal with the even then long overdue restructuring of processes and the consolidation and integration of information systems. When the lack of security, availability, reliability and process integration, together with flawed business models, resulted in the burst of the dot.com bubble, the years of omissions and the weaknesses of the prevailing information system architectures became obvious. The lessons learned by many companies the hard way make them think twice before embarking on what they consider another risky adventure, in this case UMTS. Experiments with the customer are a bad memory of the recent past, still haunting and slowing down development.

Confidence is very slowly coming back and technologies that once had a reputation for being rather experimental, brittle and unreliable, such as WAP, are maturing and becoming solid. Technology is not anymore the focus; the solution of business problems is regaining the center of attention. This is exactly the environment in which information technology is doing well and has in fact never seized to do so.

3   ERP, Integration, Inter-enterprise Computing: Basis for Future-Oriented Mobile Services

EAI proposals and solutions have now been discussed for several decades. Approaches developed by research and practice have lead to varying levels of success.

Revolutions very rarely take place and whenever they happen their core ideas usually are best implemented in an evolutionary approach. ERP systems have for a long time been the workhorse of enterprise information systems infrastrucutres and have served their users well (for an overview of the benefits of these systems see [SAP 2003]). Derogatory terms, such as legacy systems, have been used to discredit core database systems, integrated information systems and even ERP systems. The reality is that without these systems, industry and business could not operate anymore. The mobile revolution therefore has, as the Internet revolution had to, learn to live with these systems and benefit from their existence (an indication of how central integration is and what an IT failure may result in can be found in [Avison and Wilson 2002]). As long as network access was limited to known users on site, some issues, such as billing, 24x7 availability and security could be approached in a very lax way. When opening networks towards mobile infrastructures, outsourcing parts of network infrastructures and giving access to mobile employees, business partners and customers connecting via public networks, these issues, if not properly taken care of, could very suddenly result in serious security breaches, unacceptable downtime and billing problems. Bridges built between mobile systems and already existing infrastructures do sometimes lead to an additional layer of instability, very similar to the first generation of interfaces between databases and web-based applications. That the integration of customer front-ends with back office systems, systems of business partners, and electronic payment systems leads to increased stress on existing infrastructures is known from the effects of the Internet. Companies also have to face up to reality regarding their business processes. If they want to make full use of the opportunities provided by the technology, communication, service, brokerage and application providers will have to accept standards and will have to streamline their internal business processes accordingly (see [Bullinger and Scheer 2003] for a recent overview of service engineering). As ubiquitous mobile work is expected to become standard, environments will change, time and location independence being the major challenges. Information technology infrastructures are expected to render their services with a high level of quality, wherever the user is and whenever the user wishes to access the system. Customer, business partner and employee self service modes mean a full process and infrastructure integration, which today still is a distant dream for the majority of real world systems. Some extremely competitive areas, such as the airline industry, have already discovered the potential of mobile services, now delivering their services not only through the Internet, but also through mobile phones, for the time being primarily through WAP gateways. Pure virtual enterprises will remain the exception, but cooperation through the use of technology will enable new ways of approaching customers and business partners. The goal is to deliver the full power of ERP systems and other core business technology to mobile users.

4   Standards, Semantics, Integration Concepts

Plenty of integration models have been developed, standardization efforts are abundant, but so far relatively little has been achieved. The real world is characterized by harmonization with none of the companies willing, and that for sound financial and operational reasons, to completely replace their existing infrastructure. Fairly recent approaches, which CORBA, DNA and SOAP are excellent examples of, follow a more pragmatic paradigm, aimed at making information held in existing systems accessible and rendering existing infrastructure usable for remote, distributed and mobile applications. Advanced integration models, such as the one presented in [Tagg and Quirchmayr 2001], demonstrate how higher level integration can build on existing architectures and standards. Today .Net and Java 2 ME are the most prominent representatives of industry contributions to enabling integrated approaches for mobile settings through leveraging infrastructure that is already in place. Integration on a purely syntactic level today is achievable; the interesting research question is again semantic integration. Early ambitious approaches once more raised the issues of ontologies, schema integration and the interpretation of relationships, as stated earlier.

5   Trust – A Unique Advantage of Mobile Phones

Unlike other systems, mobile phones have not disappointed their users with instability and a wave of security breaches. That is why users on all levels trust their mobile phones. This puts providers of communication services in a position where users trust them with financial transactions, otherwise a level of confidence previously only enjoyed by banks. Many of the problems of electronic commerce can be overcome by the user authentication and secure communication features offered by mobile phone environments. The proper integration with backbone service, be it payment systems, or back office systems is still in its early stages, but will, once the technology has had a chance to fully mature, add a new dimension to electronic commerce. With electronic signatures and citizen cards, once propagated as "the" solution for the authentication problem, suffering from a terribly low acceptance, application based on mobile phone technology have gained a unique position. They are the only environment currently satisfying three core requirements, authentication, secure communication, and being trusted by users. It can therefore be expected that applications building on this solid basis will soon overtake traditional Internet-based implementations.

6 Conclusions

Integration is a key requirement for the successful development of e- and m-commerce applications. The huge investments made in enterprise resource planning systems, intranets and other infrastructure in the past decade must now be leveraged. Some of the weaknesses still to be overcome are the harmonization of systems, their interoperability, improved security and stability. It is clear that the next logical step from enterprise resource planning is towards enterprise application integration and from there on towards schema and enterprise model integration. Scenarios developed in research and industry will become practicable through the convergence of technology and standards-based integration, harmonization and interoperability.

References

[Avison and Wilson 2002] D. Avison, D. Wilson. IT Failure and the Collapse of One.Tel, in R. Traunmüller (ed.), Proceedings of the IFIP 17th World Computer Congress, TC8 Stream on Information Systems: The e-Business Challenge, Kluwer Academic Publisher, 2002.

[Bozsak et al. 2002] E. Bozsak et al. KAON - Towards a Large Scale Semantic Web. In K.Bauknecht, A M. Tjoa, G. Quirchmayr (Eds.), Proceedings of the Third International Conference, EC-Web 2002, LNCS 2455, Springer 2002; ISBN 3-540-44137-9.

[Bullinger and Scheer 2003] H.-J Bullinger and A.-W. Scheer, (Eds.). Service Engineering Entwicklung und Gestaltung innovativer Dienstleistungen. Springer 2003; ISBN 3-540-43831-9.

[ebXML]   http://www.ebxml.org

[IBM 2003]   IBM Competitive Advisor Brochure; can be accessed via http://www-1.ibm.com/mediumbusiness/seas.jsp

[Milosevic and Bond 1995] Z. Milosevic and A. Bond. Electronic Commerce on the Internet: What is Still Missing? The 5th Annual Conference of the Internet Society, INET'95, Honolulu, Hawaii, USA, June 1995.

[McNurlin and Sprague 2002] B. C. McNurlin and R. H. Sprague (Eds.). Information Systems Management, 5th edition, Prentice Hall, Pearson Education 2002, ISBN 0-13-034073-1.

[ORACLE 2003] Oracle E-Business Suite: A Roadmap to Better Business Processes, An Oracle White Paper, October 2002; can be accessed via http://www.oracle.com/applications

[SAP 2003]   mySAP Business Suite; can be accessed via http://www.sap.com/solutions

[Tagg and Quirchmayr 2001] R. Tagg, G. Quirchmayr. Towards an Interconnection Model for Evolution of Shared Workflows in a Virtual Enterprise, in Proceedings of Third Int. Conference on Information Integration and Web-Based Applications and Services, Linz, Austria, September 2001.

[UN/EDIFACT] http://www.unece.org/trade/untdid/welcome.htm

Author Index

Lecture Notes in Computer Science

For information about Vols. 1–2704
please contact your bookseller or Springer-Verlag

Vol. 2739: R. Traunmüller (Ed.), Electronic Government. Proceedings, 2003. XVIII, 511 pages. 2003.

Vol. 2740: E. Burke, P. De Causmaecker (Eds.), Practice and Theory of Automated Timetabling IV. Proceedings, 2002. XII, 361 pages. 2003.

Vol. 2741: F. Baader (Ed.), Automated Deduction – CADE-19. Proceedings, 2003. XII, 503 pages. 2003. (Subseries LNAI).

Vol. 2742: R. N. Wright (Ed.), Financial Cryptography. Proceedings, 2003. VIII, 321 pages. 2003.

Vol. 2743: L. Cardelli (Ed.), ECOOP 2003 – Object-Oriented Programming. Proceedings, 2003. X, 501 pages. 2003.

Vol. 2744: V. Mařík, D. McFarlane, P. Valckenaers (Eds.), Holonic and Multi-Agent Systems for Manufacturing. Proceedings, 2003. XI, 322 pages. 2003. (Subseries LNAI).

Vol. 2745: M. Guo, L.T. Yang (Eds.), Parallel and Distributed Processing and Applications. Proceedings, 2003. XII, 450 pages. 2003.

Vol. 2746: A. de Moor, W. Lex, B. Ganter (Eds.), Conceptual Structures for Knowledge Creation and Communication. Proceedings, 2003. XI, 405 pages. 2003. (Subseries LNAI).

Vol. 2747: B. Rovan, P. Vojtáš (Eds.), Mathematical Foundations of Computer Science 2003. Proceedings, 2003. XIII, 692 pages. 2003.

Vol. 2748: F. Dehne, J.-R. Sack, M. Smid (Eds.), Algorithms and Data Structures. Proceedings, 2003. XII, 522 pages. 2003.

Vol. 2749: J. Bigun, T. Gustavsson (Eds.), Image Analysis. Proceedings, 2003. XXII, 1174 pages. 2003.

Vol. 2750: T. Hadzilacos, Y. Manolopoulos, J.F. Roddick, Y. Theodoridis (Eds.), Advances in Spatial and Temporal Databases. Proceedings, 2003. XIII, 525 pages. 2003.

Vol. 2751: A. Lingas, B.J. Nilsson (Eds.), Fundamentals of Computation Theory. Proceedings, 2003. XII, 433 pages. 2003.

Vol. 2752: G.A. Kaminka, P.U. Lima, R. Rojas (Eds.), RoboCup 2002: Robot Soccer World Cup VI. XVI, 498 pages. 2003. (Subseries LNAI).

Vol. 2753: F. Maurer, D. Wells (Eds.), Extreme Programming and Agile Methods – XP/Agile Universe 2003. Proceedings, 2003. XI, 215 pages. 2003.

Vol. 2754: M. Schumacher, Security Engineering with Patterns. XIV, 208 pages. 2003.

Vol. 2756: N. Petkov, M.A. Westenberg (Eds.), Computer Analysis of Images and Patterns. Proceedings, 2003. XVIII, 781 pages. 2003.

Vol. 2758: D. Basin, B. Wolff (Eds.), Theorem Proving in Higher Order Logics. Proceedings, 2003. X, 367 pages. 2003.

Vol. 2759: O.H. Ibarra, Z. Dang (Eds.), Implementation and Application of Automata. Proceedings, 2003. XI, 312 pages. 2003.

Vol. 2761: R. Amadio, D. Lugiez (Eds.), CONCUR 2003 - Concurrency Theory. Proceedings, 2003. XI, 524 pages. 2003.

Vol. 2762: G. Dong, C. Tang, W. Wang (Eds.), Advances in Web-Age Information Management. Proceedings, 2003. XIII, 512 pages. 2003.

Vol. 2763: V. Malyshkin (Ed.), Parallel Computing Technologies. Proceedings, 2003. XIII, 570 pages. 2003.

Vol. 2764: S. Arora, K. Jansen, J.D.P. Rolim, A. Sahai (Eds.), Approximation, Randomization, and Combinatorial Optimization. Proceedings, 2003. IX, 409 pages. 2003.

Vol. 2765: R. Conradi, A.I. Wang (Eds.), Empirical Methods and Studies in Software Engineering. VIII, 279 pages. 2003.

Vol. 2766: S. Behnke, Hierarchical Neural Networks for Image Interpretation. XII, 224 pages. 2003.

Vol. 2769: T. Koch, I. T. Sølvberg (Eds.), Research and Advanced Technology for Digital Libraries. Proceedings, 2003. XV, 536 pages. 2003.

Vol. 2776: V. Gorodetsky, L. Popyack, V. Skormin (Eds.), Computer Network Security. Proceedings, 2003. XIV, 470 pages. 2003.

Vol. 2777: B. Schölkopf, M.K. Warmuth (Eds.), Learning Theory and Kernel Machines. Proceedings, 2003. XIV, 746 pages. 2003. (Subseries LNAI).

Vol. 2779: C.D. Walter, Ç.K. Koç, C. Paar (Eds.), Cryptographic Hardware and Embedded Systems – CHES 2003. Proceedings, 2003. XIII, 441 pages. 2003.

Vol. 2782: M. Klusch, A. Omicini, S. Ossowski, H. Laamanen (Eds.), Cooperative Information Agents VII. Proceedings, 2003. XI, 345 pages. 2003. (Subseries LNAI).

Vol. 2783: W. Zhou, P. Nicholson, B. Corbitt, J. Fong (Eds.), Advances in Web-Based Learning – ICWL 2003. Proceedings, 2003. XV, 552 pages. 2003.

Vol. 2786: F. Oquendo (Ed.), Software Process Technology. Proceedings, 2003. X, 173 pages. 2003.

Vol. 2787: J. Timmis, P. Bentley, E. Hart (Eds.), Artificial Immune Systems. Proceedings, 2003. XI, 299 pages. 2003.

Vol. 2789: L. Böszörményi, P. Schojer (Eds.), Modular Programming Languages. Proceedings, 2003. XIII, 271 pages. 2003.

Vol. 2790: H. Kosch, L. Böszörményi, H. Hellwagner (Eds.), Euro-Par 2003 Parallel Processing. Proceedings, 2003. XXXV, 1320 pages. 2003.

Vol. 2794: P. Kemper, W. H. Sanders (Eds.), Computer Performance Evaluation. Proceedings, 2003. X, 309 pages. 2003.

Vol. 2795: L. Chittaro (Ed.), Human-Computer Interaction with Mobile Devices and Services. Proceedings, 2003. XV, 494 pages. 2003.

Vol. 2796: M. Cialdea Mayer, F. Pirri (Eds.), Automated Reasoning with Analytic Tableaux and Related Methods. Proceedings, 2003. X, 271 pages. 2003. (Subseries LNAI).

Vol. 2803: M. Baaz, J.A. Makowsky (Eds.), Computer Science Logic. Proceedings, 2003. XII, 589 pages. 2003.

Vol. 2805: K. Araki, S. Gnesi, D. Mandrioli (Eds.), FME 2003: Formal Methods. Proceedings, 2003. XVII, 942 pages. 2003.

Vol. 2810: M.R. Berthold, H.-J. Lenz, E. Bradley, R. Kruse, C. Borgelt (Eds.), Advances in Intelligent Data Analysis V. Proceedings, 2003. XV, 624 pages. 2003.

Vol. 2817: D. Konstantas, M. Leonard, Y. Pigneur, S. Patel (Eds.), Object-Oriented Information Systems. Proceedings, 2003. XII, 426 pages. 2003.